Hunter-Gatherer Adaptation and Resilience

A Bioarchaeological Perspective

Hunter-gatherer lifestyles defined the origins of modern humans and for tens of thousands of years were the only form of subsistence our species knew. This changed with the advent of food production, which occurred at different times throughout the world.

The chapters in this volume explore the different ways that hunter-gatherer societies around the world adapted to changing social and ecological circumstances while still maintaining a predominantly hunter-gatherer lifestyle.

Couched specifically within the framework of resilience theory, the authors use contextualized bioarchaeological analyses of health, diet, mobility, and funerary practices to explore how hunter-gatherers responded to challenges and actively resisted change that diminished the core of their social identity and worldview.

Daniel H. Temple is an Associate Professor of Anthropology at George Mason University. His research focuses on the life history, diet, mortuary ritual, and evolutionary morphology of hunter-gatherer populations from Northeast Asia and North America, specifically Japan, Siberia, Alaska, and Florida. He has published more than 30 peer-reviewed journal articles and book chapters on topics including growth and development, life history theory, enamel microstructures and stress, hunter-gatherer mortuary ritual, ecogeographic adaptation, functional adaptation, biodistance analysis, and prehistoric diet.

Christopher M. Stojanowski is a Professor of Anthropology at Arizona State University. He has written on diverse topics in anthropology including the bioarchaeology of colonial period peoples of southeastern America, on early and middle Holocene populations of North Africa, and on dental anthropology and biological distance. His work is bioarchaeological in focus, specializing in the analysis of human remains and dentition. He has authored over 60 peer-reviewed articles and chapters and has written three single-authored books, one of which, *The Bioarchaeology of Ethnogenesis in the Colonial Southeast*, was awarded the James Mooney Prize of the Southern Anthropological Society in 2010.

Cambridge Studies in Biological and Evolutionary Anthropology

Consulting editors

C. G. Nicholas Mascie-Taylor, *University of Cambridge*

Robert A. Foley, *University of Cambridge*

Series editors

Agustín Fuentes, *University of Notre Dame*

Nina G. Jablonski, *Pennsylvania State University*

Clark Spencer Larsen, *The Ohio State University*

Michael P. Muehlenbein, *The University of Texas at San Antonio*

Dennis H. O'Rourke, *The University of Utah*

Karen B. Strier, *University of Wisconsin*

David P. Watts, *Yale University*

Also available in the series

Hunter-Gatherer Adaptation and Resilience

A Bioarchaeological Perspective

Edited by

DANIEL H. TEMPLE
George Mason University, Virginia

CHRISTOPHER M. STOJANOWSKI
Arizona State University

CAMBRIDGE
UNIVERSITY PRESS

CAMBRIDGE
UNIVERSITY PRESS

University Printing House, Cambridge CB2 8BS, United Kingdom

One Liberty Plaza, 20th Floor, New York, NY 10006, USA

477 Williamstown Road, Port Melbourne, VIC 3207, Australia

314–321, 3rd Floor, Plot 3, Splendor Forum, Jasola District Centre, New Delhi – 110025, India

79 Anson Road, #06–04/06, Singapore 079906

Cambridge University Press is part of the University of Cambridge.

It furthers the University's mission by disseminating knowledge in the pursuit of education, learning, and research at the highest international levels of excellence.

www.cambridge.org
Information on this title: www.cambridge.org/9781107187351
DOI: 10.1017/9781316941256

© Cambridge University Press 2019

First published 2019

Printed in the United Kingdom by TJ International Ltd., Padstow, Cornwall

A catalogue record for this publication is available from the British Library.

Library of Congress Cataloging-in-Publication Data
Names: Temple, Daniel Howard, 1979– editor. | Stojanowski, Christopher M. (Christopher Michael), 1973– editor.
Title: Hunter-gatherer adaptation and resilience : a bioarchaeological perspective / edited by Daniel H. Temple, Christopher M. Stojanowski.
Description: Cambridge, United Kingdom ; New York, NY : Cambridge University Press, 2018. | Series: Cambridge studies in biological and evolutionary anthropology ; 81 | Includes bibliographical references and index.
Identifiers: LCCN 2018030097| ISBN 9781107187351 (hardback) | ISBN 9781316637999 (paperback)
Subjects: LCSH: Hunting and gathering societies. | Prehistoric peoples–Food. | Prehistoric peoples–Health and hygiene. | Paleoanthropology. | Human remains (Archaeology)
Classification: LCC GN388 .H835 2018 | DDC 306.3/64–dc23
LC record available at https://lccn.loc.gov/2018030097

ISBN 978-1-107-18735-1 Hardback

Contents

Contributors

Valerie A. Andrushko
Department of Anthropology, Southern Connecticut State University, New Haven, CT, USA

Eric J. Bartelink
Department of Anthropology, California State University, Chico, CA, USA

Viviana I. Bellifemine
The Old Schools, University of Cambridge, Cambridge, United Kingdom

Valeria Bernal
División Antropología, Facultad de Ciencias Naturales y Museo, Universidad Nacional de La Plata, Buenos Aires, Argentina

Erin E. Bornemann
Department of Anthropology, University of California, Santa Barbara, CA, USA

Lucas Bueno
Department of History, Federal University of Santa Catarina, Santa Catarina, Brazil

Jane E. Buikstra
School of Human Evolution and Social Change, Arizona State University, Tempe, AZ, USA

Michelle E. Cameron
Department of Anthropology, University of Toronto, Toronto, ON, Canada

Gary Coupland
Department of Anthropology, University of Toronto, Toronto, ON, Canada

Pedro Da-Gloria
Programa de Pós-Graduação em Antropologia, Instituto de Filosofia e Ciências Humanas, Universidade Federal do Pará, Umarizal, Belém, Brazil

Lynn H. Gamble
Department of Anthropology, University of California, Santa Barbara, CA, USA

Lesley Harrington
Department of Anthropology, University of Alberta, Edmonton, AB, Canada

Robert Jurmain
Department of Anthropology, San Jose State University, San Jose, CA, USA

Lauryn C. Justice
Department of Sociology and Anthropology, George Mason University, Fairfax, VA, USA

Bryn Letham
Department of Anthropology, University of British Columbia, Vancouver, BC, Canada

Alan Leventhal
Department of Anthropology, San Jose State University, San Jose, CA, USA

Judith Littleton
Department of Anthropology, University of Auckland, Auckland, New Zealand

Charles F. Merbs
School of Human Evolution and Social Change, Arizona State University, Tempe, AZ, USA

Irina Nechayev
Ohlone Community College, Fremont, CA, USA

S. Ivan Perez
División Antropología, Facultad de Ciencias Naturales y Museo, Universidad Nacional de La Plata, Consejo Nacional de Investigaciones Científicas y Técnicas, Buenos Aires, Argentina

Susan Pfeiffer
Department of Anthropology, University of Toronto, Toronto, ON, Canada

María Bárbara Postillone
División Antropología, Facultad de Ciencias Naturales y Museo, Universidad Nacional de La Plata, Consejo Nacional de Investigaciones Científicas y Técnicas, Buenos Aires, Argentina

Diego D. Rindel
Instituto Nacional de Antropología y Pensamiento Latinoamericana, Universidad de Buenos Aires, Capital Federal, Argentina

Rick J. Schulting
School of Archaeology, University of Oxford, Oxford, United Kingdom

Jay Stock
Department of Anthropology, University of Western Ontario, London, ON, Canada

Christopher M. Stojanowski
School of Human Evolution and Social Change, Arizona State University, Tempe, AZ, USA

Daniel H. Temple
Department of Sociology and Anthropology, George Mason University, Fairfax, VA, USA

1 Interrogating the Alterity of Hunter-Gatherers in Bioarchaeological Context: Adaptability, Transformability, and Resilience of Hunter-Gatherers in the Past

Daniel H. Temple and Christopher M. Stojanowski

1.1 Initium

This chapter presents a social history for the conceptualization of hunter-gatherers in anthropological and bioarchaeological research. Hunter-gatherers are of great interest to anthropologists and bioarchaeologists because these populations represent a lifestyle that dramatically contrasts with Western industrialized capitalism. It is on the basis of alterity that hunter-gatherers were targeted by Western scholars (Barnard, 2014; Pluciennik, 2002). Despite the fact that hunter-gatherer lifestyles are often constructed based on the practice of othering, there exists compelling evidence for an integrated pattern of transformation and endurance found among hunter-gatherers. These populations experience cultural transformation and endurance in ways that approximate cultures that adopt agricultural lifestyles, while maintaining resource procurement as a primary mode of subsistence. This suggests that cultural evolution is relevant to hunter-gatherer populations, but may be acting in ways that substantially differ from the unilineal or progressive notion espoused by cultural evolutionists over the past 150 years. Here, cultural evolution is defined as the myriad ways in which culture changes and acknowledges human agency and intentionality in this process – that is, culture change is not dependent upon environmental pressures alone, and the broader endurance or transformation of social behavior is contingent upon human intentionality *and* environmental context. Bioarchaeological research infrequently integrates the concepts of adaptation *and* resilience (see below for exceptions) when interacting with hunter-gatherer assemblages and frequently relegates these groups to comparative samples, usually stepping stones to agriculture. The goal of this book is to discard the notion of alterity that is attached to the hunter-gatherer lifestyle and orient these populations within the broader auspices of resilience and adaptation. This volume uses bioarchaeological data to understand the integration and persistence of hunter-gatherer cultural and socioecological identities as well as the circumstances acting to promote whole-scale change within these systems. Thus, this volume synthesizes hunter-gatherer adaptation, resilience, and transformation within the context of cultural and environmental challenges, while militating against what Fitzhugh (2003: 8) referenced as the facile notion that evolution requires hunter-gatherers to transform into agricultural economies. This approach embraces the idea that culture change in hunter-gatherers is an intentional and purposeful act that occurs in response to a variety of cultural and environmental catalysts, while the enduring legacy of hunter-gatherer identities remains a unifying theme.

Hunter-gatherers are frequently defined by the absence of domesticated foods and the presence of small-scale, mobile settlements (Lee and Daly, 1993). Others report that hunter-gatherers exist on a continuum of behavioral variability from high levels of mobility and loosely organized social structure to sedentary populations with elevated complexity in social organization (Binford, 1981). Hunter-gatherers are labeled "foragers" and "collectors" based on relative degrees of mobility and complexity on this continuum. Dialectical arguments juxtapose the term "forager" against "hunter-gatherer" with the goal of more precisely defining the lifestyle in question and differentiating the uniqueness of human perception and intentionality compared with the extractive goals of non-human animals (Ingold, 1988a). Hunter-gatherers, in this sense, are differentiated from foragers based on the idea that hunter-gatherers produce subsistence economies via the objectification of work.[1]

Hunter-gatherers occupy myriad ecological zones, and the productivity of these ecosystems is often reflected by mode of food procurement (Harris, 1969; Kelly, 1995). Diversity in the mode of food procurement among hunter-gatherers is associated with the continuum of delayed- versus immediate-return economies (Hayden, 1995; Woodburn, 1982). Immediate-return hunter-gatherers have smaller population densities, egalitarian social systems, and procure resources that are immediately available. Conversely, delayed-return hunter-gatherers have complex levels of social structure, live in larger, more sedentary communities, intensively harvest and store wild resources, and sometimes domesticate plants. The placement of hunter-gatherers within the continuum of delayed- and immediate-return economies adds diversity to communities that represent a *broad spectrum* of lifestyles.

Critical analyses of the hunter-gatherer concept as applied to populations who domesticate plants compellingly argues that anthropological studies are often trapped by the hegemony of dualistic epistemology (Crawford, 2008). Specifically, many populations exist in a transitional zone between hunting and gathering and agricultural economies via the existence of complex social structures and domestication. Importantly, this work suggests that these populations represent transitional phases between hunter-gatherer and intensive agricultural economies, and anthropologists are missing events in the evolution of cultural complexity by rendering these populations as socially constructed categories (hunter-gatherer/agriculturalist). This critique is of great interest to hunter-gatherer studies because it addresses the oversimplification of human cultural complexity into binary oppositions by suggesting that there are numerous subsistence groups who transcend categorization. The problem here is the underlying assumption that these transitional societies are

---

[1] The objectification of work references the reciprocal relationship (see below) between hunter-gatherers and the natural environment. This term emphasizes the socially and ecologically embedded networks in which hunting and gathering are produced and reproduced.

moving toward a progressive goal rather than existing in a cultural state that was produced through local knowledge and intentionality (i.e., Ingold, 1998). In addition, this work also assumes that the hunter-gatherer construct exists as a singular category rather than a working definition that applies to populations who vary along a lifestyle continuum (e.g., Binford, 1981; Hayden, 1995; Woodburn, 1982). This volume and others (e.g., Bettinger, 1991; Fitzhugh, 2003; Kent, 2002a) argue that agricultural economies are not the end-product of all hunter-gatherer economies, even among communities who seemingly exist in a transitional state. There are, in fact, many examples of delayed- and immediate-return hunter-gatherers who maintain contact with intensive agriculturalists and herders, yet consciously choose not to adopt these lifestyles (e.g., Kent, 2002b; Marlowe, 2002; Walker and Hewlett, 1990). Archaeological examples of populations who intensively consumed and likely domesticated plant foods or coexisted with animal herders are also numerous (e.g., Crawford, 2006; Da-Gloria and Larsen, 2014; Humphrey *et al.*, 2014; Rowley-Conwy and Layton, 2011; Stojanowski and Knudson, 2014; Temple, 2007; Turner and Machado, 1983; Walker and Erlandson, 1986). Furthermore, there exists a marked contrast in the production of hunter-gatherer subsistence economies through practice and ideology. Specifically, hunter-gatherers conceptualize relationships with nature in a far different way than that observed among agriculturalists. This conceptualization reflects worldviews surrounding dominance and care versus incorporation. The relationship between agriculturalists and domesticates is conceived as a singular transaction – humans care for plants and animals, and rituals associated with these organisms are associated with this dominion (Ingold, 1988b; but see Rindos, 1984). By contrast, hunter-gatherer relationships with nature are tethered to what might be called an eternal ontology of interactions – one in which humans and nature are tethered to a cyclical, ever unfolding set of material and spiritual relationships (Atuy, 1997; Ingold, 1988a, b, 1998). These findings militate against the "transitional" nature of delayed-return hunter-gatherers who domesticate plants or herd animals, and instead suggest that these populations fit best within the broader continuum of the hunter-gatherer construct. This construct resists singular definition, but encompasses diverse communities in which the primary mode of production revolves around food procurement, while this mode of production is objectified through the construction of ideologies (*sensu* Shanks and Tilley, 1982).

1.2   Hunters-Gatherers: An Anthropological History

The conceptualization of hunter-gatherers within the academic world has an extended history with pre-Enlightenment roots (Pluciennik, 2002). Specifically, ideations of hunter-gatherers were constructed by Western scholars attempting to contrast economic systems with early forms of capitalism (Barnard, 2014). It is within these writings that a lifestyle of capriciousness was established as the binary opposition to capitalistic society: complex/simple, active/lazy, progressive/regressive, and wealthy/destitute were ways in which the social institutions that are often attributed to hunter-gatherers were compared to industrial states. These contrasts were personified by the infamous epithet of "nasty, brutish, and short" in an attempt to define lifestyles that contrast with industrialized capitalism (Hobbes, 1651). The political philosophy of Jean-Jacques Rousseau depicted hunter-gatherers as an ideal state of human nature. In particular, philosophers such as Rousseau (1754) argued that human morality experienced a zenith in the "primitive" past because these groups were free from the corrupting influences of materiality. While Rousseau clearly held a view of hunter-gatherer cultures that was similar to cultural evolutionists, for example juxtaposing these cultures as intermediate stages between ape-men [sic] and civilization, the idea that these groups held key insights to human morality was novel. This conceptualization of human nature reflects an ideology that is often given the derisive appellation Noble Savage, and in some cultures tied to collective fetishizations of authenticity, where the ability to identify with an indigenous past empowers nationalist revisions of history (Hudson, 2004). Thus, the Romantic depiction of hunter-gatherers serves as the binary opposition to the "nasty, brutish, and short" narrative, yet remains mired in unilineal paradigms that are used to privilege nationalist identities.

Anthropological conceptualizations of hunter-gatherers date to the founding of the discipline. Hunter-gatherer economies were included as the "savagery" stage in the unilineal evolutionary schematic of "savagery, barbarism, and civilization" (Morgan, 1877). These phases described human cultural progress based on subsistence economies, marriage residence, and political organization. The existence of contemporary hunter-gatherers was, however, a confounding variable – how could a progressive world produce populations that represented the lower stages of culture? In *Ancient Society*, Morgan (1877) cites the work of Samuel Morton, suggesting that the apparent stasis of contemporary hunter-gatherers, and specifically American Indian cultures, was explained by inferior brain sizes. Hunter-gatherers were also included in the primitive echelon of Frazer's (1890) unilineal classification of religious belief in human societies. The work argues that the savage mind cannot distinguish between the material and spiritual worlds, and that this worldview is defined based on a belief that human actions control nature.

These anthropological works were not to be outdone by Darwin (1890), who described hunter-gatherers as an initial template for civilization, but erroneously suggested that contemporary hunter-gatherers existed in an arrested state of social development. For example, Darwin (1890) argued that environmental constraints limit cultural progress and cites the impact of cold on Esquimaux [sic] hunter-gatherers as an example. These conceptualizations of hunter-gatherers are contextualized within the paradigm of transmutationism. In particular, numerous examples of how energy and perseverance produce successful, progressive societies are provided, including references to the success of American colonists, and the apparent inheritance of this energetic perseverance by future citizens of the United States.

The response of cultural evolutionists to the existence of contemporary hunter-gatherers is comparable to the approach of early Darwinian naturalists when confronted by creationists about the dearth of fossil evidence for transitional phases (Marks, 2012). Darwinian evolutionists argued that human ethnic groups represented transitional phases leading from African apes to modern civilizations to parry against the argument that fossil evidence was lacking. In so doing, these early evolutionists permitted and even advocated for white European supremacy, when the ethical choice was to acknowledge the veracity of the creationist critique. The same paradox confronted cultural evolutionists when attempting to explain coexistence of industrial nation states and egalitarian hunter-gatherers. Cultural evolutionists argued that contemporary hunter-gatherers existed in a state of arrested development – a context in which cultural and ecological forces acted to produce human communities that relied on food procurement as a primary subsistence economy, but still maintained flexibility in response to the broader cultural and ecological landscape.

The paradigms of cultural evolutionists were questioned by historical particularists who viewed culture, including hunter-gatherers, as a unique process that was governed by historical experience and local knowledge – cultural similarities were seen as a result of diffusion, and environmental factors producing similarity in behavior were discounted or minimized (Boas, 1911). The work of Boas (1911), in particular, sought to combat what might be termed inequalities of complexity by demonstrating porousness in the expression of complexity between "primitive" and "civilized" communities. Historical particularists argued that hunter-gatherers were products of a unique past that helped populations adjust cultural traditions to local circumstances through shared knowledge and/or collective experience. This approach valued the knowledge-base of hunter-gatherer communities as equally important to the knowledge-base of industrialized nations and sought to diminish the idea that human culture existed on a ranked scale.

Cultural ecologists were critical of historical particularism inasmuch as this theoretical paradigm argued that parallels in culture might be useful to disentangling broader patterns of human adaptation to the environment (Steward, 1955). Specifically, facets of shared culture among geographically disparate hunter-gatherers were conceptualized as having a unique origin within communities (one that was part of shared collective knowledge), but could represent a general pattern of adaptation among hunter-gatherers in a broader geographical spectrum. The opportunity to test the hypotheses of cultural ecology on the rich ethnographic record prompted the *Man the Hunter* symposium in 1968. The seminar produced a large edited volume that integrated social, archaeological, and biological approaches to the study of hunter-gatherers (Lee and DeVore, 1968). One of the most important contributions in that volume addressed the integrated and varied lifestyles of hunter-gatherers, arguing that hunter-gatherer biological and cultural variability was part of an integrated pattern of knowledge accumulated into the mind and body during the developmental process (Laughlin, 1968). This essay provided key insights into the concept of human culture as a social tradition (see below) by tracing the developmental and socioecological context for hunting and gathering behavior from a life history perspective.

The contemporary analog to this approach is human behavioral ecology, which evaluates the role of "socioenvironmental" variables in producing behavioral diversity and similarity across a range of human populations (Winterhalder and Smith, 2000). The underlying assumption of this research is that human behavioral choices are optimized by natural selection based on the benefits and costs of behavioral choices within each environment. Winterhalder and Smith (2000) note that human behavioral ecology is distinct from most approaches in cultural anthropology because the approach relies on Neo-Darwinian and hypothetico-deductive reasoning. The work emphasizes the considerable plasticity in human behavioral choices, while simultaneously recognizing that these choices are constrained by environmental context and represent long-term adaptations shaped by natural selection – the currency of choices varies depending on environment (Laland and Brown, 2003). By and large, this approach values environment as a primary driver of socioecological and cultural transformation in hunter-gatherer lifestyles and does not interact with persistence, outside the auspices of evolutionary stable strategies. In addition, behavioral ecology does not differentiate between the deeper processes of change such as internally directed changes that promote sustainability or whole-scale transformations that render previous systems unrecognizable. Finally, behavioral ecology does not interact with the agencies and historical contingencies that structure human interactions with the natural world (Smith, 2013).

While these evolutionary paradigms are important mechanisms for interpreting culture change, the present volume also focuses on the enduring legacy of hunter-gatherer economies and how persistence may facilitate change within socioecological or cultural systems. In addition, the ways in which agency, learning, perception, and worldviews help structure these responses are emphasized (Cannon, 2011). This volume endeavors to demonstrate how hunter-gatherers produced enduring legacies in terms of subsistence (as materialistic and symbolic modes of production) and broader expressions of social identities such as mortuary rituals, embodied components of the self, relationships with nature, and ethnicity. Hunting and gathering requires intentionality and planning, specifically reflecting the individual perception of the environment in which organisms are defined according to essential attributes, and the individual controls interactions with the environment – Ingold (1988a: 274) labels this process "purposive social action," referencing the production of subsistence economy *and* social interactions through hunting and gathering. This approach does not assume any particular social organization is tethered to hunter-gatherer lifestyles, but that the subsistence mode is tied to human relational boundaries. Here, hunter-gatherers are granted a broader agency through intentionality and identities that are symbolically bound to hunting and gathering as a way of life.

Cultural transmission among hunter-gatherers begins at a young age where visual observation, teaching, and copying form the basis for social learning (Jordan, 2014; Kamei, 2005; Muraki, 1999). Cultural transmission is seen as a conserved process and coherence of social traditions may follow predictable pathways. Items of a strictly functional purpose are more frequently subjected to modification in construction, while items with high levels of ritual or symbolic value as well as those with design constraints have greater levels of coherence (Jordan, 2014). Within this framework, culture is seen as having a high level of ontological fidelity, and this fidelity likely helps maintain cultural transmission across generations. Of course, as pointed out by evolutionary ecologists, all populations are challenged by cultural and ecological imperatives that threaten survival. Under these circumstances, anthropologists must understand how these challenges are met. However, the dynamics of change are complex, and the deeply ontological nature of behavioral learning suggests that the framework for collective social action has both internal and external mediators. Cultures may transform or persist, and within persistence and transformation, the processes must be differentiated as having internal or external mediation.

Resilience theory provides an additional and useful theoretical lens through which hunter-gatherers must be evaluated and one that places hunter-gatherers within the framework of collective social action. The development of the resilience paradigm is associated with ecological systems theory, where this paradigm was first derived as an alternative to the study of extinction (Holling, 1973). The term resilience references the capacity of relationships within a system to absorb external stressors and persist (Holling, 1973). Examples of ecological resilience include circumstances in which organisms encounter changing landscapes, yet demonstrate persistence in terms of population size or foraging strategies. Socioecological resilience is the target of a vast majority of studies, and the socioecological system references the mutually dependent relationship formed by humans and the biosphere (Berkes and Folke, 1998). That is, the nature of the biosphere is determined by the behavior of surrounding animals, including humans, while human behavior is, in turn, influenced by the nature of the biosphere. The concept of resilience is often organized into adaptive cycles (Gunderson and Holling, 2002). These cycles are illustrated as a figure-eight, infinity symbol – adaptive cycles are associated with four specific phases: growth (use of the land for natural resources), conservation (accretion of natural resources from the land), release (sudden change within the panarchy[2]), and reorganization (returning to or building new basins of attraction[3]) (Figure 1.1).

Walker *et al.* (2004) differentiated between resilience, adaptability, and transformability as terms that respectively differentiate between *what* is maintained, *how* it is maintained, and the *capacity* to fundamentally alter the system in the face of failure. Thus, resilience focuses on persistence, while adaptation references the broader trade-offs or flexibilities that permit the preservation of cultural or ecological continuity. By contrast, transformability focuses on drastic alterations that render previous socioecological or cultural systems unrecognizable. Models of the adaptive cycle emphasize "revolt" and "remember" phases of reorganization that reproduce or produce newly resilient populations (Folke, 2006). Here, "remember" represents a

---

[2] Panarchy is a term that references the role and source of change within systems, and by turn, influences the capacity for resilience, adaptability, and transformation (Holling and Gunderson, 2002).

[3] Basin of attraction is the region in state space in which a system *tends* to remain (Walker *et al.*, 2004). The term may be used to describe persistent behaviors, socioecological conditions, or landscapes. Basins of attraction are featured during the reorganization phase of the adaptive cycle and may be reproduced or newly produced through transformation.

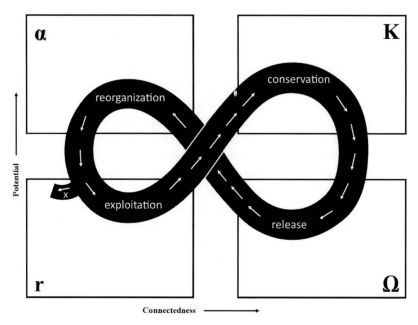

Figure 1.1. Model of the adaptive cycle after Holling and Gunderson (2002). Image produced by Brandie S. Temple.

pattern of adaptability and resilience within the system, while "revolt" represents transformation of the system. Conceptual models of resilience/adaptability and transformation provide a useful way to differentiate these processes (Pearson and Pearson, 2012): Resilience/adaptability is associated with adaptive shifts that are derived from the internal components of system identity. By contrast, transformative change is associated with movement away from the preexisting system, often highlighted by external solutions to problems that make a system untenable.

Archaeological research focuses on sustained time periods, and therefore provides unique contexts for incorporating resilience theory (Redman, 2005). Examples of this incorporation are demonstrated by studies evaluating the persistence of salmonid fishing over a 7000-year period in the Pacific Northwest, as well as those challenging the myth of collapse in some of the most famous anthropological examples of social disintegration (Campbell and Butler, 2010; McAnany and Yoffee, 2012). Overall, the use of resilience theory has great importance in explaining how humans use local knowledge and behavioral plasticity to mitigate the stressors of environmental perturbations, while maintaining unifying themes in cultural identity. The concept is flexible enough that populations are not viewed within the linear vacuum of replacement versus stasis, but instead are seen through a lens of complexity that is willing to grant that cultures experience environmental transitions in myriad ways and behavioral changes permit the persistence of important hallmarks of cultural identity. Thus, the reorganization of populations following environmental change does not necessitate collapse or whole-scale changes to the cultural identity of local populations, but instead revolves around persistence and plasticity: persistence of behaviors that are important to the maintenance of cultural identity and plasticity in behaviors that permit survival in a changing world.

As noted above, a comprehensive study of hunter-gatherers relies heavily on knowledge, historical contingencies, perceptions, and worldviews structuring behavior (Cannon, 2011). In this sense, resilience theory should also be applied to hunter-gatherer cultural systems. The concept of cultural resilience is defined as "the capacity to maintain livelihoods that satisfy material and moral (normative) needs in the face of major environmental or sociopolitical shocks" (Crane, 2010: 2). Cultural resilience frequently interacts with ethnicity as ethnicity references a group of individuals who are defined based on common cultural beliefs, practices, and values (Kent, 2002a). The persistence of ethnic identity, in particular, receives special attention in terms of cultural resilience because these affiliations buffer against stress through the maintenance of broad networks of social support (Clauss-Ehlers *et al.*, 2006). In addition, resilient cultural systems also grant agency to flexibility within socioecological systems or interact with these systems to produce socioecological resilience (Adger, 2000; Daskon, 2010). One way that ethnic identity interacts with resilience theory is through cultural memory (Redman and Kinzig, 2003). Archaeological research has the capacity to uncover evidence for the use of memory in a variety of contexts reflecting the material and symbolic components of social structure in the past, and the deep time perspective afforded to this research is particularly informative regarding persistence and transformation (Redman, 2005).

This volume also explores collapse as an end-point for some adaptive cycles and tries to understand how resilience may be associated with this process. Collapse is defined as a significant and rapid loss of sociopolitical complexity (Tainter, 1988: 4). Collapse is traditionally studied in complex socioeconomic systems, particularly in communities with evidence for massive redistribution networks and state-level governmental structures. However, the increasing number of studies in resilience, transformability, and collapse demonstrate that this process occurs across the spectrum of cultural complexity and also incorporates socioecological and cultural systems (Butzer, 2012; Butzer and Endfield, 2012). Thus, collapse is possible within hunter-gatherer frameworks. Collapse entails deconstruction of the system, usually reductions in complexity or diversity (Tainter, 1988). Populations experience demographic collapse through declining numbers or extinction, sociopolitical collapse in the form of eroded institutional complexity, socioecological collapse through contractions in subsistence diversity, and cultural collapse in the form of lost coherency (Butzer, 2012). Some attempts at exploring collapse emphasize transformation as an important component of this process: "Societal collapse represents transformation at a large social or spatial scale, with long term impact on combinations of interdependent variables" (Butzer and Enfield, 2012: 3628). However, many transformations lead to improved systems, or at the very least, systems that allow populations the ability to continue living within a specific environment, even under severe duress (Hegmon *et al.*, 2008; Pearson and Pearson, 2012). Collapse is, in this sense, differentiated from transformation. In including collapse in this volume it is also important to note that populations experience stress from multiple external agents including disease or aggressive neighboring populations (Solich and Bradtmöller, 2017). Thus, even in circumstances in which populations appear resilient to challenges that arise through ecological perturbation, additional agents may challenge populations in ways that diminish population size and structure.

One important criticism levied upon resilience theory is that the paradigm strongly resembles systems theory, and in fact, initial explorations of resilience theory are derivative of this paradigm (Holling, 1973). Systems theory assumes that a series of interrelated hypotheses may be subsumed under a broad generalization, and that broad generalizations act as a primary starting point for understanding differentiation within organizations (Blau, 1972). This approach relies on a top-down process of deductive reasoning in which the confirmation of hypotheses at higher levels of generalization acts to prove those at lower scales (Hempel and Oppenheim, 1948). Faulseit (2016) points out that resilience theory is differentiated from systems theory by a "bottom-up" approach, addressing interactions of increasing scale. In addition, it is noted that the adaptive cycle includes differentiated systems within the panarchy, specifically how small/rapid and large/slow changes produce varied, often unpredictable outcomes (Faulseit, 2016).

In addition, systems theory views broad generalizations (i.e., systems) as mutually exclusive epi-phenomena linked through independent, increasingly small-scale observations (Blau, 1972; Hempel and Oppenheim, 1948). The strength of this approach is interconnectedness within each system. However, this remains problematic for the practice of anthropology as it presumes that "humanness" is compartmentalized into non-interacting, bounded systems, reinforcing a so-called science–theory divide in the evaluation of human culture in one instance and socioecological systems in the other. By contrast, approaches associated with practice theory focus on human agency as producing and reproducing variation and interaction within and between institutions, ecosystems, and even bodies (Bourdieu, 1972). Resilience theory has addressed this problem, specifically through the introduction of cultural resilience (see above) as an independent *or* interactive agency. Cultural resilience may be found under circumstances of transformation in socioecological systems, demonstrating the persistence of behavior as a social tradition. Cultural resilience may interact with socioecological conditions acting to legitimize transformations in behavior, thus demonstrating flexibility in system function through collective action and agency (Daskon, 2010). Cultural resilience also exists independent of socioecological resilience by responding to social, political, or environmental change through behaviors outside the domain of the socioecological system (Adger, 2000). Socioecological resilience is dependent upon entire cultural systems established around and supported by the biosphere (Berkes and Folke, 1998; Folke, 2006; Walker *et al.*, 2004). In terms of studying hunter-gatherers, the interactive component of the cultural and socioecological system is emphasized as this behavior helps demonstrate the broader production of hunting and gathering through collective social action (*sensu* Ingold, 1988a), or what might be termed the reciprocal relationship between socioecological and cultural practices in hunter-gatherer worlds. In this sense, resilience theory, as applied to bioarchaeological contexts involving hunter-gatherers, interacts with the human element of socioecological and cultural practices.

1.3   Archaeological Analysis of Persistent Hunter-Gatherers and Social Memory

Resilience theory is centered on the concept of persistence, or the ability to thrive in response to perturbations. Numerous archaeological studies (see below) engage with the idea of persistence in socioecological and cultural systems as well as endurance between the two. *The Oxford Handbook of the Archaeology and Anthropology of Hunter-Gatherers* (Cummings *et al.*, 2014) sets forth a series of chapters that outline the persistence of hunter-gather socioecological systems through the agricultural transition in a variety of locations. These chapters represent an important contribution to the study of hunter-gatherer lifeways by demonstrating the longstanding, enduring legacy of hunting and gathering economies across one of the most transformative events in human history. The chapters evaluate hunter-gatherers in terms of subsistence strategies and include novel conceptualizations of the agricultural transition including *in situ* cultural developments that incorporated local hunter-gatherer knowledge of surrounding ecological systems. An entire subsection is devoted to the Neolithization [sic] of Europe, and these works focus on various iterations of a diffusion versus replacement model of agricultural adoption. Many of these works do not directly invoke resilience theory, but the idea of hunter-gatherers as persistent populations as opposed to those groups thriving in a state of arrested development is clear, as is the integration of culture as a social tradition (Cummings, 2014).

Archaeological research also explores the persistence of hunter-gatherers through social memories. Persistent places may be defined as landscapes of renewal where populations migrated into and away from particular locations, often coming together at designated times or for specific purposes (Schlanger, 1992). Social memories are associated with collective population-wide memories of events, places, or individuals that are invoked through various figures such as stories, images, or other sensationalizing experiences (Assman, 1995; Halbwachs, 1925). Persistent hunter-gatherers in North America altered the landscape to construct burial mounds that acted as immediately visible citations of the past, in many cases referencing ancient inhabitants of the landscape during subsequent agricultural periods (e.g., Buikstra and Charles, 1999; Thompson and Pluckhahn, 2010). The powerful nature of cultural memory in the mortuary context is exemplified by the deep roots of the ethnohistorically documented feasting rituals of the Huron and Algonkian people, which have archaeologically visible ties to prehistoric mortuary ritual among earlier Hopewellian people (Carr, 2005).

Archaeological mortuary practices are also deeply tethered to the practice of collective memory and cultural identity in a variety of contexts. Prehistoric Yayoi-period farmers from Japan produced cemeteries with spatial structuring that required funeral processions to walk past earlier burials, demonstrating an acknowledgment of genealogy among these prehistoric populations (Mizoguchi, 2001). In using a macro-regional perspective, Thompson (2010) argues for the production of persistent places in the form of large-scale shell mounds during the southeastern US Middle Archaic as a variable process. These sites were produced through variable temporal rhythms including short-term events repeated over long-term occupations as well as short-term events with evidence for a hiatus between occupations. In a more recent intensive study of the El Montón site on Santa Cruz Island, evidence for persistent occupation is found in dwelling structures, burial practices, feasting, and the accumulation of material debris over a 4000-year period (Gamble, 2017). As a whole, the site preserved large-scale features that were visible from great distances and acted as daily reminders of earlier occupations, with evidence for rituals that reference these ancestral behaviors. In another example, hunter-gatherers along the Okeechobee River Basin, Florida modified local landscapes over a 2000-year period. The persistent nature of this behavior was sustained by the production of resource surpluses across these communities, suggesting interaction between cultural and socioecological resilience (Thompson, 2016). As a whole, archaeological studies of persistent behaviors and landscapes offer an important glimpse into the resilience of past populations – while some of these studies do not reference resilience specifically, the enduring nature of practice across transformative events suggests resilience was an omnipresent theme in the lives and lifestyles of these populations. In some instances, these behaviors collapse in response to drastic changes in the panarchy (e.g., Thompson, 2010), but the overall story is one in which behaviors and places acted to preserve the enduring legacy of ancestors.

1.4   Bioarchaeological Analyses of Hunter-Gatherers

Bioarchaeological research uses human skeletal remains and their associated mortuary contexts to explore the biocultural dimensions of the human past (Buikstra, 1977). A number of bioarchaeological studies evaluate the consequences for culture change among hunter-gatherers, specifically addressing the impact of climate change, ecological variability, hostile environments, and contact on the skeletal manifestations of physiological stress, activity, diet, and disease (Bernal *et al.*, 2007; Cybulski, 1994; Hilton *et al.*, 2014; Hoover and Matsumura, 2008; Lambert, 1993; Lieverse *et al.*, 2007; Merbs, 1983; Temple, 2007; Walker and Lambert, 1989). In addition, morphological analyses of hunter-gatherer skeletal remains elucidate the broader process of functional and climatic adaptation to regional landscapes and subsistence activity (Auerbach, 2014; Stock, 2006; Stock and Pfeiffer, 2001, 2004; Temple and Matsumura, 2011; Weiss, 2003). These projects contribute to a greater understanding of hunter-gatherer diversity and adaptation. Hunter-gatherer communities also have important ceremonial and symbolic components tied to subsistence economies, mortuary ritual, and embodied aspects of identity (Fitzhugh, 2014; Kusaka *et al.*, 2008; Losey, 2010; Losey *et al.*, 2011; Maher *et al.*, 2011; Stojanowski *et al.*, 2014; Temple *et al.*, 2011). The persistence of these behaviors in total is an important target of bioarchaeological inquiry.

The bioarchaeological approach also uses skeletal and dental indicators of stress among hunter-gatherers to evaluate biological and cultural variability across major adaptive transitions. This approach draws upon data collected from hunter-gatherer skeletal remains as a source of comparison. The initial bioarchaeological studies of the agricultural transition found that this period was associated with a degeneration of human well-being, exemplified by increases in dental caries, chronic systemic infection, growth disruption, and metabolic disease when compared to hunter-gatherer skeletal samples (Cohen, 2007; Cohen and Armelagos, 1984; Larsen, 1987, 1995). These findings allowed bioarchaeological research to question the Hobbesian view of civilization, while embracing the romanticized view of hunter-gatherer economies as highly efficient and exuberant communities, a theoretical paradigm resurrected by Sahlins (1968) and provided the appellation *Original Affluent Society*. A spate of later studies questioned the broader applicability of these findings, reporting that growth disruption, dental caries prevalence, evidence for chronic infection, and micronutrient deficiencies did not increase between hunter-gatherers and agriculturalists, and in many cases, agricultural economies acted to diminish local stressors through trade-offs with elevated fertility (Clark *et al.*, 2014; Eshed *et al.*, 2006; Lambert, 2009; Pietrusewsky and Douglas, 2002; Temple, 2010; Temple and Larsen, 2013). The findings of these more recent inquiries suggest that the agricultural transition, and hunter-gatherer biological variation specifically, cannot be categorized into the binary oppositions (healthy/unhealthy, mobile/stationary) created by Enlightenment and Romantic era philosophers. Instead, differences in mobility and well-being between hunter-gatherers and agriculturalists more likely represent regionally specific constellations of biocultural variability that were constrained by local environments. This approach clearly reflects a historical particularist paradigm. However, the idea that these populations experienced a mosaic of cultural adaptations that were guided by local ecologies should not be understated, as it is within the context of these regionally specific events that the broader process of cultural evolution and resilience is observable.

Bioarchaeological research that used hunter-gatherers as a benchmark to measure the relative success of the agricultural transition sought to elucidate the impact of culture change on human biological and cultural variability. Because hunter-gatherers acted as the earliest template for all agricultural societies, hunter-gatherer skeletal samples were invariably incorporated as the "before" snapshot in the range of human biocultural variation. The consequence of this paradigm for hunter-gatherers is unfortunate. Hunter-gatherers were inadvertently treated as a progressive phase leading toward agricultural economies, existing as a novelty or sample by which to measure the relative success of agriculture. While it is a truism that all agricultural and state-level societies are traceable to hunter-gatherer beginnings, it does not follow that an agricultural revolution is the only attainable form of cultural evolution available to hunter-gatherer communities (Bettinger, 1991; Fitzhugh, 2003; Jordan, 2014; Kent, 2002a; Marlowe, 2002; Steward, 1955).

The social history of bioarchaeology explains the inadvertent relegation of hunter-gatherers to "before" snapshots in the story of human evolution. Bioarchaeology was developed as a contextual application of skeletal biology – it incorporated the theoretical paradigms of cultural ecology and processual archaeology to data collected using the methods of skeletal biology and paleopathology (Armelagos, 2003; Buikstra, 1977). This approach represented a radical departure from the essentialist, racial proscriptions of early twentieth-century skeletal biology, and this period of intellectual development represented the rise of a new theoretical paradigm following the intellectual crises of racial anthropology. The approach was largely successful as bioarchaeological research increasingly emphasized hypothesis testing and a process-based approach – one interested in testing the impacts of culture change and evaluating evidence for social complexity (Larsen, 2005). At the same time, the new approach received criticism for failing to interact with archaeological context (Goldstein, 2006) and an overreliance on a binary approach (positive/negative) to understanding the consequences of culture change (Temple and Goodman, 2014). These critiques should be reconciled against the idea that modern bioarchaeological theory was born out of a paradigm that privileged the causes and consequences of culture change, while unintentionally discounting the importance of persistence or interrogating the deeper internal versus external nature of these changes. In this sense, past bioarchaeological treatments of hunter-gatherers represent a historically progressive event, but one that was tethered to a cultural ecological paradigm. Despite this shortcoming, past bioarchaeological treatments of hunter-gatherers represent an important starting point for interrogating the evolution and endurance of hunter-gatherers as these approaches embraced hypothesis testing and resistance of racist typologies.

Bioarchaeological evidence for adaptation and resilience in the face of ecological disturbance is reported and represents an important theoretical foundation for ideas expressed in this volume, though not all of these studies explicitly interact with resilience theory (Baker and Kealhofer, 1996; Hoover and Hudson, 2016; Klaus and Tam, 2009a). An interest in adaptation *and* resilience in bioarchaeological context first appears in an edited volume that sought to highlight the idea that American Indians were not passive actors in the process of contact (Baker and Kealhofer, 1996). Instead, American Indians adapted to the culture changes associated with European colonization of the New World, and in many cases experienced persistence of cultural identities. Baker and Kealhofer (1996) argue that culture change does not necessitate collapse, and that adaptation combined with persistence is a normative hallmark of such processes.

In early historic Peru, the chapel of San Pedro de Mórrope yields evidence for mortuary practices that demonstrate the persistence of Moche ceremonial behavior within colonial rituals (Klaus and Tam, 2009a). Resilience of local beliefs and integration into Catholic doctrine represents a process of ethnogenesis for the colonial Muchik people who actively manipulated traditional beliefs during a time of unprecedented and generally negative social, political, economic, and ecological change. It is important to note that this trend is documented during a period of increased systemic stress. Klaus and Tam (2009b) report evidence for increased growth suppression in prepubertal children, chronic infectious disease, and suppressed fertility.

Thus, this work documents persistence of culture in increasingly vulnerable popula-tions. The work (Klaus and Tam, 2009a) also emphasizes ethnogenesis, but the merging of identities found in the construction of colonial Muchik culture certainly represents the enduring legacy of earlier Moche communities.

More recently, resilience was explored among prehistoric Jomon foragers from northwestern Kyushu, Japan in relation to the introduction of wet-rice agriculture (Hoover and Hudson, 2016). The work uses archaeological evidence for the persist-ence of Jomon hunting and gathering for several centuries into the Yayoi cultural phase. Few changes in the frequency of dental and skeletal indicators of stress are reported during a period in which agricultural economies were introduced to the region from Northeast Asia. These results suggest that the persistence of an autono-mous Jomon culture forestalled the shifts in stress patterning that are common in many studies of the agricultural transition (e.g., Cohen and Armelagos, 1984; Larsen, 1987, 1995) – here, similarities in stress experiences are used to evidence resilience on the part of indigenous Jomon cultures across the transition to wet-rice agriculture. Findings reported by Hoover and Hudson (2016) are integral to the themes of this volume because this work demonstrates that the replacement of hunter-gatherer economies is not an inevitable result of contact with agricultural populations and that autonomous hunter-gatherer cultures resist biocultural changes associated with agricultural economies.

Taken as a whole, findings from these studies suggest that the application of resilience theory to bioarchaeological research provides an opportunity to under-stand how populations absorb the stressors of cultural and ecological transitions and persist or transform. Bioarchaeological evidence of behavior elicited through studies of diet, mobility, stress, disease, mortality, and/or mortuary practices may provide evidence for sudden/drastic or slow/gradual behavioral changes and the extent to which such changes involve internal or external mediations of the system. In particular, populations are often challenged by abrupt cultural or ecological disruptions, and bioarchaeological research has the capacity to explain where shifts occur in socioecological and cultural systems in response to stressors and whether internal or external remedies are sought.

Bioarchaeological research can also evaluate precariousness. Precariousness refer-ences the threshold for change within a socioecological or cultural system (Walker *et al.*, 2004). Bioarchaeological evidence for the stressors absorbed as well as mortal-ity risk may provide evidence for latitude (maximum change a system may sustain) or resistance (the relative ease or difficulty in changing a system). Specifically, the circumstances in which evidence for stress is found may increase the precariousness of a population yet still promote resilience and adaptability through varying degrees of latitude and resistance. Stressors that exact mortality may help push populations beyond this threshold and promote transformation as the system becomes untenable.

Finally, bioarchaeologists have the capacity to identify collapse and understand how this process fits within resilience theory. Bioarchaeologists may highlight the context for collapse and transformation by evaluating rigidity and vulnerabil-ity. Rigidity and diminished quality of life may increase the precariousness of socioecological and cultural systems and increase the likelihood of collapse as these populations may be less responsive to sudden or drastic changes within the panarchy (Folke, 2006; Hegmon *et al.*, 2008; Walker *et al.*, 2004). Bioarchaeological studies may also see evidence for persistence following collapse or transformation, adding further complexity to the issue of culture change. These studies dare to ask if collapse is ever truly observed (McAnay and Yoffee, 2010).

1.5   Edited Volume Organization

The chapters in this volume provide an initial step in identifying how bioarchaeological research has the capacity to answer questions surrounding resilience of socioecological and cultural systems. The volume is organized into three sections: socioecological resilience, cultural resilience, and collapse. These works address how human populations face challenges to socioecological and cultural systems. Internal and external changes represent trade-offs between resilience/adaptability and transformability, while in some cases collapse of the system reveals underlying vulnerabilities that were imposed by drastic change.

Socioecological resilience is explored by a number of chapters in this volume and is associated with patterns of diet and mobility (Pfieffer and Harrington, Bernal *et al.*, Schulting, Temple, Cameron and Stock). Pfieffer and Harrington provide a broad overview of lifestyle including environmental stress exposure, interpersonal violence, and habitual activity in Late Stone Age hunter-gatherers from the South African Cape. The work uses human skeletal remains to provide a *longue durée* viewpoint on the capacity for population persistence, survival of tradition, and the environmentally specific nature of adaptation in groups from this region. The work also seeks to place variation in morphology such as body size and skeletal growth in the context of a resilient population, one in which environmental challenges were abated by material technology. Bernal *et al.* explore questions of socioecological and demographic resilience using zooarchaeological data and mitochondrial DNA analysis during the Pleistocene–Holocene transition in Patagonia. Often referenced based on demographic collapse during the late nineteenth and early twentieth centuries, this work explains how populations adapted to change during intense climatic oscillations while maintaining the demographic character of the population over an approximately 10 000-year period. Importantly, the work speaks to the broader themes of resilience/adaptability and transformation by exploring how shifts in local behaviors helped maintain population survival. Evidence for persistence in these indigenous hunter-gatherers is of particular importance since European colonialism wrought incredible suffering and eventual extinction in this region. In Northwestern Europe, Schulting explores how populations exposed to climatic changes and agricultural economies responded to these challenges. Here, Schulting uses stable isotope analysis to understand how flexibility and rigidity in dietary behavior may be associated with persistence and transformation of socioecological systems. Thus, the work speaks to how the internal systems of populations may render these groups vulnerable to change or permit persistence in changing environments.

In another instance, Temple uses dental caries prevalence and long bone diaphyseal morphology to explore questions regarding resilience/adaptability or transformation of socioecological systems in response to climatic cooling during the Late/Final phase of the Jomon period. The work seeks to understand whether these populations experienced whole-scale change in terms of diet and mobility patterns, or if changes were experienced within the internal parameters of the preexisting socioecological system. In addition, archaeological mortuary analysis is used to understand whether shifts in burial practices represent transformation of the cultural system, or whether these changes were grounded in internally resilient components of the Jomon socioecological system. Finally, tooth extraction patterns between the two phases of the Jomon period are also used to explore questions regarding how ethnic identity may persist across time and space and how collective cultural memory produces cultural resilience. Cameron and Stock explore how long bone diaphyseal morphology corresponds to differing phases of the adaptive cycle during the introduction of herding economies to South African hunter-gatherers. The work seeks to characterize functional adaptation to hunting and gathering environments as a baseline for diaphyseal morphology. The chapter then seeks to differentiate between resilience/adaptability and transformation during the arrival of herding practices from southern Africa, particularly as it corresponds to habitual activity.

Cultural resilience as expressed through mortuary practices, dietary behavior, skeletal indicators of stress and disease, mobility, and evidence for interpersonal violence is also explored by a variety of chapters (Da-Gloria and Bueno, Latham and Coupland, Bornemann and Gamble, Stojanowski, Justice and Temple, and Bartelink *et al.*). Da-Gloria and Bueno use bioarchaeological data to explore the question of persistent places and resilience in the hunter-gatherers from the Lagoa Santa karst formation in Brazil. This geological formation was continuously, though variably, occupied over a 7000-year period, and populations thriving within this landscape between 9000 and 7500 BP left evidence for intensive mortuary programs. The chapter utilizes these skeletal remains to evaluate bioarchaeological evidence for stress, diet, disease, and interpersonal violence. These data help explain whether the populations of this region bear similar bioarchaeological signatures to other persistent hunter-gatherers, or if there are unique bioarchaeological signatures in the Lagoa Santa remains that are particular to time and space. In addition, the chapter challenges interpretations of abandonment of the region with archaeological evidence for changes in territorial strategies aimed at maintaining persistence of place.

Bornemann and Gamble evaluate cultural resilience in prehistoric indigenous populations from California during the earliest stages of contact with European colonialists using archaeological mortuary analysis. The work draws upon theoretical paradigms emphasizing socioeconomic inequality as well as ritual and symbol in the structuring of these behaviors, and explores how these rituals shifted due to interaction with new cultures, yet remained anchored to preexisting cultural systems.

Stojanowski approaches resilience in a sample of hunter-gatherers from the Gobero paleolake formation in Niger through the evaluation of dietary practices as an embodied form of cultural identity. The work compares oral indicators of diet and disease between Early and Middle Holocene occupations of the sites to one another and three pastoralist economies to understand whether a dietary shift to pastoralism is possible to detect. The work incorporates archaeological evidence for diet and ritual practice to further tease apart this question, focusing on the idea that the hunting and gathering/pastoralism dichotomy is a deeper reflection of cultural practices.

Letham and Coupland evaluate lavish burial practices in hunter-gatherers from the Pacific Northwest to understand whether mortuary ritual among these populations helped promote cultural resilience. Hunter-gatherers from the Pacific Northwest Coast are well known for lavish ceremonial practices that include ritual displays of wealth through gift giving and disposal of material items. These ceremonies often manifested as funerary rituals, and the chapter by Letham and Coupland explores how these rituals promoted social stability during times of environmental stress and social turmoil. Thus, the chapter seeks to demonstrate that funerary rituals acted as a primary way to reinforce and perpetuate cultural traditions in these hunter-gatherers.

Justice and Temple use archaeological mortuary practices to explore the concept of cultural resilience following population migration away from, and back to, Point Hope, Alaska. These migrations resulted in the production of the Tigara culture, a population event associated with ethnogenesis between Ipiutak and Birnirk cultures. The chapter focuses on Ipiutak and Tigara pre-adult skeletal remains and mortuary treatment. The chapter tests the hypothesis that the two populations demonstrate a shared disposition toward the use of mortuary symbols that reflect a reciprocal relationship between hunting and gathering and cultural behavior, as well as the possibility of a shared spiritual landscape. In addition, the chapter tests a second hypothesis that predicts the ontology of personhood was similar between the two groups and that these similarities will be reflected in the archaeological mortuary record.

Bartelink and colleagues use skeletal indicators of interpersonal violence to challenge long-held assumptions regarding the relationship between violence and environmental challenges. Here, the work evaluates evidence for violence from contexts of diminished ecological productivity (Little Ice Age) as well as during periods of social turmoil associated with the introduction of new cultural traditions between the Early and Middle periods. Comparing evidence for interpersonal violence over time and space ultimately helps to explain how socioecological resilience and drastic cultural transformation may impact the expression of violent behavior.

Population collapse and extinction is explored by the final two chapters. The Sadlermiut Inuit people were lost to epidemic disease waves in the early twentieth century. The chapter by Merbs provides bioarchaeological, archaeological, and ethnohistorical evidence for the identity, subsistence economy, behavior, and disease experience of the Sadlermiut population. These data represent the culmination of more than 50 years of research among these hunter-gatherers. The work establishes evidence for isolation and intensification in socioecological practices, while documenting demographic collapse. In a second case, Littleton provides a bioarchaeological and ethnohistoric account of demographic and cultural collapse among the Australian Aboriginal populations of the Western Riverina. The chapter uses bioarchaeological and ethnohistorical accounts to portray a population that produced a highly resilient socioecological and cultural system. Bioarchaeological and ethnohistoric evidence is presented to understand how contact with Europeans eroded resilience within these populations, leading to collapse. These works strongly refute notions of vulnerability rooted in cultural evolutionist paradigms surrounding collapse, vulnerability, and technology. Instead, these chapters are included to illustrate that longstanding, intensive adaptation to a highly specialized environment and diminishment of resilience through colonial practices established the context for demographic collapse in these populations. It should be emphasized that in both instances, Littleton and Merbs effectively portray populations that were well adapted to harsh ecological conditions. Yet in both circumstances, collapse was accelerated by newly introduced agents (disease and aggressive colonization) that disrupted and diminished population size and structure. Thus, cycles of resilience are complex and must be considered across multi-causal states.

References

Adger, W. N. (2000). Social and ecological resilience: Are they related? *Progress in Human Geography*, **24**, 347–364.

Armelagos, G. J. (2003). Bioarchaeology as anthropology. *Archaeological Papers of the American Anthropological Association*, **13**, 27–41.

Assman, J. (1995). Collective memory and cultural identity. *New German Critique*, **65**, 123–133.

Atuy, M. T. (1997). Coexistence with nature and the "Third Philosophy": Learning from the spirit of the Ainu. In T. Yamada and T. Irimoto, eds., *Circumpolar Animism and Shamanism*. Sapporo: Hokkaido University Press, pp. 3–8.

Auerbach, B. M. (2014). Morphologies from the edge: Perspectives on biological variation among the late Holocene inhabitants of the northwestern North American Arctic. In C. E. Hilton, B. M. Auerbach, and L. W. Cowgill, eds., *The Foragers of Point Hope: The Biology and Archaeology of Humans on the Edge of the Alaskan Arctic*. Cambridge: Cambridge University Press, pp. 235–265.

Baker, B. J. and Kealhofer, L. (1996). Assessing the impact of European contact on aboriginal populations. In B. J. Baker and L. Kealhofer, eds., *Bioarchaeology of Native American Adaptation in Spanish Borderlands*. Gainesville, FL: University Press of Florida, pp. 1–14.

Barnard, A. (2014). Defining hunter-gatherers: Enlightenment, Romantic, and social evolutionary perspectives. In V. Cummings, P. Jordan, and M. Zvelebil, eds., *The Oxford Handbook of the Archaeology and Anthropology of Hunter-Gatherers*. Oxford: Oxford University Press, pp. 43–54.

Berkes, F. and Folke, C., eds. (1998). *Linking Social and Ecological Systems: Management Practices and Social Mechanisms for Building Resilience*. Cambridge: Cambridge University Press.

Bernal, V., Novellino, P., Gonzalez, P. N., *et al.* (2007). Role of wild plant foods among Late Holocene hunter-gatherers from Central and North Patagonia (South America): An approach from dental evidence. *American Journal of Physical Anthropology*, **133**, 1047–1059.

Bettinger, R. L. (1991). *Hunter-Gatherers: Archaeological and Evolutionary Theory*. New York, NY: Springer.

Binford, L. R. (1981). Willow smoke and dogs' tails: Hunter-gatherer settlement systems and archaeological site formation. *American Antiquity*, **45**, 4–20.

Blau, P. M. (1972). A formal theory of differentiation in organizations. *American Sociological Review*, 35, 201–218.

Boas, F. (1911). *The Mind of Primitive Man*. New York, NY: MacMillan.

Bourdieu, P. (1972). *Outline of a Theory of Practice*. Cambridge: Cambridge University Press.

Buikstra, J. E. (1977). Biocultural dimensions of archaeological study: A regional perspective. In R. L. Blakely, ed., *Biocultural Adaptation in Prehistoric America*. Athens, GA: University of Georgia Press, pp. 67–84.

Buikstra, J. E. and Charles, D. K. (1999). Centering the ancestors: Cemeteries, mounds, and sacred landscapes of the North American midcontinent. In W. Ashmore and A. B. Knapp, eds., *Archaeologies of Landscape: Contemporary Perspectives*. Oxford: Blackwell Publishers, pp. 201–228.

Butzer, K. W. (2012). Collapse, environment, and society. *Proceedings of the National Academy of Sciences*, 109, 3632–3639.

Butzer, K. W. and Endfield, G. H. (2012). Critical perspectives on historical collapse. *Proceedings of the National Academy of Sciences*, 109, 3628–3631.

Campbell, S. K. and Butler, V. L. (2010). Archaeological evidence for resilience of Pacific Northwest salmon populations and the socioecological system over the last ~7500 years. *Ecology and Society*, 15, 1.

Cannon, A. (2011). Introduction. In A. Cannon, ed., *Structured Worlds: The Archaeology of Hunter-Gatherer Thought and Action*. London: Routledge. pp. 1–10.

Carr, C. (2005). Scioto Hopewell ritual gatherings: A review and discussion of previous interpretations and data. In C. Carr and D. T. Case, eds., *Gathering Hopewell: Society, Ritual, and Ritual Interaction*. New York, NY: Kluwer Academic/Plenum Publishing, pp. 463–469.

Clark, A. I., Tayles, N., and Halcrow, S. (2014). Aspects of health in prehistoric mainland Southeast Asia: indicators of stress in response to the intensification of rice agriculture. *American Journal of Physical Anthropology*, 153, 484–495.

Clauss-Ehlers, C. S., Yang, Y-T. T., and Chen, W-C. J. (2006). Resilience from childhood stressors: The role of cultural resilience, ethnic identity, and gender identity. *Journal of Infant, Child, and Adolescent Psychotherapy*, 5, 124–138.

Cohen, M. N. (2007). Introduction. In M. N. Cohen and G. Crane-Kramer, eds., *Ancient Health: Skeletal Indicators of Agricultural and Economic Intensification*. Gainesville, FL: University Press of Florida, pp. 10–19.

Cohen, M. N. and Armelagos, G. J. (1984). Paleopathology at the origin of agriculture: Editors' summation. In M. N. Cohen and G. J. Armelagos, eds., *Paleopathology at the Origins of Agriculture*. Orlando, FL: Academic Press, pp. 585–602.

Crane, T. A. (2010). Of models and meanings: Cultural resilience in social-ecological systems. *Ecology and Society*, 15, 19.

Crawford, G. (2006). East Asian plant domestication. In M. Stark, ed., *Archaeology of Asia*. New York, NY: Wiley-Blackwell, pp. 77–95.

Crawford, G. W. (2008). The Jomon in early agriculture discourse: Issues arising from Matsui, Kanehara, and Peterson. *World Archaeology*, 40, 445–465.

Cummings, V. (2014). Hunting and gathering in a farmers' world. In V. Cummings, P. Jordan, and M. Zvelebil, eds., *The Oxford Handbook of the Archaeology and Anthropology of Hunter-Gatherers*. Oxford: Oxford University Press, pp. 767–786.

Cummings, V., Jordan, P., and Zvelebil, M., eds. (2014). *The Oxford Handbook of the Archaeology and Anthropology of Hunter-Gatherers*. Oxford: Oxford University Press.

Cybulski, J. (1994). Culture change, demographic history, and health and disease on the Northwest Coast. In C. S. Larsen and G. R. Milner, eds., *In the Wake of Contact*. New York, NY: Wiley-Liss, pp. 75–85.

Da-Gloria, P. and Larsen, C. S. (2014). Oral health of the Paleoamericans of Lagoa Santa, central Brazil. *American Journal of Physical Anthropology*, 154, 11–26.

Darwin, C. (1890). *The Descent of Man and Selection in Relation to Sex*. London: John Murray, Albemarle Street.

Daskon, C. D. (2010). Cultural resilience: The roles of cultural traditions in sustaining rural livelihoods – a case study from rural Kandyan villages in Central Sri Lanka. *Sustainability*, 2, 1080–1100.

Eshed, V., Gopher A., and Hershkovitz, I. (2006). Tooth wear and dental pathology at the advent of agriculture: New evidence from the Levant. *American Journal of Physical Anthropology*, 130, 145–159.

Faulseit, R. K. (2016). Collapse, resilience, and transformation in complex societies: Modeling trends and understanding diversity. In R. K. Faulseit, ed., *Beyond Collapse: Archaeological Perspectives on Resilience, Revitalization, and Transformation in Complex Societies*. Carbondale, IL: Southern Illinois University Press, pp. 3–26.

Fitzhugh, B. (2003). *The Evolution of Complex Hunter-Gatherers of the North Pacific*. Berlin: Kluwer Academic/Plenum Publishers.

Fitzhugh, W. (2014). The Ipiutak spirit-scape: An archaeological phenomenon. In C. E. Hilton, B. M. Auerbach, and L. W. Cowgill, eds., *The Foragers of Point Hope: The Biology and Archaeology of Humans on the Edge of the Alaskan Arctic*. Cambridge: Cambridge University Press, pp. 266–290

Folke, C. (2006). Resilience: The emergence of a perspective for social-ecological systems analyses. *Global Environmental Change*, 16, 253–267.

Frazer, J. G. (1890). *The Golden Bough*. London: MacMillan.

Gamble, L. (2017). Feasting, ritual practices, social memory, and persistent places: New interpretations of shell mounds in Southern California. *American Antiquity*, 82, 427–451.

Goldstein, L. (2006). Mortuary analysis and bioarchaeology. In J. E. Buikstra and L. A. Beck, eds., *Bioarchaeology: A Contextual Approach*. Amsterdam: Elsevier, pp. 375–388.

Halbwachs, M. (1925). *Les Cadres Sociaux de la Mémoire*. Paris: Librairie Félix Alcan.

Harris, D. R. (1969). Agricultural systems, ecosystems, and the origins of agriculture. In P. J. Ucko and G. W. Dimbleby, eds., *The Domestication and Exploitation of Plants and Animals*. London: University of London, Institute of Archaeology, pp. 3–15.

Hayden, B. (1995). Pathways to power: Principles to creating socioeconomic inequalities. In T. D. Price and G. M. Feinman, eds., *Foundations of Social Inequality*. New York, NY: Plenum Press, pp. 15–86.

Hegmon, M., Peeples, M. A., Kinzig, A. P., et al. (2008). Social transformation and its human costs in the Prehispanic U.S. Southwest. *American Anthropologist*, 110, 313–324.

Hempel, C. G. and Oppenheim, P. (1940). Studies in the logic of explanation. *Philosophy and Science*, 15, 135–175.

Hilton, C. E., Ogilvie, M. D., Czarniecki, M. D., et al. (2014). Postcranial pathological lesions in precontact Ipiutak and Tigara skeletal remains of Point Hope, Alaska. In C. E. Hilton, B. M. Auerbach, and L. W. Cowgill, eds., *The Foragers of Point Hope: The Biology and Archaeology of Humans on the Edge of the Alaskan Arctic*. Cambridge: Cambridge University Press, pp. 138–180.

Hobbes, T. (1651). *Leviathan*. London: Andrew Crooke.

Holling, C. S. (1973). Resilience and stability of ecological systems. *Annual Review of Ecological Systems*, 4, 1–23.

Holling, C. S. and Gunderson, L. H. (2002). Resilience and adaptive cycles. In L. H. Gunderson and C. S. Holling, eds., *Panarchy: Understanding Transformations in Human and Natural Systems*. Washington, DC: Island Press, pp. 25–62.

Hoover, K. C. and Hudson, M. J. (2016). Resilience in prehistoric persistent hunter-gatherers in northwestern Kyushu, Japan as assessed by population health. *Quaternary International*, 405B, 22–33.

Hoover, K. C. and Matsumura H. (2008). Temporal variation and interaction between nutritional and developmental instability in prehistoric Japanese populations. *American Journal of Physical Anthropology*, **137**, 469–478.

Hudson, M. J. (2004). Foragers as fetish in modern Japan. *Hunter-Gatherers of the North Pacific Rim: Senri Ethnological Studies*, **63**, 263–274.

Humphrey, L. T., DeGroote, I., Morales, J., *et al.* (2014). Earliest evidence for caries and exploitation of starchy plant foods in Pleistocene hunter-gatherers from Morocco. *Proceedings of the National Academy of Sciences*, **111**, 954–959.

Ingold, T. (1988a). Notes on the foraging mode of production. In T. Ingold, D. Riches, and J. Woodburn, eds., *Hunters and Gatherers 1: History, Evolution, and Social Change*. Oxford: Berg, pp. 269–285.

Ingold, T. (1988b). *The Appropriation of Nature*. Iowa City, IA: University of Iowa.

Ingold, T. (1998). *The Perception of the Environment: Essays on Livelihood, Dwelling, and Skill*. London: Routledge.

Jordan, P. D. (2014). *Technology as Human Social Tradition: Cultural Transmission among Hunter-Gatherers*. Berkeley, CA: University of California Press.

Kamei, N. (2005). Play among the Baka children in Cameroon. In B. S. Hewlett and M. B. Lamb, eds., *Hunter-Gatherer Childhoods: Evolutionary, Developmental, and Cultural Perspectives*. New Brunswick, NJ: Aldine Publishing Company, pp. 343–362.

Kelly, R. L. (1995). *The Foraging Spectrum*. Washington, DC: Smithsonian Institution Press.

Kent, S. (2002a). Interethnic encounters of the first kind: An introduction. In S. Kent, ed., *Ethnicity, Hunter-Gatherers, and the "Other": Association or Assimilation in Africa*. Washington, DC: Smithsonian Institution Press, pp. 1–27.

Kent, S., ed. (2002b). *Ethnicity, Hunter-Gatherers, and the "Other": Association or Assimilation in Africa*. Washington, DC: Smithsonian Institution Press.

Klaus, H. D. and Tam M. E. (2009a). Surviving contact: Biological transformation, burial, and ethnogenesis in the colonial Lambayeque Valley of North Coast Peru. In K. J. Knudson and C. M. Stojanowski, eds., *Bioarchaeology and Identity in the Americas*. Gainesville, FL: University Press of Florida, pp. 126–154.

Klaus, H. D. and Tam M. E. (2009b). Contact in the Andes: Bioarchaeology of systemic stress in colonial Mórrope, Peru. *American Journal of Physical Anthropology*, **138**, 356–368.

Kusaka, S., Ikarashi, T., Hyodo, F., *et al.* (2008). Variability in stable isotope ratios in two Late-Final Jomon communities in the Tokai coastal region and its relation to sex and ritual tooth ablation. *Anthropological Science*, **116**, 171–181.

Laland, K. N. and Brown, G. R. (2003). *Sense and Nonsense: Evolutionary Perspectives on Human Behavior*. Oxford: Oxford University Press.

Lambert, P. M. (1993). Health in prehistoric populations of the Channel Islands. *American Antiquity*, **58**, 509–522.

Lambert, P. M. (2009). Health versus fitness: Competing themes in the origins and spread of agriculture. *Current Anthropology*, **50**, 603–608.

Larsen, C. S. (1987). Bioarchaeological intepretations of subsistence economy and behavior from human skeletal remains. In M. B. Schiffer, ed., *Advances in Archaeological Method and Theory*. New York, NY: Academic Press, pp. 339–445.

Larsen, C. S. (1995). Biological changes in human populations with agriculture. *Annual Review of Anthropology*, **24**, 185–214.

Larsen, C. S. (2005). Description, hypothesis testing, and conceptual advances in physical anthropology: Have we moved on? In M. A. Little and K. A. R. Kennedy, eds., *Histories of American Physical Anthropology in the Twentieth Century*. Lanham, MD: Lexington Books, pp. 243–242.

Laughlin, W. S. (1968). Hunting: An integrating biobehavioral system and its evolutionary importance. In R. B. Lee and I. DeVore, eds., *Man the Hunter*. Chicago, IL: Aldine Publishing Company, pp. 304–320.

Lee, R. B. and Daly, R. (1993). Foragers and others. In R. B. Lee and R. Daly, eds., *The Cambridge Encyclopedia of Hunters and Gatherers*. Cambridge: Cambridge University Press, pp. 1–19.

Lee, R. B. and DeVore, I., eds. (1968). *Man the Hunter*. Chicago, IL: Aldine Publishing Company.

Lieverse, A. R., Link, D. W., Bazaliiskii, V. I., *et al.* (2007). Dental health indicators of adaptation and culture change in Siberia's Cis-Baikal. *American Journal of Physical Anthropology*, **134**, 323–339.

Losey, R. (2010). Animism as a means of exploring local fishing structures on Willapa Bay, Washington, U.S.A. *Cambridge Archaeological Journal*, **20**, 17–32.

Losey, R., Bazaliiskii, V. I., Garvie-Loc, S., *et al.* (2011). Canids as persons: Early Neolithic dog and wolf burials, Cis-Baikal, Siberia. *Journal of Anthropological Archaeology*, **30**, 174–189.

Maher, L., Stock, J. T., Finney, S., *et al.* (2011). A unique human–fox burial from a Pre-Natufian cemetery in the Levant (Jordan). *PLoS One*, **6**, e15815.

Marks, J. (2012). Why be against Darwin? Creationism, racism, and the roots of anthropology. *Yearbook of Anthropology*, **149**, 95–104.

Marlowe, F. (2002). Why the Hadza are still hunter-gatherers. In S. Kent, ed., *Ethnicity, Hunter-Gatherers, and the "Other": Association or Assimilation in Africa*. Washington, DC: Smithsonian Institution Press, pp. 247–275.

McAnany, P. A. and Yoffee, N., eds. (2012). *Questioning Collapse: Human Resilience, Ecological Vulnerability, and the Aftermath of Empire*. Cambridge: Cambridge University Press.

Merbs, C. F. (1983). *Patterns of Activity-Induced Pathology in a Canadian Inuit Population*. Ottawa: Archaeological Survey of Canada.

Mizoguchi, K. (2001). Time and genealogical consciousness in the mortuary practices of the Yayoi period. *Journal of East Asian Archaeology*, **3**, 173–197.

Morgan, L. H. (1877). *Ancient Society*. New York, NY: Henry Holt and Company.

Muraki, M. (1999). Ainu children's play. In W. Fitzhugh and C. O. Dubreuil, eds., *Ainu: Spirit of a Northern People*. Washington, DC: Smithsonian Institution Press, pp. 246–247.

Pearson, L. J. and Pearson, C. J. (2012). Letter: Societal collapse or transformation, and resilience. *Proceedings of the National Academy of Sciences*, **109**, E2030–E2031.

Pietrusewsky, M. and Douglas, M. T. (2002). Intensification of agriculture at Ban Chiang: Is there evidence from the skeletons? *Asian Perspectives*, **40**, 157–178.

Pluciennik, M. (2002). The invention of hunter-gatherers in seventeenth-century Europe. *Archaeological Dialogues*, **9**, 98–118.

Redman, C. R. (2005). Resilience theory in archaeology. *American Anthropologist*, **107**, 70–77.

Redman, C. L. and Kinzig, A. P. (2003). Resilience of past landscapes: Resilience theory, society, and the *Longue Durée. Ecology and Society*, **7**, 14.

Rindos, D. (1984). *The Origins of Agriculture: An Evolutionary Perspective*. Orlando, FL: Academic Press.

Rousseau, J. J. (1754). *Discours sur l'Origine et Les Fondemens de l'Inégalité parmi les Hommes*. Amsterdam: Marc Michel Rev.

Rowley-Conwy, P. A. and Layton, R. H. (2011). Foraging and farming as niche construction: Stable and unstable adaptations. *Philosophical Transactions of the Royal Society B: Biological Sciences*, **366**, 849–862.

Sahlins, M. A. (1968). Notes on the original affluent society. In R. B. Lee and I. DeVore, eds., *Man the Hunter*. Chicago, IL: Aldine Publishing Company, pp. 85–88.

Schlanger, S. H. (1992). Recognizing persistent places in Anasazi settlement systems. In J. Rossignol and L. Wandsnider, eds., *Space, Time, and Archaeological Landscapes*. New York, NY: Plenum Press, pp. 91–113.

Shanks, M. and Tilley, C. (1982). Ideology, symbolic power, and ritual communication: A reinterpretation of Neolithic mortuary practices. In I. Hodder, ed., *Symbolic and Structural Archaeology*. Cambridge: Cambridge University Press, pp. 129–154.

Smith, E. A. (2013). Agency and adaptation: New directions in evolutionary anthropology. *Annual Review of Anthropology*, 42, 103–120.

Solich, M. and Bradtmöller M. (2017). Socioeconomic complexity and the resilience of hunter-gatherer societies. *Quaternary International*, 446, 109–127.

Steward, J. H. (1955). *Theory of Culture Change*. Urbana-Champaign, IL: University of Illinois Press.

Stock, J. T. (2006). Hunter-gatherer postcranial robusticity relative to patterns of mobility, climatic adaptation, and selection for tissue economy. *American Journal of Physical Anthropology*, 131, 194–204.

Stock, J. T. and Pfieffer, S. (2001). Linking structural variability in long bone diaphyses to habitual behaviors: Foragers from the southern African Later Stone Age and the Andaman Islands. *American Journal of Physical Anthropology*, 115, 337–348.

Stock, J. T. and Pfieffer, S. (2004). Long bone robusticity and subsistence behavior among Later Stone Age foragers of the forest and fynbos biomes of South Africa. *Journal of Archaeological Science*, 31, 999–1013.

Stojanowski, C. M. and Knudson, K. J. (2014). Changing patterns of mobility in response to climatic deterioration and aridification in the Middle Holocene Southern Sahara. *American Journal of Physical Anthropology*, 154, 79–93.

Stojanowski, C. M., Carver, C. L., and Miller, K. A. (2014) Incisor avulsion, social identity, and Saharan population history: New data from the Early Holocene southern Sahara. *Journal of Anthropological Archaeology*, 35, 79–91.

Tainter, J. A. (1988). *The Collapse of Complex Societies*. Cambridge: Cambridge University Press.

Temple, D. H. (2007). Dietary variation and stress among prehistoric Jomon foragers from Japan. *American Journal of Physical Anthropology*, 133, 1035–1046.

Temple, D. H. (2010). Patterns of systemic stress during the agricultural transition in prehistoric Japan. *American Journal of Physical Anthropology*, 142, 112–124.

Temple, D. H. and Goodman, A. H. (2014). Bioarchaeology has a health problem: Conceptualizing "stress" and "health" in bioarchaeological research. *American Journal of Physical Anthropology*, 155, 186–191.

Temple, D. H. and Larsen, C. S. (2013). Bioarchaeological perspectives on systemic stress during the agricultural transition in prehistoric Japan. In E. Pechenkina and M. F. Oxenham, eds., *Bioarchaeology of East Asia: Movement, Contact, Health*. Gainesville, FL: University Press of Florida, pp. 344–367.

Temple, D. H. and Matsumura, H. (2011). Do body proportions among prehistoric foragers from Hokkaido conform to ecogeographic expectations? Evolutionary implications of size and shape variation among northerly hunter-gatherers. *International Journal of Osteoarchaeology*, 21, 268–282.

Temple, D. H., Kusaka, S., and Sciulli, P. W. (2011). Patterns of social identity in relation to ritual tooth ablation among prehistoric Jomon foragers from the Yoshigo site, Aichi prefecture, Japan. *International Journal of Osteoarchaeology*, 21, 323–335.

Thompson, V. D. (2010). The rhythms of space-time and the making of monuments and places during the Archaic. In D. H. Thomas and M. C. Sanger, eds., *Trend, Tradition, and Turmoil: What Happened to the Southeastern Archaic?* New York, NY: American Museum of Natural History Anthropological Papers 93, pp. 217–227.

Thompson, V. D. (2016). Finding resilience in ritual and history in the Lake Okeechobee Basin. In R. K. Faulseit, ed., *Beyond Collapse: Archaeological Perspectives on Resilience, Revitalization, and Transformation in Complex Societies*. Carbondale, IL: Southern Illinois University Press, pp. 313–342.

Thompson, V. D. and Pluckhahn, T. J. (2010). History, complex hunter-gatherers, and the mounds and monuments of Crystal River, Florida, USA: A geophysical survey. *Journal of Island and Coastal Archaeology*, 5, 33–51.

Turner, C. G. and Machado, L. M. C. (1983). A new dental wear pattern and evidence for high carbohydrate consumption in a Brazilian Archaic skeletal population. *American Journal of Physical Anthropology*, 61, 125–130.

Walker, B., Holling, C. S., Carpenter, S. R., *et al.* (2004). Resilience, adaptability, and transformability in social-ecological systems. *Ecology and Society*, **9**, 5.

Walker, P. L. and Erlandson, J. M. (1986). Dental evidence for prehistoric dietary change on the northern Channel Islands, California. *American Antiquity*, **51**, 375–383.

Walker, P. L. and Hewlett B. S. (1990). Dental health, diet, and social status among Central African foragers and farmers. *American Anthropologist*, **92**, 383–398.

Walker, P. L. and Lambert, P. M. (1989). Skeletal evidence for stress during a period of culture change in prehistoric California. *Journal of Paleopathology*, **1**, 207–212.

Weiss, E. (2003). Effects of rowing on humeral strength. *American Journal of Physical Anthropology*, **121**, 293–302.

Winterhalder, B. D. and Smith E. A. (2000). Analyzing adaptive strategies: Human behavioral ecology at twenty-five. *Evolutionary Anthropology*, **9**, 51–72.

Woodburn, J. (1982). Egalitarian societies. *Man* (N.S.), **17**, 431–451.

2 Regional Continuity and Local Challenges to Resilience among Holocene Hunter-Gatherers of the Greater Cape Floristic Region, South Africa

Susan Pfeiffer and Lesley Harrington

2.1 Introduction

2.1.1 Resilience in the South African Landscape

The southern African landscape yields evidence of human evolution that dates from long before the emergence of our species. It is also the site of early evidence for the complex behaviors associated with contemporary humans. The southerly region that provides the earliest, most complete record of our species is the Greater Cape Floristic Region (GCFR). This is an area of roughly 80 000 km², characterized by floristic diversity, abundance of geophytic plants, and other associated terrestrial food resources, abutting a resource-rich coastline (Allsopp et al., 2014). It is a region where the resilience of hunter-gatherer adaptations is apparent through diverse lines of evidence, including archaeology, genetics, and bioarchaeology.

There is archaeological evidence for the resilience of the knowledge needed to exploit the GCFR. Aspects of that knowledge are reflected in artifacts and in skeletal biology. The earliest evidence of sustained human success in the GCFR dates from MIS6 (from about 195 000 BP) (Marean et al., 2014). Perhaps the earliest distinctive characteristic of the GCFR Stone Age behavioral package is regular exploitation of marine resources. For this, nuanced understanding of lunar cycles and tides is required. From subsequent millennia, there is evidence of knowledge regarding the mental mapping needed to exploit patchy plant resources (Bradshaw and Cowling, 2014), including the skills needed to harvest underground storage organs; the ability to exploit plant and animal toxins (Deacon, 1992; Wooding et al., 2017); and the connectivity needed to maintain a social safety net. Taken together, this conceptual tool kit was unique to the GCFR and appears to have been relatively resistant to change during the Middle and Later Stone Ages (Barham and Mitchell, 2008; Deacon and Deacon, 1999; Marean et al., 2014; Mitchell, 2002). The continuity in distinctive technologies and ecogeographic decisions (about how to use and move about the landscape) can be used to provide evidence of the resilience of cultural traits in hunter-gatherer populations living in southern Africa, particularly between about 40 000 BP and the present period known archaeologically as the Later Stone Age (d'Errico et al., 2012, 2016; Marean et al., 2014).

This narrative meshes well with genomic evidence that consistently dates the divergence of the indigenous populations of southern Africa from about 160 000 to

110 000 BP (Nielsen *et al.*, 2017). Archaeological and genetic lines of evidence complement one another (Schlebusch *et al.*, 2012, 2013). Human burials add another line of direct physical evidence of people who lived in the GCFR. Though the bulk of the human skeletal record dates to the mid-Holocene, the homogeneity of cranial shape (Stynder, 2006; Stynder *et al.*, 2007a, 2007b), dental size and shape (Black, 2014; Black *et al.*, 2009), and diverse skeletal dimensions (Ginter, 2011) are consistent with the evidence that the population existed for many millennia, relatively undisturbed by major perturbations from new peoples or changes to regional climate (Bradshaw and Cowling, 2014). Insofar as resilience is defined as the property or the ability to maintain "healthy functioning" in response to external stressors (Bradtmöller *et al.*, 2017), peoples of this region provide a superb example.

Bioarchaeology adds new dimensions to how resilience can be documented among people from the GCFR. Assessment of skeletons for the timing of growth disruption and evidence of stress markers, provides insights into the success of past lifeways. Aspects of the specific GCFR behavioral package are reflected in skeletal and paleodemographic characteristics. Reliance on trekking for exploitation of resource patches, exploitation of plant and animal toxins for hunting (facilitating light-draw bows), and use of tools for geophyte extraction can all be studied through biomechanical analyses. Reliance on marine protein sources can be evaluated using stable isotopes. Additionally, human skeletons provide evidence of biological stress during which challenges to resilience were addressed. Evidence for stress that appears to have arisen from population density in the second half of the Holocene includes transient variability in adult body size, territoriality, and interpersonal violence. These disruptions could have marked the end of the Late Stone Age, but seem not to have done so. Later Holocene responses to the arrival of a new subsistence option (pastoralism) were diverse, but hunting and gathering within the GCFR persisted until the historic era.

2.1.2   Population Continuity

Modern genetic diversity among descendants indicates that KhoeSan[1] peoples were numerous since the origin of the lineage, with evidence of substantial numbers since at least 120 000 BP (Kim *et al.*, 2014; Pugach and Stoneking, 2015; Tishkoff *et al.*, 2007). Genomic studies have identified a tripartite, ancient KhoeSan population structure, with inner divisions variably attributed to linguistic (Scheinfeldt *et al.*, 2010) and geographic (distance) (Montinaro *et al.*, 2017). KhoeSan hunter-gatherer lifeways continued until European colonization (450 BP), after which time warfare,

---

[1] As contemporary authors attempt to be sensitive to the wishes of Khoe and San descendant groups, variations on nomenclature have been proposed with some regularity. Sometimes proposals for new terms are accompanied by negative interpretations of prior terminology, like "Bushman" – a term that falls in and out of favor. Terminology in most of the cited literature refers to the KhoeSan language group, as per Crawhall (2006). Depending on the archaeological theory followed, the ancestors described herein may be more appropriately characterized simply as San. Whatever the nomenclature, the intent is to acknowledge the right of descendants to a voice in the matter.

disease, and enslavement eroded the lifeways of GCFR groups at the Cape. Northern and more interior regions were less directly affected by the European newcomers. Descendant San-speaking groups in more interior locales have continued to follow lifeways that include hunting and gathering to some extent. These populations now live in the modern states of Botswana, Namibia, Zimbabwe, and Angola, especially in the Kalahari.

While the GCFR groups known archaeologically may represent lineages that were somewhat distinct from the survivors of historic times (Morris *et al.*, 2014), core components of the genome, tool kit, and subsistence approaches show strong links with ethnographically/historically known groups (Deacon and Deacon, 1999; d'Errico *et al.*, 2012). Most descriptions of San-speaking peoples are observations from interior, semi-desert landscapes (the Kalahari and adjoining regions). The best-known works focus on the Ju/'hoansi (or !Kung), G/wi, and /Xam (Lee, 1979; Marshall, 1958; Silberbauer, 1981; Skotnes, 2007). When drawing on this literature, one must avoid "reading back" the ethnographically documented situation into the prehistoric past, thus assuming rather than investigating similarities between recent and ancient societies (Barham, 1992; Wadley, 1992). While recognizing that the information is historically contingent, ethnographic and historic observations provide a framework for hypothesis formation in archaeology and bioarchaeology.

2.1.3   The Geographic Setting

The GCFR (Born *et al.*, 2007), with its rich archaeological evidence of the Later Stone Age, is predominantly within the Western Cape Province, although it extends into the Eastern Cape Province along the coast. It reaches from the coast to the Cape Fold Mountains, which form a partial barrier between the coastal forelands and the higher, drier, more climatically variable interior of South Africa (Figure 2.1).

The GCFR is home of the fynbos (pronounced fain'boss, meaning fine bush in Afrikaans) and other unique plant communities. The region is characterized by restios (reeds), ericas, proteas, aloes, and plants with underground storage organs (known as geophytes or corms) (Cramer *et al.*, 2014; Day *et al.*, 1979). Differences in bedrock substrate and precipitation lead to locally distinct patterns of abundance, but throughout the area available plants provided food, bedding, medicinal products, and poisons used for hunting. The very high diversity of plants in the GCFR is one of the important distinctions between this environment and the Kalahari, where KhoeSan descendant groups are found today (Marean *et al.*, 2014). Throughout the GCFR, small to medium-sized mammals could be exploited. The size and diversity of prey animals declined from the late glacial period to the Holocene, reflecting a drying of the climate throughout the region (Faith, 2013). Hunting technology included hafted, light poison-tipped arrows that delivered a neurotoxin, likely combined with the practice of persistence tracking (Wadley *et al.*, 2009). Based on both the excavated material and dietary stable isotope studies, marine protein sources may have been more important than terrestrial sources for most communities. The frequently rocky shores reliably yielded food, through action of the cold Benguela oceanic current on

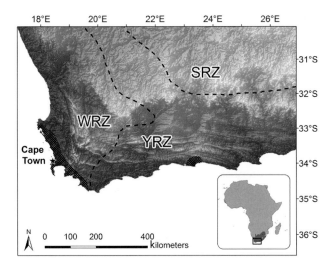

Figure 2.1 The southern African Cape and the Cape Fold Mountains. Zones of winter (WRZ), summer (SRZ), and year-round (YRZ) rainfall are identified. The shaded region with Cape Town as its focus (to the left) is the region from which perimortem trauma cases have come. The small shaded area along the south coast (to the right) marks the location of Plettenberg Bay, the Robberg Peninsula, and Matjes River Rock Shelter. Map prepared by Robert Gustas.

the Atlantic side and the warm Agulhas current on the Indian Ocean side (Jerardino, 2016; Jerardino *et al.*, 2013). These are strong currents, with sharks, stingrays, and other hazards. Perhaps the absence of appropriate raw materials is a further explanation for the absence of boats (Marean *et al.*, 2014). This was a coastal, not maritime, adaptation. There is no evidence for watercraft.

The cultural stage known as the Later Stone Age (LSA) of southern Africa, from ca. 40 000 BP to historic times, developed *in situ* from Middle Stone Age (MSA) antecedents (Ambrose, 1998), with some divergence of opinion about when to mark the LSA's beginning (Barham and Mitchell, 2008; Deacon and Deacon, 1999; Mitchell, 2002; Villa *et al.*, 2012; Wadley, 2015) and about the nature of the transition (Mackay *et al.*, 2012). While archaeological evidence of the LSA can be found throughout southern Africa, the comparatively mild, stable climate and availability of resources made the GCFR region an important focus of hunter-gatherer exploitation. Both MSA and LSA populations are characterized as immediate-return hunter-gatherers (as per Woodburn, 1982). The most informative sites are found in rock shelters, many of which were used as habitation sites, sometimes for prolonged periods (but see Mackay, 2016).

Features of LSA material culture traced to the MSA (d'Errico *et al.*, 2012) include hunting with bows and arrows, the use of composite poisoned bone arrowheads, relatively short and light spears, digging sticks weighted with bored stones, and the presence of standardized ostrich eggshell beads that were prepared using grooved stones (but see Pargeter, 2014; Pargeter *et al.*, 2014). The exploitation of ostrich eggshells for water storage and the use of ochre for mastic and decorative arts are other practices that originated in the MSA (Wadley, 2015). Rock art panels are also said to provide linkages with KhoeSan people (Lewis-Williams and Dowson, 1999). Lithic technology has been used to separate the archaeological record into traditions, although transitions are not abrupt. Both the number of sites and the number of human skeletons indicate that population sizes increased throughout the Holocene (Deacon, 1984; Mitchell, 2002). The sparsity of grasses within the GCFR made the region relatively unattractive to the Bantu-speaking farmers who reached the eastern regions of southern Africa by about 1800 BP (Huffman, 2007). At around the same time, ovicaprine bones and pottery reach the GCFR, which are interpreted as evidence of pastoralism (Henshilwood, 1996). There is considerable debate about the chronology (Horsburgh *et al.*, 2016) and dynamics of this new subsistence option, including the extent to which the presence of herd animals disrupted hunter-gatherer lifeways (Sadr, 2008; Smith, 2008). Genomic studies of descendants indicate that it was primarily a cultural process with limited genetic impact (Uren *et al.*, 2017). Hunter-gatherer lifeways, perhaps intermixed with some herding, continued throughout the GCFR until European incursions.

2.1.4   Human Remains from the Later Stone Age

Most human remains from the LSA are derived from recent millennia, rarely extending past 10 000 BP. The absence of earlier skeletal material reflects a period during which high sea levels destroyed most evidence of human activities (Compton, 2011; Fisher *et al.*, 2010; Herbert and Compton, 2007). Human burials recovered from the coastal forelands and the Cape Fold Mountains of South Africa have been explored and excavated since the early twentieth century. Through both purposeful archaeological excavations and chance discoveries, hundreds of human skeletons have been reported and retained in collections. All are primary interments, and almost all are individual burials. Deceased LSA hunter-gatherers were most commonly interred as individual burials, unmarked, usually in a tightly flexed posture and without grave goods. They appear to have been buried near where they lived. Some rock shelters include many single interments. For example, over 100 skeletons were removed from the Matjes River Rock Shelter, with dates extending over 3000 years (L'Abbe *et al.*, 2008). Such sites are occasionally characterized as cemeteries (cf. Marean *et al.*, 2014). KhoeSan genetic distinctiveness, combined with the absence of genetic evidence for intrusive migrations, suggests that these individual interments can be collectively treated as an assemblage derived from a single population. Nevertheless, examination of the temporal and spatial variability of burial features is also relevant. Possible patterns in sex, age at death, body position, and burial inclusions have been compared to Kalahari ethnographies (Hall, 2000; Hall and Binneman, 1987; Inskeep, 1986; Pearce, 2008; Pfeiffer and Harrington, 2011; Wadley, 1996, 1997). Few patterns arise, except that grave goods are found more commonly in rock shelter burials than in sand dune burials. There are no cemeteries, in the sense of a physical space set aside solely for interment of the dead. Assessing those human burials with radiocarbon dates, burials dating from 9800 to

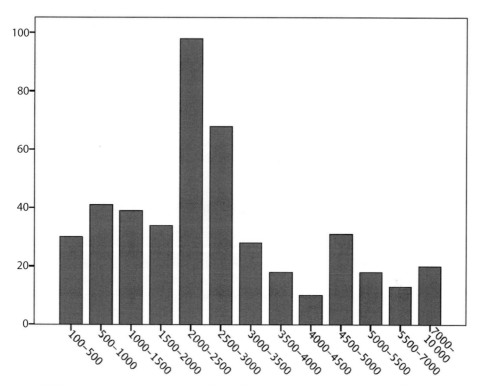

Figure 2.2 Bars indicate the number of individually dated skeletons (uncalibrated ^{14}C, BP) in 500-year time periods. N = 448. There is a peak in population between 2500 and 2000 BP, followed by a drop in numbers. Dates are uncalibrated because of variable amounts of marine protein in people's diets. The presence of this older marine carbon may bias some dates by as much as 200 years (Dewar and Pfeiffer, 2010; Dewar et al., 2012).

6000 BP have been found exclusively in rock shelters. The absence of sand dune burials from this early period probably reflects shore erosion of archaeological features. From 6000 to 1800 BP, burials are known from rock shelters and from open, sand dune contexts, the latter including shell middens. All burials dated later than 1800 BP are derived from open contexts. The west coast is distinctive in having a small number of rock shelters and an almost complete absence of infant burials (Pfeiffer, 2013; Pfeiffer and Harrington, 2011).

Early excavators tended to retain only the adult crania, now held in institutions around the world (Legassick and Rassool, 2000; Morris, 2013; Steyn et al., 2013). More recent practice has shifted toward curating all skeletal material. Collections of relatively complete archaeologically documented skeletons of diverse ages at death are held at several South African institutions (Iziko Museums, University of Cape Town Human Biology, University of the Witwatersrand, National Museum Bloem-fontein, KwaZulu-Natal Museum, Albany Museum) (Morris, 1992). Newly discovered skeletons are normally radiocarbon dated, so the number of dated skeletons slowly increases. A recent histogram (Figure 2.2) plots dates from 448 LSA skeletons (including 76 pre-adults), with the largest number dated between 3000 and 2000 BP

(Pfeiffer, 2016). This does not include those skeletons associated (through archaeological context) with pastoralism and the era after European contact. As an approximate tally, there are 500–600 well-contextualized LSA skeletons, of which about 150 are pre-adults. Relative to the many thousands of KhoeSan people estimated from genetic evidence to have occupied the Cape during the Holocene, this is a small sample. However, evidence from immediate-return hunter-gatherers is scarce worldwide. Consistent features of the sample presumably characterize those of the population. Features that are temporally or spatially unique provide opportunities for insights into the challenges faced by these communities.

2.2   Bioarchaeological Perspectives on Hunter-Gatherer Lifeways in the GCFR

2.2.1   Body Size in Southern African Hunter-Gatherers

The distinctive feature of LSA skeletons from southern Africa is small body size. Based on a large sample of femoral lengths ($n = 185$), no adults achieved a stature of more than 178 cm (formula of Feldesman *et al.*, 1990). The mean femur length for the assemblage is 409 mm (s.d. 25.7 mm), estimating a stature of about 153 cm. The consistency of small body size concomitant with particular aspects of pelvic shape suggests an adaptive quality to this body type. Body breadth, measured by bi-iliac diameter in combination with linear measures, indicates that body mass was quite low. Outcomes of various estimation methods average slightly below 45 kg (Kurki *et al.*, 2010). Kurki (2007) has demonstrated that despite narrow bi-iliac breadth, in comparison to other populations LSA women had relatively large pelvic mid-planes and outlet canal planes. This implies adaptive allometric remodeling, through selective pressures (Kurki, 2007; Kurki *et al.*, 2008; Pfeiffer *et al.*, 2014). It is clear that obstetric accommodation is adaptive. It is less clear whether small body size is the result of natural selection or drift, although arguments for the potential selective value of this body shape can be made (Pfeiffer, 2012a).

As first reported when sample sizes were smaller (Pfeiffer and Sealy, 2006; Sealy and Pfeiffer, 2000; Smith *et al.*, 1992; Wilson and Lundy, 1994), stature and mass estimates remain similar to measurements taken on KhoeSan descendants in more recent times (Dart, 1937; Tobias, 1962; Truswell and Hanson, 1976). Temporal and spatial variability in linear measures are consistent with expectations of human biology – that adult stature is the product of the interaction of environment and inheritance. However, this isolated group had a set point that tended toward small body size. The nature of this body size can be evaluated bioarchaeologically through study of linear growth in the pre-adult portion of the LSA skeletal assemblage. Evidence for growth stunting is examined by considering stature-for-age. When stature is plotted against dental age in pre-adults spanning the neonatal period to the end of adolescence, hunter-gatherer infants are of similar size to European infants. As children, southern African hunter-gatherers appear to have experienced growth faltering from about two years of age onward when assessed against stature norms from North American growth curves (Denver Growth Study; Maresh, 1955, 1970).

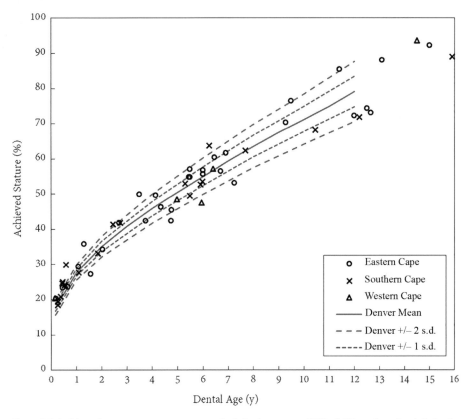

Figure 2.3 Achieved stature as a percentage of adult size among LSA children from burials in the Eastern, Southern, and Western Cape regions relative to a modern growth standard.

However, when juvenile stature-for-age is evaluated as a proportion of adult size using mean LSA adult stature as the standard (following the method of Humphrey, 2000), hunter-gatherer children grow in stature with a tempo that matches Denver Growth Study cohorts (Figure 2.3; Pfeiffer and Harrington, 2011). This indicates an absence of evidence for growth stunting in non-surviving children when growth is standardized by adult survivors of childhood from within the population. Notably, the absence of growth disruption prior to death distinguishes LSA children from the children of Iron Age farmers of southern Africa (Harrington and Pfeiffer, 2008), who, using the same comparative approach, show evidence of growth faltering prior to death. Small body size in GCFR hunter-gatherers, viewed through the lens of child growth, would seem to be the outcome of stable rather than variably disturbed development.

2.2.2 Osteological Indicators of the GCFR Hunting and Gathering Lifeway

Isotopic values from bone collagen for $\delta^{13}C$ and $\delta^{15}N$ are available for a large proportion of the adult LSA skeletons. There are some differences between the western and southern regions in soil substrate and plant communities, so comparisons are regional. The overarching pattern is of reliance on combinations of terrestrial protein – including tortoise, small mammals, occasionally larger mammals – and marine protein, with trophic values reflecting a continuum from seal to mussels (Sealy, 2010; Sealy and Pfeiffer, 2000). The location of each burial relative to the coast seems to be the strongest predictor of dietary protein source. That is, people buried along the coast have values indicating diverse marine protein sources, and people buried further inland have more terrestrial dietary isotopes (Sealy and van der Merwe, 1986, 1988; Sealy *et al.*, 1987).

The physical activities engaged in by hunter-gatherers in the procurement of GCFR resources are marked by plastic responses in cortical bone. Studies of bone functional adaptation (methods as per Ruff, 2008 and others) describe the skeletons of southern African hunter-gatherers as having characteristically strong lower limbs relative to body size. This is a consistent feature through time and space. Using biomechanical analysis of femoral shaft cross-sections, Stock demonstrated evidence for high levels of terrestrial mobility among adults of both sexes (Stock and Pfeiffer, 2001). Bone functional adaptation in the upper limb provides information about task differentiation within the highly mobile hunting and gathering lifeway. Looking at humeral antimeres, women show balanced cortical bone strength, while men show dominance asymmetry that differs between zones within the GCFR. The more forested southern region with archaeological evidence of hunting with spears shows higher asymmetry, and the more open western region where light-draw bows were used shows less asymmetry (Stock and Pfeiffer, 2004). Studies based on external shaft dimensions (Stock and Shaw, 2007) demonstrate that the femora of both sexes show high torsional strength relative to other populations, and humeral asymmetry is greater among males compared to females (Cameron and Pfeiffer, 2014).

These results have been interpreted as indicating a number of behavioral patterns: Substantial time was spent by both sexes trekking over the landscape; women used digging sticks that required balanced arm strength for accessing roots and corms; men's hunting activities required different patterns of asymmetric arm strength, depending on the weapons used. Biomechanical research supports an argument for gender-based division of labor throughout time and space. This is consistent with Holocene rock art (Parkington and Dlamini, 2015), and with ethnographically observed behaviors of Kalahari descendants. As this research approach is applied to skeletal remains of past peoples from other parts of the world, it is apparent that the hunter-gatherers of the GCFR are distinctive. Early work showed gender differences in upper arm symmetry among adults with a maritime subsistence economy (Stock and Pfeiffer, 2001). A recent comparison of humeri from GCFR hunter-gatherers to other southern African hunter-gatherers (interior and Namib regions) confirms that the GCFR females show the most symmetrical upper arm strength (Cameron, 2017). This feature may be distinctive to GCFR hunter-gatherers. Cameron also compared southern African hunter-gatherers with published values for lower limb cross-sectional geometric properties. Both sexes from the GCFR show stronger limbs than like-sex skeletons from diverse habitats and subsistence contexts (Cameron, 2017).

The uniquely robust lower limbs of GCFR hunter-gatherers may reflect habitual travel over exceptionally rugged terrain, featuring both vertical relief and unstable rocky surfaces.

Examining the developmental timing of patterns of limb strength, Harrington (2010) quantified the accrual of lower limb strength in the juvenile subset of the LSA assemblage and demonstrated that the sexual differentiation in activities is emergent in adolescence. These patterns were recently examined in a comparative study of hunter-gatherer children from diverse environments (Osipov *et al.*, 2016). Children from the GCFR show the highest levels of lower relative to upper limb strength, in comparison to contemporaneous pre-adult assemblages from Alaska, Japan, and the Cis-Baikal region. A follow-up study (Osipov *et al.*, 2017) examining levels of upper limb asymmetry in these groups highlighted the distinctiveness of the LSA body form, with high levels of male limb strength being evident in adolescence. The study of bone functional adaptation in juvenile LSA skeletons reinforces the impression that the hunting and gathering lifeway was well established throughout the Holocene in the GCFR. The process of developing the knowledge, skill, and stamina required for resource procurement is marked in the skeleton through the plastic response of cortical bone.

2.3   Challenges and Resilience

2.3.1   Bioarchaeological Evidence

The topics introduced thus far demonstrate pervasive features that characterize South African LSA hunter-gatherers across a broad spatial and temporal swath. Throughout the Holocene, these hunter-gatherers were exploiting GCFR landscapes, following a social system that had at least some gender-defined activities. Although some behaviors reflect local adaptations (such as differences in humeral strength between males and females), most skeletal traits parallel other lines of archaeological evidence for connectivity across the GCFR region, probably maintained through movement and exchange of goods and people. Through successful reproduction and childcare, hunter-gatherers increased in numbers until about 2000 BP. The distribution of sites suggests that as numbers increased, groups populated favorable spaces more densely, rather than moving into the interior of the country, where the climate was colder and drier (Marean *et al.*, 2014). Genomic evidence, too, indicates that ecogeographic boundaries – not social or linguistic boundaries – created fine-scale population structure (Uren *et al.*, 2017). However, there is bioarchaeological evidence of social disruption dated to around 2500 BP.

2.3.2   Regional Dietary Differentiation

In contrast to populations with marine-rich diets, there is one region where a sharp dietary distinction is found between neighboring coastal groups. Rock shelter burials along the rocky southern coast dating between 4500 and 2000 BP demonstrate clear evidence for dietary diversity. Those from the Robberg area of Plettenberg Bay ingested marine protein from higher trophic levels than populations at Matjes River Rock Shelter, just 14 km further east along the coast. In the former neighborhood there was a seal rookery ("Robberg" means seal mountain) (Figure 2.1). Sealy has argued that the large, consistent disparity in types of protein represents the maintenance of territories (Sealy, 2006). The people from Matjes River did not consume foods from the rookery. Instead, "Later Stone Age material culture, including the assemblages from these sites, shows many similarities to that of twentieth-century Kalahari hunter-gatherers, but settlement pattern and social organization were sometimes very different" (Sealy, 2006: 569).

2.3.3   Are Changes to Adult Body Size and Episodes of Interpersonal Violence Linked?

An intriguing aspect of the small adult body size of the GCFR population is the presence of a transient period of even smaller stature from roughly 3500 to 2000 BP. This was first noted many years ago, when few firmly dated skeletons were available for study (Smith *et al.*, 1992; Wilson and Lundy, 1994). The initial thought was that hunter-gatherers were gradually failing to thrive, until being eclipsed by a pastoralist economy. As sample sizes have increased, the pattern has held: There is an increase in variability created by a few very small adults, then a disappearance of those outliers. It has been argued that the up-tick began substantially earlier than evidence for pastoralism (Pfeiffer and Sealy, 2006), and it has become apparent that the decline in stature parallels an increase in the number of skeletons (Figure 2.2). The juvenile subset of the LSA assemblage bears no signs of increased frequency of non-specific stress indicators, nor deviations from normal child growth (Pfeiffer, 2007). These results suggest that the causes underlying persistent smaller body size in adults were not associated with growth disruption.

Burials of people who were victims of interpersonal violence also date to this period of apparent distress, but these burials are found from only one part of the region. Skeletons with perimortem lesions are limited to the southwestern territory (south of about 33°S, west of 20°E) at dates around 2500 to 2200 BP. Most of these individuals are women and children (Pfeiffer, 2016). The clearest documented incidents include a woman with an infant found with bone projectiles in her spine (Morris and Parkington, 1982), a woman and adolescent girl with cranial breaks and cut marks (Pfeiffer *et al.*, 1999), and three children with cranial punctures from a rounded weapon with a small diameter, akin to a digging stick (Pfeiffer and van der Merwe, 2004). The apparent focus on women and children has no ethnographic parallel. While KhoeSan peoples were documented to sometimes settle disputes through violence leading to death, disputes among men were by far the most common (Lee, 1979). When adult femoral lengths (proxies for stature) are compared across regions, the southwestern region shows no statistically significant decline and recovery, unlike areas to the north and to the east, where decline and recovery are seen. There may be a causative link between the anomalous violence in this region and the consistency of adult stature (Pfeiffer, 2016). At present, however, causal factors surrounding the relationship between reduced stature and interpersonal violence are elusive. The time period between 3500 and 2200 BP appears to be one characterized by increasing systemic stress and violence. However, it remains important to emphasize population socioecological and cultural persistence following these events, though there is evidence for demographic contraction.

2.3.4   Health, Hazards, and Reproduction

An interesting feature of LSA skeletons is the absence of evidence of chronic infectious disease, such as osteomyelitis and tuberculosis. That non-surviving children lack signs of growth faltering prior to death raises questions about the frailty of individuals who do not survive until adulthood. Considering statural growth achievement in the context of other skeletal and dental markers of growth disruption sheds further light on the biological resilience of GCFR hunter-gatherers. A survey of 43 juveniles for *cribra orbitalia* (CO) and growth arrest lines found 13 with slight to moderate CO. Both CO and growth arrest are seen mainly between the ages of 6 and 12 years (Pfeiffer, 2007), suggesting possible parasitic infections (Perry, 2014; Walker *et al.*, 2009) and short-term health issues in mid-childhood.

Developmental defects of enamel provide an opportunity to consider the timing and frequency of disruptions to normal growth. A study of linear enamel defects in a subset of the juvenile assemblage suggests that children experienced regular, minor interruptions to growth in early childhood as evidenced by accentuated perikymata spacing (Harrington and Pfeiffer, 2016). Larger furrow-form hypoplastic defects involving multiple growth increments are rarely observed in LSA dentitions (Figure 2.4). This suggests that hunter-gatherer childhood, irrespective of whether an individual died early in life, was not marked by pervasive illness or malnutrition. The skeletal markers, taken together with the study of growth

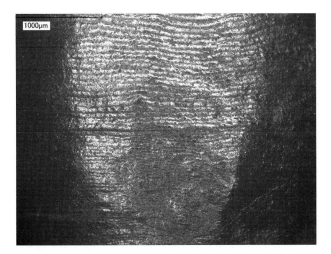

Figure 2.4 The surface of a replica of an upper lateral permanent incisor, mid-crown region, viewed at 100×, showing disrupted perikymata in the center of the field of view.

increments in enamel, suggest children faced insults to health that were overcome. Although cause of death cannot be known, the remains of non-surviving juveniles do not bear indictors of severe illness. Common causes of mortality among hunter-gatherers were probably acute events (accidents of various kinds), as compared to the more chronic conditions (disease/nutrition related) reported among horticulturists.

A survey of 152 adults found 8 percent had healed long bone fractures, with the radius and ulna most commonly affected (Pfeiffer, 2007, 2016). Instances of survival after substantial cranial trauma have been noted (Pfeiffer, 2016) as have instances of prolonged care associated with health disruptions (Pfeiffer, 2012b; Pfeiffer and Crowder, 2004) and pelvic stress injuries (Pfeiffer, 2011). The latter is a case study of a woman from about 2000 BP whose pelvis shows eburnation on all joint surfaces, thought to be the sequellae of parturition trauma. Such clear pelvic joint laxity and eburnation may illustrate the tension between small body size and obstetric adequacy.

2.4   Times of Disruption

Throughout the mid-Holocene, hunter-gatherers were exploiting the extensive GCFR landscape. Marean and colleagues argue that there exist parallels with other coastal hunting and gathering economies such as those of Australia and central California, as "closely packed and small territories and regionally specialized economies" became more complex (Marean *et al.*, 2014: 193). The deviations from prior behavioral patterns described above seem to have ended as population numbers dramatically declined. Based on current evidence, anomalous behaviors began and ended within the GCFR hunter-gatherer landscape. However, an alternative interpretation in which the introduction of pastoralism is pivotal has some support. Because pastoralism is hard to distinguish archaeologically, there is debate about exactly when, where, and with what impact ovicaprines were introduced to the region.

During the past 2000 years, the isolation of the LSA hunter-gatherers of southern Africa was disrupted by three waves of new ideas and people: Pastoralism entered from the northwest; African farmers entered from the northeast; and European explorers arrived by sea. Genomic (Pugach and Stoneking, 2015) and craniometric studies (Ribot *et al.*, 2010) provide evidence that KhoeSan people interbred to some extent with the newcomers, both African and European.

However, at the same time, there continues to be archaeological and bioarchaeological evidence within the GCFR for people whose lives had not changed, behaviorally or dietarily, until well into the European era. Indeed, while European accounts from the seventeenth and eighteenth centuries describe Khoekhoe pastoralists with extensive herds of cattle and sheep at the Cape, the archaeological evidence for those pastoralists is slim, even from that historic time period. Because cattle are grazers and few native grazers were a part of hunter-gatherer diets, Sealy (2010) explored dietary isotopes of dated skeletons to look for a shift toward protein from grazing stock. From 2000 to 1000 BP, domesticated animals did not alter the overall dietary isotopic patterning. Among the skeletons dating from 1000 to 380 BP, values from some skeletons deviate from the previous pattern in ways that suggest a shift toward the products of grazers (probably milk) (Sealy, 2010).

Archaeological data from the historic period is scant, and many questions remain. Current evidence suggests that the arrival of new subsistence approaches did not generate dramatic cultural change. By the historic period, Khoekhoe were known to bury the dead in seated positions, topped by rock cairns, and sometimes with rocks filling the grave shaft. However, one of the skeletons found by Sealy to have a "pastoralist" diet (with a date of 560 BP) was documented in a flexed, seated position, but without rock infill or cairn (Morris *et al.*, 2005). One hypothesis suggests that Khoekhoe culture did not achieve its historic form until European sailors' demand for meat to re-stock ships (Sadr, 1998). This suggests continuity in burial practices from the prehistoric to historic Khoekhoe culture.

Returning to the story of KhoeSan hunter-gatherers in the GCFR, historic European accounts describe the presence of "strandlopers" (beach walkers), although it is not clear to what extent these individuals practiced a hunting and gathering economy. By the end of the nineteenth century, "Bushmen" were gone from the Cape, having been hunted, imprisoned, enslaved, exposed to disease, and to some extent integrated into the dominant society. The continuation of the hunting and gathering lifeway was, however, variably maintained to the north, in the interior of the continent.

2.5   Conclusion

The skeletons of LSA hunter-gatherers show patterns that would be expected from immediate-return hunter-gatherers, considered broadly: highly mobile people whose home bases shifted frequently and whose diets were diverse, nutritionally balanced, and relatively reliable. The combined information from child growth and non-specific stress indicators suggests that parasites may have presented some challenges, and there is limited evidence of traumatic injury caused by accidents, animal attacks, and interpersonal violence. There is also evidence of mutual care and attention that helped maintain this population. Examples of recovery from dramatic injury and health challenges surely reflect strong ties among group members. The maintenance of normal growth in children who subsequently failed to survive is an indicator of cultural adaptation to daily challenges. In these ways, the LSA skeletons may illustrate the resilient world of highly mobile hunter-gatherers, broadly considered.

In other ways, these skeletons have features that are unique to time and place. Consistently small adult body size and adaptively shaped pelves reflect long-term isolation. It has been hypothesized that both natural selection and sexual selection may favor taller stature in humans (Stulp and Barrett, 2016; Walker and Hamilton, 2008; Walker *et al.*, 2006), but pelvic shape differences may mitigate selection through parturition, and technology may mitigate the benefit of greater body mass in male–male competition. In an environment where persistence tracking was adaptive, smallness may also have been adaptive. Behaviorally, the clearest examples of continuity with descendants are the evidence for terrestrial mobility and the antiquity of men hunting and women gathering, as documented in the cross-sectional geometric properties of long bones.

The overall picture is of a lifeway characterized by resilience. On the other hand, there is bioarchaeological evidence for times and places when things happened that challenged these identities. The occasional evidence for territoriality and/or defense of resources suggests aspects of social organization that differed from immediate-return hunting and gathering, as narrowly defined. This territoriality is not analogous to any ethnographically described KhoeSan behavior. The evidence from one part of the GCFR for the episodic traumatic deaths of women and children is also inconsistent with expectations. These examples of regional disparities arise through study of the human remains and may help to guide broader archaeological investigations of artifacts, landscape use, and other indicators of past lives.

The research summarized here was made possible by the excellent preservation of the human remains, sustained efforts to generate radiocarbon dates for each isolated burial, and dedicated curation at several institutions. The resulting archaeologically derived data are complemented by the ethnographic/historic documents about the lives of descendants. The many living descendants of this lineage seek to know more about their ancestors, and the remarkable resilience of their cultural and biological strategies. More research is underway, with a growing focus on ancient DNA. Themes of this chapter emphasize the study of skeletal morphology and the linkage of excavation records with features of the human remains. This type of work remains crucial for the interpretation of aDNA patterns. As issues of proper consultation and repatriation arise in South Africa, it is important that the evidence of hunter-gatherers, including skeletal remains, be seen as particularly valuable to global understandings of human evolution. Collectively, these strategies and adaptations form the behavioral basis of what it means to be human.

Acknowledgments

The research summarized in this chapter could not have been undertaken without the sustained engagement and support of the South African archaeological community. This group includes archaeologists, curators, and scholars who have established protocols for monitoring heritage and ensuring accountability in research practices. Much of the research was supported by funding from the Social Sciences and Humanities Research Council of Canada.

References

Allsopp, N., Colville, J. F., and Verboom, G. A., eds. (2014). *Fynbos: Ecology, Evolution, and Conservation of a Megadiverse Region.* Oxford: Oxford University Press.

Ambrose, S. H. (1998). Chronology of the Later Stone Age and food production in East Africa. *Journal of Archaeological Science,* 25, 377–392.

Barham, L. and Mitchell, P. (2008). *The First Africans: African Archaeology from the Earliest Toolmakers to the Most Recent Foragers.* Cambridge: Cambridge University Press.

Barham, L. S. (1992). Let's walk before we run: An appraisal of historical materialist approaches to the Later Stone Age. *South African Archaeological Bulletin*, **47**, 44–51.

Black, W. (2014). *Dental Morphology and Variation across Holocene Khoesan People of Southern Africa*. PhD dissertation, University of Cape Town.

Black, W., Ackermann, R. R., and Sealy, J. C. (2009). Variation in Holocene Khoesan dentition. *American Journal of Physical Anthropology*, **S48**, 92–93.

Born, J., Linder, H. P., and Desmet, P. (2007). The Greater Cape Floristic Region. *Journal of Biogeography*, **34**, 147–162.

Bradshaw, P. L. and Cowling, R. M. (2014). Landscapes, rock types, and climate of the Greater Cape Floristic Region. In N. Allsopp, J. F. Colville, and G. A. Verboom, eds., *Fynbos: Ecology, Evolution and Conservation of a Megadiverse Region*. Oxford: Oxford University Press, pp. 26–46.

Bradtmöller, M., Grimm, S., and Riel-Salvatore, J. (2017). Resilience theory in archaeological practice: An annotated review. *Quaternary International*, **446**, 3–16.

Cameron, M. E. (2017). *Behaviour, Biology, and Ecology: Investigating the Impact of Ecological Constraints on Prehistoric Southern African Skeletal Phenotypes*. PhD dissertation, Cambridge University.

Cameron, M. E. and Pfeiffer, S. (2014). Long bone cross-sectional geometric properties of Later Stone Age foragers and herder-foragers. *South African Journal of Science*, **110**, http://dx.doi.org/10.1590/sajs.2014/20130369

Compton, J. S. (2011). Pleistocene sea-level fluctuations and human evolution on the southern coastal plain of South Africa. *Quaternary Science Reviews*, **30**, 506–527.

Cramer, M. D., West, A. G., Powee, S. C., and Stock, W. D. (2014). Plant ecophysiological diversity. In N. Allsopp, J. F. Colville, and G. A. Verboom, eds., *Fynbos: Ecology, Evolution and Conservation of a Megadiverse Region*. Oxford: Oxford University Press, pp. 248–270.

Crawhall, N. (2006). Languages, genetics and archaeology: Problems and the possibilities in Africa. In H. Soodyall, ed., *The Prehistory of Africa*. Johannesburg: Jonathan Ball Publishers.

d'Errico, F., Backwell, L., Villa, P., *et al.* (2012). Early evidence of San material culture represented by organic artifacts from Border Cave, South Africa. *Proceedings of the National Academy of Sciences*, **109**, 13214–13219.

d'Errico, F., Villa, P., Degano, I., *et al.* (2016). The "to be or not to be" of archaeological enquiry. *Antiquity*, **90**, 1079–1082.

Dart, R. A. (1937). The physical characters of the /?auni-/=khomani Bushmen: Appendices A–W. *Bantu Studies*, **11**, 175–246.

Day, J., Siegfried, W. R., Louw, G. N., and Jarman, M. L., eds. (1979). *Fynbos Ecology: A Preliminary Synthesis*. Pretoria: Council for Scientific and Industrial Research.

Deacon, H. J. and Deacon, J. (1999). *Human Beginnings in South Africa*. Cape Town: David Philip Publishers.

Deacon, J. (1984). Later Stone Age people and their descendants in southern Africa. In R. G. Klein, ed., *Southern African Prehistory and Paleoenvironments*. Rotterdam: Balkema, pp. 221–328.

Deacon, J. (1992). *Arrows as Agents of Belief amongst the /Xam Bushmen*. Cape Town: South African Museum.

Dewar, G. and Pfeiffer, S. (2010). Methods for estimating the relative proportion of marine protein in human collagen affect radiocarbon date calibration. *Radiocarbon*, **52**, 1611–1625.

Dewar, G., Reimer, P. J., Sealy, J., and Woodborne, S. (2012). Late-Holocene marine radiocarbon reservoir correction (ΔR) for the west coast of South Africa. *The Holocene*, **22**, 1481–1489.

Faith, J. T. (2013). Ungulate diversity and precipitation history since the Last Glacial Maximum in the Western Cape, South Africa. *Quaternary Science Reviews*, **68**, 191–199.

Feldesman, M. R., Kleckner, J. G., and Lundy, J. K. (1990). The femur/stature ratio and estimates of stature in mid- and late-Pleistocene fossil hominids. *American Journal of Physical Anthropology*, **83**, 359–372.

Fisher, E. C., Bar-Matthews, M., Jerardino, A., and Marean, C. W. (2010). Middle and Late Pleistocene paleoscape modeling along the southern coast of South Africa. *Quaternary Science Reviews*, **29**, 1382–1398.

Ginter, J. (2011). Using a bioarchaeological approach to explore subsistence transitions in the Eastern Cape, South Africa during the mid- to late Holocene. In R. Pinhasi and J. T. Stock, eds., *Human Bioarchaeology of the Transition to Agriculture*. New York, NY: John Wiley & Sons, pp. 107–149.

Hall, S. (2000). Burial and sequence in the Later Stone Age of the Eastern Cape province, South Africa. *South African Archaeological Bulletin*, 55, 137–146.

Hall, S. and Binneman, J. (1987). Later Stone Age burial variability in the Cape: A social interpretation. *South African Archaeological Bulletin*, 42, 140–152.

Harrington, L. (2010). *Ontogeny of Post-cranial Robusticity among Holocene Hunter-Gatherers of Southernmost Africa*. PhD dissertation, University of Toronto.

Harrington, L. and Pfeiffer, S. (2008). Juvenile mortality in southern African archaeological contexts. *South African Archaeological Bulletin*, 63, 95–101.

Harrington, L. and Pfeiffer, S. (2016). Developmental variation in perikymata expression in co-interred child foragers. *American Journal of Physical Anthropology*, 159(S62), 168.

Henshilwood, C. (1996). A revised chronology for pastoralism in southernmost Africa: New evidence of sheep at c. 2000 b.p. from Blombos Cave, South Africa. *Antiquity*, 70, 945–949.

Herbert, C. T. and Compton, J. S. (2007). Geochronology of Holocene sediments on the western margin of South Africa. *South African Journal of Geology*, 110, 327–338.

Horsburgh, K. A., Orton, J., and Klein, R. G. (2016). Beware the springbok in sheep's clothing: How secure are the faunal identifications upon which we build our models? *African Archaeological Review*, 33, 353–361.

Huffman, T. N. (2007). *Handbook to the Iron Age: The Archaeology of Pre-colonial Farming Societies in Southern Africa*. Scottsville: University of KwaZulu-Natal Press.

Humphrey, L. (2000). Growth studies of past populations: An overview and an example. In M. Cox and S. Mays, eds., *Human Osteology in Archaeology and Forensic Science*. London: Greenwich Medical Media, pp. 23–38.

Inskeep, R. (1986). A preliminary survey of burial practices in the Later Stone Age, from the Orange River to the Cape coast. In R. Singers and J. K. Lundy, eds., *Variation, Culture and Evolution in African Populations*. Johannesburg: Witwatersrand University Press, pp. 221–240.

Jerardino, A. (2016). On the origins and significance of Pleistocene coastal resource use in southern Africa with particular reference to shellfish gathering. *Journal of Anthropological Archaeology*, 41, 213–230.

Jerardino, A., Klein, R. G., Navarro, R., Orton, J., and Horwitz, L. (2013). Settlement and subsistence patterns since the terminal Pleistocene in the Elands Bay and Lamberts Bay areas. In A. Jerardino, A. Malan, and D. Braun, eds., *The Archaeology of the West Coast of South Africa*. Cambridge: Archaeopress, pp. 85–108.

Kim, H. L., Ratan, A., Perry, G. H., *et al.* (2014). Khoisan hunter-gatherers have been the largest population throughout most of modern-human demographic history. *Nature Communications*, 5, 5692.

Kurki, H. K. (2007). Protection of obstetric dimensions in a small-bodied human sample. *American Journal of Physical Anthropology*, 133, 1152–1165.

Kurki, H. K., Ginter, J. K., Stock, J. T., and Pfeiffer, S. (2008). Adult proportionality in small-bodied foragers: A test of ecogeographic expectations. *American Journal of Physical Anthropology*, 136, 28–38.

Kurki, H. K., Ginter, J., Stock, J., and Pfeiffer, S. (2010). Body size estimation of small-bodied humans: Applicability of current methods. *American Journal of Physical Anthropology*, 141, 169–180.

L'Abbe, E. N., Loots, M., and Keough, N. (2008). The Matjes River Rock Shelter: A description of the skeletal assemblage. *South African Archaeological Bulletin*, 63, 61–68.

Lee, R. B. (1979). *The !Kung San: Men, Women and Work in a Foraging Society*. Cambridge: Cambridge University Press.

Legassick, M. and Rassool, C. (2000). *Skeletons in the Cupboard: South African Museums and the Trade in Human Remains 1907–1917*, Cape Town: South African Museum.

Lewis-Williams, J. D. and Dowson, T. A. (1999). *Images of Power: Understanding San Rock Art.* Johannesburg: Southern Book Publishers.

Mackay, A. (2016). Three arcs: Observations of the Elands Bay and northern Cederberg landscapes. *Southern African Humanities*, **29**, 1–15.

Mackay, A., Stewart, B., and Chase, B. M. (2012). Coalescence and fragmentation in the last Pleistocene archaeology of southernmost Africa. *Journal of Human Evolution*, **72**, 26–51.

Marean, C. W., Cawthra, H. C., Cowling, R. M., *et al.* (2014). Stone Age people in a changing South African Greater Cape Floristic Region. In N. Allsopp, J. F. Colville, and G. A. Verboom, eds., *Fynbos: Ecology, Evolution, and Conservation of a Megadiverse Region.* Oxford: Oxford University Press, pp. 164–199.

Maresh, M. M. (1955). Linear growth of long bones of extremities from infancy through adolescence: Continuing studies. *AMA American Journal of Diseases in Children*, **89**, 725–742.

Maresh, M. M. (1970). Measurements from roentgenograms. In R. W. McCammon, ed., *Human Growth and Development.* Springfield, IL: Charles C. Thomas, pp. 157–200.

Marshall, E. M. (1958). *The Harmless People.* New York, NY: Knopf.

Mitchell, P. (2002). *The Archaeology of Southern Africa.* Cambridge: Cambridge University Press.

Montinaro, F., Busby, G. B. J., Gonzalez-Santos, M., *et al.* (2017). Complex ancient genetic structure and cultural transitions in southern African populations. *Genetics*, **205**, 303–316.

Morris, A. G. (1992). *A Master Catalogue: Holocene Human Skeletons from South Africa.* Johannesburg: Witwatersrand University Press.

Morris, A. G., ed. (2013). *Skeletal Identity of Past Southern African Populations: Lessons from Outside South Africa.* Cape Town: South African Archaeological Society.

Morris, A. G. and Parkington, J. (1982). Prehistoric homicide: A case of violent death on the Cape South Coast, South Africa. *South African Journal of Science*, **78**, 167–169.

Morris, A. G., Dlamini, N., Joseph, J., *et al.* (2005). Later Stone Age burials from the Western Cape province, South Africa. Part 1: Voelvlei. *Southern African Field Archaeology*, **13/14**, 19–26.

Morris, A. G., Heinze, A., Chan, E. K. F., *et al.* (2014). First ancient mitochondrial human genome from a prepastoralist southern African. *Genome Biology and Evolution*, **6**, 2647–2653.

Nielsen, R., Akey, J. M., Jakobsson, M., *et al.* (2017). Tracing the peopling of the world through genomics. *Nature*, **541**, 302–310.

Osipov, B., Temple, D., Cowgill, L., *et al.* (2016). Evidence for genetic and behavioral adaptations in the ontogeny of prehistoric hunter-gatherer limb robusticity. *Quaternary International*, **405**, Part B, 134–146.

Osipov, B., Harrington, L., Cowgill, L., *et al.* (2017). Regional variation and sexual dimorphism in the ontogeny of humeral asymmetry among prehistoric hunter-gatherers. *American Journal of Physical Anthropology*, **162**(S64), 306.

Pargeter, J. (2014). The Later Stone Age is not San prehistory. *The Digging Stick*, **31**, 1–4.

Pargeter, J., MacKay, A., Mitchell, P., and Shea, J. (2014). Primordialism and the "Pleistocene San" of southern Africa. *Antiquity*, **90**, 1072–1079.

Parkington, J. E. and Dlamini, N. (2015). *First People.* Cape Town: Krakadouw Trust.

Pearce, D. G. (2008). *Later Stone Age Burial Practice in the Eastern Cape Province, South Africa.* PhD dissertation, University of the Witwatersrand.

Perry, G. H. (2014). Parasites and human evolution. *Evolutionary Anthropology*, **23**, 218–228.

Pfeiffer, S. (2007). The health of foragers: People of the Later Stone Age, southern Africa. In M. N. Cohen and G. Crane-Kramer, eds., *Ancient Health: Skeletal Indicators of Agricultural and Economic Intensification.* Gainesville, FL: University Press of Florida, pp. 223–236.

Pfeiffer, S. (2011). Pelvic stress injuries in a small-bodied forager. *International Journal of Osteoarchaeology*, **21**, 694–703.

Pfeiffer, S. (2012a). Conditions for evolution of small adult body size in southern Africa. *Current Anthropology*, **53**, S383–S394.

Pfeiffer, S. (2012b). Two disparate instances of healed cranial trauma from the Later Stone Age of South Africa. *South African Archaeological Bulletin*, **67**, 256–261.

Pfeiffer, S. (2013). Population dynamics in the Southern African Holocene: Human burials from the West Coast. In A. Jerardino, D. Braun and A. Malan, eds., *The Archaeology of the West Coast of South Africa*. Oxford: Archaeopress, pp. 143–154.

Pfeiffer, S. (2016). An exploration of interpersonal violence among Holocene foragers of southern Africa. *International Journal of Paleopathology*, **13**, 27–38.

Pfeiffer, S. and Crowder, C. (2004). An ill child among mid-Holocene foragers of southern Africa. *American Journal of Physical Anthropology*, **123**, 23–29.

Pfeiffer, S. and Harrington, L. (2011). Bioarchaeological evidence for the basis of small adult stature in southern Africa: Growth, mortality, and small stature. *Current Anthropology*, **52**, 449–461.

Pfeiffer, S. and Sealy, J. (2006). Body size among Holocene foragers of the Cape ecozone, southern Africa. *American Journal of Physical Anthropology*, **129**, 1–11.

Pfeiffer, S. and van der Merwe, N. J. (2004). Cranial injuries to Later Stone Age children from the Modder River Mouth, Southwestern Cape, South Africa. *South African Archaeological Bulletin*, **59**, 59–65.

Pfeiffer, S., van der Merwe, N. J., Parkington, J. E., and Yates, R. (1999). Violent human death in the past: A case from the Western Cape. *South African Journal of Science*, **95**, 137–140.

Pfeiffer, S., Doyle, L. E., Kurki, H. K., *et al.* (2014). Discernment of mortality risk associated with childbirth in archaeologically derived forager skeletons. *International Journal of Paleopathology*, **7**, 15–24.

Pugach, I. and Stoneking, M. (2015). Genome-wide insights into the genetic history of human populations. *Investigative Genetics*, **6**, 6. DOI: 10.1186/s13323-015-0024-0

Ribot, I., Morris, A. G., Sealy, J. C., and Maggs, T. (2010). Population history and economic change in the last 2000 years in KwaZulu-Natal, RSA. *Southern African Humanities, Natal Museum*, **22**, 89–112.

Ruff, C. B. (2008). Biomechanical analyses of archaeological human skeletons. In M. A. Katzenberg and S. R. Saunders, eds., *Biological Anthropology of the Human Skeleton*. 2nd edn. New York, NY: Wiley-Liss, pp. 183–206.

Sadr, K. (1998). The first herders at the Cape of Good Hope. *African Archaeological Review*, **15**, 101–132.

Sadr, K. (2008). Invisible herders? The archaeology of Khoekhoe pastoralists. *Southern African Humanities*, **20**, 179–203.

Scheinfeldt, L. B., Soi, S., and Tishkoff, S. A. (2010). Working toward a synthesis of archaeological, linguistic and genetic data for inferring African population history. *Proceedings of the National Academy of Sciences*, **107**, 8931–8938.

Schlebusch, C. M., Skoglund, P., Sjödin, P., *et al.* (2012) Genomic variation in seven Khoe-San groups reveals adaptation and complex African history. *Science*, **338**, 374–379.

Schlebusch, C. M., Lombard, M., and Soodyall, H. (2013). MtDNA control region variation affirms diversity and deep sub-structure in populations from southern Africa. *BMC Evolutionary Biology*, **13**, 56.

Sealy, J. (2006). Diet, mobility and settlement pattern among Holocene hunter-gatherers in southernmost Africa. *Current Anthropology*, **47**, 569–595.

Sealy, J. and Pfeiffer, S. (2000). Diet, body size and landscape use among Holocene peoples in the Southern Cape, South Africa. *Current Anthropology*, **41**, 642–655.

Sealy, J. C. (2010). Isotopic evidence for the antiquity of cattle-based pastoralism in southernmost Africa. *Journal of African Archaeology*, **8**, 65–81.

Sealy, J. C. and van der Merwe, N. J. (1986). Isotope assessment and the seasonal-mobility hypothesis in the southwestern Cape of South Africa. *Current Anthropology*, **27**, 135–150.

Sealy, J. C. and van der Merwe, N. J. (1988). Social, spatial and chronological patterning in marine food use as determined by ^{13}C measurements of Holocene human skeletons from the southwestern Cape, South Africa. *World Archaeology*, 20, 87–102.

Sealy, J. C., van der Merwe, N. J., Lee-Thorp, J. A. and Lanham, J. L. (1987). Nitrogen isotopic ecology in southern Africa: Implications for environmental and dietary tracing. *Geochemica et Cosmochimica Acta*, 51, 2707–2717.

Silberbauer, G. (1981). *Hunter and Habitat in the Central Kalahari Desert*. Cambridge: Cambridge University Press.

Skotnes, P. (2007). *Claim to the Country: The Archive of Wilhelm Bleek and Lucy Lloyd*. Athens, OH: Ohio University Press.

Smith, A. B. (2008). Pastoral origins at the Cape, South Africa: Influences and arguments. *Southern African Humanities*, 20, 49–60.

Smith, P., Horwitz, L. K., and Kaplan, E. (1992). Skeletal evidence for population change in the Late Holocene of the South-Western Cape: A radiological study. *South African Archaeological Bulletin*, 47, 82–88.

Steyn, M., Morris, A. G., Mosothwane, M. N., Nienaber, W. C., and Maat, G. J. R. (2013). *Introduction: Opening the Cupboard – Lessons in Biology and History from African Skeletons*. Cape Town: South African Archaeological Society.

Stock, J. and Pfeiffer, S. (2001). Linking structural variability in long bone diaphyses to habitual behaviors: Foragers from the southern African Later Stone Age and the Andaman Islands. *American Journal of Physical Anthropology*, 115, 337–348.

Stock, J. and Pfeiffer, S. K. (2004). Long bone robusticity and subsistence behaviour among Later Stone Age foragers of the forest and fynbos biomes of South Africa. *Journal of Archaeological Science*, 31, 999–1013.

Stock, J. T. and Shaw, C. N. (2007). Which measures of diaphyseal robusticity are robust? A comparison of external methods of quantifying the strength of long bone diaphyses to cross-sectional geometric properties. *American Journal of Physical Anthropology*, 134, 412–423.

Stulp, G. and Barrett, L. (2016). Evolutionary perspectives on human height variation. *Biological Reviews*, 91, 206–234.

Stynder, D. D. (2006). *A Quantitative Assessment of Variation in Holocene Khoesan Crania from South Africa's Western, South-western, Southern and South-eastern Coasts and Coastal Forelands*. PhD dissertation, University of Cape Town.

Stynder, D. D., Ackermann, R. R., and Sealy, J. C. (2007a). Craniofacial variation and population continuity during the South African Holocene. *American Journal of Physical Anthropology*, 134, 489–500.

Stynder, D. D., Ackermann, R. R., and Sealy, J. C. (2007b). Early to mid-Holocene South African Later Stone Age human crania exhibit a distinctly Khoesan morphological pattern. *South African Journal of Science*, 103, 349–352.

Tishkoff, S. A., Gonder, M. K., Henn, B. M., *et al.* (2007). History of click-speaking populations of Africa inferred from mtDNA and Y chromosome genetic variation. *Molecular Biology and Evolution*, 24, 2180–2195.

Tobias, P. V. (1962). On the increasing stature of the Bushmen. *Anthropos*, 57, 801–810.

Truswell, A. S. and Hanson, J. D. L. (1976). Medical research among the !Kung. In R. B. Lee and I. DeVore, eds., *Kalahari Hunter-Gatherers*. Cambridge, MA: Harvard University Press, pp. 166–194.

Uren, C., Kim, M., Martin, A. R., *et al.* (2017). Fine-scale human population structure in southern Africa reflects ecogeographic boundaries. *Genetics*, 204, 303–314.

Villa, P., Soriano, S., Tsanova, T., *et al.* (2012). Border Cave and the beginning of the Later Stone Age in South Africa. *Proceedings of the National Academy of Sciences*, 109, 13208–13213.

Wadley, L. (1992). Reply to Barham: Aggregation and dispersal sites in the Later Stone Age. *South African Archaeological Bulletin*, 47, 52–55.

Wadley, L. (1996). The Bleek and Lloyd records of death and burial: The problems that these present for archaeologists. In J. Deacon and T. A. Dowson, eds., *Voices from the Past: /Xam Bushmen and the Bleek and Lloyd Collection.* Johannesburg: Witwatersrand University Press, pp. 271–286.

Wadley, L. (1997). Where have all the dead men gone? In L. Wadley, ed., *Our Gendered Past: Archaeological Studies of Gender in Southern Africa.* Johannesburg: Witwatersrand University Press, pp. 107–134.

Wadley, L. (2015). Those marvelous millennia: The Middle Stone Age of Southern Africa. *Azania: Archaeological Research in Africa,* **50,** 155–226.

Wadley, L., Hidgskiss, T., and Grant, M. (2009). Implications for complex cognition from the hafting of tools with compound adhesives in the Middle Stone Age, South Africa. *Proceedings of the National Academy of Sciences,* **106,** 9590–9594.

Walker, P. L., Bathurst, R. R., Richman, R., Gjerdrum, T., and Andrushko, V. (2009). The causes of porotic hyperostosis and cribra orbitalia: A reappraisal of the iron-deficiency-anemia hypothesis. *American Journal of Physical Anthropology,* **135,** 109–125.

Walker, R. S. and Hamilton, M. J. (2008). Life-history consequences of density dependence and the evolution of human body size. *Current Anthropology,* **49,** 115–122.

Walker, R. S., Gurven, M., Hill, K., *et al.* (2006). Growth rates and life histories in small-scale societies. *American Journal of Human Biology,* **18,** 295–311.

Wilson, M. L. and Lundy, J. K. (1994). Estimated living statures of dated Khoisan skeletons from the south-western coastal region of South Africa. *South African Archaeological Bulletin,* **49,** 2–8.

Woodburn, J. (1982). Social dimensions of death in four African hunting and gathering societies. In M. Bloch and J. Parry, eds., *Death and the Regeneration of Life.* Cambridge: Cambridge University Press, pp. 187–210.

Wooding, M., Bradfield, J., Maharaj, V., *et al.* (2017). Potential for identifying plant-based toxins on San hunter-gatherer arrowheads. *South African Journal of Science,* **113,** 1–10.

3 Hunter-Gatherer Persistence and Demography in Patagonia (Southern South America): The Impact of Ecological Changes during the Pleistocene and Holocene

Valeria Bernal, S. Ivan Perez, María Bárbara Postillone, and Diego D. Rindel

3.1 Introduction

Human populations were exposed to significant environmental and ecological changes during the Pleistocene–Holocene transition. In particular, changes in temperature and rainfall occurring at the end of the last glacial period greatly influenced the dynamics of ecological communities and led to spectacular changes in faunal diversity (Barnosky *et al.*, 2004; Haynes, 2009; Lorenzen *et al.*, 2011). Almost all mega-mammals and numerous large mammals became extinct in Eurasia, Oceania, and the Americas, reaching maximum extinction rates around 10 000 BP (Haynes, 2009; Koch and Barnosky, 2006). After the megafaunal extinction, mammalian assemblages became impoverished, although a few remaining mega-mammals survived (e.g., *Bison* and *Rangifer* in temperate North America and Eurasia; *Tapirus* and *Pecari* in tropical South and Central America; *Lama* in temperate South America) and probably became the dominant species throughout the Holocene (Haynes, 2009). As a consequence, the diversity and amount of animal resources available for hunter-gatherers underwent significant fluctuations, which in turn may have induced varied responses in these populations.

Dramatic changes in resource availability may have had a negative impact on human population demography due to declines in population size or variance in population growth rate. Fluctuations in growth rate can generate a reduction in population density that can lead to population extinction if the system does not re-establish a stable state (Inchausti and Halley, 2003; Turelli, 1978). In this context, the persistence of a population depends on the capacity to absorb the impact of exogenous disturbances ("resistance") as well as endogenous processes that pull demographic population parameters back toward an equilibrium ("recovery"). Overall, these two components determine the resilience of populations (Hogdson *et al.*, 2015). Despite a strong ecological and evolutionary relevance, the capacity of small hunter-gatherer populations to respond to perturbations by resisting damage and/or recovering remains largely unknown (Hoover and Hudson, 2016). Investigating the causes of persistence and the population dynamics that lead to resistance and recovery of socioecological and cultural systems is key to understanding resilience in past human populations.

Hunter-gatherers from Patagonia (southern South America) are an excellent model for studying these processes because these populations persisted until historical times. These populations thrived in spite of the severe climatic and ecological changes documented in southern South America since the Late Pleistocene. The Patagonia region was peopled around 15 000 BP by small groups of hunter-gatherers who shared a recent common ancestor (Bodner *et al.*, 2012; de Saint Pierre *et al.*, 2012a, 2012b). Palynological and glacial studies suggest that, in the final Late Pleistocene, climatic conditions in Patagonia were relatively warm and humid, with high primary productivity generating a favorable environment that could support a large diversity of mega-herbivores and predators (nearly 37 species; Cione *et al.*, 2009; McCulloch *et al.*, 2000; Rabassa, 2008; Tonni and Carlini, 2008). After approximately 10 000 to 8000 BP, all megafaunal species from Patagonia were extinct, with only two large mammalian herbivores – the guanaco (*Lama guanicoe*) and huemul (*Hippocamelus bisulcus*) – surviving to the present (Borrero, 2009; Cione *et al.*, 2009). Archaeological evidence suggests that large and mega-mammals, mainly the guanaco, were primary food sources of Patagonian hunter-gatherers from the Late Pleistocene to 400 BP (Borrero, 2009).

Despite the fact that Patagonian hunter-gatherer groups have been the focus of numerous studies, the responses of these populations to drastic climatic and ecological changes at the Pleistocene/Holocene transition remain largely unexplored. This chapter evaluates the persistence of hunter-gatherer demography as evidence of resilience in response to ecological disturbances, specifically mega-mammal extinction in south and northwest Patagonia during the Late Pleistocene–Holocene transition (Figure 3.1). These two areas were selected because the regions represent the extremes of environmental, ecological, and cultural variation in Patagonia. Compared to the southern area, northwest Patagonia is characterized by a higher diversity of resources during the Pleistocene–Holocene transition as well as by higher cultural variation, including the early incorporation of ceramic technology and domestic vegetables (Borrero, 2009; Perez *et al.*, 2017). This chapter explores the relationship between variation in faunal composition and changes in population size during the Pleistocene–Holocene transition. More specifically, this chapter analyzes ancient and modern mitochondrial DNA (mtDNA), employing Bayesian genealogical reconstructions and Skyline Plot methods to assess changes in the size of human populations during this drastic period of climate change. Zooarchaeological data are also incorporated, with measurements of individual and species abundance to gain insight into the ecological changes that challenged human populations over the last 15 000 years. This work predicts that human dynamics during the Late Pleistocene and Holocene will be correlated with changes in the availability of resources, being strongly impacted by the megafaunal extinctions ca. 10 000 BP.

3.2   Materials and Methods

3.2.1   Reconstructing Changes in Trophic Interactions and Faunal Consumption

To explore changes in the faunal composition and diet of prehistoric hunter-gatherers from Patagonia, zooarchaeological assemblages derived from several sites from south and northwest Patagonia were analyzed (Figure 3.1). These sites were

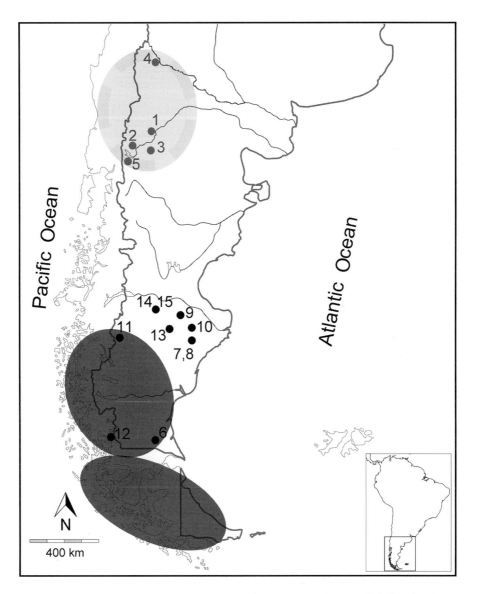

Figure 3.1 Map showing the geographic locations of archaeological sites included in this chapter Light and dark gray represent source populations for mtDNA for northwest and southwest Patagonia respectively. See references in Table 3.1. The map was modified from the d-maps website: http://dmaps.com/carte.php?num_car=1463&lang=en.

Table 3.1 Archaeological sites included in this chapter.

	Site	Map Reference	Reference
Northwest	Cueva Epullán Grande	1	Cordero, 2009, 2010
	Cueva Traful	2	Cordero 2010, 2011
	Cueva and Paredón Loncomán	3	Cordero, 2007, 2010
	Cueva Huenúl	4	Barberena *et al.*, 2015
	Cueva El Trébol	5	Lezcano *et al.*, 2010
South	Cueva Fell	6	Emperaire *et al.*, 1963
	Cueva Tunel	7	Paunero *et al.*, 2005
	Casa Minero	8	Paunero *et al.*, 2007
	Cueva 3 de Los Toldos	9	Cardich *et al.*, 1973
	Piedra Museo	10	Miotti, 1996; Marchionni, 2013
	Cerro Casa de Piedra 7	11	De Nigris, 2004
	Cueva del Medio	12	Nami and Menegaz, 1991
	Cueva Maripe	13	Marchionni, 2013
	Cueva de las Manos	14	Mengoni Goñalons and Silveira, 1976
	Cueva Grande del Arroyo Feo	15	Silveira, 1979

dated between the Late Pleistocene and late Holocene periods (Table 3.1) (Borrero, 2009; Miotti and Salemme, 2003; Prates *et al.*, 2013; Perez *et al.*, 2016). Only cave sites with a long sequence of occupation and zooarchaeological assemblages of large sample sizes were included in this study. Because this study only used cave sites, a general similarity in the depositional environment for all assemblages was assured. This is particularly relevant because of differences in the presence and incidence of taphonomic agents between caves and open-air sites (Surovell *et al.*, 2009; Torfing, 2015). Moreover, caves in Patagonia are generally the only sites that sample the whole chronological range of human occupation from the Late Pleistocene to the Late Holocene. For the northern region, samples were collected from five caves, while ten caves were included for the southern region (Figure 3.1; Table 3.1). The total faunal sample comprised 37 850 specimens, 15 826 from northwest Patagonia and 22 024 from south Patagonia.

First, changes in the diversity of species in the assemblages were evaluated, enumerating the species observed and estimating the Shannon diversity index (Shannon, 1948). For assessing temporal changes in diversity, the number of species for different temporal strata from each archaeological site were obtained. Changes in species diversity over time provide the most direct estimate of the impact of ecological disturbances on human population dynamics. Second, changes in the size of the faunal assemblages over time were estimated as an indirect measurement of the changes in the intensity of animal consumption. For this analysis, the number of identified specimens (NISP; Lyman, 2008) of faunal species for different temporal strata at each archaeological site were enumerated. The size of the faunal assemblages was calculated as the sum of the NISP of the different sites for each temporal stratum.

Third, proportional changes in the primary prey exploited by humans in Patagonia (guanaco, *Lama guanicoe*) were estimated (Borrero, 2009). The relative frequency of guanaco over other faunal species using the NISP guanaco/NTAXA index was measured (number of species; Grayson and Delpech, 1998). The minimum number of individuals (MNI; Lyman, 2008) for each stratum was estimated because this measure is more robust than NISP/NTAXA when the assemblages are fragmented (Grayson and Delpech, 1998). Additionally, an alternative percentage of the relative frequency of guanaco was measured by dividing the NISP of this species by the total NISP of the stratum (percent NISP). This step estimated the relative importance of guanaco in the diet of the prehistoric human populations compared to the other potential prey. Temporal changes in species diversity, the size of faunal assemblages, and the relative contribution of guanaco to the human diet were explored, plotting the Shannon index, NISP, and the NISP guanaco/NTAXA against the mean time of each stratum.

3.2.2   Inferring the Demographic History of Patagonian Hunter-Gatherers

To explore the demographic history of prehistoric human populations from south and northwest Patagonia (Figure 3.1), ancient and modern mtDNA sequences from the descendants of aboriginal populations carrying variants (haplotypes) with high frequencies and/or those mainly restricted to the southern regions of South America were analyzed (Bodner *et al.*, 2012; de Saint Pierre *et al.*, 2012a; Perego *et al.*, 2009). mtDNA sequences of 305 individuals from northwest Patagonia and 85 individuals from south Patagonia were obtained from previous publications and GenBank (Bobillo *et al.*, 2010; Bodner *et al.*, 2012; Catelli *et al.*, 2011; de Saint Pierre *et al.*, 2012a, 2012b; de la Fuente *et al.*, 2015; García-Bour *et al.*, 2004; Ginther *et al.*, 1993; Moraga *et al.*, 2000, 2010; Perego *et al.*, 2009). The studied sequences comprise 1131 base pairs (bp), corresponding to the mtDNA control region, and were aligned with MAFFT v7.012b (Katoh and Standley, 2013). The model of sequence substitution was estimated using the Akaike Information Criterion with correction for sample size (AICc) as implemented in Mega 6 software (Tamura *et al.*, 2013).

mtDNA sequences were used to estimate changes in population size over time in south and northwest Patagonia, employing the Bayesian Skyline Plot (BSP) method (Drummond *et al.*, 2005; Ho and Shapiro, 2011). This method relates the shape of a molecular genealogy to the demographic changes of the population in the past, and its algorithms are based on coalescent theory (Drummond *et al.*, 2005; Ho and Shapiro, 2011). The reconstruction of the demographic curve comprises the estimation of a genealogy or chrono-phylogenetic tree and the inference of the effective population size at different points along the phylogenetic tree. The effective population size is estimated for each coalescent interval (i.e., the time interval between nodes of the phylogenetic tree) considering that effective population size is proportional to the number of molecular lineages and length of the coalescent interval (Ho and Shapiro, 2011). A general introduction to the methods can be found in

Ho and Shapiro (2011). The assumptions, strengths, and weaknesses of the application of these methods in the region under study are discussed by Perez *et al.* (2016).

The demographic curve was generated using the BSP approach implemented in BEAST 1.6.1 (Drummond and Rambaut, 2007). Markov chain Monte Carlo (MCMC) sampling procedures of 50 000 000 generations, sampling with a frequency of 5000 generations, was used to co-estimate a genealogy, time of sequence coalescence, and demographic changes through time. The average and credibility intervals that represent both genealogical and coalescent uncertainty were also included (Drummond *et al.*, 2005). These analyses were performed assuming the HKY substitution model, a rate of substitutions of 3.02E–7 by site by year (de Saint Pierre *et al.*, 2012a; Endicott and Ho, 2008), and an uncorrelated log-normal relaxed molecular clock model (Drummond and Rambaut, 2007; Drummond *et al.*, 2006). The Bayesian demographic curves and convergence in the MCMC simulations were reconstructed in the program Tracer v1.5 (Rambaut and Drummond, 2007).

3.3   Results

3.3.1   Faunal Turnover and Socioecological Adaptation

Figure 3.2 displays the temporal changes in the Shannon diversity index. A decreasing pattern in the Shannon values is observed from the Pleistocene–Holocene transition to the present time for both northwest and south Patagonia. Greater intensity of change is, however, observed in the northwest region. In both regions, during the Pleistocene–Holocene transition, the diversity of species was higher as a result of the presence of extinct taxa (*Mylodon* sp., *Dusycion avus*, and deer extinct in the northwest, and *Lama gracilis*, *Hemiauchenia paradoxa*, *Hippidion saldiasi*, *Mylodon* sp., *Megatherium* sp., *Panthera onca mesembrina*, and *Rhea americana* in the south) (Borrero, 2009). Moreover, the Shannon index values were higher in the northwest than in southern Patagonia during all of the periods under investigation, indicating a greater diversity of species exploitation in northwest compared to southern Patagonia. In the case of northwest Patagonia, taxa such as dasipodidos, fish, flightless birds, mollusks, carnivores (felines, canids, and mustelids), and rheids were exploited, while in the south the range of species was smaller. These results are concordant with the expectation of a higher species diversity for north Patagonia, since species diversity decreases with increasing latitude (Adams, 2010; Willig *et al.*, 2003). In northwest Patagonia, more species were always included in the assemblages, but this diversity was rapidly lost, while in south Patagonia, after the process of megafaunal extinction, diversity remained narrow throughout the Holocene.

Figure 3.3 shows temporal changes in the Shannon diversity index for the faunal assemblages from northwest and south Patagonia. The total quantity of osseous specimens assigned to different species displayed a general increase from the Pleistocene–Holocene transition to the late Holocene in both regions. However, a

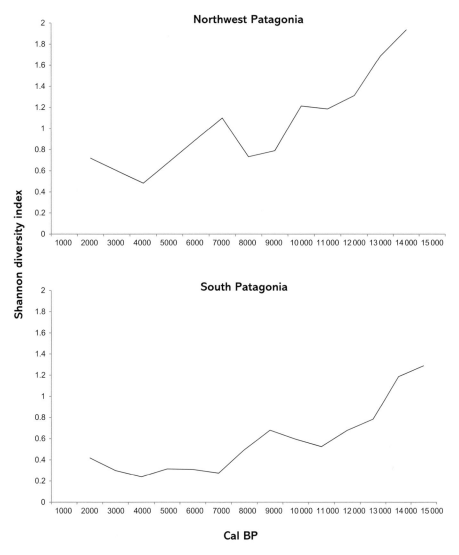

Figure 3.2 Temporal changes in the Shannon diversity index for the faunal assemblages from northwest and south Patagonia.

significant increase, together with gaps, was observed in the middle Holocene in both regions. In this sense, the first great increase in the size of the assemblage occurred in northwest Patagonia during the Late Pleistocene, followed by a relatively stable pattern until the Late Holocene. In south Patagonia, the first increase in the size of the assemblage is observed ca. 10 000 BP.

The proportion of NISP guanaco/NTAXA shows that the contribution of guanaco to the assemblages grew over time in the two areas (Figure 3.4). It should be noted that other measures of abundance, such as the MNI or NISP guanaco/total NISP (results not shown), also displayed a similar pattern. However, the pattern of relative

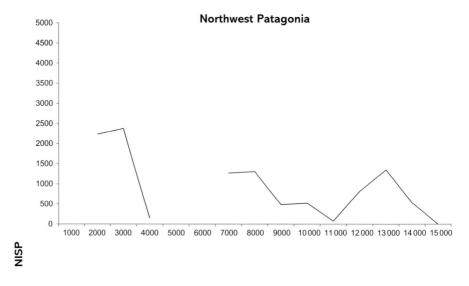

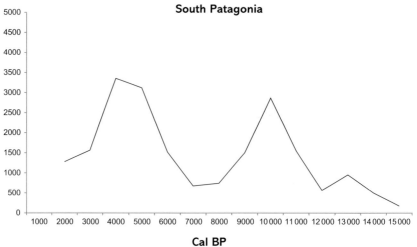

Figure 3.3 Temporal changes in the size (NISP) of faunal assemblages from northwest and south Patagonia.

increase in the guanaco contribution was stronger in south Patagonia. Moreover, it is interesting to note that the guanaco was more important during the Pleistocene–Holocene transition in northwest compared to south Patagonia. In this regard, there are several archaeological sites with evidence of megafaunal exploitation in south Patagonia (Los Toldos 3 Cave, Piedra Museo U6, Casa del Minero, Tunel Cave, El Ceibo, Fell Cave, Palli Aike, Cueva del Medio, Lago Sofía 1 Cave, and Tres Arroyos, among others) (Borrero, 2009; Pires *et al.*, 2016), but only one site with evidence of human exploitation of megafauna in the northwest (El Trébol) (Borrero, 2009). The lower quantity of megafaunal remains in northwest Patagonia could be due to differences in the sampling effort in each area, problems with preservation, the

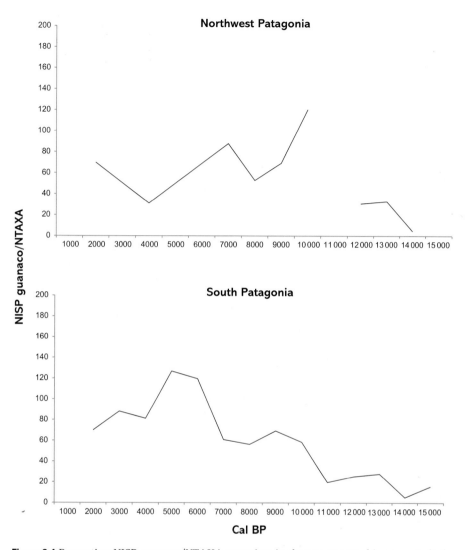

Figure 3.4 Proportion NISP guanaco/NTAXA over time in the two geographic areas studied.

absence of suitable habitats for megafauna, or the exploitation of other species. Finally, the increase in the contribution of guanaco to the total NISP was more marked in the south compared to northwest Patagonia.

3.3.2   Effective Population Size during Pleistocene–Holocene Transition

The BSP plots show that human populations from both south and northwest Patagonia had a female effective population size of ca. 1100 individuals during the Late Pleistocene, between 15 000 and 13 000 BP (Figure 3.5). This value increased slowly between 12 500 and 6000 BP, reaching an effective population size of ca. 3500 individuals. After this time, these two areas display some differences in estimated

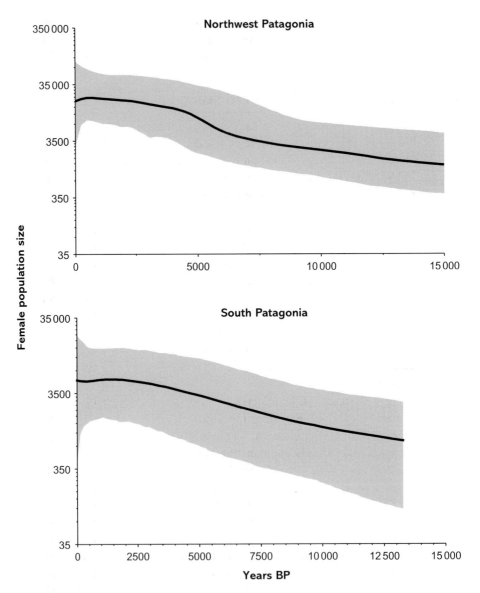

Figure 3.5 BSP plots for human populations from northwest and south Patagonia.

demographic curves. In northwest Patagonia, the human population steeply increased after 6000 BP, and an estimated female effective population size of approximately 20 000 individuals was reached by 1100 BP (Figure 3.5). The confidence intervals generated by the BSP progressively increase in northwest Patagonia from 700 to 10 000 individuals by 15 000 BP, 2000 to 30 000 individuals by 6000 BP, and 7000 to 70 000 individuals by 1100 BP (Figure 3.5). Conversely, the population from south Patagonia grew at a constant rate, reaching an estimated maximum female effective population size of 6000 individuals at around 1200 BP.

The confidence intervals generated by the BSP progressively increased in south Patagonia from 100 to 3500 individuals by 12 500 BP, 700 to 10 000 individuals by 6000 BP, and 1700 to 14 000 individuals by 1100 BP (Figure 3.5).

3.4   Ecological Transformation and Demographic Resilience

The analyses of faunal assemblages from archaeological sites in northwest and south Patagonia show a clear trend toward a decrease in the diversity of species from the Pleistocene–Holocene transition to around 7000 years BP, and remained relatively stable after that date. This decrease in faunal diversity is likely a consequence of megafaunal exinctions initiated around 12 000 BP. The available evidence suggests that, unlike other regions such as North America where most species went abruptly extinct, the process in Pampa and Patagonia was gradual and spanned around 5000 years (Borrero, 2009; Hubbe *et al.*, 2007; Prates *et al.*, 2013). Overall, these results are consistent with previous studies indicating that as faunal diversity decreased, the subsistence practices of hunter-gatherers changed. Previous studies have interpreted the reduction in diversity in faunal assemblages as a change from generalist to more specialized subsistence strategies (Miotti and Salemme, 2003; Prates *et al.*, 2013). However, if the decrease in diversity during the Late Pleistocene and Early Holocene is considered, it is clear that Holocene human populations shifted subsistence practices to target surviving species, mainly guanaco (Cione *et al.*, 2009; Pires *et al.*, 2016).

These changes can be understood in the context of processes favoring ecosystem stability – for example, the adjustments in species densities maintaining overall community biomass. These processes reinforce the resistance of the ecological community and constituent populations to disturbance, and thus favor stability and persistence (Connell and Ghedini, 2015). Interestingly, the amount of biomass consumed by human populations in Patagonia, as measured by the NISP, grew at a constant rate throughout the Late Pleistocene until the Late Holocene. Such an inverse relationship between the diversity of species and biomass suggests that hunter-gatherers not only consumed a progressively smaller number of species, but that these species were more intensively exploited. Future studies should explore whether the increase in the number of specimens was associated with the intensification of anatomical elements with lower caloric returns.

Despite the sustained decrease in faunal diversity, the size of human populations, as estimated by molecular data, displayed a consistent, positive trend between the Pleistocene and Holocene in both geographic regions. Overall, these results demonstrate the persistence of human population density in Patagonia after the megafaunal extinction. Moreover, the molecular data, as well as previous radiocarbon studies (Perez *et al.*, 2016, 2017), show no evidence for the attenuation of population density after the Pleistocene–Holocene transition. This suggests that the persistence of hunter-gatherer populations in Patagonia during the Holocene results from the ability of these groups to absorb the impact of such exogenous disturbances, (i.e., population resistance), rather than from an endogenous process that recovers demographic population parameters (recovery).

Although both populations in northwest and south Patagonia increased effective population size throughout ecological disturbances during the Late Pleistocene and Holocene, differences in population growth between the two regions are noted. In northwest Patagonia, the rate of population growth displayed a notable acceleration between 7000 and 6000 BP, when the diversity of faunal resources reached a stable value. Similar changes in the human population growth of northwest Patagonia have been previously documented on the basis of site frequency distributions uncorrected and corrected by taphonomic bias (Perez *et al.*, 2016), suggesting that the demographic pattern observed by this study is broadly supported. The ecological factors underlying human population growth after the Early Holocene remains to be investigated. According to results reported here, changes in population size cannot be fully explained in terms of faunal resources because the rate of increase in faunal biomass is lower in this region compared to south Patagonia. There exists higher diversity in ecological settings at lower latitudes, including the diversity of fauna in northwest compared to south Patagonia. On this basis hunter-gatherers from northwest Patagonia might have broadened ecological niches by incorporating resources other than fauna. Carbon and nitrogen isotope values from human remains suggest the incorporation of plants into the diet of these groups around 6500 BP (Fernandez and Panarello, 2001; Gordón *et al.*, 2017). The use of plants is also supported by the high concentration of grinding stones in the archaeological record of northwest Patagonia around 4500 BP (Bernal *et al.*, 2016; Della Negra *et al.*, 2014; Lema *et al.*, 2012; Perez *et al.*, 2009). Another technological change that may reflect a broader niche is the use of pottery. Pottery was first used around 1900 BP (Della Negra, 2008), a few hundred years prior to the achievement of maximum population size. These technological innovations might have contributed to food processing (grinding and cooking), resulting in the incorporation of a larger quantity of nutrients (Carmody *et al.*, 2011), and more importantly, helped sustain demographic resilience during a period fraught with ecological challenges

In south Patagonia, demographic growth is associated with an increase in the faunal biomass that was dominated by guanaco. Previous studies show that the guanaco population experienced sustained growth after approximately 8000 BP, and this expansion may have been favored by the gradual occupation of geographical areas previously dominated by mega-mammals (Pires *et al.*, 2016), a compensatory process that allows ecosystem stability. Accordingly, isotopic and zooarchaeological data suggest that south Patagonian hunter-gatherers' dietary habits included faunal resources, with guanaco targeted as the main prey throughout the Pleistocene–Holocene, together with the incorporation of marine resources (Borrero, 2009; Tessone *et al.*, 2009). Along with the increasing importance of guanaco in the diet, several technological changes took place. Especially remarkable is the predominant use of stone balls around 7000 BP, a hunting technology used until historical times (Cardich *et al.*, 1973). The incorporation of stone balls, a thrown weapon, during the middle Holocene allowed an expanded exploitation of large herbivores who survived the initial megafaunal extinction, such as guanaco and ñandú. It is worth noting that the first evidence of grinding tools and pottery is documented thousands of years later in south rather than northwest Patagonia, with these tools seemingly used for meat processing (Cassiodoro and Tessone, 2014; Pallo and Borrero, 2015). This finding further supports the stronger dependence on hunting by southern compared to northern populations, which in turn might account for the slower growth and lower density attained by these populations. Other indirect evidence related to a decline in mobility and an increase in population density, such as the presence of formal burial areas, is also dated later in south compared to northwest Patagonia, at 2000 and 5000 BP, respectively (Della Negra *et al.*, 2014; García Guraieb *et al.*, 2015; Perez *et al.*, 2016). These results suggest that demographic resilience in south Patagonia was maintained by a socioecological system focused on hunting diverse mammalian fauna. This difference in subsistence practices between southern and northwestern populations may help explain variation in the rate of population expansion between these two groups.

3.5 Conclusion

The results of this chapter suggest that hunter-gatherers from northwest and south Patagonia were resilient to the significant ecological changes that took place during the Late Pleistocene and Early Holocene. In particular, the rate of population growth was resistant to reduction in the diversity of available resources as a consequence of megafaunal extinctions around 10 000 BP. The resistance of hunter-gatherers from northwest and south Patagonia could be related to the ability of human populations to absorb the impact of relatively slow ecological changes. The chronological association between the demographic dynamics and archaeological evidence suggests that cultural responses (i.e., technological changes) might have helped maintain and even increase human population density. Thus, the two populations used ecological adaptations as a way to maintain, and even grow, effective population sizes during a period of ecological turnover.

Despite evidence for population growth during the Pleistocene–Holocene transition, the human populations living in these two regions responded in different ways to megafaunal extinctions. Populations in south Patagonia persisted through a low but constant rate of population growth that mirrored the demographic expansion of highly valued prey. The northwestern population experienced a faster rate of growth, probably sustained by an increase in the carrying capacity of the environment mediated by cultural changes that expanded dietary breadth. These results demonstrate that demographic resilience is mediated by differing modes of cultural adaptation to environmental challenges.

Acknowledgments

This work was supported by grants from FONCyT ("Dinámica poblacional humana y variación en el nicho ecológico en el Noroeste de Patagonia durante el Holoceno."

PICT 2014/2017–2134), CONICET ("Dinámica poblacional humana y cambios en el nicho ecológico en el Noroeste de Patagonia durante el Holoceno." PIP 729- 2015-2017), and Universidad Nacional de La Plata ("Ecología y evolución de las poblaciones humanas del Noroeste de Patagonia [Pcia. del Neuquén] durante el Holoceno." UNLP. 2016–2019).

References

Adams, J. (2010). *Species Richness: Patterns in the Diversity of Life.* Heidelberg: Springer.

Barberena, R., Borrazzo, K., Rughini, A. A., *et al.* (2015). Perspectivas arqueológicas para Patagonia Septentrional: Sitio Cueva Huenul 1 (Provincia del Neuquén, Argentina). *Magallania*, **43**, 137–163.

Barnosky, A. D., Koch, P. L., Feranec, R. S., Wing, S. L., and Shabel, A. B. (2004). Assessing the causes of late Pleistocene extinctions on the continents. *Science*, **306**, 70–75.

Bernal, V., Gonzalez, P. N., Gordón, F., and Perez, S. I. (2016). Exploring dietary patterns in the southernmost limit of pre-Hispanic agriculture in America by using Bayesian stable isotope mixing models. *Current Anthropology*, **57**, 230–239.

Bobillo, M. C., Zimmermann, B., Sala, A., *et al.* (2010). Amerindian mitochondrial DNA haplogroups predominate in the population of Argentina: Towards a first nationwide forensic mitochondrial DNA sequence database. *International Journal of Legal Medicine*, **124**, 263–268.

Bodner, M., Perego, U. A., Huber, G., *et al.* (2012). Rapid coastal spread of First Americans: Novel insights from South America's Southern Cone mitochondrial genomes. *Genome Research*, **22**, 811–820.

Borrero, L. A. (2009). The elusive evidence: The archeological record of the South American extinct megafauna. In G. Haynes, ed., *American Megafaunal Extinctions at the End of the Pleistocene*, Dordrecht: Springer, pp. 145–168.

Cardich, A. R., Cardich, L. A., and Hajduk, A. (1973). Secuencia arqueológica y cronológica radiocarbónica de la cueva 3 de Los Toldos (Santa Cruz, Argentina). *Relaciones de la Sociedad Argentina de Antropología*, **7**, 85–123.

Carmody, R. N, Weintraub, G. S., and Wrangham R. W. (2011). Energetic consequences of thermal and nonthermal food processing. *Proceedings of the National Academy of Sciences*, **108**, 19199–19203.

Cassiodoro, G. and Tessone, A. (2014). Análisis radiocarbónico y de isótopos estables en residuos cerámicos del centro-oeste de Santa Cruz (Patagonia). *Relaciones de la Sociedad Argentina de Antropología*, **39**, 293–299.

Catelli, M. L., Álvarez-Iglesias, V., Gómez-Carballa, A., *et al.* (2011). The impact of modern migrations on present-day multi-ethnic Argentina as recorded on the mitochondrial DNA genome. *BMC Genetics*, **12**, 77

Cione, A. L., Tonni, E. P., and Soibelzon, L. (2009). Did humans cause the Late Pleistocene–Early Holocene mammalian extinctions in South America in a context of shrinking open areas? In G. Haynes, ed., *American Megafaunal Extinctions at the End of the Pleistocene*. Dordrecht: Springer, pp. 125–144.

Connell, S. D. and Ghedini, G. (2015). Resisting regime-shifts: The stabilising effect of compensatory processes. *Trends in Ecology & Evolution*, **30**, 513–515.

Cordero, A. (2007). Cambios en la amplitud de dieta de cazadores recolectores de Patagonia septentrional desde c. 10 000 AP hasta el presente. In M. Ramos and E. Néspolo, eds., *Signos en el Tiempo y Rastros en la Tierra*, Lujan: Universidad Nacional de Luján, pp. 127–134.

Cordero, A. (2009). Arqueofauna de las primeras ocupaciones de cueva Epullán Grande. *Cuadernos de Antropología*, **5**, 159–188.

Cordero, A. (2010). *Explotación animal en el Holoceno del noroeste de la Patagonia Argentina. Cambios climáticos y transformaciones del comportamiento humano: Una primera aproximación.* Doctoral dissertation, Facultad de Filosofía y Letras, Universidad de Buenos Aires.

Cordero, A. (2011). Subsistencia y movilidad de los cazadores-recolecto res que ocuparon Cueva Traful I durante el Holoceno Medio y Tardío. *Comechingonia Virtual* **5**, 158–202.

de la Fuente, C., Galimany, J., Kemp, B. M., *et al.* (2015). Ancient marine hunter-gatherers from Patagonia and Tierra Del Fuego: Diversity and differentiation using uniparentally inherited genetic markers. *American Journal of Physical Anthropology*, **158**, 719–729.

De Nigris, M. E. (2004). *El consumo en grupos cazadores recolectores: Un ejemplo zooarqueológico de Patagonia Meridional.* Buenos Aires: Sociedad Argentina de Antropología.

de Saint Pierre, M., Bravi, C. M., Motti, J. M., *et al.* (2012a). An alternative model for the early peopling of southern South America revealed by analyses of three mitochondrial DNA haplogroups. *PLoS One*, **7**, e43486.

de Saint Pierre, M., Gandini, F., Perego, U. A., *et al.* (2012b). Arrival of Paleo-Indians to the southern cone of South America: New clues from mitogenomes. *PLoS One*, **7**, e51311.

Della Negra, C. E. (2008). Gubevi I: Un sitio con restos óseos humanos asociados a cerámica en el departamento de Minas, zona norte de la provincia del Neuquén. In P. F. Azar, E. M. Cuneo, and S. N. Rodríguez, eds., *Tras la senda de los ancestros: Arqueología de Patagonia.* San Carlos de Bariloche: 3° Jornadas de Historia de la Patagonia. CD publication.

Della Negra, C., Novellino, P., Gordón, F., *et al.* (2014). Áreas de entierro en cazadores-recolectores del Noroeste de Patagonia: Sitio Hermanos Lazcano (Chos Malal, Neuquén). *RUNA*, **35**, 5–19

Drummond, A. J. and Rambaut, A. (2007). BEAST: Bayesian evolutionary analysis by sampling trees. *BMC Evolutionary Biology*, **7**, 214.

Drummond, A. J., Rambaut, A., Shapiro, B., and Pybus, O. G. (2005). Bayesian coalescent inference of past population dynamics from molecular sequences. *Molecular Biology and Evolution*, **22**, 1185e1192

Drummond, A. J., Ho, S. Y. W., Phillips, M. J., *et al.* (2006). Relaxed phylogenetics and dating with confidence. *PLoS Biology*, **4**, e88.

Emperaire, J., Laming-Emperaire, A., Reichlen, H., and Poulain-Josien, T. (1963). La grotte Fell et autres sites de la région volcanique de la Patagonie chilienne. *Journal de la Société des Américanistes*, **52**, 167–254.

Endicott, P. and Ho, S. Y. W. (2008). A Bayesian evaluation of human mitochondrial substitution rates. *American Journal of Human Genetics*, **82**, 895–902.

Fernández, J. and Panarello, H. (2001). Cazadores recolectores del holoceno medio y superior de la cueva Haichol, región cordillerana central del Neuquén, República Argentina: Cronología 14 C-AMS sobre colágeno óseo y su conversión a tiempo calendario. Signaturas isotópicas del carbono y del nitrógeno en el colágeno óseo, en función de trazadores paleodietéticos. *Relaciones de la Sociedad Argentina de Antropología*, **26**, 9–30

García-Bour J., Pérez-Pérez, A., Álvarez, S., *et al.* (2004). Early population differentiation in extinct aborigines from Tierra del Fuego-Patagonia: Ancient mtDNA sequence and Y chromosome STR characterization. *American Journal of Physical Anthropology*, **123**, 361–370.

García Guraieb, S., Goñi, R., and Tessone, A. (2015). Paleodemography of Late Holocene hunter-gatherers from Patagonia (Santa Cruz, Argentina): An approach using multiple archaeological and bioarchaelogical indicators. *Quaternary International*, **356**, 147–158.

Ginther, C., Corach, D., Penacino, G. A., *et al.* (1993). Genetic variation among Mapuche Indians from the Patagonia region of Argentina: Mitochondrial DNA sequence variation and allele frequencies of several nuclear genes. In S. D. J. Pena, R. Chakraborty, J. T. Epplen, and A. J. Jeffreys, eds., *DNA Fingerprinting: State of the Science.* Basel: Birkhauser Verlag, pp. 211–219.

Gordón, F., Perez, S. I., Hajduk, A., Lezcano, M., and Bernal V. (2017). Dietary patterns in human populations from Northwest Patagonia during Holocene: An approach using Binford's frames of reference and Bayesian isotope mixing models. *Archaeological and Anthropological Science.* DOI: 10.1007/s12520-016-0459-0.

Grayson, D. K. and Delpech, F. (1998). Changing diet breadth in the early Upper Palaeolithic of southwestern France. *Journal of Archaeological Science*, **25**, 1119–1129.

Haynes, G. (2009). *American Megafaunal Extinctions at the End of the Pleistocene.* Dordrecht: Springer.

Ho, S. Y. W. and Shapiro, B. (2011). Skyline-plot methods for estimating demographic history from nucleotide sequences. *Molecular Ecology Resources*, **11**, 423e434.

Hodgson, D., McDonald, J. L., and Hosken, D. J. (2015). What do you mean, "resilient"? *Trends in Ecology & Evolution*, **30**, 503–506.

Hoover, K. C. and Hudson, M. J. (2016). Resilience in prehistoric persistent hunter-gatherers in northwest Kyushu, Japan as assessed by population health and archaeological evidence. *Quaternary International*, **405**B, 22–33.

Hubbe, A., Hubbe, M., and Neves, W. (2007). Early Holocene survival of megafauna in South America. *Journal of Biogeography*, **34**, 1642–1646.

Inchausti, P. and Halley, J. (2003). On the relation between temporal variability and persistence time in animal populations. *Journal of Animal Ecology*, **72**, 899–908.

Katoh, K. and Standley, D. M. (2013). MAFFT multiple sequence alignment software version 7: Improvements in performance and usability. *Molecular Biology and Evolution*, **30**, 772–780.

Koch, P. L. and Barnosky, A. D. (2006). Late Quaternary extinctions: State of the debate. *Annual Review in Ecology, Evolution and Systematics*, **37**, 215–250.

Lema, V. S., Della Negra, C., and Bernal, V. (2012). Explotaci on de recursos vegetales silvestres y domesticados en Neuqu en: Implicancias del hallazgo de restos de maíz y algarrobo en artefactos de molienda del Holoceno tardío. *Magallania*, **40**, 229–247.

Lezcano, M. J., Hajduk, A., and Albornoz, A. M. (2010). El menú a la carta en el bosque¿ entrada o plato fuerte?: Una perspectiva comparada desde la zooarqueología del sitio El Trébol (lago Nahuel Huapi, Pcia. de Río Negro). In M. Gutiérrez, M. De Nigris, P. Fernández, *et al.*, eds., *Zooarqueología a principios del siglo XXI: aportes teóricos, metodológicos y casos de estudio.* Buenos Aires: Ediciones del Espinillo, pp. 243–257.

Lorenzen, E. D., Nogués-Bravo, D., Orlando, L., *et al.* (2011). Species-specific responses of Late Quaternary megafauna to climate and humans. *Nature*, **479**, 359–365.

Lyman, R. L. (2008). *Quantitative Paleozoology.* Cambridge: Cambridge University Press.

Marchionni, L. (2013). *Comparación de las distintas historias tafonómicas en conjuntos zooarqueo-lógicos provenientes de la Meseta Central de la provincia de Santa Cruz.* Doctoral dissertation, Facultad de Ciencias Naturales y Museo, Universidad Nacional de La Plata.

McCulloch, R. D., Bentley, M. J., Purves, R. S., *et al.* (2000) Climatic inferences from glacial and palaeoecological evidence at the last glacial termination, southern South America. *Journal of Quaternary Science*, **15**, 409–417.

Mengoni Goñalons, G. L. and Silveira, M. J. (1976). Análisis e interpretación de los restos faunísticos de la Cueva de las Manos, Estancia Alto Río Pinturas (Provincia de Santa Cruz). *Relaciones de la Sociedad Argentina de Antropología*, **10**, 261–270.

Miotti, L. (1996). Piedra Museo (Santa Cruz), nuevos datos para la ocupación Pleistocénica en Patagonia. In J. Gomez Otero, ed., *Arqueología: Solo Patagonia.* Puerto Madryn: Universidad Nacional de la Patagonia, 27–38.

Miotti, L. and Salemme, M. C. (2003). When Patagonia was colonized: People mobility at high-latitudes during Pleistocene/Holocene transition. *Quaternary International*, **109–110**, 95–111.

Moraga, M., Rocco, P., Miquel J. F., *et al.* (2000). Mitochondrial DNA polymorphisms in Chilean aboriginal populations: Implications for the peopling of the southern cone of the continent. *American Journal of Physical Anthropology*, **113**, 19–29.

Moraga, M., de Saint Pierre, M., Torres, F., and Ríos, J. (2010). Vínculos de parentesco por vía materna entre los últimos descendientes de la etnia Kawésqar y algunos entierros en los canales patagónicos: Evidencia desde el estudio de linajes mitocondriales. *Magallania*, 38, 103–114.

Nami, H. G. and Menegaz, A. (1991). Cueva del Medio: Aportes para el conocimiento de la diversidad faunística hacia el Pleistoceno-Holoceno en la Patagonia austral. *Anales del Instituto de la Patagonia*, 20, 117–132.

Pallo, C. and Borrero, L. (2015). Arqueología de corredores boscosos en Patagonia Meridional: el caso del río Guillermo (SO de la provincia de Santa Cruz, Argentina). *Intersecciones en Antropología*, 16, 313–326.

Paunero, R. S., Frank, A., Skarbun, F., *et al.* (2005). Arte rupestre en Estancia La María, meseta central de Santa Cruz: Sectorización y contextos. *Relaciones de la Sociedad Argentina de Antropología*, 30, 147–168.

Paunero, R. S., Frank, A. D., Skarbun, F., *et al.* (2007). Investigaciones arqueológicas en sitio Casa del Minero 1, Estancia La María, Meseta Central de Santa Cruz. In F. Morello, M. Martinic, A. Prieto, and G. Bahamonde, eds., *Arqueología de Fuego Patagonia. Levantando piedras, desenterrando huesos ... y develando arcanos*. Punta Arenas: CEQUA, pp. 577–588.

Perego, U. A., Achilli, A., Angerhofer, N., *et al.* (2009). Distinctive Paleo-Indian migration routes from Beringia marked by two rare mtDNA haplogroups. *Current Biology*, 19, 1–8.

Perez, S. I., Della Negra, C., Novellino, P., *et al.* (2009). Deformaciones artificiales del cráneo en cazadores-recolectores del Holoceno medio-tardío del noroeste de Patagonia. *Magallania*, 37, 7–20

Perez, S. I., Bernal, V., and Gonzalez, P. N. (2016). Past population dynamics in Northwest Patagonia: An estimation using molecular and radiocarbon data. *Journal of Archaeological Science*, 65, 154–160.

Perez, S. I., Postillone, M. B., and Rindel, D. (2017). Domestication and human demographic history in South America. *American Journal of Physical Anthropology*, 163, 44–62.

Pires, M. M., Koch, P. L., Fariña, R. A., *et al.* (2016). The structure and dynamics of South American megafaunal assemblages and the aftermath of megafaunal extinctions in Patagonia. Paper presented at the IX Latin American Paleontology Conference, Lima, Peru.

Prates, L., Politis, G., and Steele, J. (2013). Radiocarbon chronology of the early human occupation of Argentina. *Quaternary International*, 301, 104–122.

Rabassa, J. (2008). *Late Cenozoic of Patagonia and Tierra del Fuego*. Amsterdam: Elsevier.

Rambaut, A. and Drummond, A. J. (2007). Tracer v1.5. Available at: http://tree.bio.ed.ac.uk/soft ware/tracer.

Shannon, C. E. (1948). A mathematical theory of communication. *Bell System Technical Journal*, 27, 379 423.

Silveira, M. J. (1979). Análisis de los restos faunísticos de la Cueva Grande del Arroyo Feo (Santa Cruz). *Relaciones de la Sociedad Argentina de Antropología*, 13, 229–247.

Surovell, T. A., Byrd Finley, J., Smith, G. M., Brantingham, P. J., and Kelly, R. (2009). Correcting temporal frequency distributions for taphonomic bias. *Journal of Archaeological Science*, 36, 1715–1724.

Tamura, K., Stecher, G., Peterson, D., Filipski, A., and Kumar, S. (2013). MEGA6: Molecular Evolutionary Genetics Analysis Version 6.0. *Molecular Biology and Evolution*, 30, 2725–2729.

Tessone, A., Zangrando, A. F., Barrientos, G., *et al.* (2009). Stable isotope studies in the Salitroso Lake Basin (southern Patagonia, Argentina): Assessing diet of Late Holocene hunter-gatherers. *International Journal of Osteoarchaeology*, 19, 297–308.

Tonni, E. P. and Carlini, A. A. (2008). Neogene vertebrates from Argentine Patagonia: Their relationship with the most significant climatic changes. In J. Rabassa, ed., *Late Cenozoic of Patagonia and Tierra del Fuego*. Amsterdam: Elsevier, pp. 269–282.

Torfing, T. (2015). Neolithic population and summed probability distribution of ^{14}C dates. *Journal of Archaeological Science*, 63, 193–198.

Turelli, M. (1978). A reexamination of stability in randomly varying versus deterministic environments with comments on the stochastic theory of limiting similarity. *Theoretical Population Biology*, 13, 244–267.

Walker, B., Holling, C. S., Carpenter, S. R., and Kinzig, A. (2004). Resilience, adaptability and transformability in social–ecological systems. *Ecology and Society*, 9, 5.

Willig, M. R., Kaufman, D. M., and Stevens, R. D. (2003). Latitudinal gradients of biodiversity: Pattern, process, scale, and synthesis. *Annual Review of Ecology, Evolution, and Systematics*, 34, 273–309.

4 The Success and Failure of Resilience in the European Mesolithic

Rick J. Schulting

4.1 Introduction

4.1.1 Resilience Theory

Resilience theory is situated at the interface of society and the environment (Adger, 2000). It offers one way to explore the effects of environmental change on human communities, or indeed other forms of social, economic, or political change. The extension of resilience theory to the archaeological record offers a framework within which to investigate human responses to changing circumstances in the past. As has often been noted, archaeology – and prehistoric archaeology in particular – offers a long-term perspective that is lacking in other human-centered disciplines (Bailey, 1983). What this means in the context of resilience theory is that archaeologists can see the long-term outcomes of choices made by individuals and communities (Redman, 2005). This is not to say that the application of resilience theory to the archaeological record is straightforward. Potential areas for concern include how resilience is defined in an archaeological context (part of a wider debate concerning the utility of the concept in the social sciences; Olsson *et al.*, 2015) and how its investigation can be operationalized. In this chapter, resilience among the fisher-hunter-gatherers of Mesolithic Europe is explored through stable carbon and nitrogen isotope analysis of human remains, and the insights provided by these isotopes are used to interpret rapid changes in foodways. Foodways, in turn, are seen as intimately linked with sociocultural identity – a core aspect of resilience in human communities (Cumming and Collier, 2005; Cumming *et al.*, 2005) – and so provide a means of applying the concept that permits an assessment of the success and failure of resilience under different circumstances and challenges. The focus is on two periods: the 8.2 kya cal BP climatic event, and the transition to farming that marks the end of the Mesolithic (11 500 to 8800/6000 cal BP).

4.1.2 Resilience to What?

What is meant by resilience, and at what levels does it operate? While the term has a much older currency in both the natural and social sciences (Rival, 2009), resilience theory as currently understood was introduced in a seminal paper by C. S. Holling, which outlined a new approach to ecological systems in which multiple stable states were possible (Holling, 1973). This perspective challenged the then-prevailing model of ideal static climax states toward which systems strived (Holling, 1973). Resilience refers to the amount of disturbance an ecosystem can withstand before shifting to a new stable state, a process termed transformation (Gunderson, 2000; Holling, 1973, 1987). Adapting the term from ecology, Adger (2000: 361) defines social resilience as, "the ability of communities to withstand external shocks to their social infrastructure." Social and ecological resilience are explicitly and inextricably linked in the notion of a socioecological system (SES) (Adger, 2000; Carpenter *et al.*, 2001; Cumming *et al.*, 2005; Gallopín 2006; Redman, 2005; Widlok *et al.*, 2012), providing a framework within which to consider the kinds, levels, and frequencies of stresses to which individuals and communities might respond. If the ecosystem is resilient, then human communities are more likely to be buffered against external stressors. Ecosystem resilience may be exceeded when major social changes are implicated, whether generated internally or externally (e.g., through significant population immigration), leading to a change in the system state followed by a new adaptive cycle. While there are parallels in the use of the concept of resilience in the ecological and social sciences literature, the relationship is by no means straightforward (cf. Cote and Nightingale, 2012; Davidson, 2010; Olsson *et al.*, 2015).

For the purposes of this chapter it is useful to make a broad distinction between the aquatic (mainly marine, but including certain productive inland waterways) and inland habitats exploited by hunter-gatherers. In the absence of modern damming, pollution, and overfishing, many marine ecosystems are resilient compared to terrestrial counterparts (Costanza *et al.*, 1995; Mann, 1982). The extent to which this translates directly into the resilience of human communities depends, in part, on the technology employed. A complicating factor is that access to the best marine resources may be spatially (and temporally) heterogeneous, leading to a greater degree of sedentism, which in turn creates a greater investment in specialized capture technology (e.g., boats, large nets, stationary fishing facilities), and an even greater reliance on marine environments for subsistence, frequently articulated as a positive-feedback loop (Yesner, 1987). Combined with the high population densities seen in productive coastal zones, this can lead to greater vulnerability to perturbations affecting either marine resources directly, or the capacity for humans to access these resources. An example of this situation is considered below.

Minor environmental shifts are unlikely to result in transformational challenges to the SES. Changing weather patterns and ocean currents can impact the abundance of various marine species, but people can usually adjust fishing and harvesting strategies to target other species without affecting the overall system to the degree that requires its major reorganization. A more serious event such as a tsunami might deplete resources for a substantial period (e.g., by covering shellfish beds with sand), which could result in populations temporarily relocating, and/or calling upon support networks in adjacent inland territories that would be less affected. Such relatively short-term events would not generally be discernible archaeologically, and again would probably not lead to a loss of resilience and hence a transformation of the system (buffered by individual and social memory, with an ecological analogue in terms of deeply rooted plants, seed banks, repopulation from neighboring regions, etc.). A potential exception to this is the final catastrophic flooding of Doggerland, which was likely submerged by a tsunami (Weninger *et al.*, 2008).

Terrestrial environments are comparatively more vulnerable. Optimal foraging theory predicts that game is preferentially targeted according to criteria of body size and encounter rate, the latter a function of density. Thus, aurochs (*Bos primigenius*) and moose (*Alces alces*), being the largest terrestrial herbivores across northern Eurasia, should be pursued whenever encountered by hunters. But because large terrestrial mammals are K-selected, these species are more vulnerable to overexploitation (MacArthur and Wilson, 1967). Indeed, it is likely that human hunting pressure combined with habitat loss as a result of isostatic sea-level rise led to the local extinction of aurochs (*Bos primigenius*) on the large Danish island of Zealand by the Late Mesolithic (Aaris-Sørenson, 1999). The much smaller roe deer, by contrast, should only be pursued when the encounter rates for larger game fall below a certain threshold (or in situations in which returning to a camp with any game is preferable to returning empty-handed) (Mithen, 1990). While populations may encourage different hunting practices, and the social formations underlying these behaviors, a shift from large to medium-size terrestrial mammals would probably not bring about a change in the SES, though this is a matter that would benefit from further research.

Importantly, the simple persistence of a population need not imply resilience as defined here (cf. Cumming *et al.*, 2005; see below), since it may have undergone a significant step change or transformation to a new adaptive strategy, and hence have a different set of relationships with the natural and social environment (accepting that the distinction can be seen as largely artificial). Conversely, and perhaps counter-intuitively, the abandonment of a region also need not imply a lack of resilience, since mobility may be a highly successful strategy, particularly for those hunter-gatherers at low population densities and with minimal investment in fixed facilities (Testart, 1982). There is a crucial distinction – especially for those involved – between local extinction and group migration. Population migration or displacement is ambiguous in terms of resilience. It could refer to the failure of the socioeconomic/ sociocultural system to adapt to changing conditions, or, considered at another spatial scale, it could be seen as an integral part of those adaptations, and hence a prime example of resilience. The deciding factor is whether or not the community is reconstructed elsewhere in a form that is still recognizable in terms of institutions and practices (Adger, 2000). Unfortunately, these distinctions may not be detectable in the prehistoric archaeological record. The appropriate spatiotemporal scale of the units of analysis is another problematic area (Cumming and Collier, 2005).

Resilience is a function of cycles operating at different scales. At one end of the scale it can be seen as simply referring to the ability of an individual organism to survive adverse environmental and/or social conditions (e.g., psychological resilience; Maclean *et al.*, 2017). While archaeology does deal with individuals – by definition when considering human skeletal data – it is usually more concerned with the survival of sociocultural systems, or of particular institutions within those systems (even though, of course, this ultimately comes down to the behavior of individuals – nested scales of analysis being a feature of panarchy theory, which draws heavily on notions of resilience at different levels of complex systems; Allen *et al.*, 2014). A relevant example in the present context would be the persistence of a strong sharing ethic, often taken to be a defining social institution in low-density hunter-gatherers or foragers (Bird-David, 1990; Cashdan, 1980; Peterson, 1993; Woodburn, 1998). Sharing, for these groups, forms part of what can be termed livelihood strategies (Lancelotti *et al.*, 2016), involving day-to-day subsistence and other economic activities. Subsistence is perhaps too restricted a term here, given the complex and multifaceted elements of technology, social organization, resource acquisition, preparation, and consumption that constitute foodways in a wider sense (Schulting, 2008). These in turn can be argued to form a large part of identity at various levels from the individual to the community and society. Thus, at the scale of analysis of particular interest here, resilience refers to the persistence of a recognizable cultural identity (Adger, 2000; Cumming *et al.*, 2005; Forbes *et al.*, 2009), in which foodways, especially for small-scale societies, are an integral component (Fernández-Armestto, 2002; Schulting, 2008; Twiss, 2007).

4.1.3   Operationalizing Resilience in the Prehistoric Archaeological Record

Applying resilience theory in any empirical study, let alone in the prehistoric archaeological record, is not straightforward (Carpenter *et al.*, 2001, 2005; Cumming and Collier, 2005; Cumming *et al.*, 2005). Following the above discussion, social resilience is defined as a society's ability to maintain a recognizable core of identity in the face of environmental and/or social perturbations. This focus on identity departs from the usual definition of resilience in ecology (Cumming *et al.*, 2005; cf. Cumming and Collier, 2005). Identity is maintained through repositories of knowledge held by individuals in the form of personal memory, stories, myths, etc., operating over increasing timescales, but with concomitant loss of specificity. Proficiency in many tasks, for example, is only gained through long repetition, to the extent that the required bodily motions become habitualized – this is not the kind of knowledge that can be easily transmitted through disembodied oral transmission, and is inherently different from memory in ecological contexts, where it refers to seed banks, soil nutrients, repopulation from neighboring regions. Of course identity is complex and multifaceted; some aspects of identity might change while others remain more or less intact (Dìaz-Andreu *et al.*, 2006). Language, for example, is a core element, but even when this is lost individuals and communities can maintain a distinct identity, as is seen with many indigenous communities around the world today. Rather than attempting to consider identity as a single concept and to recognize retention or loss, the investigator can select some aspect of the socioecological system that is likely to have important ramifications for identity, termed identity thresholds by Cumming *et al.* (2005). The example of a ranching system has been used in the social resilience literature: A shift from keeping sheep to keeping goats would likely entail only limited restructuring of the SES and thus maintain rancher identity, while any breakdown of the dynamic between ranchers, stock, and the presence of a harvesting relationship would constitute a transformation of identity, and hence the failure of the resilience of the ranching system (Carpenter *et al.*, 2001; Cumming *et al.*, 2005). This example is particularly *apropos* here, since it also makes an intimate connection between the subsistence economy, lifeways, and identity (cf. Strang, 1997).

4.2   Stable Carbon and Nitrogen Analysis of Human Bone

This chapter focuses on the use of maritime versus terrestrial resources using stable carbon and nitrogen isotope analysis of human bone collagen. Foodways are central to identity in small-scale societies. This is particularly so for hunter-gatherers, since there is often a strong food-sharing ethic and there are generally far fewer opportunities for full-time specialists than in agricultural societies that could form the basis for alternative identities. Thus, most individuals are involved at some level in the acquisition of food and/or food preparation (Fernández-Armestto, 2002; Schulting, 2008; Twiss, 2007). This suggests that foodways are integral to the socioecological system, and to emic understandings of identity.

Stable carbon (δ^{13}C) and nitrogen (δ^{15}N) isotope measurements on human bone collagen are well suited to an investigation of the consumption of marine/aquatic protein. The proportion of the heavier ^{13}C isotope is higher in marine ecosystems, resulting in bone collagen values in human consumers of ca. $-12 \pm 1‰$, compared to values of ca. $-21 \pm 1‰$ for the consumption of terrestrial plants and animals in a C_3 ecosystem (Richards and Hedges, 1999). Stable nitrogen isotope values increase with trophic level, and so tend to be significantly higher in both marine and freshwater aquatic systems, since food chains tend to be far longer than in the terrestrial systems on which humans tend to focus (primary producers and first-order consumers, i.e., plants and herbivores) (Minagawa and Wada, 1984). Measurements on human bone collagen reflect the foods consumed over the last decade or so of life, depending on the skeletal element analyzed and on the age of the individual. Thus, these data provide the averaged, long-term isotopic signature of individual diet, the cumulative outcome of many thousands of meals, and hence reflect underlying daily subsistence practices and cuisines. This is particularly appropriate in the context of this discussion, since it imparts a time frame that is not only relevant to human experience, but also resonates with the notion of (literally) embodied knowledge touched upon above.

While a number of other factors should be considered (e.g., aridity effects), in a European context δ^{13}C and δ^{15}N measurements primarily reflect diet. This, in turn, serves as a powerful proxy for livelihood strategies. While the details will vary, communities focused on marine resources to any great extent will share certain practices that will form identity. The rhythms of the sea, the affordances offered (Ingold, 2000), and the demands the sea makes differ from terrestrial environments. Thus, a significant shift in δ^{13}C and δ^{15}N values at the community level (defined here as multiple individuals from a reasonably constrained spatiotemporal context) represents a change in lifeways, and hence the loss of resilience resulting in a change to a new system state, or regime. This is not to say that some aspects of identity may not persist, but does represent a fundamental transformation in system identities. For the purposes of this discussion, three δ^{13}C ranges reflecting different levels of reliance on marine protein are defined, with shifts of more than 3‰ indicating a threshold for transformation, and thus a significant change in livelihood strategy and identity.

1. −21 to −18‰: a predominantly terrestrial diet, albeit with the possibility of some minor use of marine resources;
2. −17.9 to −15‰: a balanced use of terrestrial and marine resources, potentially involving a greater degree of movement between coast and interior;
3. −14.9 to −12‰: a strong focus on marine resources, implying a settlement pattern oriented almost exclusively on the coast, and the presence of distinct coastal and (where present) inland identities (see Schulting, 2010a).

Ethnographic parallels could be found for groups with all of the above adaptations, with the distinctions clearly recognized by the groups (e.g., Yesner *et al.*, 2003). The movement of individuals between groups (e.g., as marriage partners) does not obviate this distinctiveness. While the specifics can be debated, this scheme has the advantage of clearly setting out criteria by which a transformation in the SES may be identified. It allows a degree of adaptive flexibility within each system, such that there can be considerable movement within the basin of attraction (Walker et al., 2004). Equally, it provides conditions for a system state change, so that the retention of a minor component of marine resource exploitation, while perhaps constituting a degree of continuity, still suggests that transformation occurred. An example of this is discussed below in relation to the Mesolithic–Neolithic transition in northwest Europe. An important corollary of the approach is the need to demonstrate a relatively rapid change in stable isotope values – on the meso-scale of no more than a few human generations. Any gradual trends observed over a longer period of time than this would probably not be discernable to the communities involved and so cannot constitute a loss of resilience/identity (cf. Cumming and Collier, 2005). Ideally this approach would be linked with classic osteological indicators of stress, such as linear enamel hypoplasia, Harris lines, non-specific infections, adult stature. But the reality for the present study is that, at least across much of northwestern Europe, sample sizes are very small and skeletal remains are often incomplete and highly fragmentary. Isotopic approaches provide a means of using data even from the smallest human skeletal fragments, as long as these fragments represent distinct individuals and either derive from secure stratigraphic contexts or have been directly AMS radiocarbon dated (Schulting and Richards, 2002a; Schulting *et al.*, 2013). The recent development and application of ZooMS (zooarchaeology by mass spectrometry) offers even more potential through the ability to identify the species of previously unidentifiable bone fragments (e.g., Charlton *et al.*, 2016).

4.3   Resilience in Mesolithic Europe

4.3.1   The Archaeological Record

In a European context, the Mesolithic refers to the time between the onset of the Holocene and the adoption of agro-pastoralism as the dominant subsistence economy. While the start is thus fixed, the latter is a moveable feast, with a general diachronic trend from southeastern to northern Europe (Pinhasi *et al.*, 2005). No domestic species other than dog was present, though the management of some wild species, most notably wild boar, has been proposed (Zvelebil, 1995). The degree to which socioeconomic inequality existed is an area of active debate: A limited degree of institutionalized inequality is proposed for certain places at certain times, based mainly on the burial record, while for other regions and periods such evidence is largely lacking. This is relevant in the present discussion, since greater organizational complexity, which includes specialization and socioeconomic inequality, can be argued to make a society more vulnerable to perturbations. In chiefdom and state-level societies, for example, the loss of resilience may be differentially distributed throughout society, affecting the elite (e.g., the collapse of the Classic Maya), while practices of the general population persist (Dunning *et al.*, 2012). The implications of power and inequality relations have yet to be fully integrated into social resilience theory (Abel *et al.*, 2006; Cote and Nightingale, 2012; Cretney, 2014; Davidson, 2010; Hatt, 2013).

Another consideration is that, while the archaeological record has the benefit of a long timescale, it still suffers from imprecision in both absolute and relative chronology, often making the ordering of events problematic. To some extent these problems are addressed by increased precision of radiocarbon dating combined with Bayesian modeling, as well as the use of other dating techniques such as tephrochronology, which are particularly well suited to linking spatially discrete locations together into a single time horizon (Lowe, 2011). Even so, chronologies remain very general. Moreover, since the archaeological record must be compared with environmental proxies, the chronological imprecision of the latter introduces an additional source of uncertainty. Thus, the problem of linking changes in the archaeological and environmental records is far from trivial (Robinson *et al.*, 2013; Schulting, 2010b). This makes it difficult to know whether human communities are responding to environmental perturbations or some other unknown mechanism. Given that external stressors are often placed at the core of resilience theory, connecting these links is crucial in terms of identifying particular sequences of events, or adaptive cycles, and so presents a real challenge in archaeological applications. Nevertheless, archaeologists can deploy resilience theory to explore and think through data in novel ways, and this can be a very useful exercise (cf. Cote and Nightingale, 2012).

Two approaches are considered in this section, illustrated by case studies drawn from Mesolithic Europe. The first is a known climatic event, evidence for the impact of which may be sought on contemporaneous societies in the archaeological record. Depending on the extent of observed changes, the chapter considers whether the pre- and post-event societies were sufficiently similar to constitute adaptive flexibility in what is still recognizably the same society, and in what specific ways these communities changed, or whether the society's capacity for resilience was exceeded and underwent a more significant transformation leading to a new SES. Of course, knowing where to draw the line between these and other possibilities is not straightforward, and will to some extent be subjective. But it does provide grounds for discussion, and potentially for hypothesis building and testing.

4.3.2   The 8.2 kya cal BP Event

The best-known and most widespread environmentally driven change impacting on the early and mid-Holocene in the northern hemisphere is the 8.2 kya cal BP climatic downturn, caused by the last major meltwater pulse from the Laurentide ice sheet and the resulting impact on North Atlantic thermohaline circulation (Alley *et al.*, 1997). Despite the indication that this event would have been experienced most strongly in the North Atlantic region (Thomas *et al.*, 2007), discussions have primarily focused on potential effects on early farmers, who were at this time restricted to southwest Asia and southeast Europe (Biehl and Nieuwenhuyse, 2016; Budja, 2007; Flohr *et al.*, 2016; Pross *et al.*, 2009; Weninger *et al.*, 2006). However, as discussed below, some attempts have been made to identify the impact of this event on Mesolithic hunter-gatherers, with conflicting or at least ambiguous results.

A considerable amount of work has focused on the Iberian Peninsula, where the 8.2 kya cal BP event manifests through slightly colder but more arid conditions. This resulted in Mesolithic hunter-gatherers abandoning certain areas and restructuring settlement organization on a regional level (García-Martínez de Lagrán *et al.*, 2016; González-Sampériz *et al.*, 2009; López de Pablo and Jochim, 2010). There is no evidence, however, that this was accompanied by a significant change in the SES, and so this arguably serves as a good example of resilience. A caveat to note here is that this observation is based on a limited view provided by lithics and settlement patterns. It might be that this shift entailed the emergence of significantly different lifeways, gender relations, or ideas of land tenure, that are simply not visible with the available evidence.

Another approach is to begin with observed changes in some aspect of the archaeological record, and then attempt to situate this within an environmental and social context. Much research on the Mesolithic has focused on stone tool traditions, with a number of recognized shifts over time, such that much of Western Europe fits into a broad tripartite scheme of Early, Middle, and Late Mesolithic. Robinson *et al.* (2013) observe that the Middle Mesolithic in the Rhine–Meuse–Scheldt area of the Netherlands is bracketed by two climate events at 9.3 kya and 8.2 kya cal BP. This certainly suggests that human populations might be reacting to environmental changes, but it is difficult to determine the extent to which relatively minor changes – even if very clear in typochronological terms – in the form and size of microliths reflect a substantial shift in the SES. Furthermore, continuity in landscape use at least in the broad sense and in population suggests resilience/adaptability rather than transformation.

The interpretive challenge comes into sharper focus when evaluating the dating of comparable changes in stone tool typologies elsewhere in northwest Europe. For example, the shift from Early to Late Mesolithic (the latter broadly equivalent to the Middle Mesolithic on the Continent) microlith traditions in Britain occurs at ca. 9700 cal BP (Tolan-Smith, 2008), well before either of the abovementioned climate events. What is arguably a more dramatic shift is seen in the change from an Early Mesolithic microlithic tradition in Ireland to a macrolithic tradition in the Late Mesolithic; yet this occurred at ca. 9000 cal BP (Costa *et al.*, 2005) and so again appears unrelated to any known climate change event *per se*. It is likely that it instead relates to Ireland's insular position and impoverished terrestrial fauna. While this may indeed represent a shift in the SES, it does not appear to be have been climate-driven.

One recent study that considers the effect of the 8.2 kya cal BP event on north-temperate hunter-gatherers is that by Wicks and Mithen (2014). Using radiocarbon dates as a proxy for population size, the authors note a marked decline in the summed probability distribution for dates from the west coast of Scotland seemingly coinciding with this climatic downturn (Wicks and Mithen, 2014). It is not clear why coastally adapted hunter-gatherers would be so strongly affected by a temperature drop of a few degrees, since the marine environment would presumably be resilient to a shift of this order, and indeed might even be expected to see higher fish productivity, as colder water holds more oxygen (Keeling *et al.*, 2010). To address this, Wicks and Mithen refer to paleoenvironmental studies supporting a concomitant increase in storminess at this time (Clarke and Rendell, 2009), which may have physically impeded the exploitation of marine resources as well as adversely affected near-shore shell beds. But what is even more striking is that no recovery is seen in the summed probability distribution of radiocarbon dates until after ca. 7000 cal BP. It is hard to understand how a relatively short-lived climatic downturn lasting no more than a century should lead to the apparent near-abandonment of the region for a millennium. It may be more a matter of archaeological visibility that is driving this pattern, though this remains a matter for future research. Taken at face value, this is a good candidate for the loss of resilience. The time frame seems too long for this to be simply a matter of temporarily readjusting the nature of activities across the landscape, while retaining sufficient knowledge though cultural memory to return to the same coastally focused SES many centuries later.

Unfortunately, human remains on the Scottish west coast are currently only available for the last few centuries of the Mesolithic, ca. 6200 to 5800 cal BP, and are also restricted to the small island of Oronsay. Nevertheless, it can be noted that diets here fall into the category of extremely high reliance on marine resources (Charlton *et al.*, 2016; Richards and Mellars, 1998; Richards and Sheridan, 2000; Schulting and Richards, 2002b). Thus, if increased storminess from ca. 8.2 kya cal BP adversely affected the ability to pursue the kind of strongly marine-oriented economy seen toward the end of the Mesolithic, then this could provide an example of an environmental perturbation that exceeded the ability of hunter-gatherers to cope, presumably leading to a new SES focused elsewhere on the regional landscape. Unfortunately, the character and even existence of this new adaptation is purely hypothetical, since the region is largely bereft of evidence of human presence during the period in question. The implication is that the population here, if present at all, was highly mobile and left minimal archaeological traces. Given the existence of the sizeable Late Mesolithic shell middens on Oronsay, the high marine diets seen in human stable isotope values, and the concomitant implication of some degree of sedentism and attachment to place, a major shift in lifeways can be proposed. But, unlike the previous shift, it is possible to debate whether this should be termed a loss of resilience, since it implies a more successful (i.e., larger) population on the west coast of Scotland. Nevertheless, assuming that coast resources were largely abandoned, and following the methods outlined above, the shift should also be understood as a transformation of the SES, and hence a loss of resilience of the previous system in favor of a new basin of attraction. The success of the new SES is irrelevant to the loss of the old since transformation moves populations into new adaptive cycles, and thus is representative of adaptation. A sudden influx of new resources can be as disruptive to a system, whether social or ecological, as a sudden decline. In this particular case it is the millennium-long gap between the two systems that makes it difficult to accept any meaningful persistence of identity, given the terms of reference employed in this chapter (cf. Cumming and Collier, 2005). This is not to deny that an alternative interpretation, employing a difference frame of reference, could legitimately see this as an example of successful adaptation, moving between basins of attraction, rather than one of transformation. The difference comes down to the questions being asked, the selected identity criteria, and the chosen spatiotemporal scales of analysis.

South Wales is currently the only region in Britain or Ireland with a series of directly radiocarbon dated human remains spanning the 8.2 kya cal BP event. Moreover, most of the sites from which these remains derive are described as near-coastal (i.e., within approximately 5–10 km), and thus provide an opportunity to investigate whether any isotopic changes can be seen at this time that might imply a shift in the SES to the degree required for crossing an identity threshold. While the sample size is limited, it is apparent that there is no difference pre- and post-8.2 kya cal BP, with $\delta^{13}C$ values remaining relatively high throughout, averaging $-16.1 \pm 1.2‰$ ($n = 12$), indicating a balanced use of marine and terrestrial resources (Figure 4.1). This provides a sharp contrast to the west coast of Scotland, despite the fact that increased storminess also affected southern Britain, and indeed the entire Atlantic façade (Clarke and Rendell, 2009). One means, albeit a speculative one, of reconciling these two outcomes is that the more balanced use of marine and terrestrial resources seen in south Wales may have provided communities with the flexibility to shift adaptive strategies within the same general SES. If communities on the Scottish west coast were more committed to a fully marine specialization, and this option became unviable, then the population may have had to abandon the region in favor of a new landscape.

4.3.3   The Mesolithic–Neolithic Transition

There continues to be considerable debate over whether or not there was any meaningful "continuity" across the Mesolithic–Neolithic transition in parts of North-west Europe, particularly Britain, Ireland, and southern Scandinavia (Cummings and Harris, 2011; Milner et al., 2004; Richards and Schulting, 2006; Richards et al., 2003b; Sheridan, 2010; Thomas, 2013). One line of evidence featured in this debate

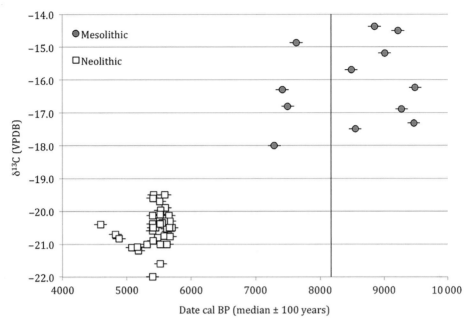

Figure 4.1 Stable carbon isotope results and radiocarbon dates on human remains from coastal south Wales. The vertical line indicates the 8.2 kya cal BP event. Dates calibrated in OxCal 4.2 using the IntCal13 and Marine13 calibration curves (Bronk Ramsey, 2013; Reimer *et al.*, 2013). Mesolithic dates are corrected for the marine reservoir effect, proportional to the estimated contribution of marine dietary protein (cf. Schulting *et al.*, 2013).

is the continued use of coastal resources in the Neolithic. This is inferred from the presence of coastal site locations, as well as the persistence of shell middens and evidence for fishing (Milner *et al.*, 2004). More recently, direct evidence for marine products has been identified in residues in Early Neolithic pottery in Denmark (Craig *et al.*, 2011). Conversely, no such evidence has been found in Britain or Ireland, despite a large-scale study aimed at just this (Cramp *et al.*, 2014a, b).

But in both regions, the human bone collagen stable isotope evidence unequivocally supports a reversal in the relative importance of marine and terrestrial resources (Fischer *et al.*, 2007; Price *et al.*, 2007; Richards *et al.*, 2003a; Schulting, 2013; Tauber, 1986). Following the three ranges proposed above, the majority of coastal Mesolithic individuals from Denmark exhibit $\delta^{13}C$ values indicating diets strongly focused on marine resources, constituting more than half of the signal. By contrast, and with only very few exceptions (concerning which see discussion in Schulting, 2011, 2015, 2018), coastal Neolithic individuals exhibit $\delta^{13}C$ values consistent with the dominance of terrestrial resources, accompanied by the appearance of domestic animals and plants in the region. A comparable shift is seen in $\delta^{15}N$ values, which become significantly lower in the Neolithic (Figure 4.2). This need not be seen as conflicting with evidence for the continued use of marine resources, since the inclusion of these resources as a minor component of the diet (constituting no more than ~10–15 percent of dietary protein) is not precluded by the stable

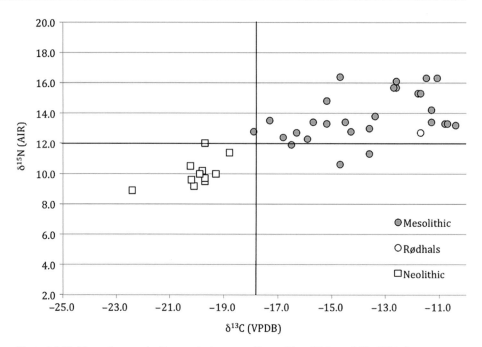

Figure 4.2 Stable carbon and nitrogen isotope results on Mesolithic and Neolithic human remains from coastal Denmark. The individual from Rødhals dates to the transition period, but clearly shows a strongly marine diet entirely typical of the Mesolithic and atypical of the Neolithic (data from Fischer *et al.*, 2007; Price *et al.*, 2007). The lines at −18‰ and 12‰ demarcate predominantly terrestrial (lower left quadrant) and balanced/predominantly marine (upper right quadrant) diets (see Schulting, 2015, in press).

isotope data. The lines of evidence refer to different temporal scales: measurements on adult bone collagen reflect averaged diet over a decade or more of life, reflecting literally thousands of meals (10 950 if one assumes three meals a day over ten years), while marine contents in a pot could potentially refer to just a single meal. The step change in emphasis from marine to terrestrial resources, and all this implies concerning lifeways and identity, is argued here to constitute a clear transformation in the SES.

The picture is even clearer in Britain, though finds of Mesolithic human remains from coastal sites are limited to south Wales and to the west coast of Scotland. There is still a gap of over a millennium between the latest known Mesolithic and earliest Neolithic individuals in south Wales (Figure 4.1). While it would be very useful to fill this gap (and this has been the focus of ongoing research by the author), the isotope signals from Neolithic remains are very clear: Dietary practices in these populations were completely dominated by a terrestrial signal (Schulting and Borić, 2017). While some minor contribution of marine foods is likely, this is on a different order entirely from that seen in the Mesolithic. This is particularly striking because a number of directly dated Mesolithic and Neolithic human remains derive from nearby locations (e.g., Caldey Island) or even from the same site (e.g., Foxhole Cave) (Schulting and

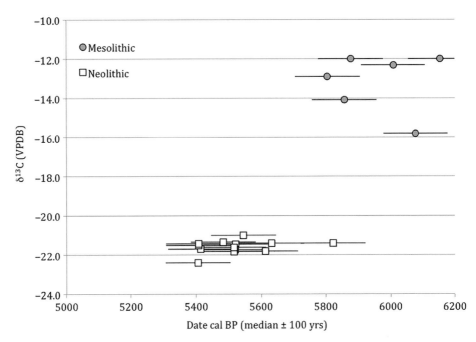

Figure 4.3 Stable carbon isotope results and radiocarbon dates on human remains from the west coast of Scotland (data from Charlton et al., 2016; Richards and Sheridan, 2000; Schulting and Richards, 2002b). Dates calibrated in OxCal4.2 using the IntCal13 and Marine13 calibration curves (Bronk Ramsey, 2013; Reimer et al., 2013). Mesolithic dates are corrected for the marine reservoir effect, proportional to the estimated contribution of marine dietary protein.

Richards, 2002a; Schulting et al., 2013). Furthermore, due to rising sea levels, the coast would actually have been somewhat more distant from these locations in the Mesolithic than in the Neolithic. As discussed in more detail below, this is strongly suggestive of a loss of resilience by Late Mesolithic communities, prompting entry into a new adaptive cycle marked by the beginning of the Neolithic in the region.

The west coast of Scotland provides the clearest case for a rapid shift from the dominance of marine to that of terrestrial resources (Schulting and Richards, 2002b). More recent research has only strengthened this view (Armit et al., 2016; Charlton et al., 2016) (Figure 4.3). The available radiocarbon dates overlap, raising the intriguing possibility of the coexistence of two very distinct lifeways (Charlton et al., 2015; Richards and Sheridan, 2000; Schulting and Richards, 2002b). If so, the marine adaptation appears to have disappeared very quickly. It should be noted that the earliest Neolithic individual shown on Figure 4.3, at ca. 5800 cal BP, is from Macarthur Cave, Oban, and is not in association with diagnostic Neolithic material culture. Thus, pending the outcome of ongoing DNA analysis, the provisional assignment of these remains to a Neolithic time period relies on the $\delta^{13}C$ ratio. While this could be seen as a circular argument, previous research has shown the utility of using $\delta^{13}C$ as an independent means of identifying Mesolithic and post-Mesolithic humans from coastal contexts in Britain (Schulting and Richards, 2002a;

Schulting *et al.*, 2013). The later individuals in Figure 4.3 derive from caves and a series of Neolithic mortuary monuments on the Scottish west coast (Armit *et al.*, 2016; Schulting and Richards, 2002b; Schulting in Ashmore, 2004). As mentioned above, there is also an absence of marine biomarkers in Early Neolithic pottery in the region (Cramp *et al.*, 2014a, b). It is hard to imagine a sharper shift in diet, and hence associated lifeways, occurring within the span of a few generations, i.e., the period encompassed by social memory. It is, furthermore, accompanied by concomitant changes in material culture, technology, living and funerary architecture, and in the scale of ceremonial activity. In this sense, the rehabilitation of the long-discarded term revolution seems warranted, entailing, "among other things, rapid redefinitions between past and future, between shared memories and shared expectations" (Tilly, 1994: 247).

The question remains as to whether this was the result of the rapid adoption of introduced domesticated plants and animals, largely by indigenous hunter-gatherers, or whether there was actually a substantial incursion by a new incoming population with an established farming economy. The results of a number of large-scale projects on ancient DNA, including British and Irish Mesolithic and Neolithic human remains, are starting to appear (Armit *et al.*, 2016; Brace *et al.*, 2018; Cassidy *et al.*, 2016; Olalde *et al.*, 2018), and the results will make an important contribution to the debate. The aDNA data for Neolithic Britain and Ireland show surprisingly strong genetic affiliation with contemporary farmers in continental Europe, who in turn show affinity with the Near East (Brace *et al.*, 2018; Cassidy *et al.*, 2016; Olalde *et al.*, 2018), a finding consistent with the picture emerging across Europe (Mathieson *et al.*, 2015). Thus, there appears to have been a large element of population replacement associated with the initial spread of farming, significantly changing the nature of the debate.

Regardless of the outcome of the genetic studies, the isotopic and archaeological evidence indicates a step change in lifeways across the Mesolithic–Neolithic transition in Denmark, and even more so in south Wales and on the west coast of Scotland. The focus of the subsistence economy clearly underwent a major change, along with concomitant changes in technology, settlement, and mortuary practices, all of which point toward a transformation of the SES and loss of the previous fisher-hunter-gatherer way of life, i.e., the resilience of that system was exceeded and failed. Drawing upon the previous discussion, it is important to emphasize that this does not imply that individuals or even entire communities failed to adapt to new circumstances, but rather that, in doing so, these populations significantly altered lifeways and entered a new adaptive cycle in which new identities and relationships were created. Some of these consequences may have been unintended. The ownership of cleared horticultural plots and of animals, for example, may have transformed the nature of social relations, while the new plants and animals themselves would have modified local environments in partnership with humans as part of a process of niche construction (Rowley-Conwy and Layton, 2011).

An environmental trigger for the transition to farming in northwest Europe has been proposed (Bonsall *et al.*, 2002; Macklin *et al.*, 2000; Rowley-Conwy, 1984), but there are problems both with the chronological imprecision of the archaeological and environmental evidence, and with the scale at which this explanation is intended to apply (see discussion in Schulting, 2010b). Alternatively, the transition here could be viewed as the result of purely or largely social factors (Schulting, 2010b; see also Lemmen and Wirtz, 2012). This explanation becomes more compelling if the accumulating genetic data continue to support a major population influx at this juncture, although ultimately this may have had an underlying climatic driver (Warner, 2011). This presents an interesting example, since it highlights two ways in which resilience may be exceeded, one emphasizing mainly indigenous change in the face of environmental factors, and the other emphasizing a clash of two different cultures and ways of life. The exciting thing is that archaeologists and bioarchaeologists are in a position to discuss this in increasingly nuanced detail compared to what was possible before the turn of the millennium.

4.4   Conclusion

Identifying resilience in the past is a very challenging prospect. This chapter offers one potentially fruitful approach based on the use of stable carbon and nitrogen isotope data to argue for the persistence of livelihood strategies and identities in south Wales across the 8.2 kya cal BP event, the largest climatic downturn known in the Holocene record of the northern hemisphere. The persistence of this lifestyle was facilitated by a broad-spectrum economy that allowed flexibility during periods of environmental turmoil. That the west coast of Scotland appears, on present evidence, to have been largely depopulated at this time presents an interesting contrast, one that requires explanation. It is possible that these populations abandoned the basin of attraction and experienced complete transformation of the SES due to excessive rigidity. However, few pieces of this complicated puzzle are available, suggesting that this question is unlikely to be resolved in the near future. The second example draws upon the marked changes observed in stable isotope results across the Mesolithic–Neolithic transition in northwest Europe, focusing on Denmark and Britain. The previously proposed sharp shift is re-affirmed, and it is argued that this is a potential candidate for the loss of hunter-gatherer resilience and the instigation of a new adaptive cycle focused on mixed farming. The interesting question – possibly one on the verge of being at least partly answered through ancient DNA – is whether this occurred largely within an indigenous context, or whether it was primarily due to a substantial (however defined) incoming population of farmers.

Acknowledgments

Many thanks to Dan Temple for the invitation to contribute to this volume, as well as for discussions concerning resilience. Thanks also to Amy Bogaard, Nicki Whitehouse, and an anonymous reviewer for their very useful comments on a draft of this chapter. They are in no way culpable for the final result.

References

Aaris-Sørenson, K. (1999). The Holocene history of the Scandinavian aurochs (*Bos primigenius Bojanus*, 1827). In G.-C. Weniger, ed., *Archäologie und Biologie des Auerochsen.* Mettmann: Neanderthal Museum, pp. 49–57.

Abel, N., Cumming, D. H. M., and Anderies, J. M. (2006). Collapse and reorganization in social-ecological systems: Questions, some ideas, and policy implications. *Ecology and Society,* 11, e17.

Adger, W. N. (2000). Social and ecological resilience: Are they related? *Progress in Human Geography,* 24, 347–364.

Allen, C. R., Angeler, D. G., Garmestani, A. S., Gunderson, L. H., and Holling, C. S. (2014). Panarchy: Theory and application. *Ecosystems,* 17, 578–589.

Alley, R. B., Mayewski, P. A., Sowers, T., *et al.* (1997). Holocene climate instability: A prominent, widespread event 8200 yr ago. *Geology,* 25, 843–486.

Armit, I., Sheridan, A., Reich, D., Cook, G., and Naysmith, P. (2016). Radiocarbon dates obtained for the GENSCOT ancient DNA project, 2016. *Discovery and Excavation in Scotland,* 17, 195–198.

Ashmore, P. J. (2004). A list of archaeological radiocarbon dates. *Discovery and Excavation in Scotland,* 5, 155–176.

Bailey, G. N. (1983). Concepts of time in Quaternary prehistory. *Annual Review of Anthropology,* 12, 165–192.

Biehl, P. F. and Nieuwenhuyse, O. P. (2016). *Climate and Cultural Change in Prehistoric Europe.* New York: State University of New York Press.

Bird-David, N. (1990). The giving environment: Another perspective on the economic system of hunter-gatherers. *Current Anthropology,* 31, 183–196.

Bonsall, C., Anderson, D. E., and Macklin, M. G. (2002). The Mesolithic–Neolithic transition in western Scotland and its European context. *Documenta Praehistorica,* 29, 1–19.

Brace, S., Diekmann, Y., Booth, T. J., *et al.* (2018). Population replacement in Early Neolithic Britain. *bioRxiv.*

Bronk Ramsey, C. (2013). OxCal 4.2. https://c14.arch.ox.ac.uk.

Budja, M. (2007). The 8200 cal BP "climate event" and the process of neolithisation in south-eastern Europe. *Documenta Praehistorica,* 34, 191–201.

Carpenter, S, Walker, B., Anderies, J. M., and Abe, N. (2001). From metaphor to measurement: Resilience of what to what? *Ecosystems,* 4, 765–871.

Carpenter, S., Westley, F., and Turner, M. (2005). Surrogates for resilience of social-ecological systems. *Ecosystems,* 8, 941–944.

Cashdan, E. A. (1980). Egalitarianism among hunters and gatherers. *American Anthropologist,* 82, 116–120.

Cassidy, L., Martiniano, R., Murphy, E. M., *et al.* (2016). Neolithic and Bronze Age migration to Ireland and establishment of the insular Atlantic genome. *Proceedings of the National Academy of Sciences,* 113, 368–373.

Charlton, S., Alexander, M., Collins, M. J., *et al.* (2016). Finding Britain's last hunter-gatherers: A new biomolecular approach to "unidentifiable" bone fragments utilising bone collagen. *Journal of Archaeological Science,* 73, 55–61.

Clarke, M. L. and Rendell, H. M. (2009). The impact of North Atlantic storminess on western European coasts: A review. *Quaternary International,* 195, 31–41.

Costa, L. J., Sternke, F., and Woodman, P. C. (2005). Microlith to macrolith: The reasons behind the transformation of production in the Irish Mesolithic. *Antiquity,* 79, 19–33.

Costanza, R., Kemp, W. M., and Boynton, W. R. (1995). Predictability, scale and biodiversity in coastal and estuarine ecosystems: Implications for management. *Ambio,* 22, 88–96.

Cote, M. and Nightingale, A. J. (2012). Resilience thinking meets social theory: Situating social change in socio-ecological systems (SES) research. *Progress in Human Geography,* 36, 475–489.

Craig, O. E., Steele, V. J., Fischer, A., *et al.* (2011). Ancient lipids reveal continuity in culinary practices across the transition to agriculture in northern Europe. *Proceedings of the National Academy of Sciences*, **108**, 17910–17915.

Cramp, L. J. E., Evershed, R. P., Lavento, M., *et al.* (2014a). Neolithic dairy farming at the extreme of agriculture in northern Europe. *Proceedings of the Royal Society B*, **281**, 20140819.

Cramp, L. J. E., Jones, J. R., Sheridan, A., *et al.* (2014b). Immediate replacement of fishing with dairying by the earliest farmers of the northeast Atlantic archipelagos. *Proceedings of the Royal Society B*, **281**, e20132372.

Cretney, R. (2014). Resilience for whom? Emerging critical geographies of socio-ecological resilience. *Geography Compass*, **8**, 627–640.

Cumming, G. S. and Collier, J. (2005). Change and identity in complex systems. *Ecology and Society*, **10**, 29.

Cumming, G. S., Barnes, G., Perz, S., *et al.* (2005). An exploratory framework for the empirical measurement of resilience. *Ecosystems*, **8**, 975–987.

Cummings, V. and Harris, O. (2011). Animals, people and places: The continuity of hunting and gathering practices across the Mesolithic–Neolithic transition in Britain. *European Journal of Archaeology*, **14**, 361–382.

Davidson, D. J. (2010). The applicability of the concept of resilience to social systems: Some sources of optimism and nagging doubts. *Society and Natural Resources*, **23**, 1135–1149.

Díaz-Andreu, M., Lucy, S., Babić, S., and Edwards, D. N. (2006). *The Archaeology of Identity: Approaches to Gender, Age, Status, Ethnicity and Religion*. London: Routledge.

Dunning, N. P., Beach, T. P., and Luzzadder-Beach, S. (2012). Kax and kol: Collapse and resilience in lowland Maya civilization. *Proceeding of the National Academy of Sciences*, **109**, 3652–3657.

Fernández-Armestto, F. (2002). *Food: A History*. London: Pan Macmillan.

Fischer, A., Olsen, J., Richards, M. P., *et al.* (2007). Coast–inland mobility and diet in the Danish Mesolithic and Neolithic: Evidence from stable isotope values of humans and dogs. *Journal of Archaeological Science*, **34**, 2125–2150.

Flohr, P., Fleitmann, D., Matthews, R., Matthews, W., and Black, S. (2016). Evidence of resilience to past climate change in Southwest Asia: Early farming communities and the 9.2 and 8.2 ka events. *Quaternary Science Reviews*, **136**, 23–39.

Forbes, B. B., Stammler, F., Kumpula, T., *et al.* (2009). High resilience in the Yamal-Nenets social-ecological system, West Siberian Arctic, Russia. *Proceedings of the National Academy of Sciences*, **106**, 22041–22048.

Gallopín, G. C. (2006). Linkages between vulnerability, resilience, and adaptive capacity. *Global Environmental Change*, **16**, 293–303.

García Martínez de Lagrán, I., Tejedor-Rodríguez, C., Iriarte, F., *et al.* (2016). 8.2 ka BP paleoclimatic event and the Ebro Valley Mesolithic groups: Preliminary data from Artusia rock shelter (Unzué, Navarra, Spain). *Quaternary International*, **403**, 151–173.

Garmestani, A. S. and Benson, M. H. (2013). A framework for resilience-based governance of social-ecological systems, *Ecology and Society*, **18**, article 9.

González-Sampériz, P., Utrilla, P., Mazo, C., *et al.* (2009). Patterns of human occupation during the early Holocene in the Central Ebro Basin (NE Spain) in response to the 8.2 ka climatic event. *Quaternary Research*, **71**, 121–132.

Gunderson, L. H. (2000). Ecological resilience – in theory and application. *Annual Review of Ecology and Systematics*, **31**, 425–439.

Hatt, K. (2013). Social attractors: A proposal to enhance "resilience thinking" about the social. *Society and Natural Resources*, **26**, 30–43.

Holling, C. S. (1973). Resilience and stability of ecological systems. *Annual Review of Ecology and Systematics*, **4**, 1–24.

Holling, C. S. (1987). Simplifying the complex: The paradigms of ecological function and structure. *European Journal of Operational Research*, **30**, 139–146.

Ingold, T., ed. (2000). *The Perception of the Environment: Essays in Livelihood, Dwelling and Skill*. London: Routledge.

Keeling, R. F., Körtzinger, A., and Gruber N. (2010). Ocean deoxygenation in a warming world. *Annual Review of Marine Science*, 2, 199–229.

Lancelotti, C., Zurro, D., Whitehouse, N., *et al.* (2016). Resilience of small-scale societies' livelihoods: A framework for studying the transition from food gathering to food production. *Ecology and Society*, 21, 8.

Lemmen, C. and Wirtz, K. W. (2012). On the sensitivity of the simulated European Neolithic transition to climate extremes. *Journal of Archaeological Science*, 51, 65–72.

López de Pablo, J. F. and Jochim, M. A. (2010). The impact of the 8,200 cal BP climatic event on human mobility strategies during the Iberian Late Mesolithic. *Journal of Anthropological Research*, 66, 39–68.

Lowe, D. J. (2011). Tephrochronology and its application: A review. *Quaternary Geochronology*, 6, 107–153.

MacArthur, R. H. and Wilson, E. O. (1967). *The Theory of Island Biogeography*. Princeton, NJ: Princeton University Press.

Macklin, M. G., Bonsall, C., Robinson, M. R., and Davies, F. M. (2000). Human–environment interactions during the Holocene: New data and interpretations from the Oban Area, Argyll, Scotland. *The Holocene*, 10, 109–121.

Maclean, K., Ross, H., Cuthill, M., and Witt, B. (2017). Converging disciplinary understandings of social aspects of resilience. *Journal of Environmental Planning and Management*, 60, 1–19.

Mann, K. H. (1982). *Ecology of Coastal Waters*. Berkeley, CA: University of California Press.

Mathieson, I., Lazaridis, I., Rohland, N., *et al.* (2015). Genome-wide patterns of selection in 230 ancient Eurasians. *Nature*, 528, 499–503.

Milner, N., Craig, O. E., Bailey, G. N., Pedersen, K., and Andersen, S. H. (2004). Something fishy in the Neolithic? A re-evaluation of stable isotope analysis of Mesolithic and Neolithic coastal populations. *Antiquity*, 78, 9–22.

Minagawa, M. and Wada, E. (1984). Stepwise enrichment of ^{15}N along food chains: Further evidence and the relation between δ^{15}N and animal age. *Geochimica et Cosmochimica Acta*, 48, 1135–1140.

Mithen, S. J. (1990). *Thoughtful Foragers: A Study of Prehistoric Decision Making*. Cambridge: Cambridge University Press.

Olalde, I., Brace, S., Allentoft, M. E., *et al.* (2018). The Beaker phenomenon and the genomic transformation of northwest Europe. *Nature*, 555, 190–197.

Olsson, L., Jerneck, A., Thoren, H., Persson, J., and O'Byrne, D. (2015). Why resilience is unappealing to social science: Theoretical and empirical investigations of the scientific use of resilience. *Science Advances*, 1(4), e1400217.

Peterson, N. (1993). Demand sharing: Reciprocity and the pressure for generosity among foragers. *American Anthropologist*, 95, 860–874.

Pinhasi, R., Fort, J., and Ammerman, A. J. (2005). Tracing the origin and spread of agriculture in Europe. *PLoS Biology*, 3(12), e410.

Price, T. D., Ambrose, S. H., Bennike, P., *et al.* (2007). New information on the Stone Age graves at Dragsholm, Denmark. *Acta Archaeologica*, 78, 193–219.

Pross, J., Kotthoff, U., Müller, U. C., *et al.* (2009). Massive perturbation in terrestrial ecosystems of the Eastern Mediterranean region associated with the 8.2 kyr B.P. climatic event. *Geology*, 37, 887–890.

Redman, C. L. (2005). Resilience theory in archaeology. *American Anthropologist*, 107, 70–77.

Reimer, P. J., Bard, E., Bayliss, A., *et al.* (2013). IntCal13 and Marine13 radiocarbon age calibration curves 0–50,000 years cal BP. *Radiocarbon*, 55, 1869–1887.

Richards, M. P. and Hedges, R. E. M. (1999). Stable isotope evidence for similarities in the types of marine foods used by Late Mesolithic humans on the Atlantic coast of Europe. *Journal of Archaeological Science*, 26, 717–722.

Richards, M. P. and Mellars, P. A. (1998). Stable isotopes and the seasonality of the Oronsay middens. *Antiquity*, **72**, 178–184.

Richards, M. P. and Schulting, R. J. (2006). Against the grain? A response to Milner *et al.* (2004). *Antiquity*, **80**, 444–458.

Richards, M. P. and Sheridan, J. A. (2000). New AMS dates on human bone from Mesolithic Oronsay. *Antiquity*, **74**, 313–315.

Richards, M. P., Price, T. D., and Koch, E. (2003a). Mesolithic and Neolithic subsistence in Denmark: New stable isotope data. *Current Anthropology*, **44**, 288–295.

Richards, M. P., Schulting, R. J., and Hedges, R. E. M. (2003b). Sharp shift in diet at onset of Neolithic. *Nature*, **425**, 366.

Rival, L. (2009). The resilience of indigenous intelligence. In K. Hastrup, ed., *The Question of Resilience: Social Responses to Climate Change*. Viborg: Det Kongelige Danske Videnskabernes Selskab, pp. 293–313.

Robinson, E., Van Strydonck, M., Gelorini, V., and Crombé, P. (2013). Radiocarbon chronology and the correlation of hunter-gatherer sociocultural change with abrupt palaeoclimate change: The Middle Mesolithic in the Rhine–Meuse–Scheldt area of northwest Europe. *Journal of Archaeological Science*, **40**, 755–763.

Rowley-Conwy, P. (1984). The laziness of the short-distance hunter: The origins of agriculture in western Denmark. *Journal of Anthropological Archaeology*, **4**, 300–324.

Rowley-Conwy, P. and Layton, R. (2011). Foraging and farming as niche construction: Stable and unstable adaptations. *Philosophical Transactions of the Royal Society B*, **366**, 849–862.

Schulting, R. J. (2008). Foodways and social ecologies: Early Mesolithic to the Early Bronze Age. In J. Pollard, ed., *Prehistoric Britain*. London: Blackwell, pp. 90–120.

Schulting, R. J. (2010a). Staying home for dinner: An isotopic approach to regionality in Mesolithic Atlantic Europe. In R. Barndon, A. Engevik, and I. Øye, eds., *The Archaeology of Regional Technologies: Case Studies from the Palaeolithic to the Age of the Vikings*. Lewiston: Edwin Mellen Press, pp. 69–88.

Schulting, R. J. (2010b). Holocene environmental change and the Mesolithic–Neolithic transition in northwest Europe: Revisiting two models. *Environmental Archaeology*, **15**, 160–172.

Schulting, R. J. (2011). Mesolithic–Neolithic transitions: An isotopic tour through Europe. In R. Pinhasi and J. Stock, eds., *The Bioarchaeology of the Transition to Agriculture*. New York, NY: Wiley-Liss, pp. 17–41.

Schulting, R. J. (2013). On the northwestern fringes: Earlier Neolithic subsistence in Britain and Ireland as seen through faunal remains and stable isotopes. In S. Colledge, J. Conolly, K. Dobney, K. Manning, and S. Shennan, eds., *The Origins and Spread of Stock-Keeping in the Near East and Europe*. Walnut Creek, CA: Left Coast Press, pp. 313–338.

Schulting, R. J. (2015). Sweet or salty? Isotopic evidence for the use of aquatic resources in Mesolithic Europe. In N. Bicho, C. Detry, T. D. Price, and E. Cunha, eds., *Muge 150th: The 150th Anniversary of the Discovery of Mesolithic Shellmiddens*, vol. 2. Cambridge: Cambridge Scholars, pp. 153–172.

Schulting, R. J. (2018). Dietary shifts at the Mesolithic–Neolithic transition in Europe: An overview of the stable isotope data. In J. Lee-Thorp and M. A. Katzenberg, eds., *Oxford Handbook of the Archaeology of Diet*. Oxford: Oxford University Press.

Schulting, R. J. and Borić, D. (2017). A tale of two processes of Neolithisation: Southeast Europe and Britain/Ireland. In P. Bickle, V. Cummings, D. Hofmann, and J. Pollard, eds., *Neolithic Europe: Essays in Honour of Professor Alasdair Whittle*. Oxford: Oxbow Books, pp. 82–104.

Schulting, R. J. and Richards, M. P. (2002a). Finding the coastal Mesolithic in southwest Britain: AMS dates and stable isotope results on human remains from Caldey Island, Pembrokeshire, South Wales. *Antiquity*, **76**, 1011–1025.

Schulting, R. J. and Richards, M. P. (2002b). The wet, the wild and the domesticated: The Mesolithic–Neolithic transition on the west coast of Scotland. *European Journal of Archaeology*, **5**, 147–189.

Schulting, R. J., Fibiger, L., Macphail, R. I., *et al.* (2013). Mesolithic and Neolithic human remains from Foxhole Cave (Gower, South Wales). *Antiquaries Journal*, **93**, 1–23.

Sheridan, A. (2010). The Neolithization of Britain and Ireland: The "big picture." In B. Finlayson and G. Warren, eds., *Landscapes in Transition*. Oxford: Oxbow, pp. 89–105.

Strang, V. (1997). *Uncommon Ground: Landscape, Values and the Environment*. Oxford: Berg.

Tauber, H. (1986). Analysis of stable isotopes in prehistoric populations. *Mitteilungen der Berliner Gesellschaft für Anthropologie, Ethnologie und Urgeschichte*, **7**, 31–38.

Testart, A. (1982). The significance of food storage among hunter-gatherers: Residence patterns, population densities, and social inequalities. *Current Anthropology*, **23**, 523–537.

Thomas, E. R., Wolff, E., Mulvaney, R., *et al.* (2007). The 8.2 ka BP event from Greenland ice cores. *Quaternary Science Review*, **26**, 70–81.

Thomas, J. (2013). *The Birth of Neolithic Britain: An Interpretive Account*. Oxford: Oxford University Press.

Tilly, C. (1994). Political memories in time and space. In J. Boyarin, ed., *Remapping Memory: The Politics of Timespace*. Minneapolis, MN: University of Minnesota Press.

Tolan-Smith, C. (2008). Mesolithic Britain. In G. N. Bailey and P. A. Spikins, eds., *Mesolithic Europe*. Cambridge: Cambridge University Press, pp. 132–157.

Twiss, K. C., ed. (2007). *The Archaeology of Food and Identity*. Carbondale, IL: Centre for Archaeological Investigations, Southern Illinois University.

Walker, B., Holling, C. S., Carpenter, S. R., and Kinzig, A. (2004). Resilience, adaptability and transformability in social-ecological systems. *Ecology and Society*, **9**, e5.

Warner, K. (2011). Environmental change and migration: Methodological considerations from ground-breaking global survey. *Population & Environment*, **33**, 3–27.

Weninger, B., Alram-Stern, E., Bauer, E., *et al.* (2006). Climate forcing due to the 8200 cal yr BP event observed at Early Neolithic sites in the eastern Mediterranean. *Quaternary Research*, **66**, 401–420.

Weninger, B., Schulting, R. J., Bradtmöller, M., *et al.* (2008). Catastrophic final flooding of Doggerland by the Storegga slide tsunami. *Documenta Praehistorica*, **35**, 1–24.

Wicks, K. and Mithen, S. (2014). The impact of the abrupt 8.2 ka cold event on the Mesolithic population of western Scotland: A Bayesian chronological analysis using "activity events" as a population proxy. *Journal of Archaeological Science*, **45**, 240–269.

Widlok, T., Aufgebauer, A., Bradtmöller, M., *et al.* (2012). Towards a theoretical framework for analyzing integrated socio-environmental systems. *Quaternary International*, **274**, 259–272.

Woodburn, J. (1998). "Sharing is not a form of exchange": An analysis of property-sharing in immediate-return hunter-gatherer societies. In C. M. Hann, ed., *Property Relations: Renewing the Anthropological Tradition*. Cambridge: Cambridge University Press, pp. 48–63.

Yesner, D. R. (1987). Life in the "Garden of Eden": Causes and consequences of the adoption of marine diets by human societies. In M. Harris and E. B. Ross, eds., *Food and Evolution: Toward a Theory of Human Food Habit*. Philadelphia, PA: Temple University Press, pp. 285–310.

Yesner, D. R., Figuerero Torres, M. J., Guichon, R. A., and Borrero, L. A. (2003). Stable isotope analysis of human bone and ethnohistoric subsistence patterns in Tierra del Fuego. *Journal of Anthropological Archaeology*, **22**, 279–291.

Zvelebil, M. (1995). Hunting, gathering, or husbandry? Management of food resources by the Late Mesolithic communities of temperate Europe. In D. V. Campana, ed., *Before Farming: Hunter-Gatherer Society and Subsistence*. Philadelphia, PA: Museum of Applied Science Center for Archaeology (MASCA), pp. 79–104.

5 Persistence of Time: Resilience and Adaptability in Prehistoric Jomon Hunter-Gatherers from the Inland Sea Region of Southwestern Honshu, Japan

Daniel H. Temple

5.1 Introduction

The Jomon culture is one of the longest continuous phases of complex hunter-gatherer populations in world prehistory (Habu, 2004; Imamura, 1996). Jomon culture extends to approximately 16 500 BP and terminates with the introduction of wet-rice agriculture around 2400 BP on Honshu and Kyushu Islands (Habu, 2014a). These populations survived volcanic eruptions, climatic oscillations, and eventually migrations that resulted in a merging of cultures to produce the incipient agricultural complex of the Yayoi period (Habu, 2004; Hudson, 1999; Imamura, 1996; Kobayashi, 2005). How did these populations actively resist and survive so many challenges? What anthropological and evolutionary paradigms may help explain this persistence? This chapter uses bioarchaeological evidence to explore resilience/adaptability and transformation in the socioecological and cultural systems of Middle (5500 to 4300 BP) and Late/Final (4300 to 2400 BP) Jomon period hunter-gatherers during a period of intense, sustained cooling along the Inland Sea region of Japan.

Bioarchaeological research has long emphasized the culturally and biologically disruptive nature of changing environments, including ecological shifts, subsistence transitions, or contact (Armelagos, 2003; Larsen, 1987, 1994, 2002). A typical approach to exploring these issues within bioarchaeological research is to compare the frequency of skeletal or dental lesions associated with stress experiences or to evaluate some manner of change in the archaeological mortuary record (Larsen, 2015). This approach may produce binary categories for populations as relatively healthy versus unhealthy (Temple and Goodman, 2014). Another unintended consequence of this research is that hunter-gatherers are often treated as a starting point for comparative research, when in fact the random, nonlinear nature of both biological and cultural evolution does not augur directionality in cultural and ecological transitions. Persistence in response to potentially disruptive events is of equal importance and should be emphasized by bioarchaeological studies of hunter-gatherers. This process helps explain the maintenance of deeper cultural identities and removes the veneer of teleology in the study of cultural evolution. The integration of resilience theory and the human adaptive cycle offers a useful approach to exploring the interconnectedness of behavioral flexibility and persistence in the past (Redman, 2005; Redman and Kinzig, 2003).

Resilience theory was derived as an alternative to extinction in ecological contexts (Holling, 1973). This theoretical framework evaluates populations in terms of adaptive cycles, with periods of growth (exploitation of natural resources), conservation (accumulation of resources), release (sudden change within the panarchy), and reorganization (return to or production of new basins of attraction) (Gunderson and Holling, 2002; Holling, 1986). The ability to differentiate between resilience/ adaptability and transformation as well as the broader contexts that drive these processes is a focus of social and ecological science research (Butzer and Endfield, 2012; Cumming et al., 2006; Faulseit, 2016; McAnany and Yoffee, 2010; Redman, 2005; Redman and Kinzig, 2003; Walker et al., 2004). Results from this work provide evidence for the nonlinear nature of socioecological and cultural evolution, as well as the conditions that drive resilience/adaptability and transformation within socioecological and cultural systems. Resilience/adaptability is associated with behavioral shifts and persistence that are pointed toward the internal components of the socioecological and cultural system; on the other hand, transformation requires the adoption of external modes of production and practice that render the previous system unrecognizable (Cumming et al., 2006; Folke, 2006; Pearson and Pearson, 2012; Walker et al., 2004). Transformations occur when precariousness within socioecological and cultural systems increases due to rigidity or overgeneralization (Folke, 2006).

Archaeological research frequently focuses on release and reorganization as these phases of the adaptive cycle include adaptation and transformation (Redman, 2005). Resilience is often ignored, despite comprising an essential role in the adaptive cycle: Where reorganization produces shifts within the socioecological and cultural system, it remains important to understand the internally versus externally directed nature of these shifts. Differentiating between these events helps define the structure of changes within the adaptive cycle as those based on memory within the system or revolt against preexisting agencies. Archaeological studies benefit from a deep-time perspective, and therefore act as important contexts for the study of resilience/ adaptability and transformation (Redman, 2005; Redman and Kinzig, 2003).

Jomon culture is named after the chord-impressed, linear applique pottery produced by these populations (Imamura, 1996). Archaeological evidence suggests that Jomon cultural origins are derived from a microblade technology that arrived in the Japanese Islands around 20 000 BP (Imamura, 1996). These technologies were related to the Paleolithic Yubetsu culture of Siberia (Ikawa-Smith, 2004, 2007). Linear applique pottery is associated variously with microlithic technologies in Kyushu and the lack of surviving microblade technologies on Honshu and Hokkaido (Figure 5.1) (Imamura, 1996). Dates for linear applique pottery are currently listed at around 13 800 BP on Kyushu and 12 000 BP in southwestern Honshu (Habu, 2014a). Evidence for plain-bottom Jomon-stylized ceramics were, however, found associated with Chokajubo-Mikoshiba lithic technologies, which date to the earliest stages of the Initial Jomon period in northeastern Honshu: Radiocarbon dates

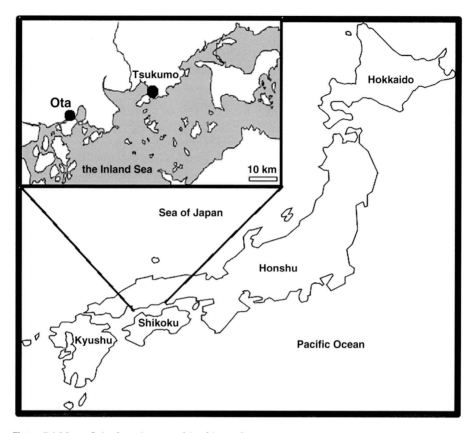

Figure 5.1 Map of site locations used in this study.

obtained from carbonized remains place these ceramics between 16 500 to 15 170 cal BP (Nakamura *et al.*, 2001). On this basis, the Jomon period is defined according to Incipient (16 500 to 11 000 BP), Initial (11 000 to 7000 BP), Early (7000 to 5500 BP), Middle (5500 to 4300 BP), Late (4300 to 3300), and Final (3300 to 2400 BP) phases (Habu, 2014a).

Shifts in mobility and site size are the primary behavioral differences between the Incipient through Early phases of the Jomon periods, with population aggregation and centralized communal habitation sites appearing during the Early and Middle phases (Habu, 2004; Imamura, 1996). Climatic cooling around 4000 BP marks the transition from the Middle to Late phase of the Jomon period. Cooling trends between the Middle and Late/Final phase of the Jomon period are associated with a rise in beech (*Fagus*), hemlock (*Tsuga soeboldii*), Japanese fir (*Abies firma*), and general coniferous forests (Tsukada, 1986). C_{37} alkenone cores recovered from coastal sites off the northern coast of Honshu (20 km from the Sannai Maruyama archaeological site) in Mutsu Bay were used to reconstruct sea surface temperatures (Kawahata *et al.*, 2009). Higher temperatures occurred between 8400 and 4100 BP, while a period of intensive, sustained cooling was noted between 4100 and 2300 BP, with an average decline in ambient temperature of two to three degrees Celsius.

Zooarchaeological research centered around this climatic cooling event documents the consumption of smaller, younger deer across Honshu (Koike, 1992; Koike and Ohtaishi, 1985), but no change in the size of gastropods and bivalves (Koike, 1986). It is noted that these temperature shifts likely impaired the capacity of chestnut (*Castanea*) cultivation in northeastern Japan (Kawahata *et al.*, 2009). Studies from this region emphasize diminished population size and site abandonment following the Middle Jomon period (Habu, 2004, 2008; Koyama, 1978). Tool kit density at Sannai Maruyama shows a rapid increase in grinding stones and a decline in arrowheads toward the end of the Middle Jomon period (Habu and Hall, 2013). Increasing specialization within this socioecological system may have rendered these populations vulnerable to ecological turnovers (Habu, 2014b). It is, however, noted that Jomon populations consumed *Castanea hansaibai* (chestnuts) following climatic cooling in regions at slightly lower latitudes, and in regions where *C. hansaibai* production was impaired, many populations consumed *Aesculus* species as a fallback source (Kitagawa and Yasuda, 2008). When contextualized in terms of the adaptive cycle, the Early/Middle phases of the Jomon period can be loosely understood as part of a growth/accumulation phase, while the transition between the Middle and Late/Final phases of the Jomon period may be attributed to release and reorganization. In northeastern Japan, increasing precariousness associated with socioecological and cultural rigidity led to full-scale transformation of the socioecological and cultural systems.

Bioarchaeological research in Kyushu (Figure 5.1) suggests that Jomon culture persisted beyond the introduction of wet-rice agriculture at the onset of the Yayoi period (Hoover and Hudson, 2016). Skeletal and dental indicators of stress suggest little change over time within these samples. Thus, the precariousness of the Jomon socioecological and cultural systems did not increase during the transition to agriculture in this region. Instead, persistence of the system was facilitated. Less is known, however, about resilience/adaptability and transformations within these systems during climatic cooling dated to the transition between the Middle and Late/Final phases of the Jomon period in populations from southwestern Honshu. This chapter tests the hypothesis that the socioecological and cultural systems of the Late/Final phase of the Jomon period in the Inland Sea region resisted transformation. Diversity in subsistence practices likely provided sustainability in food choices, while continuity in cultural practices was maintained. Patterns of stress were likely similar between the two time periods, hinting at the likelihood of a persistent, sustainable hunter-gatherer occupation.

5.2   Materials and Methods

5.2.1   Materials

The data for this study focus on human skeletal remains excavated from the southwestern district of Sanyo, along the Inland Sea coast. These remains were excavated from two sites, Ota and Tsukumo (Figure 5.1), both of which are

Table 5.1 Sample sizes by site and sex.

Comparison	N
Ota: anterior teeth	129
Tsukumo: anterior teeth	151
Ota: premolars	149
Tsukumo: premolars	225
Ota: molars	227
Tsukumo: molars	408
Ota: male cross-sectional geometry	11
Tsukumo: male cross-sectional geometry	16
Ota: male body mass/stature	14 / 11
Tsukumo: male body mass/stature	16 / 16
Ota: female body mass stature	6 / 5
Tsukumo: female body mass/stature	10 / 11
Ota: burials	55
Tsukumo: burials	72
Ota: Tooth extraction	52
Tsukumo: tooth extraction	68

considered pattern A sites (Kiyono, 1969), following Kobayashi (1992). Pattern A sites represent the "model Jomon village" and include 100 or more pit dwellings, tools used for both functional and ritual purposes, and several styles of pottery. Pattern A sites also have cemeteries with carefully delineated boundaries between the living and spiritual world. The diversity of tools and pottery, accumulations of human skeletal remains, and number of pit dwellings are important in demonstrating longstanding occupation of the sites. The Ota site was excavated in 1926 by Professor Kenji Kiyono of Kyoto University and dated between 5000 and 4300 BP based on pottery chronologies (Shiomi *et al.*, 1971). The site is located in Onamichi City within Hiroshima Province. The Tsukumo site was excavated between 1920 and 1922 by Professor Kenji Kiyono and dated between 4300 and 2400 BP (Late/Final phase of the Jomon period) based on pottery chronologies (Kiyono, 1969). The two sites are located approximately 40 km from one another and both face the Inland Sea. Similarity in geographic landscape also suggests that the two sites are comparable. Sample sizes for the sites are listed in Table 5.1.

5.2.2   Estimation of Age and Determination of Sex

Morphological features of the os pubis and greater sciatic notch were recorded to determine sex using standard protocols (Buikstra and Ubelaker, 1994). To overcome reference sample mimicry and underrepresentation of older adults, this work used transition analysis to estimate age at death in adult skeletal remains (Boldsen *et al.*, 2002). Morphological features of the pubic symphysis and auricular surface were recorded according to protocols published by Boldsen and colleagues (2002). These features were entered into the ABDOU 2.1.046, which calculates point estimates and 95 percent confidence intervals for age at death.

5.2.3   Diet

Diet was evaluated based on the prevalence of carious lesions between the samples. Dental caries is a disease process associated with the focal demineralization of enamel by organic acids (Hillson, 2001, 2008; Larsen, 1987, 2015). Organic acids are produced by bacteria that consume fermentable carbohydrates in the oral cavity. As a result, dental caries prevalence is often characterized as a reflection of diet. This study compared the prevalence of carious lesions to explore the possibility that differences in cariogenic food consumption may be associated with climate change between the Middle and Late/Final phases of the Jomon period. Carious lesions were defined as pits or dark discolorations that ranged in size from destruction of the majority of the tooth crown to pin-prick lesions. Dental caries is age progressive and the condition is more frequently recorded on molar compared to anterior or premolar teeth (Hillson, 2001). Because this chapter compares carious tooth frequencies between only two sites, there is prohibitively limited statistical power in comparing carious tooth frequencies by age group. Therefore, carious lesions were compared between the Ota and Tsukumo samples by tooth group only. Tooth groups were defined as anterior (incisors and canines), premolars, and molars. Significant differences in dental caries prevalence between the two groups were compared using a chi-square statistic.

5.2.4   Mobility

Long bone diaphyses are modeled as hollow beams based on the premise that the strength and rigidity of these structures is responsive to mechanical stimuli (Ruff et al., 2006). This responsiveness is part of a complex feedback system that finds mechanical loading experienced during ontogeny and adulthood prompt the growth and maintenance of bone strength/rigidity and shape through modeling and remodeling respectively (Bass et al., 2002; Lieberman and Pearson, 2001; Lieberman et al., 2003; Ruff et al., 1994, 2006). Greater loading intensity is associated with greater bone strength and rigidity, while differences in the anatomical distribution of bone about a neutral axis reflect directionality of loading in the anteroposterior and mediolateral planes (Ruff, 2008).

Long bone diaphyseal morphology was used to explore differences in mobility between the Middle and Late/Final phases of the Jomon period. Cross-sections of Jomon femora were produced using an XCT Research SA+ model peripheral quantitative computerized tomographic (PQCT) machine produced by Stratec Medizintechnik (Pforzeim, Germany). Planar resolution was set between 68 and 80 μm per pixel. Tube voltage was 50 kV and the current was 300 μA. Slice thickness was set at 100 μm. Femoral cross-sections were taken at 50 percent of biomechanical length in fused, mature elements. All Jomon cross-sectional properties were derived using Image J (NIH, Washington, DC) combined with MomentMacro, an IML syntax that calculates cross-sectional properties from CT slices (www.hopkinsmedicine.org/fae/mmacro.htm).

Cross-sectional properties evaluated by this study include cortical area (CA), total subperiosteal area (TA), medullary area (MA), polar second moment of area (J), second moment of area about the mediolateral plane (I_x), and second moment of area about the anteroposterior plane (I_y). CA measures the total amount of bone in the cross-section and reflects compressive/tensile strength, while TA measures area about the outer perimeter of the section. MA is the total amount of space within the medullary cavity. J is the polar second moment of area, which is the sum of I_{min} and I_{max} or I_x and I_y, which are always perpendicular to one another. I_x measures bending rigidity in the anteroposterior plane, while I_y measures bending rigidity in the mediolateral plane. The mobility index I_x/I_y is a ratio that evaluates bending strength in the anteroposterior relative to the mediolateral plane, and by many measures provides an index of strain experienced in this direction (Ruff, 2008).

The product of body mass and bone length^2 was used to standardize femoral second moments of area, while body mass alone was used for femoral moments of area (Ruff, 2008). Standardized moments of area were multiplied by 10^2 and second moments of area were multiplied by 10^4 to reflect mm^2 and mm^4 for each measurement, respectively. Comparisons of mean cross-sectional properties between the Jomon samples were performed using two-tailed *t*-tests for independence, except in the case of the mobility index, which was compared using Mann–Whitney *U* tests. Owing to prohibitively small numbers of females available from the Ota sample, these comparisons are reported for males only.

5.2.5   Tooth Extraction and Mortuary Practices

Tooth extraction is a form of physical alteration that is immediately observable and symbolically conveys information about individual affiliations (Hrdlička, 1940; Milner and Larsen, 1991; Robb, 1997; Stojanowski *et al.*, 2014). This study traces tooth extraction between the Middle and Late/Final Jomon period to understand whether these symbolic affiliations persisted, were altered, or newly emerged during this time period. Tooth extraction styles were recorded for each individual. These styles include the removal of four mandibular incisors (4I) or two mandibular canines (2C). Identification of tooth extraction was made based on styles reported by previous studies (Harunari, 1986) and the identification of alveolar resorption in each tooth crypt.

Mortuary practices reflect the beliefs, social structuring, and ritual behavior of prehistoric human populations (Binford, 1971; Carr, 1995; Hodder, 1982; Shanks and Tilley, 1982; Rakita and Buikstra, 2008). This study explores variation in mortuary ritual between the Middle and Late/Final Jomon period to better understand whether this transition was typified by shifting social structures and ritual practices. Grave goods at the Ota and Tsukumo sites are described by Kiyono (1969). Grave goods were divided into two types, including animal implements and hip ornaments. Following Justice (2017), animal implements are defined as grave goods that are directly derived from the anatomical processing of an animal or material objects fashioned into an animal shape. In the case of these cemeteries, funerary offerings are limited to the former, though numerous instances of ceramic animal depictions are found at ritual and habitation sites (Matsumoto, 2011; Nagamine, 1986). The second grave good category includes hip ornaments. Hip ornaments are deer antlers of various fashions that were ceremonially placed at the right hip of individuals within graves (Kiyono, 1969). Hip ornaments are found throughout Jomon burials on south-central and southwestern Honshu Island (Harunari, 1986).

5.2.6   Stress

Stressors are external perturbations that disrupt physiological homeostasis (Goodman *et al.*, 1988). Exposure to stressors during growth and development is frequently measured using comparisons of estimated body size (Larsen, 2015). The association between body size and mortality helps explain the broader life history trade-offs associated with these experiences and provides a lifespan perspective on stress experience (DeWitte and Hughes-Morey, 2012; Temple and Goodman, 2014). This study uses evidence for changes in body size and mortality risk as measures reflecting severity of transformation – specifically, as evidence to understand the relative degree of change experienced by the Late/Final Jomon people. Body mass was estimated using equations based on femoral head breadth (Ruff *et al.*, 1991). Bioarchaeological studies estimate stature based on equations that predict height from long bone measurements (Ubelaker, 1989). Estimation of stature requires equations that are derived from populations with similar intralimb proportions (Auerbach and Ruff, 2010; Sciulli *et al.*, 1990). Jomon samples have similar crural indices to populations from Europe, and stature estimation equations for these samples perform well when applied to Jomon individuals (Saeki, 2006). Equations derived from European samples were used by this study to estimate stature among the Jomon samples (Pearson, 1899).

Two-tailed *t*-tests were used to evaluate differences in body mass and stature for males and females. Estimates of stature and body mass were also evaluated in association with point estimates of age at death to clarify the risk of mortality associated with body size. Here, z-scores of body size were separately calculated for the male and female samples. Risk of death in association with z-scores for body size was evaluated using Cox's proportional hazard model. Age at death was listed as the time series variable, and the z-scores for stature and body mass were listed as covariates.

5.3   Results

Table 5.2 lists the percentage of carious teeth within each tooth group for the Ota and Tsukumo sites. Significant differences in carious tooth frequencies for the anterior

Table 5.2 Frequencies of carious teeth between the Ota and Tsukumo sites.

Group	N anterior	% carious	N premolar	% carious	N molar	% carious
Ota	129	0.7	149	1.3	227	7.0
Tsukumo	151	2.6	225	2.7	408	13.5

(χ^2 = 1.39, $p \leq 0.238$) and premolar (χ^2 = 0.75, $p \leq 0.396$) tooth groups were not found between the sites, though these rates doubled over time. Significantly greater carious tooth frequencies were found for the molar teeth in the Tsukumo compared to Ota sample (χ^2 = 6.08, $p \leq 0.014$). This difference represents an approximately twofold increase in the percentage of molar teeth with carious lesions (Table 5.2).

Box plots for femoral moments and second moments of area are shown in Figure 5.2. Boxes are associated with the interquartile ranges of the data, while the line within each box represents the mean for each sample. Whiskers reflect 95 percent confidence intervals. No significant differences in CA (t = −1.03, $p \leq 0.313$), TA (t = 0.266, $p \leq 0.79$), MA (t = 1.364, $p \leq 0.185$), or J (t = 0.74, $p \leq 0.735$) were found. The mobility index ($p \leq 0.42$) did not differ between the two samples.

Figure 5.3 shows the number of burials containing animal implements and hip ornaments at each site, as well as the number of graves lacking animal implements. No burials at the Ota site included animal implements or hip ornaments. Animal implements were found in approximately 33 percent of burials at the Tsukumo site. Hip ornaments were recovered from three burials at the Tsukumo site. These findings suggest no differentiation of identities in death at the Ota site, while identity differentiation existed for at least three subsets of individuals (those buried with animal implements, those with hip ornaments, and those lacking grave goods) at the Tsukumo site.

Percentages of individuals with tooth extraction relative to individuals with observable tooth sockets are shown in Figure 5.4. The frequency of individuals with tooth extraction remarkably increases between the Ota and Tsukumo site. The 2C style of tooth extraction persists between the two sites, while the 4I style of tooth extraction represents a new stylistic form.

Males and females from the Tsukumo site were significantly smaller in stature (t = −3.84, $p < 0.0008$; t = −3.04, $p \leq 0.0088$) and body mass (t = 2.76, $p < 0.01$; t = 3.21, $p \leq 0.006$) respectively when compared to Ota (Figures 5.5 and 5.6). Z-scores for body mass and stature were not associated with mortality risk at either of these sites (Table 5.3).

5.4   Discussion

5.4.1   Diet, Mobility, and Socioecological Resilience

A significantly greater frequency of carious molar teeth were found in the Tsukumo compared to Ota sample. Increased caries prevalence reflects an intensification of carbohydrate-heavy plant foods within the Late/Final Jomon diet and is consistent with the results of previous studies from across the Japanese Islands (Fujita, 1995;

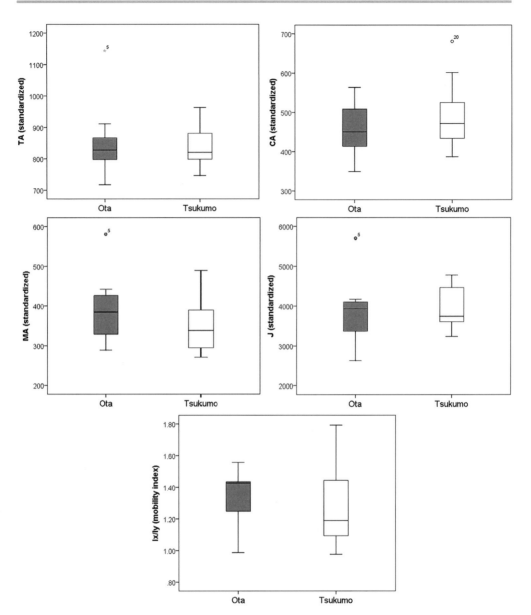

Figure 5.2 Areas, polar second moment of area, and mobility index for femora.

Temple, 2007). These results are also consistent with earlier works that found higher nitrogen relative to carbon ratios in bone collagen and tooth enamel at the Ota compared to Tsukumo sites (Kusaka *et al.*, 2010, 2015). Such findings suggest increased consumption of plant foods and reduced consumption of terrestrial mammals as well as maritime resources among the Tsukumo compared to Ota communities.

Early studies of dental caries prevalence among prehistoric Jomon people suggest that starchy roots or tubers such as taro may have been exploited by these

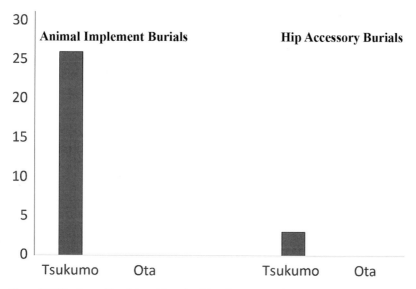

Figure 5.3 Number of burials with animal implements and hip ornaments by site.

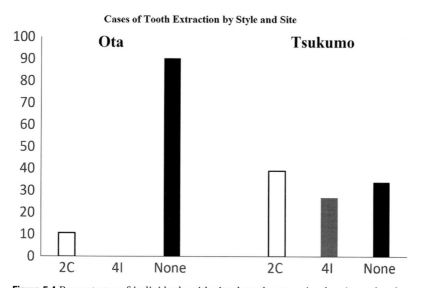

Figure 5.4 Percentages of individuals with ritual tooth extraction by site and style.

populations (Turner, 1979). However, little evidence for root exploitation is reported in the paleoethnobotanical record (Crawford, 2006; Habu, 2004). Alternatively, evidence for intensive management of acorn, chestnut, and walnut trees is documented (Kawashima, 2016; Kitagawa and Yasuda, 2008; Nishida, 1983; Tsuji, 1995). These plants have elevated starch content (Yoo *et al.*, 2012). Grenby (1997) and Lingström *et al.* (1989, 2000) note that starch has a low cariogenic potential compared to other carbohydrates, though boiling and processing increase this potential

Table 5.3 Cox's proportional hazards analysis for mortality risk, stature, and body mass.

Group	B	SE	Wald	Df	Significance	Exp (B)
Stature	0.078	0.194	0.163	1	0.687	1.081
Body mass	0.031	0.219	0.019	1	0.899	1.031

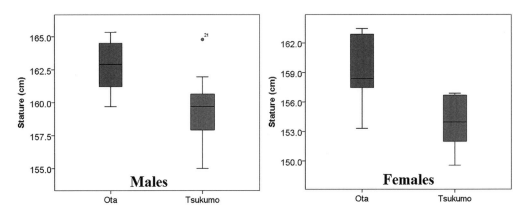

Figure 5.5 Box plots of stature distribution by sex and site.

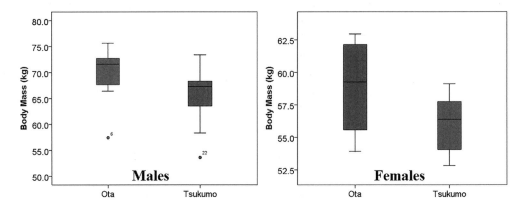

Figure 5.6 Box plots of body mass by sex and site.

by enhancing gelatinization. Gelatinization occurs when starchy foods are boiled above a particular temperature, causing the granules to swell and water to be absorbed into the food. This produces a gelatinous material surrounding the granule, which increases the adhesiveness and cariogenic potential of starch (Grenby, 1990, 1997; Lingström *et al.*, 2000). Traditional processing techniques including grinding and drying increase the susceptibility of starches to gelatinization through mechanical reduction of the starch molecule (Lingström *et al.*, 1989, 2000). Acorns and chestnuts require considerable processing prior to consumption, and the starch of these nuts gelatinizes when subjected to boiling and roasting (Attanasio *et al.*, 2004; Chung *et al.*, 1998; Mert, 2010; Silva *et al.*, 2016).

Increases in acorn-storage pits are found throughout Japan during the Late/Final phases of the Jomon period (Kawashima, 2016). Acorns were intensively processed, including leeching of tannins by boiling and processing. Deep ceramic pots and stone hearths were used to boil acorns with ash (Kawashima, 2016; Kobayashi, 2005). Stone querns and grinding slabs were likely used to grind nuts into dumplings, which were boiled or baked. Carbonized remains of these dumplings have been identified at a number of sites (Kobayashi, 2005). These findings suggest that Jomon people processed and prepared nuts in ways that enhance cariogenicity. Increased carious tooth frequencies are likely associated with the intensification of these behaviors, though it remains important to understand whether these dietary behaviors reflect internally or externally oriented shifts in the Jomon socioecological system.

Resilience is facilitated by socioecological memory (Cumming *et al.*, 2006; Folke, 2006; Walker *et al.*, 2004). The facilitation of resilience through socioecological memory references the transmission of knowledge regarding the care and management of an ecosystem across generations. Domestication of nuts is observed among Early Jomon cultures (Crawford, 2006), while exploitation of nuts dates to the Incipient Jomon period (Nishida, 1983). In one instance, evidence for modification of the natural environment to exploit these resources is reported: Jomon people burned local oak trees and preserved chestnut trees at the Sannai Maruyama site (Tsuji, 1995). Evidence for increased emphasis on nut storage, processing, and cooking is found in the Late/Final Jomon period in southwestern Honshu (Imamura, 1996; Kawashima, 2016). This suggests that increases in cariogenic food consumption, likely processed nuts, during the Late/Final Jomon period was based on institutional knowledge and represents socioecological memory among these prehistoric hunter-gatherers. Dental caries prevalence does, however, attest to changes in the intensity of consumption of these food products, indicating that Late/Final Jomon people in this region adapted to changes within the panarchy through shifting dietary behavior. These changes reflect a process of resilience and adaptability in the dietary spectrum of Jomon people rather than whole-scale transformation – adaptability through intensified consumption of cariogenic resources and resilience in the exploitation of a product that long served as a basin of attraction for Jomon hunter-gatherers.

No changes in the areas or second moments of area were observed in the femora of the Ota and Tsukumo people. Significant reductions in femoral robusticity are observed in populations that undergo transformative change in subsistence behavior (Bridges, 1995; Holt, 2003; Larsen, 1981, 2015; Ruff, 1999, 2008; Ruff and Larsen, 1990; Ruff *et al.*, 1984; Stock and Pinhasi, 2011). By contrast, little change is observed between Natufian and Pre-Pottery Neolithic B periods in the Levant, though significant changes are found when these samples are compared to groups from the Pre-Pottery Neolithic C period (May and Ruff, 2016). This continuity is likely attributable to patterns of resilience and persistence between Natufian and Pre-Pottery

Neolithic populations: Pre-Pottery Neolithic B culture represents the onset of rigidity and transformation toward an agricultural economy (Rosen and Rivera-Collazo, 2012), though persistence of mobility patterns is documented in these samples (May and Ruff, 2016). One note of caution is required. Recent studies of long bone diaphyseal morphology report increases in anteroposterior strain among indigenous populations from Australia following climate change (Hill *et al.*, 2016). The authors argue that increased anteroposterior strain was associated with the expansion of foraging radii. Expanded foraging radii allowed these populations to continue hunting high-value resources within the same socioecological system. This suggests that changes in cross-sectional geometry may be seen under circumstances of socio-ecological resilience, and paleodietary analysis must accompany data associated with long bone diaphyseal morphology so that results are appropriately contextualized. Late/Final Jomon period populations consumed greater amounts of cariogenic plant foods. However, this dietary shift occurred within the preexisting socioecological system of Jomon communities. Considered within this context, the lack of differences in femoral diaphyseal robusticity supports persistence of the socioecological system.

5.4.2   Mortuary Practices, Tooth Extraction, and Cultural Resilience

Increasing use of grave goods was found at the Tsukumo site. Mortuary grave goods found at these sites include deer antlers placed at the right hip of individuals, boar tusks, deer crania and postcrania, bear teeth, fox mandibles, shark teeth, shell bracelets, earrings fashioned from monkey radii, and boar postcrania (Kiyono, 1969). This pattern is contrasted by mortuary behavior in northeastern Honshu, where lavish child burials and the construction of funerary architecture suggest a deeper expression of ceremonial practice and socioeconomic inequality (Kodama, 2003; Mizoguchi, 2002; Nakamura, 1999). Jomon funerary treatment in eastern Honshu increases in complexity during the Late/Final Jomon period with the inclusion of more individuals in grave pits, movement away from household burials, and intensified ancestor worship (Kawashima, 2011). Similar trends are observed between the Ota and Tsukumo sites, where animal-implement grave goods and hip ornaments appear during the Late/Final phase of the Jomon period. Importantly, because these sites are similar in scale and purpose, it is possible that these trends are associated with a concept introduced by Imamura (1999), termed the swelling of ideology. Here, ritual and symbolic components of daily practice receive greater emphasis and increase in diversity, while sociopolitical equality (lack of exploitation) is maintained. However, recent isotopic studies note that individuals from the Late/Final Jomon period with hip ornaments ate comparatively more maritime resources than other members of the population (Kiriyama and Kusaka, 2017). These findings are specific to the Atsumi Peninsula, but do indicate the possibility of rising socioeconomic inequalities.

Ingold (2005) points to the objectification of memory as an important starting point in the evolution of ownership societies. This objectification frequently takes the form of items or objects that come into being through actions that produce memories and help identify individuals as members of descendant populations. These products are separated from the past but tethered to its relational nature through beliefs, customs, and traditions. Ingold (2005) states that animal remains among hunter-gatherers fit within this model as objects that came into being through human interactions with nature and elicit memories of these events. Grave goods are indicators of the social lifespan, symbolizing the persistence of social identity after death (Sofaer, 2011), and are associated with rituals that act as symbolically commemorative events (Carr, 1995; Hodder, 1982; Shanks and Tilley, 1982). Commemorative rituals are important to the social memory of a population as these behaviors serve to legitimize and maintain social order (Connerton, 1989). In this sense, what is seen in Late/Final Jomon period funerary rights may provide tantalizing evidence of a population at the edge of social transformation and demonstrate an important cultural reaction to ecological change – increasing social complexity through the objectification of memory into funerary ritual.

Despite the possibility that these populations may have been on the verge of social transformation, it is important to point out that ritual behavior in transformed societies draws on collective social memory (see below) (Connerton, 1989). This point picks up on a meta-referential component of resilience studies: Resilient landscapes frequently rely on deeply internal symbols to maintain social order during periods of stress. The material symbols used in mortuary ritual were derived from the Jomon socioecological system. Jomon hunter-gatherers actively exploited deer, boar, high-trophic fish, and shellfish (Kobayashi, 2005). Zooarchaeological analysis of age at death in many of these animals suggests seasonal consumption (Koike, 1986, 1992; Koike and Ohtaishi, 1985; Komiya et al., 2003), ordaining these beings as de facto members of cyclical interactions between the Jomon people and nature. Ethnological studies of the Ainu people emphasize interdependent relationships between humans and nature as well as the eternal ontologies attached to these relationships (Atuy, 1997). Ethnoarchaeological studies find that these relationships are reproduced in death rituals through the inclusion of animal implements in graves and ceremonies that invoke animal spirits (Fujimura, 1999; Obayashi, 1997; Watanabe, 1972). Among the Jomon people, animal figurines are found at ceremonial sites and may be tied to deeper rituals involving the interaction between human and animal spirits (Matsumoto, 2011; Nagamine, 1986). All of this suggests a longstanding spiritual role for animals within Jomon communities and points toward increasing social complexity at the Tsukumo cemetery as an internally reflective event – one that hints at a transformation in the social structure of the Late/Final Jomon period people, while demonstrating cultural resilience through the appropriation of symbols tethered to the Jomon socioecological system.

The 2C style of tooth extraction persists across time periods between the Ota and Tsukumo sites, while the 4I style of tooth extraction is specific to Tsukumo. The persistence of 2C tooth ablation at the Tsukumo site suggests a pattern of resilience in group identity/ethnicity, where embodied indicators of identity transcend time and space and may be associated with collective (or social) memory. Collective memories are remembrances shared among a group and are granted historical momentum through repeated points of reference (Halbwachs, 1925). These are differentiated from individual memories by the shared experience of collective agents. Collective memory is associated with performance rituals that serve to convey and sustain memories within a population narrative (Connerton, 1989). These memories are embodied as visual cues and incorporated by the body through ritual performance. This body of work is supported by theoretical explorations that suggest collective memory is tethered to symbolic artifacts or practices – these include "figures of memory" such as epics, poems, or images – that are maintained through production and practice (Assman, 1995: 29).

Examples of collective memory in the archaeological record include alterations of the landscape that reference ancestral generations in death rituals (Bradley, 2000; Buikstra and Charles, 1999; Cannon, 2002; Carr, 2005a, b; Charles and Buikstra, 2002; Gamble, 2017; Mizoguchi, 2001; Thompson and Pluckhahn, 2010). While these archaeological studies demonstrate ancestral affiliation through alteration of landscapes affiliated with the dead, it is also possible to alter the living body in ways that commemorate ancestral affiliations. Alterations of the body demonstrate the transformation of social identity into the physical being, which then acts as a symbolic message to the viewer and may also be tied to a broader performance, either public or private (Joyce, 2005). Tooth extraction is a form of physical alteration that is immediately observable and symbolically conveys information about individual affiliations (Hrdlička, 1940; Milner and Larsen, 1991; Robb, 1997; Stojanowski et al., 2014). Because the process is distributed throughout populations and produces an immediately recognizable indicator of group affiliation, tooth extraction is also arguably an embodied symbol of ethnic identity, establishing membership and "otherness" based on presence/absence and style within individuals. Tooth extraction among prehistoric Jomon people was performed around 13.0 years of age and teeth were removed using a traumatic method of avulsion, suggesting that the practice was tethered to deeper communal ritual (Funahashi, 2003; Takenaka et al., 2001). In addition, results of this study suggest that the behavior was sustained over a broad time frame, involving individuals from both the Middle Jomon period site of Ota and Late/Final Jomon period site of Tsukumo. These displays preserve ethnic heritage through affiliation with previous generations, and thus demonstrate cultural resilience through the persistence of embodied figures of memory.

The appearance of 4I tooth extraction at Tsukumo represents a new style of tooth extraction between the two sites. As mentioned above, tooth extraction may be associated with a symbolic ethnic affiliation and ties to ancestral populations through evocation of social memory. Individuals with the 4I style of tooth extraction are found at sites throughout south-central Honshu, and in some cases these individuals are affiliated with the earliest occupations of sites (Kusaka et al., 2018). It is possible that this style of tooth extraction represented contested affiliations with ancestral populations at the Tsukumo site, or alternately, ancestral ties with populations from a different region. It is equally likely that this new style of tooth extraction represents a reorientation in symbolic meaning (e.g., Buikstra, 2005). It is necessary to collect more data regarding tooth extraction from Middle Jomon sites within and outside the Inland Sea area to arrive at a more resolute answer. Interpreted either way, however, the appearance of 4I tooth extraction represents an expansion of identities within these two communities and further hints at cultural transformation within this social world.

5.4.3   Stress, Resilience, Adaptability, and Transformability

No associations between mortality risk and body size are found at the Ota and Tsukumo sites, though a reduction in stature and body mass is observed over time. Previous studies document relationships between skeletal and dental indicators of early life stress and severe environmental deterioration or epidemics. For example, individuals with shorter stature were at greater risk of death from the Black Plague, but these trends did not persist in populations that were not exposed to epidemic disease (DeWitte and Hughes-Morey, 2012). In addition, linear enamel hypoplasia is associated with greater mortality risk in samples exposed to famine (Yaussy *et al.*, 2016), while the same trend is observed in pre-Columbian populations on the verge of climatic deterioration and collapse (Wilson, 2014). By contrast, zooarchaeological studies of the Middle to Late/Final phases of the Jomon period have argued for a period of resource stress and adaptation in the absence of collapse (Koike, 1986, 1992), while others suggest reorganization through migration (Habu, 2004). Results of this study are consistent with these findings: Evidence for early life stress among prehistoric Late/Final Jomon period hunter-gatherers suggests reductions in body size associated with this transition, though there is no evidence that these experiences impacted mortality. These experiences are more closely affiliated with small-scale changes within the preexisting socioecological and cultural system as opposed to whole-scale transformation.

Archaeological research in the American Southwest documents how systemic stress may be tethered to the resilience/adaptability or transformation of socioecological or cultural systems (Hegmon *et al.*, 2008). Severity of transformation among Mimbres populations was low, and the reorganization phase of this period suggests great coherency in socioecological and cultural systems. In two contrasting case studies, the Mesa Verde and Hohokom populations experienced severe transformation that included declining/emigrating populations, reorganization of ceremonial structures, elevated violence, and increases in skeletal evidence of stress (Hegmon *et al.*, 2008). In the case of prehistoric Jomon hunter-gatherers, it would appear that climatic cooling presented a less severe challenge to these populations. Flexibility in diet and mobility likely helped offset the long-term consequences of this process. Thus, while there is some indication for increasing stress associated with climatic changes dated to the Middle/Late/Final Jomon period transition, this experience appears to have elicited small-scale, internally driven adaptive change, while the socioecological and cultural identity of the population was maintained.

5.5   Conclusion

Results of this chapter are similar to those of previous studies that demonstrate resilience/adaptability as opposed to full-scale transformation of the Jomon system in response to climate change and the introduction of agricultural economies (Hoover and Hudson, 2016; Kawashima, 2013). This chapter found repeated evidence that resilience was fueled by adaptability within the socioecological and cultural systems of these prehistoric hunter-gatherers. Jomon people relied on internally directed changes including flexibility of preexisting dietary structures, while maintaining similar levels of mobility. Increasing cultural complexity in mortuary treatment is found, though this practice remained tethered to an internal socioecological system. Persistence of 2C tooth extraction may be associated with ritual performance and embodied symbols of ethnicity that were referential of ancestral populations, though the appearance of 4I tooth extraction suggests increasing complexity in these symbols. Patterns of systemic stress may help further explain adaptability and resilience within these populations. There was a decline in body size from the Middle to Late/Final Jomon period, but no evidence that reduced body size exacerbated mortality. Such findings are consistent with an increase in the precariousness of the socio-ecological and cultural systems of Late/Final Jomon period hunter-gatherers, but one that did not push the system past a threshold for transformation.

It is, however, important to note that the Japanese Islands include a large number of ecological zones, where minor differences in temperature produce diversity in biota, and therefore food availability and subsistence practices (Akazawa, 1999; Kitagawa and Yasuda, 2008). Evidence for socioecological and cultural transformation is reported among Jomon hunter-gatherers from northeastern Japan as rigidity within these systems increased vulnerability to changes within the panarchy (Habu, 2014b). Further bioarchaeological explorations of this event will help explain how climate change produced diversity in the Jomon adaptive cycle across the Japanese Islands.

Acknowledgments

The author thanks Masato Nakatsukasa for allowing access to and assistance with the skeletal collections included in this chapter. Nawa Sugiyama assisted with translation of the original archaeological documents for these sites. The author is grateful to Haagen Klaus, Clark Larsen, and Lauryn Justice for reading drafts of this manuscript. Jane Buikstra provided helpful feedback on an earlier iteration of this work. Christopher Stojanowski and one anonymous reviewer also provided helpful comments that greatly improved the manuscript.

References

Akazawa, T. (1999). Regional variation in the Jomon hunting-fishing-gathering societies. In K. Omoto, ed., *Interdisciplinary Perspectives on the Origins of the Japanese*. Kyoto: International Research Center for Japanese Studies, pp. 223–231.

Armelagos, G. J. (2003). Bioarchaeology as anthropology. In D. L. Nichols, R. A. Joyce, and S. D. Gillespie, eds., *Archaeology is Anthropology*. Washington, DC: American Anthropological Association, pp. 27–41.

Assman, J. (1995). Collective memory and cultural identity. *New German Critique*, 65, 123–133.

Attanasio, G., Cinquanta, L., Albanese, D., and Di Matteo, M. (2004). Effects of drying temperatures on physico-chemical properties of dried and rehydrated chestnuts (*Castanea sativa*). *Food Chemistry*, 88, 583–590.

Atuy, M. T. (1997). Coexistence with nature and the "Third Philosophy": Learning from the spirit of the Ainu. In T. Yamada and T. Irimoto, eds., *Circumpolar Animism and Shamanism*. Sapporo: Hokkaido University Press, pp. 3–8.

Auerbach, B. M. and Ruff, C. B. (2010). Stature estimation formulae for indigenous North American populations. *American Journal of Physical Anthropology*, 141, 190–207.

Bass, S. L., Saxon, L., Daly, R. M., *et al.* (2002). The effect of mechanical loading on the size and shape of bone in pre-, peri-, and postpubertal girls: A study in tennis players. *Journal of Bone and Mineral Research*, 17, 2274–2280.

Binford, L. R. (1971). Mortuary practices: Their study and potential. *Memoirs of the Society for American Archaeology*, 25, 6–29.

Boldsen, J. L., Milner, G. R., Konigsberg, L. W., and Wood, J. W. (2002) Transition analysis: A new way of estimating age from skeletons. In R. D. Hoppa and J. W. Vaupel, eds., *Paleodemography: Age Distributions from Skeletal Samples*. Cambridge: Cambridge University Press, pp. 73–106.

Bradley, R. (2000). *An Archaeology of Natural Places*. London: Routledge.

Bridges, P. S. (1995). Skeletal biology and behavior in ancient humans. *Evolutionary Anthropology*, 4, 112–120.

Buikstra, J. E. (2005). Discussion: Ethnogenesis and ethnicity in the Andes. In R. M. Reycraft, ed., *Us and Them: Archaeology and Ethnicity in the Andes*. Los Angeles, CA: Cotsen Institute of Archaeology, pp. 233–238.

Buikstra, J. E. and Charles, D. K. (1999). Centering the ancestors: Cemeteries, mounds, and sacred landscapes of the North American midcontinent. In W. Ashmore and A. B. Knapp, eds., *Archaeologies of Landscape: Contemporary Perspectives*. Oxford: Blackwell Publishers, Ltd, pp. 201–228.

Buikstra, J. E. and Ubelaker, D. H. (1994). *Standards for Data Collection from Human Skeletal Remains*. Fayetteville, AR: Arkansas Archaeological Survey.

Butzer, K. W. and Endfield, G. H. (2012). Critical perspectives on historical collapse. *Proceedings of the National Academy of Sciences*, 109, 3628–3631.

Cannon, A. (2002). Spatial narratives of death, memory, and transcendence. *Archaeological Papers of the American Anthropological Association*, 11, 191–199.

Carr, C. (1995). Mortuary practices: Their social, philosophical-religious, circumstantial, and physical determinants. *Journal of Archaeological Method and Theory*, 2, 105–200.

Carr, C. (2005a). Rethinking interregional Hopewellian "Interaction." In C. Carr and D. T. Case, eds., *Gathering Hopewell: Society, Ritual, and Ritual Interaction*. New York, NY: Kluwer Academic/Plenum Publishing, pp. 575–623.

Carr, C. (2005b). Scioto Hopewell ritual gatherings: A review and discussion of previous interpretations and data. In C. Carr and D. T. Case, eds., *Gathering Hopewell: Society, Ritual, and Ritual Interaction*. New York, NY: Kluwer Academic/Plenum Publishing, pp. 463–469.

Charles, D. K. and Buikstra, J. E. (2002). Siting, sighting, and citing the dead. *Archaeological Papers of the American Anthropological Association*, 11, 13–25.

Chung, H., Cho, S., Shin, T., Son, H., and Lim, S.-T. (1998). Physical and molecular characteristics of cowpea and acorn starches in comparison with corn and potato. *Food Science and Biotechnology*, 7, 41–47.

Connerton, P. (1989). *How Societies Remember*. Cambridge: Cambridge University Press.

Crawford, G. (2006). East Asian plant domestication. In M. Stark, ed., *Archaeology of Asia*. New York, NY: Wiley-Blackwell, pp. 77–95.

Cumming G. S., Barnes, G., Perz, S., *et al.* (2006). An exploratory framework for the empirical measurement of resilience. *Ecosystems*, 8, 975–987.

DeWitte, S. N. and Hughes-Morey, G. (2012). Stature and frailty during the Black Death: The effect of stature on risks of epidemic mortality. *Journal of Archaeological Science*, 39, 1412–1419.

Faulseit, R. K. (2016). *Beyond Collapse: Archaeological Perspectives on Resilience, Revitalization, and Transformation in Complex Societies*. Carbondale, IL: Southern Illinois University Press.

Folke, C. (2006). Resilience: The emergence of a perspective for social-ecological systems analyses. *Global Environmental Change*, 16, 253–267.

Fujimura, H. (1999). Life and death. In W. W. Fitzhugh and C. O. Dubreuil, eds., *Ainu: Spirit of a Northern People*. Washington, DC: Smithsonian Institution Press, pp. 268–273.

Fujita, H. (1995). Geographical and chronological differences in dental caries in the Neolithic Jomon period of Japan. *Anthropological Science*, 103, 23–37.

Funahashi, K. (2003). A study of the timing of ritual tooth ablation and its meaning as rights of passage in Final Jomon period. *Quarterly of Archaeological Studies*, 50, 56–76.

Gamble, L. (2017). Feasting, ritual practices, social memory, and persistent places: New interpretations of shell mounds in Southern California. *American Antiquity*, 82, 427–451.

Goodman, A. H., Thomas, R. B., Swedlund, A. C., and Armelagos, G. J. (1988). Biocultural perspectives on stress in prehistoric, historic, and contemporary populations. *Yearbook of Physical Anthropology*, 31, 169–202.

Grenby, T. H. (1990). Snack foods and dental caries: Investigations using laboratory animals. *British Dental Journal*, 168, 353–361.

Grenby, T. H. (1997). Summary of the dental effects of starch. *International Journal of Food Sciences and Nutrition*, 48, 411–416.

Gunderson, L. H. and Holling, C. S. (2002). *Panarchy: Understanding Transformations in Human and Natural Systems*. Washington, DC: Island Press.

Habu, J. (2004). *Ancient Jomon of Japan*. Cambridge: Cambridge University Press.

Habu, J. (2008). Growth and decline in complex hunter-gatherer societies: A case study from the Jomon period, Sannai Maruyama site, Japan. *Antiquity*, 82, 571–584.

Habu, J. (2014a). Early sedentism in East Asia: From Late Paleolithic to early agricultural societies in Insular East Asia. In C. Renfrew and P. Bahn, eds., *The Cambridge World Prehistory*. Cambridge: Cambridge University Press, pp. 724–741.

Habu, J. (2014b). Post-Pleistocene transformations of hunter-gatherers in East Asia: The Jomon and Chulumun. In V. Cummings, P. Jordan, and M. Zvelebil, eds., *The Oxford Handbook of the Archaeology and Anthropology of Hunter-Gatherers*. Oxford: Oxford University Press, pp. 504–520.

Habu, J. and Hall, M. E. (2013). Climate change, human impacts on the landscape, and subsistence specialization: Historical ecology and changes in Jomon hunter-gatherer lifeways. In V. D. Thompson and J. C. Waggoner, eds., *The Archaeology and Historical Ecology of Small Scale Economies*. Gainesville, FL: University Press of Florida, pp. 65–78.

Halbwachs, M. (1925). *Les Cadres Sociaux de la Mémoire*. Paris: Librairie Félix Alcan.

Harunari, H. (1986). Rules of residence in the Jomon period based on the analysis of tooth extraction. In R. Pearson, G. Barnes, and K. Hutterer, eds., *Windows on the Japanese Past: Studies in Archaeology and Prehistory*. Ann Arbor, MI: Center for Japanese Studies, University of Michigan, pp. 293–310.

Hegmon, M., Peeples, M. A., Kinzig, A. P., *et al.* (2008). Social transformation and its human costs in the Prehispanic U.S. Southwest. *American Anthropologist*, 110, 313–324.

Hill, E. C., Durband, A. C., and Walshe, K. (2016). Risk minimization and a Late Holocene increase in mobility at Roonka Flat, Australia: An analysis of lower limb diaphyseal shape. *American Journal of Physical Anthropology*, 161, 94–103.

Hillson, S. W. (2001). Recording dental caries in archaeological human remains. *International Journal of Osteoarchaeology*, 11, 249–289.

Hillson, S. W. (2008). Dental pathology. In M. A. Katzenberg and S. R. Saunders, eds., *Biological Anthropology of the Human Skeleton*. New York, NY: Wiley-Liss, pp. 249–286.

Hodder, I. (1982). The identification and interpretation of ranking in prehistory: A contextual perspective. In C. Renfrew and S. Shennan, eds., *Ranking, Resource, and Exchange*. Cambridge: Cambridge University Press, pp. 150–156.

Holling, C. S. (1973). Resilience and stability of ecological systems. *Annual Review of Ecology and Systematics*, 4, 1–23.

Holling, C. S. (1986). The resilience of terrestrial ecosystems: Local surprise and global change. In W. C. Clark, ed., *Sustainable Development of the Biosphere: Interactions between the World Economy and Global Environment*. Cambridge: Cambridge University Press, pp. 292–317.

Holt, B. M. (2003). Mobility in Upper Paleolithic and Mesolithic Europe: Evidence from the lower limb. *American Journal of Physical Anthropology*, 122, 200–215.

Hoover, K. C. and Hudson, M. (2016). Resilience in prehistoric persistent hunter-gatherers in Northwest Kyushu, Japan as assessed by population health and archaeological evidence. *Quaternary International*, 405B, 22–33.

Hrdlička A. (1940). Ritual ablation of front teeth in Siberia and America. *Smithsonian Miscellaneous Collections*, 69, 1–32.

Hudson, M. J. (1999). *Ruins of Identity: Ethnogenesis in the Japanese Islands*. Honolulu: University of Hawaii Press.

Ikawa-Smith, F. (2004). Humans along the Pacific margin of Northeast Asia before the Last Glacial Maximum. In D. B. Madsen, ed., *Entering America: Northeast Asia and Beringia before the Last Glacial Maximum*. Salt Lake City, UT: University of Utah Press, pp. 285–309.

Ikawa-Smith, F. (2007). Conclusion: In search of the origins of microblades and microblade technology. In Y. V. Kuzmin, S. G. Keates, and C. Shen, eds., *Origin and Spread of Microblade Technology in Northern Asia and North America*. Burnaby: Simon Fraser University, pp. 189–198.

Imamura, K. (1996). *Prehistoric Japan: New Perspectives on Insular East Asia*. Honolulu: University of Hawaii Press.

Imamura, K. (1999). *In Pursuit of the Real Image of the Jomon*. Tokyo: Yoshikawa Kobunkan. (In Japanese.)

Ingold, T. (2005). Time, memory, and property. In T. Widlock and W. Gossa Tadesse, eds., *Property and Equality*, vol. 1. New York, NY: Berghan Books, pp. 165–174.

Joyce R. A. (2005). Archaeology of the body. *Annual Review of Anthropology*, 34, 139–158.

Justice, L. C. (2017). *Biological and Cultural Evidence for Social Maturation at Point Hope, Alaska: Integrating Data from Archaeological Mortuary Practices and Human Skeletal Biology*. MA thesis, George Mason University.

Kusaka, S., Yamada, Y., and Yoneda, M. (2018). Ecological and cultural shifts of hunter-gatherers of the Jomon period paralleled with environmental changes. *American Journal of Physical Anthropology*. In press.

Kawahata, H., Yamamoto, H., Ohkushi, K., *et al.* (2009). Changes of environments and human activity at the Sannai-Maruyama ruins in Japan during the mid-Holocene Hypsithermal climatic interval. *Quaternary Science Review*, 28, 964–974.

Kawashima, T. (2011). Bural practices and social complexity: Jomon examples. *Documenta Prehistorica*, 38, 109–115.

Kawashima, T. (2013). Social change at the end of the Middle Jomon: A perspective from resilience theory. *Documenta Prehistorica*, 40, 227–232.

Kawashima, T. (2016). Food processing and consumption in the Jomon. *Quaternary International*, 404, 16–24.

Kiriyama, K. and Kusaka, S. (2017). Prehistoric diet and mortuary practices in the Jomon Period: Isotopic evidence from human skeletal remains from the Yoshigo Shell Mounds. *Journal of Archaeological Science Reports*, **11**, 200–210.

Kitagawa, J. and Yasuda, Y. (2008). Development and distribution of *Castanea* and *Aesculus* culture during the Jomon period in Japan. *Quaternary International*, **184**, 41–55.

Kiyono, K. (1969). *Study of Japanese Shell Middens*. Tokyo: Iwanami Shoten. (In Japanese.)

Kobayashi, T. (1992). Patterns and levels of social complexity in Jomon Japan. In C. M. Aikens and S. Nai Rhee, eds., *Pacific Northeast Asia in Prehistory: Hunter-Fisher-Gatherers, Farmers, and Sociopolitical Elites*. Pullman, WA: Washington State University Press, pp. 91–98.

Kobayashi, T. (2005). *Jomon Reflections: Forager Life and Culture in the Prehistoric Japanese Archipelago*. Oxford: Oxbow Publishers.

Kodama, D. (2003). Komakino stone circle and its significance for the study of Jomon social structure. *Senri Ethnological Studies*, **63**, 235–262.

Koike, H. (1986). Jomon shell mounds and growth line analysis of molluscan shells. In R. Pearson, G. Barnes, and K. Huterrer, eds., *Windows on the Japanese Past: Studies in Archaeology and Prehistory*. Ann Arbor, MI: Center for Japanese Studies, University of Michigan, pp. 267–279.

Koike, H. (1992). Exploitation dynamics of the Jomon period. In C. M. Aikens and S. Nai Rhee, eds., *Pacific Northwest Asia in Prehistory: Hunter-Fisher-Gatherers, Farmers, and Sociopolitical Elites*. Pullman, WA: Washington State University Press, pp. 53–67.

Koike, H. and Ohtaishi, N. (1985). Prehistoric hunting pressure estimated by the age composition of excavated sika deer (*Cervus nippon*) using annual layer of tooth cement. *Journal of Archaeological Science*, **12**, 443–456.

Komiya, H., Kobayashi, R., and Abe, M. (2003). Examination of slaughter season and age composition of wild boar from the Late Jomon Takeshi site, Chiba prefecture, Japan, based on the analysis of tooth eruption and wear patterns. *Anthropological Science* (Japanese Series), **111**, 131–142.

Koyama, S. (1978). Jomon subsistence and population. *Senri Ethnological Studies*, **2**, 1–65.

Kusaka, S., Hyodo, F., Yumoto, T., and Nakatsukasa, M. (2010). Carbon and stable isotope analysis on the diet of Jomon populations from two coastal regions of Japan. *Journal of Archaeological Science*, **37**, 1968–1977.

Kusaka, S., Uno, K. T., Nakano, T., Nakatsukasa, M., and Cerling, T. (2015). Carbon ratios of human tooth enamel record evidence of terrestrial resource consumption during the Jomon period, Japan. *American Journal of Physical Anthropology*, **158**, 300–311.

Larsen, C. S. (1981). Functional implications of postcranial size reduction on the prehistoric Georgia Coast, U.S.A. *Journal of Human Evolution*, **10**, 489–502.

Larsen, C. S. (1987). Bioarchaeological interpretations of subsistence economy and behavior from human skeletal remains. In M. B. Schiffer, ed., *Advances in Archaeological Method and Theory*. New York, NY: Academic Press, pp. 339–445.

Larsen, C. S. (1994). In the wake of Columbus: Postcontact native population biology in the Americas. *Yearbook of Physical Anthropology*, **37**, 109–154.

Larsen, C. S. (2002). Post-Pleistocene human evolution: Bioarchaeology of the agricultural transition. In P. S. Ungar and M. F. Teaford, eds., *Human Diet: Its Origin and Evolution*. West Port: Bergin & Garvey, pp. 19–35.

Larsen, C. S. (2015). *Bioarchaeology: Interpreting Behavior from the Human Skeleton*. Cambridge: Cambridge University Press.

Lieberman, D. E. and Pearson, O. M. (2001). Trade-off between modeling and remodeling responses to loading in the mammalian limb. *Bulletin of the Museum of Comparative Zoology*, **156**, 269–282.

Lieberman, D. E., Pearson, O. M., Polk, J. D., Demes, B., and Crompton A. W. (2003). Optimization of bone growth and remodeling in response to loading in tapered mammalian limbs. *Journal of Experimental Biology*, **206**, 3125–3138.

Lingström, P., Holm, J., Birkhed, D., and Björck, I. (1989). The effect of variously processed foods on pH of human dental plaque formation. *Scandinavian Journal of Dental Research*, **97**, 392–400.

Lingström, P., Van Houte, J., and Kashket, S. (2000). Food, starches, and dental caries. *Critical Reviews in Oral Biology and Medicine*, **11**, 366–380.

Matsumoto, N. (2011). Figurines, circular settlements, and Jomon worldviews. In A. Cannon, ed., *Structured Worlds: The Archaeology of Hunter-Gatherer Thought and Action*. Oxford: Oxbow Books, pp. 168–182.

May, H. and Ruff, C. B. (2016). Physical burden and lower limb structure at the origin of agriculture in the Levant. *American Journal of Physical Anthropology*, **161**, 26–36.

McAnany, P. A. and Yoffee, N. (2010). *Questioning Collapse: Human Resilience, Ecological Vulnerability, and the Aftermath of Empire*. Cambridge: Cambridge University Press.

Mert, C. (2010). Proximate content and starch granule structure in raw and boiled chestnuts with different aptitude to candying. *Acta Horticulturae*, **866**, 667–674.

Milner, G. R. and Larsen, C. S. (1991). Teeth as artifacts of human behavior: Intentional mutilation and accidental modification. In M. A. Kelley and C. S. Larsen, eds., *Advances in Dental Anthropology*. New York, NY: Wiley-Liss, pp. 357–387.

Mizoguchi, K. (2001). Time and genealogical consciousness in the mortuary practices of the Yayoi period. *Journal of East Asian Archaeology*, **3**, 173–197.

Mizoguchi, K. (2002). *An Archaeological History of Japan: 30,000 B.C. to A.D. 700*. Philadelphia, PA: University of Pennsylvania Press.

Nagamine, M. (1986). Clay figurines and Jomon society. In R. Pearson, G. Barnes, and K. Huterrer, eds., *Windows on the Japanese Past: Studies in Archaeology and Prehistory*. Ann Arbor, MI: Center for Japanese Studies, University of Michigan, pp. 255–266.

Nakamura, O. (1999). Burials and cemetery structures: Western-Japan. *Kikan Kokogaku*, **69**, 6064. (In Japanese.)

Nakamura, T., Taniguchi, Y., Tsuji, S., and Oda, H. (2001). Radiocarbon dating of charred residues on the earliest pottery in Japan. *Radiocarbon*, **43**, 1129–1148.

Nishida, M. (1983). The emergence of food production in Neolithic Japan. *Journal of Anthropological Archaeology*, **2**, 305–322.

Obayashi, T. (1997). The Ainu concept of the soul. In T. Yamada, and T. Irimoto, eds., *Circumpolar Animism and Shamanism*. Sapporo: Hokkaido University Press, pp. 8–20.

Pearson, K. (1899). Mathematical contributions to the theory of evolution: V. On the reconstruction of stature of the prehistoric races. *Philosophical Transactions of the Royal Society of London (A)*, **192**, 169–244.

Pearson, L. J. and Pearson, C. J. (2012). Letter: Societal collapse or transformation, and resilience. *Proceedings of the National Academy of Sciences*, **109**, E2030–E2031.

Rakita, G. F. M. and Buikstra, J. E. (2008). Introduction. In G. F. M. Rakita, J. E. Buikstra, L. A. Beck, and S. R. Williams, eds., *Interacting with the Dead: Perspectives on Mortuary Archaeology for the New Millennium*. Gainesville, FL: University Press of Florida, pp. 1–11.

Redman, C. L. (2005). Resilience theory in archaeology. *American Anthropologist*, **107**, 70–77.

Redman, C. L. and Kinzig, A. P. (2003). Resilience of past landscapes: Resilience theory, society, and the *Longue Durée. Ecology and Society*, **7**, 14.

Robb, J. (1997). Intentional tooth removal in Neolithic Italian women. *Antiquity*, **71**, 659–669.

Rosen, A. and Rivera-Collazo, I. (2012). Climate change, adaptive cycles, and the persistence of foraging economies during the Late Pleistocene/Holocene transition in the Levant. *Proceedings of the National Academy of Sciences*, **109**, 3640–3645.

Ruff, C. B. (1999). Skeletal structural and behavioral patterns of the prehistoric Great Basin populations. In B. Hemphill, ed., *Prehistoric Lifeways in the Great Basin Wetlands: Bioarchaeological Reconstruction and Interpretation*. Salt Lake City, UT: University of Utah Press, pp. 290–320.

Ruff, C. B. (2008). Biomechanical analyses of archaeological human skeletons. In M. A. Katzenberg and S. R. Saunders, eds., *Biological Anthropology of the Human Skeleton*. New York, NY: Alan R. Liss, pp. 183–206.

Ruff, C. B. and Larsen, C. S. (1990). Postcranial biomechanical adaptations to subsistence strategy changes on the Georgia Coast. In C. S. Larsen, ed., *The Archaeology of Mission Santa Catalina de Guale, Part 2: Biocultural Interpretations of a Population in Transition*. New York, NY: American Museum of Natural History, pp. 94–120.

Ruff, C. B., Larsen, C. S., and Hayes, W. C. (1984). Structural changes in the femur with the transition to agriculture on the Georgia coast. *American Journal of Physical Anthropology*, **64**, 125–136.

Ruff, C. B., Scott, W. W., and Liu A. Y. C. (1991). Articular and diaphyseal remodeling of the proximal femur with changes in body mass in adults. *American Journal of Physical Anthropology*, **86**, 397–413.

Ruff, C. B., Walker, A., and Trinkaus, E. (1994). Postcranial robusticity in *Homo* III: Ontogeny. *American Journal of Physical Anthropology*, **93**, 35–54.

Ruff, C. B., Holt, B., and Trinkaus, E. (2006). Who's afraid of the big, bad, Wolff? "Wolff's Law" and bone functional adaptation. *American Journal of Physical Anthropology*, **129**, 484–498.

Saeki, F. (2006). Estimation of stature and lower limb proportion of the prehistoric Jomon based on an anatomical method. *Anthropological Science (Japanese Series)*, **114**, 17–33.

Sciulli, P. W., Schneider, K. M., and Mahaney, M. C. (1990). Stature estimation in prehistoric Native Americans of Ohio. *American Journal of Physical Anthropology*, **83**, 275–280.

Shanks, M. and Tilley, C. (1982). Ideology, symbolic power, and ritual communication: A reinterpretation of Neolithic mortuary practices. In I. Hodder, ed., *Symbolic and Structural Archaeology*. Cambridge: Cambridge University Press, pp. 129–154.

Shiomi, H., Kawagoshi, T., and Kawse, M. (1971). Report on the excavation of Ota Shell Mound of the Onomichi City, Hiroshima Prefecture. In H. Shiomi, ed., *Report on the Research of Cultural Heritage of Hiroshima Prefecture 9*. Hiroshima: Educational Board of Hiroshima. (In Japanese.)

Silva, A., Oliveira, I., Silva, M. E., *et al.* (2016). Starch characterization in seven raw, boiled and roasted chestnuts (*Castanea sativa* Mill.) cultivars from Portugal. *Journal of Food Science and Technology*, **53**, 348–358.

Sofaer, J. (2011). Towards a social bioarchaeology of age. In S. C. Agarwal and P. Beauchesne, ed., *Social Bioarchaeology*. New York, NY: Wiley-Blackwell, pp. 285–311.

Stock, J. T. and Pinhasi, R. (2011). *Human Bioarchaeology of the Agricultural Transition*. New York, NY: Wiley.

Stojanowski, C. M., Carver, C. L., and Miller, K. M. (2014). Incisor avulsion, social identity, and Saharan population history: New data from the early Holocene Southern Sahara. *Journal of Anthropological Archaeology*, **35**, 79–91.

Takenaka, M., Mine, K., Tsuchimochi, K., and Shimada, K. (2001). Tooth removal during ritual tooth ablation in the Jomon period. *Bulletin of the Indo-Pacific Prehistory Association*, **21**, 49–52.

Temple, D. H. (2007). Dietary variation and stress among prehistoric Jomon foragers from Japan. *American Journal of Physical Anthropology*, **133**, 1035–1046.

Temple, D. H. and Goodman, A. H. (2014). Bioarchaeology has a "health" problem: Conceptualizing "stress" and "health" in bioarchaeological research. *American Journal of Physical Anthropology*, **155**, 186–191.

Thompson, V. D. and Pluckhahn, T. J. (2010). History, complex hunter-gatherers, and the mounds and monuments of Crystal River, Florida, USA: A geophysical survey. *Journal of Island and Coastal Archaeology*, **5**, 33–51.

Tsuji, S. (1995). On the paleoenvironment. In Aomoriken Kyoiku Iiknai, ed., *Sannai Maruyama Iseki 6*. Aomori: Aomoriken Kyoiku Iinkai, pp. 81–83. (In Japanese.)

Tsukada, M. (1986). Vegetation in prehistoric Japan: The last 20,000 years. In R. Pearson, G. Barnes, and K. Huterrer, eds., *Windows on the Japanese Past: Studies in Archaeology and Prehistory*. Ann Arbor, MI: Center for Japanese Studies, University of Michigan, pp. 11–56.

Turner, C. G. (1979). Dental anthropological indications of agriculture among the Jomon people of central Japan. *American Journal of Physical Anthropology*, 51, 619–636.

Ubelaker, D. H. (1989). *Human Skeletal Remains: Excavation, Analysis, Intepretation*. Washington, DC: Taraxacum Press.

Walker, B., Holling, C. S., Carpenter, S. R., and Kinzig, A. P. (2004). Resilience, adaptability, and transformability in socioecological systems. *Ecology and Society*, 9, 5.

Watanabe, H. (1972). *The Ainu Ecosystem: Environment and Group Structure*. Tokyo: University of Tokyo Press.

Wilson, J. J. (2014). Paradox and promise: Research on the role of recent advances in paleodemography and paleoepidemiology to the study of "health" in Pre-Columbian societies. *American Journal of Physical Anthropology*, 155, 268–280.

Yaussy, S. L., DeWitte, S. N., and Redfern, R. C. (2016). Frailty and famine: Patterns of mortality and physiological stress among victims of famine in Medieval London. *American Journal of Physical Anthropology*, 160, 272–283.

Yoo, S., Lee, S., and Shin, M. (2012). The properties and molecular structures of gusiljatbam starch compared to those of acorn and chestnut starches. *Starch-Stärke*, 64, 339–347.

6 Biomechanics, Habitual Activity, and Resilience among Southern African Hunter-Gatherers and Herders

Michelle E. Cameron and Jay Stock

6.1 Introduction

Resilience theory may be used to interpret the sources and roles of transformative changes in adaptive systems (Folke, 2006; Redman, 2005). This theory is increasingly applied by archaeological researchers to help explain how past populations responded to external disturbances (Davies and Moore, 2016; Hoover and Hudson, 2016; Redman, 2005; Rick, 2011; Thompson and Turck, 2009). Archaeologists are uniquely positioned to apply resilience theory when evaluating behavioral and cultural variation over long timescales when examining instances of change in prehistory. The temporal depth provided by archaeological contexts allows researchers to investigate patterns of stasis and change that may occur in response to social, ecological, and economic perturbations (Redman, 2005; Rick, 2011; Thompson and Turck, 2009). Southern African Later Stone Age (LSA) groups provide the opportunity to test whether habitual physical behaviors vary in response to economic changes. LSA human skeletal remains from southernmost Africa have been recovered from archaeological contexts spanning the Holocene (approximately 10 000 to 250 BP; all dates expressed in uncalibrated radiocarbon years) and originate from sites encompassing a broad geographic range (Figure 6.1; Ginter, 2011; Mitchell, 2002; Morris, 1992; Pfeiffer and Sealy, 2006; Pfeiffer *et al.*, 2014). For the majority of the Holocene, LSA populations hunted and gathered resources including medium- to large-sized grazers and browsers, birds, fish, small mammals, fruits, underground storage organs, and shellfish (Deacon and Deacon, 1999; Mitchell, 2002).

However, domesticated livestock and herding practices were introduced to the region between approximately 2500 and 2000 BP (Barham and Mitchell, 2008; Kinahan, 1991; Mitchell, 2002; Russell and Lander, 2015; Sadr, 1998, 2003, 2015; Sadr and Plug, 2001; Sadr *et al.*, 2003; Sampson, 1974, 1986, 2010; Smith, 1984, 1992, 1998, 2009). Eastern Africa is the most likely source for the livestock and practices associated with herding in southernmost Africa (Sadr, 2013, 2015). The introduction of herding represents a perturbation of preexisting southern African subsistence systems. During this transition, herding practices were incorporated into local hunter-gatherer lifeways (Sadr, 1998, 2003, 2015), resulting in changes to LSA material cultures and subsistence strategies (Barham and Mitchell, 2008; Deacon and Deacon, 1999; Klein, 1986; Mitchell, 2002; Sadr, 1998, 2003, 2015;

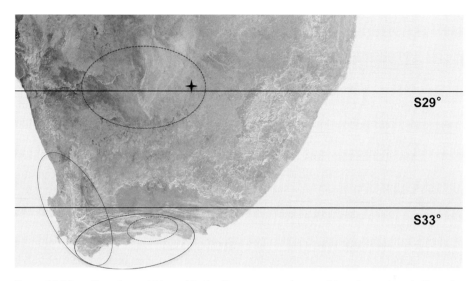

Figure 6.1 Map of southern Africa with the Cape coast and central interior regions indicated. The fynbos ecology of the Cape coast region is indicated by the solid outline, the Cape coast forest region is indicated by the small dotted outline. The central interior region is indicated by the dashed outline. Black lines indicate approximate latitude markers and the star indicates the approximate location of Koffiefontein. From Cameron and Pfeiffer (2014).

Sampson, 1974, 1986, 2010). The occurrence of this transition within the well-documented LSA archaeological context allows for the impact of this event on human behavior and morphology to be assessed.

Population resilience in response to the introduction of domesticated livestock to southern Africa may be investigated through multiple lines of archaeological evidence (Redman, 2005; Rick, 2011; Thompson and Turck, 2009). However, bioarchaeology also helps explain how human biology is impacted by such disturbances. Resilience theory is used to interpret data collected from human skeletal remains, particularly when analyzing population stress and demography before, during, and after periods of change (Hegmon et al., 2008; Hoover and Hudson, 2016; Redman and Kinzig, 2003). However, analyses of habitual physical behaviors, as inferred from human long bone biomechanical properties, may also inform interpretations of resilience in prehistory as groups negotiate economic perturbations.

Habitual physical behaviors undertaken during the lifespan can be inferred from human skeletal morphology using analyses of long bone biomechanical properties (Jones et al., 1977; Ruff, 2000, 2008; Ruff and Hayes, 1983a, b; Ruff et al., 1993, 2006; Shaw and Stock, 2009a, b; Stock and Pfeiffer, 2001). Inferences of prehistoric physical behaviors based on biomechanical data are most informative when interpreted alongside other lines of archaeological and bioarchaeological evidence. Consequently, bioarchaeologists may analyze long bone biomechanical properties to assess whether physical behaviors vary in response to subsistence strategy changes.

Long bone biomechanical properties have been examined in the context of hunter-gatherers transitioning to agriculture; however, the influence of herding on physical activity patterns is frequently overlooked. Biomechanical properties associated with decreased mobility and differences in manual activity patterns are noted across the transition to agriculture in several regions (Bridges, 1989; Bridges *et al.*, 2000; Macintosh *et al.*, 2014a, b; Ruff and Hayes, 1983a, b; Ruff *et al.*, 1984; Stock *et al.*, 2011). Studies examining the transition from hunting and gathering to herding report diverse results, reflecting the deeper cultural and ecological contingences mediating this transition. Stock *et al.* (2011) found that herding groups had decreased terrestrial mobility compared to hunter-gatherers, while Marchi *et al.* (2006) noted that herding groups had higher indicators of terrestrial mobility, likely due to transhumance activities in a mountainous region. Southern African groups that transitioned from hunting and gathering to herding provide a test case through which the influence of herding practices on physical behavior may be assessed further.

Subsistence practice changes among LSA groups that adopted herding may have impacted the physical behaviors and activities undertaken by LSA populations after the introduction of herding. Habitual physical behaviors linked to LSA hunting and gathering activities have previously been inferred from biomechanical analyses of long bone cross-sectional geometric properties (Cameron and Pfeiffer, 2014; Stock and Pfeiffer, 2001, 2004). As such, the biomechanical properties of individuals before and after the introduction of herding may be compared to assess whether physical behaviors associated with hunting and gathering persisted or changed before and after this transition.

The aim of this chapter is to assess whether physical behavioral patterns differed among groups before and after the introduction of herding in southern Africa. Temporal variation before and after the introduction of herding will be explored on the Cape coast, where skeletal remains that pre- and post-date this transition are available. Spatial variation following this transition will be explored among groups from the Cape coast and from the central interior of southern Africa to explore the influence of diverse environments on reorganized post-herding behaviors. LSA biomechanical properties indicative of hunting and gathering activities may have remained static across this transition and persisted into post-herding subsistence practices. Alternatively, populations may have adapted to this transition by changing subsistence behaviors and physical activities, resulting in different biomechanical properties from preceding hunter-gatherer groups. Results will be contextualized with information from other bioarchaeological studies of this transition and will be grounded in resilience theory.

6.2   Context

6.2.1   The Southern African Later Stone Age Archaeological Context

Holocene LSA sites and human skeletal remains have been found throughout southern Africa, but the Cape coast represents the most densely occupied and highly exploited region (Figure 6.1; Barham and Mitchell, 2008; Deacon and Deacon,

1999; Mitchell, 2002; Pfeiffer, 2013). Sites are also known from more interior regions of southern Africa, but population sizes were constrained in these regions due to higher aridity during the middle Holocene (Figure 6.1; Deacon, 1984; Lee-Thorp and Ecker, 2015). High population densities along the coast were likely due to high resource availability and the temperate climate. Coastal hunter-gatherers used digging sticks, leather clothing, firesticks, netting for fishing, as well as stone-tipped and fletched arrows (Binneman, 1994a, b; Deacon, 1976; Deacon and Deacon, 1999; Manhire, 1993; Mitchell, 2002). Social organization changed during the late Holocene around 4500 BP, with increased regionalization of material culture, increased territoriality in terms of landscape use, and the development of more formal burial practices (Hall, 1990; Pfeiffer and Sealy, 2006). However, the identifying characteristics of LSA populations, including a predominantly hunting and gathering subsistence strategy, show continuity from the Middle Stone Age through the majority of the Holocene.

Southern African LSA groups underwent large-scale changes due to the introduction of herding across southern Africa between 2500 and 2000 BP (Barham and Mitchell, 2008; Kinahan, 1991; Klein, 1986; Mitchell, 2002; Russell and Lander, 2015; Sadr, 1998, 2003, 2015; Sadr and Plug, 2001; Sadr et al., 2003; Sampson, 1974, 1986, 2010; Smith, 1984, 1992, 1998, 2009). Herding likely entered southern Africa via multiple small-scale incursions from eastern Africa, with one incursion occurring along the Atlantic coast and a smaller infiltration across the Limpopo/Zambezi watershed (Barham and Mitchell, 2008; Mitchell, 2002; Sadr, 1998, 2003, 2015). These incursions resulted in the introduction of domesticated livestock, including sheep, goats, and cattle; domesticated dogs; the construction of livestock-keeping enclosures; ceramic vessels; and higher proportions of backed lithics. Populations adopted aspects of this incoming package, yet maintained some hunting and gathering characteristics, as groups who possessed livestock still engaged in the hunting and gathering of wild resources (Kinahan, 1991; Klein, 1978; Klein and Cruz-Uribe, 1989; Sadr, 1998; Schweitzer, 1979; Smith et al., 1991).

6.2.2   Bioarchaeological Perspectives on the Introduction of Herding in Southern Africa

Previous bioarchaeological studies have used various lines of evidence from human skeletal remains to identify instances of biological stasis and change across this transition, including stable isotopic, zooarchaeological, osteological, and contemporary genetic research. The results of these studies will briefly be outlined to provide a bioarchaeological context for interpreting analyses of LSA biomechanical properties before and after the introduction of herding.

Stable isotopic data from southern African Cape coast skeletons indicate that terrestrial sources of protein increased after 1000 BP (Pfeiffer and Sealy, 2006; Sealy, 2010). This may reflect a higher reliance on domesticated livestock as herding became consolidated in LSA lifeways (Pfeiffer and Sealy, 2006; Sealy, 2010). However, zooarchaeological data from the Cape coast indicate that hunting wild game remained important after the introduction of herding (Kinahan, 1991; Klein, 1978;

Klein and Cruz-Uribe, 1989; Sadr, 1998; Schweitzer, 1979; Smith *et al.*, 1991). Additionally, the gathering of plant resources likely remained important after the introduction of herding as plant cultivation was not part of this incoming package (Dahl and Hjort, 1976; Kinahan, 1991, 2000; Maggs, 1971; Sadr, 1998, 2003, Sealy, 2010; Smith, 1992). In the semiarid central interior of southern Africa (Figure 6.1), isotopic data indicate populations with livestock still consumed a broad spectrum of wild resources (Masemula, 2015). These studies suggest that dietary changes occurred after the introduction of herding as populations consumed domesticated livestock. However, this change was not absolute as mixed hunter-gatherer/herding economies emerged.

Body size variation before and after the introduction of herding has also been examined (Doyle, 2015; Pfeiffer and Sealy, 2006; Pfeiffer *et al.*, 2014; Sealy and Pfeiffer, 2000; Smith *et al.*, 1992). There are no significant differences in the stature or body mass of individuals pre-dating and post-dating the introduction of domesticated livestock on the Cape coast (Pfeiffer and Sealy, 2006). Stature was larger after the introduction of herding, which may relate to the greater nutritional sufficiency and reliability provided by domesticated livestock (Doyle, 2015). However, these differences do not consistently reach statistical significance (Doyle, 2015; Pfeiffer and Sealy, 2006). Consequently, while dietary composition may have changed as herding entered southernmost Africa, body sizes remained relatively static – LSA individuals did not experience secular increases in stature or body mass after the introduction of herding.

Cranial and dental remains have also been used to assess population continuity across this transition in southern Africa. Dental phenetic analyses indicate unique characteristics among some post-herding individuals. These morphological variants may have been introduced to southern African groups by interaction with herders from more northern and eastern regions (Irish *et al.*, 2014). However, there is little temporal variation in dental morphologies pre- and post-dating the introduction of herding (Irish *et al.*, 2014). There is craniometric evidence of admixture between herding and non-herding populations in southern Africa (Morris, 1984), but overall, dental and craniometric evidence indicate continuity between pre- and post-herding communities (Black, 2014; Black *et al.*, 2009; Irish *et al.*, 2014; Stynder, 2006, 2009; Stynder *et al.*, 2007). These results are supported by genetic studies of descendant KhoeSan groups, who have mitochondrial haplotypes from east African herding populations, yet are best characterized as members of a deep, contiguous genetic lineage (Barbieri *et al.*, 2014; Macholdt *et al.*, 2014, 2015; Schlebusch *et al.*, 2012). As such, herding was likely incorporated into the subsistence practices of LSA hunter-gatherers through a reorganization of behaviors and cultural practices that reflect interaction rather than replacement.

Consequently, isotopic, body size, craniometric, and dental phenetic data indicate that many biological characteristics of LSA hunter-gatherers who pre-dated the introduction of herding remained static following this transition. These data speak to instances of continuity and stasis as southern Africans reorganized with the introduction of herding. However, stable isotopic and zooarchaeological data indicate that dietary composition changed as herding entered southern Africa. Subsistence changes may have affected the physical behavioral patterns associated with subsistence practices. Biomechanical analyses of LSA long bones pre- and post-dating this transition may clarify whether habitual behaviors changed as LSA populations adopted herding.

6.2.3   Biomechanical Research in Southern Africa

Bioarchaeological researchers may infer habitual physical behaviors from human skeletal remains using biomechanical analyses of long bone diaphyses (Holt, 2003; Shaw and Stock, 2009a, b; Ruff, 2008; Ruff et al., 2006). Bending, compressional, and torsional deformations due to muscular recruitment stimulate bone remodeling, resulting in bones with greater strength and rigidity (Cowin, 2001; Huiskes, 1982; Lanyon et al., 1982; Lovejoy et al., 1976; Ruff, 2008; Ruff et al., 2006). Long bone cross-sectional geometric properties (CSGPs) measure the distribution of bone tissue around long bone shafts at specific section locations perpendicular to the long axis of a bone. Variation in diaphyseal morphology is partly attributed to remodeling in response to the strains and deformations experienced by bone during adulthood, while modeling drifts during growth and development are associated with periosteal and medullary deposition (Ruff, 2000, 2008; Ruff and Hayes, 1983a, b; Ruff et al., 1993, 2006). CSGPs may therefore inform on the strength and shape characteristics of long bones due to muscular recruitment. Consequently, analyses of biomechanical properties may be coupled with archaeological information to infer the habitual physical behaviors of past individuals.

Biomechanical analyses have previously been used to investigate variation in manipulative activities and terrestrial mobility patterns in southern Africa. Stock and Pfeiffer (2004) compared the CSGPs of LSA hunter-gatherers from the fynbos and forest biomes of the Cape coast to test whether habitual physical behaviors differed in these two regions. There were no differences among females; however, forest males had higher bilateral asymmetry and upper arm strength than fynbos males. This pattern may be attributed to a higher reliance on spear projectiles rather than bows and arrows for hunting medium- to large-sized bovids in the forest region (Stock and Pfeiffer, 2004). Fynbos and forest males and females had strong, robust femora, indicating a high degree of terrestrial mobility with no significant differences between these regions (Stock and Pfeiffer, 2001, 2004). The ecological similarities between the fynbos and forest regions, namely high terrestrial resources and marine accessibility, may have overridden local ecological differences resulting in broadly similar upper and lower limb biomechanical properties among these groups. In recent years, a larger number of Cape coast individuals have become available for analysis (Cameron and Pfeiffer, 2014), allowing for more comprehensive analyses of biomechanical datasets with greater temporal coverage across the Holocene. Consequently, variation in the physical behaviors of individuals before and after the transition to a herding socioecological system may be further explored.

Biomechanical studies have also been conducted for LSA individuals from the semiarid central interior of southern Africa. Central interior individuals post-dating the introduction of herding to southern Africa practiced a mixed herding and hunter-gatherer subsistence strategy (Cameron and Pfeiffer, 2014; Morris, 1984). Cameron and Pfeiffer (2014) compared central interior males and females to coastal fynbos and forest males and females to assess whether the environmental contexts of these regions impacted biomechanical indicators of physical behaviors. Central interior individuals had stronger and more robust upper limbs, but these differences were not statistically significant. Lower limb biomechanical properties were similar among all southern African groups. However, in these comparisons, Cape coast individuals pre- and post-dating the introduction of herding were analyzed as a single group. This grouping may have masked variation among pre- and post-herding Cape coast individuals. Differences observed between the central interior and Cape coast groups may be attributable to the incorporation of herding practices among central interior communities. Additionally, subsistence strategy variation after 2000 BP may have impacted habitual behaviors and biomechanical properties on the Cape coast, resulting in temporally based intragroup variation.

In a broader bioarchaeological context, the transition from hunting and gathering to herding may be accompanied by changes in habitual physical activity patterns. Examinations of hunter-gatherer and herding groups from the Nile Valley and Neolithic Italy have obtained contrasting results. Indicators of physical activity intensity decreased in the Nile Valley as groups in this region transitioned from hunting and gathering to nomadic pastoralism (Stock *et al.*, 2011). Conversely, Neolithic herding groups in the mountainous Liguria region of Italy have more robust long bone diaphyses relative to earlier hunter-gatherers, which may reflect transhumance patterns in a mountainous region (Marchi, 2008).

These two contexts yielded diverse results, yet may inform predictions regarding southern African pre- and post-herding biomechanical properties. The Nile Valley groups indicate that herding may be associated with decreases in activity intensity relative to hunting and gathering. These groups present an accurate comparative population for southern African individuals. Nile Valley herders were nomadic and represent a mobile population (Stock *et al.*, 2011), and post-herding southern Africans were also relatively mobile as they engaged in some hunter-gatherer activities. However, Nile Valley herders still displayed decreased indicators of activity relative to hunter-gatherers. Consequently, this study predicts that southern African post-herding groups may have engaged in less intense manual activities and a lower degree of terrestrial mobility.

By contrast, greater indicators of terrestrial mobility among Neolithic Italian pastoralists may have been driven by the influence of terrain on lower limb mobility indicators. The mountainous terrain of the Cape coast relative to the central interior may pose an additional challenge to individuals navigating this region. As such, diverse patterns may emerge between Cape coast and central interior post-herding groups due to their different environmental contexts. Cape coast and central interior post-herding groups will be considered separately and compared to assess whether environmental variation may impact physical behaviors within post-herding groups.

Overall, biomechanical data previously collected for southern African groups may provide evidence regarding how behaviors reorganized after herding was introduced to southern Africa. Southern African pre- and post-herding groups are ideal for such comparisons based on the strong archaeological context of this region, the availability of skeletal remains from across the Holocene, and their distribution across a broad geographic range encompassing diverse environmental challenges.

6.3   Aims of the Present Study

Resilience theory may be used to interpret the transition from hunting and gathering to herding in southern Africa by placing this transition in the context of an adaptive cycle (Figure 6.2; Folke, 2006; Hoover and Hudson, 2016; Redman, 2005; Thompson and Turck, 2009). An adaptive cycle consists of four cyclical and interconnected phases: growth (r-phase), conservation (K-phase), release (omega-phase), and reorganization (alpha-phase) (Folke, 2006; Redman, 2005; Thompson and Turck, 2009). The introduction of herding may have instigated the release phase of the cycle among southern African LSA populations by initiating a period of rapid change as populations adopted elements of the incoming herder socioecological and cultural system. The reorganization of lifeways after this transition resulted in new cultural elements and practices associated with herding integrating with preexisting

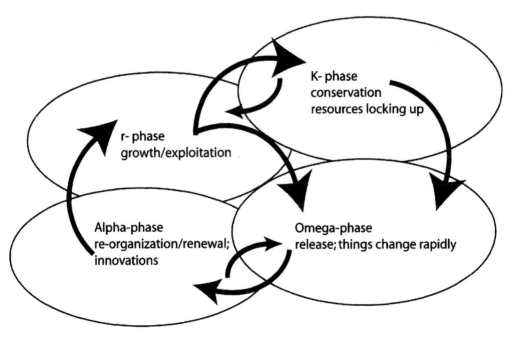

Figure 6.2 Rendering of the adaptive cycle, after Redman (2005).

hunter-gatherer behaviors. This transformation and reorganization process may have affected physical behavioral patterns as groups developed new subsistence strategies. This development of new behavioral patterns may have morphological implications that may be evaluated using biomechanical analyses.

Consequently, resilience theory provides a framework within which variation between pre- and post-herding habitual activity patterns may be interpreted. Habitual physical behaviors may have adapted to new subsistence practices, resulting in unique long bone biomechanical properties after this transition. Alternatively, physical behaviors and biomechanical properties associated with hunter-gatherers may have persisted among LSA groups, as these behaviors have remained an essential component of post-herding lifeways.

Biomechanical properties indicative of physical behaviors in Cape coast and central interior LSA groups may be re-analyzed, taking subsistence strategy variation and resilience theory into account. Physical behaviors may have changed around 2000 BP on the Cape coast due to the reorganization of subsistence behaviors associated with herding. This may be assessed by comparing individuals from archaeological contexts dated before and after this transition on the Cape coast. Additionally, the biomechanical properties of post-herding Cape coast groups may be compared to those of post-herding central interior males and females to assess whether there is a suite of biomechanical properties that may be associated with mixed herding and hunting and gathering LSA economies in diverse environments.

In summary, analyses of biomechanical properties before and after the introduction of herding on the Cape coast may clarify how LSA groups behaviorally responded to this transition. Comparisons among post-herding groups from the Cape coast and the central interior may further indicate whether behaviors associated with emergent mixed hunter-gatherer and herding economies remain consistent in diverse geographic contexts. Biomechanical datasets for the upper and lower limbs of Cape coast and central interior individuals from previous studies (Cameron and Pfeiffer, 2014; Stock and Pfeiffer, 2001, 2004) will be analyzed. Sample sizes are small, but these individuals provide the opportunity to test whether behaviors adapted or remained consistent across subsistence transitions in prehistoric southernmost Africa.

6.4   Materials and Methods

6.4.1   Materials

The skeletal remains analyzed in this study were derived from Cape coast and central interior Holocene LSA archaeological contexts. Cape coast individuals from throughout the Holocene (approximately 10 000 to 250 BP) were included to ensure that individuals pre- and post-dating the introduction of herding at approximately 2000 BP could be compared to assess whether physical behaviors changed with this transition. There is debate regarding precisely when herding became established in southern Africa (Sadr, 2015; Sealy, 2010). However, the time point of 2000 BP was used in this study to allow for comparability with other research that adopts this date

Table 6.1 Number of individuals included in this study.

| | Number of individuals | | |
Region	Male	Female	Total
Cape coast pre-herding (pre-2000 BP)	28	24	52
Cape coast post-herding (post-2000 BP)	6	6	12
Central interior post-herding	6	12	18
Total	40	42	82

as a cut-off point between hunting and gathering and herding socioecological systems (Irish *et al.*, 2014; Sealy, 2010). Central interior individuals post-dating the introduction of herding were available and included in the present study. No individuals predating the introduction of herding in the central interior have been recovered to allow for a temporal comparison between herding and non-herding groups in this region.

Sample sizes are listed in Table 6.1. In total, 82 individuals were analyzed: 64 (34 male, 30 female) individuals from the Cape coast, with 52 (28 male, 24 female) predating the introduction of herding and 12 (6 male, 6 female) post-dating this transition, as well as 18 (6 male, 12 female) individuals from the central interior. Few radiocarbon dates are available for central interior individuals; however, diagnostic materials recovered from the burials and associated archaeological sites indicate that these individuals post-date 2000 BP and engaged in herding activities (Humphreys, 1972; Humphreys and Maggs, 1970; Maggs, 1971; Morris, 1984). This study only examined skeletally mature adults. Age and sex estimations are derived from observations by the authors and previous studies (Cameron and Pfeiffer, 2014; Doyle, 2015; Stock and Pfeiffer, 2004).

Long bone biomechanical properties were assessed for the humeri and femora of Cape coast and central interior individuals. The humerus was used to infer upper limb manual activities, while femora were used to infer lower limb terrestrial mobility (Davies and Stock, 2014; Ruff, 2008; Stock, 2006; Stock and Pfeiffer, 2001). Left and right humeri were analyzed where available to assess bilateral asymmetry. Femur CSGPs were quantified unilaterally assuming symmetry of the lower limbs (Auerbach and Ruff, 2006). Right femora were preferred; however, values from left femora and tibiae were used if the right element was not available. Additionally, postcranial dimensions including maximum femoral head diameters and long bone lengths were assessed to facilitate the standardization of CSGPs.

6.4.2 Methods

The CSGP data were collected using molds of the periosteal contour (Davies *et al.*, 2012; Stock and Shaw, 2007). This method has been found to produce accurate estimates of long bone biomechanical properties, is cost-effective, and may be undertaken in remote research locales (Cameron and Pfeiffer, 2014; Davies *et al.*, 2012; Stock and Shaw, 2007). Periosteal molds were produced using Exaflex Regular Body silicone impression material at the mid-distal (35 percent) location of humeri, and the midshaft (50 percent) location of femora. Molds were taken bilaterally for humeri where both left and right humeri were available to facilitate analyses of bilateral strength and robusticity asymmetries.

Anatomical planes of orientation were marked on each mold during the molding process to maintain correct orientation during digitization. The molds were digitized using an Epson flatbed scanner, with a ruler included for scale. Periosteal contours were manually traced along the edges of digitized molds using a drawing tablet in ImageJ.[1] The traced images were analyzed using the ImageJ platform, with the Moment Macro v1.3 plug-in.[2]

The CSGP variables examined in this study are listed in Table 6.2. Total subperiosteal area (*TA*) values were calculated as these values reflect the strength and rigidity of long bone diaphyses (Table 6.2; Ruff, 2008; Stock and Shaw, 2007). Long bones also experience bending and torsional forces, which may be indicated by second moments of area (*I*) (Table 6.2; Ruff, 2008). *I* values were calculated around specific anatomical axes, including the anteroposterior axis (AP, I_x), the mediolateral (ML; I_y) axis, the axis of maximum bending strength (I_{max}), and the axis of minimum bending strength (I_{min}). Circularity indices (I_x/I_y and I_{max}/I_{min}) characterize the shape of a long bone shaft as well as bending strength in multiple directions. *I* values from perpendicular directions may be combined to reflect the bone's ability to resist bending in multiple directions: the resultant value is the polar second moment of area (*J*), which indicates diaphyseal robusticity and torsional strength.

Bilateral asymmetry may be used to further investigate activity types (Ruff, 2008). Bilateral asymmetry is a non-directional measure that indicates the loading of one arm relative to the other, and may inform on the types of activities undertaken (Ruff, 2008). Some manual activities recruit one limb preferentially (unimanual tasks), while others recruit both upper limbs in an equivalent manner (bimanual tasks). Humeral bilateral asymmetry (BA) in *TA* and *J* may be quantified as a percentage value (Table 6.2; Ruff, 2008).

To facilitate comparisons between individuals, CSGP values were standardized to body size, as body mass and bone length may impact axial, bending, and torsional loading in weight-bearing and non-weight-bearing long bones (Ruff, 2000, 2008; Ruff *et al.*, 1984, 1993). Standardization formulae are provided in Table 6.2. *TA* values were standardized to body mass as it affects the axial compression and tension forces experienced during life. *J* values were standardized using formulae that incorporated estimated body mass and bone length to account for the length of the loading moment arm (Ruff, 2000). Estimated body masses were calculated from maximum femoral head diameters using the McHenry (1992) formula (Table 6.2). This formula represents the most appropriate body mass estimation formula for small-bodied southern African

---

[1] US National Institutes of Health. Available at: http://imagej.nih.gov/ij.
[2] Available at: http://dx.doi.org/10.1002/ajpa.1330910103.

Table 6.2 Description of cross-sectional geometric properties and standardization formulae used.

Cross-sectional property	Abbreviation	Biomechanical significance	Unit of measurement
Total subperiosteal area	TA	Influences second moments of area	mm^2
Anteroposterior (AP) second moment of area	I_x	AP bending strength	mm^4
Mediolateral (ML) second moment of area	I_y	ML bending strength	mm^4
Maximum second moment of area	I_{max}	Maximum bending strength	mm^4
Minimum second moment of area	I_{min}	Minimum bending strength	mm^4
AP to ML diaphyseal circularity index	I_x/I_y	Directionality of bending strength	
Absolute diaphyseal circularity index	I_{max}/I_{min}	Generic ratio of bending strength	
Polar second moment of area	J	Torsional strength	mm^4

Formulae used to calculate and standardize cross-sectional geometric properties			
Bilateral asymmetry (%)	% BA	$100 \times$ [(maximum − minimum)/ minimum]	Ruff (2008)
Body size standardization:			
Body mass estimation	BM	$2.239 \times FH - 39.9$	McHenry (1992)
Total subperiosteal area	TA	(Total area/estimated body mass in kg) $\times 10^2$	Ruff (2000)
Polar second moment of area	J	[Torsional strength/(estimated body mass in kg $\times$ (bone length in mm)^2)] $\times 10^5$	Ruff (2000)

FH = maximum femur head diameter.

LSA individuals (Auerbach and Ruff, 2004; Kurki *et al.*, 2010). Maximum long bone lengths were measured to the nearest 0.5 mm using an osteometric board. Femoral head diameters were measured to the nearest 0.1 mm using Mitutoyo digital sliding calipers. In the CSGP analyses, some individuals could not be included due to missing femoral head dimensions, resulting in variation in the number of individuals included in different analyses.

One-way ANOVAs were used to determine whether there were significant differences in the biomechanical properties of Cape coast individuals pre- and post-dating the introduction of herding, and between the Cape coast and central interior groups post-dating the introduction of herding. Welch's one-way ANOVAs were used when comparisons violated Levene's homogeneity of variances test. Results were graphically visualized using box-and-whisker plots (box plots). For all comparisons, males and females were analyzed separately as sex-based differences in activity patterns among southern African populations have previously been detected (Cameron and Pfeiffer, 2014; Stock and Pfeiffer, 2004).

6.5   Results

6.5.1   Pre- and Post-Herding Biomechanical Properties on the Cape Coast

Upper limb diaphyseal strength (TA) and rigidity (J) are higher among post-herding males and females when compared to males and females pre-dating the introduction of herding (Table 6.3; Figures 6.3 and 6.4). However, the differences between these groups are not significant (Table 6.4). Upper limb circularity indices (I_x/I_y and I_{max}/I_{min}) are similar between pre- and post-herding males and females (Table 6.3), and there are no clear patterns of increase and decrease (Tables 6.3 and 6.4; Figures 6.3 and 6.4). Bilateral asymmetry in TA and J are relatively similar among females pre- and post-dating the introduction of herding (Tables 6.3 and 6.4; Figure 6.5). Bilateral asymmetry values are higher among pre-herding males; however, this difference is not significant. Overall, upper limb CSGP values are similar among pre- and post-herding groups.

Lower limb diaphyseal strength and rigidity are similar among pre- and post-herding males, and there are no significant differences between these groups (Tables 6.5 and 6.6; Figure 6.6). However, pre-herding females have significantly higher diaphyseal strength than post-herding females on the Cape coast. Lower limb circularity indices are similar between pre- and post-herding males and females, and there are no clear patterns of increase and decrease (Tables 6.5 and 6.6; Figure 6.6). Overall, lower limb strength and robusticity are higher among pre-herding individuals, particularly among females, yet both groups experienced similar loading directionality.

6.5.2   Post-Herding Biomechanical Properties among Cape Coast and Central Interior Groups

Upper limb diaphyseal strength and rigidity are higher among post-herding central interior males and females than post-herding Cape coast males and females

Table 6.3 Upper limb cross-sectional geometric property summary statistics.

Property	n	Cape coast pre-herding (pre-2000 BP) Mean	S.D.	n	Cape coast post-herding (post-2000 BP) Mean	S.D.	n	Central interior post-herding Mean	S.D.
				Males					
				Right humerus					
TA	18	429.2	56.9	6	457.6	69.1	3	468.8	64.0
J	17	172.5	35.0	6	188.2	53.7	3	210.7	49.3
I_x/I_y	18	1.06	0.15	6	1.11	0.21	5	1.11	0.14
I_{max}/I_{min}	18	1.19	0.11	6	1.18	0.18	5	1.22	0.12
				Left humerus					
TA	17	383.6	41.8	5	387.7	22.9	3	431.0	77.8
J	19	144.8	42.5	5	142.6	22.2	3	181.2	58.7
I_x/I_y	19	1.05	0.15	5	1.00	0.18	5	1.10	0.11
I_{max}/I_{min}	20	1.23	0.15	5	1.21	0.13	5	1.21	0.07
				Bilateral asymmetry					
% BA of TA	14	12.2	7.43	4	8.15	5.49	5	7.94	4.99
% BA of J	15	24.1	17.0	4	11.2	11.1	3	18.5	13.3
				Females					
				Right humerus					
TA	15	361.9	43.7	6	365.9	37.5	9	408.5	40.0
J	15	119.0	24.2	6	137.1	39.7	9	158.0	35.3
I_x/I_y	16	1.24	0.13	6	1.25	0.16	9	1.23	0.06
I_{max}/I_{min}	17	1.35	0.15	6	1.35	0.20	9	1.37	0.22
				Left humerus					
TA	14	338.4	39.0	5	353.1	30.9	11	389.7	45.8
J	14	111.6	26.9	5	123.1	27.4	11	143.2	38.0
I_x/I_y	16	1.25	0.18	5	1.24	0.13	11	1.19	0.12
I_{max}/I_{min}	16	1.31	0.19	5	1.30	0.15	11	1.28	0.12
				Bilateral asymmetry					
% BA of TA	10	2.92	3.90	5	2.38	0.65	9	3.84	1.53
% BA of J	11	5.83	6.02	5	3.84	1.54	9	12.6	9.94

(Table 6.4; Figures 6.7 and 6.8). However, these differences are not significant (Table 6.4). Upper limb circularity indices are similar between post-herding central interior and Cape coast males and females, with no clear patterns of increase or decrease between these groups (Tables 6.3 and 6.4; Figure 6.7 and 6.8). Bilateral asymmetry in TA and J are relatively similar among males post-dating the introduction of herding in both regions (Table 6.3; Figure 6.9). However, bilateral asymmetry

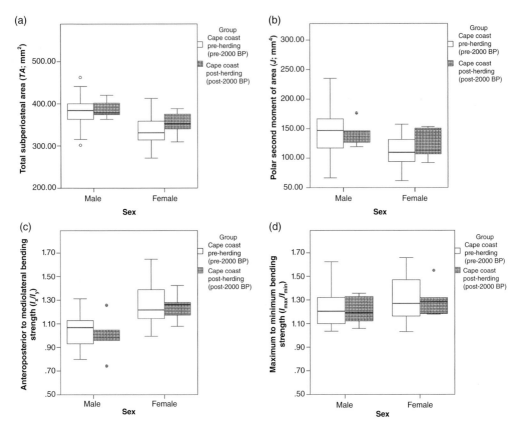

Figure 6.3 Temporal comparisons of left humerus mid-distal box plots by sex and region for: (a) total subperiosteal area (TA); (b) polar second moment of area (J); (c) anteroposterior to mediolateral bending strength (I_x/I_y); and (d) maximum to minimum bending strength (I_{max}/I_{min}). TA is standardized to body mass, while J is standardized to body mass and bone length.

in TA and J are significantly lower among Cape coast females relative to central interior females (Table 6.4; Figure 6.9). Overall, upper limb CSGP values are similar among central interior and Cape coast post-herding groups, except for lower bilateral asymmetry values among coastal females.

Lower limb diaphyseal strength and rigidity are similar between post-herding central interior and Cape coast males, and there are no significant differences between these groups (Tables 6.5 and 6.6; Figure 6.10). However, central interior females have significantly higher diaphyseal strength than post-herding females on the Cape coast. Lower limb circularity indices are similar between post-herding central interior and Cape coast males and females (Table 6.5 and 6.6; Figure 6.10). Overall, lower limb strength and robusticity are higher among central interior individuals, particularly among females, yet both groups experienced similar loading directionality.

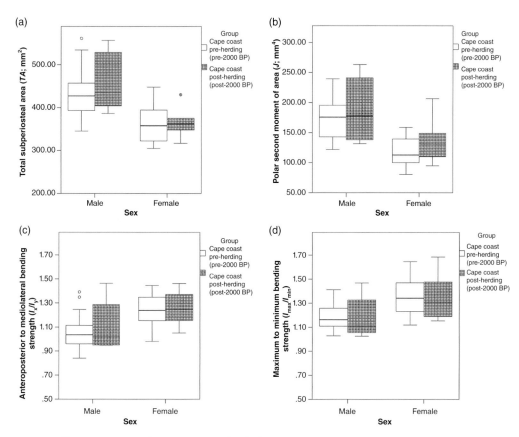

Figure 6.4 Temporal comparisons of right humerus mid-distal box plots by sex and region for: (a) total subperiosteal area (TA); (b) polar second moment of area (J); (c) anteroposterior to mediolateral bending strength (I_x/I_y); and (d) maximum to minimum bending strength (I_{max}/I_{min}). TA is standardized to body mass, while J is standardized to body mass and bone length.

6.6   Discussion

The aim of this chapter was to assess whether the introduction of herding in southern Africa resulted in a reorganization of physical behaviors and consequently long bone biomechanical properties among LSA southern Africans. Previous studies of biomechanical properties among herding and hunter-gatherer groups in other geographic contexts have obtained contradictory results. Southernmost Africa represents an ideal area for examining whether the shift from hunting and gathering to herding impacted long bone biomechanical properties. This was done by comparing humeral and femoral CSGPs among Cape coast individuals that pre- and post-dated the introduction of herding, and by comparing post-herding groups from the Cape coast and the central interior to explore whether diverse environments impacted behavioral variation.

Table 6.4 Upper limb cross-sectional geometric property one-way ANOVA results.

Property	Males			Females		
	Levene p	ANOVA p	Post hoc	Levene p	ANOVA p	Post hoc
Cape coast temporal comparisons (comparing pre-herding to post-herding)						
Right humerus						
TA	0.378	0.326		0.385	0.845	
J	0.172	0.422		0.258	0.215	
I_x/I_y	0.228	0.510		0.393	0.794	
I_{max}/I_{min}	0.130	0.857		0.626	0.953	
Left humerus						
TA	0.317	0.839		0.423	0.459	
J	0.260	0.912		0.737	0.427	
I_x/I_y	0.869	0.505		0.380	0.902	
I_{max}/I_{min}	0.702	0.801		0.221	0.910	
Bilateral asymmetry						
% BA of TA	0.536	0.335		0.194	0.765	
% BA of J	0.279	0.172		0.103	0.485	
Post-herding comparisons (post-herding Cape coast to central interior)						
Right humerus						
TA	0.570	0.822		0.549	0.059	
J	0.670	0.563		0.981	0.303	
I_x/I_y	0.222	0.985		0.004	0.749	
I_{max}/I_{min}	0.353	0.719		0.943	0.887	
Left humerus						
TA	0.030	0.438		0.426	0.130	
J	0.051	0.218		0.561	0.309	
I_x/I_y	0.610	0.316		0.913	0.405	
I_{max}/I_{min}	0.131	0.991		0.645	0.736	
Bilateral asymmetry						
% BA of TA	0.613	0.956		0.003	**0.030**	CI > PostH
% BA of J	0.977	0.463		0.028	**0.030**	CI > PostH

PreH = Cape coast pre-herding; PostH = Cape coast post-herding; CI = Central interior
Bold results indicate significant differences between groups ($\alpha < 0.05$).

Humeral and femoral biomechanical properties were not different between pre- and post-herding groups on the Cape coast. Upper limb biomechanical properties were similar between post-herding Cape coast and central interior groups; however, bilateral asymmetry values were lower among Cape coast females. Lower limb

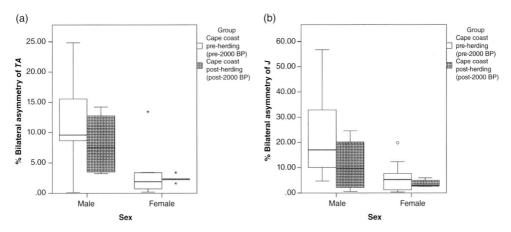

Figure 6.5 Temporal comparisons of humerus mid-distal box plots by sex and region for: (a) percentage bilateral asymmetry of total subperiosteal area (percentage BA of *TA*); and (b) percentage bilateral asymmetry of polar second moment of area (percentage BA of *J*).

strength and robusticity were decreased among post-herding Cape coast individuals relative to both coastal pre-herding and post-herding central interior individuals, particularly among females. There were no differences in loading directionality. These results are unlike those previously obtained for the Nile Valley (Stock *et al.*, 2011) or Neolithic Italy (Marchi, 2008) groups.

The similar biomechanical properties of Cape coast pre- and post-herding groups suggest that physical activities associated with pre-herding hunter-gatherer behaviors persisted after the incorporation of herding in coastal lifeways. Previous studies of coastal LSA biomechanical properties indicated a sex-based division of labor related to hunting and gathering activities: Male upper limb strength, robusticity, and bilateral asymmetry were associated with spear or bow and arrow use, while female upper limb bilateral symmetry and anteroposterior loading were associated with gathering and digging stick use (Stock and Pfeiffer, 2004). These biomechanical characteristics are evident among coastal pre- and post-herding males and females, suggesting that hunting and gathering activities continued to influence upper limb morphologies after the introduction of herding.

Comparisons between post-herding Cape coast and central interior upper limb biomechanical properties suggest broad similarities in the activities undertaken in both regions after the introduction of herding. Upper limb strength and robusticity are similar in post-herding central interior and post-herding Cape coast groups. As the upper limb biomechanical properties observed among Cape coast males and females have been associated with hunting and gathering activities, these subsistence activities were also likely important in the central interior. This is consistent with a mixed herding and hunter-gatherer economy inferred by archaeological and stable isotopic data (Humphreys, 1972; Maggs, 1971; Masemula, 2015). Humeral bilateral asymmetry in post-herding Cape coast females relative to central interior females suggests greater digging stick use on the Cape coast, as this activity requires very

Table 6.5 Femur cross-sectional geometric property summary statistics.

Property	n	Cape coast pre-herding (pre-2000 BP) Mean	S.D.	n	Cape coast post-herding (post-2000 BP) Mean	S.D.	n	Central interior post-herding Mean	S.D.
					Males				
TA	23	935.7	62.2	6	939.4	57.1	3	947.7	57.4
J	27	434.2	74.9	6	415.3	31.2	3	425.2	27.0
I_x/I_y	26	1.68	0.20	6	1.68	0.31	3	1.38	0.21
I_{max}/I_{min}	26	1.74	0.19	5	1.64	0.20	3	1.51	0.18
					Females				
TA	19	923.7	103.4	5	799.2	33.3	12	887.1	80.9
J	19	369.3	76.6	5	307.1	44.4	12	346.7	62.4
I_x/I_y	20	1.45	0.20	5	1.31	0.39	12	1.34	0.30
I_{max}/I_{min}	20	1.53	0.22	5	1.39	0.34	12	1.42	0.28

Table 6.6 Femur cross-sectional geometric property one-way ANOVA results.

Property	Males Levene p	ANOVA p	Post hoc	Females Levene p	ANOVA p	Post hoc
	Cape coast temporal comparisons (comparing pre-herding to post-herding)					
TA	0.925	0.922		0.031	**0.001**	Pre > Post
J	0.087	0.553		0.262	0.099	
I_x/I_y	0.125	0.983		0.231	0.261	
I_{max}/I_{min}	0.841	0.286		0.290	0.272	
	Post-herding comparisons (post-herding Cape coast to central interior)					
TA	0.850	0.843		0.280	**0.035**	CI > PostH
J	0.511	0.656		0.483	0.221	
I_x/I_y	0.443	0.180		0.889	0.867	
I_{max}/I_{min}	0.677	0.390		0.646	0.884	

Bold results indicate significant differences between groups ($\alpha < 0.05$).

symmetrical upper arm use (Stock and Pfeiffer, 2004). The use of other tools in the central interior, such as grindstones (Humphreys, 1972; Maggs, 1971), may have resulted in less bilaterally symmetrical loading patterns among females in this region.

Previous studies attributed high LSA femoral strength properties to intensive terrestrial hunting and gathering and high mobility across complex terrain

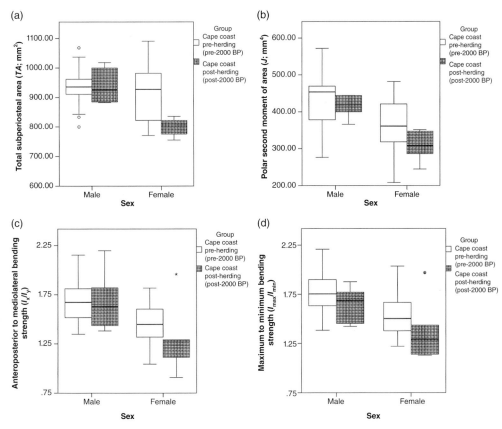

Figure 6.6 Temporal comparisons of femur midshaft box plots by sex and region for: (a) total subperiosteal area (TA); (b) polar second moment of area (J); (c) anteroposterior to mediolateral bending strength (I_x/I_y); and (d) maximum to minimum bending strength (I_{max}/I_{min}). TA is standardized to body mass, while J is standardized to body mass and bone length.

(Shaw and Stock, 2013; Stock and Pfeiffer, 2001, 2004). There is some variation in the femoral biomechanical properties of pre- and post-herding males and females, as indicators of diaphyseal strength values are lower among coastal post-herding females relative to both coastal pre-herding and central interior females. Terrestrial mobility may have been lower among post-herding females on the Cape coast as these populations became more sedentary due to reliance on a predictable, stable source of nutrition. However, the overall similarities in femoral biomechanical properties suggest that high terrestrial mobility may be a characteristic of all LSA groups. This pattern may be attributable to intensive hunter-gatherers and those from mixed economies. That said, high femoral strength and robusticity indicators have been identified in herding populations from other archaeological contexts (Marchi, 2008). It is therefore possible that higher central interior values may be related to herding activities rather than hunting and gathering. As small numbers of individuals were included in this study and there are no significant differences in

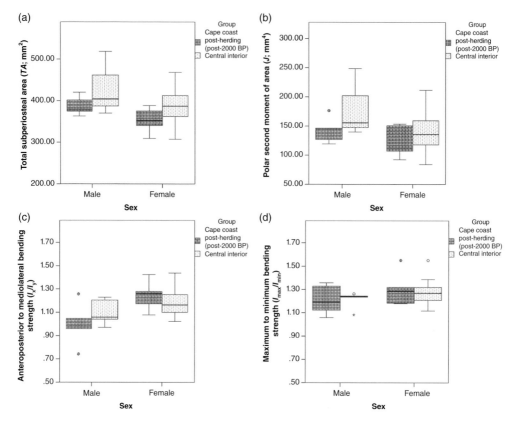

Figure 6.7 Post-herding comparisons of left humerus mid-distal box plots by sex and region for: (a) total subperiosteal area (*TA*); (b) polar second moment of area (*J*); (c) anteroposterior to mediolateral bending strength (I_x/I_y); and (d) maximum to minimum bending strength (I_{max}/I_{min}). *TA* is standardized to body mass, while *J* is standardized to body mass and bone length.

lower limb robusticity, sampling errors may have affected the representativeness and accuracy of the aforementioned comparisons. Consequently, it is difficult to determine whether stronger femora were observed among pre-herding Cape coast groups and central interior individuals due to intensive hunting and gathering among coastal pre-herding groups, herding in the central interior, or high mobility due to hunting and gathering in both contexts.

Resilience theory and the adaptive cycle may enrich interpretations of biomechanical and other archaeological data regarding the transformative changes that occurred in southern Africa with the introduction of herding (Davies and Moore, 2016; Hoover and Hudson, 2016; Redman, 2005; Rick, 2011; Thompson and Turck, 2009). In the context of southern African herding, the growth and conservation phases would represent the long-flourishing hunter-gatherer lifeways in this region, particularly on the densely populated Cape coast. These phases would encompass the spread of LSA cultural elements and the development of regional entities. In terms of

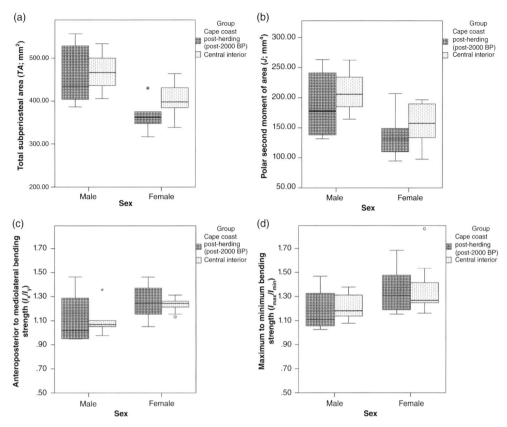

Figure 6.8 Post-herding comparisons of right humerus mid-distal box plots by sex and region for: (a) total subperiosteal area (*TA*); (b) polar second moment of area (*J*); (c) anteroposterior to mediolateral bending strength (I_x/I_y); and (d) maximum to minimum bending strength (I_{max}/I_{min}). *TA* is standardized to body mass, while *J* is standardized to body mass and bone length.

skeletal biology and morphological indicators of behavior, the maintenance of high terrestrial mobility, relatively low-intensity manual labor, and a sex-based division of labor until 2000 BP characterizes these phases.

The initial introduction of herding from eastern Africa would mark the beginning of the release phase of the adaptive cycle. The arrival of herding and associated practices are archaeologically marked by the presence of domesticate remains in zooarchaeological assemblages as well as ceramic vessels. This phase likely did not impact physical activity patterns as groups maintained predominantly hunter-gatherer practices, while herding was gradually incorporated. Skeletal remains associated with the release phase are best represented by Cape coast individuals, though there remain insufficient numbers of long bones to evaluate biomechanical variation immediately before and after the introduction of herding. However, this interpretation of a gradual incorporation of domesticated livestock into southern African lifeways is supported by isotopic evidence among Cape coast individuals. Sealy

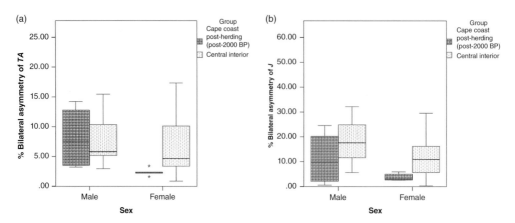

Figure 6.9 Post-herding comparisons of humerus mid-distal box plots by sex and region for: (a) percentage bilateral asymmetry of total subperiosteal area (% BA of *TA*); and (b) percentage bilateral asymmetry of polar second moment of area (% BA of *J*).

(2010) noted that stable isotope values potentially associated with the consumption of domesticates are not evident for the first 1000 years after the introduction of herding. Consequently, while changes in habitual physical behaviors during the release phase are difficult to establish, alternate lines of evidence indicate a temporal gap between the arrival of livestock and changes in skeletal biology associated with the use of domesticated animals.

Finally, the reorganization phase of the adaptive cycle encompasses the consolidation of herding practices and strategies alongside hunting and gathering in southernmost Africa. Localities associated with post-1000 BP expressions of herding practices demonstrate regional variation and diversification (Mitchell, 2002; Sadr, 2013). In terms of skeletal biology, this diversification is evident in isotopic evidence suggesting differential use of domesticated livestock on the Cape coast (Sealy, 2010) and in the central interior (Masemula, 2015), as well as dental phenetic evidence indicating some genetic differentiation of groups from these regions (Irish *et al.*, 2014). However, similarities in the biomechanical properties of post-herding groups from the Cape coast and the central interior suggest that physical activities related to subsistence practices were not strongly influenced by these broader social and demographic transformations.

LSA groups appear to have absorbed the disturbance associated with the introduction of herding by integrating herding and hunting and gathering subsistence practices into habitual activity patterns. Isotopic and zooarchaeological data suggest that products from domesticated livestock were incorporated into southern African LSA diets, albeit in differing proportions across the Cape region. However, biomechanical data suggest that hunting and gathering remained a key contributor to habitual physical activity patterns. This is likely due to the demands of herding lifeways that are similar to those experienced by hunter-gatherers.

Herd maintenance requires a high degree of activity, as herders must circulate animals across the landscape to prevent overgrazing and ensure sufficient freshwater

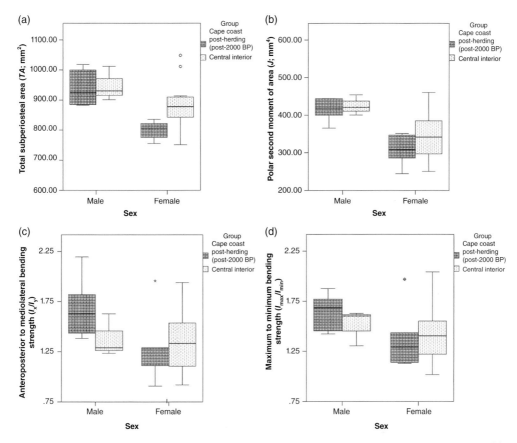

Figure 6.10 Post-herding comparisons of femur midshaft box plots by sex and region for: (a) total subperiosteal area (*TA*); (b) polar second moment of area (*J*); (c) anteroposterior to mediolateral bending strength (I_x/I_y); and (d) maximum to minimum bending strength (I_{max}/I_{min}). *TA* is standardized to body mass, while *J* is standardized to body mass and bone length.

access. Additionally, ethnographically documented herders in southern Africa frequently hunt and consume wild game alongside domesticates to meet nutritional landmarks (Barnard, 1992; Kent, 1990, 1992, 1993, 1996; Russell and Lander, 2015; Sadr, 1998, 2003). This is archaeologically evidenced by the high proportions of wild faunal remains in zooarchaeological assemblages from herding contexts (Kinahan, 1991; Klein, 1978; Klein and Cruz-Uribe, 1989; Sadr, 1998; Schweitzer, 1979; Smith *et al.*, 1991). The introduction of herding in southernmost Africa along the coast and in the central interior was not associated with the cultivation of domesticated plants. As such, these groups must have gathered plant resources to maintain nutritional sufficiency while also undertaking the activities required to maintain healthy livestock.

Additionally, ethnographically documented herders in southern Africa do not regularly consume livestock, for cultural and spiritual reasons (Barnard, 1992;

Russell and Lander, 2015). In ethnographically documented herding communities from southern Africa and farther afield, there are taboos and a degree of spiritual significance associated with consuming domesticated livestock (Barnard, 1992; Russell and Lander, 2015). For example, some groups may maintain larger herds yet rarely consume these animals. Instead, the animals are adopted for trade, social exchange, or other human–animal relationships outside of subsistence (Russell and Lander, 2015). These social and cultural behaviors may result in similar consumption patterns to hunter-gatherer groups despite differences in livestock availability and human–animal relationships. Consequently, the need to consume plant resources coupled with the infrequent consumption of domesticated livestock for non-subsistence reasons may have resulted in similar physical activity patterns before and after the introduction of herding.

The introduction of herding may have instigated the release phase of the cycle among southern African LSA populations by initiating a period of rapid change as populations adopted elements of the incoming herder package. The reorganization of lifeways after this transition resulted in new cultural elements and practices associated with herding integrating with preexisting hunter-gatherer behaviors. This transformation and reorganization process may have affected physical behavioral patterns as groups developed new subsistence strategies that were likely maintained subsequent to this reorganization during the growth and conservation phases of the adaptive cycle.

There are, however, limitations to this study. The small number of post-herding individuals available from the Cape coast and the central interior may have reduced the statistical power of all comparisons. The small number of individuals in these two groups relative to those pre-dating the introduction of herding on the Cape coast may have impacted the applicability of these biomechanical comparisons. Additionally, while femoral biomechanical properties are indicative of terrestrial mobility, tibia biomechanical properties, which were not addressed in the present study, may reflect mobility patterns and lower limb activities more accurately (Davies and Stock, 2014; Stock, 2006). Consequently, future analyses of southern African LSA biomechanical properties should try to incorporate larger sample sizes and a greater number of skeletal elements.

Additionally, the inherent overlap in activities undertaken by hunter-gatherer and herding groups may obscure any differentiation between groups engaging in these two strategies. Studies identifying significant changes in biomechanical properties across subsistence transitions often compare hunter-gatherer and agricultural groups. As herding still represents a relatively mobile strategy, it is possible that the differences between hunter-gatherers and herders are too nuanced to be detected using CSGP biomechanical analyses. Incorporating a greater diversity of hunter-gatherers and herders from other contexts could further enrich analyses of how physical behaviors reorganize after the transition to herding. Consequently, future work may also examine a broader range of hunter-gatherer and herding groups to clarify how well individuals engaging in these strategies may be differentiated using biomechanical analyses.

6.7   Conclusion

The introduction of herding represents a major economic transition that impacted LSA southern Africans. This transition may be interpreted using resilience theory, with groups post-dating the introduction of herding reorganizing subsistence behaviors and physical activity patterns to incorporate elements of herding and hunter-gatherer strategies. This chapter sought to examine whether biomechanical properties, which may be used to infer habitual physical activities, varied between pre- and post-herding groups on the Cape coast, and among post-herding groups from the Cape coast and the central interior.

Overall, there is little variation in the upper and lower limb biomechanical properties of pre- and post-herding southern African LSA groups: Physical behaviors and biomechanical properties associated with hunting and gathering remained static on the Cape coast across this transition. Additionally, similar biomechanical properties are observed in post-herding groups from the Cape coast and central interior environments. Coastal post-herding femora have lower strength values than either pre-herding or central interior individuals. Biomechanical similarities are evident despite isotopic and zooarchaeological evidence suggesting changes in southern African subsistence practices and resource consumption patterns after the introduction of herding. Collectively, these results suggest that hunting and gathering remained central to subsistence economies after lifeways reorganized due to the introduction of herding.

The maintenance of habitual physical behaviors associated with hunter-gatherer activities alongside evidence for dietary changes with the introduction of herding, such as increased terrestrial protein intake, may be interpreted within a resilience theory framework. Change occurs within the lifeways of many biological systems, though continuity through resilience following disturbance remains an important component to understanding the complexities of these interactions (Hoover and Hudson, 2016). In the southern African LSA context, dietary changes may have occurred as populations incorporated domesticated livestock yet maintained hunter gatherer activities to supplement these diets with wild game and plant resources. Future work that may clarify the impact of the introduction of herding on human skeletal biology may include further analyses of stress patterns and demographic changes across this transition. In summary, the results of this study indicate the utility of resilience theory in interpreting instances of change when assessing habitual physical behavior in prehistory.

References

Auerbach, B. M. and Ruff, C. B. (2004). Human body mass estimation: A comparison of "morpho-metric" and "mechanical" methods. *American Journal of Physical Anthropology*, 125, 331–342.

Auerbach, B. M. and Ruff, C. B. (2006). Limb bone bilateral asymmetry: Variability and commonality among modern humans. *Journal of Human Evolution*, 50, 203–18.

Barbieri, C., Vicente, M., Rocha, J., *et al.* (2013). Ancient substructure in early mtDNA lineages of Southern Africa. *American Journal of Human Genetics*, 92, 285–292.

Barbieri, C., Guldemann, T., Neumann, C., *et al.* (2014). Unravelling the complex maternal history of southern African Khoisan populations. *American Journal of Physical Anthropology*, 153, 435–440.

Barham, L. and Mitchell, P. (2008). *The First Africans: African Archaeology from the Earliest Toolmakers to Most Recent Foragers*. Cambridge: Cambridge University Press.

Barnard, A. (1992). *Hunters and Herders of Southern Africa*. Cambridge: Cambridge University Press.

Binneman, J. (1994a). Note on a digging stick from Augussie Shelter, eastern Cape. *South African Field Archaeology*, 3, 112–113.

Binneman, J. (1994b). A unique stone tipped arrowhead from Adam's Kranz Cave, Eastern Cape. *South African Field Archaeology*, 3, 58–60.

Black, W. (2014). *Dental Morphology and Variation across Holocene Khoesan People of Southern Africa*. PhD dissertation, University of Cape Town.

Black, W., Ackermann, R. R., and Sealy, J. (2009). Variation in Holocene KhoeSan dentition. *American Journal of Physical Anthropology*, 138, 92–93.

Bridges, P. S. (1989). Changes in activities with the shift to agriculture in the southeastern United States. *Current Anthropology*, 30, 385.

Bridges, P. S., Blitz, J. H., and Solano, M. C. (2000). Changes in long bone diaphyseal strength with horticultural intensification in west-central Illinois. *American Journal of Physical Anthropology*, 112, 217–238.

Cameron, M. E. and Pfeiffer, S. (2014). Long bone cross-sectional geometric properties of Later Stone Age foragers and herder-foragers. *South African Journal of Science*, 110, 1–11.

Cowin, S. C. (2001). *Bone Biomechanics Handbook*. 2nd edn. Boca Raton, FL: CRC Press.

Dahl, G. and Hjort, A. (1976). *Having Herds: Pastoral Herd Growth and Household Economy*. Stockholm: Department of Social Anthropology, University of Stockholm.

Davies, M. I. J. and Moore, H. L. (2016). Landscape, time and cultural resilience: A brief history of agriculture in Pokot and Marakwet, Kenya. *Journal of East African Studies*, 10, 67–87.

Davies, T. G. and Stock, J. T. (2014). Human variation in the periosteal geometry of the lower limb: Signatures of behavior among human Holocene populations. In K. J. Carlson and D. Marchi, eds., *Reconstructing Mobility: Environmental, Behavioral, and Morphological Determinants*. New York, NY: Springer. pp. 67–90.

Davies, T. G., Shaw, C. N., and Stock, J. T. (2012). A test of a new method and software for the rapid estimation of cross-sectional geometric properties of long bone diaphyses from 3D laser surface scans. *Archaeological and Anthropological Sciences*, 4, 77–290.

Deacon, H. J. (1976). *Where Hunters Gathered: A Study of Holocene Stone Age People in the Eastern Cape*. Claremont: South African Archaeological Society Monographs.

Deacon, H. J. and Deacon, J. (1999). *Human Beginnings in South Africa: Uncovering the Secrets of the Stone Age*. Walnut Creek, CA: Altamira Press.

Deacon, J. (1984). *The Later Stone Age of Southernmost Africa*. Oxford: British Archaeological Reports.

Doyle, L. E. (2015). *Population Stress, Growth Deficit, and Degenerative Joint Disease in Foragers from South Africa's Later Stone Age*. PhD dissertation, University of Toronto.

Folke, C. (2006). Resilience: The emergence of a perspective for social–ecological systems analyses. *Global Environmental Change*, 16, 253–267.

Ginter, J. K. (2011). Using a bioarchaeological approach to explore subsistence transitions in the Eastern Cape, South Africa during the mid- to late Holocene. In R. Pinhasi and J. T. Stock, eds., *Human Bioarchaeology of the Transition to Agriculture*. Chichester: Wiley-Blackwell. pp. 107–149.

Hall, S. (1990). *Hunter-Gatherer-Fishers of the Fish River Basin: A Contribution to the Holocene Prehistory of the Eastern Cape*. DPhil thesis, University of Stellenbosch.

Hegmon, M., Peeples, M. A., Kinzig, A. P., *et al.* (2008). Social transformation and its human costs in the prehispanic US southwest. *American Anthropologist*, 110, 313–324.

Holt, B. M. (2003). Mobility in Upper Paleolithic and Mesolithic Europe: Evidence from the lower limb. *American Journal of Physical Anthropology*, **122**, 200–215.

Hoover, K. C. and Hudson, M. J. (2016). Resilience in prehistoric persistent hunter-gatherers in northwest Kyushu, Japan as assessed by population health and archaeological evidence. *Quaternary International*, **405**, 22–33.

Huiskes, R. (1982). On the modeling of long bones in structural analyses. *Journal of Biomechanics*, **15**, 65–69.

Humphreys, A. J. B. (1972). *The Type R Settlements in the Context of the Later Prehistory and Early History of the Riet River Valley*. MA thesis, University of Cape Town.

Humphreys, A. J. B. and Maggs, T. M. O. (1970). Further graves and cultural material from the banks of the Riet River. *South African Archaeological Bulletin*, **25**, 116–126.

Irish, J. D., Black, W., Sealy, J., and Ackermann, R. R. (2014). Questions of Khoesan continuity: Dental affinities among the indigenous Holocene peoples of South Africa. *American Journal of Physical Anthropology*, **155**, 33–44.

Jones, H., Priest, J., Hayes, W., Tichenor, C., and Nagel, D. (1977). Humeral hypertrophy in response to exercise. *Journal of Bone and Joint Surgery*, **59**, 204–212.

Kent, S. (1990). Comments on Solway and Lee 1990. *Current Anthropology*, **31**, 131–132.

Kent, S. (1992). The current forager controversy: Real versus ideal views of hunter-gatherers. *Man*, **27**, 45–70.

Kent, S. (1993). Sharing in an egalitarian Kalahari community. *Man*, **28**, 479–514.

Kent, S. (1996). *Cultural Diversity among Twentieth-Century Foragers: An African Perspective*. Cambridge: Cambridge University Press.

Kinahan, J. (1991). *Pastoral Nomads of the Central Namib Desert: The People History Forgot*. Windhoek: Namibia Archaeological Trust.

Kinahan, J. H. A. (2000). *Cattle for Beads: The Archaeology of Historical Contact and Trade on the Namib Coast*. Windhoek: Namibia Archaeological Trust.

Klein, R. G. (1978). A preliminary report on the larger mammals from Boomplaas Stone Age cave site, Cango Valley, Oudtshoorn District, South Africa. *South African Archaeological Bulletin*, **33**, 66–75.

Klein, R. G. (1986). The prehistory of Stone Age herders in the Cape Province of South Africa. *South African Archaeological Society Goodwin Series*, **5**, 5–12.

Klein, R. G. and Cruz-Uribe, K. (1989). Faunal evidence for prehistoric herder-forager activities at Kasteelberg, western Cape Province, South Africa. *South African Archaeological Bulletin*, **44**, 82–97.

Kurki, H. K., Ginter, J. K., Stock, J. T., and Pfeiffer, S. (2010). Body size estimation of small-bodied humans: Applicability of current methods. *American Journal of Physical Anthropology*, **141**, 169–180.

Lanyon, L. E., Goodship, A., Pye, C., and MacFie, J. (1982). Mechanically adaptive bone remodeling. *Journal of Biomechanics*, **15**, 141–154.

Lee-Thorp, J. A. and Ecker, M. (2015). Holocene environmental change at Wonderwerk Cave, South Africa: Insights from stable light isotopes in ostrich eggshell. *African Archaeological Review*, **32**, 793–811.

Lovejoy, C. O., Burstein, A. H., and Heiple, K. G. (1976). The biomechanical analysis of bone strength: A method and its application to platycnemia. *American Journal of Physical Anthropology*, **44**, 489–506.

Macholdt, E., Lede, V., Barbieri, C., *et al.* (2014). Tracing pastoralist migrations to southern Africa with lactase persistence alleles. *Current Biology*, **24**, 875–879.

Macholdt, E., Slatkin, M., Pakendorf, B., and Stoneking, M. (2015). Brief communication: New insights into the history of the C-14010 lactase persistence variant in eastern and southern Africa. *American Journal of Physical Anthropology*, **156**, 661–664.

Macintosh, A. A., Pinhasi, R., and Stock, J. T. (2014a). Lower limb skeletal biomechanics track long-term decline in mobility across ~6150 years of agriculture in Central Europe. *Journal of Archaeological Science*, **52**, 376–390.

Macintosh, A. A., Pinhasi, R., and Stock, J. T. (2014b). Divergence in male and female manipulative behaviors with the intensification of metallurgy in Central Europe. *PLoS One*, **9**, e112116.

Maggs, T. M. O. (1971). Pastoral settlements on the Riet River. *South African Archaeological Bulletin*, **26**, 37–63.

Manhire, A. (1993). A report on the excavations at Faraoskop rock shelter in the Graafwater district of the south-western Cape. *South African Field Archaeology*, **2**, 3–23.

Marchi, D. (2008). Relationships between lower limb cross-sectional geometry and mobility: The case of a Neolithic sample from Italy. *American Journal of Physical Anthropology*, **137**, 188–200.

Marchi, D., Sparacello, V. S., Holt, B. M., and Formicola, V. (2006). Biomechanical approach to the reconstruction of activity patterns in Neolithic western Liguria, Italy. *American Journal of Physical Anthropology*, **131**, 447–455.

Marshall, L. (1976). *The !Kung of Nyae Nyae*. Cambridge: Harvard University Press.

Masemula, N. (2015). *An Investigation of Skeletons from Type-R Settlements along the Riet and Orange Rivers, South Africa, Using Stable Isotope Analysis*. MSc thesis, University of Cape Town.

McHenry, H. M. (1992). Body size and proportions in early hominids. *American Journal of Physical Anthropology*, **87**, 407–431.

Mitchell, P. (2002). *The Archaeology of Southern Africa*. Cambridge: Cambridge University Press.

Morris, A. G. (1984). *An Osteological Analysis of the Proto-historic Populations of the Northern Cape and Western Orange Free State, South Africa*. PhD dissertation, University of Cape Town.

Morris, A. G. (1992). *A Master Catalogue: Holocene Human Skeletons from South Africa*. Johannesburg: Witwatersrand University Press.

Pfeiffer, S. (2013). Population dynamics in the Southern African Holocene: Human burials from the West Coast. In A. M. Jerardino, A. Malan, and D. R. Braun, eds., *Archaeology of the West Coast of South Africa*. Cambridge: Archaeopress. pp. 143–154.

Pfeiffer, S. and Sealy, J. (2006). Body size among Holocene foragers of the Cape ecozone, southern Africa. *American Journal of Physical Anthropology*, **129**, 1–11.

Pfeiffer, S., Doyle, L. E., Kurki, H. K., *et al.* (2014). Discernment of mortality risk associated with childbirth in archaeologically derived forager skeletons. *International Journal of Paleopathology*, **7**, 15–24.

Redman, C. L. (2005). Resilience theory in archaeology. *American Anthropologist*, **107**, 70–77.

Redman, C. L. and Kinzig, A. P. (2003). Resilience of past landscapes: Resilience theory, society, and the *Longue Dureé*. *Ecology and Society*, **7**, 14.

Rick, T. C. (2011). Weathering the storm: Coastal subsistence and ecological resilience on Late Holocene Santa Rosa Island, California. *Quaternary International*, **239**, 135–146.

Ruff, C. B. (2000). Body size, body shape, and long bone strength in modern humans. *Journal of Human Evolution*, **38**, 269–290.

Ruff, C. B. (2008). Biomechanical analyses of archaeological human skeletons. In M. A. Katzenberg and S. R. Saunders, eds., *Biological Anthropology of the Human Skeleton*. 2nd edn. New York, NY: Wiley-Liss, Inc. pp. 183–206.

Ruff, C. B. and Hayes, W. C. (1983a). Cross-sectional geometry of Pecos Pueblo femora and tibiae: A biomechanical investigation: I. Method and general patterns of variation. *American Journal of Physical Anthropology*, **60**, 359–382.

Ruff, C. B. and Hayes, W. C. (1983b). Cross-sectional geometry of Pecos Pueblo femora and tibiae: A biomechanical investigation: II. Sex, age, and side differences. *American Journal of Physical Anthropology*, **60**, 383–400.

Ruff, C. B., Larsen, C. S., and Hayes, W. (1984). Structural changes in the femur with the transition to agriculture on the Georgia coast. *American Journal of Physical Anthropology*, **64**, 125–136.

Ruff, C. B., Trinkaus, E., Walker, A., and Larsen, C. S. (1993). Postcranial robusticity in *Homo*. I : Temporal trends and mechanical interpretation. *American Journal of Physical Anthropology*, **91**, 21–53.

Ruff, C. B., Holt, B., and Trinkaus, E. (2006). Who's afraid of the big bad Wolff? "Wolff's law" and bone functional adaptation. *American Journal of Physical Anthropology*, **129**, 484–498.

Russell, T. and Lander, F. (2015). "What is consumed is wasted": From foraging to herding in the southern African Later Stone Age. *Azania: Archaeological Research in Africa*, 50, 267–317.

Sadr, K. (1998). The first herders at the Cape of Good Hope. *African Archaeological Review*, 15, 101–132.

Sadr, K. (2003). The Neolithic of southern Africa. *Journal of African History*, 44, 195–209.

Sadr, K. (2013). The archaeology of herding in southernmost Africa. In P. Mitchell and P. J. Lane, eds., *The Oxford Handbook of African Archaeology*. Oxford: Oxford University Press. pp. 645–656.

Sadr, K. (2015). Livestock first reached southern Africa in two separate events. *PLoS One*, 10, e0134215.

Sadr, K. and Plug, I. (2001). Faunal remains in the transition from hunting to herding in southeastern Botswana. *South African Archaeological Bulletin*, 56, 76–82.

Sadr, K., Smith, A., Plug, I., Orton, J., and Mutti, B. (2003). Herders and foragers on Kasteelberg: Interim report of excavations 1992–2002. *South African Archaeological Bulletin*, 58, 27–32.

Sampson, C. G. (1974). *The Stone Age Archaeology of Southern Africa*. New York, NY: Academic Press.

Sampson, C. G. (1986). Model of a prehistoric herder–hunter contact zone: A first approximation. *South African Archaeological Society Goodwin Series*, 5, 50–56.

Sampson, C. G. (2010). Chronology and dynamics of Later Stone Age herders in the upper Seacow River valley, South Africa. *Journal of Arid Environments*, 74, 842–848.

Schlebusch, C. M., Skoglund, P., Sjödin, P., *et al.* (2012). Genomic variation in seven Khoe-San groups reveals adaptation and complex African history. *Science*, 338, 374–379.

Schweitzer, F. R. (1979). Excavations at Die Kelders, Cape Province, South Africa: The Holocene deposits. *Annals of the South African Museum*, 78, 101–233.

Sealy, J. C. (2010). Isotopic evidence for the antiquity of cattle-based pastoralism in southernmost Africa. *Journal of African Archaeology*, 8, 65–81.

Sealy, J. C. and Pfeiffer, S. (2000). Diet, body size, and landscape use among Holocene people in the Southern Cape, South Africa. *Current Anthropology*, 4, 642–655.

Shaw, C. N. and Stock, J. T. (2009a). Intensity, repetitiveness, and directionality of habitual adolescent mobility patterns influence the tibial diaphysis morphology of athletes. *American Journal of Physical Anthropology*, 140, 149–159.

Shaw, C. N. and Stock, J. T. (2009b). Habitual throwing and swimming correspond with upper limb diaphyseal strength and shape in modern human athletes. *American Journal of Physical Anthropology*, 140, 160–172.

Shaw, C. N. and Stock, J. T. (2013). Extreme mobility in the Late Pleistocene? Comparing limb biomechanics among fossil *Homo*, varsity athletes and Holocene foragers. *Journal of Human Evolution*, 64, 242–249.

Smith, A. B. (1984). Environmental limitations on prehistoric pastoralism in Africa. *African Archaeological Review*, 2, 99–111.

Smith, A. B. (1992). *Pastoralism in Africa: Origins and Development Ecology*. Johannesburg: Witwatersrand University Press.

Smith, A. B. (1998). Keeping people on the periphery : The ideology of social hierarchies between hunters and herders. *Journal of Anthropological Archaeology*, 17, 201–215.

Smith, A. B. (2009). Pastoralism in the Western Cape Province, South Africa: A retrospective review. *Journal of African Archaeology*, 7, 239–252.

Smith, A. B., Sadr, K., Gribble, J., and Yates, R. (1991). Excavations in the south-western Cape, South Africa, and the archaeological identity of prehistoric hunter-gatherers within the last 2000 years. *South African Archaeological Bulletin*, 46, 71–91.

Smith, P., Horwitz, L. K., and Kaplan, E. (1992). Skeletal evidence for population change in the late Holocene of the south-western Cape: A radiological study. *South African Archaeological Bulletin*, 47, 82–88.

Stock, J. T. (2006). Hunter-gatherer postcranial robusticity relative to patterns of mobility, climatic adaptation, and selection for tissue economy. *American Journal of Physical Anthropology*, 131, 194–204.

Stock, J. T. and Pfeiffer, S. (2001). Linking structural variability in long bone diaphyses to habitual behaviors: Foragers from the southern African Later Stone Age and the Andaman Islands. *American Journal of Physical Anthropology*, 115, 337–348.

Stock, J. T. and Pfeiffer, S. (2004). Long bone robusticity and subsistence behavior among Later Stone Age foragers of the forest and fynbos biomes of South Africa. *Journal of Archaeological Science*, 31, 999–1013.

Stock, J. T. and Shaw, C. N. (2007). Which measures of diaphyseal robusticity are robust? A comparison of external methods of quantifying the strength of long bone diaphyses to cross-sectional geometric properties. *American Journal of Physical Anthropology*, 134, 412–423.

Stock, J. T., O'Neill, M. C., Ruff, C. B., *et al.* (2011). Body size, skeletal biomechanics, mobility and habitual activity from the late Palaeolithic to the mid-Dynastic Nile Valley. In R. Pinhasi and J. T. Stock, eds., *Human Bioarchaeology of the Transition to Agriculture*. Chichester: Wiley-Blackwell. pp. 347–367.

Stynder, D. D. (2006). *A Quantitative Assessment of Variation in Holocene Khoesan Crania from South Africa's Western, South-western, Southern and South-eastern coasts and Coastal Forelands*. PhD dissertation, University of Cape Town.

Stynder, D. D. (2009). Craniometric evidence for South African Later Stone Age herders and hunter-gatherers being a single biological population. *Journal of Archaeological Science*, 36, 798–806.

Stynder, D. D., Ackermann, R. R., and Sealy, J. (2007). Craniofacial variation and population continuity during the South African Holocene. *American Journal of Physical Anthropology*, 134, 489–500.

Thompson, V. D. and Turck, J. A. (2009). Adaptive cycles of coastal hunter-gatherers. *American Antiquity*, 74, 255–278.

7 Biocultural Adaptation and Resilience in the Hunter-Gatherers of Lagoa Santa, Central-Eastern Brazil

Pedro Da-Gloria and Lucas Bueno

7.1 Introduction

The region of Lagoa Santa, Central-Eastern Brazil (Figure 7.1) is crucial to understanding the ancient occupation of the New World (Neves *et al.*, 2013). The preservation of a large number of human skeletons in the region is unique in the context of the Early Holocene. Doran (2007) compiled a database of North American skeletons, dividing the data by chronological periods. The period between 9999 and 7500 BP[1] in North America is associated with 44 human skeletons, while in Lagoa Santa, a region of only 356 km^2 (Patrus, 1998), 155 human skeletons dated between 9000 and 7000 BP were found at 16 archaeological sites (Da-Gloria, 2012).

Exceptional archaeological and paleontological preservation at Lagoa Santa has allowed the material to be studied for more than 180 years (Da-Gloria *et al.*, 2017). This research is primarily affiliated with craniometrics, which were associated with descriptive, racial paradigms (Lacerda and Peixoto, 1876) but now involve biodistance studies aimed at reconstructing population history and the first migrations to South America (Hubbe *et al.*, 2010, 2014, 2015; Neves and Hubbe, 2005; Neves and Pucciarelli, 1991; Neves *et al.*, 1999, 2004, 2005, 2007, 2013). Until very recently, few studies approached health and lifestyle in Lagoa Santa from the perspective of biocultural adaptation (Da-Gloria and Larsen, 2014, 2017; Da-Gloria, 2012; Neves and Kipnis, 2004).

This chapter uses bioarchaeological data to better understand biocultural adaptation and population resilience within the Lagoa Santa karst formation. To achieve this goal, the chapter provides a diachronic perspective of regional occupation and uses bioarchaeological evidence of health and behavior to explore evidence for intensive, persistent site usage between 10 500 and 7000 BP in the Lagoa Santa formation. Next, a regional perspective is provided to help explain a diminished archaeological signal, including the disappearance of burials during the Middle Holocene. The goal here is to explore the possibility that Lagoa Santa was a resilient landscape maintained through persistent occupation.

---

[1] All the radiocarbon dates in this chapter are non-calibrated and provided in years before present (yr. BP), establishing the present as CE 1950.

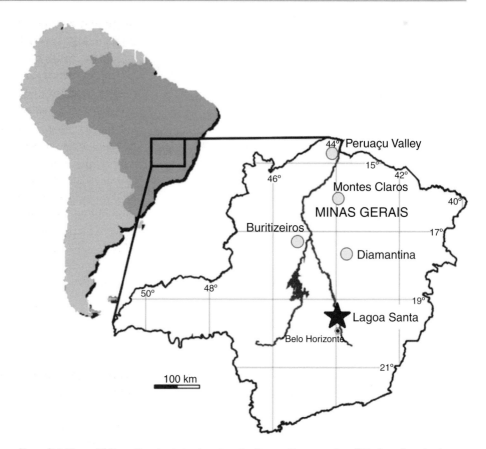

Figure 7.1 Map of Minas Gerais state showing the Lagoa Santa region (filled star) and other archaeological regions (light gray circles) cited in the text. Lagoa Santa karst region: Lapa das Boleiras, Lapa do Santo, Sumidouro, and Coqueirinho; sites around (60 km) Lagoa Santa karst: Santana do Riacho and Lapa Grande de Taquaraçu; Diamantina region: Lapa do Caboclo and Lapa do Peixe Gordo sites; Peruaçu Valley region: Lapa do Boquete and Lapa do Dragão sites; Pirapora region: Buritizeiros site. Montalvânia region is around 100 km northwest of Peruaçu Valley.

7.2   Archaeology and Bioarchaeology of Persistent Places in Hunter-Gatherers

The concept of persistent place in archaeology was developed to understand recurrent occupations of space. Persistent places are defined as "places that are repeatedly used during long-term occupations of regions" (Schlanger, 1992: 97). These places have three main characteristics: unique qualities for a recurrent occupation; features that favor repeated occupations; and a long process of repeated human occupations. Evidence for population recurrence is found at several hunter-gatherer sites across the New World. Some examples include large-scale shell middens in the Santa Barbara Channel Islands, California (Gamble, 2017) and Southern Brazil (Gaspar *et al.*, 2008), as well as the earth mounds of the southeastern United States

(Thompson, 2010). These places are interpreted as important sites for the production of social memory and symbolic meaning through spatial occupation and usage. Burials are often found in persistent places, and these features reveal the appropriation of territory by hunter-gatherer populations. As seen in Australian Aboriginal populations, burial location is interpreted as a persistent place, with constant re-occupation of the area through many generations (Littleton and Allen, 2007).

Another perspective comes from the concept of special-place disposal, practiced in "[h]unter-gatherers with restricted territories and intensive economic systems based upon predictable and abundant resources which allow long-term occupation of particular localities, [special-place disposal areas] are often associated with more complex mortuary practices when compared to highly mobile foragers" (Walthall, 1999: 4). Special-place disposal posits that secondary rituals are associated with delayed burial due to annual cycles of aggregation at and dispersion from persistent locations. That is, depending on the moment of death, populations delay burial until a return to these persistent places is possible, leading to strategies of body manipulation. As Walthall (1999: 23) writes, "the use of secondary burial and special-place cemeteries may also be linked to other factors such as reduction in territory size and seasonal, and predictable, use of particular landscape zones." Although statistical tests using a cross-cultural sample did not support a clear relationship between mobility and secondary burial (Schroeder, 2001), burial locations and rituals are intimately related to spatial dynamics and territory use by populations (Charles and Buikstra, 2002).

Another important way to understand persistence of hunter-gatherers is derived from resilience theory (Redman, 2005; Redman and Kinzig, 2003). Spatial-temporal changes in hunter-gatherers follow an adaptive cycle, which includes growth, conservation, release, and reorganization. In this sense, it is possible to understand changes in the function of persistent places by understanding how these locations were appropriated into socioecological and cultural systems over time. It is worth noting the complexity involved in abandonment behavior, especially when considered within the context of territorial strategies and the possibility of incorporating permanence and change in the same process (Cameron and Tomka, 1993; Nelson, 2000). This chapter approaches the archaeological evidence of hunter-gatherer occupation at Lagoa Santa using the concepts of persistent place, resilience, territorial strategies, and biocultural adaptation.

7.3   Diachronic Perspectives

7.3.1   Initial Occupations

Initial colonization processes of eastern South America included different routes of dispersion and displacement dynamics. Researchers propose that this region was occupied by a stable and diverse population of hunter-gatherers between 13 000 and 7000 BP (Bueno, 2011; Bueno et al., 2013; Dias, 2004; Dias and Bueno, 2013). Evidence for this occupation is derived from the tropical forests and savannahs present in northern, central, and northeastern Brazil between 13 000 and 11 000 BP (Dias and Bueno, 2013). Based on chronology, geographical distribution, and cultural material from archaeological sites, the authors (i.e., Dias and Bueno, 2013) propose that river systems served as access routes to the interior of the continent. The Itaparica cultures are associated with the Brazilian savannahs (*cerrado*) during this time period. Itaparica hunter-gatherers maintained a broad-based subsistence economy linked to vast terrestrial mobility, where regional lithic styles and rock art acted as boundary markers (Bueno *et al.*, 2013).

Based on lithic analysis of the older period of occupation in sites of central-northern Minas Gerais (e.g., Grande Abrigo de Santana do Riacho[2] in southern Serra do Espinhaço and Lapa do Caboclo and Lapa do Peixe Gordo sites [Diamantina] in northern Serra do Espinhaço mountain chains; Figure 7.1), it is possible to propose a connection between the first occupation of Lagoa Santa to groups related to the Itaparica tradition. The lithic assemblage from the Early Holocene level of Santana do Riacho (southern Serra do Espinhaço) exhibits similarities with the Lagoa Santa karst industry, considering that the assemblages are coeval and separated by only 60 km. In addition, artifacts derived from the Late Pleistocene levels of Santana do Riacho were similar to Itaparica assemblages. These similarities include retouched scrapers made of quartzite and limaces (Prous, 1991b). In turn, the deeper layers of Lapa do Santo (Lagoa Santa karst) revealed quartzite flakes related to the production of artifacts that were similar to retouched scrapers found at Santana do Riacho and at archaeological sites of Diamantina region (northern Serra do Espinhaço), dated to the Early Holocene. Based on these similarities, a connection between the first occupations of Lagoa Santa, Serra do Espinhaço sites, and groups related to the Itaparica tradition is proposed. This connection between the Itaparica culture and initial occupants of Lagoa Santa may reflect exchange systems or exploratory displacement related to an early stage of the colonization process in this region. Unfortunately, the data are still too scarce to comprehensively test either hypothesis (Bueno, 2013a).

In Lagoa Santa, the first evidence of human occupation is associated with a single skeleton found at Lapa Vermelha IV site in the 1970s. The French–Brazilian mission led by Annette Laming-Emperaire exhumed a disarticulated female skeleton in a stratigraphic level dated between 10 220 and 12 960 BP (Laming-Emperaire, 1979). This individual was later named "Luzia" and is one of the oldest human skeletons in the Americas. The specimen was dated to 9330 ± 60 BP using accelerator mass spectrometry (AMS) methods (Neves *et al.*, 1999).[3] Feathers *et al.* (2010), using optically stimulated luminescence (OSL) dating techniques, found consistency with

---

[2] We call this site Santana do Riacho throughout this text.

[3] These dates are reported by the laboratory BETA Analytic Inc. as performed on less than good-quality collagen or unidentifiable "bone organics." As reported to us (Ron Hartfield, personal communication, 2015), "there is a likelihood that humic acids (if present) may bias the age. This bias usually produces younger dates as the humic acids tend to be washed down through the sedimentary profile from the overlying sediments." Furthermore, "It is true that the age could also be too old ... but as it takes a significant amount of very old carbon by weight to change the age by much, this is a less likely scenario." This is the reason why these dates are considered minimum ages.

the indirect dating of Luzia. In another dating attempt, Fontugne (2013) found a charcoal fragment close to the skull, resulting in an indirect date of 10 030 ± 60 BP. Studies of biological affinities connected Luzia to the population of Early Holocene skeletons found in the region (Hubbe *et al.*, 2015; Neves and Hubbe, 2005; Neves *et al.*, 1999), suggesting continuity between these initial populations and those associated with the Early Holocene inhabitants of Lagoa Santa.

7.3.2   Occupation of the Lagoa Santa Karst (10 500 to 9000 BP)

The archaeological excavations in the Lagoa Santa karst before 1950 were carried out by Cassio Lanari, Jorge Padberg-Drenkpol, José Bastos de Ávila, Harold Walter, and Josaphat Penna, among others (Da-Gloria *et al.*, 2017). All of these excavations represent work done prior to the professionalization of archaeology in Brazil. In the 1950s, with the American–Brazilian mission at Lagoa Santa led by Wesley Hurt, the first radiometric dates were obtained at the complex of sites of Cerca Grande (9028 ± 120 BP and 9720 ± 128 BP), formally demonstrating the antiquity of occupation in the region (Hurt, 1964; Hurt and Blasi, 1969). In the 1970s, the French–Brazilian archaeological mission coordinated by Annete Lamming-Emperaire recovered Late Pleistocene human skeletal remains at Lapa Vermelha IV (see above) (Laming-Emperaire, 1979). In 2000, under the direction of Walter Neves, Early Holocene rock shelters and open-air sites were systematically excavated and examined by an interdisciplinary team, resulting in the recovery of plant remains, fauna, and lithics, in addition to human skeletons. The oldest dates for the systematic occupation of the Lagoa Santa region were derived from the rock shelter of Lapa do Santo (10 490 ± 50 BP) and Lapa das Boleiras (9990 ± 60 BP), and the open-air site of Coqueirinho (10 460 ± 60 BP) (Araujo *et al.*, 2012). These findings date the occupation of Lagoa Santa to the Pleistocene/Holocene boundary.

Almost every site excavated in this region was associated with a rock shelter. The lithic assemblage is mainly composed of quartz crystal flakes, with a low frequency of flint, concentrated in the deeper layers. Most of the lithics are small, measuring less than 4 cm, and the tools are informal, with only one or two well-defined small edges. Although scarce, some artifacts show evidence of re-sharpening and reuse. There is also some evidence of hafting, even in the small and unifacially flaked tools. Bifacial projectile points made of flint and limestone are associated with these assemblages (Araujo and Pugliese, 2010; Moreno de Souza, 2014) and polished hand-axes made of hematite and igneous rocks at Cerca Grande, Lapa das Boleiras, and Lapa do Santo sites were also found (Bueno, 2012; Bueno and Isnardis, 2016; Moreno de Souza, 2014).

The interaction between sheltered and open-air sites is very important for understanding the occupation at Lagoa Santa. Despite the low number of sites, Bueno (2012) showed that the rock shelter lithic assemblages are characterized by the presence of cores, complete flakes, and natural fragments, while the open-air sites show assemblages with more artifacts and fragmented flakes. In addition, the density of rock shelter lithic assemblages is several times larger than the material from open-air sites. These differences suggest that rock shelters in the region were places of long-term occupation, where all steps of lithic reduction are found, while the open-air sites represent specialized locales.

The use of bone as a raw material was also found in archaeological assemblages from Lagoa Santa. At the Lapa do Santo site, for example, 198 bone instruments were discovered. These instruments fall into the category of spatula and perforator, and were made predominantly of deer bones (Santos, 2011). At the Lapa das Boleiras and Lapa do Santo sites, several bone hooks were also found in the Early Holocene stratum (Kipnis et al., 2010b; Santos, 2011), indicating some reliance on fishing activities. A single marine gastropod shell (Olivella sp.) was found in a prehistoric context at the Cerca Grande site in the Lagoa Santa region, indicating an exchange route with coastal populations (Hurt and Blasi, 1969).

The zooarchaeological material found at Lapa das Boleiras and Lapa do Santo includes deer (Mazama sp.), armadillos (e.g., Dasypus novemcinctus), pacas (Cuniculus paca), peccaries (Tayassu sp.), cavies (Cavia sp.), tapitis (Silvylagos brasiliensis), reptiles (e.g., Ameiva ameiva), birds, and fishes, among others (Kipnis et al., 2010a; Perez, 2009). This material points to a diet based on small- to medium-sized animals (Mingatos and Okumura, 2016), which suggests that a regionally specific socio-ecological system was established since the first systematic occupations of Central Brazil.

Preliminary analyses of the botanical record at Lapa do Santo recovered 40 morphological types of macro-remains (Silva, personal communication). At Lapa das Boleiras, high frequencies of palm seeds (Syagrus flexuosa), jatobá (Hymenaea sp.), pequi (Caryocar brasiliense), araticum (Annona classiflora), and xixá (Sterculia chicha) fruits were found in Early Holocene strata. The fact that these fruits have different periods of fructification and many were recovered from the same archaeological level suggest year-round occupation of the rock shelters (Nakamura et al., 2010).

Physical, chemical, and micro-morphological analyses of the sediment of Lapa das Boleiras demonstrate the importance of an anthropic component in the formation of the archaeological deposit – gray sediments at the site that were, for example, accumulated by vegetal burning (Araujo et al., 2008). The southern part of the site accumulated 2.10 m of archaeological deposit. In the Early Holocene, the sediment accumulation rate was 8.81 cm per 100 calibrated years (Araujo et al., 2010). The same gray sediment was found at Lapa do Santo, which shows an archaeological deposit of 4 m for the Early Holocene component. Villagran et al. (2017) recovered fragments of termite mounds in the sediment, which were used to continuously burn fires, achieving temperatures of 500–800°C. An anthracological study showed the presence of taxa derived from denser woods at Lapa do Santo, which suggests the selection of wood with high calorific value (Melo and Magalhães, 2015). In short, these data show the intensive and persistent occupation of rock shelters in this region during the Early Holocene.

Neves et al. (2012) dated a rock engraving covered by sediment at the base of the Lapa do Santo site, obtaining a minimum age of 9370 ± 40 BP. This engravement is a threadlike anthropomorphic figure with three digits on the hands, a head in "C" form, and an erect phallus. Similar figures are seen at the Lapa das Caieiras and Lapa do Ballet sites of Lagoa Santa karst, as well as an engraved rock from a site in the Rio Grande do Norte state, northeast Brazil. This finding suggests that stylistic themes were also widespread in the Brazilian territory and date to the Early Holocene.

7.3.3   Persistent Occupation at Lagoa Santa (9000 to 7000 BP)

The lithic assemblages associated with the Lagoa Santa region in the Early Holocene were predominantly formed from quartz crystal flakes. The chronological analysis of lithic technology at Lapa do Santo and Lapa das Boleiras showed that flint was more frequent before 9000 BP, along with a wider range of raw materials and a relatively higher frequency of resharpened flakes (Araujo and Pugliese, 2010; Pugliese, 2007). Flint is an exotic material in the Lagoa Santa karst, being found about 60 km away, possibly in the São Francisco River. These findings seem to imply changes toward low mobility and less regional exchange over the Early Holocene at Lagoa Santa. Although there are no faunal or botanical studies investigating temporal distinctions within the Early Holocene period, the analyses of these remains show that the whole Early Holocene can be characterized by a similar subsistence strategy based on medium- to small-sized game and on local wild fruits and seeds (see above).

After the establishment of systematic occupation at Lagoa Santa, evidence of the first burials in the rock shelters are reported (Araujo *et al.*, 2012). The oldest date for human skeletons is associated with Burial 27 from Lapa do Santo (9245 ± 40 BP).[4] The next oldest dates for these burials are from Lapa Mortuária de Confins (8810 ± 50 BP), the Harold Walter collection[5] (8800 ± 40 BP), and Lapa do Santo (8840 ± 60 BP). The dead were buried in the rock shelters for almost 2000 years, with the most recent date from Lapa da Amoreira (7070 ± 40 BP).[6] More than 40 skeletons were exhumed and dated to the Early Holocene period at the Lapa do Santo site. At present, more than 200 skeletons have been excavated from the period following 9000 BP (Da-Gloria *et al.*, 2016; Mello e Alvim, 1977).

The burials in Lagoa Santa illustrate diverse mortuary treatment with intense manipulation of the body and no associated funerary goods. The first evidence of these mortuary rituals came with the excavation of a secondary burial at Lapa das Boleiras (Burial III). Funerary treatment included postmortem breakage of long bones

---

[4] There is also a date of 9680 ± 70 of a human proximal humerus from Lapa do Braga. This bone fragment was exhumed in the nineteenth century by Peter Lund, and there is no archaeological context. If this skeleton was buried in the rock shelter, it would indicate some sporadic use of the rock shelters for burials before 9000 BP.

[5] The Harold Walter collection was excavated in the 1930s to 1950s, including seven archaeological sites: Abrigo de Limeira, Abrigo de Mãe Rosa, Abrigo de Samambaia, Abrigo do Eucalipto, Abrigo do Galinheiro, Abrigo do Sumidouro, and Lagoa Funda (Walter, 1958).

[6] There are dates of 5990 ± 40 from Lapa do Santo and 6660 ± 50 from the Harold Walter collection. They were obtained from small amounts of degraded collagen or humic acids (see footnote 3), which are likely subject to younger carbon source contamination. They are not reliable dates to infer the youngest skeletons of the sample.

and the parallel alignment of these elements in addition to abundant application of red ochre (Neves *et al.*, 2002). At Lapa do Santo, diverse funerary patterns were observed among 26 exhumed burials, including cases of decapitation, anatomical selection, removal of teeth, cut marks, intentional fragmentation of bones, burials with multiple individuals, ochre use, and cremation (Strauss *et al.*, 2015, 2016). Revisiting the Harold Walter collection, 23 cut bone ends showed a similar pattern to that found at some burials at Lapa do Santo, adding more evidence of ritual manipulation of the dead at Lagoa Santa (Da-Gloria *et al.*, 2011).

The Lagoa Santa mortuary record between 9000 and 7000 BP can be interpreted in multiple ways. Strauss *et al.* (2016) classified six mortuary patterns at Lagoa Santa, with Mortuary Patterns Two and Three being the most prominently featured. Mortuary Pattern Two is interpreted as the result of funerary rites, including visual displays of manipulated burials such as the case of a decapitated skeleton with its hands on its face. Mortuary Pattern Three consists of "shallow, circular pits completely filled with mostly disarticulated bones of single individuals of various ages and sexes." These were interpreted as delayed burials, in which the individual died away from the site and the body was returned at a later date. In addition to the symbolic perspective emphasized by Strauss *et al.* (2016), it is important to emphasize territoriality. The presence of secondary burials in the rock shelters of Lagoa Santa might indicate a well-established occupation of the territory and a cyclical return to bury the dead and partake in rituals. A strontium isotopic analysis (^{87}Sr/^{86}Sr) of 23 dental samples from Lapa do Santo shows similar geographical origin for the Lagoa Santa population in this period (Strauss *et al.*, 2015). Overall, the Lagoa Santa formation shows a shift in occupational strategy from a more mobile population with exotically sourced raw materials to a sedentary population that intensively occupied the land. The presence of highly ritualized burials, large numbers of occupied sites, thick archaeological deposits, large amounts of archaeological material, and local strontium isotope values indicate intensive, persistent occupation of the Lagoa Santa space by a local population.

7.4   Health, Lifestyle, and Persistence at Lagoa Santa (9000 to 7000 BP)

The data presented in this chapter are based on a comprehensive study focusing on health and biocultural adaptation at Lagoa Santa (Da-Gloria, 2012). In reality, health is a holistic concept that cannot be operationalized by comparing lesion prevalence (Reitsema and McIlvaine, 2014; Temple and Goodman, 2014). On the other hand, the goal of this chapter is to understand whether these indicators of health and lifestyle are consistent with a persistent occupation, focusing on the integration of skeletal markers with the archaeological record, rather than comparing prevalence of disease to understand "consequences" of transition.

Skeletal indicators of activity, diet, disease, and developmental stress were collected using the protocols of the Western Hemisphere database (Steckel *et al.*, 2002). This chapter primarily reports aggregated data, without age and sex divisions. The aggregated data consist of skeletons of all ages and both sexes, except the dental

Table 7.1 Prevalence (percentage) and sample size (*N*) of Lagoa Santa sample compared to Western Hemisphere prehistoric database for each variable.

Variables	Lagoa Santa		Agriculturalists		Hunter-gatherers	
	N	%	*N*	%	*N*	%
Dental caries	829	7.36	15 142	13.74	8777	4.69
Periapical abscesses	1167	8.78	32 346	4.95	19 522	3.51
Systemic infection	26	3.85	3557	6.69	2585	1.16
Cribra orbitalia	41	7.32	2118	21.2	888	9.91
Porotic hyperostosis	51	0	2367	17.57	799	14.39

data, which only include the permanent dentition. Additionally, femoral measurements were collected from adults (closed epiphyses). This sample is derived from 16 archaeological sites within the Lagoa Santa karst, with an estimated number of 155 individuals dated between 9000 to 7000 BP. The sites have varied numbers of skeletons, ranging from four skeletons at Lapa Mortuária to 44 skeletons at the rock shelters of Cerca Grande. Sample sizes for each dataset are listed in Table 7.1.

Dental caries is defined as "a disease process characterized by the focal demineralization of dental hard tissues by organic acids produced by bacterial fermentation of dietary carbohydrates, especially sugars and (to a lesser extent) starches" (Larsen, 2015: 67). Even though dental caries has a multifactorial etiology (see Lukacs, 2008), there is a large literature correlating dental caries with carbohydrate consumption (Hillson, 2005; Larsen, 2015). Periapical abscesses are inflammations in the periapical region of the root apex due to the death of tooth pulp. Periapical abscesses may be caused by carious lesions, tooth wear, or fractured teeth (Hillson, 2005). Carious lesions were recorded as present or absent on all permanent teeth, while periapical abscesses were recorded using each alveolus of the permanent dentition.

Femoral midshaft diaphyseal shape (FMS) is calculated as the ratio of anteroposterior (D_{ap}) and mediolateral (D_{ml}) diameter of the femoral midshaft (FMS = D_{ap}/D_{ml}) (Wescott, 2006). These measurements were collected using sliding calipers. A lower value (< 1) indicates a more circular shape of the femoral section, while a higher value (> 1) points to an oval shape with anteroposterior elongation. The latter scenario results from bone strain caused by muscles that insert on the posterior region of the femoral diaphysis, such as *biceps femoris*. Elevated index scores are associated with greater mobility of the lower limb. This index was chosen because it is shape-dependent, and therefore independent of body mass.

Osteoperiostitis is defined as "the osseous manifestation of periosteal inflammatory responses resulting from bacterial infection or traumatic injury and other pathological processes" (Steckel *et al.*, 2006). Ortner (2003) described these lesions as the appearance of woven bone on the periosteal surface, which is characterized typically by porosity and bone deposition in irregular orientation and distribution. Only evidence for systemic infection is reported in this chapter. Systemic infection is defined as more than one bone with evidence of osteoperiostitis. All long bones were inspected for osteoperiostitis, but only skeletons with at least three long bones with more than 75 percent of bone preservation were recorded. Skull, ribs, vertebrae, and pelvic bones were also surveyed for osteoperiostitis.

Two osteological skeletal indicators of stress were also collected at Lagoa Santa: porotic hyperostosis and reduced stature. Porotic hyperostosis refers to the expansion of the marrow cavity through the periosteal surface of the orbit (called cribra orbitalia) and on the cranial vault (porotic hyperostosis), generating porosity of the bony outer table. The etiology of these conditions is linked to iron deprivation during childhood (Stuart-Macadam, 1985, 1987) and may be caused by low dietary intake or intestinal absorption problems related to infection and parasitism (Holland and O'Brien, 1997). Alternatively, Walker *et al.* (2009) suggested that the lack of vitamin B12 may be the cause of these lesions, while histological studies showed that other conditions – such as scurvy, rickets, and infection – also produce similar lesions (Schultz, 2001; Wapler *et al.*, 2004). Therefore, in the absence of histological or radiological analysis, these osteological markers are interpreted as non-specific indicators of nutritional stress.

Stature is the result of a complex combination of genetic and environmental factors. Reduced stature is found under circumstances of malnutrition or chronic infection. Reduced stature results from life history trade-offs: The expenditure of energy to survive stress episodes is redirected from growth, resulting in diminished adult body size following the survival of stress events (Kuzawa, 2005; Temple, 2008; Worthman and Kuzara, 2005). Boldsen (1995) and Jantz and Jantz (1999) showed significant increases in stature in the last century in European and North American populations, respectively, indicating a strong relationship between nutritional status and bone growth. Femoral length is a reasonable proxy for stature in genetically continuous populations, assuming continuity in intralimb indices (Holliday and Ruff, 1997). Maximum femoral length is used as a proxy for stature as this measurement was recorded in the Western Hemisphere database.

This chapter evaluates the prevalence and distribution of skeletal indicators of activity, diet, disease, and developmental stress with a comparative database. Comparisons were made with the Global History of Health database, which includes 36 prehistoric agricultural and hunter-gatherer populations comprising 6733 skeletons excavated throughout the Americas (Steckel *et al.*, 2002). The division of the database into two categories (farmers and hunter-gatherers) is a simplification of the diversity of subsistence strategies (Smith, 2001). This division is, however, justified to facilitate the analytical interpretation of the data and in light of the extensive literature showing the large impact of the transition from a hunter-gather to agriculturalist lifeway. The hunter-gatherer sample includes populations that lacked plant domesticates, while the agricultural sample includes several degrees of mixed subsistence. Comparisons between the Lagoa Santa sample with those in the Western Hemisphere database were performed using box plots and the relative location of Lagoa Santa on these plots. The goal is to reconstruct biocultural adaptation at Lagoa Santa within the context of hunter-gatherer and agricultural populations. It is expected that the Lagoa Santa sample will better resemble those groups who intensively and persistently occupied the same landscapes.

7.5 Results

Prevalence of skeletal indicators of developmental stress, diet, and disease are listed in Tables 7.1 and 7.2. Periapical abscess prevalence at Lagoa Santa is reported in Table 7.1 as a mean of two values (maximum periapical abscess = 10.88 percent; minimum periapical abscess = 6.68 percent). A high prevalence of carious lesions and periapical abscesses compared to other hunter-gatherer samples in the Americas is found in the Lagoa Santa group (Table 7.1; Figures 7.2 and 7.3). The population with the highest prevalence of caries and periapical abscesses in the Western Hemisphere database is from the Real Alto site, Ecuador (OSCH-12), which is an early Formative site dated between 5400 and 3500 BP (Ubelaker and Newson 2002). Although the inhabitants of that site were characterized as hunter-gatherers, recent studies report evidence for domestication of maize (*Zea mays*), manioc (*Manihot esculenta*), arrowroot (*Maranta arundinacea*), and llerén (*Calathea* sp.) (Chandler-Ezell et al., 2006; Pearsall et al., 2004), which might explain the higher prevalence of caries at this location. Taking this information into account, oral health at Lagoa Santa appears to be a pronounced outlier among hunter-gatherer populations in the Western Hemisphere database. Instead, frequencies of carious lesions and periapical abscesses are comparable to agricultural populations.

The FMS calculation from 27 individuals at Lagoa Santa resulted in a lower value compared to other hunter-gatherer populations in the Americas (Table 7.2; Figure 7.4). These results indicate relatively low mobility at Lagoa Santa, particularly when considered within the spectrum of prehistoric hunter-gatherer societies in the Americas. Some authors question the efficacy of the external measurements to indicate differences in mobility (Wescott, 2006), while others show these indices are reasonable approximations (Stock and Shaw, 2007). The Western Hemisphere database used here corroborates the latter interpretation, since the data are able to discriminate FMS of hunter-gatherers and agriculturalists, at least at the level of central tendencies (Table 7.2; Figure 7.4). The only hunter-gatherer population that shows lower FMS values than Lagoa Santa is the coastal southern California

Table 7.2 Femoral shape indices, standard deviation, and sample size of Lagoa Santa bones compared to the Western Hemisphere prehistoric database.

Samples	Femoral circumference			Maximum femoral length		
	N	FMS[a]	S.D	N	Length (mm)	S.D.
Lagoa Santa	27	1.10	0.08	12	404	23.72
Agriculturalists	1124	1.09	0.11	1165	420	29.71
Hunter-gatherers	323	1.15	0.11	320	422	29.95

[a] FMS = femoral midshaft diaphyseal shape (FMS)

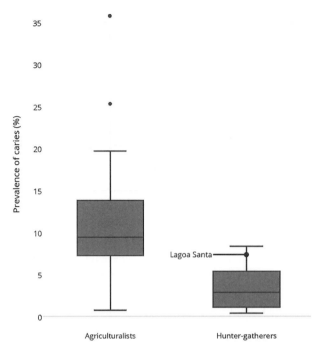

Figure 7.2 Distribution of caries prevalence in Western Hemisphere prehistoric samples. The figure shows the Lagoa Santa position among the hunter-gatherer distribution.

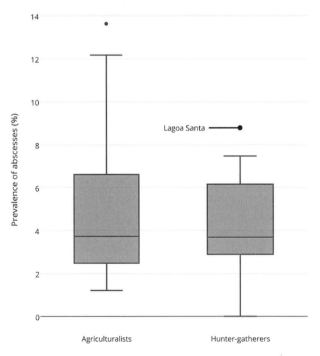

Figure 7.3 Distribution of periapical abscess prevalence in Western Hemisphere prehistoric samples. The figure shows the Lagoa Santa position among the hunter-gatherer distribution.

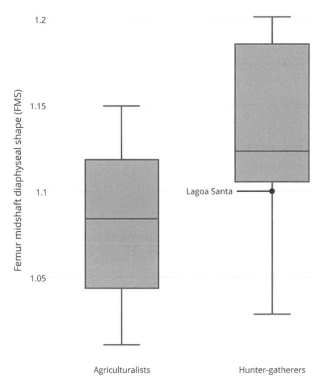

Figure 7.4 Distribution of FMS values in the Western Hemisphere prehistoric samples. The figure shows the Lagoa Santa position among the hunter-gatherer distribution.

hunter-gatherers (FMS = 1.03). This sample is composed of human skeletons from 18 sites with dates ranging from 7500 to 204 BP. These populations are described in the database as living in small- to medium-sized villages in a semi-desert environment with elevations from 0 to 100 m above sea level. Other coastal populations from California in the database, described as mobile instead of living in villages, show higher FMS values than Lagoa Santa. Importantly, these populations are associated with the Chumash culture, a population of hunter-gatherers who persistently occupied the landscapes of this region (Gamble, 2017).

The prevalence of systemic infection at Lagoa Santa is high compared to other hunter-gatherer samples in the Americas (Table 7.1; Figure 7.5). The only hunter-gatherer population that showed a higher prevalence of systemic infection than Lagoa Santa is the sample from Windover, Florida, which is dated between 8120 and 6990 BP (Dickel, 2002). This Florida cemetery includes the largest concentration of North American skeletons dated to the Early Archaic period (Wentz, 2006).

The prevalence of cribra orbitalia is unremarkable at Lagoa Santa when compared with other hunter-gatherer samples (Figure 7.6). Cribra orbitalia prevalence at Lagoa Santa is higher than samples from southern California, Ecuador, and part of the Georgia Bight pre-agricultural group. On the other hand, Lagoa Santa had a lower prevalence of cribra orbitalia than part of the pre-agricultural sample from the

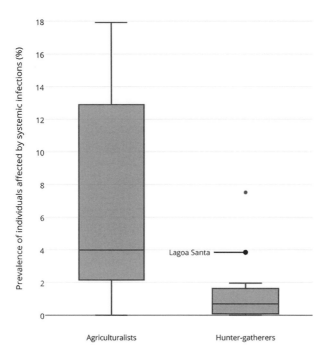

Figure 7.5 Distribution of systemic infection prevalence in Western Hemisphere prehistoric samples. The figure shows the Lagoa Santa position among the hunter-gatherer distribution.

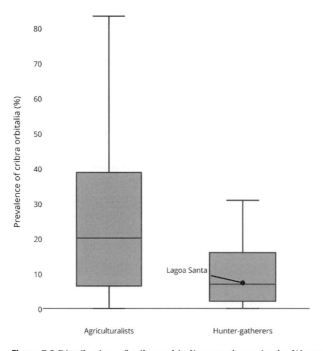

Figure 7.6 Distribution of cribra orbitalia prevalence in the Western Hemisphere prehistoric samples. The figure shows the Lagoa Santa position among the hunter-gatherer distribution.

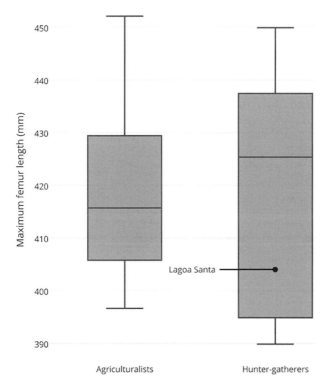

Figure 7.7 Distribution of maximum femoral length in the Western Hemisphere prehistoric samples. The Lagoa Santa sample is shown among the hunter-gatherer groups.

Georgia Bight, coastal Chile, and southern California. Cribra orbitalia frequency at Lagoa Santa was similar to samples from Real Alto, Ecuador, a population associated with a horticultural socioecological system.

The inhabitants of Lagoa Santa have shortened femora compared to other hunter-gatherers in the Western Hemisphere database (Figure 7.7). South American samples, in general, have the lowest values among hunter-gatherers (Ecuador and coastal Chile), below the average of Lagoa Santa. Populations from coastal California and coastal South Carolina show higher femoral length averages than Lagoa Santa.

7.6   Skeletal Indicators of Activity, Disease, and Stress: Bioarchaeological Evidence for Persistent Occupation (9000 to 7000 BP)

Bioarchaeological indicators of diet, developmental stress, and disease in Lagoa Santa suggest intensive carbohydrate consumption, low mobility, and high frequencies of chronic stress. Regarding subsistence, a high prevalence of dental caries reflects elevated consumption of carbohydrates, especially simple sugars (Larsen, 2015). Carious lesions also contribute to the development of abscesses, which are also observed at Lagoa Santa at a relatively high frequency. The archaeobotanical evidence suggests one source of these carbohydrates could have been the consumption of local fruits such as araticum, jatobá, pequi, palm nuts, and xixá. Furthermore, at the site Lapa Grande de Taquaraçu, a few kilometers from the Lagoa Santa karst, several types of starch granules were found on quartz flakes, suggesting the importance of plant resources for these hunter-gatherers (Flores, 2015). Indeed, the early inhabitants of Lagoa Santa relied on a combination of non-domesticated fruits and tubers (Da-Gloria and Larsen, 2014). Although the skeletal evidence is restricted to the period between 9000 and 7000 BP, the archaeological record of deeper strata also indicate the presence of similar technology, reinforcing the inference of persistence in this subsistence strategy across the region.

External dimensions of the femur indicate relatively low mobility in the Lagoa Santa inhabitants. Geographical terrain also needs to be considered in this interpretation (Ruff, 1999). The Lagoa Santa region has a terrain that suggests an intermediate load level for its inhabitants, consisting predominantly of undulating relief with some limestone cliffs. This landscape does not indicate that terrain was a major contributor to the relatively rounded shape of the Lagoa Santa femora. In addition, the comparative sample of hunter-gatherers from the Western Hemisphere database is composed of mostly coastal populations. Even compared to these populations living in relatively flat terrain, the shape of the Lagoa Santa femur indicated less mechanical demand. This diaphyseal morphology is not compatible with a population of mobile hunter-gatherers. Additional evidence of a less mobile foraging strategy comes from the settlement pattern of the region. There is evidence that the inhabitants of Lagoa Santa continuously occupied the rock shelters during the Early Holocene, as shown by thick sediment deposits at the local archaeological sites (see above). Furthermore, ethnographic studies of hunter-gatherers show that higher proportions of plant consumption are associated with lower mobility (Kelly, 2013: 95). Taken together, evidence associated with oral health and diet as well as mobility are consistent with a population that consumed high levels of plant foods and had limited terrestrial mobility, two traits consistent with persistent occupation.

Reduced mobility is also an important element for understanding the osteological indicators of disease and stress during growth and development. Aggregation and persistent occupation of the same site are important factors to explain disease experience through the challenges it creates for waste disposal, pathogen transmission, and biocultural stress (Larsen, 2015). The high prevalence of systemic infections at Lagoa Santa indicates a more aggregated and dense occupation compared to other hunter-gatherer populations. The presence of infections also contributes to deficiencies in absorption of iron and vitamins, which may help explain the presence of cribra orbitalia at Lagoa Santa. The small size of the femur at Lagoa Santa might also be connected to a high prevalence of infectious disease and nutritional stress during development. These results again suggest a persistent occupation of the landscape – one in which long-term aggregation produced increased infectious disease and conditions leading to developmental stress.

No remarkable trend in porotic hyperostosis was found – the frequency of this condition at Lagoa Santa was similar to other hunter-gatherer populations. This may reflect the complex environmental interactions associated with porotic hyperostosis.

For example, porotic hyperostosis was once thought to reflect agricultural lifestyles, specifically iron-deficiency anemia associated with poor bioavailability of this protein in domesticated plants such as maize (El-Najjar *et al.*, 1976). However, later studies found elevated porotic hyperostosis in agricultural populations from the American Southwest and hunter-fisher-gatherers from coastal southern California (Walker, 1985, 1986). In addition, the condition, once thought to reflect iron-deficiency anemia, is now associated with scurvy, rickets, chronic infection, iron-deficiency anemia, and quite possibly megaloblastic anemia (Schultz, 2001; Walker *et al.*, 2009; Wapler *et al.*, 2004). As a result, porotic hyperostosis may provide evidence for population aggregation, dietary insufficiency, or some combination of the two. Owing to this complex environmental etiology and apparent similarity in distribution between the occupants of Lagoa Santa and many hunter-gatherer populations (Figure 7.6), porotic hyperostosis is unlikely to provide evidence for persistent site occupation.

The results of the analysis of osteological markers of health and lifestyle suggest a stable and persistent occupation of the Lagoa Santa karst between 9000 and 7000 BP, based on elements that approximate indicators of activity, diet, stress, and disease with agriculturalists from the Americas. This biological profile indicates that the Lagoa Santa population lived in a more circumscribed territory, with low individual mobility, high reliance on plants, and presence of nutritional, infectious, and social stressors. Also, these characteristics may represent continuation of an existing lifestyle initiated in the beginning of the systematic occupation in the region at 10 500 BP. In fact, the archaeological record at Lagoa Santa shows clear continuity throughout the Early Holocene in terms of technology and subsistence. Furthermore, cranial morphology of Lagoa Santa inhabitants and neighboring areas dated to between 11 000 to 7000 BP showed biological continuity throughout the Late Pleistocene and Early Holocene (Hubbe *et al.*, 2015; Neves and Hubbe, 2005). On the other hand, the beginning of the practice of burying individuals in rock shelters and changes in the lithic raw material sources, occurring after 9000 BP, indicate a shift toward established territories. In summary, the evidence compiled here clearly indicates the presence of a persistent occupation of hunter-gatherers in the region, with an intensification period between 9000 and 7000 BP. Results of this study further suggest that persistent occupations of landscapes among hunter-gatherers may be identified using bioarchaeological indicators of aggregation, sedentism, and diet. These indicators, once primarily used to define "consequences" of transition (Temple and Goodman, 2014), may be incorporated to further clarify the human experience with local landscapes.

7.7   Local Abandonment and Resilience: What Happened after 7000 BP?

After 3500 years of continuous occupation, evidence of human presence in the rock shelters significantly diminished around 7000 BP at sites such as Lapa do Santo and Lapa das Boleiras. Few occupation periods were detected for the Middle Holocene: 3830 ± 60 BP for Lapa das Boleiras and between 4290 ± 90 and 3810 ± 50 BP for

Lapa do Santo (Araujo *et al.*, 2010, 2012). The comparison of lithic and bone technology, and of the zooarchaeological record at Lapa do Santo, showed that Middle Holocene occupation shares similar material culture with the Early Holocene occupation. Ash accumulation in the Middle Holocene stratum is also similar to the older period. Despite diminished site occupation in the region following 7000 BP, cultural continuity between the Early and Middle Holocene occupants of these sites suggests that the Lagoa Santa culture persisted for more than 8000 years (Araujo *et al.*, 2017).

There exists evidence for continuity between the Early and Middle Holocene occupations at Lagoa Santa, though it is also clear that there is a general decline in the number of sites associated with the Middle Holocene occupation of the region. Furthermore, the rock shelters were used differently between the Early and Middle Holocene. No human skeletons are found at Lagoa Santa between 7000 and 2000 BP. The current explanation for this archaeological event was associated with abandonment or an "Archaic Gap" found across Central Brazil. The number of radiocarbon dates during the Middle Holocene in Central Brazil decreases abruptly during this time period. In addition, paleoenvironmental data reveal evidence of climatic instability. Indeed, climatic stressors have been raised as an explanation for depopulation at Lagoa Santa (Araujo *et al.*, 2005, 2013; Raczka *et al.*, 2013).

In order to better understand this process, it is important to incorporate a regional perspective. This chapter proposes an alternative hypothesis to abandonment of the region, based on concepts of territoriality (Zedeňo, 1997, 2008) and resilience of hunter-gatherer populations (Redman, 2005). Globally, hunter-gatherer groups show a wide amplitude of territorial coverage. This coverage varies from 25 000 km^2 to 8 km^2 of total area used over the course of one year, with an average of 2448.33 km^2 and a median of 700 km^2 (Kelly, 2013). These data suggest that the 356 km^2 area covered by the Lagoa Santa karst (Patrus, 1998) may be only part of the territory occupied by the Lagoa Santa hunter-gatherers. Indeed, the territory of Lagoa Santa hunter-gatherers fluctuated over time, with a larger territorial range in the Late Pleistocene and a progressively diminished range during the Early Holocene. This trend reversed during the Middle Holocene, with a return to larger territory sizes.

There are eight archaeological areas in central-northern Minas Gerais (Montalvânia, Unaí, Diamantina, Montes Claros, Lagoa Santa, Peruaçu, Varzelândia, and Pirapora), covering an area of almost 300 000 km^2. Considering the number of radiocarbon dates over time for four of these regions (using an interval of 500 years, following Araujo *et al.*, 2005), a pattern of alternating occupation emerges (Figure 7.8). This pattern is found between 8000 and 4000 BP, while between 10 000 and 8000 BP the region of Lagoa Santa shows a higher intensity of occupation. Certainly, these data should be interpreted cautiously, but, assuming this pattern is a real representation of human occupation, these data suggest integration between areas, with alternating basins of attraction.

Two other sources of data suggest a regional integration in the central and northern areas of Minas Gerais State – lithics and rock art. Besides regional

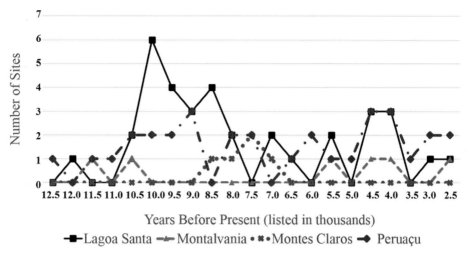

Figure 7.8 Number of sites identified from 12 500 to 2000 BP in four archaeological regions of central-northern Minas Gerais.

variations of the lithic assemblage, there are technological similarities during the Middle Holocene in the region. These similarities include lack of formal artifacts, use of local raw materials, small-sized artifacts with few retouched edges, low frequency of re-sharpening, and evidence of hafting (Bueno, 2010, 2013b; Bueno *et al.*, 2008; Isnardis, 2009; Prous, 1991a; Rodet, 2007). These characteristics are distributed in wider areas compared to previous periods. Considering rock art, the Planalto tradition occurs in rock shelters from central Minas Gerais, especially in Lagoa Santa, Santana do Riacho, and Diamantina regions (Baeta and Prous, 2016; Isnardis, 2004, 2009; Linke, 2013, 2014; Prous, 1991a, b; Ribeiro, 2007). Although scarce, two buried painted figures of the Planalto tradition were dated to around 4000 BP at the sites of Lapa Vermelha IV and Santana do Riacho (Prous, 1991a; Prous and Baeta, 1992/ 1993). In fact, rock art styles associated with this tradition are identified at sites 300 km apart from each other (Linke, 2014), demonstrative of a large-scale geographic distribution. The occurrence of rock art in central Minas Gerais is not exclusive to the Middle Holocene. There is evidence of a buried painted fragment in a stratum dated to 8000 BP at Santana do Riacho, even though there is no stylistic affiliation (Prous and Baeta, 1992/1993). Moreover, a pecked figure at Lapa do Santo is dated to the Early Holocene (Neves *et al.*, 2012), which suggests an early occurrence for the Planalto tradition iconography. Even considering these early examples, the Planalto tradition is characterized as a Middle Holocene tradition, and large painted panels occurring in multiple localities in the central-northern Minas Gerais state during this period are attributed to this culture (Baeta and Prous, 2016; Linke, 2014; Prous, 1991a). Based on this evidence, it is possible that, instead of using rock shelters as a space to engage in daily practices, bury the dead, and perform rituals – as done in the Early Holocene period – the Lagoa Santa rock shelter became a central place to produce rock art during the Middle Holocene. These data suggest that changes in territoriality, mobility patterns, and conceptions of maintaining territory occurred in the central-northern Minas Gerais region during the Middle Holocene. Instead of thinking about abandonment as a process involving population movements across vast spaces, this chapter proposes alternative behavioral strategies such as dispersion of small social units into wider regions, which then aggregate in specific areas. This dynamic use of space produces an archaeological record with low visibility, but it does not imply regional abandonment.

Another central issue is the need to evaluate the complexity associated with abandonment in terms of collapsing socioecological and cultural systems (Cameron and Tomka, 1993; Nelson, 2000). The central point is that the archaeological record of Lagoa Santa must be interpreted within the occupation of central-northern Minas Gerais broadly. Only then is it possible to construct interpretative alternatives in which a mechanistic relationship between environmental change and human behavior is not privileged. As argued by Tomka and Stevenson (1993: 192), "Although it would be tempting to see abandonment as driven purely by ecological factors, the system does not operate in a cultural vacuum. Cultural mechanisms responsible for channeling the energy input and maintaining the structure of society also need to be considered." In short, cultural and ecological factors interacted to produce the changes observed in the Middle Holocene archaeological record at Lagoa Santa, and in this sense, abandonment of a persistently occupied region requires shifting both socioecological and cultural narratives of a population.

Resilience theory provides a context for interpretation that allows for such changes to occur, while considering how the deeper cultural and socioecological identity of a population may have been maintained (Redman, 2005; Redman and Kinzig, 2003). The spatiotemporal changes in the hunter-gatherers of Lagoa Santa show elements of an adaptive cycle, which includes growth, conservation, release, and reorganization. Note that growth begins in the Pleistocene/Holocene, with the beginning of the systematic occupation of the rock shelters. The next phase, conservation, was a period of accumulation of energy and material during the Early Holocene. This slow process of accumulation is not continuous, since around 9000 BP the use of rock shelters occurs in episodic moments connected to territorial or social/cultural processes. Another change is the release phase around 7000 BP, when the occupation of the rock shelters ended and the population reorganized around periodically occupied regional landscapes combined with returns to the Lagoa Santa formation for ritual purposes. This transition seems to be related to climatic changes, though other additional elements such as regional changes in cultural, social, or demographic factors should be considered. Diminished site use does not equate to abandonment, and in this instance it implies initiation of a new adaptive cycle still focused on Lagoa Santa as a geographic basin of attraction. In this sense, changes during the Holocene represent participation in a population reorganization that maintained a central emphasis on the Lagoa Santa landscape, albeit one associated with newly contrived population structures.

7.8   Conclusion

This chapter synthesizes the bioarchaeological evidence for the hunter-gatherer occupation at Lagoa Santa, central Minas Gerais, within the context of persistent place and resilience theory. The occupation of this region began with exploratory hunter-gatherer groups, probably associated with the skeleton of Luzia, by 11 000 BP. Although the origin of these pioneer groups remains unknown, lower layers of the Santana do Riacho site and some archaeological material of the rock shelters of the Diamantina region (both in Serra do Espinhaço) show evidence of unifacial lithic production, which may be associated with hunter-gatherers of the Itaparica tradition.

After 10 500 BP, the Lagoa Santa region was more intensively occupied, but without evidence of burial practices. Intensive occupation defined by burial appears in the archaeological record around 9000 BP, is documented across many sites, and solidifies over a short time frame. During this time, there are indications of decreasing territory size and a lower degree of contact with other regions. Human skeletal remains found in this period suggest a diet with high reliance on plants, low individual mobility, and the occurrence of development stress. This biocultural profile might be associated with a more intensive use of a persistent landscape. Thus, the occupation of Lagoa Santa was not episodic. Instead, the region is associated with hunter-gatherer groups building a social landscape and adapting to the regional environment.

After 7000 BP, evidence for intensive, persistent occupation disappears from the archaeological record in Lagoa Santa. A regional perspective provides some explanation for what may have happened. Specifically, there appears to be shifts in territoriality, with a return to high mobility and lower population aggregation. Based on aspects of lithic technology, rock art distribution, chronology, and burial practices, it is likely that the Lagoa Santa hunter-gatherer groups adopted a high-mobility pattern and dispersed across larger territories, living in smaller groups and sharing knowledge to abate climatic instability typical of the Middle Holocene in central Brazil. Thus, instead of interpreting this weak archaeological signal as a result of an abandonment process, it likely represents social strategies aimed at maintaining permanence of the landscape (Nelson and Hegmon, 2001).

References

Araujo, A. G. M. and Pugliese, F. (2010). A indústria lítica. In A. G. M. Araujo and W. A. Neves, eds., *Lapa das Boleiras: Um Sítio Paleoíndio do Carste de Lagoa Santa, MG, Brasil.* São Paulo: Editora Annablume, pp. 75–106.

Araujo, A. G. M., Neves, W. A., Piló, L. B., and Atui, J. P. V. (2005). Holocene dryness and human occupation in Brazil during the "Archaic Gap." *Quaternary Research*, 64, 298–307.

Araujo, A. G. M., Feathers, J. K., Arroyo-Kalin, M., and Tizuka, M. M. (2008). Lapa das Boleiras rockshelter: Stratigraphy and formation processes at a Paleoamerican site in Central Brazil. *Journal of Archaeological Science*, 35, 3186–3202.

Araujo, A. G. M., Piló, L. B., and Neves, W. A. (2010). Estratigrafia e processos de formação do sítio. In A. G. M. Araujo and W. A. Neves, eds., *Lapa das Boleiras: Um Sítio Paleoíndio do Carste de Lagoa Santa, MG, Brasil.* São Paulo: Editora Annablume, pp. 35–74.

Araujo, A. G. M., Neves, W. A., and Kipnis, R. (2012). Lagoa Santa revisited: An overview of the chronology, subsistence, and material culture of Paleoindian sites in Eastern Central Brazil. *Latin American Antiquity*, **23**, 533–550.

Araujo, A. G. M., Strauss, A., Feathers, J., Paisani, J. C., and Schrage, T. J. (2013). Paleoindian open-air sites in tropical settings: A case study in formation processes, dating methods, and paleoenvironmental models. *Geoarchaeology*, **28**, 195–220.

Araujo, A. G. M., Pugliese, F., Santos, R. O., and Okumura, M. (2017). Extreme cultural persistence in Eastern-Central Brazil: The case of Lagoa Santa Paleoindians. *Anais da Academia Brasileira de Ciências*. DOI: /10.1590/0001-3765201720170109.

Baeta, A. and Prous, A. (2016). Os Grafismos rupestres: História dos estudos sobre o registro rupestre pré-histórico no carste de Lagoa Santa. In P. Da-Gloria, W. A. Neves, and M. Hubbe, eds., *Lagoa Santa: História das Pesquisas Arqueológicas e Paleontológicas*. São Paulo: Editora Annablume.

Boldsen, J. L. (1995). The place of plasticity in the study of the secular trend for male stature: An analysis of Danish biological population history. In C. G. N. Taylor and B. Bogin, eds., *Human Variability and Plasticity*. Cambridge: Cambridge University Press, pp. 75–90.

Bueno, L. (2010). Tecnologia lítica, cronologia e sequência de ocupação: O estudo de um sítio a céu aberto na região de Lagoa Santa, MG. *Revista do Museu de Arqueologia e Etnologia*, **20**, 91–108.

Bueno, L. (2011). L'occupation initiale du Brésil dans une perspective macro-régionale: Les cas des régions de l'Amazonie, du Nordeste et du centre du Brésil. In D. Vialou, ed., *Peuplements et Préhistoire en Amériques*. Paris: Éditions du Comité des Travaux Historiques et Scientifiques, pp. 209–220.

Bueno, L. (2012). Entre abrigos e lagoas: Tecnologia lítica e territorialidade em Lagoa Santa (Minas Gerais, Brasil). *Revista de Arqueologia*, **25**, 62–83.

Bueno, L. (2013a). Peopling the eastern South America: Occupying the landscape and constructing territories in Central Brazilian Plateau during Pleistocene/Holocene transition. Paper presented at 78th Meeting of Society for American Archaeology, Honolulu, Hawaii, USA.

Bueno, L. (2013b). Tecnologia e território no centro-norte mineiro: Um estudo de caso na região de Montes Claros, MG, Brasil. *Revista Espinhaço*, **2**, 168–186.

Bueno, L. and Isnardis, A. (2016). Tecnologia lítica em Lagoa Santa no Holoceno Inicial. In P. Da-Gloria, W. A. Neves, and M. Hubbe, eds., *Lagoa Santa: História das Pesquisas Arqueológicas e Paleontológicas*. São Paulo: Editora Annablume.

Bueno, L., Barbosa, V. and Gomes, W. (2008). Resgatando coleções: A Lapa Pequena de Montes Claros revisitada. *Canindé, Revista do Museu de Arqueologia do Xingó*, **12**, 47–80.

Bueno, L., Dias, A., and Steele, J. (2013). The Late Pleistocene/Early Holocene archaeological record in Brazil: A geo-referenced database. *Quaternary International*, **301**, 74–93.

Cameron, C. and Tomka, S., eds. (1993). *Abandonment of Settlements and Regions: Ethnoarchaeo-logical and Archaeological Approaches*. Cambridge: Cambridge University Press.

Chandler-Ezell, C., Pearsall, D. M., and Zeidler, J. A. (2006). Root and tuber phytoliths and starch grains document manioc (*Manihot esculenta*), arrowroot (*Maranta arundinacea*), and llerén (*Calathea* sp.) at the Real Alto Site, Ecuador. *Economic Botany*, **60**, 103–120.

Charles, D. K. and Buikstra, J. E. (2002). Siting, sighting, and citing the dead. *Archaeological Papers of the American Anthropological Association*, **11**, 13–25.

Da-Gloria, P. (2012). *Health and Lifestyle in the Paleoamericans: Early Holocene Biocultural Adaptation at Lagoa Santa, Central Brazil*. PhD dissertation, The Ohio State University.

Da-Gloria, P. and Larsen, C. S. (2014). Oral health of the Paleoamericans of Lagoa Santa, central Brazil. *American Journal of Physical Anthropology*, **154**, 11–26.

Da-Gloria, P. and Larsen, C. S. (2017). Subsisting at the Pleistocene/Holocene boundary in the New World: A view from the Paleoamerican mouths of Central Brazil. *Paleoamerica*, **3**, 101–121.

Da-Gloria, P., Strauss, A., and Neves, W. A. (2011). Mortuary rituals in the Early Holocene population of Lagoa Santa: The Harold Walter collection. *American Journal of Physical Anthropology*, **144** (Suppl. 52), 119–120.

Da-Gloria, P., Neves, W. A., and Hubbe, M. (2016). História das pesquisas em Lagoa Santa. Minas Gerais: Ossos humanos e patrimônio arqueológico. Paper presented at the IV Seminário de Preservação do Patrimônio Arqueológico. October 5–7, Rio de Janeiro: Museu de Astronomia e Ciências Afins, pp. 433–443.

Da-Gloria, P., Neves, W. A., and Hubbe, M., eds. (2017). *Archaeological and Paleontological Research in Lagoa Santa: The Quest for the First Americans*. Cham: Springer.

Dias, A. S. (2004). Diversificar para poblar: El contexto arqueológico Brasileño en la transición Pleistoceno-Holoceno. *Complutum*, **15**, 249–263.

Dias, A. S. and Bueno, L. (2013). The initial colonization of South America eastern lowlands: Brazilian archaeology contributions to settlement of America models. In K. Graf, C. V. Ketron, and M. R. Waters, eds., *The Paleoamerican Odyssey*. Santa Fe, NM: Center for the Study of the First Americans, pp. 339–357.

Dickel, D. N. (2002). Analysis of mortuary patterns. In G. H. Doran, ed., *Windover: Multidisciplinary Investigations of an Early Archaic Florida Cemetery*. Gainesville, FL: University Press of Florida, pp. 73–96.

Doran, G. H. (2007). A brief continental view from Windover. In M. N. Cohen and G. Crane-Kramer, eds., *Ancient Health*. Gainesville, FL: University Press of Florida, pp. 35–51.

El-Najjar, M. Y., Ryan, D. J., Turner, II, C. G., and Lozoff, B. (1976). The etiology of porotic hyperostosis among the prehistoric and historic Anasazi Indians of Southwestern United States. *American Journal of Physical Anthropology*, **44**, 477–487.

Feathers, J., Kipnis, R., Piló, L. B., Arroyo-Kalin, M., and Coblentz, D. (2010). How old is Luzia? Luminescence dating and stratigraphic integrity at Lapa Vermelha, Lagoa Santa, Brazil. *Geoarchaeology*, **25**, 395–436.

Flores, R. A. (2015). *Uso de Recursos Vegetais em Lapa Grande de Taquaraçu. Evidências Macro e Microscópicas*. Masters thesis, University of São Paulo.

Fontugne, M. (2013). New radiocarbon ages of Luzia woman, Lapa Vermelha IV site, Lagoa Santa, Minas Gerais, Brazil. *Radiocarbon*, **55**, 1187–1190.

Freire, G. Q. (2011). *Madeiras Fósseis Holocênicas de Ribeirão da Mata: Anatomia Ecológica, Relações Florísticas e Interpretação Paleoambiental da Região Arqueológica de Lagoa Santa, MG*. PhD dissertation, University of São Paulo.

Gamble, L. H. (2017). Feasting, ritual practices, social memory, and persistent places: New interpretations of shell mounds in southern California. *American Antiquity*, **82**, 427–451.

Gaspar, M. D., DeBlasis, P., Fish, S. K., and Fish, P. R. (2008). Sambaqui (Shell Mound) societies of coastal Brazil. In H. Silverman and W. Isbell, eds., *The Handbook of South American Archaeology*. New York: Springer, pp. 319–335.

Hillson, S. (2005). *Teeth*. Cambridge: Cambridge University Press.

Holland, T. D. and O'Brien, M. J. (1997). Parasites, porotic hyperostosis, and the implications of changing perspectives. *American Antiquity*, **62**, 183–193.

Holliday, T. W. and Ruff, C. B. (1997). Ecogeographical patterning and stature prediction in fossil hominids: A comment on M. R. Feldesman and R. L. Fountain. *American Journal of Physical Anthropology*, **103**, 137–140.

Hubbe, M., Neves, W. A., and Harvati, K. (2010). Testing evolutionary and dispersion scenarios for the settlement of the New World. *PLoS ONE*, **5**, e11105.

Hubbe, M., Okumura, M., Bernardo, D. V., and Neves, W. A. (2014). Cranial morphological diversity of early, middle, and late Holocene Brazilian groups: Implications for human dispersion in Brazil. *American Journal of Physical Anthropology*, **155**, 546–558.

Hubbe, M., Strauss, A., Hubbe, A., and Neves, W. A. (2015). Early South Americans cranial morphological variation and the origin of American biological diversity. *PLoS ONE*, 10, e0138090.

Hurt, W. (1964). Recent radiocarbon dates for Central and Southern Brazil. *American Antiquity*, 113, 3–10.

Hurt, W. and Blasi, O. (1969). O projeto arqueológico Lagoa Santa, Minas Gerais, Brasil. *Arquivos do Museu Paranaense, NS, Arqueologia*, 4, 1–63.

Isnardis, A. (2004). *Lapa, Parede, Painel: Distribuição Geográfica das Unidades Estilísticas (São Francisco, Norte de Minas Gerais)*. Masters thesis, University of São Paulo.

Isnardis, A. (2009). *Entre As Pedras: As Ocupações Pré-Históricas Recentes e os Grafismos Rupestres da Região de Diamantina, Minas Gerais*. PhD dissertation, University of São Paulo.

Jantz, L. M. and Jantz, R. L. (1999). Secular changes in long bone length and proportion in the United States, 1800–1970. *American Journal of Physical Anthropology*, 110, 57–67.

Kelly, R. L. (2013). *The Lifeways of Hunter-Gatherers: The Forager Spectrum*. Cambridge: Cambridge University Press.

Kipnis, R., Bissaro, M. C., and Prado, H. M. (2010a). Os restos faunísticos. In A. G. M. Araujo and W. A. Neves, eds., *Lapa das Boleiras: Um Sítio Paleoíndio do Carste de Lagoa Santa, MG, Brasil*. São Paulo: Annablume, pp. 121–147.

Kipnis, R., Santos, R. O., and Cezário, M. E. (2010b). A indústria óssea. In A. G. M. Araujo and W. A. Neves, eds., *Lapa das Boleiras: Um Sítio Paleoíndio do Carste de Lagoa Santa, MG, Brasil*. São Paulo: Annablume, pp. 111–119.

Kuzawa, C. W. (2005). Fetal origins of developmental plasticity: Are fetal cues reliable predictors of future nutritional requirements. *American Journal of Human Biology*, 17, 5–21.

Lacerda, J. B. and Peixoto, R. (1876). Contribuições para o estudo antropológico das raças indígenas do Brazil. *Archivos do Museu Nacional do Rio de Janeiro*, 1, 47–75.

Laming-Emperaire, A. (1979). Missions archéologique franco-brésiliennes en Lagoa Santa, Minas Gerais, Brésil: Le grand abri de Lapa Vermelha. *Revista de Pré-história*, 1, 54–89.

Larsen, C. S. (2015). *Bioarchaeology: Interpreting Behavior from the Human Skeleton*. 2nd edn. Cambridge: Cambridge University Press.

Linke, V. (2013). Onde é que se grafa? As relações entre os conjuntos estilísticos rupestres da região de Diamantina (Minas Gerais) e o mundo envolvente. *Revista Espinhaço*, 2, 118–131.

Linke, V. (2014). *Os conjuntos gráficos pré-históricos do centro e norte mineiros: Estilos e territórios em uma análise macro-regional*. PhD dissertation, University of São Paulo.

Littleton, J. and Allen, H. (2007). Hunter-gatherer burials and the creation of persistent places in southeastern Australia. *Journal of Anthropological Archaeology*, 26, 283–298.

Lukacs, J. R. (2008). Fertility and agriculture accentuate sex differences in dental caries rates. *Current Anthropology*, 49, 901–914.

Mello e Alvim, M. C. (1977). Os antigos habitantes da área arqueológica de Lagoa Santa, Minas Gerais, Brasil: Estudo morfológico. *Arquivos do Museu de História Natural da Universidade Federal de Minas Gerais, Belo Horizonte*, 2, 119–174.

Melo Jr., J. C. F. and Magalhães, W. L. E. (2015). Antracologia de fogueiras paleoíndias do Brasil central: Considerações tecnológicas e paleoetnobotânicas sobre o uso de recursos florestais no abrigo rupestre Lapa do Santo, Minas Gerais, Brasil. *Antipoda: Revista de Antropología y Arqueología, Bogotá*, 22, 137–161.

Mingatos, G. S. and Okumura, M. (2016). Modelo de amplitude de dieta aplicada a restos faunísticos do sítio Lapa do Santo (MG) e suas implicações para o entendimento da dieta em grupos Paleoíndios do Brasil central. *Palaeoindian Archaeology*, 1, 15–31.

Moreno de Souza, J. C. (2014). *Cognição e Cultura no Mundo Material: Os Itaparicas, os Umbus e os "Lagoassantenses."* Masters thesis. University of São Paulo.

Nakamura, C., Melo Jr., J. C. F., and Ceccantini, G. (2010). Macro-restos vegetais: Uma abordagem paleoetnobotânica e paleoambiental. In A. G. M. Araujo and W. A. Neves, eds., *Lapa das*

Boleiras: Um Sítio Paleoíndio do Carste de Lagoa Santa, MG, Brasil. São Paulo: Annablume, pp. 163–190.

Nelson, M. (2000). Abandonment: Conceptualization, representation, and social change. In M. Schiffer, ed., *Explorations in Social Theory*. Salt Lake City, UT: University of Utah Press, pp. 52–62.

Nelson, M. and Hegmon, M. (2001). Abandonment is not as it seems: An approach to the relationship between site and regional abandonment. *American Antiquity*, **66**, 213–235.

Neves, W. A. and Hubbe, M. (2005). Cranial morphology of early Americans from Lagoa Santa, Brazil: Implications for the settlement of the New World. *Proceedings of the National Academy of Sciences*, **102**, 18309–18314.

Neves, W. A. and Kipnis, R. (2004). Further evidence of a highly cariogenic diet among late Paleoindians of Central Brazil. *Current Research in the Pleistocene*, **21**, 81–83.

Neves, W. A. and Pucciarelli, H. M. (1991). Morphological affinities of the first Americans: An exploratory analysis based on early South American human remains. *Journal of Human Evolution*, **21**, 261–273.

Neves, W. A., Powell, J. F., and Ozolins, E. G. (1999). Extra-continental morphological affinities of Lapa Vermelha IV, hominid I: A multivariate analysis with progressive numbers of variables. *Homo*, **50**, 263–282.

Neves, W. A., González-José, R., Hubbe, M., *et al.* (2004). Early human skeletal remains from Cerca Grande, Lagoa Santa, Central Brazil, and the origins of the first Americans. *World Archaeology*, **36**, 479–501.

Neves, W. A., Hubbe, M., Okumura, M. M. M, *et al.* (2005). A new early Holocene human skeleton from Brazil: Implications for the settlement of the New World. *Journal of Human Evolution*, **48**, 403–414.

Neves, W. A., Hubbe, M., and Correal, G. (2007). Human skeletal remains from Sabana de Bogotá, Colombia: A case of paleoamerican morphology late survival in South America? *American Journal of Physical Anthropology*, **133**, 1080–1098.

Neves, W. A., Araujo, A. G. M., Bernardo, D. V., Kipnis, R., and Feathers, J. (2012). Rock art at the Pleistocene/Holocene boundary in Eastern South America. *PLoS One*, **7**, e32228.

Neves, W. A., Hubbe, M., and Araujo, A. G. M. (2002). A late-paleoindian secondary ritual burial from Lagoa Santa, Minas Gerais, Brazil. *Current Research in the Pleistocene*, **19**, 83–85.

Neves, W. A., Hubbe, M., Bernardo, D., *et al.* (2013). Early human occupation of Lagoa Santa, eastern central Brazil: Craniometric variation of the initial settlers of South America. In K. Graf, C. V. Ketron, and M. R. Waters, eds., *The Paleoamerican Odyssey*. Santa Fe, NM: Center for the Study of the First Americans, pp. 397–414.

Ortner, D. J. (2003). *Identification of Pathological Conditions in Human Skeletal Remains*. San Diego, CA: Academic Press.

Patrus, M. L. R. A. (1998). Estudos hidrológicos e qualidade das águas de superfície. In *APA Carste de Lagoa Santa – Meio Físico*, vol. 1. Belo Horizonte: CPRM/IBAMA.

Pearsall, D. M., Chandler-Ezell, K., and Zeidler J. A. (2004). Maize in ancient Ecuador: Results of residue analysis of stone tools from the Real Alto site. *Journal of Archaeological Science*, **31**, 423–442.

Perez, C. P. (2009). *Paleoecologia de Mamíferos Viventes Como Ferramenta na Caracterização do ambiente Holocênico de Lagoa Santa, MG*. Masters thesis, Universidade de São Paulo.

Prous, A. (1991a). *Arqueologia Brasileira*. Brasília: Editora UnB.

Prous, A. (1991b). Os instrumentos lascados. *Arquivos do Museu de História Natural da Universidade Federal de Minas Gerais*, **12**, 229–274.

Prous, A. and Baeta, A. (1992–1993). Elementos de cronologia, descrição de atributos e tipologia. *Arquivos do Museu de História Natural da Universidade Federal de Minas Gerais*, **13–14**, 241–332.

Pugliese Jr., F. A. (2007). *Os Líticos de Lagoa Santa: Um Estudo Sobre a Organização Tecnológica de Caçadores-Coletores do Brasil Central*. Masters thesis, University of São Paulo.

Raczka, M. F., Oliveira, P. E., Bush, M., and McMichael, C. H. (2013). Two paleoecological histories spanning the period of human settlement in southeastern Brazil. *Journal of Quaternary Science*, **28**, 144–151.

Redman, C. L. (2005). Resilience theory in archaeology. *American Anthropologist*, **107**, 70–77.

Redman, C. L. and Kinzig, A. P. (2003). Resilience of past landscapes: Resilience theory, society, and the longue durée. *Conservation Ecology*, **7**, 14.

Reitsema, L. J. and McIlvaine, B. K. (2014). Reconciling "stress" and "health" in physical anthropology: What can bioarchaeologists learn from the other subdisciplines? *American Journal of Physical Anthropology*, **155**, 181–185.

Ribeiro, L. (2007). *Os Significados da Similaridade e da Diferença entre os Estilos de Arte Rupestre : Um Estudo Regional das Gravuras e Pinturas do Alto-Médio Rio São Francisco*. PhD dissertation, University of São Paulo.

Rodet, M. J. (2007). *Etude Technologique des Industries Lithiques Taillées du Nord de Minas Gerais, Brésil- Depuis le Passage Pléistocène/Holocène jusqu'au Contact – XVIIIème siècle*. PhD dissertation, Université de Paris X.

Ruff, C. B. (1999). Skeletal structure and behavioral patterns of prehistoric Great Basin populations. In B. E. Hemphill and C. S. Larsen, eds., *Understanding Prehistoric Lifeways in the Great Basin Wetlands: Bioarchaeological Reconstruction and Interpretation*. Salt Lake City, UT: University of Utah Press, pp. 290–320.

Santos, R. O. (2011). *As Tecnologias Esqueletais: Uma Investigação sobre o Uso de Matérias-Primas de Origem Esqueletal por Meio de Análise Comparativa entre Coleções Arqueológicas e Etnográficas*. Masters thesis, University of São Paulo.

Schlanger, S. H. (1992). Recognizing persistent places in Anasazi settlement systems. In J. Rossignol and L. Wandsnider, eds., *Space, Time, and Archaeological Landscapes*. New York: Plenum Press. pp. 91–112.

Schroeder, S. (2001). Secondary disposal of the dead: Cross-cultural codes. *World Cultures*, **12**, 77–93.

Schultz, M. (2001). Paleohistology of bone: A new approach to the study of ancient diseases. *Yearbook of Physical Anthropology*, **33**, 106–147.

Smith, B. D. (2001). Low-level food production. *Journal of Archaeological Research*, **9**, 1–43.

Steckel, R. H., Sciulli, P. W., and Rose, J. C. (2002). A health index from skeletal remains. In R. H. Steckel and J. C. Rose, eds., *The Backbone of History: Health and Nutrition in the Western Hemisphere*. Cambridge: Cambridge University Press, pp. 61–93.

Steckel, R. H., Larsen, C. S., Sciulli, P. W., and Walker, P. L. (2006). Data collection codebook. Available at:http://global.sbs.ohio-state.edu.

Stock, J. T. and Shaw, C. N. (2007). Which measures of diaphyseal robusticity are robust? A comparison of external methods of quantifying the strength of long bone diaphyses to cross-sectional geometric properties. *American Journal of Physical Anthropology*, **134**, 412–423.

Strauss, A. M., Oliveira, R. E., Bernardo, D. V., *et al.* (2015). The oldest case of decapitation in the New World (Lapa do Santo, East-Central Brazil). *PLoS ONE*, **10**, e0137456.

Strauss, A. M., Oliveira, R. E., Villagran, X., *et al.* (2016). Early Holocene ritual complexity in South America: The archaeological record of Lapa do Santo (east-central Brazil). *Antiquity*, **90**, 1454–1473.

Stuart-Macadam, P. (1985). Porotic hyperostosis: Representative of a childhood condition. *American Journal of Physical Anthropology*, **66**, 391–398.

Stuart-Macadam, P. (1987). Porotic hyperostosis: New evidence to support the anemia theory. *American Journal of Physical Anthropology*, **74**, 521–526.

Temple, D. H. (2008). What can stature variation reveal about environmental differences between prehistoric Jomon foragers? Understanding the impact of systemic stress on developmental stability. *American Journal of Human Biology*, **20**, 431–439.

Temple, D. H. and Goodman, A. H. (2014). Bioarcheology has a "health" problem: Conceptualizing "stress" and "health" in bioarcheological research. *American Journal of Physical Anthropology*, **155**, 186–191.

Thompson, V. D. (2010). The rhythms of space-time and the making of monuments and places during the Archaic. In D. H. Thomas and M. C. Sangar, eds., *Trend, Tradition, and Turmoil: What Happened to the Southeastern Archaic?* New York: American Museum of Natural History, pp. 217–227.

Tomka, S. and Stevenson, M. (1993). Understanding abandonment processes: Summary and remaining concerns. In C. Cameron and S. Tomka, eds., *Abandonment of Settlements and Regions: Ethnoarchaeological and Archaeological Approaches*. Cambridge: Cambridge University Press, pp. 191–195.

Ubelaker, D. H., and Newson, L. A. (2002). Patterns of health and nutrition in prehistoric and historic Ecuador. In R. H. Steckel and J. C. Rose, eds. *The Backbone of History: Health and Nutrition in the Western Hemisphere*. Cambridge: Cambridge University Press, pp. 343–375.

Villagran, X. S., Strauss, A., Miller, C., Ligouis, B., and Oliveira, R. (2017). Buried in ashes: Site formation processes at Lapa do Santo rockshelter, east-central Brazil. *Journal of Archaeological Science*, **77**, 10–34.

Walker, P. L. (1985). Anemia among prehistoric Indians of the American Southwest. In C. F. Merbs and R. J. Miller, eds., *Health and Disease in the Prehistoric Southwest*. Tempe, AZ: Arizona State University, pp. 139–164.

Walker, P. L. (1986). Porotic hyperostosis in a marine-dependent California Indian population. *American Journal of Physical Anthropology*, **69**, 345–354.

Walker, P. L., Bathurst, R. R., Richman, R., Gjerdrum, T., and Andrushko, V. A. (2009). The causes of porotic hyperostosis and cribra orbitalia: A reappraisal of the iron-deficiency-anemia hypothesis. *American Journal of Physical Anthropology*, **139**, 109–125.

Walter, H. V. (1958). *Arqueologia da Região de Lagoa Santa, Minas Gerais: Índios Pré-Colombianos dos Abrigos-Rochedos*. Rio de Janeiro: Sedegra.

Walthall, J. A. (1999). Mortuary behavior and Early Holocene land use in the North American midcontinent. *North American Archaeologist*, **20**, 1–30.

Wapler, U., Crubezy, C., and Schultz, M. (2004). Is cribra orbitalia synonymous with anemia? Analysis and interpretation of cranial pathology in Sudan. *American Journal of Physical Anthropology*, **123**, 333–339.

Wentz, R. K. (2006). *A Bioarchaeological Assessment of Health from Florida's Archaic: Application of the Western Hemisphere Health Index to the Remains from Windover (8BR246)*. PhD dissertation, Florida State University.

Wescott, D. J. (2006). Effect of mobility on femur midshaft external shape and robusticity. *American Journal of Physical Anthropology*, **130**, 201–213.

Worthman, C. and Kuzara, J. (2005). Life history and the early origins of health differentials. *American Journal of Human Biology*, **17**, 95–112.

Zedeño, M. N. (1997). Landscape, land use, and the history of territory formation: An example from the Puebloan Southwest. *Journal of Archaeological Method and Theory*, **4**, 67–103.

Zedeño, M. N. (2008). The archaeology of territory and territoriality. In B. David and J. Thomas, eds., *Handbook of Landscape Archaeology*. Walnut Creek, CA: Left Coast Press, pp. 210–217.

8 Resilience among Hunter-Gatherers in Southern California before and after European Colonization: A Bioarchaeological Perspective

Erin E. Bornemann and Lynn H. Gamble

8.1 Introduction

8.1.1 Hunter-Gatherer Resilience in Situations of Culture Contact

When European explorers reached the New World, neither the local indigenous populations, nor the Europeans had any idea of the scope and long-lasting effects that this interaction and later colonization would evoke. For much of history, the central story of these encounters is European dominance over and extermination of the native populations, which subsequently led to centuries of abuse, disease, death, and relocation (Erlandson, 1998; Murphy *et al.*, 2010; Rogers, 2005). Recent scholars acknowledge the recursive relationship between indigenous groups and colonizers; these studies emphasize indigenous groups as active agents of change, resistance, rebellion, and resilience (see, for example, Dietler, 2010; Gamble, 2016; Liebmann and Murphy, 2010; Lyons and Papadopoulos, 2002; Murphy and Klaus, 2017). This perspective is imperative in gaining a full account of pre- and postcontact cultural traditions belonging to indigenous hunter-gatherer groups as well as facilitating a more nuanced account of how European contact affected the daily lives of native communities.

The theoretical concept of *resilience* initially developed by ecological studies was broadened to an interdisciplinary field of study and now includes archaeological contexts (Berkes and Folke, 2000; Folke, 2006; Holling, 1973; Levin, 1999; Redman, 2005; Redman and Kinzig, 2003). Redman and Kinzig (2003: 5) define *resilience* as "the amount of change a system can withstand while retaining certain functions and/ or structures . . . [it] is the ability of a system to remain functionally stable in the face of stress and to recover following a disturbance. Reducing this to a single word, it is the capacity to be flexible." One of the primary analytical strengths of resilience theory – when applied to archaeological contexts – is that long time scales can be examined in conjunction with the identification of relevant social patterns representing the ways in which humans respond and adapt to change. Moreover, resilience theory is useful in bioarchaeological studies for the ability to address adaptability within socioecological and cultural systems, while identifying long-standing behaviors at many levels of cultural discourse (McAnany and Yoffee, 2009; Redman, 2005).

The aim of this chapter is to combine bioarchaeological data with ethnographic and ethnohistoric accounts from the prehistoric and historic cemeteries at the site of Malibu (*Humaliwo*; CA-LAN-64) to provide dual lines of evidence that demonstrate Chumash resilience in light of European contact. Burial assemblages from the prehistoric and historic cemeteries are compared to one another to elucidate differences present in mortuary rituals, symbolism, and social complexity. Lightfoot (1995) and others (e.g., Silliman, 2009; Stojanowski, 2005) emphasize the significance of having a baseline for comparison for the postcontact period. Data from Malibu are compared to sites such as *Helo'* (CA-SBA-46), among others, as a baseline for regional parallels for the cultural resilience of the Chumash after European contact. Using dual lines of evidence, this chapter argues that individuals interred at Malibu and other sites in this region are strong examples of resilience among southern California Indians. This chapter highlights the role of the Chumash as active social agents during European contact, which is demonstrated by maintenance of traditions in the face of the drastic upheaval that occurred with European contact and colonization.

8.1.2   Coastal Chumash and European Encounters

Colonization is exemplified by asymmetrical relations of power and control and the cultural transformations that result from these relationships (Dietler, 2010). A great deal of variability exists in colonial practices, and extensive case studies, ranging from Assyrian trade colonies in Anatolia to Russian merchant colonies in northern California, provide examples of ways in which a colonized region becomes a stage for complex and unpredictable interactions (Lightfoot, 2005; Stein, 2005b). "'[H]eroic, event-oriented' colonial encounters, such as violence, disease, forced migration and settlement as well as day-to-day activities" are better understood through skeletal analyses (Murphy and Klaus, 2017: 14). Bioarchaeological evidence provides unparalleled detail regarding the ramifications of colonization at the scale of the individual, which often drastically differs from ethnohistoric accounts written from the perspectives of the colonizers (Murphy and Klaus, 2017; Stojanowski, 2005, 2013).

When investigating contact in the archaeological record, the potential for individual agency to structure larger organizational systems within a given society must be recognized (Stein, 2005a). Archaeological examples (e.g., Lightfoot, 2005; Murphy *et al.*, 2010) showcase how individual and group agency are paramount to teasing out aspects of the ways in which indigenous groups made active decisions to either change or maintain cultural traditions. This chapter incorporates conceptualizations of individual and group agency to the analysis of the Chumash at Malibu.

Archaeology provides a detailed record for long-term social change in human populations and serves as an important barometer of behavior during colonization. The nuances of these changes are often neglected in ethnohistoric accounts, but these still offer significant details of indigenous traditions such as mortuary rituals. This chapter takes a cautious approach when deciphering early accounts and instead relies on dual lines of evidence to construct a strong argument for continuity and change in the archaeological record (Rogers, 2005). This work relies on bioarchaeological data, archaeological records, and ethnohistoric accounts, informed by mortuary theory, to critically examine precontact and contact period cemeteries at Malibu for change or continuity in cultural traditions. The approach taken in this chapter allows for consideration of social relationships between individuals within the cemetery, individuals responsible for burying the deceased, and the ramifications of mortuary ritual at the societal level. Overall, evidence of cultural resiliency among the Chumash during a period of disruptive social transformation is the major theme in this chapter.

8.2   Coastal Chumash in Southern California

8.2.1   Initial Contact with Europeans

The Chumash culture represents a thriving, sociopolitically complex, hunter–gatherer population that existed in the area for more than 11 000 years prior to contact with European explorers (Erlandson, 1998; Gamble, 2008). In this chapter, the singular designation *Chumash* refers to the many separate Chumash groups for ease of discussion and comparison; it is important to note that the Chumash did not share a single language or culture, but did share many traits (Blackburn, 1975; Erlandson, 1998; Gamble, 2008). This chapter focuses primarily on the Chumash from Malibu, who are Ventureño, but this section also presents a general overview of the coastal Chumash way of life around the time of European contact.

The first historical account of European contact with the coastal Chumash dates to CE 1542, when Spanish explorer Juan Rodríguez Cabrillo – sailing with a fleet of three ships – made a record of a six-week visit to the Santa Barbara coast (Wagner, 1929). Cabrillo's encounter acts as the starting point for the protohistoric period. This period is characterized by intermittent and largely undocumented short-term interactions between local populations and European sailors (Erlandson and Bartoy, 1995; Erlandson *et al.*, 2001; Gamble, 2008). It is likely that Europeans introduced diseases that drastically reduced Chumash population size during this time (Dobyns, 1993; Erlandson, 1998; Erlandson and Bartoy, 1995; Erlandson *et al.*, 2001; Gamble, 2008; Preston, 1996; Walker and Hudson, 1993; Walker and Johnson, 1992, 1994; Walker *et al.*, 2005), although the matter is still contested for a number of reasons. Permanent European settlements in the region began soon after the Portolá Overland Expedition in CE 1769/1770 and mark the beginning of the "historic period" and sustained European contact with the implementation of the Spanish mission system in southern California (Erlandson *et al.*, 2001; Gamble, 2008).

8.2.2   Ethnohistoric and Ethnographic Accounts of Coastal Chumash

Although ethnohistoric and ethnographic records cannot be applied uncritically, when combined with an archaeological approach, these documents provide detailed accounts of burial customs and sociopolitical organization that cannot be drawn from archaeological contexts alone. Such documents include: personal records and accounts from explorers, soldiers, and priests; records from those involved in the process of colonization and missionization; and later accounts from early twentieth-century ethnographers, among others (Gamble, 2008). These accounts are crucial for interpreting aspects of mortuary customs and symbolism from the historic period cemetery in this chapter; although meanings and symbolism from the historic period cannot be applied directly to the precontact period,[1] these reports still offer a useful source for comparison.

Overall, the Chumash were sociopolitically complex hunter-gatherers that were hierarchically based, with differences in rank that were either fully or partially ascribed at birth. Each village had at least one chief who belonged to a group of political/religious specialists called the 'antap. These individuals were linked to 'antap in villages throughout Chumash territory. The 'antap and other individuals of high rank often traveled between settlements for trade and establishing marriage ties. The majority of unions observed a matrilocal post-marital residence pattern (68 percent), followed in descending order of popularity by patrilocal (22.5 percent), neolocal (5.6 percent), and bilocal (3.9 percent) residence patterns (Johnson, 1988). It is important to note that chiefs diverged from the most dominant practice and followed a patrilocal post-marital residence pattern (Johnson, 1988). Mission records offer evidence of widespread intermarriage between chiefly families as well as polygamy among chiefs (Johnson, 1988, 2000).

Chiefs – as the wealthiest and most powerful members of the community – garnered the most attention in ethnohistoric records, especially in regard to burial treatment. Chumash who were in positions of high rank had notably more elaborate burial practices than those of lower socioeconomic rank. An early reference from Costansó, prior to the establishment of the mission system or other permanent establishments by the Spanish, suggests that the burial of a chief was conducted with much pomp. High poles were erected in the cemetery during these ceremonies to signify the identity of a chief (Hemert-Engert and Teggart, 1910). In another account, Father Crespí, a priest who accompanied Costansó, recorded burial rites that took place at *Syuxtun* (within modern Santa Barbara) on 10 January 1770. Crespí's account describes lengths of beads that were placed upon the deceased's body and could have been personal possessions of the deceased or offerings from mourners (Brown, 2001). Later ethnographic accounts from John P. Harrington's research (King, 1969) suggest that a portion of the deceased's belongings were placed in the grave. Some accounts describe a mourning ceremony that took place four to five years apart, where some belongings of individuals who died within this time span were collectively burned (Hollimon, 1996; Hudson et al., 1977; Hull et al., 2013).

Other records supply clear details about the structure of Chumash cemeteries. Crespí noted that Chumash cemeteries were spatially delineated from the settlement by painted boards, poles, and whale bones (Brown, 2001). Within the confines of these cemeteries, Harrington's ethnographic notes suggest that family burial plots were maintained, and the location of a burial within the cemetery was indicative of

---

[1] The term precontact is used for the Middle Period cemetery and for any time periods prior to 1769. The contact period refers to the Historic Period cemetery at Malibu or any time after 1769.

social standing (King, 1969). In addition to burial location, depth of burials was significant in terms of wealth and rank, at least at the time of European contact. Chumash undertakers, called 'aqi, were responsible for digging graves, with the depth of the grave corresponding to the number of baskets given to the 'aqi as payment (Hollimon, 1997; King, 1969). At least at contact, burial depth was associated with material wealth. These ethnographic reports offer greater resolution regarding the mortuary customs of Chumash cultures and deeper symbolic meaning associated with grave goods.

8.2.3   Coastal Chumash: Ways of Life and Death

Chumash communities were hunter-fisher-gatherers without formal agricultural systems (Arnold et al., 2004; Gamble, 2008). Chumash diet was largely comprised of marine foods, including fish, shellfish, sea mammals, and locally obtained wild plant foods such as acorns and geophytes (Gamble, 2008; Gill, 2015). Terrestrial fauna were also consumed, but to a much lesser extent. Similar to other indigenous groups in California, the Chumash had a system of storing foodstuffs (e.g., acorns, wild cherry, chia seeds, sage, and preserved meats from both terrestrial and marine sources) (Gamble, 2005, 2008; King, 2000). Availability of food within the Chumash dietary spectrum enabled population size to remain fairly high. Estimates for Chumash population size at the time of historic contact range from 18 000 to 20 000 (Cook, 1976; Gamble, 2008; Johnson, 1998).

Chumash communities had hereditary chiefs that served as secular and religious leaders for densely populated villages (Arnold, et al., 2004; Gamble, 2008; Gamble et al., 2001; Lightfoot, 2005). These villages were areas of sociopolitical and economic importance that provided a focal point for community gatherings, trade relations, and opportunities for intermarriage between communities (Erlandson et al., 2001; Gamble, 2008). Bioarchaeological analyses document evidence for the physical ramifications of large populations and close communities: warfare, violent raiding, and illness. Paleopathological examinations indicate that Chumash and neighboring California Indian groups felt the effects of temporary resource shortages, overpopulation (crowding), and issues with sanitation due to dense populations (Erlandson and Bartoy, 1995; Erlandson et al., 2001; Lambert and Walker, 1991; Walker and Johnson, 1992, 1994).

The relatively large population size and widespread territory – including areas of coastal California along the Santa Barbara Channel, the Channel Islands, and the California mainland – set the stage for a far-reaching trade network with neighboring groups. Two primary factors that helped the Chumash establish and maintain this trade were reliance on shell beads, primarily manufactured on the Channel Islands, and the plank canoe (tomol), which was used to facilitate travel between the mainland and Channel Islands and was integral for fishing large game in deep waters (Arnold et al., 2004; Erlandson and Bartoy, 1995; Erlandson et al., 2001; Gamble, 2002, 2005, 2008). As part of this trade network, transit between the mainland and Channel Islands was important to obtain different types of shell beads that acted as markers of wealth and rank for Chumash, as well as, after about CE 1000, money (Arnold *et al.*, 2004; Gamble, 2005, 2008). Other prestige goods included in this trade network were intricately woven baskets, stone vessels (*comals* and *ollas*) shaped out of steatite, functional and decorative pestles alongside mortars, and even the *tomol* (Gamble, 2002, 2008). The aforementioned prestige items, along with items of everyday use, were commonly included in Chumash burials. Select high-ranking Chumash were interred with *tomols* and blanketed in huge quantities of beads (Gamble, 2008). Details of these mortuary contexts, when accompanied by ethnographic and ethnohistoric accounts, provide a rich picture of Chumash burial rites and customs.

8.3   Precontact and Historic Period Chumash Cemeteries at Humaliwo (Malibu, CA-LAN-64)

8.3.1   The Humaliwo Site

This chapter focuses on the *Humaliwo* (CA-LAN-64) site (Figure 8.1), the Chumash name roughly translating to "the surf sounds loudly" (King, 2000: 55). *Humaliwo* is

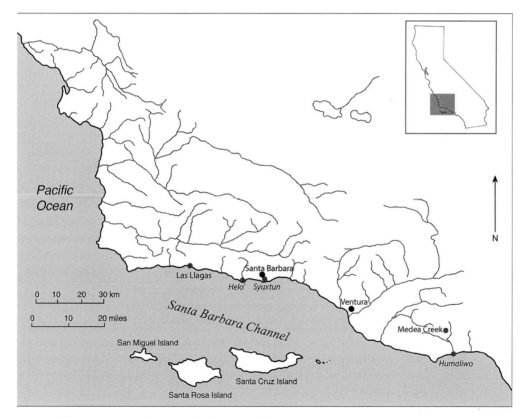

Figure 8.1 Regional map with key sites indicated.

situated along the southern California coastline on the outskirts of the Chumash region, near the southern end of the Santa Barbara Channel in the Santa Monica Mountains (Gamble, 2008). *Humaliwo*, an important political site during historic times, was the second largest coastal settlement in the Santa Monica mountains region, with nearby *Muwu* recorded as the largest (Gamble, 2008). Although a significant site for political reasons, it was smaller and more peripheral than many other Chumash sites – such as *Syuxtun* and *Helo'* near the modern towns of Goleta and Santa Barbara – in the neighboring region to the northwest, both of which had multiple chiefs overseeing populations of over 500 people (Gamble, 2008).

Humaliwo was occupied from approximately 550 BCE through European contact (Gamble, 2008); however, the cemeteries found at the site were in use for a limited time period, from about CE 950 to 1805. Both cemeteries were dated chronometrically with radiocarbon methods and with temporally diagnostic artifacts. The precontact cemetery dates between CE 950 and 1150 (Middle Period 5a, b, c, following King's chronology) (Gamble, 2008; King, 2000). This date is based on changes in the types of shell beads and ornaments associated with burial lots. In addition, two radiocarbon dates from the precontact cemetery place occupation around the ninth century (Martz, 1984). King provides additional information on one of these dates, noting it as an uncorrected bone collagen date (UCLA-1886, 1246 ± 60 RCYBP) from a burial (King, 1990). The other date was also probably uncorrected. The shell and glass beads recovered in the historic cemetery indicate that it dates from approximately CE 1775 to 1805, when mission recruitment reached completion (Gamble, 2008).

8.3.2   Excavation History of *Humaliwo*

The cemeteries at *Humaliwo* (CA-LAN-64) were first excavated during multiple seasons of UCLA field classes beginning in 1964 and continuing between 1972 and 1975 (Gamble, 2008). Most data from these excavations are in unpublished reports addressing grave goods and osteological parameters (Bickford, 1982; Davidson, 1992; Gamble et al., 1995; Gibson, 1975, 1987; Green, 1999; Martz, 1984; Meighan, 1978; Profant, 1992; Suchey et al., 1972; Walker et al., 1996), except for an article by Gamble et al. (2001). Original excavation notes document that 90 burials were excavated from the precontact cemetery and 140 burials from the historic cemetery (Accessions 572 and 573, Archaeological field notes on file at the Fowler Museum, UCLA). The historic period cemetery was excavated in entirety.

Even though *Humaliwo* was occupied into the historic period, there are some notable issues with preservation. Given the Mediterranean climate throughout coastal southern California, preservation of organic materials such as wood, cordage, and human remains is not ideal, but significant information was collected from shell, animal bone, and other more durable materials. Both cemeteries suffered from bioturbation, mostly from gophers, which displaced some aspects of the burial context. Nevertheless, it does not appear that artifact distributions were biased from these post-depositional processes. The precontact cemetery had better organic preservation with more evidence for bioturbation, while the historic cemetery had very poor organic preservation with less bioturbation. These factors, among others, have been accounted for in the subsequent analyses.

8.4   Archaeological Analysis of the Cemeteries at Malibu

A variety of grave goods were excavated from the precontact and contact components of the Malibu site. These objects were grouped into three categories: ornaments, religious objects, and utilitarian objects. Ornaments include objects used to adorn the body, such as beads. Ethnographic and ethnohistoric accounts describe these beads as material indicators of authority and wealth. In one account penned by José Longinós Martínez in 1792, strings of shell beads were worn on the top of men's heads, where these items were easily accessed for gambling and trading (Simpson, 1961).

The second category of grave goods comprises religious objects, which, based on ethnographic evidence, were often used during ritual activities (Applegate, 1978; Hudson and Blackburn, 1986; Walker and Hudson, 1993). Objects in this class include carved stone effigies, painted rocks, charm stones, quartz crystals, turtle-shell rattles, pipes, flutes, and whistles. Many of these objects – especially stone effigies and charm stones – are known throughout central and southern California as personal talismans to harness and control powerful supernatural forces (Applegate, 1978; Hudson and Blackburn, 1986; Walker and Hudson, 1993). Talismans, some of which were acquired during vision quests, were only of use to owners and would have been buried with these individuals. Other items, such as bird-shaped stone effigies, may represent particular aspects of male/female dualism as described in creation stories (Koerper and Labbé, 1987; Lee, 1981), while quartz crystals were believed to be extremely powerful stones and may have been used by magico-medical practitioners (Hudson and Blackburn, 1986). Additional objects, such as tobacco pipes, would have been used in ceremonial contexts to evoke supernatural outcomes, and similarly, turtle-shell rattles, flutes, and whistles would have been used to accompany ceremonial dancing and singing in ritual contexts (Hudson and Blackburn, 1986; King, 1982).

The third category comprises utilitarian objects such as mortars and pestles for food processing, shell fish hooks for fishing, and various stone and bone tools used for weapons, animal butchering, and basket making. These objects are classified as utilitarian due to use in daily life. However, symbolic meanings may have shifted once these items were used in funerary contexts (Ekengren, 2013).

8.5   Results

8.5.1   The Precontact Cemetery

The majority of the 90 excavated burials in the precontact cemetery had 20 or fewer beads (68 percent, $n = 61$), while nearly half of these ($n = 26$) were buried without any beads (Figure 8.2). In contrast, a small percentage (3 percent) of burials had 1000 or

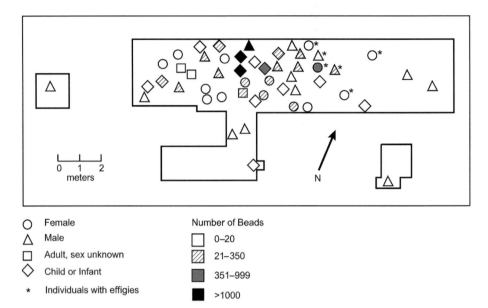

Figure 8.2 Map of Middle Period cemetery (excludes burials with insufficient information on age, location, or artifact association).

more beads. If beads are considered along with other forms of ornamentation, then there are five burials, three of which are pre-adults[2] that had 850 or more ornamental artifacts (Figure 8.2). The largest bead lot in both cemeteries was found with a pre-adult, who had 4564 beads. Approximately 80 percent of burials included beads distributed at or around the head or neck of the interred individual in both cemeteries at Malibu (Accession 573, Archaeological field notes on file at the Fowler Museum, UCLA). Spatial patterning of individuals with beads and those with few to none is also worthy of note, as those interred with many beads were located toward the center of the cemetery, while those who had few to none were located on the periphery (Figure 8.2). This pattern is also intriguing when considering the relative distribution of the number of grave goods correlated with burial depth; burials with more than 1000 artifacts have a mean depth of 236 cm, while those with less than 1000 artifacts have a mean depth of 197 cm. This is a statistically significant positive correlation ($r_s = 0.32$, $p = 0.004$), which suggests that wealthier individuals had deeper graves. A similar pattern was observed in the historic cemetery: Individuals with more grave goods had deeper burials (Table 8.1). It should be noted that the precontact cemetery was covered with 152 cm of highway fill; the mean depths presented include this fill.

Investigating these spatial relationships further, it is possible to examine the horizontal distances between burials within the cemetery, which provide a measure of burial location – relative to the center of these circular/elliptical-shaped cemeteries – as well as providing an idea of burial density. Burials with the greatest average

---

[2] We classify "pre-adults" here to be individuals under the age of 12 years.

Table 8.1 Summary of observations for each cemetery at Malibu.

	Prehistoric	Historic
Time period	CE 950–1150	CE 1775–1805
No. burials	90	140
Burial treatment	All flexed	All flexed
No. shell beads in cemetery	14 124	37 085
No. glass beads in cemetery	0	16 006
No. stone beads in cemetery	34	13
No. bone beads in cemetery	7	0
No. ornaments in cemetery	164	23
No. total beads and ornaments	14 329	53 127
Percentage of burials with 20 or fewer beads	68	45
Percentage of burials with no beads	29	21
Percentage of burials with >1000 beads	3	9
Percentage of burials with 30 or more artifacts	33	67
Percentage of burials with utilitarian items	25	4
Percentage of burials with religious artifacts	21	4
Percentage placed near/around head/neck	80	
Mean depth of burials with >1000 artifacts	236 cm	82 cm
Mean depth of burials with <1000 artifacts	197 cm	66 cm
Spatial distribution of burials with beads and ornaments	People near center have more beads	People near center have more beads
Average space between adjacent burials	~35 cm	~35 cm
Grave goods	66.6 percent largely lacked grave goods	33 percent largely lacked grave goods
Percentage of effigies with women	78 percent	No effigies in cemetery
Preservation	Better preserved	Poorly preserved
Relatedness	Women more closely related than males	Analysis not feasible
Linear enamel hypoplasias	61 percent of burials with no grave goods had hypoplasia	Tendency for burials with no grave goods to have hypoplasia, but insufficient sample size

distances from others are located along the periphery, while those with the smallest average distances are located more centrally, a pattern that is consistent across age and sex in both cemeteries. On average, burials in the precontact cemetery are approximately 35 cm apart. Furthermore, all burials are flexed, and almost all are oriented with heads to the west/southwest; as with the measure of distances between

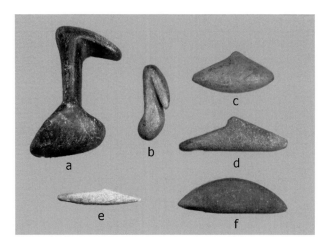

Figure 8.3 Effigies from Middle Period Malibu cemetery: (a) UCLA catalog no. 1733, dark gray chlorite schist; (b) UCLA catalog no. 1057, gray biotite schist; (c) UCLA catalog no. 1742, gray siltstone or schist; (d) UCLA catalog no. 1741 gray-brown biotite schist; (e) UCLA catalog no. 1740, siltstone; (f) UCLA catalog no. 1770, gray shale.

burials, these trends are not confounded by sex or age ($p > 0.1$). Overall, burials in the precontact cemetery largely lacked grave goods (66.6 percent had 30 or fewer items), with only 25 percent of burials having utilitarian objects, 22.2 percent religious objects, and 13.3 percent bifaces.

Of special interest to this study are the small stone effigies or talismans that are common in the precontact cemetery (Figures 8.3 and 8.4). Many of the 68 effigies found in the precontact cemetery include carved anatomical features such as eyes, mouths, and dorsal fins, and appear to be fish (Figures 8.3 and 8.4). Two of the effigies are "pelican stones" with beak-like projections (Figure 8.3(a) and (b)), and a third probably represents a whale (Figure 8.4(i); Meighan, 1976). Forty-three effigies are colored with red ochre, and a few of these may have been painted (Gamble et al., 1996). Eleven individuals were buried with effigies: five were females, four were males, and two were of unknown sex. Females had 53 (78 percent) of the total number of effigies, while males had 12 (18 percent), and two people of unknown sex had three (4 percent). Except for a child aged six years, all individuals with effigies were young adults between 17 and 30 years. Burials with effigies are clustered in the eastern portion of the cemetery, and most do not have large numbers of beads (Figure 8.2). The one exception is Burial 35, with 21 effigies and 962 beads (Gamble et al., 1996). Females had the highest frequency of effigies in our sample, and two females aged 17 years were the only individuals buried with pelican stones.

8.5.2   The Contact Era Cemetery

There are many similarities, as well as subtle differences, between the historic and precontact cemeteries, including the percentage of individuals with beads. In the

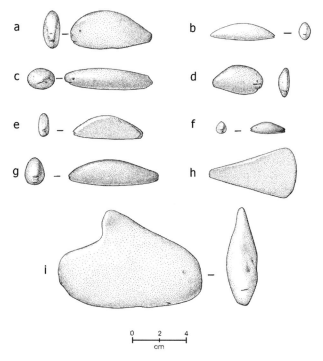

Figure 8.4 Effigies from the Middle Period Malibu cemetery: (a) UCLA catalog no. 1734, gray steatite; (b) UCLA catalog no. 1750, gray steatite; (c) UCLA catalog no. 1743, Catalina anthophyllite; (d) UCLA catalog no. 1737, gray steatite; (e) UCLA catalog no. 1771, brown shale; (f) UCLA catalog no. 1772, green serpentine; (g) UCLA catalog no. 1764, gray steatite; (h) UCLA catalog no. 1751, brown metamorphic slate, possible fish effigy; (i) UCLA catalog no. 3218, gray steatite, whale.

historic cemetery, nearly half (45 percent, $n = 65$) of the 140 excavated burials have 20 or fewer beads, while just under half of this group ($n = 30$) were buried without any beads (Figure 8.5). A small percentage (9 percent, $n = 12$) of burials had 1000 or more beads. As with the precontact cemetery, the pattern of pre-adults differs from that of adults – the majority (68 percent) of pre-adults in the historic cemetery have beads. This does not differ significantly ($\chi^2 = 0.22$, $p = 0.642$) between the cemeteries, nor does it differ significantly (Kruskal Wallis Test, $\chi^2 = 0.35$, $p = 0.5$) between infants and children in both cemeteries. The spatial patterning of those who had beads and those with few to no beads is also similar between the precontact and contact cemeteries. Except for one individual, all those buried with 1000 or more beads were interred in the southern portion of the cemetery, while people with some beads are scattered throughout the cemetery, and those with no beads were located on the periphery (Figures 8.2 and 8.5). As with the precontact cemetery, the relative distribution of number of grave goods correlated with burial depth ($r_s = 0.32$, $p = 0.006$). Burials that have more than 1000 artifacts have a mean depth of 82 cm, while those with fewer than 1000 artifacts have a mean depth of 66 cm.

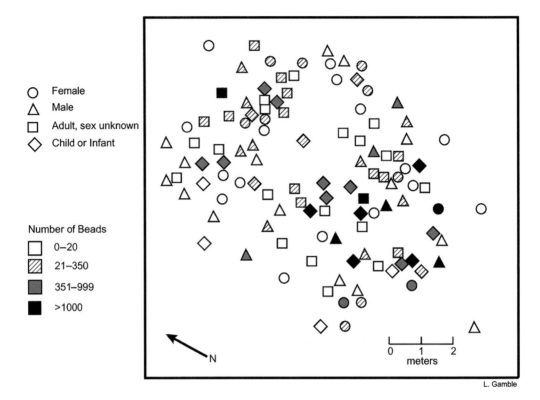

Figure 8.5 Map of historic period cemetery (excludes burials with insufficient information on age, location, or artifact association).

The placement of grave goods with individuals was also investigated to gain a deeper insight into the significance of burial practices (Baxter, 2008; Ekengren, 2013). By examining the positioning of beads, it is possible to assess whether the individual was adorned with beads before transit to the gravesite, or if these beads were deposited at a later time. If adorned with beads prior to carrying the body to the grave, beads would be expected to be around the head or neck, as most descriptions of historic Chumash note that this is how beads were worn. The notes for individuals in the historic cemetery associated with more than 1000 beads were examined for the placement of bead offerings on the individual interred. Of the 13 individuals in the historic cemetery who were buried with more than 1000 beads, two did not have adequate information. For the remaining 11 individuals, nine had the majority of beads placed around the neck or head, and seven of these were infants or children. In a few cases, even discrete strands of beads could be observed. For example, Burial 56, a male, aged 19 years, was interred in a plank canoe, had 16 strands of beads around his neck, with some spilling over to the shoulder area. The context of the burial was relatively undisturbed, so the patterns of the beads – consisting primarily of large amounts of *Olivella* rough disk beads interspersed with 11 red abalone shell beads and then more *Olivella* beads – could be distinguished for some of the strands. In one case, beads were found above the body, similar to a breast plate. This may have been a practical consideration considering that the burial was an infant. Two other individuals had some beads in the pelvis or near the legs, suggesting that these items may have been placed at the time of interment. One of the more interesting burials is nearly identical to ethnohistoric descriptions of men wearing strands of beads wrapped around the head. Burial 78, a 27-year-old male, had strands of *Olivella* disk beads still wrapped around the cranium.

When examining spatial relationships within the historic cemetery, horizontal spacing was similar to that documented in the precontact cemetery (approximately 35 cm apart); this pattern was also consistent in terms of age and sex divisions, with no significant difference between the cemeteries (analysis of variance, $F = 0.60$, $p = 0.8$). As with the precontact cemetery, all identifiable burials were recorded in a flexed position with heads oriented to the west/southwest, which did not differ for sex or age. Looking at the proportion of burials with grave goods in the historic cemetery, there was a much larger proportion ($\chi^2 = 11.3$, $p = 0.001$) of grave goods altogether (67 percent) than in the precontact cemetery, and there were more artifacts included in the burials of individuals ($\chi^2 = 6.1$, $p = 0.01$) than in the earlier cemetery. Burials in the historic period cemetery had fewer utilitarian items (3.6 percent, $\chi^2 = 24.5$, $p < 0.0005$), religious objects (3.6 percent, $\chi^2 = 19.5$, $p < 0.0005$), and bifaces (2.9 percent) than precontact burials (Table 8.1).

8.6   Discussion

This section compares the two cemeteries at Malibu in terms of mortuary rituals, symbolism, and social organization. The goal is to demonstrate how traditional Chumash culture persisted despite a period of disruptive cultural interaction.

8.6.1   Spatial Delineations for the Precontact and Contact Cemeteries

Spatial orientation of grave placement within the cemeteries appear relatively consistent through time. For both cemeteries, burials with the largest numbers of beads (1000+) tend to be clustered together near the center of the cemetery, while those with few to no grave goods are distributed along the periphery (Figures 8.2 and 8.5). In the precontact cemetery, there was a discrete grouping of burials that contained effigies, while there were no effigies documented for any of the historic period burials. This phenomenon is likely a result of shifting organization of religious and political leadership that solidified by the time of contact. In addition, individuals were closely and discretely interred within a confined area at both cemeteries; this suggests that cemeteries were circumscribed areas with sharp delineations from the living world of Chumash. It is likely that both populations in this community viewed these barriers as important dichotomies between the living and spirit worlds. Lastly, grave depth is positively correlated with the accumulation of material wealth in the grave of the deceased in both cemeteries.

8.6.2   Maintenance of Ascribed Social and Political Hierarchies

The Malibu cemetery data provide evidence for the maintenance of ascribed social and political hierarchies over time. One significant commonality between cemeteries is that only a relatively small proportion of the individuals were buried with a large number of grave goods, with a select few pre-adults buried with a multitude of beads (Table 8.1). For example, in the historic cemetery, seven of the 13 burials with over 1000 beads were pre-adults; five were infants; and two were children aged five and six years. These infants and children were treated similarly to the adults in the cemetery, indicating that these individuals were viewed as fully human and highly valued within Chumash society (Fowler, 2004; Joyce, 2000).

8.6.3   Persistence of Shell Beads as Currency in the Contact Period

Grave goods from the contact period cemetery were almost entirely (99 percent) beads, and the majority of those were the type that functioned as currency. It is important to note that the historic period had larger numbers of individuals buried with beads and increased bead counts per grave (Table 8.1). The pattern is attributable in part to the importation of glass beads by Spanish colonizers. This scenario posed an economic dilemma for Chumash communities in which shell beads were used as a form of currency. In this case, it seems that Chumash bead-makers chose to produce a much higher volume of *Olivella* rough disk shell beads to balance currency inflation. The continued manufacture, trade, and use of shell beads, despite the influx of an equivalent commodity – glass beads – attests to the persistence of traditional artifacts that have symbolic, economic, ritual, and political significance. Even within a circumscribed region, shell beads had multiple meanings depending on context. The meaning of shell beads, therefore, transcends the material object. The persistent use of shell beads in mortuary rites goes well beyond materiality and instead signifies the entanglements of the many individuals involved in the production and use of these items.

8.6.4   Evidence for Resilience in Chumash Lifeways after Contact

Grave goods in the contact period cemetery were drawn from a wider variety of contexts and include glass trade beads and metal objects related to ranching and herding. At face value, it may seem that this would suggest a discontinuity in native practices; however, this section aims to delineate ways in which the Chumash used newly available materials and goods from the Spanish as a means to continue practicing local traditions (Silliman, 2009). The presence of these artifacts also illustrates that the Chumash were willing to embody new roles and adapt to novel circumstances, with some individuals perhaps benefiting from these situations. The discrete use of the contact period cemetery between CE 1775 and 1805 provides fine-grained temporal shifts in European artifact acquisition by the Chumash.

In addition to about 15 000 glass trade beads, the historic Malibu burial offerings included some unusual objects of European origin. Metal artifacts posited in graves or in the area of the historic cemetery were typical of European tools used by the Spanish and Indian cowboys, or *vaqueros*, who worked on the *ranchos* established in the greater Los Angeles area (Gamble, 2015). These items include five *higos* (small ornaments suspended from saddle skirts), ornaments from Spanish bridles, part of an iron spur consisting of a star rowel and heel plate, and one iron *concho*, an ornament *vaqueros* wore both on the sides of their pants and on bridles or hats (Bickford, 1982). Other metal objects include four iron knives, adzes, six iron spikes or nails, pieces of firearms, a copper bead, a St. Francis medal, two metal cups (one copper, one iron), two shoe buckles, seven metal buttons, and parts of a sword. In addition to metal artifacts in and near the cemetery, there was one burial of an infant in an apothecary jar. Given the abundance of European artifacts interred with or found in the vicinity of the historic period Malibu burials, there was considerable interaction between the people of Malibu and the Spanish colonists (Bickford, 1982). The Chumash probably obtained some of these goods in exchange for work as cowboys and farm laborers.

Ethnohistoric records provide further support and describe Chumash working for Spanish colonists. On a trip between Ventura and Los Angeles in 1795, Father Vicente de Santa Maria reported seeing Indians working as "cowherds, cattlemen, irrigators, bird catchers, horsemen, etc." (Engelhardt, 1927: 9), and also cultivating watermelons, sugar melons, and corn. By this time, many Chumash not associated with the missionaries had adopted European clothing – including blankets and sombreros – and worked as muleteers for the settlers (Engelhardt, 1927). Examining the presence of metal objects at a finer timescale, even more patterning among the individuals in the historic cemetery is observable. King (1996) placed 37 of the historic era burials into rough five-year increments between 1775 and 1805, based on subtle changes of the *Olivella biplicata* disk beads. Of the 37 burials dated by this method, none had metal artifacts until after 1785. This type of patterning was not found among the individuals with glass beads, suggesting that glass beads were probably more widespread throughout the historic period than metal artifacts.

8.6.5   Shift in Religious Organization

Although many similarities exist between the precontact and contact period cemeteries, significant differences are noted in the distribution of religious objects, effigies in particular. The fact that most of the effigies were found with women can be interpreted from a variety of perspectives, but effigies need to be interpreted with the consideration that many items placed in graves may reflect the intentions of mourners, rather than those of the deceased (Gillespie, 2001). The ethnographic and ethnohistoric records indicate that fishing was not a major subsistence activity of Chumash women (Gamble, 1983). Therefore, it seems unlikely that these effigies acted as fishing talismans for the interred, though it is possible that these items were transmitted to women from males in the community. An alternative interpretation is that more women than men were ritual specialists at Malibu during the precontact period and the effigies may reflect ceremonial usage. The small number of beads associated with most of the burials that also contain effigies suggests that these individuals had less access to wealth than people buried with many beads and other grave goods. However, control and ownership of effigies likely had important social implications due to associations with shamanic activities.

The spatial clustering of burials with effigies in a restricted area of the cemetery suggests that these artifacts were reserved for select members of the community and supports the contention that ritual power may have been controlled by hereditary groups. In an artifact-based analysis of Chumash social evolution, King (1990) proposes that religious artifacts became less common as Late Period burial accompaniments when compared to earlier periods, and instead are cached outside cemeteries. This implies that the decline in effigy use was associated with the institutionalization of religion.

The role of the 'antap as a combined position of political leadership and as a ritual specialist fits well with interpreting the aforementioned patterns. In the Middle Period, evidence suggests that there was a strong division between religious and political leaders, which was not continued into the contact period. This follows suit with the absence of plank canoes in the Middle Period cemetery, and the presence of these canoes in the sumptuous burials of wealthy individuals during the contact period. Eleven burials from the contact period cemetery are associated with asphaltum or wood, suggesting that some of these individuals were buried with canoes or canoe parts. Three of these 11 burials have unmistakable associations with plank canoes and were also buried with large numbers of beads; the greatest of these (Burial 56) has 2347 shell beads and 48 glass beads. It appears that in the contact period there was a symbolic use of certain burial offerings, including plank canoes, to serve as material manifestations that further reinforced social boundaries. This is another example of a change in burial practice between periods that puts the focus on secular authorities who had the power and wealth to engage in trade and travel between communities. The 'antap position is crucial here as it provided a legitimizing way for religious, economic, and secular power to be maintained among a select few individuals from every village, and thus, away from the larger community. Data from this study further support the contention that ritual power was likely controlled by hereditary groups.

One trend that did not change at Malibu was burial position; all burials were in the flexed position, indicating continuity in traditions over time, a trait typical throughout the Chumash area. Corbett (2007) examined burial positions during the Early and Middle Periods and documented that 69 percent of the burials (808 out of 1179) were in a flexed position. By the Middle Period Phase 4, Corbett noted that all burials except reburials were flexed. Even though Malibu is situated in the southern periphery of the Chumash region, the pattern of flexed burials is widely shared, and therefore recognized by the Chumash when preparing the body for the afterlife.

8.6.6   Chumash Resilience and Adaptation: A Regional Overview

A number of the patterns discussed above are also evident from sites near Malibu, as well as in other regions within California. An example from the Pomo Indians in northern California serves as an interesting parallel for indigenous bead production practices. Manufacture of clam shell and baked magnesite beads was an important industry during the historic period in central California. In 1875, Hudson (Heizer, 1975: 9–27) wrote about the Pomo bead-makers of the time and suggested that this traditional medium of exchange was more valued than the glass beads offered by the Spanish. It is clear that both the Pomo and Chumash had access to many glass beads, but also chose to continue to use and trade shell beads. The Tongva or Gabrielino, direct neighbors of the Chumash at Malibu, are known to have maintained ritual exchanges involving shell beads with groups such as the Cahuilla in the Palm Springs area (Strong, 1929). Shell beads were used in a variety of ways in California, which changed in meaning and value across networks of people. These beads both acted as political symbols and contained economic value, but could also be used as objects to denote identities that held ritual significance (Gamble, 2016).

The cemeteries at Malibu fit squarely within regional patterns, in that religious artifacts were commonly buried with individuals in earlier periods, but later were buried in caches instead, possibly as a result of the institutionalization of religion among the Chumash (Gamble *et al.*, 2001; King, 1990). Malibu and Medea Creek cemeteries share a pattern in which religious objects are fairly numerous in the precontact period, but nearly nonexistent in the contact period, suggesting a widespread shift in religious symbolism at this time. Gamble and colleagues (2001) suggested that the disappearance of these objects as grave goods may be indicative of a power shift during the Late Period, in which religious leaders were replaced by secular authorities, but this could also be an effect of change in how the objects were used and deposited. This interpretation complements previous studies. For example, at the Las Llagas cemetery (CA-SBA-81), used in Middle Period 2a (200 BCE–CE 200), individuals who were associated with beads and ornaments were buried in different areas than those with religious objects (King, 1990). The historic period cemetery at *Helo'* (CA-SBA-46) mirrors the patterns seen at Malibu, in which burials exhibiting great wealth are found in direct association with canoes as grave goods (Gamble, 2008). Decreasing frequency in religious objects over time, along with the advent of canoes becoming a part of wealthy burial assemblages, further supports the idea that there was a consolidation of religious and political power prior to the contact period.

8.7   Conclusion

Resilience of the Chumash in the face of drastic changes during European colonization is the theme of this chapter. It has been suggested by Kintigh and colleagues (2014) that understanding human resilience in the past is one of five primary grand challenges for archaeologists in the twenty-first century. In the case of the Chumash, there exists evidence for a society that was colonized at a critical time – when these communities were supporting dense populations subsisting only on foods that were fished, hunted, and gathered. The ability of Chumash to continue traditional subsistence strategies was greatly curtailed by the Spanish, who restricted Chumash access to favored places for acquiring foods and materials used to make houses, baskets, bows and arrows, and other traditional items. Despite significant obstacles and limited access to customary resources, the Chumash continued to hold feasts (Gamble, 2015), manufacture shell beads, hold ceremonies, and produce baskets. The Malibu cemeteries provide details about this transformative period and benefit those interested in resiliency as a means to understanding what aspects of life changed rapidly, more slowly, or persisted after European contact. The pattern of flexed interments reflects long-term continuity in mortuary rituals. The continued use of shell beads in the contact cemetery demonstrates further continuity in symbolic and ritual rites surrounding the commemoration of the dead. Traits such as diversity of treatment of the dead, inequality, and inherited position are documented for both the precontact and historic eras, suggesting that even in the face of radical changes in lifeways, social norms were maintained. Implied in the persistence of traditional practices is the agency of the Chumash, who made use of European goods when convenient, while still retaining traditional lifeways (see also Gamble, 2015). Individuals buried with shell and glass beads, along with cowboy trappings, relay a complex story of human agency under the duress of outsiders attempting to eradicate indigenous belief systems.

The significance of human agency is one theme consistently stressed in resilience theory (e.g., Redman, 2005; Sauer, 2014; Walker *et al.*, 2004). As previously discussed, human agents can evoke significant change in ecological and social environments over short and long periods of time. For example, Rick (2010) identifies the importance of human agency for the adaptability and resilience of Channel Island Chumash subsistence practices over thousands of years. Evidence of resilience can also be seen at the inter- and intra-societal levels in the establishment and maintenance of exchange networks. These networks would have been responsible for the movement of goods, information, and even people as exogamous marriage partners, which is exemplified in this work especially in regard to the *'antap*. The function of such networks was to preserve particular segments of society by creating reciprocal relationships between groups within the network. These reciprocal ties were reinforced by visible demonstrations of this relationship such as ceremonies and rituals, marriages, alliances (Redman and Kinzig, 2003). As argued in this chapter, the Chumash were able, through adaptability in social practices, to withstand drastic social changes, namely European colonization (generally see Redman, 2005; Walker *et al.*, 2004).

The incorporation of European material culture and social practices into the daily lives of the Chumash must be considered in light of how these objects and practices could have been used to structure or re-structure daily lives (Silliman, 2009). Even in instances in which "European" objects are incorporated into indigenous contexts, this should not be seen as a loss of culture, but rather as a means by which indigenous practices were readjusted to allow for the persistence of cultural traditions (Silliman, 2009). Many of the European artifacts in this study relate directly or indirectly to new avenues of wealth acquisition for the Chumash by way of employment as *rancho* hands or *vaqueros* (Gamble, 2008). Examples such as these highlight the complexities and intricacies of Chumash and Spanish colonial interactions and also demonstrate active agency on the part of the Chumash (Gamble, 2008, 2015; Gamble *et al.*, 2001). Models of ethnogenesis, or "the emergence of new cultural identities" (Voss, 2015: 655), on the surface seem suitable to this analysis. However, Voss (2015) expressed concern about the broad interpretation of ethnogenesis that encompasses tactics "of resistance among subaltern communities," and suggested that the transformations of social identity in ethnogenesis are frequently hastened by substantive demographic shifts that are often seen within colonial societies. The archaeological record alone cannot substantiate the idea that Malibu Chumash who were buried with spurs, *conchos*, and other items associated with *vaqueros* were in fact taking on a new identity; instead, these individuals may have been maintaining a Chumash identity that was transposed onto items of Spanish origin.

For the Chumash, mortuary ceremonialism was an integrative process that reinforced aspects of individual social identities, especially in terms of authority and wealth. Material objects present in the Chumash burials in this study need larger social context for meaning, as these objects are inherent aspects of, as well as challenges to, concepts of daily practice (Silliman, 2009). Material goods that symbolized wealth and rank – canoes, for example – are one way that social identities of the deceased (held in life) were commemorated by the living. Examples from this study include the burial of an infant with a *higo* (Burial 95) and another interred in a Spanish apothecary jar (Burial 157), or a one-year-old with a copper cup. These cases are difficult to interpret and may have more to say about the family and other mourners that prepared the body than changing identities in a dynamic Chumash society. These items may be symbols of upward mobility, albeit ones that involve direct or indirect interactions with the new Spanish colonists. What is most significant here is that the Chumash, despite irreversible consequences due to the Spanish intrusion, continued to bury and mourn the dead according to rituals established well before Spanish contact.

The site of Malibu is one of many examples in which hunter-gatherer populations exhibited pronounced resilience while adapting to significant changes in the immediate environment. The Spanish colonial contingent that resided near Malibu in the contact period certainly produced significant change at the social level for the Chumash, but also afforded different social and economic roles not present previously in the region. The results of this analysis have many parallels in the greater region, including sites such as Las Llagas, *Helo'* on Mescalitan Island, and Medea Creek, which allow consideration of the mortuary similarities between these sites in conjunction with the extent of the Chumash sphere of influence. The many similarities between the precontact and contact period cemeteries in our study speak toward the maintenance and resilience of Chumash culture in terms of mortuary behavior, social organization, and religious beliefs over a time span of nearly a millennium.

Historical continuity and resilience is found among Chumash continuing up to today. One early example, also in the Ventureño region, is the post-mission Chumash Indian settlement of *Kamexmey*, situated just west of the mouth of the Ventura River

(Johnson, 2001). Harrington produced a sketch map of the *rancheria* in the 1840s based on information provided by Fernando Librado. Harrington mapped seven houses, including the chief's dwelling, a sweat lodge, and a semicircular structure where one of the women made beads for the village chief. There is also evidence that the canoes were produced on Santa Cruz Island. The village at *Kamexmey* and activities that occurred there serve as testimony to the continued persistence of traditional religious and economic activities. Distinct Chumash communities in Ventura persist even later in the nineteenth century. According to the 1880 Census, the Chumash continued to live in Ventura, with many families moving to a neighborhood southwest of the mission, known as "Indian Town" or "Spanish Town" (Johnson, 1994). Three well-known basket-makers from Ventura lived in this neighborhood and were friends: Petra Pico, Doniciana, and Candelaria Valenzuela, who is believed to be the last Chumash basket weaver that learned the trade from a Chumash elder (Johnson, 1994). Candelaria died in 1917, and although Candelaria did not train any basket weavers living today, basket weaving is still an active pursuit among the Chumash and other California Indians, who meet regularly to gather materials, discuss the problems associated with finding sources for materials, and weave and display baskets. Unquestionably, this continuation of basket weaving, among other practices such as traditional singing and dancing, attests to the significance and persistence of Chumash Indian culture.

Acknowledgments

The original research for the Malibu investigations was funded by California State Parks with the encouragement of Tom Wheeler. We especially acknowledge Phil Walker, who died unexpectedly in 2009, and on whose work this chapter is based. He was a co-author of the original Malibu research and a mentor who will be remembered and honored. We also thank Glenn Russell, who was another co-author of the original Malibu publication. The collections from the Malibu excavations are curated at the Fowler Museum of Cultural History Archaeological Collections facility at UCLA, and we thank Wendy Teeter for her assistance with these collections. We thank Lori Palmer for assistance with Figure 8.1, Terisa Green for assistance with Figures 8.2 and 8.5, and Lisa Pompelli for assistance with Figure 8.4. We also thank Christopher Stojanowski and Daniel Temple for inviting us to participate in this volume and doing a fine job of editing it. The comments from Jon Erlandson and one anonymous reviewer strengthened the content of this chapter, and we are grateful for their detailed suggestions and edits. Any errors or omissions in this chapter are our own.

References

Applegate, R. B. (1978). *?Atishwin: The Dream Helper in South-Central California.* Ramona, CA: Ballena Press.

Arnold, J. E., Walsh, M. R., and Hollimon, S. E. (2004). The archaeology of California. *Journal of Archaeological Research*, 12, 1–73.

Baxter, J. E. (2008). The archaeology of childhood. *Annual Review of Anthropology*, **37**, 159–175.

Berkes, F. and Folke, C. (2000). Linking social and ecological systems for resilience and sustain-ability. In F. Berkes, C. Folke, and J. Colding, eds., *Linking Social and Ecological Systems: Management Practices and Social Mechanisms for Building Resilience*. Cambridge: Cambridge University Press, pp. 1–25.

Bickford, V. (1982). *European Artifacts from a Chumash Cemetery, CA-LAN-264*. MA thesis, California State University.

Blackburn, T. C. (1975). *December's Child: A Book of Chumash Oral Narratives*. Berkeley, CA: University of California Press.

Brown, A. K. (2001). *A Description of Unpublished Roads: Original Journals of the First Expedition into California, 1769–1770 by Juan Crespí*. San Diego: San Diego State University Press.

Cook, S. F. (1976). *The Population of the California Indians, 1769–1970*. Berkeley, CA: University of California Press.

Corbett, R. (2007). *The Grammar and Syntax of the Dead: A Regional Analysis of Chumash Mortuary Practice*. PhD dissertation, University of California.

Davidson, K. (1992). *Behavioral Significance of Variations in Morphology of the Mastoid*. MA thesis, University of California.

Dietler, M. (2010). *Archaeologies of Colonialism: Consumption, Entanglement, and Violence in Ancient Mediterranean France*. Berkeley, CA: University of California Press.

Dobyns, H. F. (1993). Disease transfer at contact. *Annual Review of Anthropology*, **22**, 273–291.

Ekengren, F. (2013). Contextualizing grave goods: Theoretical perspectives and methodological implications. In L. N. Stutz and S. Tarlow, eds., *The Oxford Handbook of the Archaeology of Death and Burial*. Oxford: Oxford University Press, pp. 173–192.

Engelhardt, Z. (1927). *San Fernando Rey, the Mission of the Valley*. Chicago, IL: Herald Press.

Erlandson, J. M. (1998). The making of Chumash tradition: Replies to Haley and Wilcoxon. *Current Anthropology*, **39**, 477–510.

Erlandson, J. M. and Bartoy, K. (1995). Cabrillo, the Chumash, and Old World diseases. *Journal of California and Great Basin Archaeology*, **17**, 153–173.

Erlandson, J. M., Rick, T. C., Kennett, D. J., and Walker, P. L. (2001). Dates, demography, and disease: Cultural contacts and possible evidence for Old World epidemics among the protohistoric island Chumash. *Pacific Coast Archaeological Society Quarterly*, **37**, 11–26.

Folke, C. (2006). Resilience: The emergence of a perspective for social–ecological systems analyses. *Global Environmental Change*, **16**, 253–267.

Fowler, C. (2004). *The Archaeology of Personhood: An Anthropological Approach*. London: Routledge.

Gamble, L. H. (1983). The organization of artifacts, features, and activities at Pitas Point: A coastal Chumash village. *Journal of California and Great Basin Archaeology*, **5**, 103–129.

Gamble, L. H. (2002). Archaeological evidence for the origin of the plank canoe in North America. *American Antiquity*, **67**, 301–315.

Gamble, L. H. (2005). Culture and climate: Reconsidering the effect of palaeoclimatic variability among southern California hunter-gatherer societies. *World Archaeology*, **37**, 92–108.

Gamble, L. H. (2008). *The Chumash World at European Contact*. Berkeley, CA: University of California Press.

Gamble, L. H. (2015). Subsistence practices and feasting rites: Chumash identity after European colonization. *Historical Archaeology*, **49**, 115–135.

Gamble, L. H. (2016). The entangled life of shell beads in North America. In C. Haselgrove and S. Krmnicek, eds., *Proceedings of the Workshop "Archaeology of Money," University of Tübingen, October 2013*. Leicester: Leicester Archaeology Monograph, pp. 67–83.

Gamble, L. H., Russell, G. S., and Hudson, J. (1995). *Archaeological Site Mapping and Collections Assessment of Humaliwu (CA-LAN-264) and Muwu (CA-VEN-11)*. Sacramento, CA: California Department of Parks and Recreation.

Gamble, L. H., Russell, G. S., King, C., and Hudson J. (1996). *Distribution of Wealth and Other Items at the Malibu Site, CA-LAN-264*. Sacramento, CA: California Department of Parks and Recreation.

Gamble, L. H., Walker, P. L., and Russell, G. S. (2001). An integrative approach to mortuary analysis: Social and symbolic dimensions of Chumash burial practices. *American Antiquity*, 66, 185–212.

Gibson, R. O. (1975). The beads of Humaliwo. *The Journal of California Anthropology*, 1, 110–119.

Gibson, R. O. (1987). *A Preliminary Study of Beads from Humaliwo, 4-LAN-264 at Malibu State Park, Los Angeles County, California*. San Diego, CA: California Department of Parks and Recreation.

Gill, K. M. (2015). *Ancient Plant Use and the Importance of Geophytes among the Island Chumash of Santa Cruz Island, California*. PhD dissertation, University of California.

Gillespie, S. D. (2001). Personhood, agency, and mortuary ritual: A case study from the ancient Maya. *Journal of Anthropological Archaeology*, 20, 73–112.

Green, T. M. (1999). *Spanish Missions and Native Religion: Contact, Conflict, and Convergence*. PhD dissertation, University of California.

Heizer, R. F. (1975). *They Were Only Diggers: A Collection of Articles from California Newspapers, 1851–1866, on Indian and White Relations*. Ramona, CA: Ballena Press.

Hemert-Engert, A. V. and Teggart, F. (1910). The narrative of the Portolá expedition of 1769–1770 by Miguel Constansó. *Publications of the Academy of Pacific Coast History*, 1, 9–159.

Hollimon, S. E. (1996). Sex, gender, and health among the Chumash: An archaeological examination of prehistoric gender roles. *Proceedings of the Society for California Archaeology*, 9, 205–208.

Hollimon, S. E. (1997). The third gender in native California: Two-spirit undertakers among the Chumash and their neighbors. In C. Claassen and R. A. Joyce, eds., *Women in Prehistory: North America and Mesoamerica*. Philadelphia, PA: University of Pennsylvania Press, pp. 173–188.

Holling, C. S. (1973). Resilience and stability of ecological systems. *Annual Review of Ecology and Systematics*, 4, 1–23.

Hudson, T. and Blackburn, T. C. (1986). *The Material Culture of the Chumash Interaction Sphere*, vol. 4, *Ceremonial Paraphernalia, Games, and Amusements*. Santa Barbara, CA: Ballena Press.

Hudson, T., Blackburn, T., Curletti, R., and Timbrook, J. (1977). *The Eye of the Flute: Chumash Traditional History and Ritual as Told by Fernando Librado Kitsepawit to John P. Harrington*. Santa Barbara, CA: Santa Barbara Museum of Natural History.

Hull, K., Douglass, J., and York, A. (2013). Recognizing ritual action and intent in communal mourning features on the southern California coast. *American Antiquity*, 78, 24–47.

Johnson, J. R. (1988). *Chumash Social Organization: An Ethnohistoric Perspective*. PhD dissertation, University of California.

Johnson, J. R. (1994). Ventura's Chumash community in the early 1880s. *Ventura County Historical Society Quarterly*, 39, 39–83.

Johnson, J. R. (1998). Foreword: A bibliographic history of Chumash sites. In M. S. Holmes and J. R. Johnson, eds., *The Chumash and Their Predecessors: An Annotated Bibliography*. Santa Barbara, CA: Santa Barbara Museum of Natural History, pp. i–xi.

Johnson, J. R. (2000). Social responses to climate change among the Chumash Indians of south-central California. In R. J. McIntosh, J. A. Tainter, and S. K. McIntosh, eds., *The Way the Wind Blows: Climate, History, and Human Action*. New York, NY: Columbia University Press, pp. 301–327.

Johnson, J. R. (2001). Ethnohistoric reflections of Cruzeño Chumash society. In J. A. Arnold, ed., *The Origins of a Pacific Coast Chiefdom: The Chumash of the Channel Islands*. Salt Lake City, UT: University of Utah Press, pp. 53–70.

Joyce, R. A. (2000). Girling the girl and boying the boy: The production of adulthood in ancient Mesoamerica. *World Archaeology*, 31, 473–483.

King, C. (1990). Evolution of Chumash society: A comparative study of artifacts used for social system maintenance in the Santa Barbara Channel region before A.D. 1804. In D. H. Thomas, ed., *The Evolution of North American Indians*. New York, NY: Garland Publishing, pp. 1–296.

King, C. (1996). Appendix I: Beads and ornaments from cemetery excavations at Humaliwo (CA-LAN-264). In L. Gamble, G. Russell, C. King, and J. Hudson, eds., *Distribution of Wealth and Other Items at the Malibu Site, CA-LAN-264*. Sacramento, CA: California Department of Parks and Recreation, pp. 1–42.

King, C. (2000). *Native American Indian Cultural Sites in the Santa Monica Mountains*. Thousand Oaks, CA: Santa Monica Mountains and Seashore Foundation and the National Park Service.

King, L. B. (1969). *The Medea Creek Cemetery (Lan-243): An Investigation of Social Organization from Mortuary Practices*. Los Angeles, CA: Department of Anthropology, University of California.

King, L. B. (1982). *Medea Creek Cemetery: Late, Inland Chumash Patterns of Social Organization, Exchange and Warfare*. PhD dissertation, University of California.

Kintigh, K. W., Altschul, J. H., Beaudry, M. C., *et al.* (2014). Grand challenges for archaeology. *American Antiquity*, **79**, 5–24.

Koerper, H. C. and Labbé A. J. (1987). A birdstone from San Diego County, California: A possible example of dimorphic sexual symbolism in Luiseño iconography. *Journal of California and Great Basin Archaeology*, **9**, 110–120.

Lambert, P. M. and Walker. P. L. (1991). Physical anthropological evidence for the evolution of social complexity in coastal southern California. *Antiquity*, **65**, 963–973.

Lee, R. B. (1981). Is there a foraging mode of production? *Canadian Journal of Anthropology*, **2**, 13–19.

Levin, S. A. (1999). *Fragile Dominion: Complexity and the Commons*. Cambridge, MA: Perseus Publishing.

Liebmann, M. and Murphy, M. S., eds. (2010). *Enduring Conquests: Rethinking the Archaeology of Resistance to Spanish Colonialism in the Americas*. Santa Fe, NM: School for Advanced Research Press.

Lightfoot, K. G. (1995). Culture contact studies: Redefining the relationship between prehistoric and historical archaeology. *American Antiquity*, **60**, 199–217.

Lightfoot, K. G. (2005). The archaeology of colonization: California in cross-cultural perspective. In G. J. Stein, ed., *The Archaeology of Colonial Encounters: Comparative Perspectives*. Santa Fe, NM: School of American Research Press, pp. 207–236.

Lyons, C. L. and Papadopoulos, J. K., eds. (2002). *The Archaeology of Colonialism*. Los Angeles, CA: Getty Research Institute.

Martz, P. C. (1984). *Social Dimensions of Chumash Mortuary Populations in the Santa Monica Mountains Region*. PhD dissertation, University of California.

McAnany, P. A. and Yoffee, N. (2009). Why we question collapse and study human resilience, ecological vulnerability, and the aftermath of empire. In P. A. McAnany and N. Yoffee, eds., *Questioning Collapse: Human Resilience, Ecological Vulnerability, and the Aftermath of Empire*. Cambridge: Cambridge University Press, pp. 1–20.

Meighan, C. W. (1976). Stone effigies in Southern California. *The Masterkey*, **50**, 25–29.

Meighan, C. W. (1978). Obsidian dating of the Malibu site. In C. W. Meighan and P. I. Vanderhoeven, eds., *A Compendium of the Obsidian Hydration Determinations Made at the UCLA Obsidian Hydration Laboratory*. Los Angeles, CA: Institute of Archaeology, University of California, pp. 158–161.

Murphy, M. S. and Klaus, H. D., eds. (2017). *Colonized Bodies, Worlds Transformed: Toward a Global Bioarchaeology of Contact and Colonialism*. Gainesville, FL: University Press of Florida.

Murphy, M. S., Goycochea, E., and Cock, G. (2010). Resistance, persistence, and accommodation at Puruchuco-Huaqerones, Peru. In M. Liebmann and M. S. Murphy, eds., *Enduring Conquests: Rethinking the Archaeology of Resistance to Spanish Colonialism in the Americas*. Santa Fe, NM: School for Advanced Research Press, pp. 57–76.

Preston, W. (1996). Serpent in Eden: Dispersal of foreign diseases into pre-mission California. *Journal of California and Great Basin Archaeology*, **18**, 2–37.

Profant, L. (1992). *Craniometric Variation in Earlier Human Populations of Southern California*. MA thesis, University of California.

Redman, C. L. (2005). Resilience theory in archaeology. *American Anthropologist*, **107**, 70–77.

Redman, C. L. and Kinzig, A. P. (2003). Resilience of past landscapes: Resilience theory, society, and the *Longue Durée. Conservation Ecology*, **7**, 14.

Rick, T. C. (2010). Weathering the storm: Coastal subsistence and ecological resilience on late Holocene Santa Rosa Island, California. *Quaternary International*, **239**, 135–146.

Rogers, J. D. (2005). Archaeology and the interpretation of colonial encounters. In G. J. Stein, eds., *The Archaeology of Colonial Encounters: Comparative Perspectives*. Santa Fe, NM: School of American Research Press.

Sauer, J. J. (2014). *The Archaeology and Ethnohistory of Araucanian Resilience*. New York, NY: Springer.

Silliman, S. W. (2009). Change and continuity, practice and memory: Native American persistence in colonial New England. *American Antiquity*, **74**, 211–230.

Simpson, L. B., translator (1961). *Journal of José Longinos Martínez: Notes and Observations of the Naturalist of the Botanical Expedition in Old and New California and the South Coast, 1791–1792*. San Francisco, CA: Howell Books.

Stein, G. J. (2005a). Introduction: The comparative archaeology of colonial encounters. In G. J. Stein, ed., *The Archaeology of Colonial Encounters: Comparative Perspectives*. Santa Fe, NM: School of American Research Press, pp. 3–31.

Stein, G. J. (2005b). The political economy of Mesopotamian colonial encounters. In G. J. Stein, ed., *The Archaeology of Colonial Encounters: Comparative Perspectives*. Santa Fe, NM: School of American Research Press, pp. 143–172.

Stojanowski, C. M. (2005). The bioarchaeology of identity in Spanish colonial Florida: Social and evolutionary transformation before, during, and after demographic collapse. *American Anthropologist*, **107**, 417–431.

Stojanowski, C. M. (2013). *Mission Cemeteries, Mission Peoples: Historical and Evolutionary Dimensions of Intracemetery Bioarchaeology in Spanish Florida*. Gainesville, FL: University Press of Florida.

Strong, W. D. (1929). *Aboriginal Society in Southern California*. Berkeley, CA: University of California Press.

Suchey, J. M., Wood, M. J., and Shermis, S. (1972). Analysis of human skeletal material from Malibu, California (LAN-264). *Archaeological Survey Annual Report*, **14**, 39–78.

Voss, B. L. (2015). What's new? Rethinking ethnogenesis in the archaeology of colonialism. *American Antiquity*, **80**, 655–670.

Wagner, H. R., ed. (1929). *Spanish Voyages to the Northwest Coast of America in the Sixteenth Century*. San Francisco, CA: California Historical Society.

Walker, B., Holling, C. S., Carpenter, S. R., and Kinzig, A. (2004). Resilience, adaptability and transformability in social–ecological systems. *Ecology and Society*, **9**, 5.

Walker, P. L. and Hudson, T. (1993). *Chumash Healing: Changing Health and Medical Practices in an American Indian Society*. Banning, CA: Malki Museum Press.

Walker, P. L. and Johnson, J. R. (1992). The effects of European contact on the Chumash Indians. In J. Verano and D. Ubelaker, eds., *Disease and Demography in the Americas: Changing Patterns before and after 1492*. Washington, DC: Smithsonian Institution, pp. 127–139.

Walker, P. L. and Johnson, J. R. (1994). The decline of the Chumash Indian population. In C. S. Larsen and G. Milner, eds., *In the Wake of Contact: Biological Responses to Conquest*. New York, NY: Wiley-Liss, pp. 109–120.

Walker, P. L., Drayer, F. J., and Siefkin, S. K. (1996). *Malibu Human Skeletal Remains: A Bioarchaeological Analysis*. Sacramento, CA: California Department of Parks and Recreation.

Walker, P. L., Lambert, P. M., Schultz, M., and Erlandson, M. J. (2005). The evolution of treponemal disease in the Santa Barbara Channel area of southern California. In M. L. Powell and D. C. Cook, eds., *The Myth of Syphilis: The Natural History of Treponematosis in North America*. Gainesville, FL: University of Florida Press, pp. 281–305.

9 Persistence or Pastoralism: The Challenges of Studying Hunter-Gatherer Resilience in Africa

Christopher M. Stojanowski

9.1 Introduction

This chapter is ultimately about Africa, a continent steeped in social, linguistic, ethnic, and biological diversity. The peoples of Africa maintained this diversity up through the present, including the persistence of resilient hunter-gatherer communities that are experiencing ever-increasing pressures and stresses through the encroachment of the global world (Kent, 1996; Kusimba, 2003, 2005; Woodburn, 1988). Research on the lifestyles of these hunter-gatherer societies is highly visible in the ethnographic literature (e.g., Lee, 1979, 1984; Marlowe, 2010; Turnbull, 1983), reflecting persistence in living alongside agriculturalists and pastoralists, often in conflict or tension (Svizzero and Tisdell, 2015). Indeed, subsistence economy is one of the key aspects of identity politics in polyethnic African states (Galaty, 1986; Kenrick and Lewis, 2001; Smith, 1986a, 1998a; ten Raa, 1986; Woodburn, 1988, 1997). As such, the notion of an evolutionary drive toward subsistence change can be discarded at the outset. Identities matter, and subsistence and lifestyle are core elements of these identities throughout the continent. Because of this, the appearance of new economic modes during the Middle Holocene did not result in wholesale acceptance of these new lifestyles; subsistence mosaics and landscapes of persistence emerged instead (see Ashley, 2010; Crowther *et al.*, 2017; Gifford-Gonzalez, 2003; Jousse *et al.*, 2008; Kuper and Riemer, 2013; Kusimba, 2005; MacDonald, 1997; MacDonald and Van Neer, 1994; Prendergast and Mutundu, 2010; Sampson, 2010; Thorp, 1997; Wright, 2011). In Africa, then, persistence and resilience are in many ways the norm, and biocultural transformations within an archaeological sequence must be demonstrated and not assumed.

As Kusimba (2005: 351) commented, "pinpointing the differences between food producers and hunter-gatherers is a significant challenge. 'Transitional' societies are many and difficult to categorize." It is well known among Africanists that Near Eastern models of "Neolithization" are poor fits for African prehistory, such that differentiating and "diagnosing" hunter-gatherers and food producers is a difficult task even in regions with well-established research traditions and ethnographic analogs such as East and South Africa (cf. Smith, 1998b; Smith *et al.*, 1991, Schirer, 1992). In the Sahara the situation is more tenuous. The Middle Holocene did not witness an initial transition to agricultural food production, but rather the regional and episodic emergence of cattle and caprine pastoralism as humans responded to a deteriorating climate and increasing aridity (Blench and MacDonald, 2000; Garcea, 2004; Holl, 1998;

Marshall and Hildebrand, 2002; Smith 1986b, 1992, 2008a, b). At the same time, many hunter-gatherer groups persisted and became specialized fisher-hunter-gatherers that endured alongside pastoralists for several millennia (Arioti and Oxby, 1997; Jousse, 2004, 2006; Jousse *et al.*, 2008; Linseele, 2017; MacDonald and Van Neer, 1994; McIntosh, 1993). The real challenge is that the absence of domesticated animals at a site does not reflect the value of these beings to past human societies (recently reviewed by Russell and Lander, 2015). As such, researchers are left with little guidance for diagnosing subsistence regimes in transitional populations, including resilient hunter-gatherers. The bioarchaeological research infrastructure for studying emergent pastoralism is also just developing (see Cameron and Pfeiffer, 2014; Eng, 2007, 2016; Machicek, 2011; Machicek and Zubova, 2012; Miller, 2013; Miller *et al.*, 2014; Murphy *et al.*, 2013; Schmidt *et al.*, 2016; Zhang *et al.*, 2015), which further complicates studies of hunter-gatherer resilience in Saharan contexts.

This chapter explores the issue of hunter-gatherer resilience by considering data from the site of Gobero, located in the southern Sahara in the modern nation of Niger. Gobero preserves a number of features that make it an ideal case study to consider the diagnostic difficulties of differentiating hunter-gatherer and pastoralist communities in the archaeological record. The site preserves dozens of human burials (a rarity throughout the central and southern Sahara) associated with a once verdant paleolake basin (Sereno *et al.*, 2008). Human occupation of the region spans the Early and Middle Holocene and is securely dated between 10 000 and 4000 BP with an occupational hiatus coincident with the 8.2 kya cal BP event (Guo *et al.*, 2000; Hassan, 1997; Petit-Maire, 1986, 1989; Petit-Maire *et al.*, 1993; Walker *et al.*, 2012). The relationship between, and biocultural adaptations of, pre- and post-hiatus populations have been the subject of considerable debate. The Middle Holocene occupation phase could represent the continuation of a hunter-gatherer society adapting to an increasingly hostile Sahara (resilience), the replacement of Early Holocene hunter-gatherers by allochthonous pastoralists (failure of resilience), population continuity with indigenous populations adopting pastoralism (transformability *sensu* Walker *et al.*, 2004), or a Middle Holocene community that was "polyethnic," with distinct peoples existing in close contact but with subsistence-based markers of identity structuring interactions (resilience), a situation present throughout contemporary West, East, and southern Africa (Ashley, 2010; Denbow, 1984; Frahm *et al.*, 2017; Galaty, 1986, Kusimba and Kusimba, 2005; Manning, 2011; McIntosh, 1993; Prendergast, 2010, 2011; Prendergast and Mutundu, 2010; Sadr, 1998; Sampson, 2010; Smith, 1986a, 1998a, b, 2008a, b; Smith *et al.*, 1991; ten Raa, 1986; Turner, 1987). This chapter takes an exploratory perspective focusing on the inference of diet and oral health as the key aspect of biocultural change associated with hunter-gatherer–pastoralist interactions. Here, the challenges inherent in studying hunter-gatherer resilience in many parts of the world with emerging archaeological research programs are outlined. In addition, the chapter argues that to understand resilience using the deep-time perspective offered by archaeology (Campbell and Butler, 2010; Falseit, 2015; Hegmon *et al.*, 2008; Redman and Kinzig, 2003), bioarchaeologists must learn to identify it. Only then can causality be inferred.

9.2   The Early and Middle Holocene of Niger

This chapter focuses on human biocultural adaptations in the southern Sahara during the African Humid Period, which had profound effects on the environment and population dynamics during the Early and Middle Holocene (Drake *et al.*, 2011; Kuper and Kröpelin, 2006; Manning and Timpson, 2014). The reconstructed archaeological sequence in Niger is based on only a handful of sites that are partially deflated and fragmented (for recent reviews, see Garcea, 2013a, b; Haour, 2003). Palimpsests are a major issue, and inferences of biocultural adaptations are based on the association between artifact functions and reconstructed paleoenvironments, occasional evidence of direct consumption of animals such as cut-marked or burned fauna (Gifford-Gonzalez and Parham, 2008; Roset *et al.*, 1990), and anthropogenic faunal concentrations such as middens (Clark *et al.*, 1973; Gifford-Gonzalez and Parham, 2008; Paris, 1997, 2000; Sereno *et al.*, 2008). Until the excavation of the cemeteries at Gobero, the human skeletal record for sites older than 6500 BP was almost nonexistent (a single grave from Iwelen; Paris, 1996), with very few directly dated human burials older than 5000 BP (reviewed by Haour, 2003). As such, inference of subsistence adaptations at the populational level has been limited.

As noted by Haour (2003), the Holocene witnessed a gradual southward shift in human landscape use as the climate became more arid. For the period of interest here (roughly 10 000 to 4000 BP), archaeological sites are concentrated in the northern half of Niger, principally the Ténéré Desert, the Aïr, and the Azawagh basin. French expeditions to Niger (e.g., Hugot, 1962; Joubert and Vaufrey, 1941–1946; Mauny, 1949; Paris, 1984, 1996; Quéchon and Roset, 1974) were supplemented by Clark and colleagues' work in the Adrar Bous, which helped define two major cultural complexes – the Kiffian and the Tenerian – that reflect the material culture of hunter-gatherers and pastoralists, respectively (Clark *et al.*, 1973, 2008a; Garcea, 2008; Smith, 2008a, b).

The Kiffian was initially defined in the Adrar Bous (Clark *et al.*, 1973; Smith, 1973, 1974, 1976, 2008a) and identified at other Early Holocene sites in northern Niger (Échallier and Roset, 1986; Guibert *et al.*, 1994; Paris, 1999; Roset, 1987; Roset *et al.*, 1990). Dates cluster around 9500 to 8500 BP, associated with the onset of the more hospitable conditions of the African Humid Period, but prior to the arid spike of the 8.2 kya cal BP event. Smith (2008a) summarized the material culture inventory that includes a microlithic industry, projectile points, polished bone points, and bone harpoons. Pottery is thick and coarsely made, large and globular in form, and decorated with rocker-stamped packed zig-zag or dotted wavy-line styles (Garcea, 2008). When combined with the association with lakebed sediments and lacustrine fauna (see Gifford-Gonzalez and Parham, 2008), this suggests a subsistence base built around hunting large game, fishing (with the harpoons suggestive of *Lates niloticus* as a target), and the harvesting of wild grains. Early pottery of local manufacture and the use of grindstones are suggestive of permanent or prolonged occupations; however, the ephemeral nature of many sites suggests the contrary (cf. Échallier and Roset, 1986; Garcea, 2008, 2013b; Smith, 2008a). Garcea (2008: 282) considered the Kiffian occupations at the Adrar Bous to be seasonal camps, reflected by ceramic production, "which could occur anywhere, without a specific focus on particular places for raw materials." Kiffian sites are coeval with Early and Late Acacus hunter-gatherer sites in southwestern Libya (di Lernia, 1999, 2013) and with the early occupation phase at Gobero (see below).

The definition of the Tenerian cultural complex predates the Kiffian (Joubert and Vaufrey, 1941–1946; Reygasse, 1934; Tixier, 1962), with recent work attempting to further refine cultural attributes and modify the existing chronology. Current summaries can be found in the volume by Clark and colleagues (2008a; specifically Smith, 2008b) and Garcea (2013a, b, c). The material culture inventory indicates a greater variety of tool types for scraping hides, woodworking, processing plant materials, and hunting (Smith, 2008b); an emphasis on large core tools instead of microliths (Smith, 2008b); an elaborated groundstone industry (Crader, 2008); and distinct ceramic types and vessel forms in comparison to Kiffian sites (Garcea, 2008). Differences in lithic technology in comparison to Kiffian assemblages[1] are significant enough to suggest a dietary shift occurred. Indeed, the defining feature of the Tenerian is the undoubted presence of domesticated cattle and the transhumant settlement pattern this suggests. The identification of "Tenerian meals" may indicate feasting behavior (Gifford-Gonzalez and Parham, 2008), though this inference is controversial as ideological explanations have also been offered (Paris, 2000). Although cattle were certainly part of the Tenerian diet, the true contribution vis-à-vis hunting is difficult to determine and it is generally accepted that pastoralists rarely eat the meat of the herd (Little, 1989; Russell and Lander, 2015; Sadler *et al.*, 2010). Hunting was likely important for both cultural phases; however, the lack of lacustrine fauna associated with Tenerian contexts at the Adrar Bous suggests aquatic resources may have declined in importance (Gifford-Gonzalez and Parham, 2008). Secondary product use is suggested by vessel forms (lidded jars) (Garcea, 2008, 2013c) and confirmed in southwestern Libya around 7000 BP (Dunne *et al.*, 2012).

Dates for the Tenerian, including direct dates on cattle remains, are controversial. The most recent treatments suggest an age between 6200 and 3800 BP (Paris, 2000; Smith, 2008b), with the earliest (accepted) domesticated *Bos* dating to the end of 7000 BP (Clark *et al.*, 2008b; Smith, 2008b). Material culture similarities across a broad swath of the Sahara suggest pastoralism had taken hold throughout much of North Africa by 5000 BP (Garcea, 2008; Smith, 2005a,b, 2008b). However, it is important to stress that not all pastoralist sites in Niger are associated with the Tenerian culture. For example, Paris (1990, 1992, 1999) reported on a number of sites (Chin Tafidet, Ikawaten, Tamaya Mallet, Afunfun, In Tuduf) unrelated to the Tenerian that suggested ethnic differences in the expression of pastoral ideologies

---

[1] Smith (2008a: 236) summarizes as follows: "The Kiffian is basically a microlithic tool kit, albeit of large segments, triangles, straight-backed blades, microlithic awls and strangulated scrapers. By contrast, the Tenerian is a large tool industry that seems to have been used in woodworking and flensing, using disc and bifacial knives, axes and adzes, as well as large numbers of projectile points, presumably used in hunting."

among contemporaries. In addition, megalithic tombs appear in northern Niger between 6900 and 5000 BP, also thought to be ethnically unrelated to the makers of the Tenerian toolkit, though clearly used by pastoralists (Paris, 1990, 1996, 1997) and evidence of emergent social complexity (Brass, 2007).

In summary, the difficulty of working in northern Niger combined with the limitations of the archaeological deposits has resulted in a simplified, linear archaeological sequence that defines an Early Holocene hunting-fishing-gathering economy and a series of Middle Holocene pastoralist "ethnic groups" that begin food production in the southern Sahara around 6000 BP. However, the notion of a monolithic Nigerien "pastoral phase" is not tenable as researchers have proposed the existence of distinct ethnic groups that may have had different settlement systems and patterns of mobility. The history of Middle Holocene Saharan populations, then, is one of regional variation even within broad biocultural themes such as pastoralism. As such, one cannot simply apply a model from one part of the Sahara to another, making novel sites such as Gobero an interpretive challenge. That archaeological examples of "persistent hunter-gatherers" have been well documented (e.g., Denbow, 1984; Jousse, 2006; Kuper and Riemer, 2013; Kusimba, 2003, 2005; Kusimba and Kusimba, 2005; Macdonald, 1997; Prendergast, 2010, 2011; Prendergast and Mutundu, 2010) further complicates interpretations of the record from Gobero, as discussed below.

9.3   The Gobero Cemeteries

Gobero is a region in central Niger located at the edge of the Ténéré Desert (Figures 9.1 and 9.2). The area was once the site of a large lake basin that was the focus of human activity from around 10 000 to 4000 BP. In addition to an abundance of preserved fauna and material culture, a unique feature of Gobero is the presence of multiple discrete cemeteries located atop dunes of terminal Pleistocene age. Details of site chronology, geomorphology, zooarchaeology, and landscape reconstruction can be found in Sereno *et al.* (2008) and various chapters in Garcea (2013d). Stojanowski (2013) provides a summary of the burial program with details of age and sex, spatial patterning, and mortuary variability (these details will not be repeated here; see Figure 9.3). Multiple direct dates have been generated from the human skeletons, and when combined with inferences from mortuary practices, skeletal biology, and taphonomy, these define two principal phases of human occupation (here referred to as Early and Middle Holocene).

The earliest occupation largely associated with a single cemetery (site G3) is dated between 9500 and 8200 cal BP (Sereno *et al.*, 2008). Early-phase burials are identified as fossilized and dark-stained, reflecting a high lakestand submergence that inundated the dunes between 9000 and 8500 BP (Giraudi, 2013; Giraudi and Mercuri, 2013) (Figure 9.3(a)). The initial publication on Gobero makes a cultural association between the Early Holocene occupation and the Kiffian culture based on similarities in artifact types (a microlithic tool kit, bone harpoons, dotted wavy-line pottery) (Sereno *et al.*, 2008). More recently, Garcea (2013e) questioned this

Figure 9.1 Map of Africa showing modern cities and the location of Gobero with respect to the Adrar Bous and the Aïr. The Azawagh basin and Ténéré Desert are also indicated.

association based on differences in lithic typology and inferred settlement patterns, and there seems little value in making broad cultural associations. However, there is no doubt that the Early Holocene inhabitants of Gobero were hunter-gatherers that lived off of hunted game, fishing, and the collection of wild plant foods millennia before the earliest appearance of domesticated livestock. During this phase, the lake would have been at its deepest, thus supporting deep-water species and providing a more varied animal-based diet. A single refuse area dated to the very end of the first occupation period contained a diversity of taxa, with *Silur-formes, Clarias* sp., *Lates niloticus, Tilapinii, Trionychidae,* and *Crocodylus* dominating the assemblage (Sereno *et al.,* 2008). Wetlands and marshy lakeside environs are attested by the pollen spectra, which indicate "a mosaic of habitats mainly including a Sahelian savanna type of vegetation ... enriched with perennial trees with ... a hydro-hygrophilous vegetation near the edges" (Giraudi and Mercuri, 2013:120). That such a large cemetery existed at Gobero is suggestive of a seden-tary existence, contrary to the inferred mobile lifestyles of Early Holocene peoples living in northern Niger (Garcea, 2008; Smith, 2008a) and southern Libya (Tafuri *et al.,* 2006). Garcea (2013e) described a tethered logistical mobility settlement pattern (largely sedentary) suggestive of a delayed-return hunter-gatherer economy (Woodburn, 1982a).

Walker and colleagues (2012) proposed a formal division of the Early and Middle Holocene coincident with the widely documented cold, arid spike known as the

Figure 9.2 Gobero today is a desolate and deserted landscape, but remnants of the once vibrant landscape do remain. Mud cracks from the old lake bed are visible, with modern survey vehicles in the distance.

8.2 kya cal BP event. The effects of this arid phase have been well documented in the Sahara (Gasse, 2000; Guo *et al.*, 2000; Hassan, 1997; Petit-Maire, 1986, 1989; Petit-Maire *et al.*, 1993) and the radiocarbon record from Gobero confirms significant impacts on human communities. Dated human burials, fauna, and ceramics all point to an occupational hiatus recorded between 8200 and 7200 cal BP (Sereno *et al.*, 2008). Subsequent to this hiatus, human occupation of the lake was nearly continuous from around 7200 BP to around 4500 years BP (with an ephemeral archaeological sequence lasting until nearly 2000 BP), but the lake never reached the same extent or depth as in the previous phase.

Several factors point to population continuity across this arid phase (e.g., Kiffian-style ceramics and bone harpoons continue to be made; incisor avulsion is practiced during both phases); however, most parameters of human variation (robusticity, stature, craniometrics, and dental morphology) also increase during the Middle Holocene, suggesting a more complex population history. Whether the indigenous hunter-gatherers returned to Gobero once the climate improved has been difficult to determine; however, patterns of craniofacial and dental

Figure 9.3 (a) Burial G3B9 from the G3 cemetery at Gobero. Note the dark staining of the top of the cranial vault, which was exposed by blowing sand (and cleaned) in the year before excavation. This individual was buried in a seated position holding his knees to his face. Such variability characterizes the Early Holocene mortuary program. (b) Burial G3B5 from the G3 cemetery at Gobero. Note the light staining of the bones and the distinct burial posture in comparison to G3B9.

morphological variation suggest population continuity with the possible influx of new migrants to the region.

The most controversial aspect of site interpretation is whether the Middle Holocene inhabitants were pastoralists or persistent hunter-gatherers. The initial publication by Sereno and colleagues (2008) suggested a connection to the Tenerian further north, and Garcea's (2013e) interpretation of the site reflects a Middle Holocene pastoral phase despite noting many differences between the Gobero pastoral period and Tenerian sites (e.g., rarity of Tenerian disks, axes, and adzes; rarity of vitric greenstone lithics; pottery stylistic differences; Garcea, 2013c, e). Most critically, despite broad survey of the region, evidence for domesticated *Bos* is exceedingly rare. Only three specimens were recovered dating between 5890 and 4620 cal BP (Sereno *et al.*, 2008). This is in stark contrast to contemporaneous Tenerian sites in the Adrar Bous, where complete cattle burials were documented (Carter and Clark, 1976; Gifford-Gonzalez and Parham, 2008; Smith, 2008b), as well as sites such as Iwelen and Chin Tafidet that record extensive and ritualized burials of domesticated animals (Paris, 1990, 1992, 1996, 1997; see also di Lernia [2006] or for further west in the Tilemsi Valley, Mali, see Funicane *et al.* [2008], and for east in the Wadi Howar see Jesse *et al.* [2013]). Dating of these remains suggests cattle were present in Niger by at least 6200 BP, but cattle remains are conspicuously rare at Gobero. Three middens dating to the Middle Holocene confirm the continued importance of fishing and hunting to the peoples living there (Sereno *et al.*, 2008), although the lake was much shallower with concomitant changes in flora. Conditions were drier with an advancing desert grassland environment at the expense of Sahelian savanna (Giraudi and Mercuri, 2013). Garcea (2013e) characterized the settlement system during the Middle Holocene as logistical semi-nomadic, with long periods (years) of permanent residence at the lake and the possibility that some community members lived there on a continuous basis.

9.4   Bioarchaeology and African Pastoralism or Hunter-Gatherer Resilience?

One of the challenges of studying hunter-gatherer resilience is the variation present within the broad adaptive categories that are so commonly used in anthropology. This is true for both hunter-gatherers (Johnson, 2014; Kent, 1996; Kusimba, 2005) and pastoralists (Dyson-Hudson and Dyson-Hudson, 1980; Honeychurch and Makarewicz, 2016; Salzman, 2002), neither of which really exist in pure typological forms. Such variation precludes extrapolating expectations from one region (such as East or South Africa) to another, and it also makes effective use of ethnographic analogy difficult. So the first question to address is what form hunter-gatherer resilience will assume within a bioarchaeological dataset. Predictive data for dietary transitions are limited. Critical information on temperature, population density, demography, division of labor, and ecological constraints (see Binford, 2001) that have been used to generate predictive models of resource intensification (see

Johnson, 2014) are lacking. In temporal perspective there is clear evidence for increasing aridity and a shallower lake with concomitant changes in ecology; however, these inferences generate analytically vague expectations with respect to oral health and other bioarchaeological data.

Predictions are also difficult because of a lack of consensus on what pastoralism entails. Although the adoption of domesticated livestock certainly affects many aspects of ideology, social organization, and subsistence, it is also nearly universally the case that pastoralists rely on a broad-based economy that can include products from hunting, fishing, gathering of wild plants, and (where present) agriculture (Arioti and Oxby, 1997; Jousse, 2004; Little, 1989; Marshall, 1990; Marshall and Hildebrand, 2002; Marshall and Stewart, 1994; for a more general perspective, see Khazanov [1994]). This means that notions of "true pastoralists" as fully nomadic herders have limited value during the Middle Holocene, when herding was still emergent. The African pastoralist literature is filled with "in-betweens" offered to reflect the spectrum of dietary emphases: herder-forager, hunters with livestock, herders-who-hunt, hunter-herders, hunter-gatherer-livestock keepers, low-intensity herders, foragers with access to stock, agropastoralists, herder-farmers, herder-traders, herder-urban dwellers (Fauvelle-Aymar, 2004; Ikeya, 2005; Linseele, 2010; Russell and Lander, 2015; Sadr, 1991, 1998, 2005, 2013; Smith, 1990, 2014). Carrying this further, Hassan (2002), Ingold (1980), and MacDonald (1999), among many others, have generated typologies of pastoralist economies that highlight variations in diet, mobility, or the importance of livestock in structuring behavior. Fitting bioarchaeological data to these categories is not a useful exercise, however. Gifford-Gonzalez (2005: 188) provided a straightforward definition of pastoralism that touches on the most obvious themes in the literature: "groups who depend primarily on the products of hoofed domestic animals, and who organize settlement and mobility strategies to suit the dietary needs of livestock." Diet and mobility are key aspects, but even here the inclusion of the word "primarily" generates vague dietary expectations. But even mobility is difficult to predict and generalize beyond the fact that herd maintenance and the need for forage and water structure behavior (for ranging examples, see Hammer and Arbuckle, 2016; Honeychurch, 2014; Honeychurch and Makarewicz, 2016; Linseele, 2010). In fact, mobility may be a complete nonstarter. There are two reasons why.

The first reason is that mobility strategies are quite variable for pastoralists. For example, Di Lernia and colleagues' long-term research program on hunter-gatherer and pastoralist communities of the Libyan Sahara identified temporal changes in mobility concomitant with increasing aridity. Patterns included residential, preferential, seasonal transhumant, and large-scale mobility, all within the same basic regional ecosystem (di Lernia, 2006, 2013). A number of studies have inferred sedentary pastoralism in the Middle and Late Holocene of Niger and Mali based on the presence of large sites with residences and cemeteries (Jousse, 2003; Manning, 2008; Smith, 2002), although other explanations have been offered (Holl, 1998). The inference of distinct pastoralist ethnic groups in Niger during the Middle Holocene adds to the interpretive complexity; some are likely to have been more mobile than others. As such, it is not possible to simply assume that an increase in mobility reflects the acceptance of pastoral lifeways. For example, Tafuri *et al.* (2006) used strontium isotope analyses of hunter-gatherer and pastoralist samples from the Libyan Sahara to reconstruct temporal changes in mobility. The work documented a temporal *decrease* in variation in strontium isotope values with the transition to food production in the region. Despite this, it is emphasized that the primacy of archaeological evidence suggests that specialized husbandry had been adopted by these peoples, and that the decrease in inter-individual variation does not reflect a decrease in mobility, but rather "their returning to the same areas repeatedly" (Tafuri *et al.*, 2006: 398). Of course, Tafuri *et al.* (2006) had direct evidence of cattle and caprine pastoralism at these sites, which is not the case at Gobero. Thus, the interpretation reflects the difficulty of using changes in mobility *alone* as a marker of emergent pastoralist economies.

The second reason why mobility may not be illustrative of emergent pastoralism is that it is difficult to differentiate a resilient hunter-gatherer mobility pattern from a pastoralist pattern (cf. Hill *et al.*, 2016). For example, the near-permanent source of water at Gobero may have limited the need for mobility (assuming adequate forage) and the density of burials is suggestive of permanent (or nearly so) residence. Garcea (2013e) suggested that the primary change would have been from a tethered logistical mobility pattern (Early Holocene hunter-gatherer) to a logistical, semi-nomadic pattern (Middle Holocene pastoralist). If true, then lifecourse mobility (as measured by enamel–bone comparisons) and inter-individual variation should *increase* through time. However, even this expectation fails to differentiate the adoption of pastoralism from settlement pattern reorganization among hunter-gatherers in response to the same external, environmental stimulus – increasing aridity and a change in lake ecosystem dynamics. In fact, this is the essence of resilience – adjusting where needed while not changing core aspects of identity.

Two previous papers have been published exploring strontium isotopic variation using the data from Gobero (Stojanowski and Knudson, 2011, 2014). Stojanowski and Knudson (2011) considered strontium isotopic variation among Early Holocene individuals and found a homogeneous signal with limited lifecourse variation, which is entirely consistent with sedentism. In the subsequent paper, strontium isotopic variability was compared between occupation phases. Strontium data demonstrated an increase in inter-individual variation, which suggested Middle Holocene adults were spending more time away from the Gobero basin. Is this evidence for transhumant pastoralism? Possibly. But it could also reflect a hunter-gatherer strategy that entailed greater mobility as aridity increased and the lake environment became less predictable, shallower, and with turnover in aquatic resources. Equifinality is a major issue. Others have noted similar diagnostic vagueness when comparing activity patterns and mobility of hunter-gatherer and pastoralist populations using long bone cross-sectional geometry (e.g., Cameron and Pfeiffer, 2014; Marchi *et al.*, 2011). Neither hunter-gatherers nor pastoralists exhibit approaches to mobility and settlement organization that are universal.

For these reasons, this chapter considers diet as a key parameter of bioarchaeo-logical interest. The challenge is generating bioarchaeologically observable expect-ations of the effects of pastoralism on the human diet. This is also difficult, especially for transitional societies. Surveys of African pastoralist communities, both extant and archaeological, indicate that cattle are rarely eaten (Little, 1989; Russell and Lander, 2015; Sadler *et al.*, 2010), with the exception of feasts or other ritualized activities that are also the most archaeologically visible (see above). Instead, milk and, in some cases, blood provide sustenance while hunted game and wild plants often round out the diet within highly structured systems of exchange (Linseele, 2010; Little, 1989; Marshall, 1990; McIntosh, 1993; Sadr, 1991; Woodburn, 2016). Ingold (1980) differentiated between *milch pastoralists* and *carnivorous pastoralists*, which is a deeply ideological distinction, with the former more common throughout Africa today (Linseele, 2010; Little, 1989). It's a distinction of seeing cattle either as food or as wealth, as something to be eaten or as something to be cared for.

Garcea (2013e) suggested an emphasis on milk rather than meat explains the dearth of domesticated cattle at Gobero. However, the presence or absence of domesticated cattle is a poor indicator of whether a site was used by pastoralists or hunter-gatherers (Mutundu, 2005, 2010; Prendergast, 2010, 2011; Prendergast and Mutundu, 2010). There is tremendous variability in the percentage of domesticated animals in faunal assemblages from documented pastoralist sites, which Russell and Lander (2015) attributed, in part, to Ingold's (1980) distinction between carnivorous and *milch* pastoralists. This review of sites from across East and South Africa led to conclusions suggesting that "Faunal assemblages, while interesting, become very difficult to interpret, particularly in the middle of the continuum between pure pastoralist and forager. *As a single piece of evidence* they are a rather poor way of determining whether a site is that of a pastoralist or a hunter-gatherer" (Russell and Lander, 2015: 39 [emphasis added]). As Gifford-Gonzalez (2017: 401) commented, "Presence of domestic cattle is often interpreted as proof of pastoralism, rather than the first step in demonstrating its plausibility."

Given the decades of debates about pastoralist–hunter-gatherer relationships in other parts of the continent, it is surprising how little bioarchaeology has seemingly contributed to this literature. Is there a signature of dairying that manifests skelet-ally? Can the direct consumption of cattle meat be differentiated from hunted game or the consumption of fish? Is there a change in oral health with the hunter-gatherer-pastoralist transition similar to that documented for the hunter-gatherer–farmer transition? Few studies have attempted to address these questions in African con-texts, and more broadly it is much more common to see comparisons of pastoralists and farmers rather than hunter-gatherers (e.g., Eng, 2007; Machicek, 2011; but see Chapter 6).

Sealy (2010) used carbon and nitrogen isotope data to infer the emergence of cattle pastoralism in South Africa across a broad sample of the Holocene. She documented a relatively late shift toward more positive $\delta^{13}C$ and $\delta^{15}N$ values reflecting a transition toward a more C4-dominant diet, which she proposes is most likely the consumption of cattle or their secondary products. However, this relationship between C4 isotopic signatures and the consumption of grazing cattle is not universal, even within South Africa. Masemula (2015) found dietary signatures indicating a mix of C3 and C4 foods was consumed, which suggests the continued importance of hunting and gathering. Murphy's (2011) work with pastoralist samples from Botswana suggested limited consumption of domesticated stock despite their abundance at the site. This is similar to Funicane et al.'s (2008) work in Mali, in that domesticated animals were in abundance at the sites investigated, but were only a minor contribution to the overall diet. The archaeological invisibility of pastoralist nomads is well known (Cribb, 1991; Grillo, 2014; Honeychurch and Makarewicz, 2016; MacDonald, 1999; Mutundu, 2010; Prendergast and Mutundu, 2010; Shahack-Gross et al., 2003, 2008). Previous studies of mobility and diet using isotopic methods suggest a degree of bioarchaeological invisibility as well. For this reason, dentition and oral health are deployed as possible indicators of dietary change or stasis at Gobero.

9.5   Materials and Methods

9.5.1   Sample Composition

This chapter focuses on the Gobero cemeteries (Sereno et al., 2008) and includes data from all individuals excavated in 2005, 2006, and 2011 (Stojanowski, 2013). Because the remains were eroding from the dunes, the sample was intentionally selected to be fairly balanced, with the exception of a bias toward adult individuals. The sample includes 20 male and 16 female adults, 46 adults and 19 pre-adults, and 39 Early Holocene and 43 Middle Holocene burials.

9.5.2   Dental Indicators of Diet and Infection

Data were collected on tooth wear, carious lesion presence, periapical abscesses, antemortem tooth loss, and calculus deposits. Tooth wear was scored using the method of Smith (1984) for incisors, canines, and premolars, and that of Scott (1979) for molars. The presence of carious lesions was scored following the protocol of Buikstra and Ubelaker (1984); however, given the general low rate of severity, these data were converted to a presence/absence score for each individual. This chapter follows Lukacs (1989) in defining a minimum threshold of expression as being palpable (incipient demineralization), owing to the extensive taphonomic staining that precluded adopting a procedure targeting pre-demineralized stages of expression (Hillson, 2001). Caries were probed with a dental pick and confirmed under $30\times$ magnification. Periapical abscesses and antemortem tooth loss were both scored as binary variables; incisor antemortem tooth loss (AMTL) data are not reported due to the practice of incisor avulsion, which affected about 20 percent of individuals in each occupational phase (Stojanowski *et al.*, 2014). Finally, calculus was scored following the protocol of Brothwell (1981), and given the generally minor severity, also collapsed into a binary presence/absence score for statistical purposes. Data on linear enamel hypoplasia are not presented because these lesions were rare within the sample and morphologically difficult to score due to taphonomic issues (slight erosion of perikymata, staining, calcrete encrustation). Previously published work on localized hypoplasia of the primary canines is discussed, however (Stojanowski and Carver, 2011).

All data were recorded at the level of the individual socket, excluding those teeth not fully in occlusion at the time of death because these would not have been "at risk" for most pathological conditions. Due to small sample sizes, males and females and adults and pre-adults are combined in all analyses, and only burials that could be definitively placed within one of the occupational phases were included. To ensure comparability of data between the samples, wear scores were compared by tooth position to determine whether age structure was affecting the observability of different pathological conditions. A crude rate of wear was also estimated by comparing the wear score offsets for M1–P2, M1–M2, and M1–M3. These estimates target wear rates roughly between the ages of 6 and 12 and between 6 and 18 years of age.

Data on oral health and infection were tabulated in two ways. First, data are presented by specific tooth position (e.g., left maxillary third molar), which allows calculation of an individual count and frequency but without the biases associated with variable dental element preservation. These data reflect true individual count MNIs (minimum number of individuals). Second, all teeth of the same tooth type and number were combined (left and right, maxillary and mandibular M3s) to approximate a tooth count frequency. Fisher's exact tests were used for assessment of statistical significance.

9.6   Results

Average wear scores by tooth type are presented in Table 9.1. The Early Holocene phase burials have higher wear scores for all teeth. Scores for the P2, P1, C, and I2 were significantly higher than the Middle Holocene dataset. This is not a reflection of different rates of wear, however. The wear gradient comparison for the M1–M2 ($p = 0.308$), M1–M3 ($p = 0.243$), and M1–P2 ($p = 0.264$) are not significantly different. This, in itself, is an interesting observation because it reflects a similar rate of tooth wear during both occupation phases. It does, however, suggest a possible bias toward over-representation of age-progressive dental diseases in the Early Holocene sample, thus reducing observability for anterior tooth caries and increasing observability for anterior tooth abscesses, AMTL, and calculus.

Carious lesions were found at low frequencies in both occupation phases, with a maximum expression of 22.7 percent for the Middle Holocene sample left maxillary M1. Carious lesions were found only in the posterior dentition, as expected based on

Table 9.1 Average wear scored by tooth position, sides, and arcades combined.

	M3	M2	M1	P2	P1	C	I2	I1
EH *n*	17	20	32	35	36	39	36	32
EH mean	10.88	15.40	20.94	4.31	4.36	4.38	3.75	4.22
EH SD	7.48	7.60	9.26	1.78	1.84	1.79	1.90	1.77
MH *n*	43	48	65	61	65	59	57	52
MH mean	8.77	13.83	19.25	3.38	3.55	3.22	2.96	4.08
MH SD	5.39	8.62	9.70	1.62	1.74	1.38	1.43	1.61
p-value	0.23	0.48	0.41	0.01[**]	0.03[**]	0.00[**]	0.03[**]	0.71

EH = Early Holocene, MH = Middle Holocene, SD = standard deviation, ** = Student's *t*-test significant at the 5 percent level.

crown complexity, and there were no significant differences in degree of expression when considered by individual (Tables 9.2 and 9.3) or by tooth count (Table 9.4). The frequency of expression for all molars was 8.3 percent (24 of 290 molars) and the frequency of expression for all tooth types was 3.4 percent (25 of 732 teeth).

Periapical abscesses were rare in the Gobero sample, and there were no significant temporal differences when considered by individual (Table 9.2 and 9.3) or by tooth count (Table 9.4). The range of positive expression using the individual count was 3.8 to 8 percent for the Middle Holocene sample and 5.9 to 9.1 percent for the Early Holocene sample. Periapical abscesses were more common in the maxillary anterior dentition and in the posterior mandibular dentition. Interestingly, this idiosyncratic pattern was observed for both occupation phases, which could reflect a shared (and continued) food processing behavior or it could be related to the practice of incisor avulsion that more typically targeted the maxillary teeth (Stojanowski *et al.*, 2014). The higher frequency of AMTL in the mandibular molars (see below) is concordant with the higher frequency of abscessing, and suggests distinct etiologies for maxillary and mandibular abscesses in this sample. The frequency of expression for all teeth was 2 percent (17 of 833 sockets).

AMTL was more common during the Early Holocene occupation, with several comparisons reaching statistical significance by individual (Tables 9.2 and 9.3) and tooth count methods (Table 9.4). The range of positive expression using the individual count was 0–4 percent for the Middle Holocene sample and 5.9–20 percent for the Early Holocene sample. AMTL was found exclusively in the posterior dentition, driven by several individuals in the Early Holocene sample that were nearly edentulous. This may reflect a demographic effect, or more likely results from the age structure of the sample. That is, the edentulous individuals were among the oldest at the site and did not contribute to the wear score comparisons as a result of missing teeth. The frequency of expression for all molars was 8.3 percent (24 of 290 molars) and the frequency of expression for all teeth was 3.4 percent (25 of 732 teeth).

Table 9.2 Oral health data for the maxillary dentition by individual.

| | Left | | | | | | Right | | | | | |
| | Early Holocene | | | Middle Holocene | | | Early Holocene | | | Middle Holocene | | |
	N	P	Percent	N	P	Percent	N	P	Percent	N	P	Percent
Caries												
M3	6	0	0.0	15	1	6.3	7	1	12.5	17	1	5.6
M2	7	0	0.0	16	2	11.1	9	1	10.0	14	2	12.5
M1	8	0	0.0	17	5	22.7	9	1	10.0	17	1	5.6
P2	8	0	0.0	15	0	0.0	8	0	0.0	15	0	0.0
P1	9	0	0.0	15	0	0.0	10	0	0.0	16	0	0.0
C	8	0	0.0	16	0	0.0	12	0	0.0	14	0	0.0
I2	8	0	0.0	14	0	0.0	7	0	0.0	13	0	0.0
I1	7	0	0.0	16	0	0.0	9	0	0.0	14	1	6.7
Abscesses												
M3	5	0	0.0	12	0	0.0	5	0	0.0	12	0	0.0
M2	6	0	0.0	16	0	0.0	8	0	0.0	16	1	5.9
M1	8	0	0.0	16	0	0.0	9	0	0.0	15	0	0.0
P2	10	0	0.0	17	0	0.0	10	0	0.0	15	0	0.0
P1	12	1	7.7	19	0	0.0	10	1	9.1	16	0	0.0
C	11	0	0.0	19	1	5.0	10	0	0.0	15	0	0.0
I2	10	0	0.0	18	1	5.3	10	1	9.1	16	0	0.0
I1	9	0	0.0	15	1	6.3	9	0	0.0	14	0	0.0
Antemortem tooth loss												
M3	5	0	0.0	17	0	0.0	7	0	0.0	18	0	0.0
M2	7	1	12.5	19	0	0.0	9	0	0.0	19	0	0.0
M1	10	1	9.1	22	0	0.0	10	1	9.1	24	1	4.0
P2	11	1	8.3	20	0	0.0	12	0	0.0	18	0	0.0
P1	12	0	0.0	19	0	0.0	12	0	0.0	19	0	0.0
C	13	0	0.0	19	0	0.0	13	0	0.0	20	0	0.0
I2	na	na	na	na	na	na	na	na	na	na	na	na
I1	na	na	na	na	na	na	na	na	na	na	na	na
Calculus												
M3	6	0	0.0	14	4	22.2	4	2	33.3	12	5	29.4
M2	6	0	0.0	13	2	13.3	6	2	25.0	13	2	13.3
M1	7	0	0.0	15	3	16.7	7	0	0.0	15	5	25.0
P2	6	2	25.0	15	3	16.7	8	1	11.1	12	3	20.0
P1	7	2	22.2	15	4	21.1	8	1	11.1	15	5	25.0
C	7	1	12.5	15	4	21.1	9	3	25.0	13	5	27.8
I2	7	2	22.2	14	4	22.2	6	4	40.0	12	5	29.4
I1	6	2	25.0	13	4	23.5	5	2	28.6	12	4	25.0

N = number absent, P = number present, Percent = frequency, na = not applicable due to the practice of incisor avulsion; * = Fisher's exact test significant at the 10 percent level; ** Fisher's exact test significant at the 5 percent level.

Table 9.3 Oral health data for the mandibular dentition by individual.

| | Left | | | | | | Right | | | | | |
| | Early Holocene | | | Middle Holocene | | | Early Holocene | | | Middle Holocene | | |
	N	P	Percent	N	P	Percent	N	P	Percent	N	P	Percent
Caries												
M3	6	1	14.3	11	0	0.0	6	0	0.0	10	2	16.7
M2	8	0	0.0	16	0	0.0	8	1	11.1	14	1	6.7
M1	9	0	0.0	16	2	11.1	7	1	12.5	16	1	5.9
P2	8	0	0.0	12	0	0.0	9	0	0.0	12	0	0.0
P1	8	0	0.0	14	0	0.0	16	0	0.0	14	0	0.0
C	9	0	0.0	14	0	0.0	10	0	0.0	12	0	0.0
I2	9	0	0.0	12	0	0.0	9	0	0.0	12	0	0.0
I1	10	0	0.0	12	0	0.0	7	0	0.0	12	0	0.0
Abscesses												
M3	12	0	0.0	21	1	4.5	9	0	0.0	18	0	0.0
M2	16	0	0.0	25	1	3.8	14	1	6.7	21	0	0.0
M1	16	1	5.9	23	2	8.0	16	1	5.9	21	1	4.5
P2	15	0	0.0	19	0	0.0	15	0	0.0	16	0	0.0
P1	14	0	0.0	21	0	0.0	15	0	0.0	19	0	0.0
C	13	0	0.0	20	0	0.0	13	0	0.0	17	0	0.0
I2	11	0	0.0	16	0	0.0	12	0	0.0	15	0	0.0
I1	12	1	7.7	16	0	0.0	11	0	0.0	16	0	0.0
Antemortem tooth loss												
M3	9	2	18.2	21	0	0.0	9	2	18.2	19	0	0.0
M2	14	3	17.6*	24	0	0.0	12	3	20.0**	25	0	0.0
M1	15	3	16.7*	25	0	0.0	13	3	18.8**	27	0	0.0
P2	16	1	5.9	20	0	0.0	13	1	7.1	19	0	0.0
P1	17	0	0.0	21	0	0.0	14	0	0.0	21	0	0.0
C	14	0	0.0	21	0	0.0	13	0	0.0	18	0	0.0
I2	na	na	na	na	na	na	na	na	na	na	na	na
I1	na	na	na	na	na	na	na	na	na	na	na	na
Calculus												
M3	2	0	0.0	10	2	16.7	5	0	0.0	10	1	9.1
M2	6	0	0.0	15	1	6.3	6	0	0.0	13	1	7.1
M1	6	0	0.0	15	3	16.7	6	0	0.0	14	0	0.0
P2	6	1	14.3	12	3	20.0	6	0	0.0	10	0	0.0
P1	5	1	16.7	14	5	26.3	5	0	0.0	11	2	15.4
C	3	3	50.0	14	9	39.1	5	2	28.6	11	5	31.3
I2	3	3	50.0	11	5	31.3	3	4	57.1	10	4	28.6
I1	3	5	62.5	11	6	35.3	4	4	50.0	11	5	31.3

N = number absent, P = number present, Percent = frequency, na = not applicable due to the practice of incisor avulsion; * = Fisher's exact test significant at the 10 percent level; ** Fisher's exact test significant at the 5 percent level.

Table 9.4 Oral health data scored by tooth position, sides, and arcades combined.

	I1			I2		
	EH	MH	*p*-value	EH	MH	*p*-value
Caries	33/0	52/1	0.43	33/0	49/0	n/a
Abscesses	40/1	58/1	0.34	42/1	62/1	0.78
AMTL	na	na	na	na	na	na
Calculus	18/8/5/0	29/10/7/2	0.99	19/10/3/0	29/11/5/2	0.99

	C		
	EH	MH	*p*-value
Caries	39/0	54/0	na
Abscesses	47/0	68/1	0.41
AMTL	53/0	78/0	na
Calculus	24/7/1/0	28/14/8/1	0.10

	P1			P2		
	EH	MH	*p*-value	EH	MH	*p*-value
Caries	37/0	57/0	na	33/0	54/0	na
Abscesses	50/2	73/0	0.99	52/0	66/0	na
AMTL	55/0	80/0	na	52/3	77/0	0.07*
Calculus	25/4/0/0	37/9/6/1	0.11	26/3/2/0	41/5/4/0	0.99

	M1			M2		
	EH	MH	*p*-value	EH	MH	*p*-value
Caries	31/2	53/9	0.22	37/3	60/5	0.97
Abscesses	47/2	70/3	0.99	28/1	63/2	0.93
AMTL	48/8	98/1	0.00**	42/7	87/0	0.00**
Calculus	26/0/0/0	46/9/2/0	0.02**	24/2/0/0	46/5/0/0	0.99

	M3		
	EH	MH	*p*-value
Caries	29/1	56/4	0.52
Abscess	19/0	48/2	0.68
AMTL	30/4	75/0	0.00*
Calculus	17/2/0/0	38/6/3/0	0.49

EH = Early Holocene, MH = Middle Holocene. Data presented as number without/number with each oral health indicator. For caries and abscesses the data are binary. For calculus the data are presented for scores of 0/1/2/3 reflecting severity of calculus formation.
* = Fisher's exact test significant at the 10 percent level; ** = Fisher's exact test significant at the 5 percent level.

The patterning of calculus was complex. First, the degree of expression was generally low when considered using an individual count (Tables 9.2 and 9.3). Most values fell in the range of 20–30 percent, with the occasional higher frequency largely associated with small sample sizes. Second, there were few significant differences between the Early and Middle Holocene samples. In fact, none of the individual counts were significantly different (Tables 9.2 and 9.3) and only a single tooth count comparison was significant (first molars, see Table 9.4). Third, there were differences in the overall pattern of expression. Early Holocene dentitions exhibited calculus almost exclusively in the anterior dentition. This pattern was particularly evident for the mandible, which produced the highest frequencies of expression in the sample (50–60 percent). In contrast, the Middle Holocene sample exhibits a much more evenly distributed pattern of calculus that was low in frequency but distributed throughout the anterior and posterior dentition. The frequency of expression for all teeth was 21.4 percent (161 of 752 teeth).

9.7   Discussion

In a previous paper, Stojanowski and Carver (2011) argued for the possibility of incipient cattle pastoralism at Gobero based on a decrease in the frequency of localized hypoplasia of the primary canine (LHPC). The argument was that Early Holocene hunter-gatherers had a low-fat diet because of an emphasis on fish and hunted game that were high protein but low in fat. The decrease in LHPC frequency was interpreted as evidence of the consumption of milk, which increased dietary fat intake. Unfortunately, the etiology of LHPC is subject to considerable (and continued) debate (Skinner *et al.*, 2014), and here this chapter expands on this research by considering a full suite of oral health indicators.

The frequencies of carious lesions, periapical abscesses, and AMTL generally fell within the low range of global hunter-gatherer variation, while calculus was rarely severe and was low to moderate in frequency (cf. Eshed *et al.*, 2006; Flensborg, 2016; Lieverse *et al.*, 2007; Luna and Aranda, 2014; Turner, 1979). Importantly, there was no change in the frequency of caries or periapical abscesses through time. There was only a single significant variable indicating an increase in calculus frequency through time, and there was a significant increase in molar AMTL through time. This last observation is driven, however, by the presence of two edentulous individuals in the Early Holocene sample. In aggregate, the overall picture is of little change in oral health with the Middle Holocene transition. Furthermore, the similar rates of tooth wear exhibited by both samples suggests the factors affecting rates of enamel macrowear did not change significantly. This likely reflects a persistence in the basic core of the diet.

Is this evidence of resilience? This is difficult to say without reference to comparative data on pastoralist oral health, which are completely lacking for Africa. Data on dental health are also notoriously difficult to compare across sites and

Table 9.5. Comparative oral health data from three Old World pastoralist samples (Miller *et al.*, 2014; Murphy *et al.*, 2013; Zhang *et al.*, 2015).

	G-T	G-MH	1	2	3
Tooth count					
Caries (%)	3.4	3.8	1.9–6.4	0.0–0.1	0.8
Abscesses (%)	2.0	1.6	3.3–4.7	4.3–16.8	2.4
AMTL[1] (%)	3.4	0.2	6.4–8.9	0.7–8.2	4.1
Calculus (%)	21.4	21.7	77.2–83.8	66.0–70.9	–

G-T: Gobero, total sample, G-MH: Gobero, Middle Holocene only.

[1] The Gobero AMTL excludes the anterior dentition due to incisor avulsion. Given that AMTL would typically target high-wear posterior dentition, this exclusion has the effect of biasing these estimates upwards in comparison to the pastoralist samples summarized in this table.

observers because of differences in preservation, as well as inventorying and tabulation methods. Nonetheless, the results of three recent studies of pastoralist oral health are noteworthy (Miller *et al.*, 2014; Murphy *et al.*, 2013; Zhang *et al.*, 2015), and frequency data from these studies are normalized in Table 9.5 (limitations abound, see Temple [2016] for a critique of caries tabulation methods, for example). These data are not African, but derive from Old World populations from northern China, Siberia, and Kazakhstan, where well-documented pastoralist skeletal samples are identified. Of particular relevance is the consistency of expectations in these papers. Patterns of oral health are thought to reflect a pastoral diet that is high in protein and low in carbohydrates, resulting in a very low caries prevalence and a very high calculus frequency (for etiological discussion, see Lieverse, 1999). Pastoralist diets, in general, are considered rich in protein and fat, low in overall caloric intake, and highly seasonal (Iannotti and Lesorogol, 2014; Little, 1989; Sadler *et al.*, 2010).

In comparison, the Middle Holocene occupants of Gobero presented much lower frequencies of periapical abscesses and AMTL than pastoralist samples. This may reflect a demographic parameter more than a dietary one. However, Gobero also consistently presents a very low frequency of individuals affected by dental calculus, which is contrary to the expectations of a high-protein diet (for both pastoralists and hunter-gatherers). Gobero also has a higher frequency of individuals affected by dental caries, which suggests a greater contribution of plant-based carbohydrates to the diet. For all four oral health variables, the Middle Holocene Gobero sample is much more similar to the Early Holocene sample than it is to other documented pastoralists. While this may reflect variation in local ecologies and specific food procurement practices, it may also represent evidence for the persistence of an essentially hunter-gatherer adaptation at Gobero. That is, after the occupational hiatus the population maintained a broadly similar diet in terms of protein and carbohydrate consumption. Mobility increased (Stojanowski and Knudson,

2014) and subsistence practices were adjusted to include a greater variety of terrestrial resources with an emerging focus on the exploitation of plant-based carbohydrates.

But is this interpretation plausible? Pastoralists were certainly operating in the central Sahara throughout the Middle Holocene occupational sequence. And, based on the presence of domesticated *Bos* in the refuse middens (Sereno *et al.*, 2008), cattle likely comprised at least a small part of the diet. But this chapter argues that the hunter-gatherers of Gobero ultimately rejected a pastoral lifestyle and all that it entails. There are several utilitarian reasons that may help explain reasons for the persistence of hunting and gathering in this region. The lake ecosystem may have been rich enough, and more importantly stable enough, such that the adoption of pastoralism was not needed.[2] Pastoralists may have restricted access to early domesticates, which is consistent with the ideological importance of cattle evident from contemporaneous sites in Niger but also somewhat improbable given the thousands of years of time sampled here. The environment may have been too dry or too wet, with disease vectors preventing the successful adoption of cattle pastoralism at this time and place, thus resulting in a mosaic of subsistence practices (a process well documented in East Africa; see Gifford-Gonzalez [2017] for the latest on this topic).

Ideology and worldview are also an important factor to consider in the transition from hunting and gathering to pastoralism. Eidelberg (1986:108) provides an historical overview of this debate, emphasizing the complete change in values that pastoralism asks of hunter-gatherers: "The obstacles to the shift from hunting to pastoralism were not so much based upon the lack of knowledge as upon ideology ... In fact, as long as their economies were at all viable, animal domestication could not have appeared as an attractive option [it involved] more work hours ... personal responsibility and a new unwanted kind of labor ... to guard his animals [and] to keep constant vigilance." Andrew Smith (1990, 2016) has argued most persistently that the transition to pastoralism is ideologically difficult for hunter-gatherers. This is based on the assumption of immediate-return hunter-gatherer economies in South Africa (critiqued by Russell and Lander, 2015) and the stark differences in "modes of thought" that include "concepts of accumulation and consumption of resources, leadership, kinship models and how land is perceived and used" (Smith, 2016: 422). Smith argued that social relations and relations between people and the environment are quite different in hunter-gatherers and food producers. Simple access to domesticates is not enough, nor is practical knowledge of herd maintenance. Rather, for southern African hunter-gatherers the transition to pastoralism would have required adjustments to: (1) mode of production, (2) attitudes toward accumulation (a future-oriented ethos) and sharing (private ownership), and (3) conceptualization of the relationship between person and prey and between person and the natural world. The

[2] According to Honeychurch and Makarewicz (2016: 344), "The primary actors in African domestication and domesticate adoption processes were mobile hunter-gatherers who gradually included herds in their foraging practices to reduce subsistence uncertainty."

latter line of reasoning borrows heavily from Ingold's (1987, 2000, 2015) distinction between "trust and domination" with respect to human–animal relationships in the hunter-gatherer–pastoralist mosaic. Ingold (2000: 72) commented:

Herdsmen do indeed care for their animals, but it is care of quite a different kind from that extended by hunters. For one thing, the animals are presumed to lack the capacity to reciprocate. In the world of the hunter, animals, too, are supposed to care, to the extent of laying down their lives for humans by allowing themselves to be taken. They retain, however, full control over their own destiny. Under pastoralism, that control has been relinquished to humans.

As such, the transition to pastoralism in Ingold's view requires a realignment of the relationships between humans and animals (and the broader environment), which impacted the social relations among humans as well. Smith (2016: 430) continued: "Transforming from one system to the other [hunter-gatherer to pastoralist] requires so major a psychological jump it is probably correct to ask why it should take place at all."

There is an important distinction, however, between Smith's view and the situation at Gobero. Smith (1990, 2016) is clear that this model envisions a baseline of immediate-return hunter-gatherers. Current Gobero site interpretations suggest a relatively sedentary Early Holocene hunter-gatherer population that practiced a delayed-return economy. Cemeteries, a robust ceramic industry, and grinding equipment indicate a certain degree of sedentism, the possibility of long-term storage, and incipient social complexity. Some would argue that delayed-return hunter-gatherers are pre-adapted (or predisposed) ideologically toward the adoption of pastoralism because the "future orientation" ethos is better established (see Marshall and Hildebrand, 2002; Smith, 1986a, 1990, 1992, 2005a; Woodburn, 1982a, b, 1988). Russell and Lander (2015) contend that the shift from hunting large game to fishing and capturing smaller prey (inferred from the midden sequence at Gobero; Sereno et al., 2008) might also dismantle the "sharing ethos" barrier that Smith outlines. The logic is that small game procurement is more of an individual rather than group-level accomplishment.

Still, as a study in hunter-gatherer resilience, the data from Gobero provide important information on situations in which persistence prevailed over pastoralism. For example, the Middle Holocene inhabitants of Gobero had knowledge of, and contact with, pastoralist economies. Bioarchaeological data suggest these hunter-gatherers largely rejected this option, and further consideration of the archaeological data corroborate this interpretation. The site lacks evidence of corralling, lacks evidence of rituality or monumentality (the Cattle Cult Complex – Di Lernia et al., 2013), lacks accumulations of dung associated with open-air pastoralist sites, and lacks evidence of feasting behavior that would be expected of *milch* pastoralists (*sensu* Ingold, 1980). Furthermore, following Prendergast and Mutundu's parameters (Mutundu, 2005, 2010; Prendergast, 2010; 2011; Prendergast and Mutundu, 2010; see also Marshall and Stewart, 1994), there is no increase in the frequency of domesticated livestock through time, the taxonomic representation in the Middle

Holocene middens is predominantly wild and non-selective, and the preserved fragments of cattle (crania and dentition) are not from prime body segments. All of this speaks against the inference of herding and suggests that the scant fragments of cattle at the site could reflect theft from a non-local pastoralist group, the incidental hunting or killing of a domesticated cow, or the exchange of local products (such as fish) for cattle meat in a patron–client type of relationship.

But the presence of any cattle at all indicates some kind of interaction between different subsistence economies. In this sense, it may be best to suggest that the inhabitants of Gobero were persistent hunter-gatherers, but incorrect to say the site and the people had nothing to do with pastoralism. The presence of domesticated cattle clearly indicates some kind of interaction, and instead of seeing pastoralists and hunter-gatherers as ultimately divided, it is more productive to consider these resilient hunter-gatherers as part of a broader, expanding pastoralist landscape; just as pastoralist communities were part of an existing, dynamic hunter-gather landscape. This landscape was one of a desiccating Sahara that challenged human communities. And this is the important point about hunter-gatherer resilience. To herd or hunt or gather was not just an economic decision. It was not a decision driven solely by convenience or hardship. At Gobero, the indigenous hunter-gatherers had a choice, and these communities largely rejected that choice in favor of modifying the existing subsistence economy.

Diet was not the only (or even the most interesting) transformation to have occurred, however, if the oral health data provide an accurate portrayal of dietary behavior. Within the realm of hunter-gatherer research, Dale *et al.* (2004) argued for a middle-ground in the well-known dichotomy of delayed- and immediate-return hunter-gatherers (Woodburn, 1982a, 1988). Using ethnographic and archaeological data from East Africa, these authors argued for a third category, referred to as "moderate delayed-return hunter-gatherers" – an ownership society forming an intermediate condition between egalitarian, mobile immediate-return hunter-gatherers and non-egalitarian, sedentary, delayed-return hunter-gatherers. These intermediate groups have most of the signatures of delayed-return hunter-gatherers, but lack evidence of inequality and hierarchy. Dale and colleagues emphasized evidence of ownership (in the form of repeated site use, dense archaeological accumulations, ceramics and storage, predictable and abundant resource base, tool specialization), as well as the absence of hierarchy (reflected in prestige goods, complex architecture, elaborated material culture) in this distinction. The similarities between the description of Kansyore hunter-gatherers of East Africa and the Early Holocene occupants at Gobero is striking. Both groups practiced a lacustrine-focused subsistence economy, produced large quantities of elaborately decorated ceramics, preserved dense archaeological sites with human burials (cemeteries?), and lacked evidence of structures and prestige items. This suggests the Early Holocene hunter-gatherers of Gobero were also a moderate delayed-return hunter-gatherer society.

However, in addition to dietary resilience and adaptation, the Middle Holocene record from Gobero suggests transformation in the social realm. Although evidence

Figure 9.4 Burial G3B41 from the G3 cemetery showing *in-situ* ivory jewelry. This individual was estimated to be a 35–45-year-old female and was buried with an elaborate necklace that includes an incised ivory pendant, large ivory beads, and small ostrich eggshell beads. Only Middle Holocene burials from Gobero included grave goods.

of sociopolitical structures was still lacking, the Middle Holocene occupants of Gobero used much larger cemeteries; made amazonite jewelry, ivory bracelets and necklaces, and ostrich eggshell beads (among other exotics such as vitric greenstone lithics) (Figure 9.4); and used specialized disposal areas (Sereno *et al.*, 2008). In the work of Dale and colleagues (2004) this shift suggests an ownership society had transitioned into a delayed-return hunter-gatherer society with incipient hierarchy and social stratification. In the southern Sahara, then, hunter-gatherer resilience involved a number of transitions – a shift toward a more terrestrial, plant-based diet; an increase in mobility for some members of society, and a shift toward emergent social complexity as they navigated a drying Sahara and negotiated with pastoralist groups appearing on their northern periphery. This chapter, then, opens the possibility of discussing hunter-gatherer resilience not just in economic terms, but in social terms as well. Hunter-gatherers of the past were not monolithic baseline stages for societal advance, but distinct societies with idiosyncratic mid-Holocene trajectories that must be considered on a case-by-case basis.

9.8   Conclusion

This chapter considers hunter-gatherer resilience at the site of Gobero, an important mortuary complex that preserves over 5000 years of human activity in the southern Sahara during a time of considerable climatic transition. Coincident with increasing aridity, pastoralism appears on the landscape around 6500 years ago, creating a subsistence mosaic that would endure for millennia. Site interpretations at Gobero have been uncertain about whether the Middle Holocene occupation phase entailed pastoralism or the persistence of hunting and gathering. This chapter presents new evidence on diet and oral health that suggests continuity in subsistence practices through time, with a shift toward more terrestrial resources. Comparison of these data with other Old World pastoralist samples suggests the Middle Holocene occupants of Gobero were not pastoralists. This study, then, documents hunter-gatherer resilience across a 5000-year period that witnessed considerable climatic variation within a general trend of increasing aridity. This chapter also argues that the hunter-gatherers at Gobero were not monolithic in terms of social organization. Rather, initial steps toward hierarchy may have emerged with a shift toward an ownership society.

Acknowledgments

The Gobero cemeteries were discovered and developed by Paul Sereno with initial funding for excavations provided by private donations to him. I would like to thank Paul for inviting me to join the project. Funding for excavations in 2011 and for subsequent lab work was provided by the National Science Foundation (BCS-0820805, BCS-0636066) and the Wenner-Gren Foundation (GR-6698). I would like to thank all of the excavators and all of the students who volunteered time in my lab to clean, reconstruct, and prepare the burials for analysis. ASU graduate students Andrew Seidel, Charisse Carver, Kent Johnson, and Katherine Miller spent many hours working on the collection. Two anonymous reviewers also provided valuable comments on the chapter. Finally, I would like to thank Dan Temple for inviting me to pursue the topic of resilience with him in this volume.

References

Arioti, M. and Oxby, C. (1997). From hunter-fisher-gathering to herder-hunter-fisher-gathering in prehistoric times (Saharo-Sudanese region). *Nomadic Peoples*, 1, 98–119.

Ashley, C. Z. (2010). Towards a socialised archaeology of ceramics in Great Lakes Africa. *African Archaeological Review*, 27, 135–163.

Binford, L. R. (2001). *Constructing Frames of Reference: An Analytical Method for Archaeological Theory Building Using Ethnographic and Environmental Data Sets.* Los Angeles, CA: University of California Press.

Blench, R. and MacDonald, K. C. (2000). *The Origins and Development of African Livestock: Archaeology, Genetics, Linguistics, and Ethnography.* London: UCL Press.

Brass, M. (2007). Reconsidering the emergence of social complexity in early Saharan pastoral societies, 5000–2500 B.C. *Sahara*, 18, 7–22.

Brothwell, D. R. (1981). *Digging Up Bones.* 3rd edn. Ithaca, NY: Cornell University Press.

Buikstra, J. E. and Ubelaker, D. H. (1984) *Standards for Data Collection from Human Skeletal Remains*. Fayetteville, AR: Arkansas Archeological Survey.

Cameron, M. E. and Pfeiffer, S. (2014). Long bone cross-sectional geometric properties of later Stone Age foragers and herder-foragers. *South African Journal of Science*, **110**, 1–11.

Campbell, S. K. and Butler, V. L. (2010). Archaeological evidence for resilience of Pacific Northwest salmon populations and the socioecological system over the last ~7,500 years. *Ecology and Society*, **15**, 17.

Carter, P. L. and Clark, J. D. (1976). Adrar Bous and African cattle. In B. Abebe, J. Chavaillon, and J. E. G. Sutton, eds., *Proceedings of the Pan-African Congress of Prehistory and Quaternary Studies*. Addis Ababa: Provisional Military Government of Socialist Ethiopia Ministry of Culture, pp. 487–493.

Clark, J. D., Williams, M. A. J., and Smith, A. B. (1973). The geomorphology and archeology of Adrar Bous, central Sahara: A preliminary report. *Quaternaria*, **17**, 245–297.

Clark, J. D., Agrilla, E. J., Crader, D. C., *et al.* (2008a). *Adrar Bous. Archaeology of a Central Saharan Granitic Ring Complex in Niger*. Tervuren: Royal Museum for Central Africa.

Clark, J. D., Carter, P. L., Gifford-Gonzalez, D., and Smith, A. B. (2008b). The Adrar Bous cow and African cattle. In J. D. Clark and D. Gifford-Gonzalez, eds., *Adrar Bous: Archaeology of a Central Saharan Granitic Ring Complex in Niger*. Tervuren: Royal Museum for Central Africa, pp. 355–368.

Crader, D. C. (2008). Technology and classification of the grinding equipment. In J. D. Clark and D. Gifford-Gonzalez, eds., *Adrar Bous: Archaeology of a Central Saharan Granitic Ring Complex in Niger*. Tervuren: Royal Museum for Central Africa, pp. 291–311.

Cribb, R. (1991). *Nomads in Archaeology*. Albuquerque, NM: University of New Mexico Press.

Crowther, A., Prendergast, M. E., Fuller D. Q., and Boivin, N. (2017). Subsistence mosaics, forager–farmer interactions, and the transition to food production in eastern African. *Quaternary International*. DOI: 10.1016/j.quaint.2017.01.014.

Dale, D., Marshall, F., and Pilgram, T. (2004). Delayed-return hunter-gatherers in Africa? Historic perspectives from the Okiek and archaeological perspectives from the Kansyore. In G. M. Crothers, ed., *Hunters and Gatherers in Theory and Archaeology*. Cardondale, IL: Southern Illinois University, pp. 340–375.

Denbow, J. R. (1984). Prehistoric herders and foragers of the Kalahari: The evidence for 1500 years of interaction. In C. Schirer, ed., *Past and Present in Hunter Gatherer Studies*. Orlando, FL: Academic Press, pp. 175–193.

di Lernia, S. (1999). *The Uan Afuda Cave: Hunter-Gatherer Societies of Central Sahara*. Rome: All'Insegna del Giglio.

di Lernia, S. (2006). Building monuments, creating identity: Cattle cult as a social response to rapid environmental changes in the Holocene Sahara. *Quaternary International*, **151**, 50–62.

di Lernia, S. (2013). Places, monuments, and landscape: Evidence from the Holocene central Sahara. *Azania: Archaeological Research in Africa*, **48**, 173–192.

di Lernia, S., Tafuri, M. A., Gallinaro, M., *et al.* (2013). "Inside the African cattle complex": animal burials in the Holocene Central Sahara. *PLoS One* 8(2), e56879.

Drake, N. A., Blench, R. M., Armitage, S. J., Bristow, C. S., and White, K. H. (2011). Ancient watercourses and biogeography of the Sahara explain the peopling of the desert. *Proceedings of the National Academy of Sciences*, **108**, 458–462.

Dunne, J., Evershed R. P., Salque M., *et al.* (2012). First dairying in green Saharan African in the fifth millennium BC, *Nature*, **486**, 390–394.

Dyson-Hudson, R. and Dyson-Hudson, N. (1980). Nomadic pastoralism. *Annual Review of Anthropology*, **9**, 15–61.

Échallier, J. -C. and Roset, J.- P. (1986). La céramique des gisements de Tagalagal et de l'Adrar Bous 10 (Air, République du Niger). *Cahiers des Sciences Humaines*, **22**, 151–158.

Eidelberg, P. G. (1986). Hunters, horticulturalists, herders and "developmental inertia": Resistance to technological change in South Africa and North America. *South African Historical Journal*, **18**, 99–124.

Eng, J. T. (2007). *Nomadic Pastoralism and the Chinese Empire: A Bioarchaeological Study of China's Northern Frontier*. PhD dissertation, University of California.

Eng, J. T. (2016). A bioarchaeological study of osteoarthritis among populations of northern China and Mongolia during the Bronze Age to Iron Age transition to nomadic pastoralism. *Quaternary International*, 405B, 172–185.

Eshed, V., Gopher, A., and Hershkovitz, I. (2006). Tooth wear and dental pathology at the advent of agriculture: New evidence from the Levant. *American Journal of Physical Anthropology*, 130, 145–159.

Falseit, R. K. (2015). *Beyond Collapse: Archaeological Perspectives on Resilience, Revitalization, and Transformation in Complex Societies*. Carbondale, IL: Southern Illinois University Press.

Fauvelle-Aymar, F.-X. (2004). Between the first herders and the last herders: Are the Khoekhoe descendants of the Neolithic "hunters-with-sheep"? *Before Farming*, 4, 1–11.

Flensborg, G. (2016). Health and disease of hunter-gatherer groups from the eastern Pampa–Patagonia transition (Argentina) during the Late Holocene. *Anthropological Science*, 124, 29–44.

Frahm, E., Goldstein, S. T., and Tryon, C. A. (2017). Late Holocene forager-fisher and pastoralist interactions along the Lake Victoria shores, Kenya: Perspectives from portable XRF of obsidian artifacts. *Journal of Archaeological Science*, 11, 717–742.

Funicane, B., Manning, K., and Touré, M. (2008). Late Stone Age subsistence in the Tilemsi Valley, Mali: Stable isotope analysis of human and animal remains from the site of Karkar-ichinkat Nord (KN05) and Karkarichinkat Sud (KS05). *Journal of Anthropological Archaeology*, 27, 82–92.

Galaty, J. G. (1986). East African hunters and pastoralists in a regional perspective: An "ethno-archaeological" approach. *Sprache und Geschichte in Afrika*, 7, 105–131.

Garcea E. A. A. (2004). An alternative way towards food production: The perspective from the Libyan Sahara. *Journal of World Prehistory*, 18, 107–154.

Garcea, E. A. A. (2008). The ceramics from Adrar Bous and surrounding areas. In J. D. Clark and D. Gifford-Gonzalez, eds., *Adrar Bous: Archaeology of a Central Saharan Granitic Ring Complex in Niger*. Tervuren: Royal Museum for Central Africa, pp. 245–298.

Garcea, E. A. A. (2013a). The archaeological significance of Gobero. In E. A. A. Garcea, ed., *Gobero: The No-Return Frontier. Archaeology and Landscape at the Saharo-Sahelian Borderland*. Frankfurt am Main: Africa Magna Verlag, pp. 5–18.

Garcea, E. A. A. (2013b). Regional overview during the time frame of the Gobero occupation. In E. A. A. Garcea, ed., *Gobero: The No-Return Frontier. Archaeology and Landscape at the Saharo-Sahelian Borderland*. Frankfurt am Main: Africa Magna Verlag, pp. 251–270.

Garcea, E. A. A. (2013c). Manufacturing technology of the ceramic assemblages. In E. A. A. Garcea, ed., *Gobero: The No-Return Frontier. Archaeology and Landscape at the Saharo-Sahelian Borderland*. Frankfurt am Main: Africa Magna Verlag, pp. 209–240.

Garcea, E. A. A., ed. (2013d). *Gobero: The No-Return Frontier. Archaeology and Landscape at the Saharo-Sahelian Borderland*. Frankfurt am Main: Africa Magna Verlag.

Garcea, E. A. A. (2013e). Gobero: The secular and sacred place. In E. A. A. Garcea, ed., *Gobero: The No-Return Frontier. Archaeology and Landscape at the Saharo-Sahelian Borderland*. Frankfurt am Main: Africa Magna Verlag, pp. 271–293.

Gasse, F. (2000). Hydrological changes in the African tropics since the Last Glacial Maximum. *Quaternary Science Reviews*, 19, 189–211.

Gifford-Gonzalez, D. (2003). The fauna from Ele Bor: Evidence for the persistence of foragers into the later Holocene of arid north Kenya. *African Archaeological Review*, 20, 81–119.

Gifford-Gonzalez, D. (2005). Pastoralism and its consequences. In A. B. Stahl, ed., *African Archaeology: A Critical Introduction*. Malden, MA: Blackwell, pp. 187–224.

Gifford-Gonzalez, D. (2017). "Animal disease challenges" fifteen years later: The hypothesis in light of new data. *Quaternary International*, 436, 283–293.

Gifford-Gonzalez, D. and Parham, J. F. (2008). The fauna from Adrar Bous and surrounding areas. In J. D. Clark and D. Gifford-Gonzalez, eds., *Adrar Bous. Archaeology of a Central Saharan Granitic Ring Complex in Niger*. Tervuren: Royal Museum for Central Africa, pp. 313–354.

Giraudi, C. (2013). Late Upper Pleistocene and Holocene stratigraphy of the palaeolakes in the Gobero basin. In E. A. A. Garcea, ed., *Gobero: The No-Return Frontier. Archaeology and Landscape at the Saharo-Sahelian Borderland*. Frankfurt am Main: Africa Magna Verlag, pp. 67–81.

Giraudi, C. and Mercuri, A. M. (2013). Early to Middle Holocene environmental variations in the Gobero basin. In E. A. A. Garcea, ed., *Gobero: The No-Return Frontier. Archaeology and Landscape at the Saharo-Sahelian Borderland*. Frankfurt am Main: Africa Magna Verlag, pp. 114–126.

Grillo, K. M. (2014). Pastoralism and pottery use: An ethnoarchaeological study in Samburu, Kenya. *African Archaeological Review*, **31**, 105–130.

Guibert, P., Schvoerer, M., Etcheverry, M. P., Szepertyski, B., and Ney, C. (1994). IXth millenium B.C. ceramics from Niger: Detection of a U-series disequilibrium and TL dating. *Quaternary Science Reviews*, **13**, 555–561.

Guo, Z., Petit-Maire, N., and Kröpelin, S. (2000). Holocene non-orbital climatic events in present-day arid areas of northern Africa and China. *Global and Planetary Change*, **26**, 97–103.

Hammer, E. and Arbuckle, B. (2016). 10,000 years of pastoralism in Anatolia: A review of evidence for variability in pastoral lifeways. *Nomadic Peoples*, **21**, 214–267.

Haour, A. C. (2003). One hundred years of archaeology in Niger. *Journal of World Prehistory*, **17**, 181–234.

Hassan, F. A. (1997). Holocene paleoclimates of Africa. *African Archaeological Review*, **14**, 213–230.

Hassan, F. A. (2002). Paleoclimate, food and culture change in Africa: An overview. In F. A. Hassan, ed., *Droughts, Food and Culture: Ecological Change and Food Security in Africa's Later Prehistory*. Dordrecht: Kluwer Academic Publishers, pp. 11–26.

Hegmon, M. E., Peeples, M. A., Kinzig, A. P., *et al.* (2008). Social transformation and its human costs in the Prehispanic U.S. Southwest. *American Anthropologist*, **110**, 313–324.

Hill, E. C., Durband, A. C., and Walshe, K. (2016). Risk minimization and a Late Holocene increase in mobility at Roonka Flat, South Australia: An analysis of lower limb diaphyseal shape. *American Journal of Physical Anthropology*, **161**, 94–103.

Hillson, S. (2001). Recording dental caries in archaeological human remains. *International Journal of Osteoarchaeology*, **11**, 249–289.

Holl, A. F. C. (1998) Livestock, husbandry, pastoralisms, and territoriality: The West African record. *Journal of Anthropological Archaeology*, **17**, 143–165.

Honeychurch, W. (2014). Alternative complexities: The archaeology of pastoral nomadic states. *Journal of Archaeological Research*, **22**, 277–326.

Honeychurch, W. and Makarewicz, C. A. (2016). The archaeology of pastoral nomadism. *Annual Review of Anthropology*, **45**, 341–359.

Hugot, H.-J. (1962). Premier aperçu sur la préhistoire du Ténéré du Tefassasset. In H. Hugot, ed., *Missions Berliet Ténéré-Tchad*. Paris: Arts et Métiers Graphiques, pp. 149–178.

Iannotti, L. and Lesorogol, C. (2014). Animal milk sustains micronutrient nutrition and child anthropometry among pastoralists in Samburu, Kenya. *American Journal of Physical Anthropology*, **155**, 66–76.

Ikeya, K. (2005). Socioeconomic relationships between herders and hunters: A comparison of the Kalahari Desert and northeastern Siberia. *Senri Ethnological Studies*, **69**, 31–44.

Ingold, T. (1980). *Hunters, Pastoralists and Ranchers: Reindeer Economies and Their Transformation*. Cambridge: Cambridge University Press.

Ingold, T. (1987). Hunting, sacrifice and the domestication of animals. In T. Ingold, ed., *The Appropriation of Nature: Essays on Human Ecology and Social Relations*. Iowa City, IA: University of Iowa Press, pp. 243–276.

Ingold, T. (2000). From trust to domination. An alternative history of human–animal relations. In T. Ingold, ed., *Perceptions of the Environment: Essays on Livelihood, Dwelling and Skill.* London: Routledge, pp. 61–76.

Ingold, T. (2015). From the master's point of view: Hunting *is* sacrifice. *Journal of the Royal Anthropological Institute*, **21**, 24–27.

Jesse, F., Keding, B., Lenssen-Erz, T., and Pollath, N. (2013). "I hope your cattle are well": Archaeological evidence for early cattle-centred behaviour in the eastern Sahara of Sudan and Chad. In M. Bollig, M. Schnegg, and H.-P. Wotzka, eds., *Pastoralism in Africa: Past, Present and Future.* New York, NY: Berghahn. pp. 66–103.

Johnson, A. L. (2014). Exploring adaptive variation among hunter-gatherers with Binford's frames of reference. *Journal of Archaeological Research*, **22**, 1–42.

Joubert, G. and Vaufrey, R. (1941–1946). Le néolithique de Ténéré. *L'Anthropologie*, **50**, 325–330.

Jousse, H. (2003). *Impact des Variations Environmentales sur la Structure des Communautés Mammaliennes et l'Anthropisation des Milieu: Exemple des Faunes Holocènes du Sahara Occidental.* Lyon: Laboratoires de Géologie de Lyon.

Jousse, H. (2006). What is the impact of Holocene climatic changes on human societies? Analysis of West African Neolithic populations dietary customs. *Quaternary International*, **151**, 63–73.

Jousse, H., Obermaier, H., Raimbault, M., and Peters, J. (2008). Late Holocene economic specialisation through aquatic resource exploitation in the Méma, Mali. *International Journal of Osteoarchaeology*, **18**, 549–572.

Kenrick, J. and Lewis, J. (2001). Discrimination against the forest peoples ["Pygmies"] of Central Africa. In S. Chakma and M. Jensen, eds., *Racism against Indigenous Peoples.* Copenhagen: International Work Group for Indigenous Affairs, pp. 312–325.

Kent, S. (1996). *Cultural Diversity among Twentieth Century Foragers: An African Perspective.* Cambridge: Cambridge University Press.

Khazanov, A. (1994). *Nomads and the Outside World.* Madison, WI: University of Wisconsin Press.

Kuper, R. and Kröpelin, S. (2006). Climate-controlled Holocene occupation in the Sahara: Motor of Africa's evolution. *Science*, **313**, 803–807.

Kuper, R. and Riemer, H. (2013). Herders before pastoralism: Prehistoric prelude in the eastern Sahara. In M. Bollig, M. Schnegg, and H.-P. Wotzka, eds., *Pastoralism in Africa: Past, Present and Future.* New York, NY: Berghahn, pp. 31–65.

Kusimba, C. M. and Kusimba, S. B. (2005). Mosaics and interactions: East Africa. 2000 b.p. to the present. In A. B. Stahl, ed., *African Archaeology: A Critical Introduction.* Malden, MA: Blackwell, pp. 392–419.

Kusimba, S. B. (2003). *African Foragers: Environment, Technology, Interactions.* Walnut Creek, CA: Altamira Press.

Kusimba, S. B. (2005). What is a hunter-gatherer? Variation in the archaeological record of eastern and southern Africa. *Journal of Archaeological Research*, **13**, 337–366.

Lee, R. B. (1979). *The !Kung San: Men, Women, and Work in a Foraging Society.* Cambridge: Cambridge University Press.

Lee, R. B. (1984). *The Dobe !Kung.* New York, NY: Holt, Rinehart and Winston.

Lieverse, A. R. (1999). Diet and aetiology of dental calculus. *International Journal of Osteoarchaeology*, **9**, 219–232.

Lieverse, A. R., Link, D. W., Bazaliiskiy, V. I., Goriunova, O. I., and Weber, A. W. (2007). Dental health indicators of hunter-gatherer adaptation and cultural change in Siberia's Cis-Baikal. *American Journal of Physical Anthropology*, **134**, 323–339.

Linseele, V. (2010). Did specialized pastoralism develop differently in Africa than in the Near East? An example from the West African Sahel. *Journal of World Prehistory*, **23**, 43–77.

Linseele, V. (2017). The exploitation of aquatic resources in Holocene West Africa. In U. Albarella, M. Rizzetto, H. Russ, K. Vickers, and S. Viner-Daniels, eds., *The Oxford Handbook of Zooarchaeology.* Oxford: Oxford University Press, pp. 439–451.

Little, M. A. (1989). Human biology of African pastoralists. *American Journal of Physical Anthropology*, 32(S10), 215–247.

Lukacs, J. R. (1989). Dental paleopathology: Methods for reconstructing dietary patterns: In M. Y. Isçan and K. A. R. Kennedy, eds., *Reconstruction of Life from the Skeleton*. New York, NY: Alan R. Liss, pp. 261–286.

Luna, L. H. and Aranda, C. M. (2014). Trends in oral pathology of hunter-gatherers from Western Pampas, Argentina. *Anthropological Science*, 122, 55–67.

MacDonald, K. C. (1997). "Korounkorokalé" revisited: The Pays Mande and the West African microlithic technocomplex. *African Archaeological Review*, 14, 161–200.

MacDonald, K. C. (1999). Invisible pastoralists: An inquiry into the origins of nomadic pastoralism in the West African Sahel. In C. Gosden and J. Hather, eds., *The Prehistory of Food: Appetites for Change*. London: Routledge, pp. 333–349.

MacDonald, K. C. and Van Neer, W. (1994). Specialised fishing peoples in the Later Holocene of the Méma Region (Mali). In W. Van Neer, ed., *Fish Exploitation in the Past: Proceedings of the 7th Meeting of the ICAZ Fish Remains Working Group*. Terverun: Annales du Musée Royal de l'Afrique Centrale, Sciences Zoologiques, pp. 243–251.

Machicek, M. L. (2011). *Reconstructing Diet, Health and Activity Patterns in Early Nomadic Pastoralist Communities of Inner Asia*. PhD dissertation, University of Sheffield.

Machicek, M. L. and Zubova, A. V. (2012). Dental wear patterns and subsistence activities in early nomadic pastoralist communities of the Central Asian steppes. *Archaeology, Ethnology & Anthropology of Eurasia*, 40, 149–157.

Manning, K. M. (2008). Mobility strategies and their social and economic implications for Late Stone Age Sahelian pastoral groups: A view from the Lower Tilemsi Valley, eastern Mali. *Archaeological Review from Cambridge*, 23, 125–145.

Manning, K. M. (2011). The first herders of the West African Sahel: Inter-site comparative analysis of zooarchaeological data from the Lower Tilemsi Valley, Mali. In H. Jousse and H. Lesur, eds., *People and Animals in Holocene Africa: Recent Advances in Archaeozoology*. Frankfurt: Africa Magna Verlag, pp. 75–85.

Manning, K. M. and Timpson, A. (2014). The demographic response to Holocene climate change in the Sahara. *Quaternary Science Reviews*, 101, 28–35.

Marchi, D., Sparacello, V., and Shaw, C. N. (2011). Mobility and lower limb robusticity of a pastoralist Neolithic population from North-Western Italy. In R. Pinhasi and J. T. Stock, eds., *Human Bioarchaeology of the Transition to Agriculture*. London: Wiley-Blackwell, pp. 317–346.

Marlowe, F. (2010). *The Hadza: Hunter-Gatherers of Tanzania*. Berkeley, CA: University of California Press.

Marshall, F. (1990). Origins of specialized pastoral production in East Africa. *American Anthropologist*, 92, 873–894.

Marshall, F. and Hildebrand, E. (2002). Cattle before crops: The beginnings of food production in Africa. *Journal of World Prehistory*, 16, 99–144.

Marshall, F. and Stewart, K. (1994). Hunting, fishing and herding pastoralists of western Kenya: The fauna from Gogo Falls. *Archaeozoologia*, 7, 7–27.

Masemula, N. (2015). *An Investigation of Skeletons from Type-R Settlements along the Riet and Orange rivers, South Africa, using Stable Isotope Analysis*. Masters thesis, University of Cape Town.

Mauny, R. (1949). Etat actuel de nos connaissances sur la préhistoire de la colonie du Niger. *Bulletin de l'IFAN*, 11, 141–158.

McIntosh, R. J. (1993). The pulse model: Genesis and accommodation of specialization in the Middle Niger. *Journal of African History*, 34, 181–220.

Miller, A. V. (2013). *Social Organization and Interaction in Bronze Age Eurasia: A Bioarchaeological and Statistical Approach to the Study of Communities*. PhD dissertation, State University of New York at Buffalo.

Miller, A. V., Usmanova, E., Logvin, V., *et al.* (2014). Dental health, diet, and social transformations in the Bronze Age: Comparative analysis of pastoral populations in northern Kazakhstan. *Quaternary International*, **348**, 130–146.

Murphy, E. M., Schulting, R., Beer, N., *et al.* (2013). Iron Age pastoral nomadism and agriculture in the eastern Eurasian steppe: Implications from dental palaeopathology and stable carbon and nitrogen isotopes. *Journal of Archaeological Science*, **40**, 2547–2560.

Murphy, M. A. (2011). A meal on the hoof or wealth in the krall? Stable isotopes at Kgaswe and Taukome in eastern Botswana. *International Journal of Osteoarchaeology*, **21**, 591–601.

Mutundu, K. K. (2005). Domestic stock age profiles and herd management practices: Ethno-archaeological implications from Maasai settlements in East Africa. *Azania: Archaeological Research in Africa*, **45**, 6–23.

Mutundu, K. K. (2010). An ethnoarchaeological framework for the identification and distinction of Late Holocene archaeological sites in East Africa. *Azania: Archaeological Research in Africa*, **45**, 6–23.

Paris, F. (1984). *La Région d'In Gall: Tegidda N Tesemt (Niger). Programme archéologique d'urgence 1977–1981, III. Les sépultures du néolithique final à l'Islam.* Niamey: Institut de Recherches en Sciences Humaines.

Paris, F. (1990). Les sépultures monumentals d'Iwelen (Niger). *Journal des Africanistes*, **60**, 47–75.

Paris, F. (1992). Chin Tafidet, village néolithique. *Journal des Africanistes*, **62**, 33–53.

Paris, F. (1996). *Les Sépultures du Sahara Nigérien du Néolithique à l'Islamisation: Coutumes Funéraires, Chronologie, Civilisations.* Paris: ORSTROM.

Paris, F. (1997). Les inhumations de *Bos* au Sahara méridional au Néolithique. *Archaeozoologia*, **9**, 113–122.

Paris, F. (1999). *Vallée de l'Azawagh (Sahara du Niger).* Saint-Maur: Ètudes Nigériennes 57.

Paris, F. (2000). African livestock remains from Saharan mortuary contexts. In R. M. Blench and K. C. Macdonald, eds., *The Origins and Development of African Livestock: Archaeology, Genetics, Linguistics, and Ethnography.* London: University College London Press, pp. 111–126.

Petit-Maire, N. (1986). Palaeoclimates in the Sahara of Mali: A multidisciplinary study. *Episodes*, **9**, 7–16.

Petit-Maire, N. (1989). Interglacial environments in the presently hyperarid Sahara: Paleoclimatic implications. In M. Leinen and M. Sarnthein, eds., *Paleoclimatology and Paleometeorology: Modern and Past Patterns of Global Atmospheric Transport.* Dordecht: Kluwer Academic Publishing, pp. 637–661.

Petit-Maire, N., Page, N., and Marchand, J. (1993). *The Sahara in the Holocene. Map 1r5.000.000.* Paris: UNESCO-CGMW.

Prendergast, M. E. (2010). Kansyore fisher-foragers and transitions to food production in East Africa: The view from Wadh Lang'o, Nyanza Province, western Kenya. *Azania: Archaeological Research in Africa*, **45**, 83–111.

Prendergast, M. E. (2011). Hunters and herders at the periphery: The spread of herding in eastern Africa. In H. Jouse and J. Lesur, eds., *People and Animals in Holocene Africa: Recent Advances in Archaeozoology.* Frankfurt am Main: Africa Magna Verlag, pp. 43–58.

Prendergast, M. E. and Mutundu, K. K. (2010). Late Holocene zooarchaeology in East Africa: Ethnographic analogues and interpretive challenges. *Documenta Archaeobiologiae*, **7**, 203–232.

Quéchon, G. and Roset, J.-P. (1974). Prospection archéologique du massif de Termit (Niger). *Cahiers ORSTOM. Série Sciences Humaines*, **11**, 85–104.

Redman, C. L. and Kinzig, A. P. (2003). Resilience of past landscapes: Resilience theory, society, and the *Longue Durée*. *Conservation Ecology*, **7**, 14.

Reygasse, M. (1934). Le Ténéréen: Observations sur un faciès nouveau di Néolithique des confins algérosoudanais. In *Compte Rendu de la Session du X Congrès Préhistorique de France, Périgueux*, pp. 577–584.

Roset, J.-P. (1987). Paleoclimatic and cultural conditions of Neolithic development in the Early Holocene of northern Niger (Air and Tenere). In A. E. Close, ed., *Prehistory of Arid North Africa*. Dallas, TX: Southern Methodist University Press, pp. 189–210.

Roset, J.-P., de Broin, J., Faure, M., *et al.* (1990). La faune de Tin Ouaffadene et d'Adrar Bous 10, deux gisements archéologiques de l'Holocène ancien au Niger nord-oriental. *Géodynamique*, 5, 67–89.

Russell, T. and Lander. F. (2015). "What is consumed is wasted". From foraging to herding in the southern African later Stone Age. *Azania: Archaeological Research in Africa*, 50, 267–317.

Sadler, K., Kerven, C., Calo, M., Manske, M., and Catley, A. (2010). The fat and the lean: Review of production and use of milk by pastoralists. *Pastoralism*, 1, 291–324.

Sadr, K. (1991). *The Development of Nomadism in Ancient Northeast Africa*. Philadelphia, PA: University of Pennsylvania Press.

Sadr, K. (1998). The first herders at the Cape of Good Hope. *African Archaeological Review*, 15, 101–132.

Sadr, K. (2005). From foraging to herding: The west coast of South Africa in the first millennium AD. *Human Evolution*, 20, 217–230.

Sadr, K. (2013). A short history of early herding in southern Africa. In M. Bollig, M. Schnegg, and H.-P. Wotzka, eds., *Pastoralism in Africa: Past, Present and Futures*. New York, NY: Berghahn, pp. 171–197.

Salzman, P. C. (2002). Pastoral nomads: some general observations based on research in Iran. *Journal of Anthropological Research*, 58, 245–264.

Sampson, C. G. (2010). Chronology and dynamics of later Stone Age herders in the Upper Seacow River Valley, South Africa. *Journal of Arid Environments*, 74, 842–848.

Schirer, C. (1992). The archaeological identity of hunters and herders at the Cape over the last 2000 years: A critique. *South African Archaeological Bulletin*, 47, 62–64.

Schmidt, C. S., Beach, J. J., McKinley, J. I., and Eng, J. T. (2016). Distinguishing dietary indicators of pastoralists and agriculturalists via dental microwear texture analysis. *Surface Topography: Metrology and Properties*, 4, 014008

Scott, E. C. (1979). Dental wear scoring technique. *American Journal of Physical Anthropology*, 51, 213–218.

Sealy, J. (2010). Isotopic evidence for the antiquity of cattle-based pastoralism in southernmost Africa. *Journal of African Archaeology*, 8, 65–81.

Sereno, P. C., Garcea, E. A. A., Jousse, H., *et al.* (2008). Lakeside cemeteries in the Sahara: 5000 years of Holocene population and environmental change. *PLoS ONE*, 3, 1–22.

Shahack-Gross, R., Marshall, F., and Weiner, S. (2003). Geoarchaeology of pastoral sites: The identification of livestock enclosures in abandoned Maasai settlements. *Journal of Archaeological Science*, 30, 439–459.

Shahack-Gross, R., Simons, A., and Ambrose, S. H. (2008). Identification of pastoral sites using stable nitrogen and carbon isotopes from bulk sediment samples: A case study in modern and archaeological pastoral settlements in Kenya. *Journal of Archaeological Science*, 35, 983–990.

Skinner, M. F., Rodrigues, A. T., and Byra, C. (2014). Developing a pig model for crypt fenestration-induced localized hypoplastic enamel defects in humans. *American Journal of Physical Anthropology*, 154, 239–250.

Smith, A. B. (1973). The Adrar n'Kiffi industry. *Quaternaria*, 17, 272–281.

Smith, A. B. (1974). *Adrar Bous and Karkarichinkat: Examples of Post-Palaeolithic Human Adaptation in the Saharan and Sahel Zones of West Africa*. PhD dissertation, University of California.

Smith, A. B. (1976). A microlithic industry from Adrar Bous, Ténéré Desert, Niger. In B. Abebe, J. Chavaillon, and J. E. G. Sutton, eds., *Proceedings of the 7th PanAfrican Congress of Prehistory and Quaternary Studies*. Addis Ababa: Ministry of Culture, pp. 181–196.

Smith, A. B. (1986a). Competition, conflict and clientship: Khoi and San relationships in the Western Cape. *Goodwin Series*, 5, 36–41.

Smith, A. B. (1986b). Cattle domestication in North Africa. *African Archaeological Review*, **4**, 197–203.

Smith, A. B. (1990). On becoming herders: Khoikhoi and San ethnicity in southern Africa. *African Studies*, **49**, 51–73.

Smith, A. B. (1992). Origins and spread of pastoralism in Africa. *Annual Review of Anthropology*, **21**, 125–141.

Smith, A. B. (1998a). Keeping people on the periphery: The ideology of social hierarchies between hunters and herders. *Journal of African Archaeology*, **17**, 201–215.

Smith, A. B. (1998b). Early domestic stock in southern Africa: A commentary. *African Archaeological Review*, **15**, 151–156.

Smith, A. B. (2002). The pastoral landscape in Saharan prehistory. In T. Lenssen-Erz, U. Tegtmeier, and S. Kröpelin, eds., *Tides of the Desert: Contributions to the Archaeology and Environmental History of Africa in Honour of Rudolph Kuper*. Cologne: Heinrich-Barth Institut, University of Cologne, pp. 447–457.

Smith, A. B. (2005a). *African Herders: Emergence of Pastoral Traditions*. Walnut Creek, CA: Altamira Press.

Smith, A. B. (2005b). Desert solitude: The evolution of ideologies among pastoralists and hunter-gatherers in arid North Africa. In P. Veth, M. Smith, and P. Hiscock, eds., *Desert Peoples: Archaeological Perspectives*. New York, NY: Blackwell Publishing, pp. 261–275.

Smith, A. B. (2008a). The Kiffian. In J. D. Clark and D. Gifford-Gonzalez, eds., *Adrar Bous: Archaeology of a Central Saharan Granitic Ring Complex in Niger*. Tervuren: Royal Museum for Central Africa, pp. 179–200.

Smith, A. B. (2008b). The Tenerian. In J. D. Clark and D. Gifford-Gonzalez, eds., *Adrar Bous: Archaeology of a Central Saharan Granitic Ring Complex in Niger*. Tervuren: Royal Museum for Central Africa, pp. 201–244.

Smith, A. B. (2014). *The Origins of Herding in Southern Africa*. Saarbrücken: Lambert Academic Publishing.

Smith, A. B. (2016). Why would southern African hunters be reluctant food producers? *Hunter Gatherer Research*, **2**, 415–435.

Smith, A. B., Sadr, K., Gribble J., and Yates, R. (1991). Excavations in the south-western Cape, South Africa, and the archaeological identity of prehistoric hunter-gatherers within the last 2000 years. *South African Archaeological Bulletin*, **46**, 71–91.

Smith, B. H. (1984). Patterns of molar wear in hunter-gatherers and agriculturalists. *American Journal of Physical Anthropology*, **63**, 39–56.

Stojanowski, C. M. (2013). An archaeological perspective on the burial record at Gobero. In E. A. A. Garcea, ed., *Gobero: The No Return Frontier. Archaeology and Landscape at the Saharo-Sahelian Borderland*. Frankfurt am Main: Africa Magna Verlag, pp. 44–64.

Stojanowski, C. M. and Carver, C. L. (2011). Inference of emergent cattle pastoralism in the southern Sahara based on localized hypoplasia of the primary canine. *International Journal of Paleopathology*, **1**, 89–97.

Stojanowski, C. M. and Knudson, K. J. (2011). Biogeochemical inferences of mobility of Early Holocene fisher-foragers from the southern Sahara desert. *American Journal of Physical Anthropology*, **146**, 49–61.

Stojanowski, C. M. and Knudson, K. J. (2014). Changing patterns of mobility as a response to climatic deterioration and aridification in the Middle Holocene southern Sahara. *American Journal of Physical Anthropology*, **154**, 79–93.

Stojanowski, C. M., Carver, C. L., and Miller, K. M. (2014). Incisor avulsion, social identity and Saharan population history: New data from the Early Holocene southern Sahara. *Journal of Anthropological Archaeology*, **35**, 79–91.

Svizzero, S. and Tisdell, C. (2015). The persistence of hunting and gathering economies. *Social Evolution & History*, **14**, 3–26.

Tafuri, M. A., Bentley, R. A., Manzi, G., and di Lernia, S. (2006). Mobility and kinship in the prehistoric Sahara: Strontium isotope analysis of Holocene human skeletons from the Acacus Mts. (southwestern Libya). *Journal of Anthropological Archaeology*, **25**, 390–402.

Temple, D. H. (2016). Caries: The ancient scourge. In J. D. Irish and G. R. Scott, eds., *A Companion to Dental Anthropology*. Chichester: Wiley-Blackwell, pp. 433–449.

ten Raa, E. (1986). The acquisition of cattle by hunter-gatherers: A traumatic experience in cultural change. *Sprache und Geschichte in Afrika*, **7**, 361–374.

Thorp, C. (1997). Evidence for interaction from recent hunter-gatherer sites in the Caledon Valley. *African Archaeological Review*, **14**, 231–256.

Tixier, J. (1962). Le Ténérén de l'Adrar Bous III. In H.-J. Hugot, ed., *Missions Berliet Ténéré-Tchad*. Paris: Arts et Métiers Graphiques, pp. 333–348.

Turnbull, C. M. (1983). *The Mbuti Pygmies: Change and Adaptation*. Orlando, FL: Harcourt Brace Jovanovich College Publishers.

Turner, C. G., II. (1979). Dental anthropological indications of agriculture among the Jomon people of central Japan: X. Peopling of the Pacific. *American Journal of Physical Anthropology*, **51**, 619–636.

Turner, G. (1987). Hunters and herders of the Okacango Delta, northern Botswana. *Botswana Notes and Records*, **19**, 25–40.

Walker, B., Holling, C. S., Carpenter, S. R., and Kinzig, A. (2004). Resilience, adaptability and transformability in social-ecological systems. *Ecology and Society*, **9**, 5.

Walker, M. J. C., Berkelhammer, M., Björck, S., et al. (2012). Formal subdivision of the Holocene series/epoch: A discussion paper by a working group of INTIMATE (Integration of ice-core, marine and terrestrial records) and the subcommission on Quaternary stratigraphy (International Commission on Stratigraphy). *Journal of Quaternary Science*, **27**, 649–659.

Woodburn, J. (1982a). Egalitarian societies. *Man*, **17**, 431–451.

Woodburn, J. (1982b). Social dimensions of death in four African hunting and gathering societies. In M. Bloch and J. Parry, eds., *Death and the Regeneration of Life*. Cambridge: Cambridge University Press, pp. 187–210.

Woodburn, J. (1988). African hunter-gatherer social organization: Is it best understood as a product of encapsulation? In T. Ingold, D. Riches, and J. Woodburn, eds., *Hunters and Gatherers 1. History, Evolution and Social Change*. Oxford: Berg. pp. 31–64.

Woodburn, J. (1997). Indigenous discrimination: The ideological basis for local discrimination against hunter-gatherer minorities in sub-Saharan Africa. *Ethnic and Racial Studies*, **20**, 345–361.

Woodburn, J. (2016). Silent trade with outsiders: Hunter-gatherers' perspectives. *HAU: Journal of Ethnographic Theory*, **6**, 473–496.

Wright, D. K. (2011). Frontier animal husbandry in the northeast and east African Neolithic: A multiproxy paleoenvironmental and paleodemographic study. *Journal of Anthropological Archaeology*, **67**, 213–244.

Zhang, H., Merrett, D. C., Xiao, X., et al. (2015). A comparative study of oral health in three Late Bronze Age populations with different subsistence practices in North China. *Quaternary International*, **405B**, 44–57.

10 Ancient Mortuary Ritual and Cultural Resilience on the Northwest Coast of North America

Bryn Letham and Gary Coupland

10.1 Introduction

10.1.1 Fisher-Hunter-Gatherers of the Northwest Coast

Fisher-hunter-gatherer societies of the Northwest Coast of North America are renowned for lavish ritual displays of wealth (Barnett, 1955; Elmendorf, 1971; Suttles, 1968). The archaeological record is increasingly showing that such practices have great time depth (Carlson *et al.*, 2017; Coupland *et al.*, 2016). Wealth was most famously displayed and given away at potlatches and other feasting ceremonies (e.g., Codere, 1950; Seguin, 1985; Suttles, 1968), including mortuary potlatches where wealth was displayed and passed beyond the realm of the living. Typically, archaeological analyses of grave goods associated with such rituals are used to assign differential levels of prestige to the deceased (e.g., Ames, 1995; Burley, 1989), and the appearance of burials exhibiting differences in these rituals is used to infer the emergence of ranked societies (Matson and Coupland, 1995). Northwest Coast mortuary rituals vary greatly through time and space, however (Burchell, 2006). Material differences in burials are observed at different times throughout this region, and the appearance of extreme differentiation is often temporary and fleeting (Coupland *et al.*, 2016). These two observations suggest that mortuary ritual may be more productively analyzed as part of localized histories influenced by the intersection of ecological/environmental change, human demographic change, interregional interactions or conflicts, cultural perceptions and belief systems, and other contingencies of history.

This chapter explores possible relationships between mortuary ritual and cultural resilience, the capacity of a society to adapt to, buffer against, endure, or successfully transform in the face of acute and chronic stresses (Faulseit, 2016; Keck and Sakda-polrak, 2013). Ritual action is often recognized in anthropology and archaeology for the capacity to reinforce, reinvent, or transform power and social relations (Swenson, 2015). Thus, ritual action may help promote cultural resilience by acting as a unifying force that strengthens social bonds (Faulseit, 2016: 7; Thompson, 2016). This chapter argues that Northwest Coast societies were resilient and sustainable for thousands of years in large part because of ritual institutions related to the potlatch system (or at least something like the potlatch). Within these systems, feasting, ceremony, and wealth display were critical to maintaining social cohesion, affirming both history and a sense of confidence in the future (Trosper, 2003, 2009). The primary hypothesis of this chapter is that funerary rituals were important ceremonial venues that contributed to cultural resilience by unifying populations, ensuring the orderly transmission of rights and responsibilities from one generation to the next, and propitiating ancestors. Especially during times of upheaval or instability, the display and offering of wealth to ancestors may have been critical to maintaining or reframing social order and instilling communal confidence in the future. This interpretation presents possible explanations for the appearance of ornate burials furnished with elaborate or abundant grave goods at certain historical moments on the Northwest Coast.

These ideas are explored through two examples in which lavish grave goods have been found in burials in formal cemeteries: (1) at the site of Kwenten Makwàli (DjRw-14) in the Salish Sea region, where several burials and a possible commemorative cache were furnished with huge numbers of ground stone disc beads and other special grave goods (Bilton and Letham, 2016; Coupland *et al.*, 2016); and (2) at the Boardwalk site (GbTo-31) near Prince Rupert on the northern coast of British Columbia, where a disproportionately high number of burials were furnished with finely crafted items of exotic raw materials (Ames, 2005; Cybulski, 1992, 2014b; MacDonald and Cybulski, 2001). The burials in both cemeteries were highly "marked." High levels of "marking" suggests that these burials may be productively analyzed to query the ways in which mortuary rituals shaped realities for individuals taking part in the ceremony and those impacted by these behaviors within the broader community (Swenson, 2015: 339). Cultural values expressed in these rituals may have operated to strengthen resilience through times of stress. The persistence of other Northwest Coast cultural attributes over the *longue durée* suggests that these strategies were likely successful in promoting cultural resilience.

10.1.2   Resilience and Ritual on the Northwest Coast

As early as the 1970s and 1980s, Ames (1979, 1981) integrated resilience theory into archaeological studies of the Northwest Coast from an evolutionary and systems theory perspective. While Ames applied Hollings' (1973) analysis of transitions from "resilient systems" to "stable systems" to explore the evolution of ranked society on the Northwest Coast, this chapter considers the very stability of certain aspects of cultures to be the result of these societies' resilient capacities. There is an emerging archaeological picture of Northwest Coast societies as resilient and sustainable, with enduring and persistent cultural practices lasting on the order of thousands of years. Archaeological evidence for continuity or persistence of cultural elements through time can be a material proxy for resilience. For example, many archaeologists report remarkable long-term continuous occupation and persistent use of places (Cannon, 2003; Mackie, 2003; Martindale and Letham, 2011; McLaren *et al.*, 2015), technological conservatism in artifact styles (Ames, 2005), sustainable long-term resource harvesting practices (Campbell and Butler, 2010), and evidence for direct genetic continuity of populations in single areas (Cui *et al.*, 2013; Lindo *et al.*, 2017). Continuity does not imply stasis, or even lack of variation, however; resilience is often maintained through the capacity of people to actively modify methods for survival (Silliman, 2009; Trosper, 2003, 2009). While the Northwest Coast is often portrayed as an environment of abundance, disturbances and upheavals such as climate and sea-level fluctuations, earthquakes (Hutchinson, 2016), tsunamis (McMillan and Hutchinson, 2002; Williams *et al.*, 2005), landslides (Samuels, 1991), and warfare (Angelbeck, 2007; Cybulski, 2014a; Marsden, 2001) occurred in the past. Therefore, persistence of occupation and cultural practice suggest resilience in the face of adversity.

Resilience on the Northwest Coast was surely the result of numerous actions and institutions through which people were able to adapt to or buffer against stress. Trosper (2003, 2009) argues that the political institutions rooted in the potlatch system – rules for inheriting and managing property, environmental ethics, reciprocal exchange, and public accountability – ensured a system that was able to buffer against uncertainty and to endure. Ames (1981: 793) argues that potlatches served to regulate the flow of food, wealth, and prestige among chiefs and brought people together to share information and resources. As observed ethnographically, potlatches and other ceremonial feasts were held for many reasons. A chief could give a potlatch to honor his name, commemorate a life event, solidify alliances, or bestow a title name on a house member. One of the most important types of potlatch was the mortuary potlatch: "After the death of a titleholder, the successor would organize a major ceremony in order to obtain recognition of the right to inherit the title and to take charge of the lands of a house. Head titleholders of other houses, by accepting the gifts of the host, recognized the host's claim" (Trosper, 2003: 3). Mortuary rituals – and ritual in general – may have been one way in which people acted toward maintaining social order. Hayden (2009) argues that ostentatious funerary feasts such as mortuary potlatches brought large groups of dispersed people together, and alliances could be established when people were emotionally malleable.

Gifts of wealth were also given to the ancestors during funerary rituals. Northwest Coast people did not maintain rigid boundaries between secular and spiritual; the spirits of ancestors were present in daily life and occupied the landscape (Mathews, 2014). Appropriate treatment of spirits and ancestors was tantamount to the maintenance of proper relations with the living. Under conditions of stress, when the future seemed uncertain, or when new relationships between social groups were negotiated, titleholders engaged in wealth displays with special elaborations to propitiate both the ancestors and living. Funerary rituals, then, were critical moments wherein the smooth transition of title rested upon the capability of the successor to provide abundantly for members of the lineage, both past and present. Interpreted as such, these rituals were likely important factors in the persistence of social order and the overall resilience of cultural traditions.

Nineteenth-century potlatch ceremonies provide excellent, if somewhat extreme, examples of the ways in which these institutions were elaborated during times of stress to increase social cohesion and resilience. Northwest Coast societies recorded by early ethnographers experienced remarkable levels of stresses and societal transformations as a result of European colonialism. During this period, people engaged in extravagant and highly competitive potlatch ceremonies that included the accumulation, subsequent consumption, and sometimes destruction of so many resources that colonial governments banned the rituals as wasteful (Cole and Chaikin, 1990). These potlatches occurred at a time when powerful chiefs were dying and lands were dispossessed. The extravagance of recorded potlatches, including mortuary potlatches, may have been part of a process in which First Nations people tried to prevent the collapse of many social pillars.

Trosper (2003, 2009) argues that the ritual system underlying the potlatch dates to approximately 2000 BP, but recent archaeological evidence suggests that elements of such a system may have even greater antiquity. For example, Cannon (1998, 2002a) argues that the existence of a surplus economy and evidence for year-round settlement by 5000 BP at Namu (ElSx-1) on the central coast may be related to the introduction of winter ceremonies, which have been documented for a much later time period in the ethnographic literature. Cannon hypothesizes that an ethos of competitive production and sharing generated institutions similar to the potlatch by this time. Farther south on the coast, the production, circulation, and ritual deposition of wealth items, including huge numbers of disc beads in the Salish Sea region dated to 4000 BP (see below) may reflect the importance of ceremonial wealth displays and exchanges (Coupland *et al.*, 2016). Additionally, many finds indicate deep time depth of Northwest Coast art traditions, which are arguably tied to persistent belief systems (Ames and Maschner, 1999: 219–248; Carlson *et al.*, 2017). Often, these art pieces are found in burials and are suggestive of other persistent aspects of Northwest Coast ideological systems. For example, Carlson and colleagues (Carlson and Hobler, 1993; Carlson *et al.*, 2017) argue that elaborately carved goat horn spoons placed near the mouths of deceased individuals around 4000 BP at Pender Canal (DeRt-2) are evidence for feeding the dead, a ritual practice that continues today. This and other archaeological evidence for "feeding the dead" (see below) may also be indicative of the general importance of feasting associated with funerals in the past. The time depth of Northwest Coast practices associated with communal rituals and reciprocal wealth displays along with other archaeological evidence for continuity suggests a link between such rituals and cultural resilience. Rituals associated with succession, such as funerary ceremonies, are likely to have worked toward structuring resilience, and funerary elaboration at particular times may have ensured the maintenance of stability.

10.1.3 Northwest Coast Mortuary Practices

Approaches to interpreting mortuary remains have a long and varied history in archaeology. Early processual archaeologists often interpreted burials and grave goods as direct representations of social complexity (e.g., Binford, 1971; Saxe, 1970). A more recent shift, influenced by the postprocessual critique, emphasizes the rituals surrounding burial events (Ekengren, 2013). This involves a more context-sensitive and practice-oriented approach, wherein mortuary rituals are analyzed as events enacted by the living that may indicate attitudes toward death and the dead, but which are also shaped by the emotions, beliefs, or even strategies of the practitioners (Nilsson Stutz and Tarlow, 2013). Drawing on theories of the efficacy of ritual and performativity (e.g., Bell, 1992; Turner, 1969), mortuary ritual may be analyzed for transformative capacities and how these practices reinforce or revise power relations (Ekengren, 2013). Ostentatious burials may represent ritual enactments that carried people through transitional times or communally reinforced certain social organizations. This chapter uses evidence of mortuary ritual as a practice that supported cultural resilience on the Northwest Coast, though this work also entertains some inferences about social organization based on the burial data (cf. Gamble *et al.*, 2001). This section provides an overview of Northwest Coast mortuary practices. Two of the most salient aspects of mortuary ritual that contributed to resilience are detailed as loci of interest: burials with abundant, lavish grave goods; and emplacement of these burials in special cemeteries.

At the outset, it should be noted that the sample of formally analyzed and reported burial sites is unevenly distributed across the coast (see Burchell, 2006). The majority are located in the Salish Sea region including the Gulf Islands, southern Vancouver Island, the southern mainland coast, and the lower Fraser River; on the north coast nearly all excavated burial sites are from the Prince Rupert Harbour area, with the exception of Blue Jackets Creek (FlUa-4) on Haida Gwaii and Greenville (GgTj-6) on the Lower Nass River. In between these two areas, Namu (ElSx-1) is the only reported central coast cemetery (Figure 10.1).

Mortuary practices on the Northwest Coast were regionally and temporally variable, and the rituals associated with burials were likely equally diverse. The most common burial treatment was interment within shell-bearing deposits (colloquially but inaccurately referred to as "shell midden burials"). These burials were most often flexed and placed in shallow pits; some individuals were buried in wooden boxes (Curtin, 1999: 45; Cybulski, 1992). The earliest-dated example of a burial in shell-bearing deposits is 6260–5890 cal. BP[1] (Beta 317343; 5930 ± 40 BP) from Lucy Island on the north coast of British Columbia, just outside Prince Rupert Harbour (Cui *et al.*, 2013). The absence of earlier dated burials likely reflects inadequate sampling of Early Holocene sites on the Northwest Coast, rather than any historical reality.

There was an apparent decline in the frequency of below-ground burials in shell-bearing deposits in the last 1500 years, which likely correlates with an increase in above-ground placement and cremations (Ames and Maschner, 1999: 190–194; Burchell, 2006; Burley, 1989; Cybulski, 1992). However, examples of cremation and above-ground placement coincident with shell deposit cemeteries are found prior to 1500 BP (Curtin, 2002), and there are examples of below-ground interment up to the time of European contact (Cybulski, 2014a); the more recent increase in above-ground burials may simply be a result of preservation bias. Above-ground

---

[1] All radiocarbon dates discussed in the text are two-sigma calibrated ranges. Ages have been calibrated using best estimates for marine reservoir effects where necessary. All ages mentioned in text that are not directly referencing specific radiocarbon dates are in calendar years BP (Before Present, i.e., 1950). When these instances summarize or refer to radiocarbon-dated ages, those ages have been calibrated.

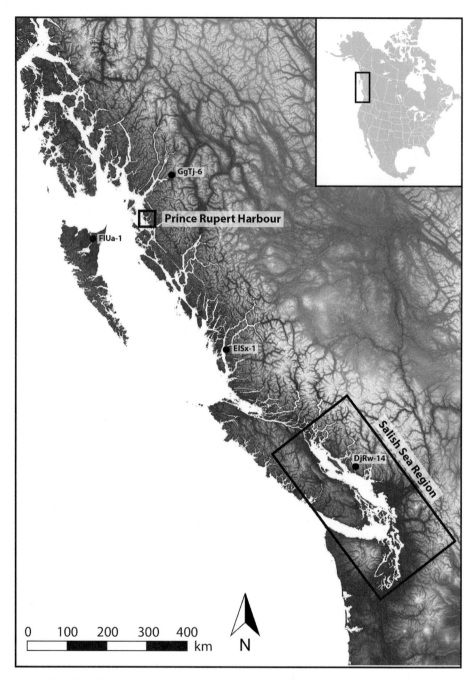

Figure 10.1 Map of the Northwest Coast, showing case study areas and several other cemetery sites mentioned in the text.

forms of body disposal included placement in caves and rock shelters, trees, canoes, and on mortuary poles, the body often being encased first within a burial box (Ames and Maschner, 1999: 192; Carlson, 1999: 43; Cybulski, 1992; MacDonald, 1973). These burials were often spatially removed from occupation areas, located on off-shore islets, or in spiritually powerful secluded places. In the Salish Sea and Lower Fraser River region, conspicuous rock cairn and earthen mound graves were introduced around 1500 BP and were in use for several centuries thereafter (Ames and Maschner, 1999: 190–194; Lepofsky *et al.*, 2000; Mathews, 2014; Thom, 1995).

The earliest identified formal cemetery on the Northwest Coast is dated between 5000 and 4000 BP, at Namu (Burchell, 2006; Curtin, 1984). Burial in cemeteries (discrete areas reserved for the interment of multiple dead) may structure cultural resilience through generating and/or signaling rootedness to places and signaling ancestral affiliations. Saxe (1970) and Goldstein (1981) developed the hypothesis that burial within cemeteries correlates with the rise of corporate group organization in areas where land or other crucial resources are restricted and where groups legitimize rights to these resources through ancestral claims (see also Morris, 1991). Repeated burial within formal cemeteries generates a tradition of legitimately passing ownership or control of land or resources down a lineage. The very existence of cemeteries may therefore also reflect a means of maintaining territorial stability through the legitimacy of historical precedent and endowment from ancestors. More recent theorizing emphasizes the role of cemeteries and mortuary rituals at cemeteries in place-making and the generation of social memory that structures persistent use of places (e.g., Fish *et al.*, 2013; Gamble, 2017; Klokler, 2014; Moore and Thompson, 2012). Emphasis on ancestral attachments to place could be a powerful means of structuring resilient cultural systems. Cemeteries are physical locations that generate and maintain social memory and attachment to the ancestral and spiritual world, which may, in turn, be used to structure political authority and stability (Cannon, 2002b). Cemeteries are also powerful physical landmarks; knowledge of location and reverence of the dead or of the social memory represented by that place may structure movement and action on the landscape.

Northwest Coast cemeteries were powerful places that were often conspicuously located (Mathews, 2014), but sometimes spatially removed from contemporaneous living areas (Curtin, 1999; Cybulski, 1992). In some cases, shell-bearing deposits associated with abandoned occupations were re-purposed as cemeteries (Brown, 1996, 2003). However, in the Prince Rupert Harbour these deposits were often placed in shell ridges immediately behind village sites, allowing for the coexistence of ancestors and the living. It has been suggested that some shell mounds were specially constructed as tumuli for the dead (Ames, 2005: 237, 249; Cybulski, 1992). "Marked" or heightened ritual acts that emphasize place- and history-making at these cemeteries may have been attempts to publically sway cosmic/ancestral forces and/or living political forces (Swenson, 2015). Long-term persistent occupation of locations where ancestors were interred may be indicative of the success of these mortuary rituals in constructing or maintaining social order (cf. Fish *et al.*, 2013; Gamble, 2017).

The practice of "marking" burials by offering grave goods as part of mortuary rituals dates to the first appearance of burials on the Northwest Coast; however, grave goods were not commonly associated with burials during any period. In a review of 1130 burials from British Columbia spanning 5000 years, Burchell (2006) found that only 17.6 percent of individuals were interred with grave goods. Where present, these goods varied widely, from utilitarian items to ornamental items such as beads or pendants, to rare prestige items such as copper and nephrite that represent specialized craftsmanship and would have been garnered through exchange. Ochre is frequently associated with burials. As mentioned earlier, it is also common to find food remains in burials, evidence of "feeding the dead" (Mathews, 2014: 117–118). In addition to the ornately carved goat horn spoons from Pender Canal (Carlson *et al.*, 2017), elderberry seeds were frequently associated with burials at Greenville on the Nass River (Cybulski, 1992), and at Namu concentrated fish remains were found near the mouths of several individuals (Curtin, 1984: 26).

Additionally, the degrees of ostentation in these burials waxed and waned through time, and there appear to be long periods in which burials were given few to no grave goods (Burchell, 2006; Coupland *et al.*, 2016). Choices behind the items placed in burials may reflect the wealth and status of the deceased, but may also act as a broader negotiation between living people regarding an idealized identity for the deceased (Cannon, 2002b). Wason (1994) and others (Cannon, 2002b; Randsborg, 1981) argue that conspicuous mortuary displays are more common during times of instability or uncertainty in political order and are used by people seeking to negotiate and legitimize that order (see also Hayden, 2009). Wealth displays during funerals could be direct statements to those participating in or observing the rituals that affirm legitimate succession or confer confidence in the right of the successor to lead.

As an example, Burchell (2006) proposes that mortuary ritual played an important role in maintaining household stability and resilience on the south coast of British Columbia in the Coast Salish region. This work finds that there are more burials with grave offerings in this region than on the north coast, and there are more ornamental grave inclusions (i.e., non-utilitarian items) on the south coast. It is noted that on the south coast, where descent was reckoned bilaterally, people had more flexibility in household membership (see Barnett, 1955; Elmendorf, 1971; Suttles, 1960, 1962), and suggests that wealth display at funerals was a strategy for attracting household members. She states that "mortuary expenditure and the destruction of wealth via burial is a means of enhancing status and prestige, and funerals provide a public venue for these displays of power" (Burchell, 2006). On the north coast house membership was more rigidly structured through unilineal descent and elaborate mortuary displays were less important for recruitment of household members. Burchell's argument is important because it highlights the potential for conspicuous and lavish funerary rituals to reinforce institutions related to maintaining social cohesion and promoting resilience.

10.2   A Hypothesis for Interpreting Mortuary Ritual on the Northwest Coast

On this basis, a hypothesis for investigating the relationship between mortuary ritual and cultural resilience is developed. Conspicuous mortuary rituals and the emplacement of lavish burials in formal cemeteries brought people together and worked to maintain or reinforce cultural resilience by: (1) treating ancestors and spirits appropriately; (2) demonstrating legitimacy of the social order through place-making and generation of social memory; and (3) establishing confidence in the future by displaying and generously distributing wealth. During times of social stress, these rituals may have been elaborated as people negotiated the future. This hypothesis is explored by presenting two case studies of cemeteries where highly "marked" mortuary rituals took place to evaluate: (1) independent evidence for cultural stress at the time of the burials; and (2) the degree to which resilience is suggested by the archaeological record during and after these burial events.

10.3   Case Studies of Northwest Coast Mortuary Ritual

10.3.1   DjRw-14 and the Salish Sea "Bead Burials"

In 2009 and 2010, during a survey of the Sechelt Inlet system, in the territory of the *shíshálh* First Nation in the northern Salish Sea, the authors discovered and excavated the remains of an individual who had been buried with over 350 000 ground stone disc beads at Kwenten Makwàli (DjRw-14) near the mouth of *Skupa* (Salmon Inlet) (Figure 10.2; Bilton and Letham, 2016; Coupland *et al.*, 2016; Letham, 2014). Subsequent excavations at this site, DjRw-14, revealed three other burials with four individuals in a ~12 × 5 m area. DjRw-14 also includes a large shell-bearing component and was the site of a mid-twentieth-century Christian Bible camp, the construction of which significantly disturbed the archaeological deposits. Radiocarbon dating on all four burials indicates that these individuals were buried between 3900 and 3400 BP, and likely during a much tighter time frame within that range (Coupland *et al.*, 2016). A basal date on a midden deposit into which one of the burials had been dug yielded an age of 6490–6350 cal. BP (Beta 309492), and two dates from overlying, fauna-rich, shell-bearing deposits yielded ages between 3000 and 2500 BP. This indicates that there was occupation of the site both before and after use as a cemetery.

DjRw-14 is located at a major nexus in the Sechelt Inlet system, a network of three intersecting inlets in the heart of *shíshálh* territory. The site enjoys a prominent location along an important transportation route and would have been regularly observed and passed by people paddling through the inlets. DjRw-14 is the largest site within the inlet system (Letham, 2014), and given its mortuary function, must have been recognized as a powerful place. People occupying the site after the cemetery was used may have affiliated with the legacy of those buried at this location.

Each burial at DjRw-14 was placed in a shallow pit that had been excavated into either preexisting cultural deposits or sterile basal gravel. Burial 1 was a male, aged approximately 50 years (Cybulski, 2011). This individual was placed in a flexed position on the right side with the body oriented east–west and the head tilted slightly and facing west toward the mouth of Salmon Inlet and the setting sun. The

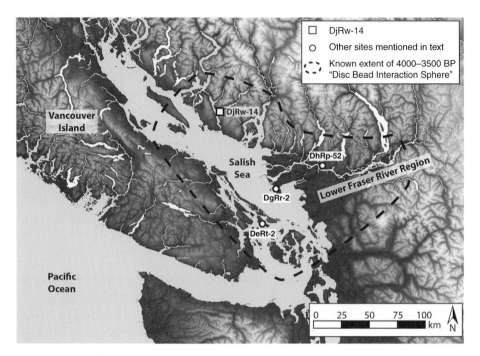

Figure 10.2 Map of the Salish Sea region, including the location of DjRw-14 and other sites mentioned in the text. Known extent of the "disc bead interaction sphere," which includes the Salish Sea and the Lower Fraser River, is highlighted.

head of the individual had been wrapped in numerous strands of ground stone disc beads, and the body was covered with strands of beads so numerous that the burial pit was filled with a layer of beads up to 5 cm thick. Approximately 350 000 ground stone disc beads and 1000 clam shell disc beads were recovered, though the west edge of the burial pit had been destroyed during the construction of the Bible camp, so the total number of beads was likely even greater. Burial 1 at DjRw-14 is likely the most "bead-rich" burial ever found on the Northwest Coast. The only other grave goods associated with this burial were a necklace of tube worm shells, a ground and notched bone piece that may have been a pendant, and ochre. Concentrations of the latter were found beneath the skull and near the left knee. The burial was capped with a thin layer of hard-packed black pebbly sediment.

Burial 2 was a young woman, aged 20 years, buried on the right side in a flexed position with the body oriented north–south and the head positioned to face in the same direction as Burial 1 (Williams, 2011). Grave goods associated with Burial 2 included ~5700 stone disc beads from the torso area and ~3175 shell disc beads from the upper torso and head area, most of which were extremely small (2–3 mm diameter) and well crafted. This individual was also buried with 40 *Olivella* shell beads that were likely a necklace, two antler ear spools, and four chipped stone stemmed projectile points. These points had all been broken at the same location near to the tip; the bases were placed side by side near the left foot, pointing toward the body, and the tips were placed below the left knee, clearly a case of intentional breakage and placement during the funerary ritual.

Burial 3 was a double burial of two young adult males, both flexed on the left side, one behind the other and facing northeast (Holland, 2014). The rear individual's flexed legs overlapped those of the other and this individual's arms were placed around the shoulder of the other individual as if embracing. Grave goods included ~650 stone disc beads and ~1550 shell disc beads.

Burial 4 contained the relatively well-preserved remains of an infant with no grave goods (Holland, 2014). However, these remains were heavily ochre-stained. The presence of individuals representing a range of ages and both sexes, each with special burial treatment, suggests that DjRw-14 could have been a cemetery for a powerful lineage.

In addition to the burials, a cache of ~6600 stone disc beads was excavated. Located in the cemetery, the cache was in a small pit, too small to have contained a burial, about 1 m below the ground surface. Two large, finely crafted stone projectile points had been placed directly on top of the beads, and a third point was recovered from the pit fill.

In addition to the finds at DjRw-14, large numbers of stone and shell disc beads were recovered from burials and other contexts at several other sites in the Salish Sea region dated between 4000 and 3500 BP (Figure 10.2; Coupland et al., 2016). Notably, in a cemetery at Tsawwassen (DgRs-2), a juvenile aged 11–14 years was buried with over 53 000 stone disc beads and a male aged 40–45 years was buried with over 11 000 beads (Arcas, 1994, 1999). Large numbers of ground stone disc beads were also recovered from non-mortuary contexts in the region that date to the same period, most notably from the Katzie Site (DhRp-52) on the Lower Fraser River, where over 100 000 beads were found in hearths and fire-cracked rock features both inside and outside houses that were occupied at the time (Katzie Development Corporation Archaeology, 2010; Wilkerson, 2010).

These finds suggest that stone and shell disc beads were mass produced, likely in the millions, and circulated throughout the southern Salish Sea and Lower Fraser River region for mortuary and non-mortuary ritual use at approximately 4000 to 3500 BP. Coupland and colleagues (2016) argue that these beads represent material wealth that accrued value through production, use life, and disposal during ritual. This work argues that the extraordinary number of beads is firm evidence for material wealth-based inequality at a time much earlier than previously proposed. Other forms of grave wealth, such as the items of adornment associated with DjRw-14 Burial 2 and the elaborately carved spoons and soapstone items at Pender Canal (Carlson and Hobler, 1993; Carlson et al., 2017), support this assertion and indicate the importance of elaborate mortuary rituals during this time. However, Coupland et al. (2016) also point out that the use of ground stone disc beads in ritual and disposal of beads in burials declined after 3500 BP and did not become common in burials again until about 2400 BP.

10.3.2   GbTo-31 and the Prince Rupert Harbour "Superordinate Elite" Burials

Nearly 700 km northwest of the Salish Sea, one of the largest archaeological burial assemblages from the Northwest Coast was excavated by the National Museum of Canada (now the Canadian Museum of History) during the 1960s and early 1970s around the Prince Rupert Harbour, in Tsimshian territory (Figure 10.3). Large-scale excavations were conducted at 11 archaeological sites in and around the harbor as part of the North Coast Prehistory Project (NCPP) (Ames, 2005; MacDonald, 1969; MacDonald and Cybulski, 2001; MacDonald and Inglis, 1981). Most of the excavated sites were large villages, and the expansive excavations recovered 288 burials (Ames, 2005: 230). Six sites each had more than ten burials, and Ames (2005: 237) argues that at least five of these sites had formal cemeteries: Boardwalk (GbTo-31), Lachane (GbTo-33), Baldwin (GbTo-36), Garden Island (GbTo-23), and Parizeau Point (GbTo-30) (Figure 10.3). These cemeteries were placed in large ridges of shell that were deposited at the back of the villages. Burials were most frequently placed in pits dug into the shell, which often disturbed earlier burials and resulted in a pattern of disarticulated human remains mixed within the shell ridge deposits. Most individuals were interred in the flexed position, though there is evidence that some were interred in burial boxes (Cybulski, 1992; MacDonald and Cybulski, 2001).

While there are individual burials at Prince Rupert Harbour that date to nearly 5000 BP, true cemeteries were not established until about 2900 BP at GbTo-33 and GbTo-36, and burials became most frequent at these sites only after 2500 BP (Cybulski, 2014a). Cemeteries also appeared around this time at GbTo-23 and GbTo-31. All Prince Rupert Harbour cemeteries fell out of use by 750 BP. Among all burials, only ~10 percent were interred with grave goods (Ames, 2005). In general, grave goods are associated with all ages and with both males and females, though there is a bias toward males (Ames, 2005).

The cemetery associated with a ridge of shell at the back of the Boardwalk site (GbTo-31, excavation Areas A and C) is particularly remarkable among the other cemetery components excavated in the Prince Rupert area. The NCPP excavated 85 burials and 1180 disturbed human bone elements at Boardwalk (Ames, 2005; Cybulski, 1992). It has the highest density of burials of any excavated cemetery in the harbor, and 18 percent of the burials have grave goods, a much higher proportion than in the other cemeteries.

In addition, 14 of 17 Prince Rupert Harbour individuals buried with items of adornment or exotic materials (e.g., copper and amber) originate from Boardwalk. These burials are furnished with rare items not found in any other Prince Rupert Harbour site, which is striking, given the scale of the NCPP excavations (Ames, 2005: 243–244). Boardwalk is the only site where copper items were found; these took the form of sheets, bracelets, and cylindrical coverings for cedar dowels that are thought to have been armor (Ames, 2005; Cybulski, 2014b).

Several of these burials had particularly elaborate assemblages. Burial 325, a male aged 12–16 years, was interred with a copper disc earring, 38 amber beads, three shell gorgets, a pendant with preserved fibers, and sheets of copper (Ames, 2005;

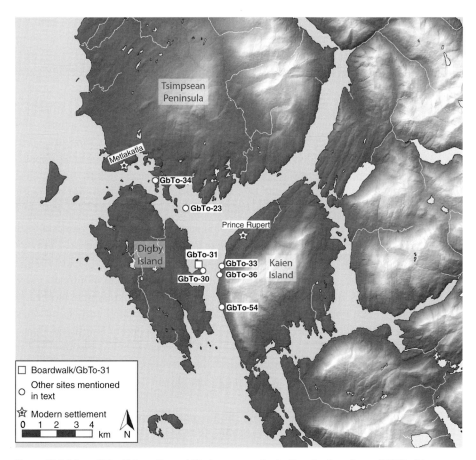

Figure 10.3 Map of the Prince Rupert Harbour area, including the location of GbTo-31 (Boardwalk) and other sites mentioned in the text.

MacDonald and Cybulski, 2001). This individual dates between 2348 and 2018 cal. BP (S-1666).[2] Burial 322 was interred with a necklace of 250 shell disc beads, 25 dentalium shells, an amber bead, an ankle bracelet of dentalium shells, a copper-wrapped wooden dowel, and other degraded copper items (Ames, 2005; MacDonald and Cybulski, 2001). This individual dates between 1522 and 1281 cal. BP (S-1667). Burial 375 dates to between 1510 to 1300 cal. BP (Beta 344287) and was interred with two trophy skulls. Burial 521 is slightly more recent (966 to 740 cal. BP, Beta 227178), and was buried with copper-wrapped cedar dowels and other deteriorated copper items, a large amber bead and a large amber pendant (Ames, 2005: 233; MacDonald and Cybulski, 2001). Other individuals had similar items of adornment, stone and bone tools or weapons, and labrets. Some individuals were buried in wooden boxes that were inlaid with sea otter teeth. The majority were young males.

---

[2] Radiocarbon dates from Boardwalk used in this analysis are taken from Ames (2005), Cybulski (2014b), and Letham *et al.* (2017).

No burials excavated at other sites in the Prince Rupert area had grave good assemblages as lavish as those found at Boardwalk, even though the majority were interred contemporaneously (Ames, 2005).

Another remarkable find at the Boardwalk cemetery is a cache of objects that has been dubbed the "warrior cache" (Ames, 2005; Cybulski, 2014b; MacDonald and Cybulski, 2001). This feature included a carved anthropomorphic whalebone club, a second club made from an orca's jaw, two copper bracelets, a large finely made ground and chipped stone blade, an oblong hammerstone or "braining stone," a shell gorget, a mountain goat horn core, and six cedar dowels wrapped in copper sheeting. There was also a copper-stained skull and articulated mandible that Cybulski (2014b) interprets as a trophy skull. This skull dates between 1000 and 755 cal. BP (Beta 200548)[3] and one of the cedar dowels dates between 1047 and 796 cal. BP (Beta 245147) (Cybulski, 2014b). Ames (2005) suggests that this was a cache of heirlooms that may have been regalia deposited as a commemorative act.

In addition to the potential trophy skulls at the site, Cybulski (1978) identified several human skeletal elements that exhibited postmortem modification by humans. These pieces include modified fragments of human skulls and worked long bone fragments. Cybulski suggests these items were associated with ritual related to the perceived powers of the dead; Cybulski notes that many Northwest Coast societies viewed the head as the vessel for the soul, and that many of the modified skulls may have been containers for spirit powers. While instances of these types of items are documented at six other sites in the Prince Rupert Harbour, the majority come from the Boardwalk cemetery.

Twenty-nine individuals from the Boardwalk cemetery have been directly radio-carbon dated (Figure 10.4; Ames, 2005; Cybulski, 2014a, 2014b; Jerome Cybulski, personal communication, 2017; Letham et al., 2017). The oldest of these burials is dated between 2705 and 2328 cal. BP (S-1284), but the majority of dated burials are between 2000 and 1300 BP (Figure 10.4; Cybulski, 2014a). A hiatus in cemetery usage occurred between 1300 and 1000 BP, which is coincident with a wider-scale abandonment of most sites in the Prince Rupert Harbour (see below). After this the cemetery was briefly reused until ~750 BP. Looking specifically at burials with grave goods, five such individuals have been dated, and along with the Warrior Cache, occurred at three "instances" or periods within the longer use life of the cemetery. Burial 410 and Burial 325 are the oldest dated burials with grave goods, both dating between 2400 and 2000 BP; Burial 375 and Burial 322 both date between 1500 and 1300 BP, and Burial 521 and the Warrior Cache both date between 1000 and 750 BP (Figure 10.4).

---

[3] Calibration of this sample differs from that of Cybulski (2014b), because this chapter uses an updated marine reservoir correction ΔR for the Prince Rupert Harbour of 273 ± 38 (Edinborough et al., 2016) and assumes a 90 percent marine contribution to the diet. In Cybulski's table 18.1, the calibrated age range for the skull is about 200 years older, and not consistent with the calibrated age range for the associated cedar dowel.

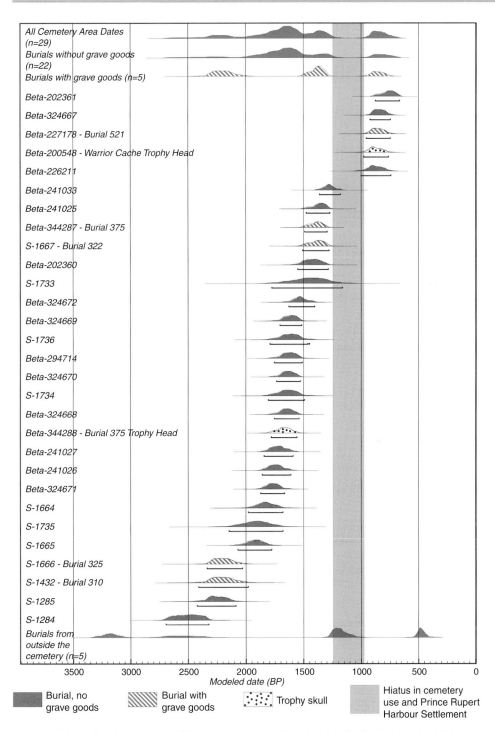

Figure 10.4 Two-sigma calibrated age ranges of all dated individuals from the GbTo-31 cemetery, and summed probability distributions (SPDs) of all cemetery dates, all dated burials without grave goods, all dated burials with grave goods, and all dated burials from outside the cemetery. Dates are from Cybulski (2014a) and Letham *et al.* (2017).

Based on the spectacular finds at Boardwalk, Ames (2005: 244) argues that individuals buried there were part of a "superordinate elite ... [who] had access to items made of exotic raw materials made by specialists" and that "these items were probably heirlooms controlled by the corporate group." The fact that many were young males buried with weaponry and trophies of war suggests that this high status was held by accomplished warriors or relatives of a warrior class. Ames argues that there may have been a site hierarchy in the Prince Rupert Harbour by as early as 3000 BP, with Boardwalk the pre-eminent site (see also Ames, 1995).[4]

10.4   Explaining Lavish Mortuary Ritual on the Northwest Coast

10.4.1   Questions Posed

How can mortuary rituals involving marked treatment of the dead at DjRw-14 and GbTo-31 be interpreted? In the Salish Sea, the pattern of bead-rich burials is observed at multiple locations but restricted temporally, although the DjRw-14 Burial 1 stands out as being an order of magnitude more "bead rich" than others recorded in the area. In the Prince Rupert area, Boardwalk appears to be a single site among many where a certain group of individuals was accorded special treatment, and this tradition lasted for a longer time. In this section the historical context for these burials is considered to explore the hypothesized connections with cultural resilience.

10.4.2   Salish Sea Bead-Rich Burials and the Cohesion of the Disc Bead Interaction Network

The manufacture and distribution of large amounts of ground stone disc beads within the Salish Sea and Lower Fraser River region, as well as the association of these beads with mortuary contexts, signals ritual importance. It is, however, important to ask: Why were so many beads produced and ultimately buried with certain individuals around the Salish Sea between 4000 and 3500 BP? Coupland and colleagues (2016) argue that the production of beads at this time was probably associated with the rise of wealth-based inequality. The formation of corporate groups with wealth-based inequality around 4000 BP created new forms of social relationships and interactions in the Salish Sea region. Control of resources and overt forms of inequality may well have been unknown in the region prior to this time. This new and unfamiliar social structure would have been promoted by some, but contested by others, likely resulting in instability and flux. At about the same time, cemeteries appear as locations for mortuary ritual and disposal of the dead. It was in this context of a changing and dynamic social milieu that mortuary ritual involving the display and disposal of thousands, sometimes hundreds of thousands, of beads and other

---

[4] More recent excavations at Ya asqalu'i (GbTo-54), across the channel from Boardwalk, unearthed an impressive assemblage of ornamental artifacts and high-status faunal remains, leading the excavators to conclude that this was a high-status site as well, though no intact burials were found at the entire site (and the *entire* site was excavated) (Eldridge *et al.*, 2014).

mortuary goods was elaborated. Corporate group leaders would have exchanged and publicly displayed beads in an effort to compete with each other for social status (cf. Burchell, 2006). The deposition of so many of these items with a single individual in a funeral ceremony could have been both an act of reverence for the deceased but also a display of wealth by mourners.

Is there other evidence suggesting that the period between 4000 and 3500 BP may have been a time of stress or instability in the Salish Sea region, beyond or in addition to the emergence of sociopolitical hierarchies? Unfortunately, little is currently known about this time period, but some region-wide demographic data allow the suggestion of a few possibilities. In a study of archaeological site frequency around the Salish Sea based on 345 radiocarbon dates, Lepofsky and colleagues (2005) report a generally stable settlement pattern for the period between 5000 and 2500 BP. However, in a more recent study focused specifically on the Lower Fraser River region (over 70 km southeast of DjRw-14) and using a sample of 599 radiocarbon dates from 95 sites, Ritchie *et al.* (2016) find a pattern of slow, steady growth from 6000 BP to 600 BP, with the exception of the period between 4000 and 3500 BP. During this 500-year period there was a decrease in the number of dated sites along the Lower Fraser (Ritchie *et al.*, 2016), suggesting a decline in population at precisely the same time that intensive mortuary ritual and the rise of the "disc bead exchange network" is observed (Figure 10.2; Coupland *et al.*, 2016). Ritchie *et al.* (2016) speculate that climate cooling around this time may be related to the decline in Lower Fraser River settlement, though this remains to be demonstrated. Whatever the cause, people may have expanded exchange networks within the broader Salish Sea region to buffer against uncertainties. Part of this process may have included increased production and circulation of disc beads, perhaps to trade for resources or to affirm strategic alliances. Broadening socioeconomic networks would very likely have increased the resilience of populations experiencing stress, and large communal rituals – including mortuary rituals – may have been part of this integrating process. Furthermore, new social relations of wealth-based inequality may have influenced the mortuary rituals that included ostentatious display and disposal of beads as communities came together.

More data are required to specifically test the relationship between resilience and the "disc bead network" in the Salish Sea between 4000 and 3500 BP. Through the Late Holocene there does, however, seem to be a pattern of fluctuating emphasis on exchange and interaction within the region (Grier, 2003; Lepofsky *et al.*, 2005), and one could posit that periodic increases or widenings in the movements of people and/or goods sometimes occurred to mitigate cultural and/or environmental uncertainties. In the context of newly emerging social inequalities and an elite class, people may have required persuasion that this new social order would best serve individual and communal needs. Furthermore, the "sharing" and disposal of wealth during funerary rituals may have served to reinforce communalism even as society became increasingly stratified (cf. Coupland *et al.*, 2009), and fits with an ethos of resisting the development of political centralization that Angelbeck and Grier (2012) suggest is characteristic of Coast Salish culture. Wealth displays and appeals to powerful ancestors in lavish funerals during these times may have affirmed cultural values of confidence in abundance in ways that could reach broader audiences and more disparate communities.

10.4.3   Prince Rupert Harbour "Superordinate Elite," Migrations, and Warfare

On the north coast, an emerging body of evidence now indicates that the Boardwalk cemetery at Prince Rupert Harbour was in use during a tumultuous period of cultural change. Tsimshian oral histories known as *adawx* refer to a time when peoples from farther north migrated into Prince Rupert Harbour and surrounding areas (Marsden, 2001; Martindale and Marsden, 2003). These outsiders were initially allowed to settle within these lands and were integrated into the fabric of local society, though the process was not without tension and occasional hostility. Eventually, these migrations culminated in a regional war that drove out the original occupants of Prince Rupert Harbour. These populations eventually moved up the Skeena River and formed an alliance to resist the invaders. Martindale and Marsden (2003) initially dated these migrations to between 3500 and 1500 BP. More recent demographic modeling for the Skeena River area using a large sample of radiocarbon dates and site frequencies suggests a population increase beginning after 2900 BP and a second major increase between 2300 and 1700 BP, followed by a dramatic decrease in population that appears to represent a near wholesale-abandonment of the area after 1300 BP (Figure 10.5; Edinborough *et al.*, 2017; Martindale *et al.*, 2017). Finally, there was a re-occupation of the harbor around 1000 BP. It is possible that these

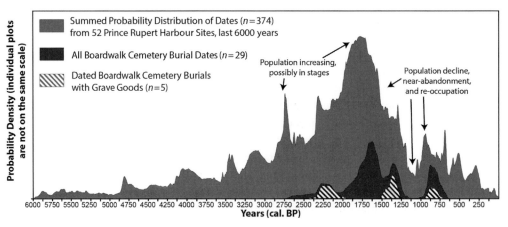

Figure 10.5 Calibrated summed probability distributions (SPDs) of all GbTo-31 cemetery burial dates and all GbTo-31 cemetery burials with grave goods and SPD of 374 non-burial dates from 52 Prince Rupert Harbour sites. The latter can be used as a coarse demographic proxy for the area. Probability plots are not on the same scale and are presented to assess contemporaneity of patterns only. Dates are from Ames (2005), Cybulski (2014a), Letham *et al.* (2017), MacDonald and Inglis (1981), and Martindale *et al.* (forthcoming).

empirically derived population estimates coincide with the in-migration events mentioned in the oral histories (Marsden, 2001).

In addition, Cybulski (2014a, b) documents a period of warfare in this area between ~3000 and 750 BP using evidence derived from human skeletal remains. Of 223 adults from the overall sample of Prince Rupert Harbour individuals, 101 (45.3 percent) had traumatic fractures to bones, and an additional seven individuals had ambiguous evidence for traumatic fractures (Cybulski, 2014a). These injuries were associated with blunt force trauma to the head and parry fractures to the forearms. Evidence of decapitations at three sites in the harbor, all dated between 1000 and 750 cal. BP, provide further evidence for interpersonal violence. Cybulski (2014b) suggests that the decapitations and the coincident deposition of the Warrior Cache at Boardwalk signal a dramatic conclusion to a long period of intermittent warfare in the area, coinciding with the proposed re-occupation of Prince Rupert Harbour.

The arrival of migrants to Prince Rupert Harbour would have required negotiations of space and territory, and clearly this was not always a peaceful process. Formal cemeteries were established at the same time as the initial wave of demographic spikes and first evidence for interpersonal violence between 2900 and 2700 BP. All cemeteries were established at sites that had been occupied prior to these demographic increases (Ames, 2005; Cybulski, 2014a), suggesting that the inhabitants explicitly marked these locations through the burial of ancestors. Migrations may have placed stress on an established system of settlement and ownership and required new assertions of hereditary legitimacy.

Though the sample size is small, dated burials with elaborate grave goods at Boardwalk all coincide with moments of dramatic change in the Prince Rupert Harbour demographic model (Figures 10.4 and 10.5), so it is tempting to consider these as potential "marked" moments within the longer history of cemetery use. The first dated burials with elaborate grave goods, around 2400 to 2000 BP, coincide with the beginning of a major population increase (Martindale *et al.*, 2017) and an increase in the frequency of interpersonal violence (Cybulski, 2014a). The second pair of burials with grave goods, dated between 1500 and 1300 BP, were interred during a precipitous decline in population as people were apparently abandoning Prince Rupert Harbour (Edinborough *et al.* 2017). Finally, the burial with grave goods and the Warrior Cache that post-date 1000 BP were emplaced during the re-occupation of the harbor. The residents at Boardwalk conducted conspicuous mortuary rituals in this cemetery during periods of violent conflict and population transition. These populations buried individuals with many items of adornment and objects of exotic raw materials often related to warfare, perhaps in an effort to assert legitimacy through wealth display or to propitiate the ancestors in a time of conflict.

Significantly, the people who re-occupied Boardwalk after 1000 BP buried individuals with the same types of items (copper and amber adornment) as the earliest-dated lavish burials. This suggests that mortuary rituals during the re-occupation made direct reference to ancestors buried in this important place prior to abandonment, potentially reconnecting with preexisting social orders. The long duration of cemetery use beyond these particular burial events suggests that part of the rituals' importance was garnered through deep-time associations with a powerful place that held generations of powerful ancestors.

Also significant, the burial of exotic materials with the dead may be suggestive of broadened exchange interactions, perhaps with migrants or other trading partners. Just as expanding social networks may have been part of a process that aided resilience in the southern Salish Sea, cementing or broadening certain relationships during the times of upheaval around the Prince Rupert Harbour – and then signaling these connections during mortuary rituals – may have been part of alliance- or community-building that maintained cohesion.

Although the osteological data suggest endemic warfare for a 2000-year period, there is evidence for cultural resilience throughout this time. Ames (2005) finds remarkable technological consistency over 5000 years; the tool kits of the occupants of the Prince Rupert Harbour were conservative and only added artifact types or styles through time. Additionally, many of the village sites show long-term occupations that span both before and after the period of warfare. For example, a sample of 66 radiocarbon dates from Boardwalk demonstrate nearly 5000 years of occupation, while 38 radiocarbon dates from GbTo-33 (Lachane) and 65 radiocarbon dates from GbTo-34 (Kitandach) present sequences of nearly 6000 years of occupation (Ames, 2005; Letham *et al.*, 2017). During turbulent times, the inhabitants of Boardwalk buried individuals in spectacular fashion, perhaps in an effort to legitimize authority and control of territories. These burials made direct reference to the ancestors through material mimicry and involved the display and deposition of wealth that would have been obtained from other regions. The persistence of occupation and mortuary ritual at Boardwalk would have contributed to cultural resilience over the long term.

10.5   Conclusion

Mortuary practices of Northwest Coast fisher-hunter-gatherer societies varied through time and space, and while burials with grave goods were rare, there were instances of lavish mortuary displays and disposals of wealth. While the burials discussed in this chapter are evidence for the existence of material wealth-based inequalities, this chapter focuses on the potential social effects attributed to the rituals surrounding these burials. These burials likely reflect communal negotiations of the social order (which were often directed toward resisting strict consolidations of hegemonic power; see Angelbeck and Grier, 2012; Coupland *et al.*, 2009), and may have been part of ancient institutions similar to the potlatch system in which people's social standings were affirmed through communal rituals that retold history and established confidence in the future.

Wealth accumulation and exchange was critical to the institutions that structured Northwest Coast societies and relationships between groups. It has been proposed that these institutions, which included inheritance of positions that was socially promoted through funeral feasts and mortuary rituals, helped maintain resilience and sustainability in Northwest Coast social systems through ancestral affiliation (Trosper, 2003, 2009). However, there may have been points in history when succession and the future were uncertain. Stresses on society, such as environmental hardships that impacted resource productivity, warfare between groups, migrations, or even the emergence of increased social inequalities may have presented challenges to established social orders and forced people to find ways to maintain, negotiate, or assert stability (cf. Cannon, 2002b).

Participation in lavish mortuary rituals in which wealth was displayed and disposed of may have helped reaffirm ties to important ancestors and legitimized the inheritance of lineage positions. The construction of cemeteries where special mortuary rituals took place may also have contributed to the assertion and maintenance of political stability. Association with these cemeteries through continued use or commemorative caching may have worked to establish real or imagined connections with powerful ancestors and structured persistent places (cf. Fish *et al.*, 2013; Gamble, 2017). In terms of resilience theory, elaborate mortuary rituals may have buffered against uncertainty during times of stress, and successful deployment of these rituals contributed to the persistence of cultural systems.

The findings of this chapter suggest that the lavish funerary rituals at Kwenten Makwàli (DjRw-14) and Boardwalk promoted cultural resilience during periods of stress, visible in the archaeological record in each area during the times when these cemeteries were in use. The available data do not allow for a full formal test of the hypotheses; a larger sample of burial data (especially from DjRw-14) and more detailed local chronologies of both cultural developments and various potential societal stresses are required. In particular, interpretations regarding the Salish Sea bead burials between 4000 and 3500 cal. BP remain speculative, as much of the contextual archaeological evidence is either unsampled or equivocal. However, the presence of lavish bead burials is indicative of the emergence of previously unknown degrees of wealth-based inequality. Shifts in social relationships with these increasing inequalities would have created turbulence within previously accepted political organizations. The disposal of large amounts of wealth during funerals may have been a means of legitimizing new social relations. There is also evidence for a decline in settlement in the Lower Fraser River region at this time and increased connections between that area and the broader Salish Sea region. This may have afforded new trade and alliance options, but also presented new circumstances in which a changing social order was negotiated through ritual.

The archaeological record around Prince Rupert Harbour is much better documented, with oral historical, archaeological, and osteological evidence for rapid population increases due to migration and interpersonal violence. These patterns occur when Boardwalk burials were most extravagant. The marked funerary rituals at Boardwalk occurred during tumultuous times, including immediately preceding and following a large-scale temporary abandonment of the harbor. The rituals that took place made direct reference to the past, likely as an attempt to negotiate certainty in the future. In both regions, many of the items deposited with the dead were likely obtained from broad exchange networks. Funerary rituals may have promoted resilience through community-building, and the disposal of exotic items suggests the coalescence of disparate groups of funerals, but these items may be indexical of even broader relationships that buffered against uncertainty.

References

Ames, K. M. (1979). Stable and resilient systems along the Skeena River: The Gitksan/Carrier boundary. In R. I. Inglis and G. F. MacDonald, eds., *Skeena River Prehistory*. Ottawa: National Museums of Canada, pp. 220–243.

Ames, K. M. (1981). The evolution of social ranking on the Northwest Coast of North America. *American Antiquity*, **46**, 789–805.

Ames, K. M. (1995). Chiefly power and household production on the Northwest Coast. In T. D. Price and G. M. Feinman, eds., *Foundations of Social Inequality*. New York, NY: Plenum Press, pp. 155–187.

Ames, K. M. (2005). *The North Coast Prehistory Project Excavations in Prince Rupert Harbour, British Columbia: The Artifacts*. Oxford: British Archaeological Reports.

Ames, K. M. and Maschner, H. D. G. (1999). *Peoples of the Northwest Coast: Their Archaeology and Prehistory*. London: Thames and Hudson.

Angelbeck, B. (2007). Conceptions of Coast Salish warfare, or Coast Salish pacifism reconsidered: Archaeology, ethnohistory, and ethnography. In B. G. Miller, ed., *Be of Good Mind: Essays on the Coast Salish*. Vancouver: University of British Columbia Press, pp. 260–283.

Angelbeck, B. and Grier, C. (2012). Anarchism and the archaeology of anarchic societies: Resistance to centralization in the Coast Salish region of the Pacific Northwest Coast. *Current Anthropology*, **53**, 547–587.

Arcas Consulting Archaeologists. (1994). Archaeological Investigations at Tsawwassen, B.C. (Volume II). Victoria, BC. Report on file, British Columbia Archaeology Branch, Permit 1989-041.

Arcas Consulting Archaeologists. (1999). Archaeological Investigations at Tsawwassen, B.C. (Volume IV). Victoria, BC. Report on file, British Columbia Archaeology Branch, Permit 1989-041.

Barnett, H. G. (1955). *The Coast Salish of British Columbia*. Portland, OR: University of Oregon Press.

Bell, C. (1992). *Ritual Theory, Ritual Practice*. New York, NY: Oxford University Press.

Bilton, D. and Letham, B. (2016). The Sechelt Archaeology Project (2008–present). *The Midden*, **46**, 5–14.

Binford, L. (1971). Mortuary practices: Their study and their potential. In J. Brown, ed., *Approaches to the Social Dimensions of Mortuary Practices*. Washington, DC: Society for American Archaeology, pp. 6–29.

Brown, D. (1996). *Disposing of the Dead: A Shell Midden Cemetery in British Columbia's Gulf of Georgia Region*. MA thesis, University of British Columbia.

Brown, D. (2003). Shell middens and midden burials in southern Strait of Georgia prehistory. In R. L. Carlson, ed., *Archaeology of Coastal British Columbia: Essays in Honour of Professor Philip M. Hobler*. Burnaby: SFU Archaeology Press, pp. 153–164.

Burchell, M. (2006). Gender, grave goods and status in British Columbia burials. *Canadian Journal of Archaeology*, **30**, 251–271.

Burley, D. V. (1989). *Senewélets: Culture History of the Nanaimo Coast Salish and the False Narrows Midden*. Victoria: Royal British Columbia Museum.

Campbell, S. K. and Butler, V. L (2010). Archaeological evidence for resilience of Pacific Northwest salmon populations and the socioecological system over the last ~7,500 years. *Ecology and Society*, **15**, 1–20.

Cannon, A. (1998). Contingency and agency in the growth of Northwest Coast maritime economies. *Arctic Anthropology*, **35**, 57–67.

Cannon, A. (2002a). Sacred power and seasonal settlement on the central Northwest Coast. In B. Fitzhugh and J. Havbu, eds., *Beyond Foraging and Collecting: Evolutionary Change in Hunter-Gatherer Settlement Systems*. New York, NY: Kluwer Academic-Plenum, pp. 311–338.

Cannon, A. (2002b). Spatial narratives of death, memory, and transcendence. *Archaeological Papers of the American Anthropological Association*, **11**, 191–199.

Cannon, A. (2003). Long-term continuity in central Northwest Coast settlement patterns. In R. L. Carlson, ed., *Archaeology of Coastal British Columbia: Essays in Honour of Professor Philip M. Hobler*. Burnaby: SFU Archaeology Press, pp. 1–12.

Carlson, R. L. (1999). Sacred sites on the Northwest Coast of North America. In B. Coles, J. Coles, and M. S. Jørgensen, eds., *Bog Bodies, Sacred Sites and Wetland Archaeology*. Exeter: University of Exeter, pp. 39–46.

Carlson, R. L. and Hobler, P. M. (1993). The Pender Canal excavations and the development of Coast Salish culture. *BC Studies*, **99**, 25–52.

Carlson, R. L., Szpak, P., and Richards, M. (2017). The Pender Canal site and the beginning of the Northwest Coast cultural system. *Canadian Journal of Archaeology*, **41**, 1–29.

Codere, H. (1950). *Fighting with Property: A Study of Kwakiutl Potlatching and Warfare, 1792–1930*. New York, NY: J. J. Augustin.

Cole, D. and Chaikin, I. (1990). *An Iron Hand upon the People: The Law Against the Potlatch on the Northwest Coast*. Vancouver: Douglas & McIntyre.

Coupland, G., Clark, T., and Palmer, A. (2009). Hierarchy, communalism and the spatial order of Northwest Coast houses: A comparative study. *American Antiquity*, **74**, 77–106.

Coupland, G., Bilton, D., Clark, T., *et al.* (2016). A wealth of beads: Evidence for material wealth-based inequality in the Salish Sea region, 4000–3500 cal. BP. *American Antiquity*, **81**, 294–315.

Cui, Y., Lindo, J., Hughes, C. E., *et al.* (2013). Ancient DNA analysis of mid-Holocene individuals from the Northwest Coast of North America reveals different evolutionary paths for mitogenomes. *PLoS ONE*, **8**, e66948.

Curtin, J. A. (1984). *Human Skeletal Remains from Namu (ElSx-1): A Descriptive Analysis*. MA thesis, Simon Fraser University.

Curtin, J. A. (1999). Mortuary practices. In Arcas Consulting Archaeologists Ltd., ed., *Archaeological Investigations at Tsawwassen, B.C. Volume IV*. Victoria, BC. Report on file, British Columbia Archaeology Branch, Permit 1989-041.

Curtin, J. A. (2002). *Prehistoric Mortuary Variability on Gabriola Island, British Columbia*. Burnaby: SFU Archaeology Press.

Cybulski, J. S. (1978). Modified human bones and skulls from Prince Rupert Harbour, British Columbia. *Canadian Journal of Archaeology*, **2**, 15–32.

Cybulski, J. S. (1992). *A Greenville Burial Ground: Human Remains and Mortuary Elements in British Columbia Coast Prehistory*. Ottawa: Archaeological Survey of Canada, Canadian Museum of Civilization.

Cybulski, J. S. (2011). The osteology of an Early Pacific human skeleton from the Bible Camp Site (DjRw-14), Sechelt, British Columbia. Gatineau, QC, Canada. Manuscript on file, Library Archives, Archaeology Ms. 5240, Canadian Museum of History.

Cybulski, J. S. (2014a). Conflict on the northern Northwest Coast: 2,000 years plus of bioarchaeological evidence. In C. Knüsel and M. J. Smith, eds., *The Routledge Handbook of the Bioarchaeology of Human Conflict*. London: Routledge, pp. 415–451.

Cybulski, J. S. (2014b). Updating the Warrior Cache: Timing the evidence for warfare at Prince Rupert Harbour. In M. W. Allen and T. L Jones, eds., *Violence and Warfare among Hunter-Gatherers*. Walnut Creek, CA: Left Coast Press, pp. 333–350.

Edinborough, K., Martindale, A., Cook, G. T., Supernant, K., and Ames, K. M. (2016). A marine reservoir effect ΔR value for Kitandach, in Prince Rupert Harbour, British Columbia, Canada. *Radiocarbon*, **58**, 885–891.

Edinborough, K., Martindale, A., Brown, T. J., Supernant, K., and Ames, K. M. (2017). A radiocarbon test for demographic events in written and oral history. *Proceedings of the National Academy of Sciences*, **114**, 12436–12441.

Ekengren, F. (2013). Contextualizing grave goods: Theoretical perspectives and methodological implications. In L. Nilsson Stutz and S. Tarlow, eds., *The Oxford Handbook of the Archaeology of Death and Burial*. Oxford: Oxford University Press, pp. 173–192.

Eldridge, M., Parker, A., Mueller, C., and Crockford, S. (2014). Archaeological Investigations at Ya asqalui'i/Kaien Siding, Prince Rupert Harbour. Report on file, Millennia Research Limited, Victoria, BC.

Elmendorf, W. W. (1971). Coast Salish status ranking and intergroup ties. *Southwest Journal of Archaeology*, **27**, 353–380.

Faulseit, R. K. (2016). Collapse, resilience, and transformation in complex societies: Modeling trends and understanding diversity. In R. S. Faulseit, ed., *Beyond Collapse: Archaeological Perspectives on Resilience, Revitalization, and Reorganization in Complex Societies*. Carbondale, IL: University of Southern Illinois Press, pp. 3–26.

Fish, P. R., Fish, S. K., Deblasis, P., and Gaspar, M. D. (2013). Monumental shell mounds as persistent places in southern coastal Brazil. In V. D. Thompson and J. C. Waggoner, Jr., eds., *The Archaeology and Historical Ecology of Small Scale Economies*. Gainesville, FL: University Press of Florida, 120–140.

Gamble, L. H. (2017). Feasting, ritual practices, social memory, and persistent places: New interpretations of shell mounds in southern California. *American Antiquity*, **82**, 427–451.

Gamble, L. H., Walker, P. L., and Russell, G. S. (2001). An integrative approach to mortuary analysis: Social and symbolic dimensions of Chumash burial practices. *American Antiquity*, **66**, 185–212.

Goldstein, L. (1981). One-dimensional archaeology and multi-dimensional people: Spatial organisation and mortuary analysis. In R. W. Chapman, I. Kinnes, and K. Randsborg, eds., *The Archaeology of Death*. Cambridge: Cambridge University Press, pp. 53–68.

Grier, C. (2003). Dimensions of regional interaction in the prehistoric Gulf of Georgia. In R. G. Matson, G. Coupland, and Q. Mackie, eds., *Emerging from the Mist: Studies in Northwest Coast Culture History*. Vancouver: UBC Press, pp. 170–187.

Hayden, B. (2009). Funerals as feasts: Why are they so important? *Cambridge Archaeological Journal*, **19**, 29–52.

Holland, A. (2014). The Osteology of Burials 3 and 4 at DjRw-14, Sechelt, British Columbia. Gatineau, QC, Canada. Manuscript on file, Archaeology and History Division, Canadian Museum of History.

Hollings, C. S. (1973). Resilience and stability of ecological systems. *Annual Review of Ecology and Systematics*, **4**, 1–23.

Hutchinson, I. (2016). Geoarchaeological perspectives on the "Millennial Series" of earthquakes in the southern Puget Lowland, Washington, USA. *Radiocarbon*, **57**, 917–941.

Katzie Development Corporation Archaeology. (2010). *Archaeological Excavations at DhRp-52: Final Report*. Victoria: British Columbia Archaeology Branch.

Keck, M. and Sakdapolrak, P. (2013). What is social resilience? Lessons learned and ways forward. *Erdkunde*, **67**, 5–19.

Klokler, D. (2014). A ritually constructed shell mound: Feasting at the Jabuticabeira II site. In M. Roksandic, S. M. de Souza, S. Eggers, M. Burchell, and D. Klokler, eds., *The Cultural Dynamics of Shell-Matrix Sites*. Albuquerque, NM: University of New Mexico Press, pp. 151–162.

Lepofsky, D., Blake, M., Brown, D., *et al.* (2000). The archaeology of the Scowlitz site, SW British Columbia. *Journal of Field Archaeology*, **27**, 391–416.

Lepofsky, D., Lertzman, K., Hallett, D., and Mathewes, R. (2005). Climate change and culture change on the southern coast of British Columbia 2400–1200 cal. B.P.: An hypothesis. *American Antiquity*, **70**, 267–293.

Letham, B. (2014). Settlement and shell-bearing site diversity in the Sechelt inlet system, British Columbia. *Canadian Journal of Archaeology*, **38**, 280–328.

Letham, B. A. Martindale, K., Supernant, T. J., *et al.* (2017). Assessing the scale and pace of large shell-bearing site occupation using percussion coring and 3D mapping: Examples from the Prince Rupert Harbour Area, British Columbia. *Journal of Island and Coastal Archaeology*. DOI: 10.1080/15564894.2017.1387621.

Lindo, J., Achilli, A., Perego, U. A., *et al.* (2017). Ancient individuals from the North American Northwest Coast reveal 10,000 years of regional genetic continuity. *Proceedings of the National Academy of Sciences*, **114**, 4093–4098.

MacDonald, G. F. (1969). Preliminary culture sequence from the Coast Tsimshian area, British Columbia. *Northwest Anthropological Research Notes*, **3**, 240–254.

MacDonald, G. F. (1973). *Haida Burial Practices: Three Archaeological Examples (The Gust Island Burial, The Skungo Cave, Mass Burials from Tanu)*. Hull, Quebec: National Museums of Canada, Archaeological Survey of Canada.

MacDonald, G. F. and Cybulski, J. S. (2001). Introduction: The Prince Rupert Harbour Project. In J. S. Cybulski, ed., *Perspectives on Northern Northwest Coast Prehistory*. Hull, Quebec: Canadian Museum of Civilization, Archaeological Survey of Canada, pp. 1–23.

MacDonald, G. F. and Inglis, R. I. (1981). An overview of the North Coast Prehistory Project (1966–1980). *BC Studies*, **48**, 37–63.

Mackie, Q. (2003). Location-allocation modelling of shell midden distribution on the west coast of Vancouver Island. In R. G. Matson, G. Coupland, and Q. Mackie, eds., *Emerging from the Mist: Studies in Northwest Coast Culture History*. Vancouver: UBC Press, pp. 260–288.

Marsden, S. (2001). Defending the mouth of the Skeena: Perspectives on Tsimshian–Tlingit relations. In J. S. Cybulski, ed., *Perspectives on Northern Northwest Coast Prehistory*. Hull, Quebec: Canadian Museum of Civilization, Archaeological Survey of Canada, pp. 61–106.

Martindale, A. and Letham, B. (2011). Causalities and models within the archaeological construction of political order on the Northwest Coast of North America. In P. G. Johansen and A. M. Bauer, eds., *The Archaeology of Politics: The Materiality of Political Practice and Action in the Past*. Newcastle: Cambridge Scholars Press, pp. 323–353.

Martindale, A. and Marsden, S. (2003). Defining the Middle Period (3500 BP-1500 BP) in Tsimshian history through a comparison of archaeological and oral records. *BC Studies*, **138**, 13–50.

Martindale, A., Letham, B., Supernant, K., *et al.* (2017). Urbanism in northern Tsimshian archaeology. *Hunter Gatherer Research*, **3**, 133–163.

Martindale, A., Letham, B., Ames, K. M., and Supernant, K. (forthcoming). Inventory and Investigation of Archaeological Sites in Order to Determine Archaeological and Paleoenvironmental History in the vicinity of Prince Rupert Harbour and Stephens Island, Prince Rupert, Northwest BC. Permit 2011-0207. Report on file, British Columbia Archaeology Branch, Victoria, BC.

Mathews, D. L. (2014). *Funerary Ritual, Ancestral Presence, and the Rocky Point Ways of Death*. PhD dissertation, University of Victoria.

Matson, R. G. and Coupland, G. (1995). *The Prehistory of the Northwest Coast*. San Diego, CA: Academic Press.

McLaren, D., Rahemtulla, F., White, G. E., and Fedje, D. (2015). Prerogatives, sea level, and the strength of persistent places: Archaeological evidence for long-term occupation of the central coast of British Columbia. *BC Studies*, **187**, 155–191.

McMillan, A. D. and Hutchinson, I. (2002). When the mountain dwarfs danced: Aboriginal traditions of paleoseismic events along the Cascadia subduction zone of western North America. *Ethnohistory*, **49**, 41–68.

Moore, C. M. and Thompson, V. D. (2012). Animism and Green River persistent places: A dwelling perspective of the Shell Mound Archaic. *Journal of Social Archaeology*, **12**, 264–284.

Morris, I. (1991). The archaeology of ancestors: The Saxe/Goldstein hypothesis revisited. *Cambridge Archaeological Journal*, **1**, 147–169.

Nilsson Stutz, L. and Tarlow, S. (2013). Beautiful things and bones of desire: Emerging issues in the archaeology of death and burial. In L. Nilsson Stutz and S. Tarlow, eds., *The Oxford Handbook of the Archaeology of Death and Burial*. Oxford: Oxford University Press, pp. 1–14.

Randsborg, K. (1981). Burial, succession and early state formation in Denmark. In R. Chapman, I. Kinnes, and K. Randsborg, eds., *The Archaeology of Death*. Cambridge: Cambridge University Press, pp. 105–121.

Ritchie, M., Lepofsky, D., Formosa, S., Porcic, M., and Edinborough, K. (2016). Beyond culture history: Coast Salish settlement patterning and demography in the Fraser Valley, BC. *Journal of Anthropological Archaeology*, **43**, 140–154.

Samuels, S. R., ed. (1991). *Ozette Archaeological Project Research Reports*. Pullman, WA: Department of Anthropology, Washington State University.

Saxe, A. A. (1970). *Social Dimensions of Mortuary Practices*. PhD dissertation, University of Michigan.

Seguin, M. (1985). *Interpretive Contexts for Traditional and Current Coast Tsimshian Feasts*. Ottawa: National Museum of Canada.

Silliman, S. (2009). Change and continuity, practice and memory: Native American persistence in colonial New England. *American Antiquity*, **74**, 211–230.

Suttles, W. (1960). Affinal ties, subsistence, and prestige among the Coast Salish. *American Anthropologist*, **62**, 296–305.

Suttles, W. (1962). Variation in habitat and culture on the Northwest Coast. In O. Grunow, ed., *Proceedings of the 34th International Congress of Americanists*. Chicago, IL: University of Chicago Press, pp. 522–537.

Suttles, W. (1968). Coping with abundance: Subsistence on the Northwest Coast. In R. B. Lee and I. DeVore, eds., *Man the Hunter*. Chicago, IL: Aldine Publishing Company, pp. 56–68.

Swenson, E. (2015). The archaeology of ritual. *Annual Reviews of Anthropology*, **44**, 329–345.

Thom, B. D. (1995). *The Dead and the Living: Burial Mounds and Cairns and the Development of Social Classes in the Gulf of Georgia Region*. MA thesis, University of British Columbia.

Thompson, V. D. (2016). Finding resilience in ritual and history in South Florida. In R. S. Faulseit, ed., *Beyond Collapse: Archaeological Perspectives on Resilience, Revitalization, and Reorganization in Complex Societies*. Carbondale, IL: University of Southern Illinois Press, pp. 313–341.

Trosper, R. L. (2003). Resilience in pre-contact Pacific Northwest social ecological systems. *Conservation Ecology (online)*, **7**, www.consecol.org/vol7/iss3/art6.

Trosper, R. L. (2009). *Resilience, Reciprocity and Ecological Economics: Northwest Coast Sustainability*. London: Routledge.

Turner, V. (1969). *The Ritual Process: Structure and Anti-Structure*. Ithaca, NY: Cornell University Press.

Wason, P. K. (1994). *The Archaeology of Rank*. Cambridge: Cambridge University Press.

Wilkerson, E. (2010). *Delineation of Site Chronology and Spatial Components Using Macroscopic Lithic Analysis at DhRp-52*. MA thesis, University of British Columbia.

Williams, G. (2011). The Osteology of Individual 2 from the Bible Camp Site, DjRw-14, Sechelt, British Columbia. Gatineau, QC, Canada. Manuscript on file, Archaeology and History Division, Canadian Museum of History.

Williams, H. F. L., Hutchinson, I., and Nelson, A. R. (2005). Multiple sources for Late-Holocene tsunamis at Discovery Bay, Washington, USA. *The Holocene*, **15**, 60–73.

11 Bioarchaeological Evidence for Cultural Resilience at Point Hope, Alaska: Persistence and Memory in the Ontology of Personhood in Northern Hunter-Gatherers

Lauryn C. Justice and Daniel H. Temple

11.1 Introduction

11.1.1 Cultural Resilience and the Reciprocal Nature of Hunting and Gathering

The goal of this chapter is to evaluate resilience in the social lifespan of prehistoric hunter-gatherers from Point Hope, Alaska using archaeological mortuary practices and to place these behaviors within a series of ecologically transformative events between two cultural groups, Ipiutak (1600 to 1100 BP) and Tigara (800 to 400 BP). Resilience theory evaluates the capacity for human populations to experience external disturbances and maintain socioecological or cultural identities (Redman, 2005; Redman and Kinzig, 2003; Walker *et al.*, 2004). Thus, resilience references persistence of preexisting systems, adaptability is associated with internal changes that maintain resilient systems, and transformation refers to the complete restructuring of a system (Walker *et al.*, 2004). Resilience theory is a conceptual framework that grants agency to human groups by emphasizing the inevitability of change *and* human adaptation to change (Redman, 2005; Redman and Kinzig, 2003). Resilience is often conceptualized in terms of an adaptive cycle (Gunderson and Holling, 2002). The adaptive cycle is depicted as a figure-eight and suggests that socioecological systems experience a sequence of events controlled by four functions: growth, conservation, release, and reorganization. Growth reflects the exploitation of land for resources. Conservation represents a slowed accretion of natural resources. Release represents periods of sudden change that influence the overarching socioecological system so that the organization becomes vulnerable to collapse. Following the release stage, human actors must respond by reorganizing and moving the socioecological system toward a renewed period of growth (Redman and Kinzig, 2003). It is in this way that human actors move socioecological systems toward internally or externally constructed basins of attraction, promoting resilience/adaptability or transformation, respectively.

Anthropology often emphasizes resilience as the capacity of a *socioecological* system to endure external changes while continuing to maintain internal function, structure, identity, and responses, mostly due to an underlying focus on adaptation (Redman, 2005; Redman and Kinzig, 2003). However, cultural systems also move through adaptive cycles and experience a release stage. On this basis, Crane (2010) advocates for a resilience framework that extends beyond ecological boundaries and constructively articulates the resilience of culture. Crane (2010) defines cultural resilience as "the ability to maintain livelihoods that satisfy both material and moral needs in the face of major stresses and shocks; environmental, political, economic, or otherwise" (Crane, 2010: 2). Thus, cultural resilience offers a theoretical mechanism to explore persistence in human social behavior as an independent phenomenon or one inextricably linked to the evolution of socioecological systems. Cultural systems allow for the exchange of ideologies and information, as well as other goods and resources. These systems are often maintained through ritual obligations or reciprocity among social groups, and this maintenance of social traditions is the heart of cultural resilience. Other studies highlight the interaction between cultural and socioecological systems (Adger, 2000). Daskon (2010) emphasizes the persistence of a deeper set of norms and values that grant agency to changes in the socioecological system. Collectively, these conceptualizations of cultural resilience reference (unintentionally) the idea of purposive social action among hunter-gatherer communities (Ingold, 1988). This (unintentional) reference makes these ideas particularly relevant and powerful theoretical frameworks for considering resilience in hunter-gatherer societies for which subsistence economy and social interactions form reciprocal relationships that are produced and reproduced through hunting and gathering behavior. The archaeological mortuary record is a useful point to understand deeper interactions between the socioecological and cultural systems as mortuary practices may reflect deeper references to the natural and symbolic world of hunter-gatherers (Atuy, 1997; Obayashi, 1997), and these behaviors may help explain persistence of culture in hunter-gatherer communities (Cannon, 2002; Gamble, 2017; Nillson Stutz, 2010; Thompson and Pluckhahn, 2010).

11.1.2   Archaeological Context of Point Hope

Point Hope is situated on a narrow strip of land that juts westward from mainland Alaska into the Chukchi Sea. Locals refer to this strip as *Tikiġaq* or *Tiagara*, which translates to "finger" in the native Iñupiaq language. Located nearly 190 miles south of the Arctic Circle, Point Hope, Alaska marks the westernmost point north of the Bering Strait. Initially excavated by Helge Larsen and Froelich Rainey from 1939 to 1941 at the discretion of Knud Rasmussen, excavations at Point Hope yielded nearly 10 000 artifacts, 500 human skeletons, and the remnants of 575 houses (Larsen and Rainey, 1948). In 1948, the two excavators published a monograph that included detailed drawings and descriptions of burials, grave goods, houses, and hunting tools. Based on differences observed between artifacts found in houses and burials, Larsen and Rainey believed that the remains of two different cultural occupations were represented at Point Hope. The scholars named this newly discovered site *Ipiutak*, the native term for a narrow sand bar that separates two lagoons.

Thanks to earlier excavations, the pair also recognized evidence for a Thule cultural occupation. Thule culture was first discovered and described primarily upon whale hunting, permanent settlements, and advanced harpoon technology (Mathiassen, 1927). Mathiassen's (1927) descriptions led Larsen and Rainey to surmise that the more recent cultural occupation at Point Hope was associated with Thule culture, owing to the discovery of harpoon heads and other whale-hunting equipment in homes and graves (Larsen and Rainey, 1948). In the 1948 monograph, Larsen and Rainey continually referred to the Thule occupation at Point Hope as the Tigara phase. Albeit spelled incorrectly, the term Tigara was chosen due to similarity with the Iñupiat word *Tiagara*, mentioned above. In an impressive feat, Rainey carbon-dated remains from the Point Hope site in 1945. Wood from the site provided dates of approximately 1000 BP for Ipiutak and 500 BP for Tigara (Larsen and Rainey, 1948). However, recent radiocarbon dates place Ipiutak cultural occupations at Point Hope between 1600 and 1100 BP and the subsequent Tigara occupation between 800 and 400 BP (Giddings, 1964).

In an initial analysis of Ipiutak culture, Larsen and Rainey (1948) proposed that Point Hope represented a locus of seasonal settlements associated with winter and early spring. More recent data based on site demography, site usage, and mortuary practices suggests Point Hope was a permanent settlement (Mason, 1998, 2014). Larsen and Rainey (1948) originally believed that a "Near-Ipiutak" culture succeeded the Ipiutak cultural period and predated Tigara occupations. However, this timeline is now considered inaccurate (Fitzhugh and Kaplan, 1982; Jensen, 2014). Based on artifactual evidence and radiocarbon dates, "Near-Ipiutak" is a misnomer. Researchers agree that what was originally conceived as "Near-Ipiutak" is actually representative of the Norton cultural tradition, which predated Ipiutak culture between 2500 and 2000 cal. BP (Giddings, 1964; Jensen, 2014). It is, thus, likely that Ipiutak culture developed *in situ* at Point Hope from nearby Norton cultural occupations at Kotzebue and Norton Sound as both cultures produced similar artifacts such as blade insets, discoidal scrapers, and bifacial knives (Jensen, 2014; Mason, 2014). By contrast, the complete absence of pottery, rubbed slate, oil lamps, and whale-hunting accouterments distinguish Ipiutak from other North Alaskan coastal cultures.

The Tigara people were part of the Thule culture. Thule is a complex whale-hunting socioecological system characterized by elaborate harpoons, and is regarded as the progenitor of modern Inuit culture. Birnirk (1500 to 1000 BP) pre-dated Thule culture and are also known for a socioecological system centered on whale hunting. Many Birnirk sites produced elaborate harpoon and marine technologies fashioned out of antlers rather than ivory (Stanford, 1976; Mason, 1998). The Birnirk culture, however, lacked art such as sculptures, carvings, and masks (Auger, 2005; Hilton *et al.*, 2014; Larsen and Rainey, 1948). Excavations of Birnirk sites indicate that only ceramic pots incorporated simplistic motifs (Larsen and Rainey, 1948). Tigara artifacts were, however, almost entirely made up of whale-hunting implements such as open boats or *umiaks*, harpoons, and whale bones (Larsen and Rainey, 1948). This particular aspect of Ipiutak and Tigara culture is of importance. Despite the Tigara relationship with Birnirk culture, Tigara inhabitants of Point Hope exhibit material proclivities similar to that of the Ipiutak, specifically the incorporation of sea mammal bones as material culture. In addition, both Ipiutak and Tigara grave goods include antler and ivory artifacts carved to resemble animals such as walrus, seals, and whales, and these arctic hunter-gatherers also exhibit an affinity for loon-related grave goods. Given the purported ancestor–descendant relationships between Birnirk and Thule cultures (see below), it seems that the Tigara peoples at Point Hope maintained whaling subsistence strategies as observed in Birnirk/Thule culture, but continued to incorporate stylistic designs in material culture as observed among the Ipiutak. Thus, Tigara populations may have been constructed based on persistence of Ipiutak cultural practices combined with transformation of the Ipiutak socioecological system through the incorporation of Birnirk whaling practices. If true, this case may represent a unique form of cultural resilience – that is, persistence of cultural systems through a deeper process of ethnogenesis.

11.1.3   Ethnogenesis and Transformation at Point Hope

Ethnogenesis is the emergence or formation of a new cultural complex (Sturtevant, 1971). Stojanowski (2009, 2013) envisions ethnogenesis in archaeological and bioarchaeological contexts as a process of ethnic emergence reflecting the interconnectedness of human populations, specifically emphasizing the idea that population formation reflects deep, polyethnic interactions. In the case of Tigara, it is important to evaluate this possibility through the lens of an emerging population that derived cultural practices from Ipiutak traditions and socioecological practices from the Birnirk following depopulation and return to the Point Hope region.

Extreme weather events depleted natural resources and caused many coastal populations to migrate away from the northern Alaskan coastline. Studies of tree rings and beach ridges suggest climatic cooling between 1000 and 800 BP, combined with increased storm activity (D'Arrigo et al., 2005; Mason and Barber, 2003; Mason and Gerlach, 1995; Mason and Jordan, 1993). This change in weather caused coastal occupations to become less sustainable and forced people to seek shelter at inland sites as environmental productivity at coastal locations diminished (Mason and Bowers, 1998). Ipiutak cultural occupations are, for example, sustained at inland locations between 1000 and 500 BP following a precipitous decline in coastal sites (Gerlach and Mason, 1992). Ipiutak coastal settlements were frequently located in close proximity to those associated with Birnirk cultures, including sites at Deering, Cape Krusenstern, and Cape Espenberg, though these interactions may have been associated with interpersonal violence (Mason, 1998). On this basis, Mason (2014) emphasizes that Thule populations migrated into the Point Hope region around 800 BP, replacing the Ipiutak people in an unoccupied landscape.

Biological distance studies suggest that the Tigara are more similar to the Birnirk at Point Barrow than to the Ipiutak, with considerable distance between Ipiutak and Birnirk (Maley, 2014, 2016). Ipiutak populations appear to have migrated along the southern Alaskan coasts following climate change, and contributed to the formation of populations along this region. Birnirk, Ipiutak, and Tigara populations are, however, distinguished from northwestern Alaskan samples based on positive residuals of observed phenotypic variation suggesting greater intensities of long-range gene flow and lower intensities of local interaction, though in the case of Ipiutak and Birnirk, the populations do represent more ancient lineages (Maley, 2014). Either way, increased residual phenotypic variance found in the Tigara sample may suggest founding events based on gene flow between populations previously isolated by distance (Maley, 2014). If true, these findings support the likelihood that Tigara represent a case of persistence through ethnogenesis. Here, Tigara culture emerged through the interaction of Ipiutak cultural traditions, Birnirk socioecological systems, and gene flow between the two groups.

As climate improved, the Tigara cultural occupation repopulated Point Hope around 800 BP (Hilton *et al.*, 2014). Contemporary studies that examine dental and skeletal remains from Point Hope shed light on ways dietary and behavioral strategies differed between Ipiutak and Tigara cultural groups and emphasize transformed socioecological systems. Ipiutak and Tigara males both exhibited low prevalence of anterior tooth loss, while females experienced high frequencies of anterior tooth loss (Costa, 1980; Madimenos, 2005). However, incisor microwear signatures of the Ipiutak and Tigara were diametrically opposed (Krueger, 2014). Ipiutak incisors were used in non-dietary tasks such as clamping and processing of caribou and seal hides. Krueger (2014) also found high textural fill volumes in the Ipiutak, suggesting consumption of dietary abrasives. By contrast, Tigara microwear suggests that anterior teeth were used comparatively less in behavioral strategies and only exposed to a moderate level of dietary abrasives. Macroscopic dental wear indicates that the majority of individuals between both populations exhibit extreme degrees of occlusal wear (Costa, 1977, 1982; El-Zaatari, 2014). Dental microwear reveals that both the Ipiutak and Tigara had significantly higher levels of occlusal molar surface complexity compared to the Aleut and Arikara populations (El-Zaatari, 2008, 2014). Beyond this, the Tigara have significantly more anisotropic surfaces when compared to the Ipiutak (El Zataari, 2014). The higher value observed among the Tigara suggests that these populations consumed tougher foods. El-Zaatari (2014) also observed age-related variation in anisotropy in the Ipiutak, but not Tigara sample. This finding suggests the Tigara group was ingesting higher amounts of abrasive particles, likely due to intensive consumption of maritime resources. In all, bioarchaeological research is consistent with previous archaeological studies that suggest the Ipiutak and Tigara cultures had significantly different diets. These reports are consistent with a hunter-fisher socioecological system among the Ipiutak and an intensive maritime socioecological system among the Tigara. Overall, these findings reflect transformation of Ipiutak socioecological systems and the incorporation of Birnirk seafaring traditions.

Hilton *et al.* (2014) found that Tigara males as a group have a higher frequency of healed upper and lower limb fractures, though the most pervasive postcranial skeletal lesion among the Tigara sample is spondylolysis. While the Ipiutak exhibited some instances of postcranial skeletal lesions, the most dramatic difference between the two cultures is the higher prevalence of postcranial skeletal lesions among Tigara relative to Ipiutak females: 66 percent versus 5.5 percent, respectively (Hilton *et al.*, 2014). Tigara males also exhibit a higher prevalence of postcranial skeletal lesions than Ipiutak males: 62 percent versus 36 percent, respectively. Hilton *et al.* (2014) posit that the high rates of postcranial skeletal lesions, most corresponding to spondylolysis and limb fractures, observed in Tigara remains are indicative of strenuous physical demands associated with whale hunting, suggesting that transformed socioecological systems became embodied in the skeletal remains of Tigara people.

The majority of bioarchaeological research associated with the Ipiutak and Tigara cultures finds evidence for a transformed socioecological system. However, some bioarchaeological research suggests similarity in lifestyle and adaptation. For example, humeral and femoral diaphyseal robusticity does not differ between Ipiutak and Tigara cultures, suggesting similar levels of strain between the two samples (Shackelford, 2014), despite clear differences in socioecological systems (see above). In addition, the development of intralimb indices suggest similar patterns of ecogeographic adaptation within the group (Cowgill, 2014), though this is likely attributed to a deeper Arctic postcranial morphotype suggesting limits on the expression of cold-adapted body form (Holliday and Hilton, 2010). Thus, despite the fact that the Tigara repopulated Point Hope as a reconstituted population, there remains some bioarchaeological evidence for persistence in lifestyle and adaptation. In addition, archaeological research demonstrates persistence of cultural systems (see above) during this period of transformed socioecological landscapes. Persistence in cultural systems often helps to maintain population identities during periods of transformation by maintaining a sense of shared norms, values, and rituals invoked through collective memory (*sensu* Halbwachs, 1925).

11.2   Archaeological Mortuary Practices and Social Maturation

Nearly a century of discourse surrounding archaeological mortuary practices emphasizes the reconstruction of social structure and symbology inherent in human burial (Binford, 1971; Hodder, 1982; Kroeber, 1927; Rakita and Buikstra, 2008). Ethnographic surveys find that mortuary practices elucidate information regarding social complexity and ritual practice in terms of grave good number and type, bodily orientation, burial location within a cemetery, cemetery location within a site, and funerary architecture (Binford, 1971; Carr, 1995; Goldstein, 1981). Mortuary practices are also important ritual events that act to solidify and maintain cultural institutions through collective memory – here, specifically, these behaviors reference past events and people through longstanding ritual enactments (Buikstra and Charles, 1999; Carr, 2005; Connerton, 1989).

Traditions surrounding maturation are deeply embodied components of cultural systems (Blurton Jones, 2006; Hewlett and Lamb, 2005; Laughlin, 1968; van Schaick *et al.*, 2006). Early studies of archaeological mortuary practices use pre-adults to evaluate evidence for achieved versus ascribed identities (Binford, 1971; Brown, 1981). Lavish pre-adult burials were associated with ascribed identity, and thus greater social complexity. Relatively sparse funerary treatment among pre-adult burials and lavish adult burials reflect achieved identities, and a more egalitarian social structure. In addition, bioarchaeologists use specific physiological markers, such as epiphyseal fusion or molar eruption, to estimate biological age, which translates to chronological age, or the number of years since an individual was born (Gowland, 2006; Halcrow and Tayles, 2008, 2011; Sofaer, 2006, 2011). Recent research in bioarchaeology advocates for an understanding of social age, which is defined as a culturally constructed understanding of age-appropriate attitudes and behaviors (Gowland, 2006; Halcrow and Tayles, 2008, 2011; Perry, 2006; Sofaer, 2006, 2011). In failing to understand age as a social event, perceptions of previous lifeways dilute maturation to a simple calendrical representation or passing of time. With this in mind, social age illustrates a conscious move away from biological determinism and aims to bridge cultural and biological aspects of the body (Halcrow and Tayles, 2011). Since the body is both a biological and a cultural product, age must be contextualized as a developmental process that transcends physiological events. Evidence for distinct social identities is found during maturation (i.e., across categories of biological age) and it is certainly possible to identify in bioarchaeological remains (Gowland, 2006; Halcrow and Tayles, 2008, 2011; Perry, 2006; Schillaci *et al.*, 2011; Sofaer, 2006, 2011; Sofaer Derevenski 2000; Yamada, 1997). Biological age must, however, be situated within a greater understanding of human development, including social relations, culturally specific life experiences, and local attitudes toward age and aging. These behaviors are preserved in the archaeological mortuary record, and the ontology of identities during maturation is one way that cultural resilience may be observed. Little is known, however, about these cultural practices at the Point Hope site, though comparisons of these practices in the archaeological mortuary record may reveal deeper persistence of culture between the two populations of Ipiutak and Tigara.

This chapter evaluates the persistence of belief systems associated with the reciprocal nature of hunting and gathering between the Ipiutak and Tigara groups and how these beliefs were incorporated into the burial ritual of pre-adults. This goal is accomplished by integrating archaeological mortuary practices with estimates of biological age to explore the expression of social age across the Ipiutak and Tigara cultures. In so doing, the hypothesis that conceptualizations of the hunter-gatherer world and social age remained consistent between the two populations is tested. Confirmation will provide further evidence that the Tigara population displays cultural resilience through ethnogenesis at the Point Hope site.

11.3   Materials and Methods

Skeletal samples used in this study were derived from the Point Hope, Alaska archaeological site, currently housed at the American Museum of Natural History (New York, NY). The Ipiutak occupation was dated between 1600 and 1100 BP. The Tigara occupation was dated between 800 and 300 BP.

Mortuary features evaluated for this study include grave goods, directional orientation of the head, burial position within the grave, and surface and underground interments. Burial information was extrapolated from Larsen and Rainey's (1948) original monograph and tabulated in an Excel spreadsheet. Grave goods surveyed among pre-adult burials from Point Hope include animal implements, which this paper defines as any grave good that is carved to emulate an animal, or any residual element from an animal such as a bone, hide, antler, or tusk (Justice, 2017). Spatial orientation within the grave references the cardinal directional orientation of the head within each burial. Burial position within the grave was recorded as prone (face-down) or supine (face-up). The original site report for Point Hope includes data on surface versus underground burials: Surface burial were not interred within the ground but were instead covered in soil along the surface (< 50 cm), while under-ground burials were greater than 50 cm (Larsen and Rainey, 1948). Previous reports note that surface burials have more lavish mortuary treatment, including a greater number of funerary offerings (Friesen, 2014). However, it is unknown whether this differentiation is associated with phases of the social lifespan, and more importantly, whether these aspects of maturation are persistent between the two cultural groups.

Radiographs were produced for 70 pre-adult mandibles associated with the Ipiutak and Tigara cultural groups. Radiographs of these mandibles were obtained using the NOMAD Pro Hand-Held X-Ray System (Aribex, Provo, UT) and Dr. Suni Plus Intraoral Digital Light Sensor (SUNI Medical Imaging Inc., San Jose, CA). Age at death was estimated using tooth formation and emergence. Mandibular tooth for-mation was recorded based on stages established for deciduous (Liversidge and Molleson, 2004) and permanent (AlQhatani *et al.*, 2010; Smith, 1991) teeth. In order to account for observer error, ages were estimated on three separate occasions and the average age obtained for all teeth was used as a final estimate of age at death in each pre-adult (per Smith, 1991). Where tooth formation was not possible to observe, tooth emergence was used to estimate age at death. Here, emergence stages were recorded as: not emerged; emerged past the alveolus; and emerged into occlusion (Hillson, 1992). These phases were compared to those derived by the London Atlas to estimate age at death (AlQhatani *et al.*, 2010).

In all, this study includes 36 pre-adults, comprising 15 Ipiutak and 21 Tigara phase burials. Overall, 34 pre-adult mandibles were excluded from this study due to a lack of corresponding burial data. Final age-at-death estimates were recorded in an Excel spreadsheet according to specimen and burial number. Visual evaluation of box plots was used to identify the distribution of age categories relative to mortuary treatment and shifts in the social lifespan of individuals at the Point Hope cemetery. Box plots list age at death as the quantitative variable and mortuary treatment as the categorical variable. Separate box plots were produced for the Ipiutak and Tigara samples to understand whether changes in mortuary treatment in accord with social lifespan differed or remained consistent between these two populations. Differences were assigned where overlap between interquartile ranges was absent or minimal. Interquartile range refers to a measure of statistical dispersion between the 75th and 25th percentiles. These differences demonstrate points at which variation in mortuary treatment is observed. Standard errors of mean age relative to burial treatment are also reported to ensure that the average ages related to a particular funerary treatment did not overlap in terms of dispersion.

11.4   Results

Results are presented as box plots (Figures 11.1–11.4). Summary statistics for each dataset are also included (Tables 11.1–11.4). Ipiutak and Tigara pre-adults from the perinatal to three-years cohort were buried in a prone position, while Ipiutak and Tigara pre-adults from 4–12 years are interred in a supine position (Figure 11.1; Table 11.1). Among Ipiutak pre-adults there is a clear delineation among supine interments, with the youngest individual interred at one year; however, the inter-quartile range suggests the majority of Ipiutak supine interments span 5–10 years. Among Tigara pre-adults, the majority of supine interments span 7–9 years, with the youngest supine individual recorded at 4 years and the oldest supine individual at 12 years.

Data concerning the directional orientation of the head within the grave (Figure 11.2; Table 11.2) indicate that Ipiutak pre-adults from 2–3 years and Tigara pre-adults between 1 and 2 years are spatially oriented toward the south. At older

Table 11.1 Summary statistics for the data represented in Figure 11.1.

Burial position	No. individuals	Mean age (years)	Standard deviation (years)	Standard error (years)
Prone Ipiutak	4	2.8	0.5	0.3
Prone Tigara	4	1.5	0.6	0.3
Supine Ipiutak	9	7.2	3.1	1.0
Supine Tigara	15	8.5	2.2	0.6
Total	32	6.5	3.4	0.6

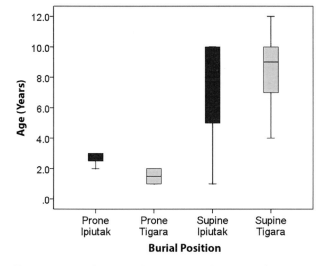

Figure 11.1 Burial position by age and cultural period.

Table 11.2 Summary statistics for the data represented in Figure 11.2.

Directional orientation	No. Individuals	Mean age (years)	Standard deviation (years)	Standard error (years)
Ipiutak south	4	2.8	0.5	0.2
Tigara south	4	1.5	0.6	0.3
Ipiutak west	11	7.3	2.8	0.9
Tigara west	16	8.0	2.5	0.6
Total	35	6.4	3.3	0.6

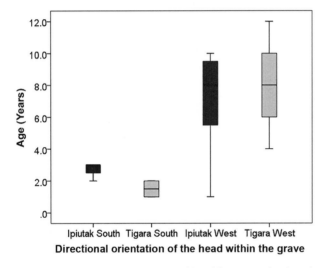

Figure 11.2 Directional orientation of head by age and cultural period.

ages, Ipiutak pre-adults aged 5–10 years are spatially oriented toward the west. Older Tigara pre-adults also mirror this pattern in that there is a clear delineation of directional orientation toward the west at 4–12 years.

Clear delineations between ages and animal implements are also observed in the dataset (Figure 11.3; Table 11.3). Ipiutak pre-adults ranging from 1 to 7 years receive only one animal implement; interquartile ranges indicate that the majority of Ipiutak pre-adults receiving one animal implement are between the ages of three and six years. Interquartile ranges suggest that Ipiutak pre-adults aged 7–10 years are interred with two or more animal implements. There is a range of data, however, that suggest some Ipiutak pre-adults aged 2–10 years do not receive any animal implements at the time of burial. Tigara pre-adults ranging from 6 to 9 years receive only one animal implement, and the delineation between Tigara individuals who receive two or more animal implements is less defined with the group consisting of Tigara pre-adults aged 7–11 years. There is a clear outline of Tigara pre-adults who

Table 11.3 Summary statistics for data represented in Figure 11.3.

Animal implements	No. individuals	Mean age (years)	Standard deviation (years)	Standard error (years)
A1 Ipiutak	6	4.5	2.2	0.9
A1 Tigara	9	7.3	1.9	0.6
A2+ Ipiutak	4	8.5	1.9	1.0
A2+ Tigara	7	8.9	3.0	1.1
None Ipiutak	5	5.4	3.8	1.7
None Tigara	5	3.0	3.4	1.5
Total	36	6.4	3.3	0.5

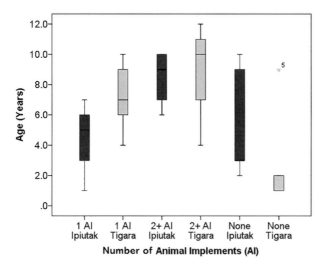

Figure 11.3 Number of animal implement (AI) grave goods by age and cultural period. The number 1 indicates one animal implement in the grave, while the 2+ distinction indicates two or more animal implements in the grave.

do not receive animal implements, aged 1–2 years; however, one individual aged nine years is an outlier in this group.

Another aspect of Ipiutak and Tigara burials that was investigated concerns surface burials and underground burials (Figure 11.4; Table 11.4). These data indicate that there is no clear delineation between age and cultural period concerning surface or underground burials. Ipiutak pre-adults that receive surface burials range from 1 to 10 years, with the majority ranging from 5 to 10 years. Ipiutak pre-adults that receive underground burials range across 2–10 years, with the majority of pre-adults in this particular group spanning 3–8 years. Tigara pre-adults receiving surface burials span ages 4–12 years; however, the interquartile range places the majority of individuals in this group between 6 and 10 years.

Table 11.4 Summary statistics for the data represented in Figure 11.4.

Surface or underground burial	No. individuals	Mean age (years)	Standard deviation (years)	Standard error (years)
Surface Burial Ipiutak	5	6.2	3.8	1.7
Surface Burial Tigara	9	8.2	2.6	0.8
Underground Burial Ipiutak	9	5.7	3.0	1.0
Underground Burial Tigara	12	5.8	3.7	1.1
Total	35	6.4	3.3	0.6

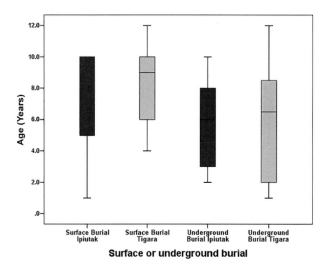

Figure 11.4 Surface or underground burial type by age and cultural period.

Tigara pre-adults that received underground burials represent a wider breadth of ages at 1–12 years.

When interpolated with the burial data from the original site report, these results indicate Ipiutak and Tigara pre-adults in the perinatal to three-year cohort were buried in a prone position, spatially oriented toward the south. Between Ipiutak and Tigara pre-adults, individuals between 4 and 12 years are interred in a supine position, spatially oriented toward the west, with animal implements such as walrus tusks or ivory animal carvings. Among Ipiutak pre-adults, there is a clear delineation concerning grave good allocations. For example, individuals ranging from 1 to 6 years are interred with only one animal implement, whereas individuals 7–10 years of age receive two animal implements. Among Tigara pre-adults, individuals are not interred with grave goods until four years of age. Tigara pre-adults between 4 and 12 years may be interred with one or two animal implements. No discernible age pattern was observed in surface versus subsurface burials for either group.

11.5   Discussion

In reconstructing funerary rituals from Point Hope, pre-adults receive prescribed mortuary treatments according to culturally recognized social identities. Most adults at Point Hope are buried supine, with hands over the pubic regions, and heads oriented toward the west. However, individuals aged between infancy and early childhood are buried prone, hands under the pubic regions, with heads oriented toward the south in both the Ipiutak and Tigara samples. Infants and young children exist prior to an "age of awareness" where the mind is incapable of forming complete memories in Inupiat and Yu'pik communities (Fienup-Riordan, 1994; Sprott, 2002). This period of development is one of great vulnerability. For example, Inupiat parents refrain from yelling or harshly chastising infants and children (Burch, 2006; Sprott, 2002). In addition, the souls of individuals in this age group are vulnerable to contamination (Birkett-Smith, 1929). Gateways for spiritual contamination include the mouth, eyes, and nose of individuals, while the soul is thought to reside in a region between the legs (Rasmussen, 1929; Fitzhugh and Kaplan, 1982; Laugrand and Oosten, 2014). It is possible that these individuals were buried prone in an effort to protect the soul from contamination through these gateways. This cohort is also directionally oriented toward the south. Previous studies of Inuit burial report changes in directional coordinates over the course of development (Boas, 1888; Merbs, 1969, 2007). Infants and young children were oriented away from directions that correspond to the afterlife, possibly to expedite reincarnation (Merbs, 1969, 2007). Infant and child death is an emotionally traumatic event in Inuit communities, and it is believed that these souls reside in those born into the family immediately following death (Nutall, 1994). It is, therefore, possible that directional orientation away from the afterlife may expedite reincarnation.

Ipiutak and Tigara pre-adults ranging from 4 to 12 years are buried face-up, supine, with hands over the pubic regions, and heads oriented toward the west. Individuals in this age group include those at the earliest stages of awareness (Fienup-Riordan, 1994; Sprott, 2002). It is possible that burial posture and directional orientation correspond to this increasing awareness and reduced vulnerability for spiritual contamination. In the Southampton Island region of Hudson Bay, male adults were oriented along easterly coordinates, while the heads of female adults were oriented along westerly coordinates (Merbs, 1969, 2007). These directional coordinates correspond to the afterlives associated with adult males and females and is symbolized by the rising and setting sun, respectively. Interviews with a Tigara man named Sam Rock provide some information regarding these practices at Point Hope: Individuals were oriented with heads toward the west and feet toward the east, which ushers the soul to a location beyond the Kuukpak River where there is always good weather (Lowenstein, 2008). Concomitant with Inuit ideas concerning the ontology of personhood, this chapter theorizes that the funerary rituals reserved for individuals of 4–12 years in the Ipiutak and Tigara communities were aimed at drawing social distinctions that correspond with age and identity. The directional orientation and burial posture of pre-adults between 4 and 12 years demonstrates a change in the complexity of identity as these individuals are interred identically to adults. In acknowledging the existence of malevolent spirits, the vulnerable nature of individuals between infancy and early childhood, and association between burial orientation and the afterlife, it may be proposed that Ipiutak and Tigara funerary rituals speak to a socially recognized boundary that is delineated by the ability to ward off impure souls and enter into an afterlife symbolized by direction. The persistence of these behaviors between the Ipiutak and Tigara cemeteries suggest resilience in the philosophical-religious beliefs of these communities as well as deeper canons associated with the unfolding of identities over the life course.

Animal implements included in Ipiutak and Tigara pre-adult burials are suggestive of culturally distinct subsistence strategies. For example, Tigara burials include whale vertebrae, whalebone shovels, and cut whale scapulae. Ipiutak animal implements, however, include walrus teeth, walrus tusks, or ivory carvings fashioned to mimic seals or walrus. While burial practices alone cannot reconstruct human consciousness, it is clear that funerary rituals concerning pre-adults ranging from 4 to 12 years emphasized the inclusion of animal implements, while those provided to infants and young children did not. Ages where one animal implement is found in the grave is around 3–6 years for the Ipiutak and Tigara, while the majority of those aged seven years and older received two or more animal implements in both samples. Personal possessions were included as grave goods in many Inuit communities (Murdoch, 1892; Rasmussen, 1931; Lantis, 1947; Fienup-Riordan, 1994). Charms or amulets were among these possessions and derived from animal figurines or residual elements (Murdoch, 1892; Rasumussen, 1931; Lantis, 1947; Rainey, 1947). These items carried deep symbolic value in ensuring hunting success, communications between humans and animal spirits, forecasting the future, and providing protection (Murdoch, 1892; Rasmussen, 1931; Rainey, 1947; Burch, 2006). The initial gifting of amulets occurs during the "age of awareness" and these items were included in funerary ritual (Lantis, 1947; Rainey, 1947). Moreover, individuals were gifted increasing numbers of amulets as the lifespan unfolded including initiation as a hunter, a person who works with animal remains, or entrance into puberty (Lantis, 1947; Rainey, 1947; Fienrup-Riordan, 1994; Laugrand and Oosten, 2014). In this sense, results from this chapter may be capturing the earliest point in development when amulets are gifted to individuals. In addition, the distinction between the age of awareness, compared with older ages when a greater number of amulets are obtained, may also be observed. Despite different types of amulets reflective of change in socioecological conditions between the Ipiutak and Tigara, cultural resilience is revealed through the incorporation of these amulets into funerary ritual as powerful symbols associated with the natural world and social maturation: Here, the hunting and gathering subsistence economy of each group is reproduced in death rituals and likely reflects comparable views surrounding relationships between humans and the natural world that unfold over the course of a lifetime.

There is no distinction concerning pre-adult age among surface burials or underground burials for either the Ipiutak or Tigara samples. The heterogeneous pattern of surface and underground burial treatment most likely reflects ecological constraints associated with the Point Hope landscape, rather than persistence or resilience. Point Hope is situated upon thick layers of permafrost; depths for permafrost at this site ranged between 0.3 and 4 m below the surface. In addition, Point Hope experiences seasonal freezing of the ground surface, a so-called thaw depth that renders burial impossible during winter months. It may, therefore, be concluded that individuals who died during different seasons were allocated burial depths based on capacity to penetrate the ground surface. This is to say that during winter thaw depth and permafrost layers are thicker and more difficult to dig through, thus surface burials might indicate a communal solution to adverse weather conditions.

As previously discussed, unforeseen ecological stressors forced the Ipiutak culture to abandon coastal residences and migrate toward interior sites. Nearly 400 years after the Ipiutak occupation at Point Hope ended, the Tigara repopulated Point Hope around 800 BP. The Tigara occupation was part of the Thule culture, which is characterized as a complex whale-hunting culture and is similar to the Birnirk culture. Studies concerning occlusal molar microwear and postcranial skeletal lesions indicate that the Tigara consumed greater proportions of frozen meat relative to the Ipiutak, and high rates of postcranial skeletal lesions resulted from strenuous physical demands brought about by whale hunting among the Tigara (Costa 1977, 1980, 1982; El-Zaatari, 2014; Hilton *et al.*, 2014). Faunal assemblages from the Ipiutak occupation at Point Hope suggest that the Ipiutak mainly relied on sea mammals such as seals and walruses, but not whales. Remains of seals and walruses make up nearly 98 percent of the faunal assemblage excavated at the Ipiutak settlement, and the remaining 2 percent constitute birds and fish (Lester and Shapiro, 1968). However, despite differences in subsistence strategies, the Tigara at Point Hope exhibited predispositions for stylized artifacts that were similar to the Ipiutak cultural occupation. The fact that there is change in surrounding socioecological landscapes is reflective of environmental stressors, or shocks, which forced the Ipiutak populations to respond and ultimately adapt through migration. When viewed in light of cultural resilience theory, it may be seen that the hunter-gatherers at Point Hope reacted to surrounding influences as a means to maintain cultural integrity and produced a new cultural group through the merging of preexisting Ipiutak cultural systems with Birnirk socioecological systems. This is to say that the Ipiutak and Tigara populations were flexible in that these groups were able to make conscious decisions to transform the socioecological system as much as cultural identity would allow and reconstitute a newly emerged population through ethnogenesis.

The move away from and later repopulation of Point Hope demonstrates resilience in that the Ipiutak were able to endure external stressors, such as extreme weather events, reorganize social structure, and initiate a move toward interior sites. After reorganizing at these inland locations, interaction between Ipiutak and Birnirk cultures produced a hybrid cultural group, Tigara. This population returned to Point Hope and engaged in a newly adopted subsistence strategy centered on whaling. The

Tigara cultural occupation demonstrates cultural resilience in that these populations were able to adapt to the surrounding ecological landscape at Point Hope, while continuing to maintain internal cultural functions associated with the ancestral Ipiutak population (*sensu* Adger, 2000; Crane, 2010; Daskon, 2010). These functions include the reproduction of hunting and gathering into mortuary rituals as well as the persistence of ritual practices that symbolically recognized boundaries in identity over the course of maturation.

That being said, cultural resilience depends on humans who adapt to the environment so that the overarching cultural and socioecological system does not collapse (Crane, 2010; Redman, 2005; Redman and Kinzig, 2003). One way that humans adapt includes invoking social memories or maintaining longstanding behavioral traditions (Crane, 2010; Daskon, 2010; Redman, 2005; Redman and Kinzig, 2003). In spite of employing whaling as a subsistence strategy, the Tigara occupation at Point Hope indicates similarities to the ancestral Ipiutak population through the persistence of mortuary treatment of pre-adults. This persistence ultimately demonstrates cultural resilience through the invocation of social memory and maintenance of cultural ideologies associated with ancestral Ipiutak communities. The conscious human actions surrounding funerary rituals as demonstrated by the Ipiutak and Tigara suggests persistence through social memory in that the data presented here imply persistence in the social boundaries of age. While it is demonstrated that the Ipiutak and Tigara populations were resilient because the cultural ideologies of these groups remained unwavering, this chapter further suggests that the Ipiutak and Tigara populations were resilient because the human actors within these populations adapted to changes so that the entire cultural system could withstand perturbations, transform, but maintain a core identity, partially rooted in ancestral concepts of maturation.

11.6   Conclusion

As previously discussed, the resilience of cultural and socioecological systems requires humans to be self-reflective, flexible, and goal-oriented, as change is inevitable. The Ipiutak socioecological system faced external pressures in the form of climatic deterioration, producing migration away from Point Hope and merging with Birnirk populations. These groups repopulated the ecological and geographic basin of attraction at Point Hope as a newly reconstituted population, Tigara, with a transformed socioecological system. Thus, the emergence of Tigara is associated with the process of ethnogenesis – one in which the Tigara population represent a newly formed polyethnic population in terms of biological and cultural identities centered in the Ipiutak ancestral homeland. Tigara populations are associated with a Birnirk-style socioecological system combined with cultural practices reminiscent of Ipiutak populations. Persistence of Ipiutak cultural systems illustrates the capacity for cultural resilience through ideas that were inherent to the identity of ancestral populations. This cultural resilience is observed in the maintenance of funerary rituals that speak to the deeper identity of a population where hunting and gathering was reproduced in rituals and symbols. Symbols differed between the Ipiutak and Tigara groups and likely had different meanings (*sensu* Buikstra, 2005), but the deeper presence of these symbols ultimately reflects continuity in the relational identities between these populations and the natural world. In addition, the persistence of funerary rituals that reflect vulnerability in pre-adult identities at early stages of the lifecourse, and the broader ontology of the social lifespan that emphasizes relationships with the natural world, are associated with a deeper symbolic persistence underlying maturation. This persistence reflects the ability of human actors to create, maintain, and pass on cultural practices when challenged by ecological perturbations.

These findings also emphasize the importance of understanding symbolic expressions of maturity in the archaeological record. The integration of estimates of biological age with archaeological mortuary practices has the capacity to reveal the social and symbolic components of maturation that define individual identities in life that transcend the living world. These symbols may persist through cultural resilience across environmental disruptions and help provide evidence regarding the preservation of cultural identities.

Acknowledgments

We thank Gisselle Garcia and Paul Beelitz for access to and assistance with the skeletal remains and archaeological records associated with the Point Hope collection at the American Museum of Natural History. Earlier iterations of this work benefited from comments by Haagen Klaus and Nawa Sugiyama. We thank Chris Stojanowski and two reviewers for comments that greatly improved this chapter.

References

Adger, W. N. (2000). Social and ecological resilience: Are they related? *Progress in Human Geography*, 24, 347–364.

AlQhatani, S. J., Hector, M. P., and Liversidge, H. M. (2010). The London Atlas of human tooth development and eruption. *American Journal of Physical Anthropology*, 142, 481–490.

Atuy, M. T. (1997). Coexistence with nature and the "Third Philosophy": Learning from the spirit of the Ainu. In T. Yamada and T. Irimoto, eds., *Circumpolar Animism and Shamanism*. Sapporo: Hokkaido University Press, pp. 3–8.

Auger, E. A. (2005). *The Way of Inuit Art: Aesthetics and History in and Beyond the Arctic*. Jefferson, NC: McFarland.

Binford, L. R. (1971). Mortuary practices: Their study and potential. *Memoirs of the Society for American Archaeology*, 25, 6–29.

Birket-Smith, K. (1929). *The Caribou Eskimo: Descriptive Part*. Report of the Fifth Thule Expedition 1921–24 5(1). Copenhagen: Gyldendalske Boghandel, Nordisk Forlag.

Blurton Jones, N. (2006). Contemporary hunter-gatherers and human life history evolution. In K. E. Hawkes and R. R. Paine, eds., *The Evolution of Human Life History*. Santa Fe, NM: School of American Research Press, pp. 231–266.

Boas, F. (1888). *The Central Eskimo*. Sixth Annual Report of the Bureau of Ethnology to the Secretary of the Smithsonian Institution. Washington: Government Printing Office.

Brown, J. E. (1981). The search for rank in prehistoric burials. In R. Chapman, I. Kinnes, and K. Randsborg, eds., *The Archaeology of Death*. Cambridge: Cambridge University Press, pp. 25–37.

Buikstra, J. E. (2005) Ethnogenesis and ethnicity in the Andes. In R. Reycraft, ed., *Us and Them: The Assignment of Ethnicity in the Andean Region – Methodological Approaches*. Los Angeles, CA: University of California Archaeological Research Facility, pp. 233–238.

Buikstra, J. E. and Charles, D. K. (1999). Centering the ancestors: Cemeteries, mounds, and sacred landscapes of the North American midcontinent. In W. Ashmore and A. B. Knapp, eds., *Archaeologies of Landscape: Contemporary Perspectives*. Oxford: Blackwell Publishers, Ltd., pp. 201–228.

Burch, E. S. (2006). *Social Life in Northwest Alaska: The Structure of Inupiaq Eskimo Nations*. Fairbanks: University of Alaska Press.

Cannon, A. (2002). Spatial narratives of death, memory, and transcendence. *Archaeological Papers of the American Anthropological Association*, 11, 191–199.

Carr, C. (1995). Mortuary practices: Their social, philosophical-religious, circumstantial, and physical determinants. *Journal of Archaeological Method and Theory*, 2, 105–200.

Carr, C. (2005). Scioto Hopewell ritual gatherings: A review and discussion of previous interpretations and data. In C. Carr and D. T. Case, eds., *Gathering Hopewell: Society, Ritual, and Ritual Interaction*. New York, NY: Kluwer Academic/Plenum Publishing, pp. 463–469.

Connerton, P. (1989). *How Societies Remember*. Cambridge: Cambridge University Press.

Costa, R. L. (1977). *Dental Pathology and Related Factors in Archaeological Eskimo Samples from Point Hope and Kodiak Island, Alaska*. PhD dissertation, University of Pennsylvania.

Costa, R. L. (1980). Incidence of caries and abscesses in archaeological Eskimo skeletal samples from Point Hope and Kodiak Island, Alaska. *American Journal of Physical Anthropology*, 52, 501–514.

Costa, R. L. (1982). Periodontal disease in the prehistoric Ipiutak and Tigara skeletal remains from Point Hope, Alaska. *American Journal of Physical Anthropology*, 59, 97–110.

Cowgill, L. W. (2014). Postcranial growth and development of immature skeletons from Point Hope, Alaska. In C. E. Hilton, B. M. Auerbach, and L. W. Cowgill, eds., *The Foragers of Point Hope: The Biology and Archaeology of Humans on the Edge of the Alaskan Arctic*. Cambridge: Cambridge University Press, pp. 212–234.

Crane, T. A. (2010). Of models and meanings: Cultural resilience in social-ecological systems. *Ecology and Society*, 15, 19.

D'Arrigo, R., Mashig, E., and Frank, D. (2005). Temperature variability over the past millennium inferred from Northwestern Alaska tree rings. *Climate Dynamics*, 25, 227–236.

Daskon, C. D. (2010). Cultural resilience: The roles of cultural traditions in sustaining rural livelihoods – a case study from rural Kandyan villages in Central Sri Lanka. *Sustainability*, 2, 1080–1100.

El-Zaatari, S. (2008). Occlusal molar microwear and the diets of the Ipiutak and Tigara populations (Point Hope) with comparisons to the Aleut and Arikara. *Journal of Archaeological Science*, 35, 2517–2522.

El-Zaatari, S. (2014). The diets of the Ipiutak and Tigara of Point Hope. In C. E. Hilton, B. M. Auerbach, and L. W. Cowgill, eds., *The Foragers of Point Hope: The Biology and Archaeology of Humans on the Edge of the Alaskan Arctic*. Cambridge: Cambridge University Press, pp. 120–137.

Fienup-Riordan, A. (1994). *Boundaries and Passages: Rule and Ritual in Yup'ik Eskimo Oral Tradition*. Norman: University of Oklahoma Press.

Fitzhugh, W. and Kaplan, S. A. (1982). *Inua Spirit World of the Bering Sea Eskimo*. Washington, DC: Smithsonian Institution Press.

Friesen, T. M. (2014). Pan-Arctic population movements: The early Paleo-Inuit and Thule Inuit migrations. In T. M. Friesen and O. K. Mason, eds., *The Oxford Handbook of the Prehistoric Arctic*. Oxford: Oxford University Press, pp. 673–692.

Gamble, L. (2017). Feasting, ritual practices, social memory, and persistent places: New interpretations of shell mounds in Southern California. *American Antiquity*, 82, 427–451.

Gerlach, S. C. and Mason, O. K. (1992). Calibrated radiocarbon dates and cultural interaction in the western Arctic. *Arctic Anthropology*, 29, 54–81.

Giddings, J. L. (1964). *The Archaeology of Cape Denbigh*. Providence, RI: Brown University Press.

Goldstein, L. (1981). One-dimensional archaeology and multi-dimensional people: Spatial organization and mortuary practices. In R. Chapman, I. Kinnes, and K. Randsborg, eds., *The Archaeology of Death*. Cambridge: Cambridge University Press, pp. 53–69.

Gowland, R. (2006). Age as an aspect of social identity. In R. Gowland and C. J. Knüsel, eds., *The Social Archaeology of Funerary Remains*. Oxford: Oxbow Books, pp. 143–154.

Gunderson, L. H., and Holling, C. S., eds. (2002). *Panarchy: Understanding Transformations in Human and Natural Systems*. Washington, DC: Island Press.

Halbwachs, M. (1925). *Les Cadres Sociaux de la Mémoire*. Paris: Librairie Félix Alcan.

Halcrow, S. E. and Tayles, N. (2008). The bioarchaeological investigation of childhood and social age: Problems and prospects. *Journal of Archaeological Method and Theory*, 15, 190–215.

Halcrow, S. E. and Tayles, N. (2011). The bioarchaeological investigation of children and childhood. In S. C. Agarwal and B. E. Glencross, eds., *Social Bioarchaeology*. Chichester: Wiley-Liss, pp. 333–360.

Hewlett, B. S. and Lamb, M. E. (2005). Emerging issues in the study of hunter-gatherer children. In B. S. Hewlett and M. E. Lamb, eds., *Hunter-Gatherer Childhoods: Evolutionary, Developmental, and Cultural Perspectives*. New Brunswick, NJ: Aldine Transaction, pp. 3–18.

Hill, E. (2011). Animals as agents: Hunting ritual and relational ontologies in prehistoric Alaska and Chukotka. *Cambridge Archaeological Journal*, 21, 407–426.

Hillson, S. W. (1992). Studies of growth in human dental tissues. *Journal of Ecology*, 2, 7–23.

Hilton, C. E., Ogilvie, M. D., Cznarniecki, M. L., and Gossett, S. (2014). Postcranial pathological lesions in precontact Ipiutak and Tigara skeletal remains, Point Hope, Alaska. In C. E. Hilton, B. M. Auerbach, and L. W. Cowgill, eds., *The Foragers of Point Hope: The Biology and Archaeology of Humans on the Edge of the Alaskan Arctic*. Cambridge: Cambridge University Press, pp. 138–180.

Hodder, I. (1982). The identification and interpretation of ranking in prehistory: A contextual perspective. In C. Renfrew, and S. Shennan, eds., *Ranking, Resource, and Exchange*. Cambridge: Cambridge University Press, pp. 150–156.

Holliday, T. W. and Hilton, C. E. (2010). Body proportions of circumpolar peoples as evidenced from skeletal data: Ipiutak and Tigara (Point Hope) versus Kodiak Island Inuit. *American Journal of Physical Anthropology*, 142, 287–302.

Ingold, T. (1988). Notes on the foraging mode of production. In T. Ingold, D. Riches, and J. Woodburn, eds., *Hunters and Gatherers 1: History, Evolution, and Social Change*. Oxford: Berg, pp. 269–285.

Jensen, A. (2014). The archaeology of north Alaska: Point Hope in context. In C. E. Hilton, B. M. Auerbach, and L. W. Cowgill, eds., *The Foragers of Point Hope: The Biology and Archaeology of Humans on the Edge of the Alaskan Arctic*. Cambridge: Cambridge University Press, pp. 11–34.

Justice, L. C. (2017). *Biological and Cultural Evidence for Social Maturation at Point Hope, Alaska: Integrating Data from Archaeological Mortuary Practices and Human Skeletal Biology*. MA thesis, George Mason University.

Kroeber, A. L. (1927). Disposal of the dead. *American Anthropologist*, 29, 308–315.

Krueger, K. L. (2014). Contrasting behavior of the Ipiutak and Tigara. In C. E. Hilton, B. M. Auerbach, and L. W. Cowgill, eds., *The Foragers of Point Hope: The Biology and Archaeology of Humans on the Edge of the Alaskan Arctic*. Cambridge: Cambridge University Press, pp. 99–119.

Lantis, M. (1947). *Alaskan Eskimo Ceremonialism*. New York: JJ Augustin Publisher.

Larsen, H. and Rainey, F. (1948). *Ipiutak and the Arctic Whale Hunting Culture*. New York, NY: American Museum of Natural History.

Laughlin, W. S. (1968). Hunting: An integrating biobehavioral system and its evolutionary importance. In R. B. Lee and I. DeVore, eds., *Man the Hunter*. Chicago, IL: Aldine Publishing Company, pp. 304–320.

Laugrand, F., and Oosten, J. G. (2014). *Hunters, Predators, and Prey: Inuit Perceptions of Animals*. New York: Berghahn Books.

Lester, C. W. and Shapiro, H. L. (1968). Vertebral arch defects in the lumbar vertebrae of pre-historic American Eskimos: A study of skeletons in the American Museum of Natural History, chiefly from Point Hope, Alaska. *American Journal of Physical Anthropology*, 28, 43–47.

Liversidge, H. and Molleson, T. (2004). Variation in crown and root formation and eruption of human deciduous teeth. *American Journal of Physical Anthropology*, 134, 329–339.

Lowenstein, T. (2008). *Ultimate Americans: Point Hope, Alaska: 1826–1909*. Fairbanks: University of Alaska Press.

Madimenos, F. (2005). *Dental Evidence for Division of Labor among the Prehistoric Ipiutak and Tigara of Point Hope, Alaska*. MA thesis, Louisiana State University.

Maley, B. (2014). Ancestor–descendant affinities between the Ipiutak and Tigara. In C. E. Hilton, B. M. Auerbach, and L. W. Cowgill, eds., *The Foragers of Point Hope: The Biology and Archaeology of Humans on the Edge of the Alaskan Arctic*. Cambridge: Cambridge University Press, pp. 71–95.

Maley, B. (2016). Examining biological continuity across the Late Holocene occupation of the Aleutian Islands using cranial morphometrics and quantitative genetic permutation. *American Journal of Physical Anthropology*, 160, 71–85.

Mason, O. K. (1998). The contest between Ipiutak, Old Bering Sea and Birnirk polities and the origin of whaling during the first millennium A.D. along the Bering Strait. *Journal of Anthropological Archaeology*, 17, 240–325.

Mason, O. K. (2014). The Ipiutak cult of shamans and its warrior protectors: An archaeological context. In C. E. Hilton, B. M. Auerbach, and L. W. Cowgill, eds., *The Foragers of Point Hope: The Biology and Archaeology of Humans on the Edge of the Alaskan Arctic*. Cambridge: Cambridge University Press, pp. 35–70.

Mason, O. K. and Barber, V. (2003). A paleogeographic preface to the origins of whaling: Cold is better. In A. P. McCartney, ed., *Indigenous Ways to the Present: Native Whaling in the Western Arctic*. Edmonton and Salt Lake City: Circumpolar Institute, University of Alberta and University of Utah Press, pp. 69–108.

Mason, O. K. and Bowers, P. M. (1998). The origin of Thule is always elsewhere: Early Thule within Kotzebue Sound, cul-de-sac or nursery? In *On the Track of Thule Culture: New Perspectives in Inuit Prehistory*. Copenhagen: SILA, Danish National Museum, pp. 25–44.

Mason, O. K. and Gerlach, S. C. (1995). Chukchi sea hot spots, paleo-polynas and caribou crashes: Climate and ecological constraints on northern Alaska prehistory. *Arctic Anthropology*, 32, 101–130.

Mason, O. K. and Jordan, J. W. (1993). Heightened North Pacific storminess and synchronous late Holocene erosion of northwest Alaska beach ridge complexes. *Quaternary Research*, 40, 55–69.

Mathiassen, T. (1927). *Archaeology of the Central Eskimos Part I: Descriptive Part. Report of the Fifth Thule Expedition 1921–1924, Volume 4*. Copenhagen: Reitzels.

Merbs, C. F. (1969). The significance of age, sex, and the time of burial in the interpretation of Thule Eskimo burial patterns. Paper presented at the annual meeting of the Society for American Archaeology, Milwaukee, WI.

Merbs, C. F. (2007). Who were the Sadlermiut? A study in bioarchaeology. Paper presented at the annual meeting of the Canadian Archaeological Association, St. Johns, Newfoundland.

Murdoch, J. (1892). *Ethnological Results of the Point Barrow Expedition*. Ninth Annual Report of the Bureau of Ethnology to the Secretary of the Smithsonian Institution. Washington: Government Printing Office.

Nillson Stutz, L. (2010). The way we bury our dead: Reflections on mortuary ritual, community, and identity at the time of the Mesolithic–Neolithic transition. *Documenta Prehistorica*, 37, 33–42.

Nutall, M. (1994). The name never dies: Greenland Inuit ideas of the person. In A. Mills and R. Slobodin, eds. *Amerindian Rebirth: Reincarnation Belief Among North American Indians and Inuit*. Toronto: University of Toronto Press, pp. 123–135.

Obayashi, T. (1997). The Ainu concept of the soul. In T. Yamada and T. Irimoto, eds., *Circumpolar Animism and Shamanism*. Sapporo: Hokkaido University Press, pp. 8–20.

Perry, M. (2006). Redefining childhood through bioarchaeology: Toward an archaeological and biological understanding of children in antiquity. *Archaeological Papers of the American Anthropological Association*, **15**, 89–111.

Rainey, F. (1947). *The Whale Hunters of Tigara*. New York: Anthropological Papers of the American Museum of Natural History.

Rakita, G. F. M. and Buikstra, J. E. (2008). Introduction. In G. F. M. Rakita, J. E. Buikstra, L. A. Beck, and S. R. Williams, eds., *Interacting with the Dead: Perspectives on Mortuary Archaeology for the New Millennium*. Gainesville, FL: University Press of Florida, pp. 1–11.

Rasmussen, K. (1929). *Intellectual Culture of the Iglulik Eskimos*. Copenhaagen: Gylndendal.

Rasmussen, K. (1931). *The Netsilik Eskimos: Social and Spiritual Culture*. New York: AMS Press.

Redman, C. R. (2005). Resilience theory in archaeology. *American Anthropologist*, **107**, 70–77.

Redman, C. R. and Kinzig, A. P. (2003). Resilience of past landscapes: resilience theory, society, and the *longue durée*. *Conservation Ecology*, **7**, 14.

Schillaci, M. A., Nikitovich, D., Akins, N. J., Tripp, L., and Palkovich, A. M. (2011). Infant and juvenile growth in ancestral Pueblo Indians. *American Journal of Physical Anthropology*, **145**, 318–326.

Shackelford, L. L. (2014). Bone strength and subsistence activities at Point Hope. In C. E. Hilton, B. M. Auerbach, and L. W. Cowgill, eds., *The Foragers of Point Hope: The Biology and Archaeology of Humans on the Edge of the Alaskan Arctic*. Cambridge: Cambridge University Press, pp. 181–211.

Smith, B. H. (1991). Standards of tooth formation and dental age assessment. In M. A. Kelley and C. S. Larsen, eds., *Advances in Dental Anthropology*. New York, NY: Wiley-Liss, pp. 143–168.

Sofaer, J. (2006). Gender, bioarchaeology, and human ontogeny. In R. Gowland and C. J. Knüsel, eds., *The Social Archaeology of Funerary Remains*. Oxford: Oxbow Books, pp. 155–167.

Sofaer, J. (2011). Towards a social bioarchaeology of age. In S. C. Agarwal and B. A. Glencross, eds., *Social Bioarchaeology*. New York, NY: Wiley-Blackwell, pp. 285–311.

Sofaer Derevenski, J. (2000). Rings of life: The role of early metalwork in mediating the gendered life course. *World Archaeology*, **31**, 389–406.

Sprott, J. W. (2002). *Raising Young Children in an Alaskan Inupiaq Village: The Family, Cultural, and Village Environment of Rearing*. Westport, CT: Bergen and Garvey.

Stanford, D. J. (1976). *Walakpa: Its Place in the Birnirk and Thule Cultures*. Washington, DC: Smithsonian Institution Press.

Stojanowski, C. M. (2009). Bridging histories: The bioarchaeology of identity in postcontact Florida. In K. J. Knudsen and C. M. Stojanowski, eds., *Bioarchaeology of Identity in the Americas*. Gainesville, FL: University Press of Florida, pp. 59–81.

Stojanowski, C. M. (2013). *Bioarchaeology of Ethnogenesis in the Colonial Southeast*. Gainesville, FL: University Press of Florida.

Sturtevant, W. C. (1971). Creek into Seminole: North American Indians. In E. Leacock and N. Lurie, eds., *Historical Perspective*. New York, NY: Random House, pp. 92–128.

Thompson, V. D. and Pluckhahn, T. J. (2010). History, complex hunter-gatherers, and the mounds and monuments of Crystal River, Florida, USA: A geophysical survey. *Journal of Island and Coastal Archaeology*, **5**, 33–51.

van Schaick, C. P., Barrickman, N., Bastian, M. L., Krakaue, E. B., and van Noordwijk, M. A. (2006). Primate life histories and the role of brains. In K. E. Hawkes and R. R. Paine, eds., *The Evolution of Human Life History*. Santa Fe, NM: School of American Research Press, pp. 127–154.

Walker, B., Holling, C. S., Carpenter, S. R., and Kinzig, A. P. (2004). Resilience, adaptability, and transformability in socioecological systems. *Ecology and Society*, **9**, 5.

Yamada, Y. (1997). Mortuary practices for children in Jomon Japan: An approach to Jomon life history. *Journal of the Japanese Archaeological Association*, **4**, 1–39.

12 Biocultural Perspectives on Interpersonal Violence in the Prehistoric San Francisco Bay Area

Eric J. Bartelink, Viviana I. Bellifemine, Irina Nechayev,
Valerie A. Andrushko, Alan Leventhal, and Robert Jurmain

12.1 Introduction

The origins and causes of violence and warfare in prehistory continue to be a contentious topic among anthropologists (Ember and Ember, 1992, 1995; Ferguson, 1984, 2000, 2013; Ferguson and Whitehead, 1992; Gat, 2000; Haas, 1990; Keeley, 1996; Kelly, 2000; Lambert, 2002; Martin and Frayer, 1997; Otterbein, 1994; Thorpe, 2003; Turney-High, 1971; Walker, 2001; Wrangham and Peterson, 1996). Researchers who perceive violence as having deep roots in the ancient past argue that aggression, violence, and warfare are part of the evolutionary package inherited from our early primate ancestry (Bowles, 2009; Pinker, 2011; Wrangham, 1999; Wrangham and Peterson, 1996). Characterized as the Hobbesian view, these researchers emphasize similarities between coalitionary killings carried out by groups of chimpanzee males against other chimpanzee communities and the warfare practices of hunter-gatherer populations (Wrangham, 1999; Wrangham and Peterson, 1996). Counter to this viewpoint, the more Rousseauian perspective emphasizes the cultural, socioeconomic, and sociopolitical dynamics of human violence, as well as the capacity for societies to resolve conflicts through cooperation (Fry, 2006; Fry and Söderberg, 2013). Many of these works de-emphasize evidence of warfare among hunter-gatherers of the past and present in favor of attributing acts of violence to raids, revenge killings, and blood feuds (Fry, 2006, 2013; Fry and Söderberg, 2013; Sussman, 2013). Some researchers have also argued that ethnographic evidence reflects intergroup conflict resulting from competition for access to foreign goods introduced by Westerners, thus providing a biased representation of indigenous patterns of violence and warfare practices (see discussions in Ferguson, 2000, 2013; Ferguson and Whitehead, 1992). Different working definitions of *warfare* also determine whether or not it is perceived to be common among hunter-gatherer populations of the past and present (see arguments in Fry, 2006 versus Keeley, 1996).

Over the past two decades, a plethora of archaeological and anthropological research has revealed convincing evidence of interpersonal violence and warfare among several prehistoric hunter-gatherer populations (Keeley, 1996; Kelly, 2013; Lambert, 1994, 1997, 2002; LeBlanc, 2007; Milner *et al.*, 1991; Smith, 1997; Walker, 1989; Webb, 1995; Willey and Emerson, 1993). While debate continues on how to classify different forms of violence (e.g., warfare versus raids versus revenge killings), osteological sources of data provide the best evidence of physical violence experienced by individuals in the past. Archaeological, ethnographic, and ethnohistoric sources of data further inform on mortuary context, markers of social inequality, and structural violence, and are thus key to contextualizing patterns of violence (Martin and Harrod, 2015).

12.2   Prehistoric Hunter-Gatherers from California

12.2.1   Bioarchaeological Evidence of Violence in Prehistoric California

The prehistoric societies of California have featured prominently in debates regarding the causes of interpersonal violence and warfare among prehistoric hunter-gatherer populations (Allen, 2012; Allen and Jones, 2014; Allen *et al.*, 2016; Keeley, 1996; Lambert, 1994, 1997, 2002; Walker, 1989, 1997, 2001). While a few early studies noted evidence of violence in osteological collections from California (Courville, 1948, 1952; Jurmain, 1991; Pastron *et al.*, 1973; Tenney, 1990), a more contextualized approach was developed by Walker (1989, 1997) and Lambert (1994, 1997) in research on violence and warfare practices among the Chumash of the Santa Barbara Channel in southern California. These influential studies documented high levels of interpersonal violence, including evidence of craniofacial trauma and projectile point injuries among both Channel Island and mainland groups. Because these studies emphasize temporal trends in skeletal trauma, they provide some of the best sources of data for understanding the relationship between patterns of interpersonal violence, climate change, and increasing social stratification and social inequality during the Late Holocene. In the Santa Barbara Channel, nonlethal healed cranial trauma peaked during the Early Middle Period (1500 cal BCE to CE 580; Colten and Erlandson, 1991; Lambert, 1994, 1997). Further, lethal violence (e.g., projectile point injuries) peaked during the Late Middle Period (ca. cal CE 580–1380; Colten and Erlandson, 1991), a time marked by the drought conditions of the Medieval Climatic Anomaly (MCA) as well as the introduction of the bow and arrow (Jones *et al.*, 1999; Kennett *et al.*, 2013; Lambert, 1994, 1997). This increase in lethal violence is commonly tied to models of resource stress associated with population pressure, MCA drought conditions, and a decline in skeletal health as measured by increases in rates of non-specific skeletal indicators of stress (Jones *et al.*, 1999; Lambert, 1993, 1994, 1997; Lambert and Walker, 1991).

Recent efforts within central California bioarchaeology have also attempted to understand demographic, regional, and temporal patterns of interpersonal violence during the Late Holocene (Allen *et al.*, 2016; Andrushko *et al.*, 2005, 2010; Bartelink *et al.*, 2013; Eerkens *et al.*, 2014a, 2014b, 2016a; Grady *et al.*, 2001; Jurmain, 2001; Jurmain and Bellifemine, 1997; Jurmain *et al.*, 2009; Nelson, 1997; Pilloud *et al.*, 2014; Schwitalla *et al.*, 2014a, 2014b; Wiberg, 2002). In addition to documenting these patterns, greater attention has been directed toward more contextualized studies focused on stable isotope analysis for differentiating intragroup from intergroup conflict by determining the provenance of victims of lethal violence as either local or non-local to the location where they were buried (Eerkens *et al.*, 2014a, 2014b, 2016a). Recent research has also focused on determining the provenance of extra skulls found within single burials to determine whether these remains likely reflect ancestor veneration or war trophies (Eerkens *et al.*, 2016b), as well as documenting patterns of cut marks associated with the postmortem removal of heads and limbs associated with trophy-taking (Andrushko *et al.*, 2005, 2010; Bartelink *et al.*, 2013; Grady *et al.*, 2001; Schwitalla *et al.*, 2014a, 2014b; Wiberg, 2002). In addition, several studies have investigated whether temporal patterns of violence were linked to changes in sociopolitical complexity, social inequality, weapon technology, climate, resource depression, or resulting from population intrusions (Allen *et al.*, 2016; Andrushko *et al.*, 2005, 2010; Bartelink *et al.*, 2013; Jurmain *et al.*, 2009; Pilloud *et al.*, 2014; Schwitalla *et al.*, 2014a, 2014b). These perspectives are all influenced to some degree by osteological studies from the Santa Barbara Channel region despite significant differences in sociopolitical complexity and environment between southern and central California.

Bioarchaeological research in central California has often identified temporal patterns of violence that are at odds with those found in the Santa Barbara Channel (Andrushko *et al.*, 2010; Bartelink *et al.*, 2013; Jurmain *et al.*, 2009; Schwitalla *et al.*, 2014b). For example, evidence of trophy-taking is not clearly documented in southern California, but peaks in the San Francisco Bay Area during the Early/Middle Period Transition (ca. 500–200 BCE) (Andrushko *et al.*, 2005, 2010; Bartelink *et al.*, 2013; Schwitalla *et al.*, 2014b). In addition, cranial trauma prevalence also peaks during this period, whereas projectile point injury only shows a slight, non-significant increase during the Late Period (ca. CE 900–1700) when the bow and arrow was introduced into the region around CE 1200 (Bartelink *et al.*, 2013). In a broader survey based on osteological data compiled from unpublished and published sources representing multiple archaeological sites from central California, evidence of elevated levels of violence, including trophy-taking/dismemberment and sharp-force trauma, was documented for the Early Middle Period (500 cal BCE–cal CE 420), whereas both blunt force trauma and sharp-force trauma showed another increase during the Protohistoric/Historic Period (cal CE 1720–1899) (Schwitalla *et al.*, 2014a). Comparisons of patterns of violence between central and southern California are further complicated by variations in the timing of the archaeological periods used in the two culture areas. In addition to these issues, there are many other reasons to expect patterns of violence to vary between these different cultural groups. For example, hunter-gatherer societies of central California were dispersed across a wider range of environmental zones (coastal, bayshore, valley, riparian, and marshland communities), were composed of multiple cultural and language groups, and lacked the hallmarks of well-developed chiefdoms like those found among the Chumash of southern California. In addition, bioarchaeological studies from different regions within central California suggest that different populations mitigated resource stress in different ways based on spatial and temporal variation in the prevalence of physiological stress and disease indicators observed on human skeletal remains (Bartelink, 2006; Dickel *et al.*, 1984; Nechayev, 2007; Schulz, 1981).

12.2.2 Resilience in Hunter-Gatherer Lifeways in Prehistoric Central California

Precontact California maintained some of the highest population densities in North America, yet native populations persisted as hunter-gatherers across the entire Holocene (Cook, 1976). Early theorists argued that California's bountiful landscape provided all the food that was needed, and that the development of agriculture was simply not necessary (Bean and Lawton, 1976; Kroeber, 1939). Indeed, in his *Handbook of the Indians of California*, noted ethnographer Alfred Kroeber stated "the food resources of California were bountiful in their variety rather than in their overwhelming overabundance along special lines. If one supply failed, there were a hundred others to fall back upon" (Kroeber, 1925: 524). Notions of resource abundance in California's prehistory have recently been challenged by a number of scholars (Bartelink, 2006; Basgall, 1987; Beaton, 1991; Broughton, 1994a, 1994b, 1997, 1999, 2002; Broughton *et al.*, 2010; Simons, 1992). Various archaeological lines of evidence suggest that the adoption of intensive acorn-storage economies during the Late Holocene (ca. 4500–200 BP) marked a major subsistence transition in California prehistory, one that resulted in greater investment in higher-cost, lower-ranked food resources, increased sedentism, and greater territorial circumscription. Framed within the context of *resource intensification*, these models predict reductions in foraging efficiency during the Late Holocene associated with a decline in the relative abundance of large mammalian prey items due to intensive hunting pressure by humans. Evidence of resource depression has been documented in numerous prehistoric contexts throughout central California, including the Sacramento Valley and San Francisco Bay Area. Notable work by Broughton (1994a, 1994b, 1997, 1999, 2002; Broughton *et al.*, 2010) at several Bay Area shell mounds has demonstrated significant declines in the relative abundance of artiodactyls relative to smaller, more costly fauna during the Late Holocene, providing robust evidence of resource depression and declining foraging efficiency.

Bioarchaeological research on Native California populations has often emphasized temporal patterns of non-specific markers of stress, dental disease, violence, and paleodiet during the Late Holocene (Bartelink, 2006, 2009; Dickel *et al.*, 1984; Eerkens and Bartelink, 2013; Eerkens *et al.*, 2013; Gardner, 2013; Griffin, 2014; Lambert, 1993, 1994, 1997; Lambert and Walker, 1991; Nechayev, 2007; Schulz, 1981; Walker, 1989). In many ways, these studies have attempted to counter notions of a static past touted by early ethnographers, such as Kroeber, who argued that California Indians lacked evidence of culture change in prehistory (Kroeber, 1925, 1936, 1939). Several studies have predicted that increased investment in acorn-storage economies and other low-ranked foodstuffs (e.g., small fauna and small seeds) during the Late Holocene resulted in a decline in skeletal health as measured by increased rates of non-specific markers of stress (e.g., enamel hypoplasia defects, cribra orbitalia and porotic hyperostosis lesions, dental disease, and periosteal bone reaction) and a reduction in stature (Bartelink, 2006; Broughton *et al.*, 2010; Lambert, 1993; Lambert and Walker, 1991; Nechayev, 2007). Recent investigations have also examined regional and temporal patterns of interpersonal violence in central

California, with the goal of understanding how these societies adapted to resource stress driven by intensification, territorial circumscription, and the severe drought conditions of the complete MCA period (CE 900 to CE 1400) (Bartelink *et al.*, 2013; Jurmain *et al.*, 2009; Pilloud *et al.*, 2014; Schwitalla *et al.*, 2014a, 2014b).

More recently, resilience theory was introduced to archaeology from ecology and has provided an informative framework from which to evaluate how populations adapt to changing environmental, social, and sociopolitical circumstances (Bradtmöller *et al.*, 2017; Hoover and Hudson, 2016; McAnany and Yoffee, 2009; Redman, 2005; Tainter, 2006; Walker *et al.*, 2004). Resilience is defined as the "capacity of a social-ecological system to maintain internal integrity against external pressure – to absorb perturbations and retain the same function, structure and feedbacks" (Hoover and Hudson, 2016: 23–24). In the formalized model (known as the Adaptive Cycle Model), resilience theory covers four phases: exploitation, conservation, release, and reorganization (Holling, 1973, 1986, 1996). The model was developed initially for ecological research and thus can be difficult to test empirically in archaeological contexts (Bradtmöller *et al.*, 2017). However, a generalized version of the Adaptive Cycle Model can be used as a heuristic device to explore evidence of population resilience, including analyses of osteological indicators of stress, disease, and violence (Hoover and Hudson, 2016). A central tenet of resilience theory is that it focuses on both stability *and* change, recognizing that societies can show plasticity in the face of external stressors while at the same time showing evidence of cultural and sociopolitical change.

The hunter-gatherer societies of the San Francisco Bay Area of central California demonstrate long-term stability in subsistence patterns (e.g., intensive acorn-storage economies) across much of the Late Holocene despite evidence of significant changes in climate, population, resource abundance, and sociopolitical complexity. In this study, we evaluate San Francisco Bay Area population resilience to resource stress and climate change using a large sample of human skeletons from 12 Late Holocene burial mounds. Using a suite of osteological markers of violence from these sites (e.g., craniofacial trauma, projectile point injuries, and trophy-taking), we identify a set of expectations for Late Holocene patterns of violence in the eastern and southern regions of the San Francisco Bay Area.

As discussed above, California bioarchaeologists have used resource intensification models to evaluate systemic stress and disease in human skeletal remains, often linking declines in skeletal health to resource depression, increased sedentism and territoriality, and the drought conditions of the MCA (Bartelink, 2006; Lambert, 1993, 1994, 1997; Schwitalla, 2014a; Walker, 1986, 1989, 1997). Previous research on Bay Area skeletal samples, however, found few temporal differences in non-specific markers of stress, such as enamel hypoplasia defects, cribra orbitalia and porotic hyperostosis, and tibial periosteal lesions (Bartelink, 2006; Nechayev, 2007), the opposite of the trends identified among the Chumash of the Santa Barbara Channel (Lambert, 1993, 1994; Lambert and Walker, 1991; Walker, 1986). These findings were unexpected, especially given the significant temporal changes in diet observed using stable carbon and nitrogen isotopes of human skeletons from the Bay Area

(Bartelink, 2009). We interpret this stability in physiological stress through time as evidence of socioecological and cultural resilience. For this study, we hypothesize that osteological indicators of interpersonal violence among San Francisco Bay Area hunter-gatherer societies will not correlate with Late Holocene resource depression trends (i.e., resource stress) or with deteriorating conditions associated with the most severe MCA drought interval documented in the Bay Area paleoclimate record (ca. CE 750–1050; Goman *et al.*, 2008; Ingram and Malamud-Roam, 2013; Malamud-Roam *et al.*, 2007). To evaluate this hypothesis, we compare temporal patterns of indicators of violence with trends in the zooarchaeological record (Broughton, 1994a, 1999) and paleoclimatic data from the Bay Area (Ingram and Malamud-Roam, 2013). If evidence of elevated levels of violence is uncorrelated with periods of resource stress or with climate change during the MCA (ca. CE 750–1050), this would support the notion of socioecological and cultural resilience in the Bay Area during the Late Holocene. However, if these groups were not resilient to resource stress or drought conditions of the MCA, we expect markers of violence to increase during these time periods, consistent with patterns found in the Santa Barbara Channel in southern California (Lambert, 1994, 1997; Walker, 1989, 1997). While these contrasting hypotheses are not mutually exclusive (e.g., drought conditions may exacerbate resource stress), this chapter argues that a lack of correlation between violence and these variables can provide support for socioecological and cultural resilience, especially when other osteological markers of physiological stress also fail to show a relationship.

Moreover, evidence that increased violence did not correlate with resource stress or drought, but rather with sociopolitical factors such as external migrations and emerging social inequality, may be indicative of transformation. Transformation, as explored in archaeological studies, looks at how cultures may have reacted to disruptive events or processes in ways that could not be internally mitigated (i.e., with resilience), but rather were met in costly ways that transformed the society (Hegmon *et al.*, 2008; Hoover and Hudson, 2016). In the California example here, this transformation may have been expressed, in part, in the form of lethal violence and trophy-taking.

12.2.3 Archaeological and Ethnohistoric Context

At the time of Spanish contact, the shoreline of the San Francisco Bay was dotted with more than 425 shell and earthen mound sites (Milliken *et al.*, 2007). Large mounds located near the bayshore reflect formal burial sites for the dead, as well as middens for food refuse and artifacts (Lightfoot and Luby, 2002). Site functions appear to have varied significantly across space and time, with some sites likely serving as mortuary mounds, locations for community feasting, and residential village locations (Leventhal, 1993; Lightfoot and Luby, 2002; Lightfoot *et al.*, 2011; Luby and Gruber, 1999; Luby *et al.*, 2006).

During the Late Holocene, three major successive cultural patterns are recognized in the Bay Area: the Lower Berkeley Pattern, the Upper Berkeley Pattern, and the

Augustine Pattern (Bennyhoff and Hughes, 1987: 149). The Lower Berkeley Pattern corresponds to the Early Period (ca. 3000–500 BCE), and is marked by the first sedentary communities as well as the establishment of clusters of between four and six shell mound sites located along either fresh water drainages or the bayshore of the upper East Bay (Lightfoot and Luby, 2002; Lightfoot *et al.*, 2011; Milliken *et al.*, 2007). Mortar and pestle technology indicates the importance of acorns, although millingstone technology also suggests investment in small seed grinding, an interpretation supported by paleobotanical analyses (Basgall, 1987; Wohlgemuth, 2002, 2004). Archaeofaunal assemblages indicate a heavy emphasis on higher-ranked prey (e.g., artiodactyls), suggesting high levels of foraging efficiency (Broughton, 1994a).

The Upper Berkeley Pattern corresponds to the Early/Middle Transition (ca. 500–200 BCE) and Middle Period (ca. 200 BCE–CE 700), and is marked by the establishment of numerous shell mound sites in the upper eastern and northern bayshore, as well as the first large earthen mound sites along the lower eastern and southern bayshore (Lightfoot and Luby, 2002). A significant increase in the number of dated site components and burials appears to reflect significant increases in population (Rosenthal, 2011), leading researchers to argue that the Middle Period represented a "golden age" of shell mound communities (Lightfoot and Luby, 2002). Burial wealth differentiation also appears to increase during this period, suggesting greater status inequality compared to the Early Period (Hylkema, 2002; Milliken and Bennyhoff, 1993). This pattern is further marked by significant changes in shell bead types, the development of a more complex bone tool industry, and greater investment in the use of acorns and smaller fauna (Milliken *et al.*, 2007). The early Middle Period is marked by the disruption of shell bead trading networks and by evidence of a population intrusion by the Meganos Culture into the East and South Bay regions from the Sacramento–San Joaquin Delta (Central Valley) to the east (Bennyhoff, 1994a, 1994b; Milliken *et al.*, 2007). These population intrusions are especially evident in the sudden appearance of new burial patterns and artifact assemblages associated with some burials from bayshore sites, and have been hypothesized to represent evidence of the influence of the Windmiller Culture from the Central Valley. Bennyhoff (1994a, 1994b) argued that Meganos traits disappear from the bayshore sites toward the end of the Middle Period, only to reappear in the San Joaquin Valley at the beginning of the Late Period.

Finally, the Augustine Pattern, corresponding to the Middle/Late Transition (ca. CE 700–900) and Late Period (ca. CE 900–1700), signifies a decline in foraging efficiency (i.e., widening of diet breadth) based on a shift toward greater intensification of acorns and small seeds, as well as an increased reliance on smaller fauna compared to earlier time periods (Broughton, 1994b, 1999; Milliken *et al.*, 2007; Wohlgemuth, 2002, 2004). The introduction of Stockton serrated series projectile points around CE 1200 provides the earliest evidence for bow and arrow technology in the Bay Area (Bettinger, 2015; Kennett *et al.*, 2013; Milliken *et al.*, 2007). Greater social complexity and perhaps ascribed status is inferred based on evidence of a greater degree of "wealth" identified among a smaller number of burials, and by an increase in cremation and pre-interment burning of grave pits (Milliken and Bennyhoff, 1993).

Banjo-shaped effigy ornaments found in burials may signify the development of a widespread ceremonial complex throughout central California, possibly associated with the *Kuksu* cult documented by early ethnographers (Milliken *et al.*, 2007). A dramatic decline in the number of bayshore sites is noted during the Late Period, suggesting a change in settlement patterns toward greater use of more inland sites as well as more seasonal occupation of the bayshore (Lightfoot and Luby, 2002); however, some bayshore sites lack evidence of disruption and appear to have been in use throughout the Late Period (Leventhal, 1993; Milliken *et al.*, 2007). Severe drought conditions associated with the MCA may have influenced settlement patterns, although poor chronological resolution of many of these sites makes it difficult to directly evaluate (Ingram and Malamud-Roam, 2013; Lightfoot and Luby, 2002).

Ethnographic and ethnohistoric sources shed light on the tribal groups living in the Bay Area at the time of Spanish contact in 1769. Seven different languages were spoken in the Bay Area, reflecting a high level of linguistic diversity. The Spanish named the local population "Costanoans" (from costaños or coast people), which included tribal groups from the San Francisco Peninsula, the Santa Clara Valley, the Southern Coast Range, and the eastern bayshore (Milliken, 1995: 24–26). The estimated population numbered between 7000 (Kroeber, 1925: 464) and 10 200 (Levy, 1978: 485), with approximately 6–10 persons per square mile (Milliken, 1995: 19–21). Costanoans were organized into small, autonomous tribes consisting of large villages linked to smaller hamlets within a circumscribed territory, approximately 8–12 miles across with populations ranging from 200 to 400 individuals (Milliken, 1995; Moratto, 1984: 225). Sources suggest that sociopolitical organization was loosely structured, but often a headman served in a leadership role and exerted some control over the group (Kroeber, 1932; Levy, 1978; Lightfoot and Parrish, 2009: 76). These leaders were responsible for settling disputes, presiding over feasts and ceremonies, and for managing economic exchanges between groups (Bean and Lawton, 1976; Lightfoot and Parrish, 2009).

Territorial boundaries were defined by geographic features and often engendered hostility between neighbors if violated (Bolton, 1930; Heizer, 1978: 487–488). Ethnographic and ethnohistoric accounts report reprisals for violations of territorial rights (e.g., trespassing or poaching of hunting and fishing grounds, theft, etc.) as the most frequent cause of war (Heizer, 1978; Kroeber, 1925; McCorkle, 1978). Acquisition of marriage partners was another cited cause for conflict (James and Graziani, 1975). Warfare took the form of prearranged encounters or surprise attacks (Broadbent, 1972: 73), and weapons included projectile point technology (e.g., atlatl, bow and arrow), sling stones, stones, and clubs. In central California, violent encounters were mostly among males; however, females and children were reported to take part in skirmishes (Beals, 1933; Du Bois, 1935; Kroeber, 1925; Merriam, 1955). This is an indication that females were not mere accidental casualties of violence, but fought alongside men in defending villages from enemies.

Evidently, village feuds or small-scale warfare occurred between Costanoan groups and neighboring tribes from time to time (Kroeber, 1925: 466). Some of these conflicts were brief and resulted in few casualties (Heizer and Whipple, 1971:

217–218), while others were more disastrous (Beechey, 1831: 77). The earliest Spanish accounts report that, although friendly in general, Native groups were highly territorial against neighboring communities (Anza *et al.*, 1930: 129).

12.3   Materials and Methods

12.3.1   Archaeological Sites and Chronology

The skeletal remains used in this study (*n* = 2230) derive from 12 archaeological sites located near the eastern and southern shore of the San Francisco Bay (Figure 12.1). The sites were excavated over the past century in present-day Alameda and Santa Clara counties by archaeologists from various local universities and cultural resource management firms. Analyses of remains from the West Berkeley Shellmound (CA-ALA-307), the Emeryville Shellmound (CA-ALA-309), the Patterson Mound (CA-ALA-328), and the Ryan Mound (CA-ALA-329) were conducted at the Phoebe

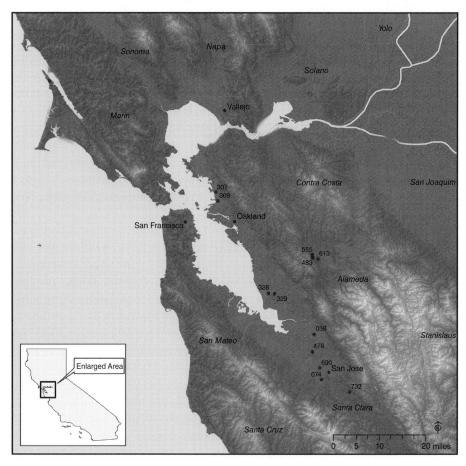

Figure 12.1 Map of the San Francisco Bay Area showing the 30 archaeological sites used in the current study. Map produced by the authors with the assistance of Kevin Dalton.

Table 12.1 Archaeological sites, dates, and data sources for the study sample.

County/site	Period	References for trauma data
Alameda County		
CA-ALA-307	Early Period, Middle Period	Bartelink *et al.*, 2013
CA-ALA-309	Middle Period, Middle/Late Transition	Bartelink *et al.*, 2013
CA-ALA-328	Early/Middle Transition, Middle Period, Late Period	Bartelink *et al.*, 2013
CA-ALA-329	Middle Period, Late Period	Jurmain *et al.*, 2009
CA-ALA-483, -483 Ext.	Late Period	Wiberg, 1996
CA-ALA-555	Late Period	Wiberg, 1996
CA-ALA-613/H	Early Period, Middle Period, Middle/Late Transition, Late Period	Strother *et al.*, 2005
Santa Clara County		
CA-SCL-038	Middle Period, Middle/Late Transition, Late Period	Bellifemine, 1997; Jurmain 2000, 2001
CA-SCL-478	Early/Middle Transition	Wiberg, 2002
CA-SCL-674	Early/Middle Transition, Middle Period, Late Period	Grady *et al.*, 2001; Andrushko *et al.*, 2005
CA-SCL-690	Middle/Late Transition	Bethard and Jurmain, 2007
CA-SCL-732	Early/Middle Transition, Middle Period	Musladin *et al.*, 1996; Cambra *et al.*, 1996

A. Hearst Museum of Anthropology at UC Berkeley, whereas the larger collection from the Ryan Mound was examined at San Jose State University. Data from the additional sites were tabulated from high-quality archaeological site reports and publications that followed similar data-collection procedures (CA-ALA-483, -483 Ext., CA-ALA-555, CA-ALA-613/H, CA-SCL-038, CA-SCL-478, CA-SCL-674, CA-SCL-690, and CA-SCL-732) (Table 12.1). The ethnographic territory under investigation is one of the best-studied in central California and is well represented in both the preservation and quantity of human skeletal remains and associated archaeological materials. In general, the majority of human skeletal remains in the sample are fairly complete. However, we controlled for degree of skeletal completeness for analyses of craniofacial trauma, projectile point injury, and trophy-taking following the same criteria used by earlier research using a wider range of archaeological sites (Bartelink *et al.*, 2013).

There are a number of chronological systems devised for central California archaeology (Milliken *et al.*, 2007). Prehistory is divided into three major and two transitional time periods following Bennyhoff and Hughes' (1987) Scheme B1: Early Period (ca. 3000–500 BCE), Early/Middle Transition (ca. 500–200 BCE), Middle Period (ca. 200 BCE–CE 700), Middle/Late Transition (ca. AD 700–900), and Late Period (ca. CE 900–1700). Temporal attribution of individuals to a particular chronological period was based on the results of various dating techniques such as seriation of time-diagnostic artifacts, stratigraphy, obsidian hydration dates, and radiocarbon dates (Table 12.2). Although all chronological periods are represented in the sample, the Early Period sample was too small to include in the statistical analysis. Thus, the comparative analysis focused on the Early/Middle Transition through the Late Period (ca. 500 BCE–CE 1700). Comparisons of indicators of violence were evaluated using chi-square and Fisher's exact test (when sample criteria for chi-square analysis was not met). All analyses were conducted using SPSS (v. 20) with *p*-values considered statistically significant at $\alpha = 0.05$.

12.3.2 Sex Determination and Age Estimation

Sex and age assessments followed standard procedures described by Buikstra and Ubelaker (1994). When possible, sex was evaluated based on the morphology of the pelvis, although sex determinations also included assessments of morphological features of the skull and, in some cases, postcranial osteometric sectioning points developed for central California samples (Dittrick and Suchey, 1986). The sample was divided into two major age categories of adult (15+ years) and pre-adult (0–14.9 years), as well as more fined-grained subcategories of infant (0–1.9 years), child (2–14.9 years), young adult (15–30 years), mature adults (30–45 years), and older adult (45+ years).

12.3.3 Indicators of Interpersonal Violence

The following indicators were analyzed based on strong associations with interpersonal violence in prehistoric California: craniofacial trauma, projectile point injury, and trophy-taking. This study followed similar previously established criteria used to study interpersonal violence in human skeletal remains by other researchers (Bartelink *et al.*, 2013; Galloway, 1999; Judd, 2006; Jurmain, 2001; Jurmain *et al.*, 2009; Lovell, 1997, 2008; Smith 1997, 2003; Walker, 1997). For all types of trauma, healed and unhealed status were recorded. Healed cases were identified by the presence of an osseous response in the injured area (Lovell, 1997, 2008). Unhealed cases without evidence of an osseous response were identified as perimortem trauma. Perimortem trauma was differentiated from postmortem damage, with ambiguous cases scored as absent of trauma.

   To control for variation in skeletal preservation that can distort prevalence calculations (Grauer and Roberts, 1996; Jurmain, 1999; Walker, 1997), only individuals with more than 50 percent of cranial and postcranial bones present were included in the analyses. To avoid double-counting cases, distinct types of trauma were analyzed separately. Thus, embedded projectile points discovered in cranial bones were only included with the analysis of projectile injuries. Similarly, cut marks that were observed on cranial vaults indicating the possibility of scalping or dismemberment were only included with other cases of trophy-taking. Cranial vault and facial

Table 12.2 Sample composition (without control for completeness).

	Early	Early/Middle	Middle	Middle/Late	Late	Indeterminate	Total
Males	11	30	129	22	329	113	634
Females	18	21	151	19	274	85	568
Indeterminate	8	62	240	107	415	196	1028
Total	37	113	520	148	1018	394	2230

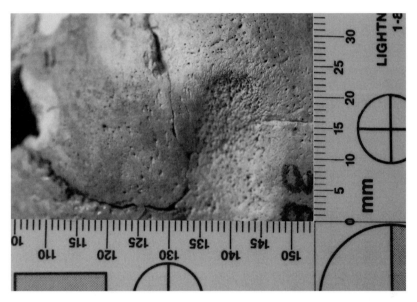

Figure 12.2 Depressed cranial vault fracture (catalog no. 12-3801, CA-ALA-309).

injuries were calculated separately to evaluate more nuanced patterns of interpersonal violence (Figures 12.2 and 12.3) (Walker, 1997).

Projectile point injuries and trophy-taking offer explicit evidence of intergroup violence, behaviors most likely directed toward a lethal outcome (Andrushko *et al.*, 2010; Bartelink *et al.*, 2013; Jurmain *et al.*, 2009; Lambert, 1994, 2002, 2007). In the analysis of projectile point injuries, only those cases with embedded stone fragments were considered as reliable indicators of this type of trauma (Figure 12.4). To reduce potential bias, those cases in which projectile points did not leave direct evidence on the bone were excluded from the sample (Jurmain, 1999; Jurmain *et al.*, 2009).

Trophy-taking, the detachment of various body parts from a defeated enemy, was a documented practice in central California that may have allowed warriors to collect evidence of victory and gain social recognition (Andrushko *et al.*, 2005, 2010; Bartelink *et al.*, 2013; Grady *et al.*, 2001; Lambert, 2007; Schwitalla *et al.*, 2014b). Instances of trophy-taking were identified on long bones by the presence of circumferential cut marks adjacent to missing elements from remains recovered in primary burial contexts (Figure 12.5) (Smith, 1997). On cranial bones, circumferential

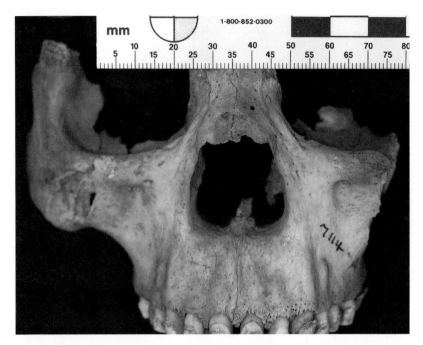

Figure 12.3 Healed nasal fracture (catalog no. 7114G, CA-ALA-329).

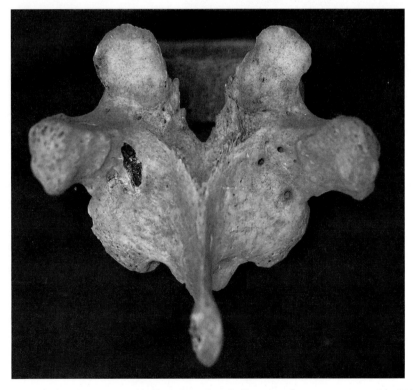

Figure 12.4 Perimortem projectile point injury in T-10 (catalog no. 12-7104, CA-ALA-329).

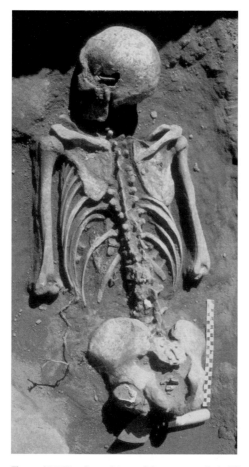

Figure 12.5 Trophy-taking of forearm and obsidian point in left rib (Burial 76, CA-SCl-674). Photograph by Andrew Gotsfield.

patterns of cut marks on the frontal, parietal, and occipital bones were recorded as evidence of scalping (Owsley *et al.*, 1977). For methodological consistency, cases of detached body parts that lacked evidence of cut marks were excluded from the sample. Thus, instances of skulls that were interred with a burial, tools fashioned from human bone, or repositioned/disturbed cranial or postcranial elements were excluded as reliable indicators of violence (cf., Schwitalla *et al.*, 2014b).

12.4   Results

12.4.1   Craniofacial Trauma

Cranial trauma (Table 12.3) was documented among 4.2 percent of individuals from the sample (50/1177). Most of these injuries represent healed depressed fractures (3.1 percent, 36/1177), followed by perimortem fractures (0.8 percent, 9/1177). Of the 50 individuals with cranial vault trauma, 6.4 percent were male (27/422), 4.6 percent were female (19/409), and 1.2 percent were of indeterminate sex (4/346). Although

Table 12.3 Distribution of interpersonal violence indicators by sex.

Sex	Cranial vault trauma Percentage	*n*	Facial trauma Percentage	*n*	Projectile injury Percentage	*n*	Trophy-taking Percentage	*n*
Male	6.4	27/422	3.0	12/398	4.0	19/473	6.0	19/317
Female	4.6	19/409	1.4	5/354	1.0	4/409	0.7	2/281

males demonstrated a slightly higher prevalence of vault injuries compared to females, these differences were not statistically significant (Fisher's exact test, $p = 0.291$). Similar patterns were documented for perimortem cranial vault trauma, with 6 percent of males (25/420) and 4.2 percent of females (17/407) affected, also a non-significant difference (Fisher's exact test, $p = 0.270$). Cranial vault injuries were most common among middle adults (30–45 years) at 6.2 percent (25/404) and older adults (46+ years) at 5.4 percent (9/166).

Healed facial trauma affected 1.5 percent of individuals in the sample (17/1100), with all injuries identified only on adult individuals (Table 12.3). These injuries were observed in 11 individuals (1 percent) with nasal bone fractures, four individuals (0.4 percent) with zygomatic fractures, and three individuals (0.3 percent) with mandibular fractures. For the total adult sample, the prevalence of facial trauma was 1.8 percent (17/922). For individuals 30–45 years of age, 2.9 percent (12/417) showed evidence of facial trauma, whereas for individuals 20–29.9 years of age, 1.2 percent (2/167) were affected. Facial trauma was not noted in the youngest (<15 years) and oldest (45+ years) age categories. No perimortem facial fractures were observed. Among individuals with healed facial injury, 3 percent were male (12/398) and 1.4 percent were female (5/354). Although males showed twice as many facial fractures as females, the difference was not statistically significant (Fisher's exact test, $p = 0.218$). The majority of observed facial injuries were nasal fractures (64.7 percent, 11/17), followed by zygomatic fractures (23.5 percent, 4/17), and mandibular fractures (11.8 percent, 2/17). Of those individuals with cranial vault trauma, 8 percent (4/50, three male and one female) also exhibited healed facial fractures.

12.4.2 Projectile Point Injury

Projectile point injuries were documented in 2 percent of the overall sample (25/1250), and 2.3 percent of all adults (25/1080) (Table 12.3). In the majority of cases (69.5 percent, 16/23), no signs of healing were observed. No individuals under 15 years of age were affected. Males showed a higher prevalence of 4 percent (19/473) compared to 1 percent (4/409) for females, a statistically significant difference (Fisher's exact test, $p = 0.005$). Among affected adults whose age could be assessed, 41.7 percent were from the 20–29.9 age category (5.1 percent, 10/198 within this age category), 50 percent were from the 30–45 age category (2.4 percent, 12/496 within this age category), and only 8.3 percent were between 15 and 19.9 years of age (2.6 percent, 2/77 within this age category). No projectile point injuries were found among individuals in the oldest adult age category (45+ years of age).

The distribution of projectile injuries between age classes is significantly different ($\chi^2 = 9.320$; $p = 0.025$). Among the 25 individuals with projectile point injuries, there were 17 cases of a single embedded point (68 percent) and eight cases of multiple embedded points (32 percent).

12.4.3 Trophy-Taking

Evidence of trophy-taking was observed in 3.3 percent of individuals in the sample (22/676) (Table 12.3). The area most affected was the forearm (15 cases), followed by the scalp (four cases) and the lower leg (two cases). In addition, one individual exhibited evidence of trophy-taking of both the forearm and the scalp. Three of the four scalping cases were healed, while all postcranial trophy-taking cases were perimortem. For males only, evidence of trophy-taking occurred in conjunction with cranial vault trauma (healed and unhealed) in 22.7 percent (5/22) of cases. Two of the five individuals also exhibited more than one projectile point injury.

Of the trophy-taking cases, 6 percent (19/317) were males, 0.7 percent were females (2/281), and 0.5 percent were of indeterminate sex (1/211). Among individuals with an estimated sex, males represented 90.5 percent (19/21) of the trophy-taking sample versus females at only 9.5 percent (2/21), a statistically significant difference (Fisher's exact test, $p < 0.001$). The age distribution of trophy-taking cases included one (4.5 percent) adolescent (15–19.9 years), seven (32 percent) young adults (20–29.9 years), and 14 (64 percent) middle adults (30–45 years).

12.4.4 Temporal Patterns of Interpersonal Violence

An analysis of temporal patterns of cranial vault trauma revealed no evidence (0/32) during the Early Period (Table 12.4). However, the prevalence during the Early/Middle Transition peaked at 12.7 percent (8/63), and then decreased to 7 percent during the Middle Period (14/201) and 0 percent (0/42) during the Middle/Late Transition. In the Late Period, the prevalence increased to 5 percent (20/401) (Figure 12.6). These temporal differences were statistically significant ($\chi^2 = 10.5$; $p = 0.032$).

Table 12.4 Distribution of interpersonal violence indicators by temporal period.

Time period	Cranial vault trauma		Facial trauma		Projectile injury		Trophy-taking	
	Percentage	n	Percentage	n	Percentage	n	Percentage	n
Late Period	5.0	20/401	1.7	8/477	3.1	17/556	0.3	1/385
Middle/Late Transition	0	0/42	0	0/71	2.8	2/72	0	0/68
Middle Period	7.0	14/201	3.7	7/190	2.4	5/205	3.9	8/207
Early/Middle Transition	12.7	8/63	0	0/60	1.6	1/62	15.3	9/59
Early Period	0	0/0	0	0/4	0	0/3	0	0/1

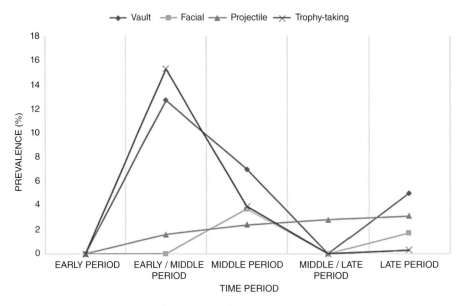

Figure 12.6 Temporal patterns of interpersonal violence indicators.

Overall, the prevalence of facial injuries among adults did not change significantly over time (x^2 = 5.361; p = 0.147). No facial injuries were identified in the small Early Period sample. In contrast to the peak in cranial vault trauma identified for the Early/Middle Transition, no cases of facial trauma were documented for that period. The prevalence of facial injuries among adults was highest during the Middle Period at 3.7 percent (7/190), and then declined to 1.7 percent (8/477) in the Late Period (Figure 12.6).

The earliest evidence of projectile injury was found for the Early/Middle Transition, where 1.6 percent (1/62) of adults were affected. The prevalence increased slightly to 2.4 percent (5/205 adults) during the Middle Period, to 2.8 percent (2/72 adults) during the Middle/Late Transition, and finally to 3.1 percent (17/556 adults) during the Late Period. This temporal pattern was not statistically significant (x^2 = 0.615; p = 0.961) (Figure 12.6).

Of the 18 cases of trophy-taking that had a temporal designation, 15.3 percent (9/59) dated to the Early/Middle Transition Period, 3.9 percent (8/207) to the Middle Period, and 0.3 percent (1/385) to the Late Period. No cases were observed that dated to either the Early Period or Middle/Late Transition. These temporal differences were statistically significant (x^2 = 50.7, p < 0.001) (Figure 12.6).

12.5   Discussion

This chapter focused on several different osteological indicators of violence observed among prehistoric hunter-gatherers of the San Francisco Bay Area, including evidence of craniofacial trauma, projectile point injuries, and trophy-taking. The results demonstrate various indicators of violence peaked at different points in time during the Late Holocene, with cranial trauma and trophy-taking showing the highest prevalence during the Early/Middle Transition (ca. 500–200 BCE), facial trauma during the Middle Period (ca. 200 BCE–CE 700), and projectile point injuries during the Late Period (ca. CE 900–1700). This study hypothesized that osteological indicators of interpersonal violence among Bay Area hunter-gatherers would not correlate either with zooarchaeologically documented patterns of resource depression or with the most severe drought conditions of the MCA (ca. CE 750–1050). The peaks in cranial trauma and trophy-taking precede evidence of significant resource depression in the Bay Area, which appears most evident about halfway through the Middle Period in the East Bay around CE 425 to 475 (Milliken *et al.*, 2007). Further, only a slight, non-significant increase in projectile point injuries was noted for the Late Period (ca. CE 900–1700), which also spans the most severe drought period documented in the MCA's Bay Area paleoclimate record (Goman *et al.*, 2008; Ingram and Malamud-Roam, 2013; Malamud-Roam *et al.*, 2007). While these comparisons are crude given the long time spans represented, these data provide little evidence to suggest that either resource stress or severe drought conditions were major drivers of interpersonal violence. Thus, the absence of a clear temporal pattern of violence provides potential support for population resilience in the Bay Area during the Late Holocene.

The application of resilience theory to our data suggests that many prehistoric events archaeologically detected in the San Francisco Bay Area, including shifts in settlement pattern, subsistence strategy, and sociopolitical system, reflect dynamic responses of the local populations to various socioecological imbalances. In the Bay Area demographic situation, these sociopolitical and economic changes appear to have been sufficient to mitigate environmental and resource stresses without resorting to violence.

Resource intensification models for the Bay Area are well supported based on significant temporal reductions in the relative abundance of large game relative to smaller fauna (Broughton, 1994a, 1997, 1999, 2002; Simons, 1992), as well as the increased intensification of low-ranked vegetal foods, such as acorns and small seeds (Basgall, 1987; Beaton, 1991; Wohlgemuth, 2002, 2004); however, these declines in foraging efficiency do not appear to have influenced rates of interpersonal violence. Further, while robust paleoclimate records for the San Francisco Bay Area clearly document drought conditions during the MCA (especially ca. CE 750–1050), these changes in climate do not correspond to patterns of violence. Evidence for a reduction in the use of several bayshore mounds throughout the East and South Bay Area during the MCA has been documented, but this may reflect greater use of interior Bay Area sites and more seasonal use of bayshore settlements rather than site abandonment (Lightfoot and Luby, 2002). This change in the settlement pattern may reflect the reorganization of the Bay Area communities rather than abandonment, as well as the adoption of the subsistence strategies that involved "more fluid seasonal movement, as described in the ethnographic literature" (Lightfoot and Luby, 2002: 279). Stable carbon and nitrogen isotopes of human skeletons support this notion, as paleodiets shifted from a heavy emphasis on high-trophic-level marine resources (e.g., marine and anadromous fish) during the Early Period toward a diet focused more on lower-trophic-level resources, such as C_3 plants (e.g., acorns and small seeds), during the Middle and Late Periods (Bartelink, 2006, 2009). Despite these patterns, bioarchaeological studies focused on physiological indicators of stress (e.g., enamel hypoplasia defects, cribra orbitalia and porotic hyperostosis, and tibial periosteal lesions) have failed to demonstrate significant changes in prevalence rates through time, suggesting population stability and resilience in this region (Bartelink, 2006; Nechayev, 2007). These trends are in stark contrast with the Chumash societies of the Santa Barbara Channel, where both indicators of physiological stress and interpersonal violence increased through time, attributed by researchers to both resource stress and the deteriorating environmental conditions of the MCA (Jones et al., 1999; Lambert, 1993, 1994, 1997; Lambert and Walker, 1991; Walker, 1986, 1989, 1997). Based on these divergent trends in central versus southern California, it seems likely that different factors influenced patterns of physiological stress and violence in these environmentally and culturally distinct regions.

Given the lack of correlation between peaks in violence, resource depression, and climate change in the Bay Area, alternative explanations invoking transformation of lifestyle should be considered to account for Late Holocene patterns of interpersonal violence. As mentioned previously, the Meganos Culture expanded into the Bay Area from the Sacramento–San Joaquin Delta (Central Valley), possibly beginning as early as the Early/Middle Transition or early Middle Period (Bennyhoff, 1994a, 1994b; Milliken et al., 2007). Meganos mortuary patterns and artifact assemblages further provide evidence of hybridization between Central Valley and Bay Area cultural groups. However, extended interactions between Bay Area and Central Valley groups may not have always been peaceful, and may have resulted in greater competition for resources and territorial circumscription, leading to higher levels of interpersonal violence (Arnold and Walsh, 2010: 72–73; Bartelink et al., 2013).

While population intrusion by Meganos peoples provides one possible explanation for higher levels of cranial trauma and trophy-taking, changes in sociopolitical organization should be considered as another potentially important factor. The Early Period demonstrates the lowest rates of violence in the Bay Area (Bartelink et al., 2013), and marks a period in which social organization was less hierarchical (Milliken and Bennyhoff, 1993). In contrast, mortuary patterns during the Middle Period appear to signify a shift toward a more hierarchical society with a higher degree of social inequality (King, 1974), which is supported by evidence that grave wealth was more unevenly distributed among a smaller segment of the population (Milliken and Bennyhoff, 1993). Further, the high rate of trophy-taking during the Early/Middle Transition may also reflect a shift toward prestige-seeking behaviors among male warriors compared to the Early Period. While sex differences were not found for craniofacial trauma, males were significantly more likely to be victims of lethal violence and trophy-taking, suggesting that males participated more extensively in warfare, raids, and other acts of violence, consistent with findings in the literature (Jurmain and Kilgore, 2007; Keeley, 1996; Knauft, 1991; Lambert, 2002). However, the fact that some females experienced lethal violence (in the form of perimortem projectile point injuries) and exhibited similar levels of craniofacial trauma as males is consistent with the notion that women also sometimes participated in interpersonal conflict (Beals, 1933; Du Bois, 1935; Kroeber, 1925; Merriam, 1955).

This chapter finds that the increased levels of violence may be evidence of transformation among these California groups. The impacts of external migrations and rising socioeconomic inequality were not ones that could be mitigated internally, through cultural buffering systems, and thus demonstrate resilience (as seen in the responses to resource stress and drought conditions). Instead, these powerful forces likely led to large-scale changes in the sociocultural system that affected a wide range of behaviors, including burial rituals and warfare practices. The emergence of trophy-taking is a particularly provocative aspect of this transformation, as bodies were butchered to remove particular parts such as arms and scalps, at times buried haphazardly or among other mutilated individuals, with the human trophies in some cases modified for possible display in rituals (Andrushko *et al.*, 2005, 2010). Such indications of heightened violence are likely to result from extreme transformations, and thus demonstrate how cultural transformation can have a demonstrable impact on human suffering (Hegmon *et al.*, 2008).

12.6   Conclusion

In the present study, the model of resource stress and climate change connected to patterns of violence was not supported for the San Francisco Bay Area. Differences in population pressure, environment, climate, and sociopolitical organization may account for these divergent patterns between the Santa Barbara Channel and the Bay Area. This chapter argues that the lack of correlation between osteological indicators of violence and resource stress or the severe drought conditions of the MCA signifies population resilience among the hunter-gatherer societies of the San Francisco Bay Area. The higher prevalence of cranial vault trauma and trophy-taking during the Early/Middle Transition may suggest that patterns of violence and warfare were linked more closely to transformations brought about by intrusive population movement into the Bay Area from the Central Valley, as well as changes in social organization, such as the development of a higher degree of social inequality. Future research should focus on examining victims of violence and mortuary contexts to tease out variables reflecting the development of social hierarchy in the Bay Area during the Late Holocene.

Acknowledgments

We would like to thank the researchers who collected much of the data compiled for this study. We are grateful to Dr. Tim White, Natasha Johnson, and the staff of the Phoebe A. Hearst Museum of Anthropology at the University of California, Berkeley, for their assistance with many of the collections used in this study. We would like to acknowledge Melynda Atwood and Diane DiGiuseppe for their assistance with data collection and input on CA-ALA-329, as well as the Muwekma Ohlone Tribal Council leadership for their support of research on many of the sites used in this study. We also thank Kevin Dalton for producing the site map. Finally, we would like to thank Christopher Stojanowski and Daniel Temple for inviting us to contribute to this volume. Funding for data collection at the Phoebe A. Hearst Museum of Anthropology, UC Berkeley, was provided to E. J. Bartelink through the California State University, Chico's Research Foundation (Internal Research Grant: Foundation Scholars) and through California State University, Chico's Grant Development Funding, College of Behavioral and Social Sciences.

References

Allen, M. W. (2012). A land of violence. In T. L. Jones and J. E. Perry, eds., *Contemporary Issues in California Archaeology*. Walnut Creek, CA: Left Coast Press, pp. 93–114.

Allen, M. W. and Jones, T. L., eds. (2014). *Violence and Warfare among Hunter-Gatherers*. Walnut Creek, CA: Left Coast Press.

Allen, M. W., Bettinger, R. L., Codding, B. F., Jones, T. L., and Schwitalla, A. W. (2016). Resource scarcity drives lethal aggression among prehistoric hunter-gatherers in central California. *Proceedings of the National Academy of Sciences*, 113, 12120–12125.

Andrushko, V. A., Latham, K. A. S., Grady, D. L., Pastron, A. G., and Walker, P. L. (2005). Bioarchaeological evidence for trophy-taking in prehistoric central California. *American Journal of Physical Anthropology*, 127, 375–384.

Andrushko, V. A., Schwitalla, A. W., and Walker, P. L. (2010). Trophy-taking and dismemberment as warfare strategies in prehistoric central California. *American Journal of Physical Anthropology*, 141, 83–93.

Anza, J. B., Díaz, J., Garcés, F., and Palou, F. (1930). *Opening a Land Route to California, Diaries: Of Anza, Díaz, Garcés and Palóu*. Translated from the Original Spanish Manuscripts and Edited by Herbert Eugene Bolton. Berkeley, CA: University of California Press.

Arnold, J. E. and Walsh, M. R. (2010). *California's Ancient Past: From the Pacific to the Range of Light*. Washington, DC: Society for American Archaeology Press.

Bartelink, E. J. (2006). *Resource Intensification in Pre-contact Central California: A Bioarchaeological Perspective on Diet and Health Patterns among Hunter-Gatherers from the Lower Sacramento Valley and San Francisco Bay*. PhD dissertation, Texas A&M University.

Bartelink, E. J. (2009). Late Holocene dietary change in the San Francisco Bay area: Stable isotope evidence for an expansion in diet breadth. *California Archaeology*, 1, 227–52.

Bartelink, E. J., Andrushko, V. A., Bellifemine, V., Nechayev, I., and Jurmain, R. (2013). Violence and warfare in the prehistoric San Francisco Bay Area, California: Regional and temporal variations in conflict. In C. Knusel and M. Smith, eds., *The Routledge Handbook of the Bioarchaeology of Human Conflict*. Oxford: Routledge, pp. 285–307.

Basgall, M. E. (1987). Resource intensification among hunter-gatherers: Acorn economies in prehistoric California. In B. L. Issac, ed., *Research in Economic Anthropology*, vol. 9. Greenwich: JAI Press, pp. 21–52.

Beals, R. L. (1933). *Ethnology of the Nisenan*. Berkeley, CA: University of California Press, pp. 335–414.

Bean, L. J. and Lawton, H. (1976). Some explanations for the rise of cultural complexity in native California with comments on proto-agriculture and agriculture. In L. J. Bean and T. C. Blackburn, eds., *Native Californians: A Theoretical Retrospective*. Socorro, NM: Ballena Press, pp. 19–48.

Beaton, J. M. (1991). Extensification and intensification in central California prehistory. *Antiquity*, 65(249), 946–952.

Beechey, F. W. (1831). *Narrative of a Voyage to the Pacific and Beering's Strait, to Cooperate with the Polar Expeditions: Performed in His Majesty's Ship Blossom, Under the Command of Captain*

F.W. Beechey, R.N., F.R.S., etc., in the Years 1825, 1826, 1827, 1828. 2 vols. Reprint 1968. New York, NY: Da Capo Press.

Bellifemine, V. (1997). Mortuary Variability in Prehistoric Central California: A Statistical Study of the Yukisma Site, CA-SCL-38. MA thesis, San Jose State University.

Bennyhoff, J. A. (1994a [1968]). A delta intrusion to the bay in the Late Middle Period in central California. In R. E. Hughes, ed., Toward a New Taxonomic Framework for Central California Archaeology. Berkeley, CA: University of California, pp. 7–13.

Bennyhoff, J. A. (1994b [1987]). Variation within the Meganos culture. In R. E. Hughes, ed., Toward a New Taxonomic Framework for Central California Archaeology. Berkeley, CA: University of California, pp. 81–9.

Bennyhoff, J. A. and Hughes, R. E. (1987). Shell Bead and Ornament Exchange Networks between California and the Western Great Basin. New York, NY: American Museum of Natural History.

Bethard, K. and Jurmain, R. (2007). The mortuary complex (physical anthropology of CA-SCL-690). In M. Hylkema, ed., Santa Clara Prehistory: Archaeological Investigations at CA-SCL-690, the Tamien Station Site. San Jose, CA: Center for Archaeological Research at Davis, pp. 185–225.

Bettinger, R. L. (2015). Orderly Anarchy: Sociopolitical Evolution in Aboriginal California. Oakland, CA: University of California Press.

Bolton, H. E. T. (1930). Anza's California Expeditions: Font's Complete Diary of the Second Anza Expedition, vol. 4. Berkeley, CA: University of California Press.

Bowles, S. (2009). Did warfare among ancestral hunter-gatherers affect the evolution of human social behaviors? Science, 324, 1293–1298.

Bradtmöller, M., Grimm, S., and Riel-Salvatore, J. (2017). Resilience theory in archaeological practice: An annotated review. Quaternary International, 446, 3–16.

Broadbent, S. M. (1972). The Rumsen of Monterey: An ethnography from historical sources. In Miscellaneous Papers on Archaeology: Contributions of the University of California Archaeological Research Facility, vol. 14. Berkeley, CA: University of California Press, pp. 45–93.

Broughton, J. M. (1994a). Declines in mammalian foraging efficiency during the Late Holocene, San Francisco Bay, California. Journal of Anthropological Archaeology, 13, 371–401.

Broughton, J. M. (1994b). Late Holocene resource intensification in the Sacramento Valley, California: The vertebrate evidence. Journal of Archaeological Science, 21, 501–514.

Broughton, J. M. (1997). Widening diet breadth, declining foraging efficiency, and prehistoric harvest pressure: Icthyofaunal evidence from the Emeryville Shellmound, California. Antiquity, 71, 845–862.

Broughton, J. M. (1999). Resource Depression and Intensification during the Late Holocene, San Francisco Bay. Berkeley, CA: University of California Press.

Broughton, J. M. (2002). Prey spatial structure and behavior affect archaeological tests of optimal foraging models: Examples from the Emeryville Shellmound vertebrate fauna. World Archaeology, 34, 60–83.

Broughton, J. M., Cannon, M. D., and Bartelink, E. J. (2010). Evolutionary ecology, resource depression, and niche construction theory in archaeology: Applications to central California hunter-gatherers and Mimbres-Mogollon agriculturalists. Journal of Archaeological Method and Theory, 17, 371–421.

Buikstra, J. E. and Ubelaker, D. H., eds. (1994). Standards for Data Collection from Human Skeletal Remains. Fayetteville, AR: Arkansas Archeological Survey.

Cambra, R., Leventhal, A., Jones, L., et al. (1996). Archaeological Investigations at Kaphan Umux (Three Wolves) Site. CA-SCL-732: A Middle Period Cemetery on Coyote Creek in Southern San Jose, Santa Clara County, California. Report prepared for the Santa Clara County Traffic Authority and the California Department of Transportation. http://works.bepress.com/alan_leventhal/76.

Colten, R. H. and Erlandson, J. M. (1991). Perspectives on early hunter-gatherers of the California coast. In J. M. Erlandson and R. Colten, eds., Hunter Gatherers of Early Holocene Coastal California, Los Angeles, CA: Cotsen Institute of Archaeology, pp. 133–139.

Cook, S. F. (1976). *The Population of the California Indians, 1769–1970*. Berkeley, CA: University of California Press.

Courville, C. B. (1948). Cranial injuries among the Indians of North America: A preliminary report. *Bulletin of the Los Angeles Neurological Society*, 13, 181–219.

Courville, C. B. (1952). Cranial injuries among the early Indians of California. *Bulletin of the Los Angeles Neurological Society*, 17, 137–162.

Dickel, D. N., Schulz, P. D., and McHenry, H. M. (1984). Central California: Prehistoric subsistence changes and health. In M. N. Cohen and G. J. Armelagos, eds., *Paleopathology at the Origins of Agriculture*. Gainesville, FL: University Press of Florida, pp. 439–461.

Dittrick, J. and Suchey, J. M. (1986). Sex determination of prehistoric central California skeletal remains using discriminant-analysis of the femur and humerus. *American Journal of Physical Anthropology*, 70, 3–9.

Du Bois, C. (1935). *Wintu Ethnography*. Berkeley, CA: University of California Press, pp 1–148.

Eerkens, J. W. and Bartelink, E. J. (2013). Sex-biased weaning and early childhood diet among middle Holocene hunter-gatherers in Central California. *American Journal of Physical Anthropology*, 152, 471–483.

Eerkens, J. W., Mackie, M., and Bartelink, E. J. (2013). Brackish water foraging: Isotopic landscapes and dietary reconstruction in Suisun Marsh, Central California. *Journal of Archaeological Science*, 40, 3270–3281.

Eerkens, J. W., Barfod, G. H., Jorgenson, G. A., and Peske, C. (2014a). Tracing the mobility of individuals using stable isotope signatures in biological tissues: "locals" and "non-locals" in an ancient case of violent death from Central California. *Journal of Archaeological Science*, 41, 474–481.

Eerkens, J. W., Bartelink, E. J., Gardner, K. S., and Carlson, T. (2014b). Stable isotope perspectives on hunter-gatherer violence: Who's fighting whom? In M. W. Allen and T. L. Jones, eds., *Violence and Warfare among Hunter-Gatherers*. Walnut Creek, CA: Left Coast Press, pp. 296–313.

Eerkens, J. W., Carlson, T., Malhi, R. S., *et al.* (2016a). Isotopic and genetic analyses of a mass grave in central California: Implications for precontact hunter-gatherer warfare. *American Journal of Physical Anthropology*, 159, 116–125.

Eerkens, J. W., Bartelink, E. J., Brink, L., *et al.* (2016b). Trophy heads or ancestor veneration? A stable isotope perspective on disassociated and modified crania in precontact central California. *American Antiquity*, 81, 114–131.

Ember, C. R. and Ember, M. (1992). Resource unpredictability, mistrust, and war: A cross-cultural study. *Journal of Conflict Resolution*, 36, 242–262.

Ember, C. R. and Ember, M. (1995). Warfare, aggression, and resource problems: SSCS Codes. *World Cultures*, 9, 17–57.

Ferguson, R. B., ed. (1984). *Warfare, Culture, and Environment*. Orlando, FL: Academic Press.

Ferguson, R. B. (2000). The causes and origins of "primitive warfare": On evolved motivations for war. *Anthropological Quarterly*, 73(3), 159–164.

Ferguson, R. B. (2013). Pinker's list: Exaggerating prehistoric war mortality. In D. P. Fry, ed., *War, Peace, and Human Nature: The Convergence of Evolutionary and Cultural Views*. New York, NY: Oxford University Press, pp. 112–150.

Ferguson, R. B. and Whitehead N. L., eds. (1992). *War in the Tribal Zone: Expanding States and Indigenous Warfare*. Santa Fe, NM: School of American Research Press.

Fry, D. P. (2006). *The Human Potential for Peace: An Anthropological Challenge to Assumptions about War and Violence*. New York, NY: Oxford University Press.

Fry, D. P., ed. (2013). *War, Peace, and Human Nature: The Convergence of Evolutionary and Cultural Views*. New York, NY: Oxford University Press.

Fry, D. P. and Söderberg, P. (2013). Lethal aggression in mobile forager bands and implications for the origins of war. *Science*, 341, 270–273.

Galloway, A., ed. (1999). *Broken Bones: Anthropological Analysis of Blunt Force Trauma*. Springfield, IL: Charles C. Thomas.

Gardner, K. S. (2013). *Diet and Identity among the Ancestral Ohlone: Integrating Stable Isotope Analysis and Mortuary Context at the Yukisma Mound (CA-SCL-38)*. MA thesis, California State University.

Gat, A. (2000). The human motivational complex: Evolutionary theory and the causes of hunter-gatherer fighting. Part 1: Primary somatic and reproductive causes. *Anthropological Quarterly*, **73**, 20–34.

Goman, M., Malamud-Roam, F., and Ingram, B. L. (2008). Holocene environmental history and evolution of a tidal salt marsh in San Francisco Bay, California. *Journal of Coastal Research*, **24**, 1126–1137.

Grady, D. L., Latham, K. A., and Andrushko, V. A. (2001). *Archaeological Investigations at CA-SCL-674, the Rubino Site, San Jose, Santa Clara County, California*. Salinas, CA: Coyote Press Archives of California Prehistory.

Grauer, A. L. and Roberts, C. A. (1996). Paleoepidemiology, healing, and possible treatment of trauma in the medieval cemetery population of St. Helen-on-the-Walls, York, England. *American Journal of Physical Anthropology*, **100**, 531–544.

Griffin, M. C. (2014). Biocultural implications of oral pathology in an ancient Central California population. *American Journal of Physical Anthropology*, **154**, 171–188.

Haas, J., ed. (1990). *The Anthropology of War*. Cambridge: Cambridge University Press.

Hegmon, M., Peeples, M. A., Kinzig, A. P., *et al.* (2008). Social transformation and its human costs in the Prehispanic US Southwest. *American Anthropologist*, **110**, 313–324.

Heizer, R. F. (1978). Introduction. In R. F. Heizer, ed., *Handbook of North American Indians*, vol. 8. Washington, DC: Smithsonian Institution Press, pp. 1–5.

Heizer, R. F. and Whipple, M. A., eds. (1971) *The California Indians: A Source Book*. Berkeley, CA: University of California Press.

Holling, C. S. (1973). Resilience and stability of ecological systems. *Annual Review of Ecology and Systematics*, **4**, 1–23.

Holling, C. S. (1986). The resilience of terrestrial ecosystems: Local surprise and global change. *Sustainable Development of the Biosphere*, **14**, 292–317.

Holling, C. S. (1996). Surprise for science, resilience for ecosystems, and incentives for people. *Ecological Applications*, **6**, 733–735.

Hoover, K. C. and Hudson, M. J. (2016). Resilience in prehistoric persistent hunter-gatherers in northwest Kyushu, Japan as assessed by population health and archaeological evidence. *Quaternary International*, **405**, 22–33.

Hylkema, M. (2002). Tidal marsh, oak woodlands, and cultural fluorescence in the southern San Francisco Bay region. In J. M. Erlandson and T. L. Jones, eds., *Catalysts to Complexity: Late Holocene Societies of the California Coast*. Los Angeles, CA: University of California, Cotsen Institute of Archaeology, pp. 263–281.

Ingram, B. L. and Malamud-Roam, F. (2013). *The West without Water: What Past Floods, Droughts, and Other Climatic Clues Tell Us about Tomorrow*. Berkeley, CA: University of California Press.

James, S. R. and Graziani, S. (1975). California Indian warfare. *Contributions of the University of California Archaeological Research Facility*, **23**, 47–109.

Jones, T. L., Brown, G. M., Raab, L. M., *et al.* (1999). Environmental imperatives reconsidered: Demographic crises in western North America during the Medieval Climatic Anomaly. *Current Anthropology*, **40**, 137–170.

Judd, M. A. (2006). Continuity of interpersonal violence between Nubian communities. *American Journal of Physical Anthropology*, **131**, 324–333.

Jurmain, R. D. (1991). Paleoepidemiology of trauma in a prehistoric central California population. In D. J. Ortner and A. C. Aufderheide, eds., *Human Paleopathology: Current Syntheses and Future Options*. Washington, DC: Smithsonian Institution Press, pp. 241–248.

Jurmain, R. D. (1999). *Stories from the Skeleton: Behavioral Reconstruction in Human Osteology*. Amsterdam: Gordon and Breach.

Jurmain, R. D. (2000). *Analysis of the Human Skeletal Remains from CA-SCL-038*. Technical report, San Jose State University Foundation and Ohlone Families Consulting Services.

Jurmain, R. D. (2001). Paleoepidemiological patterns of trauma in a prehistoric population from central California. *American Journal of Physical Anthropology*, **115**, 13–23.

Jurmain, R. D. and Bellifemine, V. I. (1997). Patterns of cranial trauma in a prehistoric population from central California. *International Journal of Osteoarchaeology*, **7**, 43–50.

Jurmain, R. D. and Kilgore, L. (2007). Skeletal evidence of aggression in humans and African apes: An evolutionary perspective. *American Journal of Physical Anthropology*, **44**, 139.

Jurmain, R., Bartelink, E. J., Leventhal, A., *et al.* (2009). Paleoepidemiological patterns of interpersonal aggression in a prehistoric central California population from CA-ALA-329. *American Journal of Physical Anthropology*, **139**, 462–473.

Keeley, L. H. (1996). *War before Civilization: The Myth of the Peaceful Savage*. Oxford: Oxford University Press.

Kelly, R. C. (2000). *Warless Societies and the Origin of War*. Ann Arbor, MI: University of Michigan Press.

Kelly, R. L. (2013). *The Lifeways of Hunter-Gatherers: The Foraging Spectrum*. Cambridge: Cambridge University Press.

Kennett, D. J., Lambert, P. M., Johnson, J. R., and Culleton, B. J. (2013). Sociopolitical effects of bow and arrow technology in prehistoric coastal California. *Evolutionary Anthropology: Issues, News, and Reviews*, **22**, 124–132.

King, T. F. (1974). The evolution of status ascription around San Francisco Bay. In L. J. Bean and T. F. King, eds., *Antap: California Indian Political and Economic Organization*. Ramona, CA: Ballena Press, pp. 35–53.

Knauft, B. M. (1991). Violence and sociality in human evolution. *Current Anthropology*, **32**, 391–428.

Kroeber, A. E. (1925). *Handbook of the Indians of California*. New York, NY: Dover Publications.

Kroeber, A. E. (1932). *The Patwin and Their Neighbors*. Berkeley, CA: University of California Press, pp. 253–423.

Kroeber, A. E. (1936). Prospects in California prehistory. *American Antiquity*, **2**, 108–116.

Kroeber, A. E. (1939). *Cultural and Natural Areas of Native North America*. Berkeley, CA: University of California Press, pp. 1–240.

Lambert, P. M. (1993). Health in prehistoric populations of the Santa Barbara Channel Islands. *American Antiquity*, **58**, 509–22.

Lambert, P. M. (1994). *War and Peace on the Western Front: A Study of Violent Conflict and its Correlates in Prehistoric Hunter-Gatherer Societies of Coastal Southern California*. PhD dissertation, University of California, Santa Barbara.

Lambert, P. M. (1997). Patterns of violence in prehistoric hunter-gatherer societies of coastal Southern California. In D. L. Martin and D. W. Frayer, eds., *Troubled Times: Violence and Warfare in the Past*. Amsterdam: Gordon and Breach, pp. 77–109.

Lambert, P. M. (2002). The archaeology of war: A North American perspective. *Journal of Archaeological Research*, **10**, 207–241.

Lambert, P. M. (2007). Ethnographic and linguistic evidence for the origins of human trophy taking in California. In R. J. Chacon and D. H. Dye, eds., *The Taking and Displaying of Human Body Parts as Trophies by Amerindians*. New York, NY: Springer, pp. 65–89.

Lambert, P. M. and Walker, P. L. (1991). Physical anthropological evidence for the evolution of social complexity in coastal Southern California. *Antiquity*, **65**, 963–973.

LeBlanc, S. A. (2007). Why warfare? Lessons from the past. *Daedalus*, **136**, 13–21.

Leventhal, A. (1993). *A Reinterpretation of Some San Francisco Bay Mound Sites: A View from the Mortuary Complex from Prehistoric Site CA-ALA-329, the Ryan Mound*. MA thesis, California State University.

Levy, R. (1978). Costanoan. In R. F. Heizer, ed., *Handbook of North American Indians*, vol. 8. Washington, DC: Smithsonian Institution Press, pp. 485–495.

Lightfoot, K. G. and Luby, E. M. (2002). Late Holocene in the San Francisco Bay area: Temporal trends in the use and abandonment of shell mounds in the East Bay. In J. M. Erlandson and T. L. Jones, eds., *Catalysts to Complexity: Late Holocene Societies of the California Coast*. Los Angeles, CA: Cotsen Institute of Archaeology, pp. 263–281.

Lightfoot, K. G. and Parrish, O. (2009). *California Indians and Their Environment: An Introduction*. Berkeley, CA: University of California Press.

Lightfoot, K. G., Luby, E. M., and Pesnichak, L. (2011). Evolutionary typologies and hunter-gatherer research: Rethinking the mounded landscapes of central California. In K. E. Sassamanan and D. H. Holly Jr., eds., *Hunter-Gatherer Archaeology as Historical Process*. Tuscon, AZ: University of Arizona Press, pp. 55–78.

Lovell, N. C. (1997). Trauma analysis in paleopathology. *Yearbook of Physical Anthropology*, **40**, 139–70.

Lovell, N. C. (2008). Analysis and interpretation of skeletal trauma. In M. A. Katzenberg and S. R. Saunders, eds., *Biological Anthropology of the Human Skeleton*. 2nd edn. Hoboken, NJ: Wiley-Liss, pp. 341–386.

Luby, E. M. and Gruber, M. F. (1999). The dead must be fed: Symbolic meanings of the shellmounds of the San Francisco Bay area. *Cambridge Archaeological Journal*, **9**, 95–108.

Luby, E. M., Drescher, C. D., and Lightfoot, K. G. (2006). Shell mounds and mounded landscapes in the San Francisco Bay area: An integrated approach. *The Journal of Island and Coastal Archaeology*, **1**, 191–214.

Malamud-Roam, F., Dettinger, M., Ingram, B. L., Hughes, M. K., and Florsheim, J. L. (2007). Holocene climates and connections between the San Francisco Bay estuary and its watershed: A review. *San Francisco Estuary and Watershed Science*, **5**(1), http://repositories.cdlib.org/jmie/sfews/vol5/iss1/art3.

Martin, D. L. and Frayer D. W., eds. (1997). *Troubled Times: Violence and Warfare in the Past*. Amsterdam: Gordon and Breach.

Martin, D. L. and Harrod, R. P. (2015). Bioarchaeological contributions to the study of violence. *American Journal of Physical Anthropology*, **156**(S59), 116–145.

McAnany, P. A. and Yoffee, N., eds. (2009). *Questioning Collapse: Human Resilience, Ecological Vulnerability, and the Aftermath of Empire*. Cambridge: Cambridge University Press.

McCorkle, T. (1978). Intergroup conflict. In: R. F. Heizer, ed., *Handbook of North American Indians*, vol. 8. Washington, DC: Smithsonian Institution Press, pp. 694–700.

Merriam, C. H. (1955). Tribes of the Wintoon stock. In: J. A. Bennyhoff, E. W. Gifford, A. L. Kroeber, and T. D. McCown, eds., *Studies of the California Indians*. Berkeley, CA: University of California Press, pp. 3–25.

Milliken, R. (1995). *A Time of Little Choice: The Disintegration of Tribal Culture in the San Francisco Bay Area, 1769–1810*. Menlo Park, CA: Ballena Press.

Milliken, R. T. and Bennyhoff, J. A. (1993). Temporal changes in beads as prehistoric California grave goods. In G. White, P. Mikkelsen, W. R. Hildebrandt, and M. E. Basgall, eds., *There Grows a Green Tree: Papers in Honor of David A. Fredrickson*. Davis, CA: University of California, Davis, pp. 381–395.

Milliken, R., Fitzgerald, R. T., Hylkema, M. G., *et al.* (2007). Punctuated culture change in the San Francisco Bay area. In T. L. Jones and K. Klar, eds., *California Prehistory: Colonization, Culture and Complexity*. Walnut Creek, CA: AltaMira Press, pp. 99–123.

Milner, G. R., Anderson, E., and Smith, V. G. (1991). Warfare in late prehistoric west-central Illinois. *American Antiquity*, **56**, 581–603.

Moratto, M. J. (1984). *California Archaeology*. New York, NY: Academic Press.

Musladin, A., Leventhal, A., Morley, S., Jurmain, R. D., and Calleri, D. (1996). Evidence of specialized burial treatment: An osteological sub-study. In R. Cambra, ed., *Archaeological Investigations at Kapahn UMUX (Three Wolves) Site, CA-SCL-732*. Sonoma, CA: Northwest Information Center, Sonoma State University, pp. 5.1–5.20.

Nechayev, I. (2007). *A Bioarchaeological Study of Health in the Prehistoric Population from CA-Ala-329*. MA thesis, San Jose State University.

Nelson, J. S. (1997). *Interpersonal Violence in Prehistoric Northern California: A Bioarchaeological Approach*. MA thesis, California State University.

Otterbein, K. F., ed. (1994). *Feuding and Warfare: Selected Works of Keith F. Otterbein*. Amsterdam: Gordon and Breach.

Owsley, D., Berryman, H. E., and Bass, W. M. (1977). Demographic and osteological evidence for intertribal warfare at the Larson Site (39WW2), Walworth County, South Dakota. *Plains Anthropologist*, **22**, 119–131.

Pastron, A. G., Clewlow, C. W. J., and Atkinson, P. T. (1973). Aboriginal warfare in northern California: Preliminary observations from skeletal material. *The Masterkey*, **47**, 136–142.

Pilloud, M. A., Schwitalla, A. W., and Jones, T. L. (2014). The bioarchaeological record of cranio-facial trauma in central California. In M. W. Allen and T. L. Jones, eds., *Violence and Warfare among Hunter-Gatherers*. New York, NY: Routledge, pp. 257–272.

Pinker, S. (2011). *The Better Angels of Our Nature: The Decline of Violence in History and Its Causes*. New York, NY: Viking.

Redman, C. L. (2005). Resilience theory in archaeology. *American Anthropologist*, **107**, 70–77.

Rosenthal, J. (2011). The function of shell bead exchange in central California. In R. E. Hughes, ed., *Perspectives on Prehistoric Trade and Exchange in California and the Great Basin*. Salt Lake City, UT: University of Utah Press, pp. 83–113.

Schulz, P. D. (1981). *Osteoarchaeology and Subsistence Change in Prehistoric Central California*. PhD dissertation, University of California, Davis.

Schwitalla, A. W., Jones, T. L., Pilloud, M. A., Codding, B. F., and Wiberg, R. S. (2014a). Violence among foragers: The bioarchaeological record from central California. *Journal of Anthropological Archaeology*, **33**, 66–83.

Schwitalla, A. W., Jones, T. L., and Wiberg, R. (2014b). Archaic violence in western North America: The bioarchaeological record of dismemberment, human bone artifacts, and trophy skulls from central California. In M. W. Allen and T. L. Jones, eds., *Violence and Warfare among Hunter-Gatherers*. Walnut Creek, CA: Left Coast Press, pp. 273–295.

Simons, D. D. (1992). Prehistoric mammal exploitation in the San Francisco Bay area. In T. Jones, ed., *Essays on the Prehistory of Maritime California*, vol. 10. Davis, CA: Center for Archaeological Research, pp. 73–103.

Smith, M. O. (1997). Osteological indicators of warfare in the Archaic period of the western Tennessee Valley. In D. L. Martin and D. W. Frayer, eds., *Troubled Times: Violence and Warfare in the Past*. Amsterdam: Gordon and Breach, pp. 241–265.

Smith, M. O. (2003). Beyond palisades: The nature and frequency of late prehistoric deliberate violent trauma in Chickamauga Reservoir of east Tennessee. *American Journal of Physical Anthropology*, **121**, 303–318.

Strother, E. C., Price, J., Arrigoni, A., *et al.* (2005). *Data Recovery, Burial Removal and Construction Monitoring at the Canyon Oaks Site (CA-ALA-613/H), Pleasanton, Alameda County, California*, vol. 2: *Human Osteology*. Report on file with the Northwest Information Center, Sonoma State.

Sussman, R. W. (2013). Why the legend of the killer ape never dies: The enduring power of cultural beliefs to distort our view of human nature. In D. P. Fry, ed., *War, Peace, and Human Nature: The Convergence of Evolutionary and Cultural Views*. Oxford: Oxford University Press, pp. 97–111.

Tainter, J. A. (2006). Social complexity and sustainability. *Ecological Complexity*, **3**, 91–103.

Tenney, J. M. (1990). Trauma among early Californians. *Human Evolution*, **5**, 397–401.

Thorpe, I. J. (2003). Anthropology, archaeology, and the origin of warfare. *World Archaeology*, **35**, 145–165.

Turney-High, H. H. (1971). *Primitive War: Its Practice and Concepts*. 2nd edn. Columbia, SC: University of South Carolina.

Walker, B., Holling, C. S., Carpenter, S., and Kinzig, A. (2004). Resilience, adaptability and transformability in social–ecological systems. *Ecology and Society*, **9**, 5.

Walker, P. L. (1986). Porotic hyperostosis in a marine-dependent California Indian population. *American Journal of Physical Anthropology*, **69**, 345–354.

Walker, P. L. (1989). Cranial injuries as evidence of violence in prehistoric Southern California. *American Journal of Physical Anthropology*, **80**, 313–323.

Walker, P. L. (1997). Wife beating, boxing, and broken noses: Skeletal evidence for the cultural patterning of violence. In D. L. Martin and D. W. Frayer, eds., *Troubled Times: Violence and Warfare in the Past*. Amsterdam: Gordon and Breach, pp. 145–163.

Walker, P. L. (2001). A bioarchaeological perspective on the history of violence. *Annual Review of Anthropology*, **30**, 573–596.

Webb, S. (1995). *Palaeopathology of Aboriginal Australians: Health and Disease across a Hunter-Gatherer Continent*. Cambridge: Cambridge University Press.

Wiberg, R. S. (1996). *Archaeological Excavations and Burial Removal at Sites CA-ALA-483, CA-ALA-483 Extension, and CA-ALA-555, Pleasanton, Alameda County, California*. Salinas, CA: Coyote Press.

Wiberg, R. S. (2002). *Archaeological Investigations: Skyport Plaza Phase I (CA-SCL-478), San Jose, Santa Clara County, California*. Report on file, Sonoma State University: Northwest Information Center, California Historical Resources Information System.

Willey, P. and Emerson, T. E. (1993). The osteology and archaeology of the Crow Creek massacre. *Plains Anthropologist*, **38**, 227–269.

Wohlgemuth, E. (2002). Late prehistoric plant resource intensification in the eastern San Francisco Bay area: plant remains from ALA-42 and ALA-555, Pleasanton, California. In S. L. R. Mason and J. G. Hather, eds., *Hunter-Gatherer Archaeobotany: Perspectives from the Northern Temperate Zone*. London: University College London Press, pp. 28–43.

Wohlgemuth, E. (2004). *The Course of Plant Food Intensification in Native Central California*. PhD dissertation, University of California, Davis.

Wrangham, R. W. (1999). Evolution of coalitionary killing. *American Journal of Physical Anthropology*, **110** (S29), 1–30.

Wrangham, R. W. and Peterson, D. (1996). *Demonic Males: Apes and the Origins of Human Violence*. New York, NY: Houghton Mifflin.

13 The Discovery and Rapid Demise of the Sadlermiut

Charles F. Merbs

13.1 Introduction

13.1.1 First Contact

Unlike the Inuit of Greenland, who came into contact with the Norse as early as CE 1000, or those of Baffinland, who first encountered English seamen in 1576, the first recorded Sadlermiut–European contact did not take place until the early nineteenth century. George F. Lyon (1825), Captain of HMS *Gripper*, reported that on August 27, 1824, while sailing along the south shore of Coats Island (which was thought to be Southampton Island) in northern Hudson Bay, loud shouting was heard on the shore and seven "natives" were seen following along the water's edge. While still a mile from the beach, "a native was seen coming off to us, and as he approached, we observed, that instead of a canoe he was seated on three inflated seal-skins, connected most ingeniously by blown intestines, so that his vessel was extremely buoyant" (Lyon, 1825: 54–55). The man's name was recorded as *Nee-a-kood-loo*, and this contact with the crew of the *Gripper* is the first known contact between Europeans and the Canadian Inuit group known as the Sadlermiut (Figure 13.1).

Although more accurate spellings based on Inuktitut pronunciation have been proposed, to avoid confusion this chapter will use the Sadlermiut spelling. The name is derived from the Inuktitut language, *Sadler* (or *Saglirn*) referring to a place and *miut* translating as "the people of that place." The place name here refers to Southampton Island, the large (15 913 square miles; 41 214 square kilometers) triangular island that forms the northern boundary of Hudson Bay. The homeland of the Sadlermiut was the southern part of this island, along with Walrus Island, Bencas Island, and Coats Island to the south (Figure 13.2).

With the beginning of commercial whaling in northwestern Hudson Bay in 1860 (Keenleyside, 1990), opportunities for contact increased. However, during 40 years of whaling and approximately 120 voyages into Hudson Bay, contacts between whalers and the Sadlermiut amounted to a half-dozen brief encounters. "Most of the whalers operated within sight of Southampton Island and wintered within a day's sail, but their bases and winter harbours were located along the mainland coast between Marble Island and Lyon Inlet rather than on the west coast of Southampton Island, which offered no safe anchorages" (Ross, 1977: 3). It must also be noted, however, that whaling was a highly competitive business and knowledge was not always shared. Also, the maps of the period were inaccurate, indicating that Southampton Island and Coats Island were a single island, directing ships around the southern

Figure 13.1 Nee-a-kood-loo paddling out for the first Sadlermiut meeting with Europeans in 1824. Etching by Captain C. B. Lyon, image used courtesy of the John Carter Brown Library, Brown University.

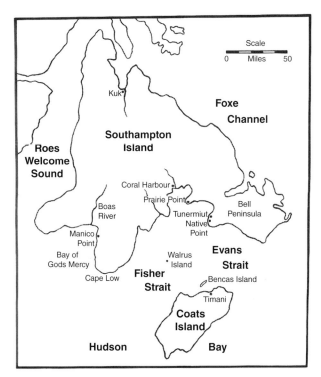

Figure 13.2 Map of Southampton Island.

coast of Coats Island instead of through the broad passage now known as Evans Strait (eastern end) and Fisher Strait (western end) that separates the islands. The first map to accurately show the two as separate islands as well as the presence of Coral Harbour on Southampton Island did not appear until 1910 (Comer, 1910). This map error effectively kept Euro-American whalers well away from the primary homeland of the Sadlermiut, thus preserving isolation between the two populations. The Sadlermiut may also have avoided contact: "They seem to have made no efforts to attract passing ships or boats" (Ross, 1977: 3).

Geography and ice conditions in Roes Welcome Sound, which separates Southampton Island from the mainland to the west, also isolated the Sadlermiut. According to Ferguson (1938: 43), when the whaling schooner *Abbie Bradford* approached the west coast of Southampton Island on September 8, 1878, and people were sighted, "An Eskimo, who was on board with us, said that he did not know of any natives being there." According to Miktok Bruce, an elderly Enuk who lived at Native Point between 1920 and 1940, "No one else – none of the mainland Inuit – knew they were here until the whalers came" (Pelly, 1987: 30). Comer (1910) related a story told by the mainland Aivillingmiut, that during a winter when the ice stretched firmly across from the island to the mainland, a party of five Southampton Island natives walked over to the mainland. Typically the strong currents of Roes Welcome Sound make this impossible. The story gains credence when during this visit one of the Sadlermiut saw a ground squirrel, sitting on a rock, which began to chatter, causing the individual to run and hide. Having never seen any of these animals, the man thought that it was one of the guardian spirits of the local Inuit. The mainlanders further relate that these Sadlermiut then returned to Southampton Island, and, as far as these local people knew, this was the first and only contact between Sadlermiut and mainland Inuit.

13.1.2   Biocultural Context and Cultural Isolation

The Sadlermiut were so much an exception to the cultural uniformity in the region that articles about these communities evoked titles such as "Vanished Mystery Men of Hudson Bay" (Collins, 1956), "The Mysterious Sadlermiut" (Taylor, 1959), and "Sadlermiut Mystery" (Pelly, 1987). The neighboring Aivillingmiut and Igloolingmiut who worked for the whalers were well aware of the cultural distinctiveness of these islanders (Taylor, 1959: 30). The Sadlermiut appear similar to the Central Arctic Thule ancestors of the contemporary Inuit, but some distinctive differences are evident. The Sadlermiut flaked blade tools out of chert instead of slate and fashioned lamps out of limestone instead of soapstone (steatite). The Sadlermiut developed a unique style of harpoon heads and a tool exclusive to the culture – a scraper made from the mandible of a polar bear (Figure 13.3). Sadlermiut men wore trousers made from polar bear hides and their hair was piled into a ball at the top of the head. The first artifact found by the author in 1959 was a small ivory object known as a *tingmiuyak*, or bird-like figure. Although this common Thule artifact, probably a gaming piece, is usually in the shape of a bird, human shapes have been found. The shoulders and

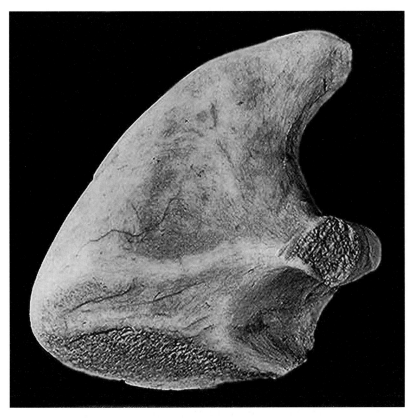

Figure 13.3 Polar bear mandible scraper, from Burial PP-2, Prairie Point, Southampton Island.

head identify this *tingmiuyak* as human, and the knob on top of the head suggests it was a male Sadlermiut (Figure 13.4).

Unlike the Thule, the Sadlermiut used stones to build inverted cone-shaped meat-drying racks (Figure 13.5). The Sadlermiut used stone tombs to bury their dead, like the Thule, but with some interesting variations. This includes often extending the body rather than flexing it, and orienting the body to the east rather than to the northeast or southwest like the Thule. The Sadlermiut constructed stone and sod winter homes like the Thule, but these houses were built from ground level rather than below ground (Figure 13.6). Taylor (1960) also notes other differences between Thule and Sadlermiut winter houses. The lack of slate tools and limestone lamps reflects the absence of these two materials on Southampton Island, and the isolation of the Sadlermiut prevented trade of these materials onto the island. Some of the other items mentioned, such as stone graves and winter houses, have a Thule origin but developed a distinctive Sadlermiut pattern in isolation.

The other theory is that the Sadlermiut were essentially Dorset, a Paleo-Eskimo population who took refuge on Southampton Island after being replaced across the Central Arctic by Thule Culture migrants from Alaska. Dorset sites are prominent at

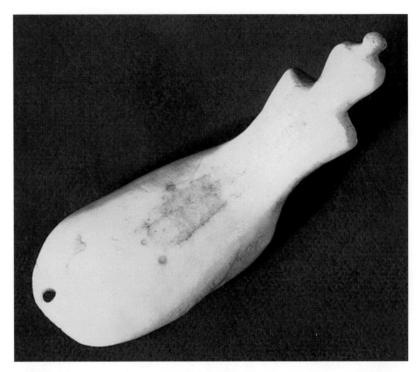

Figure 13.4 Ivory *tingmiuyak* (bird-like figure) in human form with hair in a topknot, the style worn by Sadlermiut men, from Burial PP-2, Prairie Point, Southampton Island.

Figure 13.5 Sadlermiut-style stone drying rack and the author at Timani, Coats Island.

Figure 13.6 Sadlermiut winter house at Timani, Coats Island.

Native Point. This theory, first proposed by Frederica de Laguna and supported by Henry Collins (1957), appears to be based largely on harpoon head style and winter houses on Walrus Island, which are Sadlermiut in style but contain some Dorset artifacts. However, the presence of Dorset artifacts in a Sadlermiut context must be approached with caution. Two of the graves at Native Point that are clearly late Sadlermiut contained Dorset artifacts. NP-199 of the Meat Cache Series, an infant burial, contained a small ivory harpoon head with the line hole gouged out in Dorset fashion. The Sadlermiut, like the Thule, drilled their holes. NP-131, also an infant burial, included two small triangular points, clearly of Dorset origin, and a larger point that has been tentatively identified as Pre-Dorset (M.A.P. Renouff, personal communication, 2007). It must be assumed that these artifacts were found by the Sadlermiut, recognized as distinctive, possibly the work of ancient people, and retained as talismans.

The Dorset issue is confused by the contemporary Inuit, who referred to the Sadlermiut as Tunit and the community at Native Point as Tunermiut. Inuit folklore includes many accounts of the Tunit, the people who occupied the Canadian Arctic before the arrival of Thule ancestors. The Dorset appear to be the Tunit of Inuit folklore, a people of great physical strength and hunters of the walrus. Despite this strength, the Tunit were remembered as a timid and peaceable people. These characteristics also fit the Sadlermiut, who were also seen as old-fashioned, still living in stone and sod winter houses, and using stone tools. However, when asked about

Tunit ancestry by other Inuit, the Sadlermiut are said to have replied "We have only heard of Tooniks; we are not Tooniks," but the Inuit were not convinced (Pitseolak and Eber, 1975: 33).

The Lake Site (KkHh-2), located on an old beach ridge approximately 4 km north of the Tunermiut site and approximately 0.5 km from the shore of Native Bay, may hold some clues as to the origin of the Sadlermiut. Present at this site are eight house ruins, two of which, H2 and H5, were excavated by Brenda Clark in 1977. These houses appear more Thule than Sadlermiut in appearance and construction. House 2 produced C14 dates from samples of land mammal bone ranging between CE 1325 and 1540 (Clark, 1980: 57). A single typical "spade-shaped" Sadlermiut point was found among the assemblage. Also recovered were several triangular points that may be of Dorset origin.

Of additional interest in this context are two cone-shaped, tubular ivory artifacts recovered by Mathiassen from a sleeping platform in a house ruin excavated at the Kuk site on Duke of York Bay at the north end of Southampton Island (Mathiassen, 1927: 230). Both objects have carved animal heads, which Mathiassen thought might be dogs. Maxwell (1985) identified these artifacts as shaman's tubes, with carved bear heads and skeletal engraving, and unquestionably Dorset. A typical limestone lamp of the type made and used by the Sadlermiut was also recovered (Mathiassen, 1927).

McGhee (1996: 233) states emphatically that the Sadlermiut culture "was firmly based in the Inuit tradition, and there is little reason to think of them as a remnant Dorset people." But he adds: "To the Inuit who inherited the Arctic, Paleo-Eskimos almost certainly contributed some small component of heredity. From the memories of stolen wives and adopted orphans, some minor elements of the Dorset language, culture, and view of the world may have been incorporated into those of the Inuit people." Park (1993), however, questions whether face-to-face contact between Dorset and Inuit ever took place, and contends that salvage was the sole means of contact and transfer of technology between these cultures.

Utermohle and Merbs (1979) used cranial measurements and Penrose's shape component to determine the biological relationship of the Sadlermiut to other Eskimo-Aleut and related skeletal series ranging from Siberian Eskimo and Chukchi, Aleuts and Koniags in the west and to northeast Greenlanders in the east. The Sadlermiut were found to cluster with eastern Inuit, specifically Thule-Historic Inuit from the Hudson Bay sites of Naujan, Kamarvik, and Silumiut, as well as Inuit from Labrador and northeast Greenland. The closest affinity was a cluster representing the Mackenzie Inuit from western Canada and the prehistoric Birnirk and Inugsuk from northern Alaska. The most distant were series representing northern Alaskans from Point Hope and Point Barrow, Koniags, Aleuts, and Siberian Eskimos and Chukchi. Within the eastern Inuit cluster, the Sadlermiut most closely resemble the northeast Greenlanders. Although this study confirms a basic Thule biological identity for the Sadlermiut, it suffers from an absence of Dorset crania for comparison.

13.1.3 Sadlermiut Language and Cultural Isolation

Since the Inuktitut language is spoken by Inuit over a vast distance, from the west central coast of Alaska to Greenland, it is likely that the Sadlermiut, who occupied a central position in this range, also spoke Inuktitut. A number of references pertaining to the Sadlermiut language do exist, but these references are confusing and somewhat contradictory. In the 1824 meeting with *Nee-a-kood-loo* on Coats Island, George Lyon (1825: 56) says "He understood me a little, and used a few words with which I was acquainted, yet he spoke a language differing very materially from that of any other Esquimau whom we had seen." During the September 1878 encounter of the *Abbie Bradford* with Sadlermiut along the west coast of Southampton Island, Ferguson (1938: 43) says, "Our Eskimo tried to talk to them, but they could not understand him, nor could he understand a word of their tongue." When they met again in June of 1888, Ferguson (1938: 156) says: "When they saw us they swarmed around and tried to talk to us, but we could not make out one word of their language," despite the fact that he was familiar with several Inuktitut dialects in the region.

In July 1896, boat crews from the American whaling schooner *Era*, captained by George Comer, encountered Sadlermiut south of Manico Point on Southampton Island (Ross, 1977). Comer records that the Aivillingmiut who manned the *Era*'s boats were able to understand the language of the strangers. These Inuit were Aivillingmiut from Repulse Bay, not more than 100 miles distant. Comer concluded that while the dialect was similar to that of the Aivillingmiut, the intonation was quite different. The Sadlermiut women grasped meaning much more quickly than did the men (Comer, 1910: 85). Other Inuit referred to the Sadlermiut as talking with baby voices, "unable to pronounce correctly" (Pitseolak and Eber, 1975: 33). Also, some of the words used were different. Two Sadlermiut words that survived were *nakootlik*, a sealskin hand protector for flaking chert tools, and *eetook*, the last rib of a polar bear used for flaking chert (Pitseolak and Eber, 1975: 33–34), objects that were no longer used by contemporaneous Inuit.

13.1.4 Intensification of Subsistence Behavior

Based on information from Aivillingmiut Inuit who lived with the Sadlermiut for a time, Mathiassen presented a picture of the hunting patterns of the Sadlermiut (Mathiassen, 1927). The communities hunted walrus and seal, partly from the ice edge and partly at breathing holes. During the summer the Sadlermiut lived in tents, migrating inland to hunt birds and catch fish. In September, the Sadlermiut hunted caribou at the narrows between Bell Peninsula and the main part of the island as these animals vacated the low-lying peninsula to avoid mosquitoes. As the lakes and rivers froze over at the end of September the Sadlermiut moved back into winter settlements.

The southern coast of Southampton Island is rich in marine resources today and the same appears to have been true during prehistoric times. Some impression of the intensive nature of marine resource exploitation is demonstrated by the 6538 mammal bones retrieved by Collins and Taylor during 1954 and 1956 field seasons at Tunermiut (Taylor, 1960). The largest number, 49.8 percent, were from small seals (*Phoca hispida*), followed by caribou (*Rangifer tarandus*) at 23.8 percent, walrus (*Odobenus rosmarus*) at 10.0 percent, and large seals (*Erignathus barbatus*) at 7.1 percent. The caribou remains were primarily ribs. Polar bear bones (*Ursus maritimus*) made up 1.5 percent, and whale (*Balaena mysticetus*) comprised 1.4 percent. A piece of narwhal (*Monodon monoceros*) tusk was also found. Dogs (or wolves) were represented by 260 bones (3.9 percent) and foxes (*Vulpes lagopus*) by 111 bones (1.7 percent). The Sadlermiut used dogs to pull sleds, as did the Thule and present-day Inuit. The Dorset may have had dogs, but do not appear to have used these animals for transportation. Foxes were used for clothing, primarily trim (Ferguson, 1938: 157), and a large number of perforated fox canines were found in an infant burial at Tunermiut. The Sadlermiut diet included fish (Lyon, 1825: 58) and birds (Mathiassen, 1927: 269), and the absence of these assemblages at Tunermiut probably reflects seasonality. Bird bones were found in two of the caches that had been used for infant burials, the infant skeleton in each case resting on top of the bird bones. The Sadlermiut diet likely included little if any plant food.

13.2   Mortuary Practices

The skeletal remains that produced the observations recorded in this report were recovered from Tunermiut, the primary settlement site of the Sadlermiut, by Henry B. Collins between 1954 and 1955 and William S. Laughlin along with the author in 1959 (Figure 13.7). Collins excavated 36 graves, but information is available for only 30 graves. Three of these contained a second individual, in each case an infant, bringing the total from Collins's excavation to 33 individuals. Merbs and Laughlin excavated another 135 burials at Tunermiut, eight containing a second individual, for a total of 143 individuals. One of these double graves contained an adult male and an adult female; the second individual in the other seven was an infant. The total number of individuals available for study in the Tunermiut series is thus 176, not counting various skeletal parts found scattered around the site. This includes 66 infants, 6 children, 7 adolescents, 53 adult females, 42 adult males, and 2 adults of undetermined sex. Some of the studies referenced here were carried out exclusively on the Merbs–Laughlin series before it was joined with the Collins series. Although Tunermiut is located approximately three miles north of the geographical feature known as Native Point, field burial numbers simply carry the prefix NP (Merbs–Laughlin) or NPC (Collins). Six burials were recovered by the author from the Sadlermiut site at Prairie Point, approximately 23 miles northwest of Native Point. Those burials carry the prefix PP.

The typical Sadlermiut grave consisted of a surface structure constructed of limestone rocks. Occasionally caribou antler or whale rib were used to support the roof stones. The skeleton was usually found lying on a natural gravel or loose rock

Figure 13.7 Air photo of the Tunermiut area, Southampton Island: A = Sadlermiut winter house area; B = southwest (main) meat cache area; C = northeast meat cache area; D = T1 Dorset site.

surface, often partially buried by 5–30 cm of dark humus. In several instances the floor had been paved with flat pieces of stone. Most graves showed varying degrees of disturbance, ranging from some movement of roof stones to complete removal of all roof stones. A thick turf of vegetation, which was detrimental to skeletal preservation, was found in graves where the roof had been removed. In most instances, the grave was a primary structure, built specifically to house the dead, but in many cases these structures were initially used as meat caches, being converted into graves as necessity required. The original function of these structures was belied by shape, round rather than oval or rectangular, and animal bones that were left behind when the conversion took place. Some grave structures had been dismantled, probably so the rocks could be used elsewhere, such as in house construction. One grave structure had been converted into a fox trap and several were used as tombs by later Inuit. Some of this dismantling and converting appears to have been done by the Sadlermiut; some was clearly done by later Inuit. Several subsurface graves were also found and it is likely that these had originally been constructed as caches before being converted into graves.

Although Sadlermiut burials resembled Thule-Historic Inuit burials, such as those at Kamarvik and Silumiut on the west shore of Roes Welcome Sound, several significant differences were observed. Unlike the Thule-Historic Inuit graves, which are typically short to accommodate a flexed body, Sadlermiut graves were often longer, with many skeletons in an extended position. The extended individuals were more often males and in general appeared to be more recent. The head orientation of the Thule-Historic Inuit graves presented a bimodal pattern, with graves tending to be oriented to the northeast or southwest quadrants of the compass, males more often to the northeast, females to the southwest. Head orientation of the Sadlermiut graves was heavily toward the east half of the compass, with no obvious sex difference. Some differences in quality of grave construction were noted for the Sadlermiut, with adult males receiving the best construction, followed by adult females; infants received the least attention, in some cases the body simply being placed in an unaltered meat cache on top of animal remains. Among the Thule-Historic Inuit, these age–sex categories received approximately equal attention. Many of the Thule-Historic Inuit graves had a head marker consisting of a white rock, limestone or quartz, that stood out in sharp contrast to the dark stones of the grave structure. Sadlermiut graves contained no recognizable head marker. It should, however, be noted that graves were actually constructed of limestone, making it necessary to choose some other method for demarcating the head.

Although many of the grave structures show signs of disturbance and may have been subjected to looting, the skeletons recovered, other than those of infants, were generally in good condition and relatively complete. Infant remains were often more poorly preserved owing to reduced cortical density, and incomplete because the grave floors in some areas consisted of a deep deposit of old beach rocks, where bones might be lost. In addition, lemmings, which had established residency in some of the graves, appear to have removed small bones for nesting (Merbs, 1962).

13.3   Bioarchaeological Indicators of Subsistence Intensification

13.3.1   The Dentition

Teeth were free of carious lesions, probably due to the absence of carbohydrates and sticky foods in the Sadlermiut diet. However, remarkable frequencies of enamel pressure chipping and antemortem tooth loss are present in this group. Chipping is distinguished from enamel breakage that occurs after death by signs of wear along the broken edges. Pressure chipping appears to be associated with a diet rich in frozen meat and bones. The great force generated by the Sadlermiut when masticating this food and other objects, resulted in the enamel and dentine of the tooth crown being subjected to minor and even major crushing, fracturing, and splintering, in addition to attrition and abrasion (Turner and Cadien, 1969: 303). Chipping was found in 72.7 percent of Sadlermiut aged 6–20 years, which increased to 91.1 percent in individuals aged 21 years and older ($p = 0.305$). Females had slightly more chipping than males, 81.9 percent to 77.8 ($p = 0.307$) and greater tooth wear than males (Wood, 1992).

Hrdlička (1940) published a study of anterior tooth loss in more than 8000 skulls in which he noted a high frequency of this feature in Arctic groups. Based on seven specific criteria he attributed the tooth loss to ritual ablation. Using Hrdlička's own criteria, Merbs (1968, 1983) demonstrated that the loss was due to trauma produced by unusually intense tooth use. Ethnographic accounts indicate that anterior teeth were very important to the Inuit, serving as a third hand for both men and women (Hayes, 1885; Nansen, 1893; de Poncins, 1941).

Intense tooth use for males "lies in grasping objects while the hands are otherwise occupied. The function is thus analogous to that performed by a vise or pliers, tools not present in the Eskimo's otherwise well-developed tool kit" (Merbs, 1983: 145). The strength may be slight, as when a fish is held in the teeth while another is being pursued by a leister (de Poncins, 1941: 39), or increasingly greater, as when a bird's head is crushed (Hayes, 1885: 128), a seal is towed behind a kayak (Nansen, 1890: 406), lines are tightened or untied (Birket-Smith, 1928; de Poncins, 1941), the bit of a bow drill is grasped in the teeth (Lyon, 1824), wooden kayak ribs are bent into shape (Hylander, 1977), seal bones are cracked (de Poncins, 1941), or the cover of a gasoline drum is pried off (de Poncins, 1941). A crude bone shaft, blackened at one end, apparently used as a bow drill shaft, was actually found in a Sadlermiut burial NP-9 that contained the skeletons of an adult male and an adult female.

Inuit females have been observed using teeth to prepare skins for clothing (Lyon, 1824; Nansen, 1893; Steensby, 1910), soften boot soles (Hall, 1865; Tyrrell, 1908), tear sinew for thread (Lyon, 1824), and extract blubber for lamps (Boas, 1888; Hall, 1865; Lyon, 1824). Of course anterior teeth are also engaged when eating highly abrasive and tough food, and thus pressure chipping of enamel is also possible to interpret within the context of diet.

The highest rates of incisor tooth loss in the eight Arctic and Subarctic groups studied by Hrdlička (1940) were found in Paleo-Aleut: 21 percent for maxillary and 18 percent for mandibular incisors in females, and 23 percent for maxillary and 3 percent for mandibular incisors in males. The Sadlermiut rates were even higher than those of the Paleo-Aleuts: 41 percent for maxillary and 17 percent for mandibular incisors in females, and 28 percent for maxillary and 4 percent for mandibular incisors in males (Merbs, 1983). Both sexes among the Sadlermiut show greater loss on the left side, but the difference is more pronounced in males, 19 percent to 13 percent, than in the females, 30 percent to 28 percent. One of the criteria used by Hrdlička to identify ritual ablation is that it takes place at a particular age, as part of a "coming of age" ceremony, but among the Sadlermiut the percentage of missing anterior teeth simply accumulated with age, going from 0 percent in the 12–18 years category, 44 percent in the 19–30-years category, 79 percent in the 31–40 years category, and 100 percent in individuals 41 years and over (Merbs, 1983).

13.3.2 Traumatic Injury

The Sadlermiut thrived in a harsh and dangerous environment and engaged in intensive subsistence activities. As a consequence, traumatic injuries associated with this landscape and lifestyle are often found. Three individuals experienced a fracture of the body of the sternum – two adult females (PP-1, NPC-36) and an adult male (NP-43A). In each case the fracture occurred toward the superior end of the bone, at approximately the border between the first and second sternebrae. In another adult male (NP-62) the cartilage of the right first rib ossified, fractured, and was in the process of healing when the individual died (Merbs, 1983). A healed fracture was observed in the right second and third ribs, approximately 30 mm from the chondro-costal border. The affected individual was a middle-aged adult female (NP-193).

A fracture of the spinous process of the seventh cervical vertebra in an adult male (NPC-31) healed but failed to unite. The terminal portion was not recovered. This kind of fracture is referred to as a "shoveler's fracture" and is often associated with lifting and tossing heavy objects. Although it may result from a blow to the upper back, it is more likely associated with avulsive force.

Five fractures of the clavicle were observed in the Tunermiut Sadlermiut series, three involving the left side and two the right. In all three left-side cases, two older adult females (NP-72 and NP-193) and a young adult male (NP-177), the fracture occurred in the midshaft. In the case of NP-72, some rotation had taken place between the separated parts before fusion occurred, resulting in degenerative changes at the articulation with the scapula (acromion) (Merbs, 1983). The two fractures of the right clavicle involved young males (NP-3 and NP-33), with the fracture occurring nearer the acromial end. A midshaft fracture of the left humerus was observed in a young male (NP-68) and a wrist (Colles) fracture of the left radius in an older adult male (NP-59). Both had healed with little distortion of the affected bone. Phalanges were recovered too infrequently to support meaningful observations, but a proximal right phalanx had sustained a diagonal fracture (Merbs, 1983). The Sadlermiut series contains several examples of traumatic injury involving the femur. The most dramatic example involves the head and neck of the left femur from a middle-aged adult male (NPC-31). This condition results from slipping of the femoral head epiphysis and occurs more commonly in males, usually during the teenage years. The primary injury is a stress fracture between the metaphyseal side of the growth plate and the neck of the femur (Ortner, 2003). This allows downward displacement of the femoral head and sometimes aseptic necrosis in the epiphyseal bone. Because the growth plate stays with the epiphysis, the epiphysis is little altered except through secondary degenerative changes. In this case, those changes include a wide groove that has developed on the superior–posterior surface of the neck and a broad rim of osteophyte that developed on the inferior margin of the head. Animal gnawing has destroyed much of this osteophyte, as well as the extreme proximal end of the bone. The right femur of another young adult male (NP-3) shows signs of trauma with an apparent fracture line approximating the epiphyseal margin of the head. Again, this may be an injury incurred during growth in this region. The distortion incurred in this case is much less severe.

Two individuals, a young adult male (NP-177) and an older female (NP-26), exhibit what appears to be a longitudinal fracture of the femoral shaft, the male in the left femur and the female in the right femur. Such fractures are rare (Bilreiro *et al.*, 2016). Longitudinal fractures are classified as stress or fatigue fractures, depending on whether the bone is otherwise normal or pathological. The associated disease-state is usually osteopenia, or bone mineral loss, a condition demonstrated to be prevalent in these Inuit at an early age. In the two cases noted here, the bone mineral loss may have played a bigger role in the older female (fatigue fracturing), while stress, especially caused by lifting and carrying heavy stones, an activity for which the Sadlermiut were known (Pitseolak and Eber, 1975; Marsh, 1976), is a more likely cause in the younger male.

Another adult male (NPC-20) has a right femur that is extremely bowed and much shorter than the left, with a maximum length of 392 mm compared with 427 mm. The anterior–posterior diameter at midshaft is 41 mm on the pathological right side, compared with 29 mm on the normal left side. This may be the result of a greenstick fracture sustained as a child.

A male judged to have been about 29 years of age (NP-129) suffered a fracture of the left fibula approximately 80 mm from the distal end. The break showed good union with only slight displacement and angulation, but the tibiotalar joint was affected enough to produce severe arthritis compared with this joint on the other side (Merbs, 1983). It is classically known as a Pott's fracture, after Sir Percival Pott who described it in 1765 as a fracture of the fibula associated with dislocation of the tibia. The fracture may be caused by nothing more than a slight twisting of the ankle. However, in 1963 the author met an Eskimo man in the Alaskan village of Alatna who limped very badly because of an ankle fracture sustained years earlier. The fracture occurred when the man lost control of a dog team and was hit in the ankle by the platform of the sled.

A crushing injury involving the right navicular of the foot in a male (NP-43A) approximately 43 years of age resulted in severe osteoarthritis where this bone articulates with the second and third cuneiforms. Two healed metatarsal shaft fractures were observed. One involved the right fourth metatarsal of a young adult male (NPC-17); the other involved the right fifth metatarsal of an older male (NP-167). The distal end of the left fifth metatarsal from a male (NP-112) approximately 27 years of age shows a crushing injury. All of these foot injuries could well have occurred from dropping one of the enormous rocks the Sadlermiut appear to have been so fond of carrying (Marsh, 1976).

13.3.3 Spondylolysis

Spondylolysis, a vertebral condition generally affecting the lower back, has been found to occur with high frequency in Inuit and Aleuts, and the Sadlermiut are no exception. The condition is a type of stress fracture, usually occurring between the superior and inferior articular processes. It is related to erect posture and to unusual stresses placed on the lower back, probably including excessive flexion and extension in this region. The condition first becomes visible in the bone as a stress fracture, then proceeds to full separation. This process was illustrated in Thule-Historic Inuit skeletal remains recovered from sites on the mainland, across Roes Welcome Sound from Southampton Island (Merbs, 1995), but the Sadlermiut collection also contains examples of incomplete separation.

Among the Sadlermiut, 20 individuals ranging in age from 15 to 45 years show evidence of spondylolysis (Merbs, 1983). Evidence for the condition generally occurs with higher frequencies in males, and this is also true of the Sadlermiut, with 12 of 40 males (30 percent) and seven of 52 females (13 percent) affected (Merbs, 2002). The first lumbar vertebra is affected in one case and the second lumbar vertebra in two (Merbs, 1983). In all three the separation is unilateral, which is typical for involvement at this level. In three cases the affected vertebra is a sixth lumbar, which is actually a lumbarized sacral unit, and in two it is the first unit of the sacrum. Spondylolysis of the sacrum was unknown clinically until it was described in 16 Inuit skeletons, eight from Alaska and eight from Canada (Merbs, 1996). Two of the Canadian examples are Sadlermiut, NP-68 and NPC-4. Both were estimated to have been 18–20 years of age, and both are six-unit sacra, the last unit, S6, being a fused caudal vertebra. NP-68 shows complete separation on just the left side of S1; NPC-4 shows partial separation on just the right side of S1 (Merbs, 1983). An interesting feature of spondylolysis is that the stress producing the fracture requires movement between adjacent neural arches. This means that the separation seen in the sacrum occurred while S1 and S2 were still separate, suggesting that this movement occurred during adolescence or late childhood (Merbs, 2002: 363).

Based on a study of incomplete spondylolysis in Thule-Historic Inuit skeletons where more information is available, the developing condition was more likely to occur when an individual was young, during adolescence or early adulthood (Merbs, 1995). Based on the age profile in this study, it would appear some incomplete cases actually heal by middle adulthood.

13.3.4 Vertebral Compression Fractures

Another condition that occurs with high frequency among the Inuit is compression fracturing of vertebral bodies. In the Sadlermiut vertebral column, the distribution of fracturing runs from the third thoracic to the last lumbar vertebrae. In this type of fracture the superior surface of a vertebral body is pressed downward, crushing the body. The process is resisted by the neural arch posteriorly, thus producing a body that is wedge-shaped in cross-section. In the adult Sadlermiut, some degree of body compression was found to have taken place in 9 percent of male vertebrae and 12 percent of female vertebrae (Merbs, 1983). The distribution in the two sexes was quite different, females showing greatest involvement in the mid-thoracic region

(T5–T9) and males in the lower thoracic region (T11–L2). Vertebral compression fracturing was also observed in some children and adolescents (Merbs, 1983). In general, the number of affected vertebrae increased with age.

The primary cause of vertebral compression fracturing in the Inuit is likely riding on sleds. The ride produces exceptional strain on the back, especially as the sled traverses pressure ridges. The high frequency of compression fracturing in the Inuit is in sharp contrast to the low frequency observed in the non-sledding Aleut (Yesner, 1981). The situation is analogous to riding snowmobiles over rough terrain. The result can be "snowmobiler's back," an important feature of which is vertebral compression fracturing (Merbs, 1983; Roberts *et al.*, 1971).

Cores removed from Sadlermiut femora revealed these bones to have thin cortices and increased numbers of secondary osteons, indicators of osteoporosis (Thompson *et al.*, 1985). These results are consistent with those obtained from Inuktitut-speaking Inuit. Higher levels of bone loss correlates with older age in the Sadlermiut series, as does the frequency of vertebral compression fractures. It should be noted, however, that these fractures are of the wedge-shaped variety, not the concertina type more likely to be associated with osteoporosis. A relevant factor may be the relatively short lifespan of these Inuit. Based on osteological indicators, the oldest Sadlermiut female in the series was approximately 55 years of age and the oldest male 45 years of age (Merbs, 1983).

To some extent spondylolysis and compression fracturing may be seen as two different ways bone responds to stress in the lower back. In young individuals with healthy bone, the stress is more likely to produce stress fracturing leading to spondylolysis. In older individuals suffering from osteoporosis it is more likely to produce fatigue (compression) fracturing of vertebral bodies.

13.3.5 Degenerative Joint Disease

Levels of osteoarthritis of diarthrodial joints and degenerative disk disease of the vertebrae are very high in the Sadlermiut skeletons. More interesting, however, is the patterning of these conditions in the population overall and between the sexes. Degenerative disk disease of the vertebral column can be identified through the development of osseous lipping (osteophyte) on the margins of the vertebral bodies. For that reason the condition is often simply referred to as osteophytosis. The pattern in the Sadlermiut, and likely all human groups, closely follows the curvature of the column, occurring with greatest frequency and intensity where the disks experience the greatest stress. That is, vertebral osteophytosis is most often found where the cervical, thoracic, and lumbar curves place these disks at the greatest distance from the more stable midline of the column (Merbs, 1983: 108). The two sexes show approximately equal levels of the condition in the cervical region. In the thoracic region, however, it is more prevalent in females, and in the lumbar region osteophytosis is more prevalent in males. The female pattern resembles that seen for vertebral body compression (Merbs, 1983) with the same activity factors probably responsible,

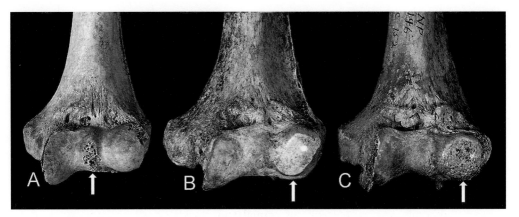

Figure 13.8 Osteoarthritis of the elbow as reflected on the articular surfaces of the humerus. (a) Female (NP-159), trochlear involvement (porosity). (b) Male (NP-43-A), primarily capitular involvement (eburnation). (c) Male (NP-146), more severe involvement of the capitulum (eburnation and exposure of underlying cancellous bone).

primarily carrying a child on the back. An interesting observation, again probably a universal in humans, is that when the disks are treated as joints, that is comparing the occurrence and degree of osteophyte development on the two osseous margins of the vertebra above the disk and the vertebra below, the greatest involvement is seen on the superior margin (inferior margin of the vertebra above) in the thoracic region and the inferior margin (superior margin of the vertebra below) in the lumbar region. The difference is likely purely mechanical, the thoracic curve being convex posteriorly, and the lumbar curve being the opposite (Merbs, 1983: 109).

Indicators of osteoarthritis (degenerative joint disease) in the Sadlermiut skeletons include marginal osteophyte development and articular surface eburnation and are far more prevalent in the joints of the upper limb than those of the lower limb. This pattern opposes that usually seen in modern populations. Affected most frequently in both sexes are the elbow joints, followed in order by those of the shoulder, wrist, pelvis, knee and ankle (Merbs, 1983: 102). The elbow presents an especially interesting dichotomy between males and females. Females show signs of osteoarthritis on the medial margin of the trochlea and males on the capitulum (Figure 13.8). This reflects activity differences, emphasis on flexion–extension at this joint complex by females, as in scraping skins, and pronation–supination by males, as in paddling a kayak or throwing a harpoon. Levels of osteoarthritis are higher in males than females for all joint complexes except the temporomandibular and costovertebral joints, with the difference being much greater at the lower half of the thorax than the upper half (Merbs, 1983: 103). The temporomandibular joint shows more osteoarthritis on the left side than the right. Greater frequencies of osteoarthritis in this joint in females is probably due primarily to chewing animal skins. Like the Inuit today, Sadlermiut women were inclined to hold skin objects with the left hand and use the left side of the dentition for chewing, while leaving the right hand free for precision tasks.

13.3.6   High-Risk Encounters in an Intensive Environment

Polar bears represented an important resource for the Sadlermiut, providing skins for trousers and sleeping mats, bones for chert-knapping tools and the distinctive bear mandible scraper, and meat for dogs as well as humans. Bears are found on all coasts of Southampton Island, but particularly those around Bell Peninsula to the east of Native Bay and the Tunermiut site. The presence of tent rings in these areas suggest the Sadlermiut made special trips during the summer to hunt bears (Bird, 1953). Thule-Historic skeletons from the western mainland of Southampton Island suggest these hunters occasionally became the hunted (Merbs, 1989, 1997), and the Sadlermiut were no exception.

The skeletal remains of an adult woman (NPC-14) excavated from a tent ring at Tunermiut showed evidence of cranial and postcranial trauma consistent with a polar bear attack (Ryan *et al.*, 2014: 493–494). Traumatic lesions in the form of comminuted fractures are present on both femora, the left breaking into three sections and the right into at least four. This type of injury typically requires direct high-energy force. A penetrating crush fracture is located toward the distal end of the right tibia and a round puncture is visible on the radius near the elbow. Fourteen injury loci were located on the cranium, with two more becoming evident during digital analysis (Ryan *et al.*, 2014). A three-dimensional model of the cranium and mandible was then created for better visualization and analysis of the lesions. The authors concluded this woman had indeed been attacked by a polar bear and that a minimum of six separate bites, in a specific chronological order, could account for the number and pattern of the lesions observed (Ryan *et al.*, 2014). No parts of the woman appear to have been consumed by the bear and none of the injuries was judged to have been immediately fatal. Nevertheless, the woman was gravely injured and certainly died as a result of the attack (Ryan *et al.*, 2014: 493–505). The bear was identified as a female or young male.

Another possible bear victim was a male (NP-144), estimated at around 45 years of age. The skeleton was found in a typical stone burial structure, but the presence of a caribou pelvis under the human remains suggest that it had originally served as a meat cache. Bones that were present include an intact skull, seven cervical vertebrae, proximal half of the right humerus, distal two-thirds of the right femur, most of the right patella, two rib fragments, and the distal ends of the left tibia and fibula, along with bones from the ankle and lateral side of the left foot. Although several roof stones appear to have been moved, it is unlikely that the skeleton had been scavenged while in the tomb. The location of the grave in an area that appears to represent the Sadlermiut at an extremely stressful time suggests that this individual was in a weakened state when attacked and largely consumed by a bear, or was scavenged by a bear after death but before burial. As noted in the case of the Thule-Historic Inuit bear victims, even partial remains were given a full grave so as not to insult the soul of the deceased (Merbs, 1997).

13.4   The Decline and Extinction of the Sadlermiut

13.4.1   European Contact

The isolation of the Sadlermiut was first disrupted in 1896 by Captain Comer, who began sending whaleboats on springtime expeditions to Southampton Island (Eber, 1989; Keenleyside, 1990). The following year, Comer established an American whaling station on the island between Manico Point and Cape Low. Contact with the Sadlermiut increased, but was still minimal. The situation changed drastically in 1899 when the Scottish firm of Robert Kinnes and Sons established a whaling station near Cape Low. Three Scots were landed to operate the station along with approximately 150 Inuit, who maintained whaleboats during the summer and trapped foxes in the winter (Ross, 1977). This economic venture did not involve the Sadlermiut, who essentially remained on the periphery of the station's operation during the next three years. Sadlermiut visited from time to time, sometimes joining the station Inuit in games of football (Mathiassen, 1927).

The situation changed drastically during the summer of 1902 with the arrival of the *Active*, a steam whaler and supply ship. Some of the crew members and passengers of the *Active* were carrying an (unknown) infectious disease that quickly spread to the Sadlermiut (Ross, 1977). Angutimarik, an Aivillingmiut eye-witness to the catastrophe, described the situation to Mathiassen (1927: 284) while visiting Southampton Island:

Several of the Aivilik at the station became ill and some of them ... lost children, who contracted severe diarrhoea and died very quickly. Some of the Sadlermiut who called at the trading station also fell ill, and some of them were so bad that they had to be sailed back to Tunermiut in the station's whaleboat. When their settlement was visited during the winter they were all dead; some of the Eskimos lay on their platforms, others outside the houses; a number of dogs were running about.

The disease must have rapidly consumed the population.

Missionary Donald B. Marsh (1976: 36) recalled a conversation from 1938 with Special Constable Jimmy Gibbons, an Aivillingmiut who, as a boy, lived close to the Sadlermiut houses at Native Point. Gibbons claimed to have been in the houses of infected Sadlermiut in the winter of 1902–1903. In many of the houses, bodies of the occupants were still lying at the location of death. The whale ribs used as roof supports were useful to the later Inuit as sled runners, and these items were removed from the houses. The removal resulted in the collapse of numerous roofs.

Two Sadlermiut houses at Tunermiut were excavated, both yielding human skeletal remains (Taylor, 1960). Three skeletons, a child, an adolescent, and an adult, lay on a sleeping platform of House 34, presumably victims of the 1902–1903 epidemic. House 49 contained the skeleton of a child. Presumably more skeletons remain in some of the houses that have not been excavated.

The station proved a failure and in 1903 Comer moved the group to Repulse Bay. Only one Sadlermiut woman and four children joined them, the sole survivors of a once numerous people.

They were adopted by the Aivilik of Repulse Bay, and when, in 1908, I left a colony of about seventy Aiviliks on Southampton Island at a point north of Cape Kendall, among them were two surviving children of the Saglernmiut – too young, however, to remember the traditions and customs of their people. (Comer, 1910: 90)

The effects of this disease apparently extended well beyond the Sadlermiut. Ross (1977) describes how the disease affected Inuit aboard the supply ship *Active* and the whaling ship *Era*, which were carrying these individuals back to their home communities. From these communities the disease quite possibly was transmitted to various hunting areas where affected individuals made contact with even more Inuit.

The identity of the disease that killed the Sadlermiut and many other Inuit in 1902 has not been identified. Mathiassen (1927) suggested typhus and Bird (1953) suggested typhoid fever, but the recorded symptoms do not fit either disease. However, Angutimarik described severe diarrhea, with death following very quickly (Mathiassen, 1927). According to the 1900 to 1902 logbook of the *Era*, the Gore Island Inuit immediately to the north of Southampton Island apparently suffered from the same disease, also experiencing "diarrhoea in which much blood passes also a white phlegm" (Ross, 1977: 6). This suggests "something like a severe dysentery, perhaps a gastric or enteric fever, would seem to fit the facts more closely," according to Ross (1977). Ross (1977) adds that a Dundee (home port of the *Active*) newspaper reported that some time during the *Active*'s voyage a seaman died of "gastric fever" and was buried at Lake Harbour (Kimmirut) on Baffin Island.

13.4.2 Demographic Collapse

In 1955 William E. Taylor studied the house ruins at Tunermiut. Of the 111 structures identified, ten are clearly of Aivilik origin and others were too overgrown to make a definitive identification (Ryan *et al.*, 2014). Fifty-eight are, however, clearly Sadlermiut, 28 single-room structures, 24 with two rooms, and six with three rooms; a total of 82 rooms. Each room could conceivably house a family. Sadlermiut winter houses also exist elsewhere on the island. Although all of these houses were obviously not occupied simultaneously, even a minimal estimate based on them stands in sharp contrast to the meager population size reported for the Sadlermiut: 70 in 1896 and 58 in 1902 (Comer, 1910). Estimates of population size based on counts of dwelling structures plus a diminished area of occupation by 1902 suggest the Sadlermiut were in decline for some time, perhaps even decades, before the final epidemic of 1902–1903 (Taylor, 1959).

13.4.3 Archaeological Evidence of Stress

Native Point burials were divided into three groups labeled Village, Peripheral, and Meat Cache. The Village burials, thought to be the oldest, tended to be in close proximity to the Sadlermiut winter houses and severe disturbance of these burials may be attributed to the removal of grave stones to construct the nearby houses.

The Peripheral burials range out from the house cluster and are thought to be of intermediate age. The Meat Cache burials were so named because these graves were located on several old beach ridges that contained many meat caches, some of which had been converted into graves. Several modern non-Sadlermiut graves were also located here. This series is at a much lower elevation than the others and is thought to be the most recent. The use of meat caches as graves and the large number of infants inside them suggest a period of great stress for the residents of Tunermiut. There is also a grouping of eight Peripheral graves (NP-34 to NP-41) that contain only infant skeletons, possibly representing another period of stress. Also of interest is a series of graves (NP-18 to NP-31) included in the Meat Cache series but located some distance east of the main meat cache area. Along with two adult females and a child of approximately six years were 11 infants. Again, all were primary graves, not converted meat caches. The presence of so many infants suggests a disease episode moved through the population, with infants rendered the most vulnerable.

Of special interest is the main meat cache area that lies northeast of the house concentration (Figures 13.9 and 13.10). It is located on a low-lying series of old beach lines that include flat terraces. This area has good access to the water, was close to the winter houses, and contained a wealth of building material in the form of limestone rocks. At the time this area was investigated in 1959 it contained 64 meat cache structures, 54 stone graves containing 58 individuals interpreted as Sadlermiut, and 5 recent graves containing wooden coffin boxes.

Twenty-five of the Sadlermiut graves show clear evidence of having once served as meat caches, thus bringing the total number of caches to 89. Because some of the

Figure 13.9 Meat Cache Area at Tunermiut (looking east). A = Sadlermiut winter house area. B = southwest (main) meat cache area. C = northeast meat cache burial area. D = T1 Dorset site.

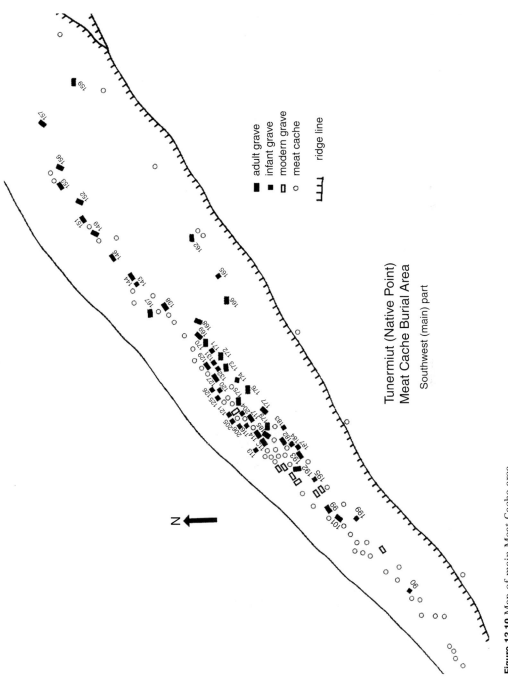

Figure 13.10 Map of main Meat Cache area.

Figure 13.11 Meat cache used for burial (NP-195). The skeleton of an infant was lying on a bed of caribou, seal, and walrus bones, shown here arranged outside the structure.

graves probably represent meat caches that were altered beyond recognition, the total number of caches likely once numbered over 100. The animal bones still present in these caches were primarily walrus, followed by seal, caribou, and bird. The Native Point meat cache area indicates that the Sadlermiut had the capacity to store a large volume of meat. The numerous animal bones still present in the unaltered caches and caches turned into graves appears to verify that the Sadlermiut did not become extinct through starvation, a belief commonly held for many years following demographic collapse in 1902 (Comer, 1910: 89–90; Mathiassen, 1927, Part 1: 284).

The fact that so many of the cache structures were utilized as graves suggests a period of considerable stress, with many individuals dying within a short period of time, thus putting a severe strain on the grave-constructing capabilities of the community. These graves contained the skeletal remains of 58 individuals, 13 adult males, 13 adult females, four adolescents, one child, and 27 infants. Some of the cache structures used as graves were not altered. The body, most often that of an infant, had been simply placed on top of whatever animal remains were still present (Figure 13.11).[1]

13.5 Conclusion

The Sadlermiut existed in relative isolation from the Inuit for many years, developing a unique variation of the Thule Culture. These communities also

---

[1] In a study by Coltrain *et al.* (2004), six meat cache graves were C14 dated using human bone. The dates ranged from CE 1557 to 1677, with an error range of 1484 to 1836. Given the degree of isostatic rebound this region is undergoing, these early dates appear impossible.

Figure 13.12 The last Sadlermiut, Etienne Kingak, in 1947. As a child Kingak survived the epidemic of 1902–1903 and was adopted by Aivillingmiut, raised in this culture, and died in 1948. Photo by C. E. Jordan.

remained isolated from European contact while other Inuit in Canada were rapidly acculturating. Contact finally occurred in 1824, when Europeans encountered a highly isolated population with a specialized, intensive subsistence economy representing adaptation to a harsh environment. Isolation and intensification are demonstrated from the persistence of material culture, including graves, lithic industries, and watercraft technology, while skeletal evidence for dental chipping and tooth wear, traumatic injuries, and degenerative joint conditions attest to the intensive lifestyle of this population. The high degree of specialization and the intensive, persistent occupation of the landscape depict a population that was resilient to harsh ecological challenges. However, additional agents outside the socioecological spectrum may also threaten and diminish population survival. This is well demonstrated by mortuary evidence for minor epidemics pre-dating the events of 1901 to 1902 and dwindling population sizes leading up to this point. In 1902 Europeans introduced a highly contagious disease into the Sadler-miut community and during the winter of 1902–1903 the population collapsed. These results suggest that population collapse during periods of contact is less a consequence of inferior technology or ability to withstand disease, but instead may reflect variation in the capacity for resilience when these instances introduce new challenges to survival. The last Sadlermiut, Etienne Kingak, who survived the epidemic as a child and was adopted by Aivillingmiut, died in 1948 (Figure 13.12). Ironically, the Sadlermiut people who were so little known in life are well known in death, thanks to the numerous well-preserved skeletons recovered from Tunermiut.

References

Bilreiro, C., Bahia, C., and Castro, M. O. E. (2016). Longitudinal stress fracture of the femur: A rare presentation. *European Journal of Radiology Open*, 3, 32–34.

Bird, J. B. (1953). *Southampton Island*. Ottawa: Canada Department of Mines and Technical Surveys.

Birket-Smith, K. (1928). The Greenlanders of the present day. In M. Vahl, G. C. Amdrup, L. Bobe, and A. S. Jansen, eds., *Greenland*. London: Oxford University Press, pp. 1–207.

Boas, F. (1888). *The Central Eskimo*. Washington, DC: Bureau of Ethnology, Smithsonian Institution.

Clark, B. (1980). The Lake Site (KkHh-2), Southampton Island, N.W.T. and its position in Sadlermiut prehistory. *Canadian Journal of Archaeology*, 4, 53–81.

Collins, H. B. (1956). Vanished mystery men of Hudson Bay. *National Geographic Magazine*, 110, 669–687.

Collins, H. B. (1957). Archaeological work in Arctic Canada. *Annual Report of the Smithsonian Institution for 1956*, 1956, 509–528.

Coltrain, J. B., Hayes, M., and O'Rourke, D. H. (2004). Sealing, whaling and caribou: The skeletal isotope chemistry of Eastern Arctic Foragers. *Journal of Archaeological Science*, 31, 39–57.

Comer, G. (1910). A geographical description of Southampton Island and notes upon the Eskimo. *Bulletin of the American Geographical Society*, 42, 84–90.

de Poncins, G. (1941). *Kabloona*. Garden City, NY: Garden City Publishing.

Eber, D. H. (1989) *When the Whalers Were Up North: Inuit Memories from the Eastern Arctic*. Montreal: McGill-Queen's University Press.

Ferguson, R. (1938). *Arctic Schooner: A Voyage on the Schooner Abbie Bradford 1878–1879*. Philadelphia, PA: University of Pennsylvania Press.

Hall, C. F. (1865) *Arctic Researches and Life among the Esquimaux*. New York, NY: Harper Brothers.

Hayes, I. I. (1885). *The Open Polar Sea: A Narrative of a Voyage of Discovery Towards the North Pole in the Schooner "U.S."* New York, NY: Hurd and Houghton.

Hrdlička, A. (1940). Ritual ablation of front teeth in Siberia and America. *Smithsonian Miscellaneous Collections*, 99, 1–32.

Hylander, W. L. (1977). The adaptive significance of Eskimo craniofacial morphology. In A. A. Dahlberg and T. M. Graber, eds., *Orofacial Growth and Development*. The Hague: Mouton Publishers, pp. 215–227.

Keenleyside, A. (1990) Euro-American whaling in the Canadian Arctic: Its effects on Eskimo health. *Arctic Anthropology*, 27, 1–19.

Lyon, G. F. (1824). *Private Journal*. London: John Murray.

Lyon, G. F. (1825) *A Brief Narrative of an Unsuccessful Attempt to Reach Repulse Bay, Through Sir Thomas Rowe's "Welcome," in His Majesty's Ship Griper, in the Year MDCCCXXIV [1824]*. London: John Murray.

Marsh, D. B. (1976). The stone winter houses of the Sadlermiut. *The Beaver*, 307, 36–39.

Mathiassen, T. (1927). *Archaeology of the Central Eskimos. Report of the Fifth Thule Expedition 1921–24, vol. 4, no. 1*. Copenhagen: Glyndendal.

Maxwell, M. S. (1985). *Prehistory of the Eastern Arctic*. Orlando, FL: Academic Press.

McGhee, R. (1996). *Ancient People of the Arctic*. Vancouver: University of British Columbia Press.

Merbs, C. F. (1962). A case of osteological thievery. *Arctic Circular*, 14, 73–74.

Merbs, C. F. (1968) Anterior tooth loss in Arctic populations. *Southwestern Journal of Anthropology*, 24, 20–32.

Merbs, C. F. (1983) *Patterns of Activity-Induced Pathology in a Canadian Inuit Population*. Ottawa: National Museums of Canada.

Merbs, C. F. (1989). Trauma. In M. Y. İşcan and K. A. R. Kennedy, eds., *Reconstruction of Life from the Skeleton*. New York, NY: Alan R. Liss, pp. 161–189.

Merbs, C. F. (1995). Incomplete spondylolysis and healing. A study of ancient Canadian Eskimo skeletons. *Spine*, 20, 2328–2334.

Merbs, C. F. (1996). Spondylolysis of the sacrum in Alaskan and Canadian Inuit skeletons. *American Journal of Physical Anthropology*, **101**, 357–367.

Merbs, C. F. (1997). Eskimo skeleton taphonomy with identification of possible polar bear victims. In W. D. Haglund and M. H. Sorg, eds., *Forensic Taphonomy: The Postmortem Fate of Human Remains*. Boca Raton, FL: CRC Press, pp. 249–262.

Merbs, C. F. (2002). Spondylolysis in Inuit skeletons from Arctic Canada. *International Journal of Osteoarchaeology*, **12**, 279–290.

Nansen, F. (1890). *The Crossing of Greenland*, vols. I and II. London: Longmans, Green and Co.

Nansen, F. (1893). *Eskimo Life*. London: Longmans, Green and Co.

Ortner, D. J. (2003). *Identification of Pathological Conditions in Human Skeletal Remains*. Boston, MA: Academic Press.

Park, R. W. (1993). The Dorset–Thule succession in Arctic North America: Assessing claims for culture contact. *American Antiquity*, **58**, 203–234.

Pelly, D. F. (1987). Sadlermiut mystery. *Canadian Geographic*, **107**, 28–32.

Pitseolak, P. and Eber, D. (1975). *People from Our Side*. Edmonton: Hurtig.

Roberts, V. L., Noyes, F. R., Hubbard, R. P., and McCabe, J. (1971). Biomechanics of snowmobile injuries. *Journal of Biomechanics*, **4**, 569–577.

Ross, W. G. (1977). Whaling and the decline of native populations. *Arctic Anthropology*, **14**, 1–8.

Ryan, K., Betts, M. W., Oliver-Lloyd, V., *et al.* (2014). Identification of pre-contact polar bear victims at Native Point, Southampton Island, Nunavut, using 3D technology and a virtual zooarchaeology collection. *Arctic*, **67**, 493–510.

Steensby, H. P. (1910). Contributions to the ethnology and anthropogeography of the polar Eskimos. *Medelellsar on Grønland*, **34**, 255–407.

Taylor, W. E., Jr. (1959). The mysterious Sadlermiut. *The Beaver*, **290**, 26–33.

Taylor, W. E., Jr. (1960). *A Description of Sadlermiut Houses Excavated at Native Point, Southampton Island, N.W.T.* Ottawa: National Museum of Canada.

Thompson, D. D., Laughlin, S. B., Laughlin, W. F., and Merbs, C. F. (1985). Bone core analysis and vertebral pathologies in Sadlermiut Eskimo skeletons. *Ossa*, **9**(11), 189–197.

Turner, C. G., II and Cadien, J. D. (1969). Dental chipping in Aleuts, Eskimos and Indians. *American Journal of Physical Anthropology*, **31**, 303–310.

Tyrrell, J. (1908). *Across the Sub-Arctics of Canada: A Journey of 3,200 Miles through the Hudson Bay Region*. Toronto: William Briggs.

Utermohle, C. J. and Merbs, C. F. (1979). Population affinities of Thule culture Eskimos in northern Hudson Bay. In A. P. McCartney, ed., *Thule Eskimo Culture: An Anthropological Retrospective*. Ottawa: National Museum of Man, pp. 435–447.

Wood. S. R. (1992). *Tooth Wear and the Sexual Division of Labour in an Inuit Population*. MA thesis, Simon Fraser University.

Yesner, D. R. (1981). Degenerative and traumatic pathologies of the Aleut vertebral column. *Archives of the California Chiropractic Association*, **5**, 45–57.

14 When Resilience Fails: Fences, Water Control, and Aboriginal History in the Western Riverina, Australia

Judith Littleton

14.1 Introduction

Resilience relates to a capacity of ecological and social systems and actors. Most work on ecological systems begins with Holling's definition of resilience as: "the persistence of systems and their ability to absorb change and disturbance and still maintain the same relationships between populations and state variables" (Holling, 1973: 14). An alternative definition by Vayda and McCay (1975: 299) is the capacity of "remaining flexible enough to change in response to whatever hazards or perturbations come along." This addition of flexibility and change in addition to persistence has led to the contemporary formulation of resilience as comprising "a system's capacity to persist in its current state of functioning while facing disturbance and change, to adapt to future challenges, and to transform in ways that enhance its functioning" (Keck and Sakdapolrak, 2013: 8).

The concept of social or cultural (Butzer, 2012) resilience emphasizes the actors while ecological resilience often focuses upon the ecological or socioecological system. As Diener (1974) points out in relation to the Hutterites, resilience of cultural practices and ecological systems does not necessarily correspond to the actions of individuals who may fail to survive, migrate, or cease to be a Hutterite. So how do these multiscalar relationships unfold in particular histories of place and time? Is it even possible to identify evidence of resilience in a very partial record of early contact histories and bioarchaeology?

Contact was initially defined by Dobyns (1983) in terms of American Indian acquisition: acquisition of disease, acquisition of epidemics, and acquisition of collapse via disease and epidemics. This concept of acquisition or consequence became the initial paradigm for studies of contact by bioarchaeological research (Murphy and Klaus, 2017). However, contact is associated with interactions between previously isolated groups that resulted in multidirectional, transformative acquisitions that include the adaptive and persistent capacities of indigenous populations (Baker and Kealhofer, 1996; Stojanowski, 2017). This chapter evaluates the loss of resilience and subsequent demographic collapse of Australian Aborigines following contact with Europeans. In this particular analysis, the arrival of European colonists constitutes a "surprise" in the sense of a change that confounds social expectations (Kates and Clark, 1996) as opposed to the ebb and flow of changes that might be expected within an environment outside the auspices of contact. Yet the temporal variability of the environment that created changing conditions for Aboriginal people did not cease with the arrival of Europeans. It is this overlay of European colonization against the normal fluctuations of the Western Riverina environment that creates the background for this analysis. This chapter argues that fine-grained historical analysis of the early period of European colonization shows a complex of adaptation and accommodation on the part of Aboriginal people at multiple levels (environmental, cultural, and personal), most especially when considered against the backdrop of archaeological and bioarchaeological research. The subsequent depopulation, movement, and pauperization of Aboriginal people did not result from a failure of transformation, but a systematic dispossession in terms of land and economic opportunity, changes that limited flexibility or response at all levels from the ecological system to personal action.

This is a story of collapse. Collapse is traditionally defined as a loss of complexity within political institutions (Tainter, 1988). However, Butzer and Endfield (2012: 3628) suggest that collapse "represents transformation at a large social or spatial scale, with long-term impact on combinations of interdependent variables: (i) environmental change and resilience; (ii) demography or settlement; (iii) socioeconomic patterns; (iv) political or societal structures; and (v) ideology or cultural memory" (Butzer and Endfield, 2012: 3628). It is, however, important to differentiate between collapse and adaptive transformation: Collapse represents the loss of coherency within socioecological and cultural systems, dwindling population sizes, or lost identities, while transformation is associated with adaptive restructuring of socioecological and cultural systems (Faulseit, 2016). In the case of the Western Riverina, European colonization disrupted and diminished all of these lifeways, but contrary to models that focus exclusively on disease or violence as prime movers, the pattern of collapse covered by this chapter reflects the role that ecological relationships had in delaying and then hastening change.

This chapter begins with a brief description of Aboriginal life in the Western Riverina and how these behaviors may suggest resilience. This is followed by a general discussion of the impact of European settlement and a consideration of the limited bioarchaeological evidence that demonstrates broad contrasts of stress and disease in the wake of colonization. Finer-grained analysis based on three local observers from 1845 to 1856 – a crucial ten-year period of change – is then used to demonstrate the variability of human responses and how exploring issues of resilience and collapse may sometimes be limited by the nature of the evidence used by bioarchaeological research.

14.2   The Western Riverina

14.2.1   The Western Riverina Landscape

Understanding the interaction between Aboriginal and European people relies upon an appreciation of the specific environment of the Western Riverina of New South Wales (Figure 14.1). The Western Riverina is located approximately 800 km west of

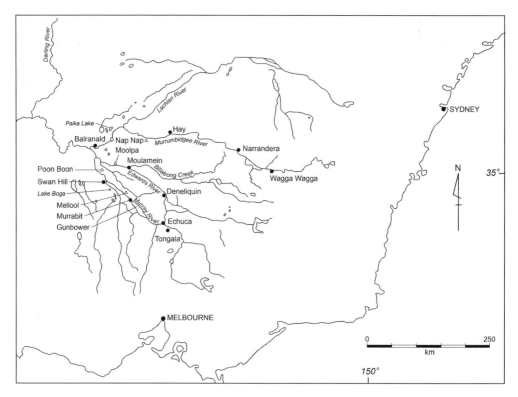

Figure 14.1 The Western Riverina.

Sydney. The landscape is a flat plain-bounded territory, bordered on the north by the Lachlan River and in the south by the much broader Murray River that forms the state border between New South Wales and Victoria. The eastern margin of the area is marked by undulating foothills, while the western margin is formed by the Lachlan River as it joins the Murrumbidgee River and by the Murrumbidgee as it joins the Murray River.

Covered initially by saltbush interspersed with *Eucalyptus* trees along the river and ephemeral creek lines, the contemporary plain is largely grassland. Currently this stretch of land is occupied by pastoral stations (both sheep and cattle) with some irrigation crops. Yet in the past, the unvarying landscape was not seen as particularly attractive by Europeans. Indeed, many settlers described the land as "repellent" (Sturt in Bride and Sayers, 1898: 365).

The rivers were fringed with a margin of *Eucalyptus camaldulensis* forest, more extensively along the Murray than the other rivers. Bordering this margin of timbered country was drier grassland shifting in the western margin to woodland vegetation sheltering grass or saltbush (Figure 14.2). The land is semiarid, with highly variable rainfall of around 30 mm per annum. The Murray and Murrumbidgee Rivers provide the major water supplies. Both fill with the flush of snowmelt from the Snowy Mountains in spring and the southern half of the area is crisscrossed by

Figure 14.2 A view of the Riverine plains.

smaller creeks. Even to the north the ephemeral lakes and creeks can be traced in the lines of black box trees against the sky line. In good years "this soil supports a rank vegetation which can feed sheep in their thousands" (Jervis, 1952: 1). However, variability in rainfall and in climate is the rule (33 percent variability in rainfall per annum). The land bakes in summer, but is bitingly cold in winter due to the prevailing southwesterly winds.

There was, and is, no reliable forecasting for drought. In 1839 heavy rains broke a three-year drought that caused the Murray and Murrumbidgee Rivers to stop flowing (Jeans, 1972). Between 1849 and 1850, there was a general inland drought, while the time between 1870 and 1890 was seasonable. In the decade between 1890 and 1900 there was an unbroken series of dry years. As John Dunmore Lang wrote in 1847 (cited in Grant, 1970: 65): "There is occasionally a great shortage of water in the extensive tract of pastoral country between the Murrumbidgee and the Hume, except near the rivers and the more permanent creeks." Even these large bodies of water could become a series of isolated water holes in drier years. The current is strongly seasonal and the full flow of the Murray and Murrumbidgee Rivers is largely a result of water control through irrigation (gradually increasing in intensity since the late nineteenth century).

14.2.2 Aboriginal Occupation

For Aboriginal people, this region encompassed several linguistic groups such as the Wamba-Wamba, Nari-Nari, and Mutti-Mutti (Figure 14.3). Each group occupied a relatively small area and was further divided into clans that acted as the land-holding unit, while bands (not necessarily from a single clan) were effectively the land-using unit (Clark, 1990). These different groups subsisted on a mixture of riverine and plain resources, including the grinding of seeds (Buchan, 1983).

Archaeological surveys indicate the importance of aquatic resources along the rivers and plain. Clay earth ovens used for the steaming of vegetable and meat resources are frequent and marked by evidence of mussel shell, bird and fish bone – resources available in the plain only when the ephemeral creek and lake systems were running (Craib, 1991; Martin, 2007). Floods also caused many old channels (billa-bongs) to fill, making riverine foods easily accessible (Humphries, 2007). Flooding was perceived as part of a good season, as described in the *Riverina Grazier* (October 12, 1867): "During a flood, Aboriginal people collected on high ground between the

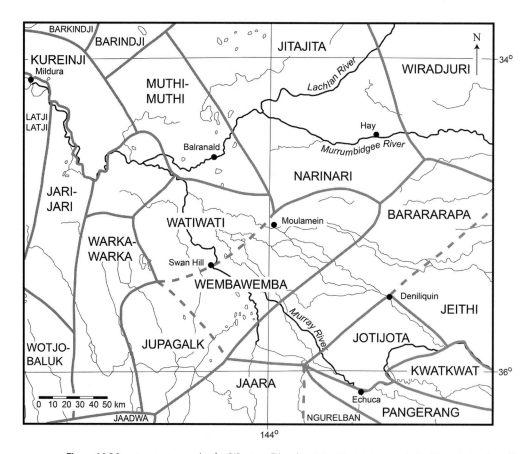

Figure 14.3 Language groups in the Western Riverina (after Tindale's map of tribal boundaries: http://archives.samuseum.sa.gov.au/tribalmap).

Edwards and the Wakool. They claimed to have plenty to eat since kangaroos and other animals were also forced back to the smaller areas of high ground."

Analyses of precontact health demonstrate that Aboriginal population density was higher in this region than in many other parts of Australia (Webb, 1995). These results are consistent with Birdsell's early estimates of population size based on the availability of water resources (Birdsell, 1953). As a result, conditions such as iron-deficiency anemia (possibly related to parasitism) and some infectious diseases (endemic syphilis has been one controversial suggestion) were present, although there is debate surrounding intensity of disease experience (Robertson, 2007; Webb, 1995). Infectious diseases dependent upon high-density populations (e.g., measles, flu, and smallpox) were, however, absent since population numbers would have been too low to sustain such conditions and there was, in Australia's relative isolation, no source of introduction.

The coalescence of people and language families along the rivers produced diversity in cultural practices and phenotypes (Pardoe, 1991). For example, numerous writers mention Aboriginal "ambassadors" accompanying early European colonialists and speaking diverse dialects as well as "postmen" liaising between groups (Curr, 1883), and intertribal conflict (e.g., Phillips, 1893). This cultural diversity was further reflected in Holocene burial customs as attested by both early observers and the archaeological record. For instance, the burial position and customs of Wati Wati were much more similar to Darling River practices than to those of Wiradjuri (Littleton, 2007; see Figure 14.3 for locations). However, it is important to note that burial position and location varied by group identity and individual (Littleton, 2002; Musgrave, 1930). The variable relationships between language groups were also marked in terms of ceremonies between different areas. Mereweather (1859) recounts meeting men at Moulamein who had attended a Wiradjuri ceremony (east of Hay). The men suggested that the ceremonial practices were similar to those found in their own community. Such markers of identity and of networks allowed for the exchange of raw materials and maintenance of land tenure over what would become critical resources (Pardoe, 1988).

Thus, prior to European arrival Aboriginal people occupied the Western Riverina more densely along the river and more intermittently in the back country. The primary socioecological focus was aquatic resources, and this allowed for a sufficient population size to also maintain a diversity of language and distinct customs. How does this relate to resilience? Flexibility in response to the highly variable environment was maintained through networks (both trade and kinship), shifting locations, and following resources as the water levels ebbed and flowed. The evidence for this is primarily based upon Martin's observation of the development of oven mounds in response to changes in water regimes and upon the persistence of Aboriginal occupation in the late Holocene (Martin, 2007). The palimpsest nature of the archaeological record makes it extremely difficult to distinguish very precise indicators of practices that relate directly to ecological resilience, nor can persistence be read as necessarily the same people in the same places (Littleton and Allen, 2007).

14.2.3 European Colonization

One feature of the Western Riverina is the relatively late arrival of European colonialists. Charles Sturt explored the lower reaches of the Murrumbidgee in 1829, 41 years after first settlement at Botany Bay (Sturt, 1833). Exploration of the remaining area was even later. Despite being the largest of the three rivers, the central Murray River was probably not explored by Europeans until overlanding parties began moving stock from Sydney to Adelaide in 1838 (Hawdon, 1952).

Despite the late arrival of Europeans, the impact of colonization began at a relatively accelerated pace. Below the junction of the Murray and Murrumbidgee Rivers, Sturt observed smallpox scars from a previous epidemic estimated to have occurred around 1828 (Sturt, 1833). Hawdon, camping near the Murray River in 1838, observed a group of Wadi Wadi whose "faces were nearly all marked with smallpox" (Hawdon, 1952: 27). Later settlers in the area also noted the scars of smallpox (Beveridge, 1883). Pulteney Mein, who settled at Moolpa Station (see Figure 14.3) on the lower Edward River (west of Moulamein) in 1858, wrote:

The Blacks must have suffered from smallpox before the advent of the Europeans in the Murray district for there was a man at Moolpa in 1858, from 35 to 40 years of age, who was perfectly blind, and he was deeply pitted with the small pox marks – [our ambassador] told me "Jimmy" became blind when he was 10 or 11 years old. – He also told me that so many Blacks died (about the time Jimmy became blind) on the Murray that they let the bodies remain in the camps, could not bury them, too many. (Mein, 1897)

The associated mortality was estimated by Dowling (1997) to be around 25 percent on average, though the experience was variable. Factors such as the pattern of group networks, location of different groups at the time, individual reactions to infection (whether to flee, contact other groups, or remain stationary), and the age composition of the group could all vary between local bands and produce differing disease experiences. It is estimated that this outbreak of smallpox in southeastern Australia took place around 1830 (Butlin, 1983; Dowling, 1997).

At the time of this outbreak, the country between the Murray and Murrumbidgee Rivers remained unoccupied by Europeans. By 1848, however, practically all of the river frontages were occupied (Jervis, 1952), though there were gaps in this settlement pattern. The late settlement was due to distance from major ports and towns, the availability of more fertile land closer to these towns, and the commonly held view, fostered by an incident in 1836 (Mitchell, 1839: II, 265–272), that violence in the region was frequent (Christie, 1979).

The earliest Europeans to settle were pastoralists with sheep and cattle. These groups were small in number. For instance, Hobler's establishment of a settlement on Paika Lake around 1840 below the junction of the Lachlan and Murrumbidgee Rivers (see Figure 14.3) involved fewer than ten men (Hobler, 1992 [1882]: March 19, 1845). Settlement was sparse. In 1846 the census of the Murray River district was approximately 1500 European settlers (Byrne, 1849), significantly fewer than estimates for Aboriginal groups in the area, which ranged between 3000 and 5000 people (Clark, 1990).

The main house of these stations was generally built close to the river. Water supplies were safeguarded and extended by enlarging Aboriginal clay pans, wells, and soaks (i.e., natural pools of water) as well as by using earthen tanks and ultimately tin and iron tanks (Calder, 1981). Other huts were dispersed on outstations (i.e., areas away from the main house, stations, and yards). There was no permanent fencing (except for the stock yards near the main house) and the flocks of sheep were moved by shepherds and placed in hurdles or yards at night. Shepherds and sheep were mobile. The sheep were herded by day and guarded at night by the hut keeper. Fences for sheep were mobile and moved every second day (Mereweather, 1859). Water was generally supplied by earthen tanks (Jeans, 1972). The ratio of sheep to shepherd tended to be one person to 1000 sheep (although this increased over time; Pickard, 2007).

With the station huts adjacent to large Aboriginal camps along the river (Mereweather, 1859), outstations close to wells and soaks (often Aboriginal water sources; Jeans, 1972), and with shepherds moving sheep across the landscape, Aboriginal and European occupation of the Western Riverina overlapped considerably in terms of flexibility – low population density, mobility, and a focus on water supplies. To a degree, despite the changes following European settlement, Aboriginal traditional forms of social control and conflict resolution through physical punishments, duels, and even ritual battles continued within and between neighboring groups (Mereweather, 1859; Phillips, 1893). There were, however, certainly violent incidents between Aboriginal groups and Europeans.

In the Western Riverina, most early European accounts from the area mention cattle killing and retaliatory violence by white settlers and native police (Baylis, 1914; Bride and Sayers, 1898; Phillips, 1893). While many overlanding parties did not encounter violence, the potential for clashes increased with greater contact. One of the earliest incidents of violence between European colonists and Aboriginal people occurred in 1843, involving Green, a squatter, who had attempted settlement on the Barham property (see Figure 14.3) (Grant, 1970). Such violence, however, varied greatly, with some colonial settlers creating and experiencing little difficulty (Phillips, 1893: 71).

Apart from the violence centered around cattle and station owners, other incidents were associated with sexual encounters between shepherds and Aboriginal women (Stuart in Bride and Sayers, 1898: 368). Such relations were widespread. In 1852 Stutchbury, a surveyor, wrote "one can scarcely visit a large camp of blacks without finding nearly one third of children to be half caste [sic]" (cited in Jeans, 1972: 75).

It is impossible to estimate the impact of violence upon the numbers of Aboriginal people living in the area. Curr (1883), living on the southern border of the Western Riverina, suggested that between 15 and 25 percent of Aboriginal deaths in more densely settled Victoria were due to violence. Corris, for the neighboring western district, has a much lower estimate of 5 percent (Corris, 1968: 153–157). There is, however, enough variation between accounts to indicate that violence was not universal or undirected, but rather depended upon the cultural contingencies of interpersonal relationships (Penney, 1979; see also Burke *et al.*, 2016).

Economic relations with Europeans did exist, with Aboriginal people being casually employed stripping bark and performing stock work (Freeman, 1985). This increased over time and in the range of activities. But this was not an unchallenged utopia for Aboriginal people. While the population may have experienced some demographic recovery from smallpox mortality, these groups were affected by violence, and even more so by diseases affecting the colonists.

Smallpox was not the only disease to travel beyond the frontiers of settlement. Venereal syphilis appeared in the lower Murray River region around 1830 (Dowling, 1997, 2017). However, once Europeans settled in the Western Riverina, a major disease exchange took place (Littleton, 2005). This exchange was determined by the nature of settlement and by the social position (and health profile) of the colonists. Most settlers were male ex-convicts: These were the shepherds, hut keepers, barkers, and bullock drivers. These individuals hosted a range of diseases acquired prior to colonization, including sexually transmitted infections (STIs) and tuberculosis.

The impact of STIs was particularly severe upon the Aboriginal population. Contemporary accounts describe the rapid and severe course of venereal syphilis (Parker, 1841). There is a debate over whether endemic syphilis was present prior to European invasion (Dowling, 2017; Hackett, 1975; Webb, 1995). However, the severity and spread of venereal syphilis was so marked that even had there been some residual immunity among the population, this clearly had little effect on lessening the impact of the disease.

14.3   Demographic History

Since smallpox occurred before Sturt traveled along the Murrumbidgee River, there are no observations of Aboriginal people before this disease impacted population dynamics. This makes it extremely difficult to obtain any indication of precontact population sizes. In 1832, Sturt (1833) observed 50 Aboriginal people on the 290 km stretch of the upper Murrumbidgee River, and 1000 on a similar stretch of the Murray River. These were generally small groups of fewer than 20 men who would join colonial expeditions, sometimes acting as guides or ambassadors. These groups of Aboriginal people were accompanied by extended families that consisted of a man, his wife or wives, children, and possibly older relatives.

This impression remains of groups of Aboriginal people moving through the area and of occasional large congregations (e.g., Phillips, 1893) until the 1860s, when a decline in absolute numbers began to be commented upon: "Blacks were very thick until 1869 and they would roam up and down the river (Murrumbidgee); often as many as 200 would arrive on the station (Berembed) at the same time" (Andrew q. in Bartley, 1892: 55).

Two sources make this clear: the *Pastoral Times* from Deniliquin, and records from blanket distributions in the same area. A blanket and a tomahawk were issued on the Queen's Birthday, May 24, each year, and declining numbers of distributed items is seen in Table 14.1. At the same time, the European population was increasing. By

Table 14.1 Blankets issued from 1861 and 1876 (incomplete).

Date	Recipients	Number	Source
August 6, 1861	District of Woorooma on Edwards R – Brian Borombe, King of the Wakool, his relatives and adherents the recipients of blankets.	–	*Pastoral Times*
May 7, 1864	At courthouse – natives from Mathoura, Morocco, Redbank, Aratula, Cornella, Werai, Thule, and Deniliquin	100	*Pastoral Times*
April–August 1867	Named individuals and stations (including Phillips 43, WH Kennedy 36, Wolsely Gibbs Co. 40, Clark [Cobran? Station] 16, Mathoura PM 6).	182	Deniliquin- Court of Petty Sessions. Register of Applications for Licences, including lists of blankets issued to Aborigines 1861–1876. State Archives, Wagga SA 215/4
April 1868	Named individuals 50, Mathoura 26	76	As above
June–July 1868	Warbeccan 10, Named individuals 8, PA Jennings 5, Watson 4, JB Caine 12	39	As above
June 1869	J.M. Graves Mathura ?-21, T.L. Parker Inampy 2, Alex McLaurin Morocco 12, Hunt and Watson 7, McKee Berennegan ? 6, JH Patterson Bownoke? 12, Do Jen? 11, Wolseley 39, Kennedy 15, named individuals 24	149	As above
May 1874	Courthouse	53	*Pastoral Times*
May 1876	Courthouse	3	*Pastoral Times*

Note: ? in text are H. Allen's – where names are not clear.

1865 there were 550 Europeans in Swan Hill district, 150 in Swan Hill proper (Calder, 1981). Deniliquin was even larger. Accompanying these changes were transformations in the mode of occupation. From having parallel mobile existences in the early period, European technology such as dams, poisoning and shooting of wild animals, and wire fencing led to greater exploitation of land and water to the exclusion of Aboriginal people.

Until 1860, a plowed furrow of land was an accepted boundary marker, but sheep pastures were being reorganized into more compact shapes (Williams, 1962). In 1850, wire became more cheaply and readily available. As a result, sheep runs were increasingly fenced. The resulting paddocks were large and sheep were moved only infrequently so labor requirements were reduced. Stocking rates increased by about 60 percent (Williams, 1962) and, subsequent to land acts that enabled free selection of land, selectors settled in the region, which increased the density of European colonialists. The change in fencing led from one man per 5000 sheep to a boundary rider caring for about 10 000 sheep. The demand for casual labor increased, while permanent employment fell (Jeans, 1972). This increase in stocking was facilitated by damming creeks and use of windmills (Jeans, 1972).

It was not only human socioecological practices that changed the prevailing environmental conditions. More sheep and cattle were moved overland. By 1864, large flocks of sheep traveled through Deniliquin and it is recorded that in one week 11 000 sheep crossed the Edward River. These herds placed additional stress upon local resources (Williams, 1962), and as these changes escalated the environment progressively deteriorated. For example, in a search for water for the herds, Phillips (1893) describes digging wells to a depth of 200 ft. While the new dams and fences allowed fenced country to be grazed evenly, this changed the distribution of wild animals and plants across the landscape. As Phillips (1893) writes, "on the fencing of the country and dispensing with the service of shepherds it became necessary to exterminate the dingo." However, the extermination of dingoes meant an increase in kangaroos, "thus proving that in the occupation of a new country, it is often unwise to interfere with the natural order of things, by the extermination of certain pests, which are generally followed by greater ones" (Phillips, 1893: 145–147).

Sheep and cattle also consumed the reed beds of rivers. By 1862 reed beds had deteriorated due to sheep and cattle grazing, while wild pigs and horses further damaged reed beds and overgrazed grasses (Williams, 1962). This rapid degradation meant that by 1865, sheep consumed the grasses on the back blocks, and stations relied upon forage production. Grasses were also affected by the appearance of Bathurst burr in 1865, and these herbs began to replace the grasses. The *Pastoral Times* (May 30, 1868) reported that on the Jerilderie to Yanco road, saltbush and cotton bush had been completely grazed out.

Government policy hastened the environmental change. The Free Selection Act of 1861 led to formerly uninhabited areas, particularly the back blocks, being settled, replacing the remote shepherds or stockman huts. The population of Europeans was growing at a rapid pace, with a more balanced sex ratio than previously reported. All of these changes led to a more intensive use of the landscape. These changes also resulted in a progressive loss of Aboriginal control over and access to resources, producing a greater reliance of Aboriginal people upon Europeans. Given the changes to the reed beds, greater competition for water resources in the back blocks, and changes to animal populations as well as greater density of Europeans, traditional Aboriginal lifestyles were disappearing. Beside towns were semi-permanent camps of Aboriginal people. These became a focus of European complaint. In 1860, it was noted in the *Pastoral Times* that "a great number of native blacks are now in the neighbourhood, and corroborees are of almost nightly occurrence" (Mulham, 1994: 1).

Inexorably, Aboriginal people were incorporated as a marginal group into European society. Similarly, the patterns of disease experienced by Aboriginal populations were a darker reflection of European lifestyles. Those without access to or control of resources or medical care experienced these conditions more frequently and generally with more severe results (Dowling, 1997). As the numbers of Aboriginal people declined both absolutely and relatively compared to European numbers, the identification of Aboriginal people as a dying population became more common. Syphilis became less of a mortality threat to Aboriginal people, but respiratory infections and outbreaks of dysentery and diphtheria, particularly in town camps, became the leading cause of mortality (Dowling, 1997). At the same time people were progressively moved to missions and other settlements. The Aboriginal population became encapsulated by Europeans. By the 1870s the relationship between colonists and the land had changed dramatically, as had the demographic balance between colonists and Aboriginal people. The preexisting resilient socioecological landscape of Aboriginal populations had also been completely altered.

14.4   Bioarchaeological Evidence of Stress and Disease

This major contrast is visible in the bioarchaeological record, but to a limited extent. Most bioarchaeological work undertaken in Australia (Pardoe, 1991; Webb, 1995) includes undated skeletal samples from museum collections, which makes it difficult to ascertain the bioarchaeological consequences of contact. However, one discrete group of human remains was found in the Western Riverina region and has been radiocarbon dated to the postcontact period (Littleton, 2005). The remains include five individuals: two young females, one older adult female, one older adult male, and one young to mid-adult male. The two males had skeletal evidence of treponemal infection: stellate lesions on the frontal bone of the younger male and caries sicca with destruction of the nasal bones in the older adult male. Three of the five (one young woman is only represented by a humerus and femur) had evidence of antemortem trauma, and postcranial indicators of chronic systemic infection. Three also had evidence of cribra orbitalia.

In addition to differences in disease experience, other changes were apparent. Tooth wear in human remains of known precontact origin was rapid and severe (Richards and Brown, 1981). The older man in the group experienced similarly rapid and severe tooth wear. Indicators of oral infection were not found in this individual. By contrast, the young adult male had much less severe wear, which occurred more slowly. Two mandibular molars had carious lesions. Periapical abscesses were found in the maxillary dentition.

Comparison between these five people and five dated samples from southern Australia show clear contrasts (Table 14.2). In precontact groups, skeletal evidence of treponemal infection is uncommon and equivocal. It is not clear whether the infectious lesions observed in the precontact sample are of endemic syphilis or some other non-specific infection (Dowling, 1997). Cribra orbitalia occurs at moderate frequencies. Most groups experienced a high frequency of trauma; depressed fractures of the crania were particularly common.

Table 14.2 Comparison of lesion frequency in the Barham remains compared to precontact Aboriginal populations of known date and place.

	Cranial treponema	Postcranial infection	Cribra orbitalia	Trauma
Barham (n = 5)	60%	60%	60%	60%
Roonka (n = 132) 7000–50 BP (Prokopec, 1972)	1%	5%	1%	14%
Broadbeach (n = 139) 1390–50 BP (Webb, 1995)	0%	3%	23%	15%
Chowilla (n = 72) 6000–170 BP (Sandison, 1973)	0%	0%	0%	2%
Pleistocene (n = 44) >9500 BP (Webb, 1995)	0%	–	17%	14%

The physical evidence recovered from the postcontact Western Riverina is suggestive of a high rate of chronic infection, particularly treponemal disease, though it seems likely that these individuals experienced multiple chronic conditions. Rates of trauma were as high as, if not higher to precontact populations. These five individuals help attest to the consequences of European contact. Skeletal evidence of stress and disease affected every person except the female, whose skeleton was poorly preserved. This stark contrast accords with other assessments of the effect of contact on Aboriginal health – without a detailed context for the remains such evidence lacks nuance and is only interpretable as before and after, not part of change.

14.5   A Finer-Grained Analysis?

14.5.1   Ethnohistory

This broader history and bioarchaeological evidence reads like many others as an inevitable and irreversible move toward Aboriginal depopulation and dispossession in common with many studies of indigenous people and settler capitalism (e.g., Kunitz, 1996; Larsen and Milner, 1994). Yet, it remains possible to analyze this record for evidence of resilience and adaptation on the part of Aboriginal people. In order to do this, three historical accounts from the region are evaluated: the 1845 to 1848 diaries of Hobler (1882), a grazer who took up residence at first in Nap Nap and then at Paika (see Figure 14.3); an account from Mereweather (1859), a Presbyterian clergyman who resided in the Moulamein district from 1851 to 1852 (see Figure 14.3); and a third account from Krefft (1865), which dates to 1856 to 1857 and was recorded from the perspective of a scientific officer on an expedition down the Murray River. These three narratives traverse a crucial period from the occupation of land to the greater spread of European people. In addition, the accounts involve particular places and observations in contrast to more generic, time-averaged sequences. The accounts form an unusually detailed sequence of change over a crucial time frame and demonstrate a diversity of responses to those changes on the part of Aboriginal people, specifically how complex changes in ecological and cultural resilience may be observed in the ethnohistoric record (see also Butzer, 2012).

14.5.2   Hobler and Nap Nap (CE 1845 to 1848)

George Hobler (born 1801) was a grazer who moved to New South Wales in 1836, living and working as a gentleman farmer. In 1844 Hobler occupied Nap Nap and then Paika, two tracts of land on the Murrumbidgee River. Hobler resided in these areas between 1845 and 1848. Hobler's diary of that period is comprehensive, although lacking daily documentation. Most of Hobler's attention was focused upon the business of agriculture, yet this diary also provides a good account of relations with Aboriginal people in the area from the perspective of employment and occasional hostility.

Hobler moved sheep herds between Nap Nap and Paika along the Murrumbidgee River. Most references to Aboriginal people in this area describe them in terms of small groups of 3–14 individuals (Table 14.3; Figure 14.4). Hobler does not give any indication of how many people were resident on both properties, though there is mention of a camp that seems semi-permanent on Paika. The average number at this camp is probably around 8–10 men and associated women and children (e.g., May 31, 1847).

People were, however, still following a mobile round in terms of food supplies. In August 1847, Hobler wrote "none of my Blacks are at their camp tonight – I fear the flood is high enough to tempt them to leave me for the sake of the ducks and other food they get among the reeds." But by late September these individuals returned and a group was observed feasting off caterpillars (Hobler, 1882).

Hobler noted the variability of language and customs between the various Aboriginal groups:

31 April 1848 Paika: their language often varies so suddenly that at a distance of say 20 miles – the most common objects have a totally different name – and some of the tribes consist only of a few families.

There are also several mentions of people from the Lachlan River who are identified as "strange blacks." The assumption is that these individuals may have been involved in violent interactions. Despite the presence of European colonists, intertribal relations were still a significant source of concern, with accounts of conflict (March 1, 1847).

Table 14.3 Number and context of Aboriginal people sighted by Hobler and Mereweather.

Date	Location	Description
Hobler (1845–1847)		
March 19, 1845	Murrumbidgee	2 parties of natives – 14 in number
May 15, 1845	Lake Paika	8 blacks looking out for emus, camped by lake
March 29, 1847	Nap Nap	River below Cunuranga? I saw more than 20 blacks chiefly belonging to the Lachlan
May 31, 1847	Paika	Visited by 8 or 10 Paika blacks
September 5, 1847	Paika	Saw a horde of blacks at the edge of the water
March 31, 1848	Paika	About 20 blacks of a tribe called the Larche larches [Lati Lati?] who inhabit the extensive plains laying between the north bank of Murrumbidgee and the Darling River
Mereweather (1851–1852)		
May 27, 1851	Moolpar	50–60 men, women, and children
May 30, 1851	Moulamein	"number of blacks at door of church"
June, 1851	General district	"thinly population by small tribes of blacks"
July 4, 1851	Mr Learmouth's station	Baptized half caste child
July 25, 1851	Moolpa	Ceremonial (corroboree?) at Moolpa
August 9, 1851	Kieta	Large tribe of blacks permanently camped in the neighborhood
August 15, 1851	Poon Boon	Black's camp – different language group
June 1, 1852	Mr Gwynne's station	Native corroboree
June 30, 1852	Mt Dispersion	Regular black's camp
July 1, 1852	Murray River	One black man fishing
August 25, 1852	Maiden's Punt	"Fine tribe of blacks temporarily camped, 25 canoes, c100 dogs"

Apart from this continuity of concern with intertribal relations, ceremonial relations were also maintained, along with burial customs (March 7, 1847), while Aboriginal people are also noted as learning English:

31 April 1848 Paika: Attended a dance or corrobora of the natives – about ¼ mile down the river a few nights ago ... It is to be regretted that no person of ability has attempted to record any account of the various tribes of blacks indigenous to this great island, they learn our language when we come upon a fresh tribe of them and the white man adopts a few of their words so as to form a jargon by which communication upon simple subjects can be kept up – but we acquire no knowledge of their history, or religious or superstitious feeling.

The majority of Hobler's descriptions refer to Aboriginal people obtaining food from the lake or surrounding area. Specific mention is made of netting fish, hunting emus, crows, and eating seasonal foods: large amounts of tadpoles and caterpillars. Food and hunting is also a major arena for interaction between Aboriginal people

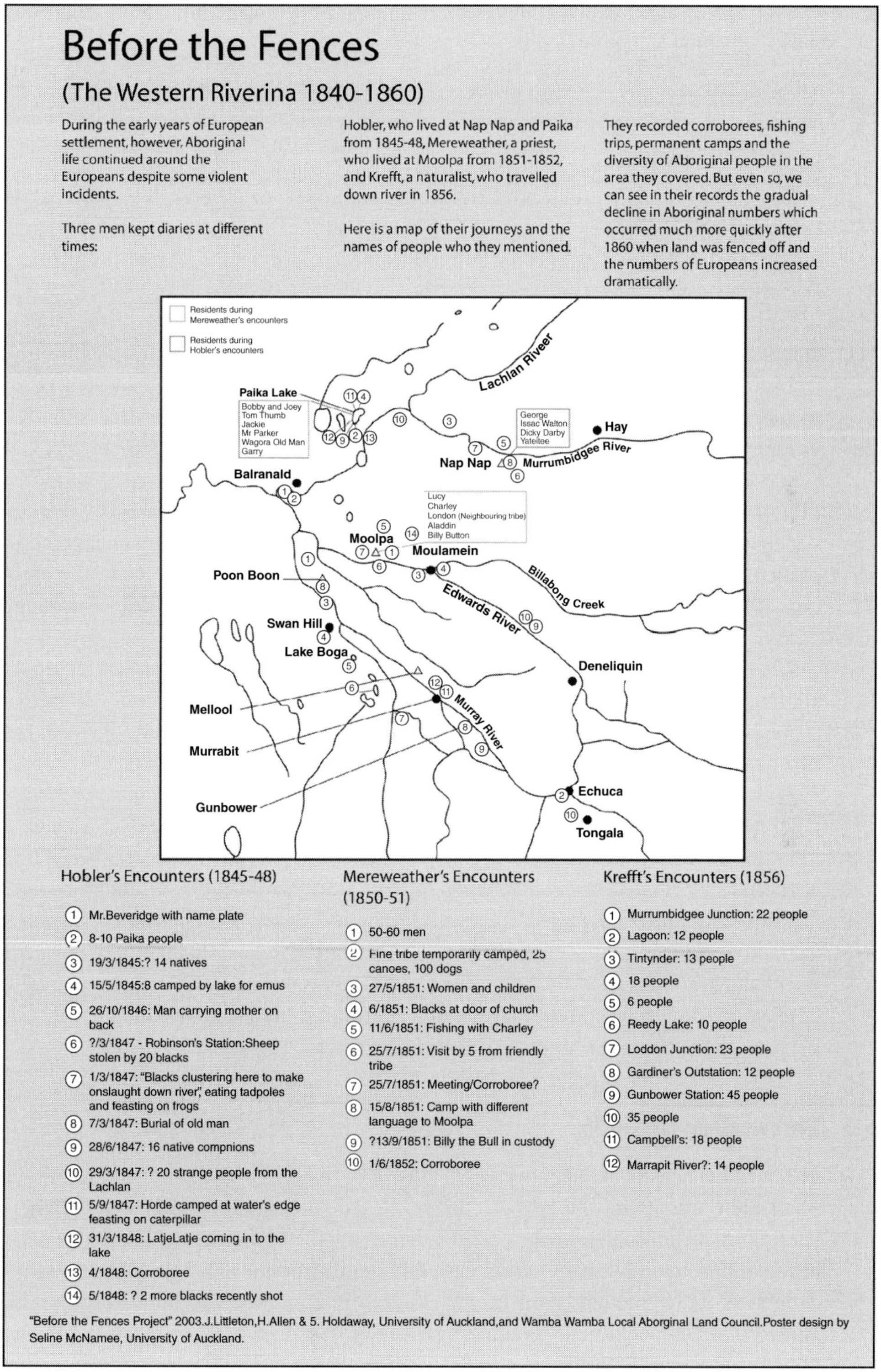

Before the Fences

(The Western Riverina 1840-1860)

During the early years of European settlement, however, Aboriginal life continued around the Europeans despite some violent incidents.

Three men kept diaries at different times:

Hobler, who lived at Nap Nap and Paika from 1845-48, Mereweather, a priest, who lived at Moolpa from 1851-1852, and Krefft, a naturalist, who travelled down river in 1856.

Here is a map of their journeys and the names of people who they mentioned.

They recorded corroborees, fishing trips, permanent camps and the diversity of Aboriginal people in the area they covered. But even so, we can see in their records the gradual decline in Aboriginal numbers which occurred much more quickly after 1860 when land was fenced off and the numbers of Europeans increased dramatically.

Residents during Mereweather's encounters

Residents during Hobler's encounters

Lachlan River

Paika Lake
Bobby and Joey
Tom Thumb
Jackie
Mr Parker
Wagora Old Man
Garry

George
Issac Walton
Dicky Darby
Yateitee

Hay

Nap Nap   Murrumbidgee River

Balranald

Lucy
Charley
London (Neighbouring tribe)
Aladdin
Billy Button

Moolpa   Moulamein

Poon Boon

Edwards River

Billabong Creek

Swan Hill

Lake Boga

Deneliquin

Mellool

Murray River

Murrabit

Echuca

Gunbower

Tongala

Hobler's Encounters (1845-48)

1. Mr.Beveridge with name plate
2. 8-10 Paika people
3. 19/3/1845:? 14 natives
4. 15/5/1845:8 camped by lake for emus
5. 26/10/1846: Man carrying mother on back
6. ?/3/1847 - Robinson's Station:Sheep stolen by 20 blacks
7. 1/3/1847: "Blacks clustering here to make onslaught down river", eating tadpoles and feasting on frogs
8. 7/3/1847: Burial of old man
9. 28/6/1847: 16 native compnions
10. 29/3/1847: ? 20 strange people from the Lachlan
11. 5/9/1847: Horde camped at water's edge feasting on caterpillar
12. 31/3/1848: LatjeLatje coming in to the lake
13. 4/1848: Corroboree
14. 5/1848: ? 2 more blacks recently shot

Mereweather's Encounters (1850-51)

1. 50-60 men
2. Fine tribe temporarily camped, 25 canoes, 100 dogs
3. 27/5/1851: Women and children
4. 6/1851: Blacks at door of church
5. 11/6/1851: Fishing with Charley
6. 25/7/1851: Visit by 5 from friendly tribe
7. 25/7/1851: Meeting/Corroboree?
8. 15/8/1851: Camp with different language to Moolpa
9. ?13/9/1851: Billy the Bull in custody
10. 1/6/1852: Corroboree

Krefft's Encounters (1856)

1. Murrumbidgee Junction: 22 people
2. Lagoon: 12 people
3. Tintynder: 13 people
4. 18 people
5. 6 people
6. Reedy Lake: 10 people
7. Loddon Junction: 23 people
8. Gardiner's Outstation: 12 people
9. Gunbower Station: 45 people
10. 35 people
11. Campbell's: 18 people
12. Marrapit River?: 14 people

"Before the Fences Project" 2003.J.Littleton,H.Allen & 5. Holdaway, University of Auckland,and Wamba Wamba Local Aboriginal Land Council.Poster design by Seline McNamee, University of Auckland.

Figure 14.4 Accounts of Aboriginal people and their location from Hobler, Mereweather, and Krefft (Littleton *et al.*, 2003).

and the Europeans. Food is given and exchanged, as is information about what food is available and how to catch it:

6 Sept 1847 Paika: Jackie brought me 10 goose eggs today seven had chicks in them and were returned as he prefers them in that state, the other three were fried for dinner and proved very fine eating.

Hobler does not mention exchanges of flour, sugar, or tobacco, but more often fishhooks and sheep carcasses, even at times fish. Taken together, these accounts suggest that the Aboriginal people at the station were still obtaining traditional forms of carbohydrates.

Personal relationships are important in Hobler's account and a distinction is drawn between people belonging to the area, with whom there are friendships and relationships of trust, and those from outside, who are defined as a source of potential trouble (e.g., July 22, 1848). Hostility was a major concern, although intermittent. Hobler only mentions two main incidents. One in October 1846 at Paika, where a hut was robbed. The other in March 1847 when sheep were stolen from the Upper Station at Nap Nap. This confirms the impression gained by Penney (1979) more generally for the area, that hostility seemed to be dependent upon particular sets of relationships between individuals. However, violence certainly escalated rapidly, as seen in Hobler's description of the killing of Andrew Beveridge (May 9, 1848).

What is more common than hostility in Hobler's account is the gradual incorporation of Aboriginal people in labor relations. Much of the employment of Aboriginal people was casual – extra hands when moving stock and sending messages are the two most common areas of employment apart from obtaining tree bark.

Overall, Hobler's concern is with establishing properties – in this endeavor Aboriginal people are often considered in terms of labor or social interactions involving food and hunting. Clearly both groups frequently encountered one another – it is never hard for Hobler to find help when moving stock, for instance, although he does mention occasional absences. However, Aboriginal people living in the area retain distinctive cultural practices – some individuals are regular inhabitants of Hobler's world and become part of the network of social and economic relations, but a greater number are only intermittent participants continuing independent practices of subsistence, movement, ceremonies, and social concerns.

14.5.3   Mereweather 1851–1852

Mereweather's account dates five years later than Hobler's and is centered around the Moulamein district on the Edwards River (Figure 14.4). Mereweather was a clergyman. Contrary to Hobler, Mereweather's diaries are focused on social life and general observations. In addition, given concern for congregational well-being, Mereweather comments more frequently on health conditions. However, the impression is also gained that the people encountered by Mereweather had been in much more sustained contact with Europeans.

Table 14.3 also lists Mereweather's encounters of Aboriginal groups between 1851 and 1852 (see also Figure 14.4). The groups encountered are larger than those described by Hobler, and the locations mentioned are native camps, including Moolpa, Kieta, and Poon Boon stations:

May 27, 1851 Molopo: Close to the head-station is a camp of the natives, consisting of 50 to 60 men women and children and innumerable mangy dogs. These poor people pick up what they can get, and make themselves useful in many ways, But they like their wild life, and cannot be prevailed on to enter into regular service. (Mereweather, 1859: 101)

Despite these large encampments near station homesteads, Aboriginal people were dispersed across the landscape and at this stage still outnumbered the Europeans (Mereweather, 1859). Aboriginal people were also concerned with customary relations, with Mereweather detailing ceremonies, meetings, and corroborees between neighboring groups as demonstrated in a description of a visit after intergroup conflict and death by men from a friendly group (Mereweather, 1859: 123).

As with Hobler, Mereweather's descriptions of hunting activities point to a lack of direct competition with Europeans and even the odd bit of cooperation. Mereweather does, however, mention several violent incidents between Aboriginal people, between Aboriginal and European groups, and between Aboriginal people and non-Europeans (e.g., Mereweather, 1859: 179).

One of the most significant aspects of Mereweather's account is, however, a discussion of the shepherds:

June 4, 1851 Moolpar: Far away in the plains at a distance of perhaps 20 miles from the head station, do these poor exiles stupidly vegetate, tending stupid sheep, for sheep are the most stupid of animals. Now and then some blacks pass by. Once a week they get their rations from the head stations . . . The shepherds about here are many of them old convicts from the Sydney side, many of them fugitives from the sea-board for some crime, but nearly all of them have brought on a premature old age from early excessive, are suffering from various chronic diseases. (Mereweather, 1859: 98)

While Mereweather does not directly address the issue of sexual relations between Europeans and Aboriginal people, he is clearly aware of the implications of such relations (Mereweather, 1859: 103). For August 15, 1851, Mereweather wrote:

Rode to a station called Poon Boon. And then it is sad to see how quickly a tribe melts away after contact with civilization. Before the whites came they were always unclothed; now they are clothed in our cast off clothes half their time and unclothed the other half; so then they catch cold, and die of consumption. And I find they cease to reproduce. I have as yet scarce seen any babies or very young children. (Mereweather, 1859: 129)

Most European commentators wrote as if Aboriginal people were fading away before the advance of a superior group due to higher death rates (often coupled with infanticide). However, Mereweather's account portrays an increasingly vulnerable population, with evidence for demographic loss, quite possibly associated with increasing STIs.

In contrast to Hobler, Mereweather references larger groups, established more closely and permanently beside stations. Despite these indications of people being drawn into more permanent economic and social relationships with Europeans and of a lessening of traditional patterns of subsistence and movement, many traditional Aboriginal practices (e.g., hunting for food, ceremonies, intertribal relations, and burials) were actively maintained.

14.5.4   Krefft 1856–1857

The final account in this series was written five years later (ca. 1865) and situated in the most populous part of the Western Riverina (Figure 14.4). Krefft was the scientific officer and second in command of an expedition down the Murray River, led by William Blandowski (Allen, 2009). The number and location of Aboriginal people sighted by Krefft are listed in Table 14.4. The extracts in Krefft's narrative address Aboriginal people living in the areas of Gunbower and Lake Boga, Victoria and are based upon a particular set of interactions involving the collection of specimens and some wider personal observations.

Unlike the accounts of Hobler, where encounters with Aboriginal people were periodic, Krefft's account portrays a population that moved in close proximity to

Table 14.4 Number and location of Aboriginal sightings recorded by Krefft.

Krefft (1857)	N
Apple's Hotel	8
Campaspe River	13
Echuca	35
Gardiner's Station	45
Gardiner's Outstation	12
Campbell's Station	18
Loddon Junction	23
Reedy Lake	10
Lake Boga	6
Murrapit River	14
Swan Hill	18
Tintindyre	13
Coghill's Station	7
Hamilton's Station	22
Lagoon near Murrumbidgee Junction	12
McCallum's and Grant's Station	31
Euston (including native police)	40
Half-way Lagoon	29
Kilkine	11
McGrath's Station	7
Jamieson's Station and William's Station	35
Darling Junction	35

the European expedition, with awareness of items such as capital and tobacco. For example:

Sunday 29th Jan we finished the camp which Mr. Bl. who had taken up his quarters at the home station superintended our doings. We had just got the place into trim when the first natives made their appearance. They were fine stalwart fellows but as I shall have occasion hereafter to describe them I will only state that these half dozen fellows soon found out who we were and the next morning a host of men women and children arrived who made their mia mias not 15 yards from our tent, though I remonstrated with Mr. Bl. and want him to order the black fellows further off . . . Almost all of the natives carried firearms and we soon found out that powder and shot was the currency of their realm. (Krefft, unpublished journal, State Library of New South Wales, Sydney)

Blandowski and Krefft employed Aboriginal people on a casual basis. By this stage, payment in money as opposed to food or tobacco is evident in Hobler's account. The desirability of European goods and the potential rewards of associating with Europeans are much more apparent motivations in Krefft's account. This is partly because Krefft represents a casual opportunity to the Aboriginal population rather than being part of the longer network of relationships described by Hobler and Mereweather. But it is also probably a reflection of the time when the interactions between Europeans and Aboriginal people are much more intense, with greater evidence of interaction and interest in material goods due to encroaching dispossession.

One of the results of increasing interaction – a greater drift to towns and drinking – is clear in Krefft's account. When Krefft arrives in town to dispatch part of his collection, three or four men, "who were going to spend the shillings they had earned, like white fellows, that is get drunk" (Krefft, 1865: 46) accompany this journey. This parallels comments in the *Pastoral Times* five years later that suggest increasing intensity in the relationships between Aboriginal communities and European settlers (cited in Mulham, 1994: 1).

Again, there is evidence in Krefft's account of semi-permanent camps near stations: "With the close of the day we arrived at Mr. Campbell's station, Mr. Blandowski went to shake hands with the proprietor and I had a turn through the paddock where I fell in with a tribe of natives. About 15 or 16 men, women, and children were encamped close to the creek" (Krefft, unpublished journal). While Krefft recounts how the group gathered materials left behind by the expedition, there is not complete economic dependence of Aboriginal people upon Europeans. Krefft makes this intermediate state clear, and also how tethered these relations were in terms of economic and sexual interactions:

I think I have proved to the reader the independence of the native (as far as food is concerned) from his white brethren, but there are several items of consumption which can only be supplied by the white men and to procure these the Aborigines of Australia are only too ready to sacrifice their own independence or give up their wives, sisters or daughters to the white man's desires. These articles are flour, tea and sugar, tobacco, powder and shot, or their equivalent money. If we look at this from a moral point of view, I do not think the native is much to blame. (Krefft, unpublished journal)

These comments echo, but also extend, Mereweather's statements from the Edward River. There is, however, one important distinction. Krefft emphasizes the interdependence between Europeans and Aboriginal people, and this seems to follow the trend that occurred as European settlement became denser and the impact of contact intensified. Nevertheless, even in 1857, Aboriginal life continued many traditional aspects such as burial customs and ceremonies (Krefft, 1865).

Aboriginal people were still living on traditional foods. Krefft (1865) notes that some communities were living on typha roots (or wargal) gathered from the nearby swamp. Yet there had been major ecological changes. Strychnine poisoning had been used to kill off dingoes, while large-scale hunting of kangaroos had taken place in some areas. Wakefield (1966) noted that many of the mammals collected in northern Victoria or southwestern New South Wales by Krefft have not been observed since 1857. Numerous species, including the rat-kangaroos, hare-wallabies, bandicoots, stick-nest rats, and nail-tailed wallabies have been locally extinct since the 1880s at least. Aboriginal numbers have also undergone a major change in more populous areas: Krefft (1865: 368) noted that the Aboriginal population in Victoria had reduced from 5000 to 1768 people between 1847 and 1858.

14.5.5 Comparison of the Accounts

Hobler, Mereweather, and Krefft each wrote 5–6 years apart, but these temporally disparate accounts include similar themes. Aboriginal people are conspicuously present, but independent of Europeans. However, there is also a succession between the accounts. In 1846, when Hobler was writing, Aboriginal people were present as part of the backdrop to settlement, available for casual labor, a source of information, and a concern in terms of hostility, but independent of European colonists. Aboriginal people clearly outnumbered European colonists in these descriptions, despite a smallpox outbreak approximately 15 years earlier. Mereweather lived and traveled five years later in an area more densely settled by Europeans. In this account, the transition to more permanent camps, more dependent relations, and certainly deteriorating health and declining fertility is apparent. Mereweather's account mirrors Krefft's in implied sexual relations between Aboriginal people and Europeans, but this account notes the potential impact of these relations on Aboriginal fertility.

Krefft emphasizes the independence of Aboriginal people, but also details quite clearly the areas of close interest: tobacco, alcohol, sugar, money, and the deleterious effects upon Aboriginal people due to reliance upon Europeans. In this account, Aboriginal people actively seek goods, though this is likely tethered to dispossession of land and the expansion of poverty due to acculturation. This diverges from Hobler's accounts, in which such goods are barely mentioned, while Mereweather only mentions tobacco. Krefft is in an even more populous area where the European population has increased even further, and the wide-ranging environmental changes associated with fencing and water control have begun.

14.6 Conclusion

These accounts demonstrate that despite the potentially devastating impact of smallpox, Aboriginal people were engaged in traditional economic and social practices. It isn't clear that the distribution of people on the landscape mirrors what it was in the past, but all accounts coherently describe larger camps located close to permanent water, as well as describing mobile bands of people. At this point, it appears that contact with European colonists was accommodated within the realms of traditional patterns of subsistence and cultural practices.

In the early stages of European colonization, colonizers and Aboriginal people occupied land in a similar fashion – focusing on the rivers with intermittent and more mobile use of the back country, continuing what was a set of flexible practices in response to a harsh, unpredictable environment. Such a pattern of land use emphasized the importance of shepherds as a point of contact with Aboriginal people. However, as the documentation shows, well into the 1850s the two lifestyles persist. While there were episodes of hostility, Aboriginal people still outnumbered Europeans and were actively incorporating these populations into economic and social relations while maintaining ceremonial and ritual practices of central importance. Thus, interactions between the two groups had not harmed the broader identity of Australian Aborigines.

The picture was not idyllic, nor can it be simply characterized as either adaptation or breakdown (Butzer, 2012). Relationships with individual Europeans were variable. Some were friendly, many were predatory. Contact resulted in disease transmission to the Aboriginal people. However, it is not until a sequence of changes in economic relations that the absolute deterioration of Aboriginal health was observed (Dowling, 1997). These changes began around 1850, with increased use of Aboriginal labor, influx of more Europeans and closer settlement, and reorganization of landscapes through fencing, water control, and increased grazing. Closure of land facilitated by technological changes and by government policy accelerated the process of marginalization of Aboriginal people, which entailed the foreclosure of traditional lifeways at the same time that these populations actively sought European goods. This was, however, reasonably late in the sequence of European occupation in the Western Riverina. Along with Penney (1979), it is clear that in regions such as Western Victoria, direct conflict and collapse of Aboriginal lifeways occurred long after contact with European colonialists. Aboriginal life appeared more resilient in this area, where both groups occupied the land at relatively low intensity and focused on essentially different resources.

The resilience and continuation of Aboriginal lifestyles is apparent from Hobler, Mereweather, and Krefft, as well as the other archival sources. The Aboriginal response to contact was complex: hostility, friendship, tolerance, mutually ignoring each other (for a parallel account, see Burke et al., 2016). Changes in economic circumstances acted to greatly marginalize and encapsulate Aboriginal people. Resilience did not dramatically fail all at once, nor was the imperial project of dispossession so complete that Aboriginal people and culture disappeared completely. As Burke *et al.* (2016) note for Central Murray, despite the inability to link modern Aboriginal inhabitants to the named indigenous people in early ethnohistoric accounts, Aboriginal traditions and occupation of the area persist. This is the parallel of Diener's observation (1974) of persistence in the Hutterite cultural system and Butzer's assessment of cultural resilience as having a "tricky quality" (Butzer, 2012: 3638).

However, the three accounts of these men provide a wealth of detail, and indicate change over a short space of time that is not apparent within bioarchaeological analyses contrasting pre- and postcontact human remains or archaeological surveys in which it has proved very difficult to isolate this particular phase (Littleton *et al.*, 2003). Populations occupying the Western Riverina environment had sustainable, resilient economies through the utilization of a wide range of plant and animal resources. These populations were, however, exposed to a variety of conditions following European colonialism that eroded this resilience, and likely accelerated collapse. These conditions included exposure to STIs at exceedingly high rates as well as exposure to violence and disease, while the colonial practice of fencing and water control restricted access to the most crucial resources, water and land. Here specifically, populations lost demographic and socioecological coherency as reproduction and subsistence practices suffered. This greatly imperiled adaptive capacity and increased the vulnerability of Aboriginal populations.

Overall, this study reveals a palimpsest of Aboriginal and European interaction. Demonstrating resilience and how it was maintained or weakened over such a dynamic period requires relating the bioarchaeological record to the historic wherever possible. These accounts provide a more fine-grained perspective than those of binary contrasts, specifically constructing a before/after scenario. Bioarchaeological analyses most commonly rely on analysis of a number of individuals argued or assumed to be in some way representative of a population over a particular period of time. The time averaging that is inherent in this approach, plus the reliance of such analyses upon central tendencies, may mask variability between individuals and can hide evidence of progressive transformation. As Butzer (2012) demonstrates, illustrating the true complexity of collapse engenders reliance upon multiple data sources and attention to the scales at which information is applicable.

Acknowledgments

The fieldwork behind this project was undertaken with the permission and assistance of the Wamba Wamba Local Aboriginal Land Council and the Hay Plains Local Aboriginal Land Council. Justin Shiner helped with some of the fieldwork while Harry Allen and Simon Holdaway were collaborators on the field project "Before the Fences," funded by the Australian Institute of Aboriginal and Torres Strait Islander Studies. This chapter was produced with the assistance of Briar Sefton, who prepared the figures, and with the input of the reviewers and the biological anthropology writing group at the University of Auckland. Thanks to all of these numerous collaborators.

References

Allen, H. (2009). Native companions: Blandowski, Krefft and the Aborigines on the Murray River expedition. *Proceedings of the Royal Society of Victoria*, **121**, 129–145.

Baker, B. J. and Kealhofer L. (1996). Introduction. In B. J. Baker and L. Kealhofer, eds., *Bioarchaeology of Native American Adaptation in Spanish Borderlands*. Gainesville, FL: University Press of Florida, pp. 1–13.

Bartley, N. (1892). *Opals and Agates*. Brisbane: Gordon and Gotch.

Baylis, J. (1914). *Early History of the Murrumbidgee*. Wagga Wagga: Wagga Wagga Express.

Beveridge, P. (1883). *Of the Aborigines inhabiting the great lacustrine and riverine depression of the Lower Murray, Lower Murrumbidgee, Lower Lachlan, and Lower Darling*. Sydney: Royal Society of New South Wales.

Birdsell, J. B. (1953). Some environmental and cultural factors influencing the structuring of Australian Aboriginal populations. *The American Naturalist*, **87**, 171–207.

Bride, T. F. and Sayers, C. E. (1898). *Letters from Victorian Pioneers*. Melbourne: Heinemann.

Buchan, R. (1983). *Report on an Archaeological Survey in the Murray Valley, NSW 1973–4*. Report to NSW National Parks and Wildlife Service.

Burke, H., Roberts, A., Morrison, M., and Sullivan, V. (2016). The space of conflict: Aboriginal/European interactions and frontier violence on the western Central Murray, South Australia, 1830–41. *Aboriginal History*, **40**, 145–179.

Butlin, N. G. (1983). *Our Original Aggression: Aboriginal Populations of Southeastern Australia, 1788–1850*. Sydney: Allen & Unwin.

Butzer, K. (2012). Collapse, environment, and society. *Proceedings of the National Academy of Sciences*, **109**, 3632–3639.

Butzer, K. and Endfield, G. (2012). Critical perspectives on historical collapse. *Proceedings of the National Academy of Sciences*, **109**, 3628–3631.

Byrne, J. (1849). *Twelve Years' Wanderings in the British Colonies from 1835–1847*. London: R.C. Bentley.

Calder, W. (1981). *Beyond the View: Our Changing Landscapes*. Melbourne: Inkata Press.

Christie, M. (1979). *Aborigines in Colonial Victoria, 1835–1886*. Sydney: Sydney University Press.

Clark, I. D. (1990). *Aboriginal Languages and Clans*. Melbourne: Monash University.

Corris, P. (1968). *Aborigines and Europeans in Western Victoria*. Canberra: Australian Institute of Aboriginal Studies.

Craib, J. (1991). Archaeological survey of the Moira-Millewa State Forests. Report to NSW National Parks and Wildlife Service, Sydney.

Curr, E. M. (1883). *Recollections of Squatting in Victoria: Then Called the Port Phillip District (from 1841 to 1851)*. Sydney: Robertson.

Diener, P. (1974). Ecology or evolution? The Hutterite case. *American Ethnologist*, **1**, 601–618.

Dobyns, H. F. (1983). *Their Number Become Thinned: Native American Population Dynamics in Eastern North America*. Knoxville, TN: University of Tennessee Press.

Dowling, P. (1997). *A Great Deal of Sickness*. PhD dissertation, Australian National University.

Dowling, P. (2017). What Charles Sturt saw in 1830: Syphilis beyond the colonial boundaries. *Health and History*, **19**, 44–59.

Faulseit, R. K. (2016). Collapse, resilience, and transformation in complex societies: Modelling trends and understanding diversity. In R. K. Faulseit, ed., *Beyond Collapse: Archaeological Perspectives on Resilience, Revitalization, and Transformation in Complex Societies*. Carbondale, IL: University of Southern Illinois Press, pp. 1–26.

Freeman, H. (1985). *Murrumbidgee Memories and Riverina Reminiscences*. Maryborough: Dominion Press.

Grant, E. (1970). *Walking with Time: The story of the Wakool Country*. Melbourne: Abadcada Press.

Hackett, C. (1975). An introduction to diagnostic criteria of syphilis, treponarid and yaws (treponematoses) in dry bones, and some implications. *Virchows Archives A: Pathology, Anatomy and Histology*, **368**, 229–241.

Hawdon, J. (1952). *The Journal of a Journey from New South Wales to Adelaide: The Capital of South Australia, Performed in 1838*. Melbourne: Georgian House.

Hobler, G. (1992 [1882]). *The Diaries of "Pioneer" George Hobler Oct 6, 1800 – Dec 13, 1882*. Sydney: C & H Reproductions.

Holling, C. S. (1973). Resilience and stability of ecological systems. *Annual Review of Ecology and Systematics*, **4**, 1–23.

Humphries, P. (2007). Historical indigenous use of aquatic resources in Australia's Murray-Darling basin and its implications for river management. *Ecological Management and Restoration*, **8**, 106–113

Jeans, D. N. (1972). *An Historical Geography of NSW to 1901*. Sydney: Reed Education.

Jervis, J. (1952). The Western Riverina. *Royal Australian Historical Society*, **38**, 1–30.

Kates, R. W. and Clark, W. C. (1996). Environmental surprise: Expecting the unexpected? *Environment: Science and Policy for Sustainable Development*, **38**, 6–34.

Keck, M. and Sakdapolrak, P. (2013). What is social resilience? Lessons learned and ways forward. *Erdkunde*, **67**, 5–19.

Krefft, G. (1865). On the manners and customs of the Aborigines of the Lower Murray and Darling. *Transactions of the Philosophical Society of New South Wales*, **1862–1865**, 357–374.

Kunitz, S. J. (1996). *Disease and Social Diversity: The European Impact on the Health of Non-Europeans*. New York, NY: Oxford University Press.

Larsen, C. S. and Milner, G. R., eds. (1994). *In the Wake of Contact: Biological Responses to Conquest*. New York, NY: Wiley-Blackwell.

Littleton, J. (2002). Mortuary behaviour on the Hay Plain: Do cemeteries exist? *Archaeology in Oceania*, **37**, 105–122.

Littleton, J. (2005). Data quarrying in the western Riverina: A regional perspective on post-contact health, In I. Macfarlane, R. Paton, and M. Mountain, eds., *Many Exchanges: Archaeology, History, Community and the Work of Isabel McBryde*. Canberra: Aboriginal History Inc., pp. 199–218.

Littleton, J. (2007). Time and memory: Historic accounts of Aboriginal burials in south-eastern Australia. *Aboriginal History*, **2007**, 103–121.

Littleton, J. and Allen, H. (2007). Hunter-gatherer burials and the creation of persistent places in southeastern Australia. *Journal of Anthropological Archaeology*, **26**, 283–298.

Littleton, J., Allen, H., Shiner, J., and Holdaway, S. (2003). *Before the Fences*. Canberra: Australian Institute of Aboriginal and Torres Strait Islander Studies.

Martin, S. (2007). *Inscribing the Plains: Constructed Landscapes*. PhD dissertation, University of New England.

Mein, P. (1897). "Letter to H.C. Russell," October 25, Mitchell Library, Sydney.

Mereweather, J. (1859). *Diary of a Working Clergyman in Australia and Tasmania*. London: Hatchard.

Mitchell, T. L. (1839). *Three Expeditions to the Interior of Eastern Australia*. London: T. & W. Boone.

Mulham, W. (1994). *The Best Crossing Place*. Deniliquin: Reliance Stationery and Printery.

Murphy, M. S. and Klaus, H. K. (2017). Transcending conquest: Bioarchaeological perspectives on conquest and culture contact for the twenty-first century. In M. S. Murphy and H. D. Klaus, eds., *Colonized Bodies, Worlds Transformed: Towards a Global Bioarchaeology of Contact and Colonialism*. Gainesville, FL: University Press of Florida, pp. 1–40.

Musgrave, S. (1930). *The Way Back*. Parramatta: Cumberland Argus.

Pardoe, C. (1988). The cemetery as symbol: The distribution of prehistoric Aboriginal burial grounds in southeastern Australia. *Archaeology in Oceania*, **23**, 1–16.

Pardoe, C. (1991). Isolation and evolution in Tasmania. *Current Anthropology*, **32**, 1–21.

Parker, E. (1841). "Letter, 15 October, to Robinson," in Public Records Office of Victoria, Melbourne.

Penney, J. (1979). *The Death of Queen Aggie: Culture Contact in the Mid-Murray Region.* Honors thesis, La Trobe University.

Phillips, J. (1893). *Reminiscences of Australian Early Life.* London: AP Marsden.

Pickard, J. (2007). The transition from shepherding to fencing in colonial Australia. *Rural History*, **18**, 143.

Prokopec, M. (1972). Demographical and morphological aspects of the Roonka population. *Archaeology and Physical Anthropology in Oceania*, **22**, 161–176.

Richards, L. and Brown, T. (1981). Dental attrition and age relationships in Australian Aboriginals. *Archaeology in Oceania*, **16**, 94–97.

Robertson, S. (2007). Sources of bias in the Murray Black collection: Implications for palaeopathological analysis. *Australian Aboriginal Studies*, **1**, 116.

Sandison, A. (1973). Palaeopathology of human bones from Murray River region between Mildura and Renmark, Australia. *Memoirs of the National Museum of Victoria*, **34**, 173–174.

Stojanowski, C. M. (2017). The bioarchaeology of colonialism: Past perspectives and future prospects. In M. S. Murphy and H. D. Klaus, eds., *Colonized Bodies, Worlds Transformed: Toward a Global Bioarchaeology of Contact and Colonialism.* Gainesville, Fl: University Press of Florida, pp. 411–446.

Sturt, C. (1833). *Two Expeditions into the Interior of Southern Australia*, vol. 4. London: Smith, Elder and Co..

Tainter, J. A. (1988). *The Collapse of Complex Societies.* Cambridge: Cambridge University Press.

Vayda, A. P. and McCay, B. J. (1975). New directions in ecology and ecological anthropology. *Annual Review of Anthropology*, **4**, 293–306.

Wakefield, N. A. (1966). Mammals of the Blandowski Expedition to north-western Victoria. *Proceedings of the Royal Society of Victoria*, **79**, 371–391.

Webb, S. G. (1995). *Palaeopathology of Australian Aborigines: Health and Disease across a Hunter-Gatherer Continent.* Oxford: Oxford University Press.

Williams, O. B. (1962). The Riverina and its pastoral industry, 1860–1869. In A. Barnard, ed., *The Simple Fleece: Studies in the Australian Wool Industry.* Melbourne: Melbourne University Press, pp. 411–434.

15 Models, Metaphors, and Measures

Jane E. Buikstra

To us in our secular modern society, the predicament in which the Greenlanders found themselves is difficult to fathom. To them, however, concerned with their social survival as much as with their biological survival, it was out of the question to invest less in churches, to imitate or intermarry with the Inuit, and thereby to face an eternity in Hell just in order to survive another winter on Earth.   Diamond, 2005: 247

"We've always been hunters here," Nayukpuq says. "We hunt regardless of the situation."   Hughes, 2018

15.1   Introduction

In the first epigraph, Jared Diamond is referring to the "collapse" of Medieval Norse settlements on Greenland, where they lacked resilience in the face of climate change, anthropogenic degradation of the environment, uneasy relations with the Inuit, and produced inadequate societal responses to all these challenges. Contemporary Inuit hunters, by contrast, undoubtedly wary of their tall, aloof, and occasionally hostile neighbors, managed very well even further north along the margins of the Greenland glacier. In this oft-cited example, it was the Inuit who showed socioecological and cultural resilience in the face of climatic and human challenges. The Norse, who Diamond (2005: 247) characterizes as "more European than Europeans themselves" in cuisine, in style of dress, and in commitment to the Church, failed to meet these challenges.

Prominent scientific accounts (e.g., Dugmore *et al.*, 2012) augment Diamond's interpretation of the Medieval Norse–Inuit Greenland experience by arguing that the Norse made thirteenth- and fourteenth-century adjustments that led them down the narrow path that ensured their inability to further adjust to the rigors of climate change in the fifteenth century (Levi, 1997; Pierson, 2000). However one wishes to interpret the situation, the Greenlandic Inuit obviously proved more resilient than the Norse.

The second epigraph reinforces the relevance of hunter-gatherer studies today. Hughes (2018) is reporting technological appropriation of a drone by Inuit to map the best ice course to the Chukchi Sea in Shismaref, western Alaska. Global warming is rapidly changing the ice front, and the drones render hunting efforts more efficient. Nayukpuq also reports changes in the animals available, but – as reinforced in the epigram – his own and his community's core identity as hunters is both ancient and persistent, even in the face of profound challenges. These Alaskan hunters, whose adaptations over millennia excite awe and respect, now hunt aided by drones and skidoos but, importantly, they *hunt*. In contrast, the Norse may have lost their resilience by maintaining a different, rigid core identity – that of Europeans.

These examples testify to the resilience of the Inuit hunter-gatherers in the face of both environmental and colonial challenges. Studying such resilience is clearly merited in the twenty-first century, as the doomsday clock edges ever closer to the probability that our species will destroy the planet. Additional rationales for studying past and contemporary hunter-gatherers include the centrality and time depth of hunter-gatherer lifeways as baselines for inferences about our unique humanity, as Jordan and Cummings (2014) stress in *The Oxford Handbook of the Archaeology and Anthropology of Hunter-Gatherers* (Cummings *et al.*, 2014). Our cultural and biological heritage developed within these groups, who for countless millennia spread globally and persisted. Today, inquiries into myriad subjects regarding the human mind by public intellectuals such as Jared Diamond and Steven Pinker are rooted in attempts to characterize humankind's past. As Lee and Daly (1999: 1) emphasize in *The Cambridge Encyclopedia of Hunters and Gatherers*, the world's hunting and gathering peoples "represent the oldest and perhaps the most successful human adaptation." As this volume amply demonstrates, however, these adaptations involve complexity at a number of levels, especially the manner in which hunter-gatherers have constructed their worlds and the manner in which they have responded to external challenges. To attempt to paint them as a primordial adaptation upon which complexity developed does a disservice to the range of globally diverse and remarkably resilient hunting and gathering lifeways.

The history of hunter-gatherer studies thus reverberates through the disciplines of archaeology and anthropology, fundamentally important to the field and popular in public representations. It is also an essential intellectual landscape for any bioarchaeological treatment of hunter-gatherers, such as that presented in this volume. A key admonition for bioarchaeologists who study hunter-gathers today, however, is to be aware of how profoundly our characterizations and methods for study, both analogical and archaeological, have changed during the past half-century. In the following section I consider this phenomenon, emphasizing two compendia, the *Cambridge Encyclopedia* (1999) and the *Oxford Handbook* (2014).

15.2   Man the Hunter

In this section, I illustrate how anthropology's perspective on hunter-gatherers in the past has changed within the last half-century by focusing upon the subject of gender and gender identity. Gender is defined here as socially constructed, not biologically determined; a gendered archaeology investigates the construction and relationships between genders in the past. More detailed discussions of gender in archaeology may be found in Conkey and Spector (1984), Conkey and Gero (1991), Hays-Gilpin and Whitley (1998), Sørensen (2000), Nelson (2004), Geller and Stockett (2007),

Battle-Baptiste (2011), and Bolger (2012). The "waves" of feminism in relationship to archaeology are detailed by Gilchrist (1999, 2012).

Both Lee and Daly (1999) and Jordan and Cummings (2014) cite the 1966 *Man the Hunter* international conference at the University of Chicago (U of C) and the ensuing edited volume (Lee and DeVore, 1968a) as a watershed for hunter-gather studies. Watershed it undoubtedly was, and the results of the conference immediately permeated scholarly discussions at both Harvard (Lee and DeVore, 1968b: viii) and the U of C. Given my personal history as a female anthropologist who entered the graduate program at U of C in 1967, between the conference and the publication, I was astonished to find Lee and Daly (1999: 8) arguing that "Gender and the importance of women's work was a second key theme of the conference." More recently, the *Oxford Handbook* (Jordan and Cummings 2014: 8) uncritically cites Lee and Daly's (1999: 8) contention that gender and female contributions were an important theme in the *Man the Hunter* volume. While Lee and DeVore (1968b: 7) do report that mammal meat, apart from "textbook examples" from Arctic and Subarctic regions, undoubtedly comprised less than 50 percent of the diet (see also Lee, 1968), they conclude that "hunting is so universal and is so consistently a male activity that it must have been a basic part of the early cultural adaptation, even if it provided only a modest proportion of the food supplies." In the same paragraph, they also note that "it is also unlikely that early woman would have remained idle during the Pleistocene and that plant foods which are so important in the diet of inland hunter-gatherers today would have played a similar role in the diet of early peoples." Thus, men's and women's roles were essentialized and relative value assigned.

While the chapter entitled "Gender relations in hunter-gatherer societies" in the *Cambridge Encyclopedia* (Endicott, 1999: 411) associates Lee and Devore (1968a) with those voices that "gradually spoke up for hunter-gatherer women," the author also recognizes the need to adjust the characterizations of the normative dominant male hunter whose persona reverberates through the pages of *Man the Hunter*. Endicott points out that symmetrical gender relations do exist in some hunter-gatherer groups, that some hunter-gatherer women hunt, notably the Agta example reported by Estioko-Griffin and Griffin (1981). She also stresses that meat-sharing was not necessarily a source of male hunter-gatherer power and argues that the anthropological term "wife exchange" attributes more control of women to others than is truly the case. In the *Oxford Handbook*, Sterling (2014: 154) points out that *Man the Hunter* was significant in that it stimulated reactions, while "the concept of gender was all but unknown to the participants."

Of the participants in *Man the Hunter*, as Endicott (1999) notes, most were male. In fact, while Lee and DeVore indicate that "some 75 scholars" attended the conference, of the 67 who are identified on pp. xiv–xvi of the publication, seven (10 percent) are identifiable as women. Of the 30 chapters, two (7 percent) were authored by women (Sally Binford and June Helm); Lorna Marshall also contributed to published discussions. Interestingly, one of the two chapters added to *Man the Hunter* (Washburn and Lancaster, 1968) following the conference is widely cited as crystalizing the manly hunter role (Slocum, 1975).

Images of early people and those who study them, created for non-specialist viewing, are available in F. Clark Howell's *Early Man* (1965), a Time-Life volume wherein early women are amply illustrated in support of hunting men. In addition, on pages 28 and 29, 12 professionals with special skills for the study of early man are represented; two are visibly women – the fossil preparator and the palynologist. The remainder are men, who excavate, study fossils, survey, photograph, conduct physical and chemical tests, and so on. The men are identified by male personal pronouns in discussions associated with the images; no personal pronouns are used in descriptions of the women. Obviously, role models for aspiring young women paleoanthropologists must be sought elsewhere.

Over time, Lee's (1968, 1978, 1979, 1984) observations became associated with an appreciation for women's roles in human evolution (Dahlberg, 1981; Tanner and Zihlman, 1976; Watson and Kennedy, 1991; Zihlman and Tanner, 1978). Developed in parallel with second-wave feminism, these contributions by recognized women anthropologists served to elevate the visibility and the roles of women as foragers, meat processors, and horticulturalists. It is clear, however, that even today there is considerable room for rebalancing perspectives on gender roles in ancient hunter-gatherer communities and the interpretative methods archaeologists employ.

In a section of the *Oxford Handbook* entitled "Future Directions in Hunter-Gatherer Research," Jarvenpa and Brumbach (2014: 1243) champion an ethnoarchaeological approach to the study of hunter-gatherer gender and identity. By this they mean "examining gender dynamics in living communities as a means of generating models, analogies, and insights for interpreting the archaeological past." They further argue that there are many archaeological assumptions about gender and tools, tool kits, and the organization of space that require empirical consideration. For example, these authors (Jarvenpa and Brumbach, 2009), in an article intriguingly entitled "Fun with Dick and Jane: Ethnoarchaeology, Circumpolar Toolkits and Gender 'Inequality,'" illustrate the gender flexibility of tool kits and spatial organization of living spaces in relationship to gender. Future directions, they argue, should empirically consider gendered landscapes, gender in relationship to cosmological and sacred power, life history approaches, alternative gender roles, and the impact of colonization. The ethnographic approach they take seems imminently useful, as does the exploration of "ethnographically consistent relationships" defined by Susan Kent (1998: 40) in her ethnoarchaeological research.

As I was beginning this chapter, strong feelings re-emerged about the *Man the Hunter* conference and publication, intertwined with my personal history. In the interest of full disclosure and reflexivity, I report them here. When I entered the U of C's Department of Anthropology in 1967, between conference and publication, the department's archaeologists and physical anthropologists drew heavily upon the volume for lectures and assignments. I immediately learned that F. Clark Howell did not include women students in field expeditions, thus stifling my nascent career as a paleoanthropologist before it began. Certainly, the significance of women in prehistory was not portrayed to myself and the remainder of the entering graduate students in archaeology and physical anthropology, all of whom by the end of the first semester were male, excepting me. In this testosterone-enriched environment, I recall having an archaeology grade lowered significantly because I had suggested that one disordered, diffuse, peripheral, and low-frequency assortment of stone debitage and broken tools might have been a children's play area. Proposing instead a re-deposition representing stone tool reduction activities (conducted by men, of course) would, I suspect, have sent my grade spiraling in a different direction.

I fared no better in attempts to recognize diversity when I returned to the U of C after 16 years at Northwestern University. My arguments for a prospective female professorial candidate who was visible within archaeology for her household studies led a colleague from the still all-male archaeology/physical anthropology faculty to enter my office on a Saturday to yell and curse at me while jabbing his index finger, much as man the hunter might have wielded a spear. He also managed to convince the Dean that household archaeology was trivial – who would want to populate the past with women, after all?! Subsequently, my household and I moved away to a more hospitable social and physical environment, as an example of my personal response to adversity and resilience. I thought that I had left behind my anger about these various experiences, but they surface readily in the current political climate.

The past half-century has indeed witnessed considerable reframing of the anthropological perception of hunter-gatherers, balancing and blurring men's and women's roles. The key advice to bioarchaeologists studying hunter-gatherers is to be very sensitive to the context and possible biases for any ethnographic or ethnohistoric data one uses. Similarly, gendered identifications of material culture and spatial divisions by archaeologists must be viewed critically.

15.3   Bioarchaeology in Hunter-Gatherer Studies: A Brief History for North America

Given that the current volume is situated within an American bioarchaeological context, it is important to consider briefly the history of hunter-gather studies within the field. Within the broad framework of osteological study in North America, we have a long history of collection and description of remains from groups that fall into the broad hunter-gatherer category. Whether or not the cranially modified, Colombia River skull figured by John Collins Warren in 1822, or perhaps the cranium from a cave above a river 60 miles "below" Marietta, Ohio (Warren, 1822: 137) represent hunter-gatherers, we shall likely never know. The skulls from the mounds, including the Adena Grave Creek site, and caves that were studied by Samuel George Morton certainly included remains of folks who experimented with agriculture, all the while hunting, fishing, and collecting. Perhaps earlier hunter-gatherers were included, as well, in cemeteries capped and thus protected by more recent earthworks, as they certainly were in Illinois (Perino, 2006). However, nuances of the archaeological record were underappreciated by these nineteenth-century medical doctors, whose research questions centered on issues of population histories and origins.

As the nineteenth century matured and cabinets of curiosities began to give way to systematic collections and contextual study, scientists such as Jeffries Wyman (1871, 1874, 1875) studied remains from shell mounds along the St. Johns River in Florida. Wyman's studies were contextually rich, discussing formation processes and stratigraphy (Randall, 2015), along with detailed study of the remains, from which he argued that cranial capacity was not an indicator of intelligence and that the evidence for cannibalism was compelling (Buikstra, 2006). The long history represented by the shell accumulations along the coasts of North America have been considered recently in studies that emphasize the "power of place" (Gamble, 2017), along with resilience and collapse (Turck and Thompson, 2016).

Graves of the "complex hunter-gatherers" of the Northwest Coast also yielded contents to no less than Franz Boas during his 1888–1894 research trips to the region. Sponsored by the British Association for the Advancement of Science, the US Bureau of American Ethnology, and the American Museum of Natural History, these collecting ventures appear to have been motivated primarily by the potential for financial gain (Pöhl, 2008). In entries for June of 1888, Boas reports that it "is most unpleasant work to steal bones from a grave, but what is the use, someone has to do it ... Yesterday I wrote to the Museum in Washington asking whether they would consider buying skulls this winter for $600; if they will, I shall collect assiduously. Without having such a connection I would not do it" (Rohner, 1969: 88). On June 9, he reports upon a collection of approximately 75 skulls which he "measured frantically all day long" and estimated a worth in Washington of "about $700" (Rohner, 1969: 89).

With the dawn of the twentieth century came the efforts of Hrdlička to gather vast collections of human remains at the US National Museum. Among the approximately 15 000 were large series of hunter-gatherers, not the least of which accrued from his ten expeditions to Alaska between 1926 and 1938. Hrdlička's work was primarily descriptive and comparative, with his research questions centering on the peopling of the world and the antiquity of our species. Hunter-gatherers figured heavily, with focal areas on the antiquity of humans in the Western Hemisphere and Neanderthals in Europe (Schultz, 1945).

Studies of health also appeared during this period, though usually as descriptive case studies, such as those by Hrdlička. The Smithsonian collections served as the basis for comparative work on dental health, including hunter-gatherers (Cook and Powell, 2006; Leigh, 1925). Few skeletal biologists, however, were interested in temporal sequences in a manner amenable to chronological modeling, although Hooton (1930) did attempt a time-sensitive study at Pecos Pueblo.

Thousands of hunter-gatherer remains were unearthed during the WPA excavations of the 1930s and early 1940s, many from the Kentucky shell mounds (Milner and Jacobi, 2006). The vast numbers of remains excavated included the well-studied Indian Knoll collection (Claassen, 1996; Johnston and Snow, 1961; Mensforth, 2001; Rothschild, 1979; Webb, 1974). The descriptive goals for physical anthropology typical of the time led to mainly the recording of skeletal measurements as well as demographic observations, if the materials were studied at all.

These collections remain a source of potential knowledge for studies of hunter-gatherer resilience.

One challenge to students of hunter-gatherer studies in North America, as elsewhere, and abundantly represented by chapters in this volume, is the small size of most cemeteries. Even when larger numbers of burials are present in "persistent places" (Littleton and Allen, 2007; Schlanger, 1992), such as the shell mounds of the southeastern United States (Thompson, 2010), most researchers have not considered carefully the deep temporal spans, frequently across millennia, that these sites represent. On the one hand, these samples hold great potential for charting the human condition across deep time, but refined chronologies are essential. Researchers must also avoid uncritically assuming that each assemblage of hunter-gathers is representative of a community's natural death assemblage (Buikstra, 1981).

As illustrated by the chapters in this volume, for the purposes of adaptation and resilience studies, data points that proxy human diet, mobility, and health, along with clues concerning social hierarchies and worldview, derived from mortuary contexts are most useful within resilience modeling. In concert with archaeological attention to subsistence and settlement in regions, bioarchaeologists have employed health-related attributes to consider the impact of changing lifeways upon health (Cohen and Armelagos, 1984; Cohen and Crane-Kramer, 2012; Steckel and Rose, 2002; Steckel et al., 2009). The most startling result of these studies was the finding that community health appeared to worsen with the adoption of agriculture. We now know that there were exceptions to this rule, especially in South and East Asia (Clark et al., 2014; Temple, 2010), and perhaps the Levant (Eshed et al., 2010). Interpretations must also be qualified by the cautions voiced by Wood et al. (1992). Even so, the simplicity and apparent universality of the models attracted considerable attention to bioarchaeology.

The impression gained from this overview is that bioarchaeological data are widely available, but that issues of small sample size and chronological control within larger accumulations continue to be challenging. To date, studies of hunter-gatherers have generally been used as single "populations" to form a baseline for comparisons with groups engaged in pastoralism, agriculture, or some combination of the two. Temporal sequences are rarely defined and studied, which makes this volume especially noteworthy.

15.4   Modeling Change in the Archaeological Record: Systems Theory, Theories of Collapse, Resilience, Disruption, and Adaptation

15.4.1   Systems Theory and Theories of Collapse

The hypothesized relationship between agricultural intensification and poor quality of life, mentioned above, is a simple model, which logically leads us to consider intervening variables, such as overall dietary quality, social hierarchies, and population aggregation. Thus, the need for more complex models becomes immediately apparent. Modeling complex relationships has led archaeologists to explore a variety of approaches, borrowed primarily from the biological and social sciences. For example, during the latter part of the twentieth century, the general systems theory (GST) of the Austrian biologist Ludwig von Bertalanffy (1968) was adapted by archaeologists to investigate relationships between variables drawn from across the technological, social, and ideological systems. These systems, first explicitly defined by Leslie White (1959) and adapted by Lewis Binford (1962) to describe technomic, sociotechnic, and ideotechnic artifacts that functioned in specific contexts, such as "coping directly with the physical environment," "articulating individuals one with another," and signifying and symbolizing "the ideological rationalizations for the social system and further provide the symbolic milieu in which individuals are enculturated." The systems approach directly influenced the New Archaeology and its practitioners (Binford and Binford, 1968), with some important and intricate explorations by researchers such as Flannery (1968), who explicitly adapted Maruyama's (1963) first (promote equilibrium) and second (amplify deviations from equilibrium) cybernetics to explain culture change. Attempting to avoid the "esoteric terminology of systems theory," this classic paper elegantly explains the development of agriculture in terms of seasonality and scheduling. His conclusions regarding the significance of cybernetics in archaeology were of note (Flannery, 1968: 85):

The use of a cybernetics model to explain prehistoric cultural change, while terminologically cumbersome, has certain advantages. For one thing, it does not attribute cultural evolution to "discoveries", "inventions", "experiments", or "genius", but instead enables us to treat prehistoric cultures as systems. It stimulates inquiry into mechanisms that counteract change or amplify it, which ultimately tells us something about the nature of adaptation. Most importantly, it allows us to view change not as something arising *de novo*, but in terms of quite minor deviations in one small part of a previously existing system, which, once set in motion, can expand greatly because of positive feedback.

The implications of this approach for the prehistorian are clear: it is vain to hope for the discovery of the first domestic corn cob, the first pottery vessel, the first hieroglyphic, or the first site where some other major breakthrough occurred. Such deviations from the pre-existing pattern almost certainly took place in such a minor and accidental way that their traces are not recoverable. More worthwhile would be an investigation of the mutual causal processes that amplify these tiny deviations into major changes in prehistoric culture.

Thus, for Flannery and many of his colleagues, change involved small increments, certainly not the sweeping migrations and diffusion that had dominated earlier explanations of differences in the archaeological record. External factors were of primary importance; ecological adaptation served as a model for humans. Importantly, the systems approach led to the explicit definition of multiple variables and their interactions. Stimuli for change were largely external to the system, and adaptation involved return to the previous systemic relationships, or nearly so. Most of these cybernetic systems approaches focused upon describing interactions, but the overall goal of explaining causality remained elusive.

The search for causality led scholars in many directions, including toward the subject of societal collapse. Collapse theorist Joseph Tainter (1988) was influenced by Leslie White's (1943, 1949, 1959) emphasis on thermodynamics and energy capture.

Tainter's volume, *The Collapse of Complex Societies*, is ostensibly focused on groups more sociopolitically complex than hunter-gatherers, who – following collapse – become

> suddenly smaller, simpler, less stratified, and less socially differentiated. Specialization decreases and there is less centralized control. The flow of information drops, people trade and interact less, and there is overall lower coordination among individuals and groups. Economic activity drops to a commensurate level, while the arts and literature experience such a quantitative decline that a dark age often ensues. (Tainter, 1988: 193)

For Tainter (1988), as human groups become more complex, they invest more energy in complexity to the point that declining marginal returns overwhelm the system. One cannot help but wonder just what this means at the individual level, what happens following the hypothesized collapse, and how this model can possibly apply to Middle Woodland (Hopewell complex) peoples of the Eastern Woodlands, whose qualifications as a "complex society" (Tainter, 2005: 15) are questionable (Brown, 1981). This volume has been lauded by some (Kando, 2014; Kardulias, 1989; Jones, 1989), cautiously evaluated by at least one scholar (Chapman, 1988), and heavily critiqued by others (Blanton, 1990; Bowersock, 1991; Rule, 1989).

Another prominent treatment of collapse is Yoffee and Cowgill's (1988) edited volume. Of particular interest is Cowgill's final chapter, which admonishes social scientists about fads and uncritical borrowing of concepts and theories from other disciplines (Cowgill, 1988: 247):

> Another persistent source of trouble is aping the shadow rather than the substance of fashionable terms that have proven genuinely useful in other fields. As long as the social sciences remain intellectually underdeveloped, they will be subject to "cargo cults" and messianic enthusiasms. The only remedy is to develop indigenous theory that is rich and successful enough to prevent our being easily seduced or bamboozled by clever, ambitious, and energetic persons spouting half-baked or half-digested versions of something that has become popular (often for good reasons) in some other discipline.

In a similar vein, Cowgill (1988: 252) critiques systems theory, especially "systems talk," as "the use of complex diagrams, full of boxes and arrows" (see Buikstra [1977: 82] for a bioarchaeological example). He argues that while systems approaches are important, many tend to direct practitioners away from central issues and to pretend, through the use of specialized vocabularies and diagrams, to be more of an advancement in resolving a research problem than is truly the case. Systems need to be addressed, but as Flannery (1968) advised, the specialized vocabulary minimized.

Cowgill also argues against both vacuous generalizations and overly detailed, particularistic studies that remain lodged firmly within the trees, having lost sight of the forest. He prefers studies that "look beyond isolated examples at a reasonable number of instances in sufficient detail and with sufficient understanding so that they can arrive at insights that, though generalizable to a useful extent, have less than cosmic pretensions and can claim to explain fairly specific aspects of specific situations" (Cowgill, 1988: 249). This is the hoped-for outcome of any thematic edited volume, such as the one presented here.

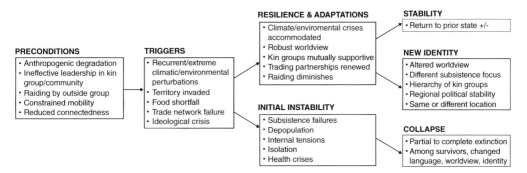

Figure 15.1 A conceptual model for hunter-gatherer collapse, situating the variables and processes of stress and interaction. Modified from Butzer (2012).

Another prominent collapse theorist, as noted at the outset of this chapter, is Jared Diamond, for whom the question is the identification of contributing factors to societal failure in the face of environmental (or other) collapse. Four such possible factors are identified, "environmental damage, climate change, hostile neighbors, and friendly trade partners," which may or may not pertain to a given circumstance (Diamond, 2005: 11). A fifth set of factors glossed in terms of the societal response to its environmental problems are considered crucial, with responses determined by a society's "political, economic, and social institutions and on its cultural values" (Diamond, 2005: 14–15). Thus, for Diamond, the thread involves external factors, followed by either a collapse or a resilient response. As illustrated in this volume, such approaches are overly simplified.

In a much more recent treatment, figured prominently in the *Proceedings of the National Academy of Sciences (PNAS)*, Butzer (2012) has argued compellingly for the significance of the social sciences in studying collapse and the response to environmental stressors. "Undue attention to stressors risks underestimating the intricate interplay of environmental, political, and sociocultural resilience in limiting the damages of collapse or in facilitating reconstruction. The conceptual model emphasizes resilience, as well as the historical roles of leaders, elites, and ideology" (Butzer, 2012: 3632). He also emphasizes that "[c]ollapse is multicausal and rarely abrupt" (Butzer, 2012: 3632; contra Tainter, 1988). With a note of optimism, he argues that "[m]uch of the current alarmist literature that claims to draw from historical experience is poorly focused, simplistic, and unhelpful. It fails to appreciate that resilience and re-adaptation depend on identified options, improved understanding, cultural solidarity, enlightened leadership, and opportunities for participation and fresh ideas" (Butzer, 2012: 3632). Figure 15.1 reframes Butzer's heuristic in a manner more suitable for hunter-gatherer groups.

15.4.2 Resilience and Panarchy

The theme of resilience, used in the title of this volume, relates to a number of models used to describe and to measure societal persistence and change in response to external and internal challenges. These include models borrowed primarily from ecology and the other social sciences. This section and the following will examine these models in their original formations, as well as examples of archaeological applications. For the latter, emphasis – though not exclusive – will be placed upon the Greater Southwest, as this is a region where chronological control has been refined due to a combination of dendrochronological and radiometric dating.

In a methodologically rigorous treatment of resilience in socioecological systems (SESs), Carpenter and colleagues (2001) emphasize that resilience and adaptive system models are frequently used as heuristic metaphors. Along with most other twenty-first-century scholarship, these authors recognize the evolutionary, dynamic nature of adaptive systems, which when challenged, may either return to resemble their pre-disruptive state or transform to another. A fully transformed system will display controls and functions (*sensu* Holling, 1973) distinctive from its earlier form. Many studies explore the system's response to external rather than internal challenges, while considering agents of internal change to be responsive innovators. When focusing upon human societies, however, one can imagine a multitude of internal factors ranging from technological advancement to messianic movements that might initiate change and attendant stresses from within. In the absence of historical records, however, as is the case for most hunter-gatherer communities and individuals, we do not presently have the fine temporal resolution necessary to consider such internal stresses. External drivers commonly cited in this volume involve such factors as episodic or directional climate change, epidemic disease, or hostile conspecifics.

The term "panarchy" is a mid-nineteenth-century construct attributed by the *Oxford English Dictionary* to the poet Philip James Bailey, who wrote of "the starry panarchy of space." The term was used by Paul Emile de Puydt in 1860 to refer to an all-encompassing form of government. It has been adopted by Holling and Gunderson (2002; see also Holling, 1986, 2000) to reference their multiscalar, overarching model of adaptation, which involves four stages: exploitation, conservation, creative destruction, and renewal as the components of an adaptive cycle. In constructing their model, the authors emphasize that change is episodic, composed of critical processes that may vary considerably, but that do cluster around a few dominant frequencies. They also contrast destabilizing forces that maintain diversity, resilience, and opportunity with stabilizing forces that maintain productivity. Thus, efficient control, constancy, and predictability are opposed to persistent adaptiveness, variability, and unpredictability. Traditionally, engineering resilience is defined in terms of return to a steady state, while the more dynamic definition, preferred by Holling and Gunderson (2002), focuses upon the magnitude of disturbance that can be absorbed prior to the system flipping to a new regime – ecosystem resilience. Engineering resilience is focused upon efficiency; maintaining existence of function is emphasized by ecosystem resilience. It is the latter that facilitates modeling system evolution. Holling and Gunderson (2002: 32) emphasize that,

The purpose of theories such as panarchy is not to explain what is: it is to give sense to what might be. We cannot predict the specifics of future possibilities, but we might be able to define the conditions that limit or expand those future possibilities. As a consequence, the properties we need to choose are not those chosen to describe the existing state of a system and its behaviors, but rather ones chosen to identify the properties and processes that shape the future.

The practical goal of Holling and Gunderson's exercise is effective ecosystem management. They emphasize not only the return to a steady state, but also the liberating nature of "creative destruction." This approach differs from traditional ecological succession theories in that both include the ecosystem functions of biomass release by external forces (omega), colonization or exploitation (r), and then conservation and accumulation of energy and material (K). To these three functions, resilience theory (RT) adds a reorganization into either a "new" system somewhat resembling the old or a fundamentally new system (Holling and Gunderson, 2002; Redman and Kinzig, 2003).

Resilience theorists argue that the responses of the system depend upon three factors: the potential available for change, the degree of connectedness between internal controlling variables and processes, and the resilience of the system in the face of unexpected or unpredictable shocks. Emphasis is placed upon measures of increasing connectedness and rigidity in the conservation phase. They also argue for the importance of conditions that occasionally encourage novelty and experimentation, when connectedness is low and resilience is high, where the progression is "wonderfully unpredictable" (Holling and Gunderson, 2002: 46). This optimism runs counter to the dark tides of collapse theory.

Recognizing the quasi-metaphorical nature of resilience modeling or adaptive cycles, it is still crucial for researchers to explicitly state how resilience is to be recognized, or as Carpenter *et al.* (2001) emphasize in their title, "Resilience of What to What?" Do we simply assume resilience if we identify hunter-gatherers persisting in a region over time? Presence alone tells us very little, if we don't consider the climatic, environmental, and social challenges groups faced over the *Longue Durée* and the manner in which they adapted over time. These and other issues are considered in reference to the archaeology of resilience, reviewed in the following section as well as in Section 15.5, which focuses on the chapters in this volume.

15.4.3 Archaeological Studies of Resilience

The twenty-first century has witnessed considerable archaeological interest in Holling and Gunderson's (2002) resilience model. There are a growing number of archaeological studies directly influenced by this approach (Gronenborn *et al.*, 2014; Hegmon *et al.*, 2008; Marsh, 2016; Nelson *et al.*, 2006; see also Bradtmöller *et al.*, 2017).

Redman and Kinzig (2003) also argue compellingly for the significance of archaeological datasets for resilience modelers. RT approaches emphasize the inevitability and repetitive nature of change. The *Longue Durée* of the archaeological record should facilitate the understanding of "true transformations," and thus identify those factors of culture and socioecological systems that persist across systems of increasing complexity and those that may be altered, as Redman and Kinzig (2003: 4) emphasize in the following passage.

Finally, the archaeological record allows us to identify those emergent features that appear to be inevitable, or at least highly probably, in societies as they become increasingly complex, including social stratification, compartmentalization of information, and, at certain scales, ecological simplification. The challenge before us will be to distinguish those features of social systems, and human interactions with the environment, that can be altered to achieve more desirable social and ecological outcomes, and those that are so much a product of history, human development, and biological, social, and cultural evolution that we must accept their constraints in fashioning our visions of the future. An archaeological perspective can contribute to meeting this challenge.

Thus, not only does RT applied in deep time aid our understanding of the past, but for Redman and Kinzig, it contributes to future well-being of humankind and therefore holds profound transdisciplinary value.

The two case studies offered by Redman and Kinzig (2003) include, first, "Adaptive Cycles of Centralization and Fragmentation in Ancient Mesopotamia." Envisioned over 1500 years of an adaptive cycle, this model offers a unifying perspective on change between 5500 and 3000 BP. A second example illustrates a Hohokam adaptive cycle in the arid US Southwest. Here, the authors argue that small- and large-scale climatic events associated with water availability, social responses, and irrigation potential drove a system that moved from a 1250 BP period of expansive irrigation, ending in approximately 850 BP, to a more recent period of fragmentation associated with monumental architecture and social and political complexity, which was able to sustain the culture until approximately 600 BP.

In another Southwest USA example, Nelson and colleagues (2006) focused on the eastern Mimbres culture of southwest New Mexico, leading up to the "Mimbres collapse." The overall outline includes a "gradual increase in aggregation culminating in the Mimbres Classic period (beginning 1000 BP), to dispersion (970 BP), to aggregation (850 BP), to regional depopulation (550 BP) (Nelson *et al.*, 2006). Both the household- and village-level expectations are derived for four socioecological foci: (1) greater wild resource utilization and household mobility during the Reorganization Phase (850 to 800 BP) than the Classic Phase (1000 to 970 BP); (2) greater similarity of households and villages during the Classic Phase than in the Reorganization Phase; that diversity in both (3) inter-household size and (4) inter-household food processing would be greater during the Reorganization Phase than the Classic Phase. Interestingly, only one of these predictions – increased residential mobility – was confirmed. The failure to support the expectations, based in RT, has led the authors to a "more nuanced" perspective on reorganization, especially at the household level, in the eastern Mimbres region. The consideration of these variables together made sense to the authors in post hoc interpretations, and they do not question, but rather continue to endorse, RT as a heuristic device.

A further comparative treatment, focusing upon the "rigidity trap" as a key concept of RT, is also centered in the Southwest, and includes the Mimbres,

Hohokam, and Mesa Verde regions (Hegmon *et al.*, 2008). The first two regions have been discussed previously; the Mesa Verde region appears to have undergone rapid depopulation, from perhaps as many as 10 000 people at 740 BP to becoming virtually abandoned by 720 BP. The authors adopt Walker *et al.*'s (2004) definition of a resilient system as one that can accept perturbations while maintaining roughly the same structure and functions. The authors then argue that while small fluctuations may positively affect resilience, humans have a tendency to resist change, or in RT terms to remain in the K stage, accumulating connectedness and rigidity in a manner that will affect the severity of transformation when the system moves to the Omega (release) stage. The stated goal of this exercise is to "evaluate the proposition that there is an association between the degree of rigidity and the severity of the transformation" (Hegmon *et al.*, 2008: 314). Drawing on RT, they develop a set of variables for assessing whether degree of rigidity and severity of transformation can be evaluated archaeologically. They assess these variables across the three study areas, developing a nominal ranking for comparative purposes.

The tone of this archaeological article differs slightly from those cited previously, in that its focal point is the people of the three regions. While material culture and architectural features dominate the list of 20 variables of interest, aspects of demography, funerary behavior, violence, and health are also assessed, the latter two under the heading of "physical suffering" (Hegmon *et al.*, 2008). For summary comparative purposes, the authors focus upon integration, hierarchy, and conformity as rigidity rankings. Their results argue for the Mimbres region having been least rigid and therefore having undergone the least disruptive and stressful transformation. The Hohokam case was the most extreme; the Mesa Verde example assumed an intermediate position. While these results conformed to expectations, the uniform (rigid) nature of the ceramics in all three regions were a surprise to the authors. In conclusion, the authors suggest implications from their assessment for people today who wish to exit, minimize, or stay out of a rigidity trap. Based primarily upon the Hohokam example, Hegmon *et al.* (2008) propose a twenty-first-century focus upon the following factors that promote rigidity: (1) absence of social options; (2) the limits of buffering strategies; (3) attachment to traditions: (4) attachment to technology; (5) attachment to place; and (6) path dependence.

Turning to international examples, Solich and Bradtmöller (2017) also consider socioeconomic complexity and resilience in hunter-gatherer societies, explicitly invoking Holling's model. They operationalize this analysis by focusing upon two dimensions of connectedness: human–environment and human–human interactions. In so doing they emphasize the special characteristics of hunter-gatherers (Solich and Bradtmöller, 2017: 115):

In comparison to societies dominated by domestication-based subsistence strategies, the outstanding feature of hunter-gatherers is the limited control of the spatial and temporal distribution and concentration of required resources. The consequence is a considerably different pattern of human–environment interactions and relations that go together with special challenges and implications for the society as a system. Here, *adaptation* represents the trend towards a higher degree of connectedness of interaction relations between humans and their environmental counterparts, individual strategies, and society level structures concentrating on process-related efficiency and not on the manipulation of environmental conditions.

The authors establish four archaeological proxies and 12 indicators for measuring human–environment and human–human relationships: (1) association with the land (maximum length of occupation, intensity of site occupations, diversity of site activities, or specialization of sites; distance of raw material transport, mobility patterns, signs of complex site structures, and signs of territoriality); (2) subsistence specializations (species, age, and sex of animals in faunal assemblage, contribution of aquatic resources, complexity of food processing and signs of storage); (3) social relations and cultural institutions (division of labor or social stratification, social network of trading); (4) demography (population density and residential group size). In general, mobility is cited as an effective strategy for coping with a release event (Solich and Bradtmöller, 2017). An example from the Upper Paleolithic in Northern Europe, dating from 36 000 and 14 000 cal BP is provided. In closing, the authors argue that archaeological studies of hunter-gatherers hold import for today's world. "Here, a better understanding of the behavior of past hunter-gatherer system developments promises to identify signals for reaching potential thresholds and how societies in a very strong human–environment relation are still able to maintain socioeconomic complexity and resilience at the same time" (Solich and Bradtmöller, 2017: 124).

One of the most compelling transdisciplinary applications of the resilience concept in archaeology is the *PNAS* article by Nelson *et al.* (2016). Here, the authors employ the lengthy archaeological record for two distinctive world areas (Southwestern USA and North Atlantic islands) to assess social and population resource variables to assess vulnerability and outcomes after significant environmental challenges. The authors conclude that social factors exerted more influence on vulnerability, especially mobility (versus embedded in landscape) and connectedness (versus isolated). The important policy implications include the need for more attention to human condition/vulnerabilities prior to disasters, rather than simple reactions to disasters and focusing upon food security afterward.

Interestingly, very few of the archaeologists explicitly cite bioarchaeological evidence. Exceptions include Hegmon *et al.*'s (2008) consideration of demography, funerary behavior, violence, and health among the many variables used to assess the strength of rigidity traps in three ancient Southwestern contexts. Freeman *et al.* (2017) note that a 6000-year-old mortuary system ceased along with other major changes due to a cascade of hunter-gatherer resource system failures.

Setting aside the health-related issues, an obvious means for considering resilience, we should pause to consider the degree to which these socioecological systems models ignore the profound changes in worldview signaled by changes in the mortuary system or the symbolic representations on ceramics. Solich and Bradtmöller (2017) emphasize relationships between humans and the environment and with each other, but what about relationships with the supernatural? They also speak of social relationships between living humans, but what about the ancestors? Changed symbols of worldview, of religions, of relationships to prior generations, and leaving behind the graves and the "sacred" places had to have profoundly reverberated through communities and individuals. A change in community identity obviously is part of an adaptive cycle and would also represent the degree to which a group had changed.

Thus, we have surveyed the current background that provides a stage for the development of this volume. Emphasis is placed on the use of ethnographic and ethnohistoric data, on the challenges inherent in the bioarchaeology of hunter-gatherers, prior approaches to resilience studies in ecology and in archaeology, with emphasis upon general systems theory (GST), resilience theory, adaptation theory (AT), and vulnerability. Table 15.1 summarizes the findings of this background discussion, with emphasis on topics relevant to resilience in hunter-gatherers, studied bioarchaeologically. Subjects range from general issues concerning the manner in which contexts should be defined and how bioarchaeological variables are used as proxies. Challenges are listed, such as small samples and temporal control. Archaeological information is essential, and researchers should be careful to precisely define the nature of environmental and climatic insults, including strength, periodicity, and timing. Archaeological, ethnoarchaeological, ethnohistoric, and ethnographic information can be useful, if critically reviewed.

15.5   The Bioarchaeology of Hunter-Gatherer Resilience and Adaptation

The contributors to this volume are to be congratulated for bringing bioarchaeology into the domain of resilience studies. Discussions of resilience, vulnerability, and transformation clearly benefit from the knowledge derived from deep time and from interdisciplinary approaches (Redman and Kinzig, 2003). In general, I think this volume amply illustrates that bioarchaeology should be a player in this field, adding inferences based upon knowledge of health, identity, and ideology to current archaeological approaches. In complementary fashion, I believe that the strongest chapters in this volume extended their knowledge base well beyond biological inferences to engage in extensive discussions of historical and archaeological contexts, along with judicious use of ethnographic and ethnohistoric data. We now truly appreciate the resilience of hunter-gatherers who maintain their identity in many challenging contexts, who transform upon some occasions, and who collapse under overwhelming external pressures.

Although theorizing resilience has attracted archaeological attention for most of the twenty-first century (see Section 15.3), bioarchaeologists have only recently been drawn to resilience models (e.g., Hoover and Hudson, 2016; Reitsema et al., 2017). Reitsema's work focuses upon diet and changing social conditions in rural and urban Medieval Europe, while Hoover and Hudson (2016) address a question with parallels in this volume: Were Jomon societies resilient in the face of the incursion of agricultural groups around 2500 BP? Hoover and Hudson (2016) argue that according to developmental health proxies (fluctuating asymmetry and linear enamel hypoplasia), the Jomon groups that persisted were not health-compromised. In this

Table 15.1 Summary background for the bioarchaeology of hunter-gatherer resilience.

General

- Archaeological/historical contexts should be fully defined.
- Knowledge of external disruptions, their magnitude, and frequency should be stated.
- Research problem should be clearly stated.
- Definitions of key variables are required.
- Assumptions about such factors as representativeness should be stated.
- Proxies for such variables as "health," "relatedness," should be stated and justified.

Bioarchaeology

- Small samples and chronological control challenges must be considered in choice of context.
- Preferable to explore a wide array of biological and archaeological variables.

Archaeology

- Temporal control is crucial.
- A combination of archaeological and biological variables is important.
- May want to explore worldview/cosmological variables more extensively than in analyses to date.
- Most of the "resilience" papers are largely descriptive. More successful are those which try to be comparative, use qualitative variables.
- Some papers try to extract a key "resilience" variable, such as "rigidity trap." Others focus upon identity or maintenance of structure and essential functions that support the structure.

Ethnohistory/ethnography

- Should be considered, although statements should be critically reviewed for bias.
- Direct analogies/direct historical approach not to be applied, but considerations of convergent relationships are useful.

Ethnoarchaeology

- Can be useful, if analyses not biased.

Theoretical approaches to systems/collapse/resilience/adaptation

---

- Change is inevitable. (Older systems approaches from ecology emphasized return to steady state.)
- Variable definition crucial!
- Most previous RT studies concentrate upon SESs, useful in policy decisions.
- Descriptive approaches, such as panarchy, are useful in isolating key variables and their interactions. Causal relationships not inherent, however.

---

volume, Temple (Chapter 5) explores aspects of hunter-gatherer health and identity of Jomon people from the Ota and Tsukumo sites, located on the Inland Sea region of southwestern Honshu, Japan. He also argues that these Jomon hunter-gathers maintained resilient socioecological and cultural adaptations well before agricultural peoples migrated into the region, as they withstood stresses attendant to a period of sustained cooling. Of particular interest are the visible displays of grave goods symbolic of hunter-gatherer identity that appear late in the Tsukumo sequence, perhaps an indication of nascent social stratification, or perhaps symbolic indicators of the deeper connection between hunter-gatherer relationships with the natural environment, a visible reference to an identity crafted to maintain order in a system experiencing stress.

A recurrent theme in this volume is identifying the persistence of hunter-gatherers in the face of contact with agriculturalists and pastoralists (Pfeiffer and Harrington, South Africa, Chapter 2; Stojanowski, North Africa, Chapter 9), yet gauging this persistence in the bioarchaeological record can be a challenge. As Stojanowski carefully points out, there is difficulty in identifying pastoralism in the archaeological record. Further, Schulting (Chapter 4), following Cumming *et al.* (2005), notes that a persistent presence of hunter-gatherers on the landscape is not necessarily an indication of resilience. A population may have undergone change or transformation and thus have an entirely new relationship with the environment, as Bartelink and co-authors (Chapter 12) infer for Bay Area hunter-gatherers.

Bartelink *et al.* (Chapter 12) also demonstrate the power of comparative approaches as they illustrate distinctly different responses in neighboring regions of present-day California. These authors contrast evidence from Bay Area hunter-gatherer sites with that from the Chumash sites along the Santa Barbara Channel. In the latter area, evidence of resource stress and violence increases through time, whereas the evidence from the Bay area is sporadic. Bartelink and co-authors suggest that the various forms of violence – craniofacial trauma, projectile wounds, and mutilation – which are not associated with climatic stress, reflect periods of societal transformation in the face of external migrations and rising socioeconomic inequality, transformations that contributed to human suffering as it responded to social stressors, not environmental or climatic ones.

Other examples of regional comparisons include Bernal *et al.* 's (Chapter 3) study of hunter-gatherer resilience in the face of megafaunal extinction, considering northern and southern Patagonian groups. They report faunal assemblage change, the presence of plants in hunter-gatherer diets, and population density estimates grounded in studies of variation in modern and ancient mitochondrial DNA haplotypes. Resilience is inferred for both groups across this major faunal change at the Pleistocene–Holocene boundary, with population increase greatest for the more northern group.

Some comparative studies, e.g., Cameron and Stock (Chapter 6), could have been strengthened by a more nuanced use of ethnographic and ethnohistorical information, much as Stojanowski employed in Chapter 9. The practice of simply comparing groups and interpreting data without the development of a formal hypothesis that is driven by expectations grounded in contextual information is unfortunately all too common in bioarchaeology. While the inferences made by Cameron and Stock may indeed be correct, providing a matrix of alternative bioarchaeological expectations for males and females and for younger and older individuals, based in knowledge derived from living hunter-gatherers and pastoralists, would yield more robust conclusions.

Two of the chapters, those by Da-Gloria and Bueno (Chapter 7) and Justice and Temple (Chapter 11), are especially amenable to adaptive cycle modeling (Figure 15.2).

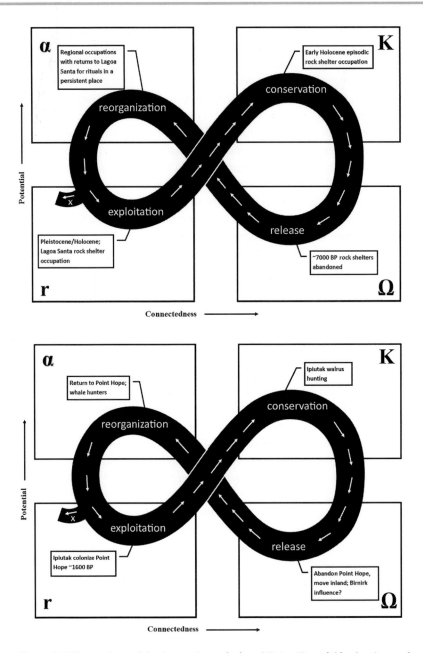

Figure 15.2 Illustrations of the Lagoa Santa (2a) and Point Hope (2b) adaptive cycles superimposed upon a stylized illustration adapted from Holling and Gunderson (2002) of four ecosystem functions: r, K, Ω, and α. The arrows vary from closely spaced, short arrows symbolizing a slowly changing process to long arrows symbolizing rapid change.

Figure produced by Brandie S. Temple, modified from Holling and Gunderson (2002).

In both the Lagoa Santa, Brazil, and the Point Hope, Alaska examples, hunter-gatherer groups have apparently abandoned a residential base. The Lagoa Santa groups, however, occasionally returned to their former home, employing the familiar landscape for ritual purposes. Their transformation was likely not as extreme as that of the Point Hope groups, who, after living in proximity with the Birnirk whaling groups, came back to Point Hope as Tigara whalers, who maintained similar beliefs and rituals pertaining to infants and children.

When dealing with complex societies, most models of collapse focus upon political disintegration or disorganization. Many hunter-gatherer communities were small, mobile groups with kin-based organization, wherein the expulsion or departure of kin lineages from the core would be the most obvious, and perhaps only, form of political disorganization expected and potentially recognizable in the best of all bioarchaeological worlds. The emergence and/or disappearance of inequalities, written in funerary contexts and perhaps in dietary differences, would provide one possible indication of a shift in community identity, as Schulting emphasizes in Chapter 4 and Stojanowski in Chapter 9.

The measured use of ethnohistorical and ethnographic sources, as illustrated by Temple (Chapter 5), Bornemann and Gamble (Chapter 8), Stojanowski (Chapter 9), Letham and Coupland (Chapter 10), Justice and Temple (Chapter 11), Merbs (Chapter 13), and Littleton (Chapter 14) holds excellent promise for enhancing our studies of hunter-gatherer resilience. Such sources figured especially heavily in discussions of both relatively recent (Chapters 8, 10, and 13) and more ancient (Chapter 9) hunter-gatherers. Both Merbs (Chapter 13) and Littleton (Chapter 14) provide chilling snapshots of the colonial experience and collapse among the Sadlermiut of Canada's Southampton Island and Australian Aborigines of the Western Riverina region. Within a century of initial contact, the groups had either transformed and collapsed (Australia) or become virtually extinct (Sadlermiut).

The chapters by Bornemann and Gamble and by Letham and Coupland amply illustrate the richness of information gained from the study of mortuary assemblages. The Chumash mortuary complexes reported by Bornemann and Gamble indeed changed in the face of colonial stressors. However, the authors also document that the Chumash were not passive following European contact, but rather were active agents who attempted to respond on their own terms, maintaining ceremonies and other aspects of their social order and belief systems. Further north, the cemeteries of Prince Rupert Harbour reported by Letham and Coupland document the maintenance of rich mortuary assemblages in times of political stress.

One of the most promising trajectories for bioarchaeology and resilience is the use of identity as a major unifying feature by which to recognize transformation. As Schulting (Chapter 4) points out, resilience scholars such as the ecologist Cumming (Cumming and Collier, 2005; Cumming et al., 2005) define identity in a manner that is amenable to modeling of complex systems. Cumming and co-workers consider adaptive systems models as one form of "metamodels," which are not predictive, but may be the source of hypotheses. System identity is defined as being composed of key components and relationships between these components (Cumming and Collier,

2005). For social systems, Cumming *et al.* (2005) specify cultural groups as components, land tenure as an example of an entity that links components, cultural and livelihood diversity as innovation variables that define prospects for resilience, and institutional memory/oral history as continuity variables. Rapid and definitive changes define significant transformations.

Cumming and Collier use the metaphor of Theseus' ship (Theseus' Paradox) to illustrate the ambiguity of the identity concept. When, in the replacement of boards and sails, does the carefully curated artifact become something else? If the form and function are the same, but the ship is sailed to another port, is this still Theseus' ship? I think most contemplating the nature of hunter-gatherer communities would say yes, but if a sail were added or the emblematic flag changed, identity would be in question.

So how might we recognize the core identities of hunter-gatherers, either as individuals or as groups? Relationships of individuals and communities, one to the other, to the environment, and to the supernatural would seem to be of key significance. Hunter-gatherer groups range either widely when resources are dispersed, or less so with aggregated resources. Symbols of identity in material culture, especially decorative aspects of material culture, are to be expected. As Temple and Stojanowski (Chapter 1) emphasize here, based upon Ingold's (2000) observations, hunter-gatherers have a partnership with animals and a relationship to the landscape that largely differs from agricultural groups. As Ingold emphasizes, based upon his primary experience with circumpolar hunters, the relationship "between hunter and prey is based on a principle of trust, which rests in turn on a combination of autonomy and dependency" (Ingold, 2015: 26).

Over and over again we encounter the idea that the environment, far from being seen as a passive container for resources that are there in abundance for the taking, is saturated with personal powers of one kind or another. It is alive. And hunter-gatherers, if they are to survive and prosper, have to maintain relationships with these powers, just as they must maintain relationships with other human persons. (Ingold, 2000: 66–67)

Similarly, Bird-David (1990, 1992) emphasizes the sharing relationship the environment has with humans. Hunter-gatherers form a partnership and frequently cosmological relationship with the animals that herders seek to subjugate. Changes in iconography are to be expected following significant reorganization of a group's identity. As Fowler and Turner (1999) emphasize, traditional ecological knowledge may be distinctive in hunter-gatherer communities. "Particularly important is the sense of place and purpose communicated by the oral tradition, and the cumulative wisdom derived from knowledge of complex ecological relationships, and the day-to-day interaction with the things of these places" (Fowler and Turner, 1999: 424).

The meaning of marked change in iconographic representations should not be undervalued in assessing resilience and identity in archaeological contexts. Although not expressly hunter-foragers, Middle Woodland horticulturalists of the lower Illinois River valley created pots and pipes with largely naturalistic animal representations

(Charles *et al.*, 1988; Perino, 2006). These contrast markedly with the stylized entities figured in more recent Mississippian artifacts (Aftandilian, 2013), underscoring identity differences. The cosmological and relational significance of animal imagery upon the ceramics of the Mimbres agriculturalists discussed earlier and the change in ceramic production after CE 1300 (Hegmon, 2002, 2010; Hegmon and Kulow, 2005) suggest an identity change, although the use of earlier ceramics in outlier contexts (Hegmon, 2002) speaks to social memory and continuity. As Shafer (2010) infers, the Mimbres universe was layered, as represented in various archaeological domains, including architecture and artifacts. This, along with an emphasis upon a persistent presence of ancestors and water, form three key Mimbres cosmological themes. Others have argued for social meaning in the Mimbres iconography, which to them speaks of gender-based links to Mexican regions where scarlet macaws are indigenous and to other faraway places with esoteric knowledge (Creel and McKusick, 1994; Hegmon, 2002; Nelson, 2010; Nelson and Gilman, 2017). The Mimbres ancestors emerged from a watery world to one in which the living dwelt in balance and harmony with their landscape and each other, including water delivered by the ancestors to fuel their agricultural existence. What happened, then, when the landscape no longer held the water vital for their agriculture and their worldview? Their response, however resilient when compared with other southwestern agriculturalists such as the Hohokam and those living at Mesa Verde (Hegmon *et al.*, 2008), doubtlessly involved significant realignments between peoples and places, along with an altered worldview.

The theme of landscape and repopulation appears in the two chapters chosen to illustrate the panarchy model (Figure 15.2). Both Lagoa Santa (Chapter 7) and Point Hope (Chapter 11) were revisited, the former sporadically for seasonal rituals and the latter more permanently as the Tigara's new subsistence regimes once more led them to ancestral lands.

This volume amply illustrates the importance of integrating worldview and ideology into human resilience modeling. As emphasized in the volume introduction by Temple and Stojanowski (Chapter 1) and discussed in Chapters 5, 7, 9, 10, and 11 hunter-gatherer worldviews are substantively different from those of pastoral, agricultural, and industrial societies. Similarly, hunter-gatherer relationships to ancestors and to landscapes are structured to emphasize associations that extend into the past and that frequently animate materials and objects we would consider inanimate and mute. Archaeological resilience modeling would be enriched by this perspective, as emphasized in Section 15.3.

Several of the chapters use non-specific markers of stress to measure health and make inferences about resilience. Such measures are difficult for a number of reasons, including the Osteological Paradox (Wood *et al.*, 1992). Temple, in Chapter 5, compares his samples for stature, body mass, and the relationship of these variable to risk of death to address the selective mortality issues raised by the Osteological Paradox. While estimates of stature and body mass differ significantly between the two groups, mortality risk was not associated with either variable in cross-site comparisons, suggesting that adaptability, rather than high-cost transformation, in the Jomon socioecological system was likely. Stature, as a variable frequently available to those working with small samples, also figures in Pfeiffer and Harrington's (Chapter 2) study of the generally small hunter-gatherers from the Greater Cape Floristic Region of South Africa. While small stature seems to co-vary with increased violence at a point of time in a specific region, the authors are reticent to propose a causal relationship for this association.

In sum, most chapters in this volume are explicit in their definition of external challenges to hunter-gatherer existence (*sensu* Carpenter *et al.*, 2001): diminished species diversity coincident with the Holocene (Chapter 3, Bernal *et al.*), the 8.2 kya BP climatic event (Chapter 4, Schulting; Chapter 9, Stojanowski), climate change, resource stress, and intensive migrations (Chapter 5, Temple; Chapter 7, Da-Gloria and Bueno; Chapter 10, Letham and Coupland; Chapter 11, Justice and Temple; Chapter 12, Bartelink *et al.*), marked subsistence change (Chapter 4, Schulting; Chapter 6, Cameron and Stock); European colonization (Chapter 8, Bornemann and Gamble; Chapter 13, Merbs; Chapter 14, Littleton).

Fewer are precise in defining how resilience should be measured (*sensu* Carpenter *et al.*, 2001). Many imply that evidence of "healthy functioning" (Chapter 2, Pfeiffer and Harrington) and/or disease is an apt measure of resilience (Chapter 5, Temple; Chapter 7, Da-Gloria and Bueno; Chapter 12, Bartelink *et al.*, who also consider evidence of violence), although only a few of these chapters define a threshold other than extinction for identifying a lack of resilience. For example, Chapter 5 (Temple) defines a threshold for identifying severity of transformation as mired in the mortality costs of growth disruption, while Bartelink and colleagues see escalations in perimortem trauma and trophy-taking as another possible indicator of this severity. Population growth is proposed by Bernal *et al.* in Chapter 3 as a positive measure of resilience. The most promising attribute available to bioarchaeologists may be identity, as proxied here by diet (Chapter 4, Schulting; Chapter 9, Stojanowski), dental modifications (Chapter 5, Temple), and burial accompaniments (Chapter 5, Temple; Chapter 8, Bornemann and Gamble; Chapter 10, Letham and Coupland; Chapter 11, Justice and Temple). Less convincing are the long bone biomechanical properties proposed by Cameron and Stock in Chapter 6, particularly in the absence of ethnographic or ethnohistoric models to support their expectations.

In future efforts to define and study resilience in hunter-gatherers, I recommend that each bioarchaeologist approaching resilience issues read the Nelson *et al.* (2016) study. While I do fault most archaeological studies to date for failing to appreciate the rich potential of bioarchaeological datasets, Nelson *et al.* (2016) is significant in its carefully constructed research design and its transdisciplinary applications. It addresses the factors that may predispose groups to resilient responses in the face of environmental challenges. Their results offer compelling advice for those who plan for social resilience prior to catastrophes and thereby ameliorate widespread human suffering. There are many further problems to be addressed in resilience studies. One that neatly follows from the research presented would be to consider the nature of transformations that lead hunter-gatherers to herd and to till the soil. Obviously significant changes in social, technological, and ideological variables result. What are the key factors that lead to a positive transformation?

15.6 Conclusion

The chapters in this volume amply illustrate the robusticity of bioarchaeological approaches to resilience. Further research needs to continue emphasizing integrated approaches drawn from ethnology, ethnoarchaeology, ethnohistory, and archaeology. Significant questions need to be clearly framed, including expectations for the recognition of resilience change and stasis. Alternative expectations need to be fully developed, variables carefully defined, and proxies, when used, cleanly linked to these variables. Assumptions must be clearly stated and justified. With such a rigorous approach, the application of bioarchaeology to questions of vulnerability, resilience, and adaptations in the past will undoubtedly further demonstrate the significance of our field.

The resilience and adaptability of hunters-gatherers reverberates throughout the pages of this volume, as it does through countless archaeological, ethnographic, and ethnohistoric accounts that range from the Pleistocene hunters of megafauna to Nayukpuq with his drones. Hunters such as Nayukpuq, who have lived in partnership with their landscapes and their prey across millennia, know that their world is currently changing and becoming increasingly fragile and less predictable. Their use of twenty-first-century technology reminds us that a lifeway that seeks balance and partnership rather than control is indeed resilient, a powerful lesson in the twenty-first century, just as it was for those who hunted mammoths.

Acknowledgments

The author deeply appreciates the constructive remarks offered by the volume editors, Katelyn Bolhofner, and Margaret (Peggy) Nelson. Comments by graduate students enrolled in Advanced Bioarchaeology ASM 491, Spring Semester 2018, also sharpened my perspective.

References

Aftandilian, D. K. (2013). Interpreting animal effigies from precontact Native American sites: Applying an interdisciplinary method to Illinois Mississippian artifacts. In M. C. Lozada and B. Ó Donnabhain, eds., *The Dead Tell Tales: Essays in Honor of Jane E. Buikstra*. Los Angeles, CA: Cotsen Institute of Archaeology Press, pp. 62–70.

Battle-Baptiste, W. (2011). *Black Feminist Archaeology*. Walnut Creek, CA: Left Coast Press.

Binford, L. (1962). Archaeology as anthropology. *American Antiquity*, 28, 217–225.

Binford, L. and Binford, S. (1968). *New Perspectives in Archaeology*. Chicago, IL: Aldine Publishing Company.

Bird-David, N. (1990). The giving environment: Another perspective on the economic system of gatherer-hunters. *Current Anthropology*, 31, 189–196.

Bird-David, N. (1992). Beyond the "original affluent society": A culturalist reformulation. *Current Anthropology*, **33**, 25–47.

Blanton, R. E. (1990). Review: *The Collapse of Complex Societies* by Joseph A. Tainter. *American Antiquity*, **55**, 421–423.

Bolger, D. (2012). *A Companion to Gender Archaeology*. New York, NY: Wiley-Blackwell.

Bowersock, G. W. (1991). Review: *The Collapse of Complex Societies* by Joseph A. Tainter. *Journal of Field Archaeology*, **18**, 119–121.

Bradtmöller, M., Grimm, S., and Riel-Salvatore, J. (2017). Resilience theory in archaeological practice: An annotated review. *Quaternary International*, **446**, 3–16.

Brown, J. A. (1981). The search for rank in prehistoric burials. In R. Chapman, I. Kinnes, and K. Randsborg, eds., *The Archaeology of Death*. Cambridge: Cambridge University Press, pp. 25–38.

Buikstra, J. E. (1977). Biocultural dimensions of archaeological study: A regional perspective. In R. L. Blakely, ed., *Biocultural Adaptation in Prehistoric America*. Athens, GA: University of Georgia Press, pp. 67–84.

Buikstra, J. E. (1981). *Prehistoric Tuberculosis in the Americas*. Evanston, IL: Northwestern University.

Buikstra, J. E. (2006). A historical introduction. In J. E. Buikstra and L. A. Beck, eds., *Bioarchaeology: The Contextual Analysis of Human Remains*. Amsterdam: Elsevier, pp. 7–26.

Butzer, K. W. (2012). Collapse, environment, and society. *Proceedings of the National Academy of Sciences*, **109**, 3632–3639.

Carpenter, S., Walker, B., Anderies J. M., and Abel, N. (2001). From metaphor to measurement: Resilience of what to what? *Ecosystems*, **4**, 765–781.

Chapman, R. W. (1988). The cost of complexity. *Nature*, **355**, 21–22.

Charles, D. K., Leigh, S., and Buikstra, J. E. (1988). *The Archaic and Woodland Cemeteries of the Elizabeth Site in the Lower Illinois Valley*. Kampsville, IL: Kampsville Archaeology Center.

Claassen, C. (1996). A consideration of the social organization of the shell mound Archaic. In D. G. Anderson and K. E. Sassaman, eds., *Archaeology of the Mid-Holocene Southeast*. Gainesville, Fl: University Press of Florida, pp. 235–258.

Clark, A. L., Tayles, N., and Halcrow, S. E. (2014). Aspects of health in prehistoric mainland Southeast Asia: Indicators of stress in response to the intensification of rice agriculture. *American Journal of Physical Anthropology*, **153**, 484–495.

Cohen, M. N. and Armelagos, G. J. (1984). *Paleopathology and the Origins of Agriculture*. Orlando, FL: Academic Press.

Cohen, M. N. and Crane-Kramer, G. M. M. (2012). *Ancient Health: Skeletal Indicators of Agricultural and Economic Intensification*. Gainesville, FL: University Press of Florida.

Conkey, M. W. and Gero, J. W. (1991). Tensions, pluralities, and engendering archaeology: An introduction to women and prehistory. In J. W. Gero and M. W Conkey, eds., *Engendering Archaeology*. London: Blackwell, pp. 3–30.

Conkey, M. W. and Spector, J. (1984). Archaeology and the study of gender. *Advances in Archaeological Method and Theory*, **7**, 1–38.

Cook, D. C., and Powell, M. L. (2006). The evolution of American paleopathology. In J. E. Buikstra and L. A. Beck, eds., *Bioarchaeology: The Contextual Analysis of Human Remains*. New York, NY: Academic Press, pp. 281–322.

Cowgill, G. (1988). Onward and upward with collapse. In N. Yoffee and G. Cowgill, eds., *The Collapse of Ancient States and Civilizations*. Tucson, AZ: University of Arizona Press, pp. 244–276.

Creel, D. G., and McKusick, C. (1994). Prehistoric macaws and parrots in the Mimbres Area, New Mexico. *American Antiquity*, **59**, 510–524.

Cumming, G. S., and Collier, J. (2005). Change and identity in complex systems. *Ecology and Society*, **10**, 29.

Cumming, G. S., Barnes, G., Perz, S., *et al.* (2005). An exploratory framework for the empirical measurement of resilience. *Ecosystems*, **8**, 975–987.

Cummings, V., Jordan, P., and Zvelebil, M. (2014). *The Oxford Handbook of the Archaeology and Anthropology of Hunter-Gatherers*. Oxford: Oxford University Press.

Dahlberg, F. (1981). *Woman the Gatherer*. New Haven, CT: Yale University Press.

Diamond, J. (2005). *Collapse: How Societies Choose to Fail or Succeed*. New York, NY: Viking.

Dugmore, A. J., McGovern, T. H., Vésteinsson, O., *et al.* (2012). Cultural adaptation, compounding vulnerabilities and conjunctures in Norse Greenland. *Proceedings of the National Academy of Sciences*, **109**, 3658–3663.

Endicott, K. (1999). Gender relations in hunter-gatherer societies. In R. B. Lee and R. Daly, eds., *The Cambridge Encyclopedia of Hunters and Gatherers*. Cambridge: Cambridge University Press, pp. 411–418.

Eshed, V., Gopher, A., Pinhasi, R., and Hershkovitz, I. (2010). Paleopathology and the origins of agriculture in the Levant. *American Journal of Physical Anthropology*, **143**, 121–143.

Estioko-Griffin, A. A., and Griffin, P. (1981). Woman the hunter: The Agta. In F. Dahlberg, ed., *Woman the Gatherer*. New Haven, CT: Yale University Press, pp. 121–151.

Flannery, K. (1968). Archaeological systems theory in early Mesoamerica. In B. Meggers, ed., *Anthropological Archaeology in the Americas*. Washington, DC: Anthropological Society of Washington, pp. 67–87.

Fowler, C. S. and Turner, N. J. (1999). Ecological/cosmological knowledge and land management among hunter-gatherers. In R. B. Lee and R. Daly, eds., *The Cambridge Encyclopedia of Hunters and Gatherers*. Cambridge: Cambridge University Press, pp. 419–425.

Freeman, J., Hard, R. J., and Mauldin, R. P. (2017). A theory of regime change on the Texas coastal plain. *Quaternary International*, **446**, 83–94.

Gamble, L. (2017). Feasting, ritual practices, social memory, and persistent places: New interpretations of shell mounds in Southern California. *American Antiquity*, **82**, 427–451.

Geller, P. L. and Stockett, M. K. (2007). *Feminist Anthropology: Past, Present, and Future*. Philadelphia, PA: University of Pennsylvania Press.

Gilchrist, R. (1999). *Gender and Archaeology: Contesting the Past*. New York, NY: Routledge.

Gilchrist, R. (2012). *Medieval Life: Archaeology and the Life Course*. Woodbridge: Boydell and Brewer.

Gronenborn, D., Strien, H. C., Dietrich, S., and Sirocko, F. (2014). Adaptive cycles and climate fluctuations: A case study from Linear Pottery Culture in western Central Europe. *Journal of Archaeological Science*, **51**, 73–83.

Hays-Gilpin, K., and Whitley, D. S. (1998). *Reader in Gender Archaeology*. New York, NY: Routledge.

Hegmon, M. (2002). Recent issues in the archaeology of the Mimbres region of the North American Southwest. *Journal of Archaeological Research*, **10**, 307–357.

Hegmon, M. (2010). Expressions in black-on-white. In M. C. Nelson and M. Hegmon, eds., *Mimbres: Lives and Landscapes*. Santa Fe, NM: School of Advanced Research Press, pp. 65–74.

Hegmon, M. and Kulow, S. (2005). Painting as agency, style as structure: Analyses of Mimbres pottery designs from southwest New Mexico. *Journal of Archaeological Method and Theory*, **12**, 313–334.

Hegmon, M., Peeples, M. A., Kinzig, A. P., *et al.* (2008). Social transformations and its human costs in the Prehispanic U.S. Southwest. *American Anthropologist*, **110**, 313–324.

Holling, C. S. (1973). Resilience and stability of ecological systems. *Annual Review of Ecological Systems*, **4**, 1–23.

Holling, C. S. (1986). The resilience of terrestrial ecosystems: Local surprise and global change. In W. C. Clark and R. E. Munn, eds., *Sustainable Development of the Biosphere*. Cambridge: Cambridge University Press, pp. 292–317.

Holling, C. S. (2000). Theories for sustainable futures. *Conservation Ecology*, **4**, 7.

Holling, C. S. and Gunderson, L. H. (2002). *Panarchy: Understanding Transformations in Systems of Humans and Nature*. Washington, DC: Island Press.

Hooton, E. A. (1930). *The Indians of Pecos Pueblo*. New Haven, CT: Yale University Press.

Hoover, K. C. and Hudson, M. J. (2016). Resilience in prehistoric persistent hunter-gatherers in northwestern Kyushu, Japan as assessed by population health. *Quaternary International*, **405B**, 22–33.

Howell, F. C. (1965). *Early Man*. New York, NY: Time, Inc.

Hughes, Z. (2018). Subsistence hunters adapt to a warming Alaska with new tools. *PRI*. www.pri.org/stories/2018-02-22/subsistence-hunters-adapt-warming-alaska-new-tools.

Ingold, T. (2000). *The Perception of the Environment: Essays on Livelihood, Dwelling and Skill*. New York, NY: Routledge.

Ingold, T. (2015). From the master's point of view: Hunting is sacrifice. *Journal of the Royal Anthropological Institute*, **21**, 24–27.

Jarvenpa, R. and Brumbach, H. (2009). Fun with Dick and Jane: Ethnoarchaeology, circumpolar toolkits, and gender "inequality." *Ethnoarchaeology*, **1**, 57–78.

Jarvenpa, R. and Brumbach, H. (2014). Future directions in hunter-gatherer research. In V. Cummings, P. Jordan, and M. Zvelebil, eds., *The Oxford Handbook of the Archaeology and Anthropology of Hunter-Gatherers*. Oxford: Oxford University Press, pp. 1243–1265.

Johnston, F. E., and Snow, C. E. (1961). The reassessment of the age and sex of the Indian Knoll skeletal population: Demographic and methodological aspects. *American Journal of Physical Anthropology*, **19**, 237–244.

Jones, E. L. (1989). Review: *The Collapse of Complex Societies* by Joseph A. Tainter. *The Economic Review*, **42**, 634.

Jordan, P. and Cummings, V. (2014). Introduction. In V. Cummings, P. Jordan, and M. Zvelebil, eds., *The Oxford Handbook of the Archaeology and Anthropology of Hunter-Gatherers*, Oxford: Oxford University Press, pp. 1–29.

Kando, T. (2014). Review: *The Collapse of Complex Societies* by Joseph A. Tainter. *International Journal on World Peace*, **31**, 107–114.

Kardulias, P. N. (1989). Review: *The Collapse of Complex Societies* by Joseph A. Tainter. *American Journal of Archaeology*, **93**, 599–601.

Kent, S. (1998). Invisible gender – invisible foragers: Hunter-gatherer spatial patterning and the southern African archaeological record. In S. Kent, ed., *Gender in African Prehistory*. Walnut Creek, CA: Alta Mira Press, pp. 39–67.

Lee, R. B. (1968). What hunters do for a living, or, how to make out on scarce resources. In R. B. Lee and I. DeVore, eds., *Man the Hunter*. Chicago, IL: Aldine Publishing Company, pp. 30–48.

Lee, R. B. (1978). Hunter-gatherers in process: The Kalahari Research Project, 1963–1976. In G. Foster, ed., *Long-Term Field Research in Social Anthropology*. New York, NY: Academic Publishing, pp. 303–321.

Lee, R. B. (1979). *The !Kung San: Men, Women and Work in a Foraging Society*. Cambridge: Cambridge University Press.

Lee, R. B. (1984). *The Dobe !Kung*. New York, NY: Holt Rinehart and Winston.

Lee, R. B. and Daly, R. (1999). *The Cambridge Encyclopedia of Hunters and Gatherers*. Cambridge: Cambridge University Press.

Lee, R. B. and DeVore, I. (1968a). *Man the Hunter*. Chicago, IL: Aldine Publishing Company.

Lee, R. B. and DeVore, I. (1968b). Problems in the study of hunters and gatherers. In R. B. Lee and I. DeVore, eds., *Man the Hunter*. Chicago, IL: Aldine, pp. 3–12.

Leigh, R. W. (1925). Dental pathology of Indian tribes of varied environmental and food conditions. *American Journal of Physical Anthropology*, **8**, 179–199.

Levi, M. (1997). A model, a method, and a map: Rational choice in comparative and historical analysis. In M. I. Lichbach and A. S. Zuckerman, eds., *Comparative Politics: Rationality, Culture, and Structure*. Cambridge: Cambridge University Press, pp. 19–41.

Littleton, J. and Allen, H. (2007). Hunter-gatherer burials and the creation of persistent places in southeastern Australia. *Journal of Anthropological Archaeology*, **26**, 283–298.

Marsh, E. J. (2016). The disappearing desert and the emergence of agropastoralism: An adaptive cycle of rapid change in the mid-Holocene Lake Titicaca Basin (Peru and Bolivia). *Quaternary International*, **422**, 123–134.

Maruyama, M. (1963). The second cybernetics: Deviation-amplifying mutual causal processes. *American Scientist*, **5**, 164–179.

Mensforth, R. P. (2001). Warfare and trophy taking in the Archaic period. In O. H. Prufer, S. E. Pedde, and R. S. Meindl, eds., *Archaic Transitions in Ohio and Kentucky Prehistory*. Kent, OH: Kent State University Press, pp. 110–138.

Milner, G. R. and Jacobi, K. P. (2006). A new deal for human osteology. In J. E. Buikstra and L. A. Beck, eds., *Bioarchaeology: The Contextual Analysis of Human Remains*. New York, NY: Academic Press, pp. 113–119.

Nelson, C. and Gilman, P. A. (2017). Mimbres archaeology. In B. Mills and S. Fowles, eds., *The Oxford Handbook of Southwest Archaeology*. Oxford: Oxford University Press, pp. 265–284.

Nelson, D. (2010). Adaptation and resilience: Responding to a changing climate. *Interdisciplinary Reviews*, **2**, 113–120.

Nelson, M. C., Hegmon, M., Kulow, S., and Schollmeyer, K. G. (2006). Archaeological and ecological perspectives on reorganization: A case study from the Mimbres region of the US Southwest. *American Antiquity*, **71**, 403–432.

Nelson, M. C., Ingram, S. E., Dugmore, A. J., *et al.* (2016). Climate challenges, vulnerabilities, and food security. *Proceedings of the National Academy of Sciences*, **113**, 298–303.

Nelson, S. (2004). *Gender in Archaeology: Analyzing Power and Prestige*. Lanham, MD: AltaMira Press.

Perino, G. (2006). *Illinois Hopewell and Late Woodland Mounds: The Excavations of Gregory Perino, 1950–1975*. Springfield, IL: Illinois Transportation Archa.

Pierson, P. (2000). Increasing returns, path dependence, and the study of politics. *The American Political Science Review*, **94**, 251–267.

Pöhl, F. (2008). Assessing Franz Boas' ethics in the Arctic and later anthropological fieldwork. *Études/Inuit/Studies*, **32**, 35–52.

Randall, A. (2015). How Jeffries Wyman put Florida and shell mounds on the map (1860–1875). *Bulletin of the History of Archaeology*, **25**, 1–12.

Redman, C. L. and Kinzig, A. P. (2003). Resilience of past landscapes: Resilience theory, society, and the *Longue Durée*. *Ecology and Society*, **7**, 14.

Reitsema, L. J., Kozlowski, T., Crews, D. E., *et al.* (2017). Resilience and local dietary adaptation in rural Poland, 1000–1400 CE. *Journal of Anthropological Archaeology*, **45**, 38–52.

Rohner, R. (1969). *The Ethnography of Franz Boas: Letters and Diaries of Franz Boas Written on the Northwest Coast from 1886 to 1931*. Chicago, IL: University of Chicago Press.

Rothschild, N. A. (1979). Mortuary behavior and social organization at Indian Knoll and Dickson Mounds. *American Antiquity*, **44**, 658–675.

Rule, J. B. (1989). Review: *The Collapse of Complex Societies* by Joseph A. Tainter. *Population and Environment*, **11**, 72–74.

Schlanger, S. H. (1992). Recognizing persistent places in Anasazi settlement systems. In J. Rossignol and L. Wandsnider, eds., *Space, Time, and Archaeological Landscapes*. New York, NY: Plenum Press, pp. 91–113.

Schultz, A. H. (1945). Biographical memoir of Ales Hrdlička, 1869–1943. *Biographical Memoirs, National Academy of Sciences*, **38**, 305–338.

Shafer, H. J. (2010). Mimbres rituals and worldview. In M. C. Nelson and M. Hegmon, eds., *Mimbres: Lives and Landscapes*. Santa Fe, NM: School for Advanced Research Press, pp. 47–56.

Slocum, S. (1975). Woman the gatherer: Male bias in anthropology. In R. Reiter, ed., *Toward an Anthropology of Women*. New York, NY: Monthly Review Press, pp. 36–50.

Solich, M. and Bradtmöller, M. (2017). Socioeconomic complexity and the resilience of hunter-gatherer societies. *Quaternary International*, **446**, 109–127.

Sørensen, M. L. S. (2000). *Gender Archaeology*. New York, NY: Wiley.

Steckel, R. H. and Rose, J. C. (2002). *The Backbone of History: Health and Nutrition in the Western Hemisphere*. Cambridge: Cambridge University Press.

Steckel, R. H., Larsen, C. S., Sciulli, P. W., and Walker, P. L. (2009). The history of the European Health Project: A history of health in Europe from the Late Paleolithic era to the present. *Acta Universitatis Carolinae Medica*, **156**, 19–25.

Sterling, K. (2014). Man the hunter, woman the gatherer? The impact of gender studies on hunter-gatherer research (a retrospective). In V. Cumming, P. Jordan, and M. Zvelebil, eds., *The Oxford Handbook of the Archaeology and Anthropology of Hunter-Gatherers*. Oxford: Oxford University Press, pp. 151–176.

Tainter, J. (1988). *The Collapse of Complex Societies*. Cambridge: Cambridge University Press.

Tainter, J. A. (2005). *The Collapse of Complex Societies*. Cambridge: Cambridge University Press.

Tanner, N., and Zihlman, A. (1976). Women in evolution. Part I: Innovation and selection in human origins. *Journal of Women in Culture and Society*, **1**, 585–608.

Temple, D. H. (2010). Patterns of systemic stress during the agricultural transition in prehistoric Japan. *American Journal of Physical Anthropology*, **142**, 112–124.

Thompson, V. D. (2010). The rhythms of space-time and the making of monuments and places during the Archaeic. In D. H. Thomas and M. C. Sanger, eds., *Trend, Tradition, and Turmoil: What Happened to the Southeastern Archaic?* New York, NY: American Museum of Natural History, pp. 217–227.

Turck, J. A., and Thompson, V. D. (2016). Revisiting the resilience of Late Archaic hunter-gatherers along the Georgia coast. *Journal of Anthropological Archaeology*, **43**, 39–55.

von Bertalanffy, A. L. (1968). *General System Theory: Foundations, Development, Applications*. New York, NY: George Braziller.

Walker, B., Holling, C. S., Carpenter, S. R., *et al.* (2004). Resilience, adaptability, and transformability in social-ecological systems. *Ecology and Society*, **9**, 5.

Warren, J. C. (1822). *A Comparative View of the Sensorial and Nervous Systems in Men and Animals; with Appendix: Account of the Crania of Some of the Aborigines of the United States*. Boston, MA: Joseph W. Ingram.

Washburn, S. and Lancaster, C. S. (1968). The evolution of hunting. In R. B. Lee and I. Devore, eds., *Man the Hunter*. Chicago, IL: Aldine Publishing Company, pp. 293–303.

Watson, P. J. and Kennedy, M. C. (1991). The development of horticulture in the Eastern Woodlands of North America: Women's role. In J. M. Gero and M. W. Conkey, eds., *Engendering Archaeology: Women and Prehistory*. Oxford: Basil Blackwell, pp. 255–275.

Webb, M. C. (1974). Exchange networks: Prehistory. *Annual Review of Anthropology*, **3**, 357–383.

White, L. (1943). Energy and the evolution of culture. *American Anthropologist*, **45**, 335–494.

White, L. (1949). *The Science of Culture: A Study of Man and Civilization*. New York, NY: Farrar, Straus and Giroux.

White, L. (1959). *The Evolution of Culture: The Development of Civilization to the Fall of Rome*. New York, NY: McGraw Hill.

Wood, J. W., Milner, G. R., Harpending, H. C., and Weiss, K. M. (1992). The osteological paradox: Problems of inferring prehistoric health from skeletal samples. *Current Anthropology*, **33**, 343–370.

Wyman, J. (1871). Report of the curator. *Reports of the Peabody Museum of American Archaeology and Ethnology*, **4**, 5–24.

Wyman, J. (1874). Report of the curator. *Reports of the Peabody Museum of American Archaeology and Ethnology*, **7**, 6–37.

Wyman, J. (1875). *Fresh-Water Shell Mounds of the St. John's River, Florida*, vol. 1. Salem, MA: Peabody Academy of Science.

Yoffee, N. and Cowgill, G. L. (1988). *The Collapse of Ancient States and Civilizations*. Tucson, AZ: University of Arizona Press.

Zihlman, A. and Tanner, N. (1978). Gathering and the hominid adaptation. In L. Tiger and H. Fowler, eds., *Female Hierarchies*. Chicago, IL: Beresford, pp. 163–194.

Index